Reading Empirical Research Studies:
The Rhetoric of Research

Reading Empirical Research Studies: The Rhetoric of Research

Edited by

John R. Hayes
Richard E. Young
Michele L. Matchett
Maggie McCaffrey
Cynthia Cochran
Thomas Hajduk
Carnegie Mellon University

LEA LAWRENCE ERLBAUM ASSOCIATES, PUBLISHERS
1992   Hillsdale, New Jersey   Hove and London

Lawrence Erlbaum Associates, Inc., Publishers
365 Broadway
Hillsdale, New Jersey 07642

Library of Congress Cataloging-in-Publication Data

Reading empirical research studies : the rhetoric of research / edited
  by John R. Hayes . . . [et al.].
      p.   cm.
    Includes bibliographical references and index.
    ISBN 0-8058-1030-7. — ISBN 0-8058-1031-5 (pbk.)
    1. English language—Composition and exercises—Study and
teaching.   2. English language—Composition and exercises—Research.
3. English language—Rhetoric—Study and teaching.   4. English
language—Rhetoric—Reseasrch.   I. Hayes, John R., 1929–   .
  PE1404.R3735   1992
  808′.042′07—dc20   91-37193
                                                              CIP

Printed in the United States of America
10 9 8 7 6 5 4 3 2 1

Table of Contents

Preface

This book has been a long time coming. Over a dozen years ago when we (Hayes and Young) first taught the introduction to research in the Rhetoric Program at Carnegie Mellon, we felt a need for it. The course we taught was designed for first-year doctoral students in rhetoric, students who typically have little experience with formal empirical research and less enthusiasm for it. The course was intended both to help students become intelligent readers of the growing body of empirical research in rhetoric and to enable them to plan and carry out relatively simple but useful empirical studies.

By presenting them with examples of this kind of research, often bad examples, we tried to clarify the principles of good design and what can go wrong if the principles are not followed. To our chagrin, we found that many of our students were becoming better critics of research than researchers. They became skillful at identifying flaws in studies but were much less skillful in making use of the studies in their own thinking. Furthermore, they appeared to believe that if a study was not perfect, then it was worthless. But we wanted them to understand that individual studies are rarely, if ever, perfect and that research is a cumulative enterprise which moves closer to adequate answers to questions through the accumulation of evidence from many flawed sources. We certainly wanted students to notice the faults in studies so that they could avoid them in their own work. But it was also important to us that they understand that most progress in research occurs through good studies rather than perfect ones.

We recognized that focussing on very good studies rather than very bad ones might be an effective approach to the problem, but as is often the case, identifying an approach didn't lead to immediate action on it. We ruminated on the problem until the Spring of 1990 when Hayes taught a course that focussed entirely on the analysis of exemplary studies, what the students began to call "neat studies." All four graduate students enrolled in the course, and co-authors of this text—Cochran, Hajduk, Matchett, and McCaffrey— found the problem interesting; to the best of our recollection, it was Tom Hajduk who first suggested that since they were going to read and evaluate a large number of studies, they should consider using this effort to produce a book. The idea was well received, and the "neat studies book project" was launched. Throughout the Spring semester of 1990, the members of the "neat studies" course asked colleagues to nominate articles for possible inclusion in the book, reviewed the articles, and winnowed the nominees to a book-size collection.

Of course, one semester was not enough to complete work on the book. So, while the graduate students continued to be involved in the project, the main work of final preparation fell to Hayes, Young, and Matchett. Hayes and Young took responsibility for editing, and Matchett for document design. As the project stretched into months, it might have been derailed by the distractions of academic life if it had not been for Joyce Young, Richard's wife, who believed in the project and understood the vagaries of academic life and of the participants. So she informed Young and Hayes that they would meet every Friday to work on the book over a lunch that she would prepare. Joyce's moral persuasion, exotic sandwiches and Twinkies (Hayes is a junkfood junkie) kept us on task. In addition to her role as motivator, Joyce Young proved to be an unusually able copy editor who read every word of the text before it went to the publisher. It is for these and many other reasons that we dedicate this volume to her.

Many others helped in producing this book, and we want to thank them as well. Muriel Fleishman spent untold hours repairing computer-scanned texts, inserting editorial changes, and dealing with the confusion that inevitably results when many people produce many drafts. John Dunn, David Fleming, George Jantzen, Christine Murphy, Mary Louise Ray, Loel Robinson, Karen Schriver, Michael Schwartz, Mark Werner, and Patricia Wojahn read drafts and contributed valuable ideas for improvement. Hollis Heimbouch, and Art Lizza at Lawrance Erlbaum Associates were always pleasant to work with no matter what problems arose. Finally, we want to thank the contributors to this volume for being very patient when we requested editorial changes.

Acknowledgements

Grateful acknowledgment is made to the following for permission to reprint previously published material:

Baumann J. F., & Serra, J. K. (1984). The frequency and placement of main ideas in children's social science textbooks: A modified replication of Braddock's research on topic sentences. *Journal of Reading Behavior*, 16(1), 27-40. Copyright 1984 by The National Reading Conference, Inc. Reprinted by permission.

Beach, R. & Wendler, L. (1987). Developmental differences in response to a story. *Research in the Teaching of English*, 21(3), 286-297. Copyright 1987 by the National Council of Teachers of English. Reprinted with permission.

Bracewell, R. J. (1983). Investigating the control of writing skills. In P. Mosenthal, L. Tamor, & S. A. Walmsley (Eds.), *Research on Writing: Principles and methods*. New York: Longman. Copyright 1983 by Longman publishing Group. Reprinted by permission of Longman Publishing Group.

Braddock, R. (1974). (The frequency and placement of topic). *Research in the Teaching of English*, 8, 287-302. Copyright 1974 by the National Council of Teachers of English. Reprinted with permission.

Enos R. L.(1986). The art of rhetoric at the Amphiareion of Oropos: A study of epigraphical evidence as written communication. *Written Communication*, 3, no. (1), 287-302. Copyright 1986 by Sage Publications, Inc. Reprinted by permission of Sage Publications, Inc.

Floreak, M. J. (1989). Designing for the real world: Using research to turn a "Target Audience" into real people. *Technical Communication*, 36, no. (4), 373-381. Reprinted with permission from *Technical Communication*, published by the Society of Technical Communication.

Freedman, S. W. (1979). How characteristics of student essays influence teacher's evaluations. *Journal of Educational Psychology*, 71(3), 328-338. Copyright 1979 by the American Psychological Association. Reprinted by permission.

Freedman, S. W. Why do teachers give the grades they do? (1979) *College Composition and Communication*, 30(2), 161-164. Copyright 1979 by the National Council of Teachers of English. Reprinted with permission.

Haas, C. & Funk, J. (1989). "Shared Information": Some observations of communication in Japanese technical settings. *Technical Communication*, 36, no.(4), 362-367. Reprinted with permission from *Technical Communication*, published by the Society of Technical Communication.

Heath, S. B., & Thomas, C. (1984). The achievement of preschool literacy for mother and child. In H. Goelman, A. A. Oberg, & F. Smith (Eds.) *Awakening to Literacy*, Oxford, England: Heinemann. Reprinted by permission of the copyright holder, Antoinette Oberg.

Hillocks, G. (1979). The effect of observational activities on student writing. *Research in the Teaching of English, 13* (1), 23-36. Copyright 1979 by the National Council of Teachers of English. Reprinted with permission.

O'Donnell, A., (1985). Cooperative writing: Direct effects and transfer. *Written Communication,* 2(3), 307-315. Copyright 1985 by Sage Publications, Inc. Reprinted by permission of Sage Publications, Inc.

Palmquist, M., & Young, R. (1992). The notion of giftedness and student expectations about writing. *Written Communication,* 9, no. (1), 137-168. Copyright 1986 by Sage Publications, Inc. Reprinted by permission of Sage Publications, Inc.

Part 1

Chapter 1   Introduction to Empirical Research and Rhetoric: Reading in a Developing Tradition

> Some months ago, one of the writers of this report mentioned to a colleague doing research in internal medicine that it was disappointing to see how little was really known about the teaching and learning of written composition, how inconclusive most of the research has been. The colleague replied that 95 percent of the research in his area was inconclusive or trivial. "Keep at it," he said. "As you learn more, you'll slowly learn to define your problems in a useful manner and to refine your techniques of analysis. Then you'll be in a position to learn something substantial."
>
> Richard Braddock, Richard Lloyd-Jones, and Lowell Schoer, *Research in Written Composition* (1963, p. 29)

> Not only have we begun to develop a research tradition, but attempts to answer questions raised by Braddock, Lloyd-Jones and Schoer have led to new breadth and depth of interest in the teaching of writing.
>
> George Hillocks, Jr., *Research on Written Composition: New Directions for Teaching* (1986, xvii)

Neat Studies

As we worked out the conception of this collection and sifted articles for inclusion, we fell into the habit of calling the book "Neat Studies." If somewhat facetious, our working title was also reasonably accurate. The studies all reveal scholars actively trying to come to grips with real problems in the discipline; the studies are all intelligently designed, carried out, and described; and they all tell us something that is new and useful. These characteristics were, in fact, the criteria we used in selecting the studies.

"Neat," though, does not mean perfect. To drive home this point, we have prefaced each of the studies with a short critique pointing out not only some of the strengths we see in the studies but weaknesses as well. Furthermore, the authors of the articles often criticize their own work in the brief essays that follow each of their works. None of the articles, then, is beyond criticism. Nor, we insist, need they be in order to have value. If perfection were a precondi-

3

tion for usefulness, it's unlikely that scholars would get very far in empirical research in rhetoric and composition, no matter what kind of method they were using. Perfection, in the sense of faultless work, is not a standard that is brought to bear in other areas of rhetorical scholarship, or for that matter in the scholarship in any other discipline. As we have all doubtless observed in so many areas of our experience, the insistence on perfection can have the effect of paralyzing action when action is needed. To put it another way, the best, which is often unobtainable, can be the enemy of the more obtainable good. Indeed, logicians (e.g., Fearnside, 1959, p. 131-2) recognize the call for perfection (that is, the establishment of impossible conditions as criteria for judgment) as an argumentative fallacy that can stifle constructive argument and consequent productive action. Whatever their shortcomings, all the articles in this collection are exemplary, in that they illustrate what it means to address genuine problems in the discipline of rhetoric with care and intelligence, and they set a standard of competence for those learning the methods of empirical research.

Empirical Research in Rhetoric

One of the most significant changes among the many significant changes in rhetorical studies over the last three decades is the growth of empirical research in rhetoric and composition. (It should be noted that Speech Communications has had a longer tradition of empirical research. Our comments here for the most part pertain to efforts by those working in English studies.) What has to be regarded as a revolution in humanistic research is readily apparent if *Research in Written Composition*, the 1963 study by Braddock, Lloyd-Jones and Schoer, is compared with George Hillocks' 1986 study, which bears nearly the same title. Both survey prior empirical research in rhetoric: Braddock, Lloyd-Jones, and Schoer sought to survey all scientific studies of written composition done in this country up to 1962; Hillocks, surveying a much shorter span of time, investigated scientific studies done between 1963 and 1982. Out of an original list of over 1,000 titles, Braddock and his colleagues identified approximately 500 studies that could be regarded as examples of scientific research, about half of which were unpublished dissertations. They also selected five studies for close scrutiny that were in their opinion not perfect but the "most soundly based of all those studies available" (1963, p. 55). However, as they say, they were tempted not to select any study because of a general failure to recognize the complexities of scientific research design (p. 55).

In contrast, Hillocks originally identified over 6,000 titles, which were then screened using a much more rigorous set of criteria than was used in the earlier study; the result was a list of over 2,000 titles. Hillocks (1986, xvi) remarks that Braddock, Lloyd-Jones, and Schoer felt that few studies were exemplary:

> "It is an unusual study," they wrote, "which does not leave several important variables uncontrolled or undescribed. . . ." While many studies included in the bibliography of this report suffer from similar flaws, there are also other studies which are, I believe, exemplary and which contribute to our knowledge of composition.

In 1963, Braddock and his colleagues likened empirical research on writing to "chemical research as it emerged from the period of alchemy" (p. 5). Whatever the shortcomings of present-day research, it has gone far beyond the rudimentary empiricism implied in their analogy. And in our comments on what it means to read empirical reports critically we acknowledge this by invoking not a special, and forgiving, set of criteria designed for applications of scientific methodology in rhetorical research ("science for humanists," so to speak), but the same criteria that are generally used in the social sciences. One point of this brief comparison between the Hillocks study and its predecessor, then, is that in the twenty-five years between the two works both the number and quality of studies making use of scientific methods have increased remarkably.

Furthermore, as Lloyd-Jones notes in the "Introduction" to Hillocks' study (1986, xiii), "the methods are also far more varied." In the 1963 survey, error counts and comparative studies dominated the book so much that without them there would have been no review. Hillocks describes other procedures for systematically refining observations. He is as governed by empiricism as are the earlier reviewers. However, the practices he describes lead in more directions by many different routes.

Many methods that have now become commonplace in our journals were rare in rhetorical research just a generation ago. The significance of this development is that those interested in rhetorical research are in a much better position now than they were earlier to match appropriate methods of research to the questions they want to investigate. Our methodological toolbox has gotten much larger. In this collection of articles, we have provided a sampling of the methods now commonly used in rhetorical research: case studies, naturalistic observation, surveys, protocol studies, correlational studies, experiments, historical studies. We might add that the questions asked by our authors and the settings in which the questions are investigated are also

5

increasingly varied: the investigations take place not only in primary, secondary, and college classrooms—the principal sites of earlier studies—but in rural black homes, inner city ghettos, and Japanese electronic firms.

Research and the Profession of English

One of the many paradoxes in the paradoxical tradition of writing instruction in departments of English is that much of the early research, whether empirical or otherwise, was carried out not in English departments but in schools of education, often by educational psychologists. That is, the teaching of writing, at least at the college level, was severed from the research on writing and on writing pedagogy. And those who did the teaching seldom were acquainted with the research, and, we might add, the researchers. However, as Anne Herrington points out (1989), the community of researchers today is growing and becoming more diverse. *Research in the Teaching of English* had a subscription of 1,171 at the time of its founding by the NCTE in 1967; ten years later the subscription had more than doubled to 2,834. In addition, those publishing in the journal are much more representative of those working in English studies. Indeed, a growing community of empirical researchers is discernible within the much larger community of scholar-teachers in English.

Such changes are encouraging to anyone interested in basing educational practices and policy on the best available knowledge. However, as encouraging as these changes are, the old division persists between, on the one hand, those who do the research on rhetoric and composition and, on the other, those who teach writing and those who make educational policy in English departments. (See, for example, Hartzog, pp. 14-71.) For the most part, those who teach writing and who administer writing programs do not do research on writing. Perhaps more significantly, they do not read the research done by others. One reason for this is that effective reading of articles on empirical research requires special knowledge and abilities that graduate training in English studies has in the past seldom sought to develop, though that tradition is changing in some schools around the country. By and large those responsible for maintaining and improving writing instruction in this country cannot, without further training, access the work that could help them carry out their responsibilities better.

Hence this book, which is designed primarily to serve as a text in graduate English programs that offer instruction in rhetoric and composition. The book has two basic purposes:

6

1. to provide models and critical methods designed to improve the reading of scientific discourse, and
2. to provide models of effective research designs and projects appropriate to those learning to do empirical research in rhetoric.

But the book is designed to serve other purposes as well. We want to demonstrate that one of the myths about empirical research commonly shared among humanists is without substance, for if you believe the myth, you will never make the effort to understand this kind of research. The myth is that empirical research never tells us anything new about rhetorical behavior and about the teaching of composition, that is, anything that isn't already known by any reasonably perceptive layman. Another variant of the myth is that the findings of empirical research may be true but they are trivial. To see that the belief is problematic, consider the widely shared assumption that the longer one works on a task the greater one's achievement will be. It is clearly not a trivial belief, but most would probably regard it as a truism, certainly not a claim requiring formal investigation. However, in one of the earliest studies in the history of teaching research, J. M. Rice found that there was no significant correlation between the amount of time devoted to spelling homework and achievement in spelling. After studying tests on 33,000 school children, Rice noted that "an increase in time. . . is not rewarded by better results. . . .The results obtained by forty or fifty minutes' daily instruction were not better than those obtained where not more than ten or fifteen minutes had been devoted to the subject" (quoted in Gage, p. 12). What seem to be truisms sometimes turn out not to be. But, as N. L. Gage remarks (1991, p.13), "even if the broad generalization is a truism, the specifics of its actualization in human affairs—to determine the magnitude of the probability and the factors that affect that magnitude—require research." We think that an open-minded reading of the studies in this collection will lay the myth to rest.

The book will also, we hope, cultivate new attitudes toward empirical research: for example, we hope that it will encourage in the reader an appreciation of the rhetorical tradition that informs the production and critical reading of empirical studies. It is a tradition that has received little scholarly attention in rhetorical studies until recently. However, once one understands that the scientist does not seek to prove beyond the possibility of objection the truth of a particular claim but instead seeks to make persuasive arguments to a particular disciplinary community, the whole enterprise has to be examined in a different light. The scientist is to be seen now as constructing arguments, within a reasonably well-defined system of rhetorical constraints, that a particular belief is warranted. That is, the scientist is to be seen as a practicing rhetorician. That change in conception of the business of the scientist opens up a whole new area of rhetorical inquiry.

One last comment on the purposes of the book: we hope that the book serves to reinforce a slowly growing realization among those working in English studies that empirical methods are not inherently alien to the humanities, rather that the methods extend the power of humanist researchers trying to solve the problems of their discipline. The methods we explore in this collection are not merely various ways of collecting data; they represent ways of reasoning about problems we confront as scholars and teachers. In particular, they represent sophisticated ways of reasoning from observations to defensible conclusions and, more broadly, of reasoning about observation as a source of knowledge.

The Organization of the Book

The organization of the book also needs comment since it is a bit unconventional. Chapter 2 is an introduction to an art of reading scientific articles. Although the effective reading of scientific discourse is not a simple and straightforward intellectual activity, some may nevertheless think it strange to speak of an art of criticism in this context, since arts of criticism have traditionally been restricted to what is commonly referred to as "imaginative discourse," that is, fictional discourse or discourse for esthetic purposes. Some of the skills associated with the effective reading of imaginative discourse are, in fact, applicable in the reading of scientific discourse. Nevertheless, the reading of scientific discourse entails more than a new application of abilities we may already have acquired in the study of literary texts. Effective readers have special skills, and these skills and their underlying principles can be taught. They are probably best taught through repeated use in the close reading of diverse texts, an approach this collection is designed to encourage.

Preceding each of the articles is a short critical analysis by the editors. The analyses are intended to help the reader see relationships among the articles, limitations and potentials of conventional designs and methods, and possible alternatives to the interpretation of the data discussed in the study. The analyses are also intended to illustrate various strategies for critical reading. In short they provide examples of the kind of analysis that a skillful reader might engage in when presented with the article.

Each of the articles in the collection is followed by a short statement by the author describing how the article came about, that is, what set the inquiry in

8

motion. These informal autobiographical accounts serve, we hope, to make the process of scientific research more accessible to the reader, who can see that it begins where all inquiry begins, scientific or otherwise, in a moment of puzzlement, or curiosity, or need to know; more generally it begins, not in some impulse peculiar to the scientist, but, as Aristotle observed when discussing the philosophic impulse, in wonder.

Then comes a brief bibliography for the reader who wants more detailed discussions of the methods and other issues exemplified in the articles. The book concludes with a glossary; in addition to doing what all glossaries do, it provides an easy way of accessing the concepts and methods that form the intellectual foundations of the book and, more generally, of empirical research.

The "neat studies" demonstrate that over the last three decades those working in rhetoric and composition have in fact been learning, as Braddock, Loyd-Jones and Schoer put it, to define their problems in a useful manner and to refine their techniques of analysis. The studies not only provide knowledge immediately useful in rhetorical studies, they also reveal a profession positioning itself to learn something substantial from this kind of research and creating conditions necessary for still more effective subsequent work. We hope that the readers of this text will share with us the sense that, in George Hillocks' words (1988, p.115), "the complex problems for study and the multi-disciplinary approaches necessary to study them are key to the excitement which the future of composition studies holds."

Works Cited

Braddock, R., Lloyd-Jones, R., & Schoer, L. (1963). *Research in written composition.* Champaign, IL: National Council of Teachers of English.

Fearnside, W. W. (1959). *Fallacy: The counterfeit of argument.* Englewood Cliffs, NJ: Prentice-Hall.

Gage, N. L. (1991). The obviousness of social and educational research results. *Educational Researcher, 20,* 10-16.

Hartzog, C. P. (1986). *Composition in the academy: A study of writing program administration.* New York: Modern Language Association of America.

Herrington, A. J. (1989). The first twenty years of *Research in the Teaching of English* and the growth of a research community in composition studies. *Research in the Teaching of English, 23,* 117-138.

Hillocks, G., Jr. (1986). *Research on written composition: New Directions for Teaching.* Urbana, IL: National Conference on Research in English and ERIC Clearinghouse on Reading and Communication Skills.

Hillocks, G., Jr. (1988). A response to the commentators. *Research in the Teaching of English, 22,* 108-116.

Chapter 2   Reading Research Reports

The purpose of this chapter is to provide you with some guidance that we hope will help you to read and evaluate research reports more easily. It consists of four sections. In Section A, we discuss how the parts of the research report are organized and provide suggestions about what is most important to attend to in each part. In Section B, we discuss the major classes of empirical studies and the sorts of conclusions that can and cannot be drawn from each. In Section C, we present some of the most useful critical strategies for evaluating empirical research studies. In Section D, the final section, we introduce a few of the measures which are very widely used in empirical studies. This section is purposely short because we prefer to introduce methods and concepts associated with empirical research in the context of actual studies. Thus, most of the concepts relevant to critical reading are introduced in our commentaries on the articles we have included in Part 2 of this volume. Our objective is not to give you extensive knowledge of subject matter or of statistical methods. Rather, we will try to give you enough information so that you can understand and evaluate the author's main line of argument. For more detailed understanding of subject matter or statistical method, you will have to consult other sources, such as those listed in the "Additional Readings" section at the end of this book.

Section A: The Format of the Research Report

As the articles in Part 2 illustrate, research reports vary in structure. Heath's article has a narrative structure, and Hunt's article is structured to help the reader empathize with the reading experience of the study's participants. Usually, though, research reports have five parts:

1. an abstract that provides a brief summary of the report,
2. an introduction that identifies the questions to be addressed in the report and provides a brief review of the most relevant literature,
3. a methods section that describes the participants, the materials, and the procedures for collecting data,
4. a results section that reports what was observed together with statistical analyses of the observations, and finally,

5. a discussion section that presents the author's claims about the meaning of the results.

Many are inclined to interpret the research report as a narrative of the research process. The structure of the report might lead one to believe that the researcher first read all of the relevant literature, then conceived a research idea, designed a study, carried it out as designed, and found the results that were later reported. What probably happened, though, was that the researcher, who was broadly familiar with the area, conceived an idea, designed a study that didn't work as expected, changed the idea, designed a new study, et cetera, and finally, after getting an interesting result, checked the relevant literature to be sure that nothing had been overlooked or misinterpreted. A research report differs, often substantially, from the events that actually took place because the author omits all of the false starts and blind alleys that were very much a part of the research process but are not needed to make the author's point. We have included authors' comments along with the articles in Part 2 to make the point that the precise, well-ordered argument in the research report may arise from a much less tidy research process, a process in which the author may have been far from clear about just where the research was going when it was carried out. Such contrasts lead to a more adequate idea of what is entailed in the process of research and the relation of research to reports about it. It also, we hope, makes empirical research on problems of literacy seem more accessible to the reader trained in the humanities.

The Abstract

The purpose of the abstract is to provide readers with just enough information so that they can decide whether or not they want to read the article. Generally, the abstract will include a statement of the issue investigated, the population in which it was investigated, and a brief summary of what was found. The abstract below, from the Wallace and Hayes article (p. 352, this volume) exemplifies the form.

> This study investigates the impact of task definition of students' revising strategies. Our primary aim was to determine if freshmen students could revise globally if instructed to do so and if those global revisions would result in improved texts. We asked two groups of freshmen to revise a text provided by the experimenters; one group was given eight minutes of instruction on how to revise globally, and the other was simply asked to make the text better. The texts written by students who received the instruction were judged both to be of significantly better quality and to have

12

included significantly more global revision. Further, the improvement appears to affect the treated population generally rather than just a small part of that population. Thus, at least for these college students, the change in task definition allowed them to tap revision skills that they already had available.

The Introduction

The purpose of the introduction is to explain to the reader what issues were investigated and why they were worth investigating. It is in this section that the author identifies the problem, or problems, that the study is designed to solve. Often, the problems to be solved are presented as clearly marked questions or hypotheses. In the Hillocks article (p. 413, this volume), for example, the hypotheses are labeled and numbered for easy recognition and reference.

Swales and Najjar (1987), who studied research reports in physics and educational psychology, found that the introduction to a research report typically involves the following four moves: First, reasons are given for being interested in an area of investigation. Then, the relevant previous research is summarized briefly. Next, a gap is identified in the previous research, and, finally, the gap is used as a rationale for the current investigation.

As the reader will find by examining the introductions of the articles in Part 2, there is considerable variation from the pattern that Swales and Najjar have described. The introduction by O'Donnell et al. (p. 374-375, this volume) fits the Swales and Najjar pattern pretty well, but, in their first move, they simply state the topic rather than arguing for its importance. On the other hand, Enos's introduction varies widely from the Swales and Najjar pattern. Enos identifies a gap with his first sentence. He elaborates on this gap and then identifies a second gap. Finally, he states the purpose of his study as contributing to filling these gaps.

While readers should expect variation in the form and content of introductions, it will still be useful to look for the moves that Swales and Najjar describe. Perhaps the most revealing move is the identification of gaps in current research because it shows us the author's representation of the problem to be solved.

The Methods Section

Methods sections are usually divided into three subsections: a "Participants" subsection, which describes the participants and how they were selected; a

"Materials" subsection, which describes any physical artifacts employed in the study such as reading material, computer software, pictures or diagrams to be examined, etc.; and a "Procedures" subsection, which describes what the participants were asked to do and how the researchers made their observations.

The primary purpose of the Methods section is to describe the study in sufficient detail so that readers are convinced that the study was conducted competently. Ideally, the Methods section should be presented in enough detail so that other researchers could repeat the study in all its essential features if they chose to do so. By describing their methods in detail, researchers offer the disciplinary community the opportunity to find fault with the study, to reinterpret its results, or, indeed, to repeat it. Researchers must do this to be credible. Critical readers would be unlikely to take a study seriously if its methods were not described clearly and in detail.

What should readers attend to while reading the methods section? Unfortunately, the answer is "many things." Critical readers would certainly want answers to the following:

1. How were the participants selected? Were they a representative sample or merely a convenient group, e.g., friends of the researcher who happened to be available?
2. What were the instructions? Could they have biased the outcome by suggesting the result that the researcher was looking for?
3. How were the results scored? Might the judges have been biased by knowing beforehand which participants were in which condition?

The last section of this chapter, "Rival Hypotheses," provides some additional guidance concerning the critical reading of both the methods and discussion sections. However, while many things are important to attend to, one is probably more important than any of the others — identifying the type of the study. Differentiating between descriptive, correlational, and experimental studies is crucial because you cannot interpret the results without knowing the type of the study. This issue is discussed in detail below in the section entitled "Types of Empirical Studies."

The Results Section

In research reports, the results section is kept separate from the discussion section for the same reason that newspapers keep the editorial section separate from the news. In both cases, the intention is to keep "observations" (those matters about which people can be expected to agree) separate from "interpretations" (those matters about which people may well disagree). The results section should present a summary of the observations of the study, e.g., "The average scores for the groups were . . ." together with a summary of the statistical analysis of the observations, e.g., "The differences among groups were significant." Interpretation of the observations should be reserved for the discussion section.

In reading the results section, you should attend carefully to information which bears on the major hypotheses of the study. Notice especially the *size* of the effects being reported. Sometimes this information is presented in sentence form, but often it is presented in a graph or in a table. (If you have trouble reading graphs, the "Visual Communication" references in the "Additional Readings" section of this book may be useful.) For example, in a study of three methods for teaching spelling, you might find a table such as this:

Table 1

Teaching Methods Studied

Teaching Method		
A	**B**	**C**
Words Spelled Correctly 125.3	127.4	143.1

Table 1. Average number of words spelled correctly in three teaching conditions.

This table shows that students in conditions A and B do about equally well (within a percent or two of each other) but that students in condition C do considerably better.

Now that you know roughly how big the differences between conditions are, you should look for information about the **reliability** of the differences. (Throughout the text, we present certain terms in boldface that we believe are both important for understanding empirical studies and perhaps unfamiliar to the reader. Each of these terms is defined in the glossary.) Information about reliability is provided by the results of statistical tests which indicate the **statistical significance** of the result.

Statistical significance and **practical significance** are very different concepts. A difference is statistically significant if it is unlikely to have occurred by chance. A difference is practically significant if it is important to

15

someone. If a difference is statistically significant at the five percent level (written p< .05), then the chances are five in a hundred or less that it occurred by accident. If the difference is significant at the one percent level (written p< .01), then the chances are less than one in a hundred that the difference would have occurred by accident. The smaller the p-value, the more significant the result. Any difference with a p-value of less than .05 is usually referred to as being statistically significant.

Looking at Table 1, we can believe that a teacher might consider the differences between condition C and the other two conditions practically significant, but not the difference between conditions A and B. However, the differences in practical significance don't necessarily correspond to differences in statistical significance. For example, if the averages in Table 1 are based on a very small number of observations, then none of the differences may be statistically significant. On the other hand, if the averages in Table 1 are based on a very large number of observations, then all of the differences may be statistically significant. The important point to remember is that the concepts of practical significance and statistical significance are different. Table 2 suggests in simplified form how you might interpret results with various combinations of practical and statistical significance.

Table 2
The Relationship Between Practical and Statistical Significance

		Practically significant?	
		Yes	No
Statistically Significant?	Yes	An important and reliable difference	A reliable difference but not an important one
	No	A potentially important difference but not definitely so because it is not reliable. It is probably worth collecting more data to establish reliability	A difference that is neither important nor reliable

Table 2: Combinations of practical and statistical significance

The Discussion Section

The discussion section and the methods section are the two parts of the research report that are most difficult to learn to read. The problem is that in these sections, authors must defend themselves against sophisticated sorts of counterarguments that may be unfamiliar to the general reader. Thus, readers may fail to see the point of certain features of the study design and of certain sorts of arguments presented in the discussion. In the final section of this chapter, "Modes of Thought and Argument in Empirical Research," we discuss some of the most important of these counterarguments or **rival hypotheses.** Familiarity with these counterarguments can help you to understand methods and discussion sections more fully, to become a more perceptive critic of research studies, and to think about studies as a researcher would.

Section B: Types of Empirical Studies

Suppose that a researcher observes that college students who have taken an argument course are more critical readers than other students. Now, one might think that an observation is an observation is an observation. But, alas, what we can conclude from an observation depends not only on the observation itself but also on the type of study the researcher was conducting when the observation was made. To evaluate research findings effectively, readers must make two important distinctions among types of empirical studies: 1. they must distinguish between **hypothesis-testing studies** and **descriptive studies**, and 2. they must distinguish, within hypothesis-testing studies, between **correlational studies** and **experimental studies**. Hypothesis-testing studies are designed to evaluate one or more hypotheses that the researcher has proposed *before* conducting the study. A hypothesis is a question for which the researcher wants to find a positive or a negative answer, e.g., "Does this training improve performance?" or "Do good writers typically use topic sentences?" Hypothesis-testing studies rarely provide an absolute "yes" or "no" answer to the question asked, but often they do provide evidence which helps us to decide whether "yes" or "no" is the more plausible answer.

In contrast to hypothesis-testing studies, descriptive studies are not designed to provide an answer to a "yes" or "no" question. Rather, they are designed to answer more open-ended, exploratory questions, such as "What happens during the process of revision?" or "How do students of various ethnic groups prepare for exams?" Descriptive studies employ various research methods including **case study analysis**, the careful and detailed description of one or a few individuals or events; **participant observation**, the description of a group by a participating member of that group; and **protocol analysis,** the moment-by-moment observation of individuals as they perform tasks. In this volume, Nelson uses the case study method to investigate students' practices in completing writing assignments. Haas and Funk use the participant observation method to study communication in a Japanese firm, and Schumacher uses protocol analysis to explore processes in journalistic writing. We should note that although case studies, participant observation, and protocol analysis are often used in descriptive studies their use is not limited to descriptive studies. A case study, for example, can be used for hypothesis testing , since a single counter instance is sufficient to disconfirm categorical claims that something is always true or never true.

Correlational and experimental studies are both classed as hypothesis-testing studies, but they differ in what researchers do in order to make their observations. In experimental studies, researchers take an active role in setting up their observations. In particular, experimental conditions are created by manipulating some aspects of the situation, called **independent variables**, to observe the effects the manipulation may have on other aspects of the situation, called the **dependent variables**. In studies of teaching, the manipulation often involves providing one kind of instruction to one group of participants and another kind of instruction to a second group. In such studies, the independent variable is the kind of instruction provided; the dependent variable might be changes in knowledge or skill resulting from instruction.

In a well-designed experimental study, participants would be assigned to experimental conditions at random. For example, in the teaching studies just mentioned, the kind of instruction that an individual would receive would be determined by a random procedure, such as drawing names from a hat or selecting numbers from a table of random numbers. The primary virtue of **random assignment** is that it is fair and unbiased. The selection is not influenced by preferences of the researchers or the participants. With random assignment, every individual has the same chance as every other of being included in a particular experimental condition. (We will have more to say about randomization later in this chapter.) Experimental studies, then, are characterized by 1. The purposeful manipulation of independent variables to create the study conditions, and 2. The selection of participants to conditions.

To illustrate the difference between experimental and correlational studies, suppose that a researcher is interested in the effect of note taking on learning from text. In an experimental study, the researcher might randomly assign,

18

say, half of the students to a group required to take notes during reading (the "notes" condition) and the other half to a group required not to take notes (the "no notes" condition). The researcher would then compare the two groups to see what effect notetaking had had on learning. However, in a correlational study the participants are not assigned to conditions; the researcher would take the world the way he finds it. For example, to study the impact of notetaking on learning from text, the researcher doing a correlational study would identify two groups of students. One of the groups would consist of students who spontaneously take notes while studying, and the other would consist of students who do not take notes. He would then compare the two groups to see if they differed in how much they learned from the reading task. The difference in procedure between these two types of studies is that in the experimental study, the researcher manipulates the conditions and assigns individuals at random to treatments; and in the correlational study, the researcher does not. As we will see below, this difference makes an important difference in what we can conclude from the two types of study.

Let's return to the observation that we discussed at the beginning of this section, namely, that college students who have taken an argument course are more critical readers than other students, and let's interpret it as if it had been made in the context of each of the three classes of study. First, suppose that the observation had been made in a descriptive study. Imagine a descriptive study in which the researcher was interested in the effects which various educational experiences in the first semester of college might have on students. To conduct this study, he administered a battery of tests to students after their first semester at college. These included tests of reasoning, memory, attitude, personality, reading and writing. The researcher then examined the data to see if he could find interesting patterns or relationships among scores and the courses that the students had taken. The relation between critical reading and enrollment in the argument course was found during this search process. That is, the observation that students who have taken argument are more critical readers was an outcome of the study.

What has the researcher learned from observing this relation? Maybe a lot and maybe nothing. Because this is a descriptive study, he can't conclude with any certainty that there really is a relation between the argument course and critical reading. Why? Because when one examines any complicated body of data, there are very likely to be some patterns in it just by accident. Students who have taken a particular physics course may happen to be taller than average. There may be more red heads than one would expect among the modern language students. Students who are taking a psychology course

19

may have especially healthy gums. The apparent relation between critical reading and taking the argument course seems to make sense, but then it may be just one of those accidents. If the researcher repeated his measurements in subsequent years, the relation might never reappear. However, the fact that we need to be cautious in drawing definite conclusions from descriptive studies doesn't mean that they are useless. The real strength of descriptive studies lies not in demonstrating the existence of such patterns but rather in identifying possibilities and in suggesting hypotheses for further investigation.

Now let's suppose that the observation had been made in a correlational study rather than in an descriptive one. As we noted above, researchers in correlational and experimental studies have sharply focused hypotheses. They are looking for particular patterns in the data. Imagine a correlational study in which the researcher hypothesized, before he collected any data, that an argument course would improve students' abilities to read critically. To test this hypothesis, he administered a critical reading test to all of the students in a college after their first semester. (Notice the use of a single test of critical reading rather than a large battery of tests reflects the narrower focus of the researcher's hypothesis.) The researcher then compared the critical reading scores of students who had taken the argument course to those who had not. He found, just as the researcher in the descriptive study had found, that the students who had taken the argument course were much more critical readers than were other students. However, while the researchers who conducted the descriptive study could only hypothesize that there might be a relation between the course and the test scores, the researcher who conducted the correlational study can argue much more convincingly that the relation is real rather than accidental. To understand why this is so, consider this analogy. Imagine that you are playing roulette. The croupier spins the wheel and the ball lands on number 27. The guy next to you says, "I knew that was going to happen!" You are not much impressed because you know lots of people who can predict things with extreme accuracy after they have happened. You would have been much more impressed if he told you before the event what the outcome was going to be. This is exactly the difference between descriptive studies, on the one hand, and correlational and experimental studies, on the other. It is much easier to believe that a result is not just an accident if it was predicted beforehand.

While correlational studies provide us with good evidence that the observed relations are not just accidents, they don't necessarily give us good evidence about the cause of the relation. We know that students who took the course scored high in critical reading, but we don't know why. It might

20

be that the course actually does improve the students' reasoning skills. However, it also might be that the course has no effect at all but that students who are naturally good at critical reading tend to sign up for such courses. A third possibility is that students who have already had argument courses in high school tend to sign up for them again in college perhaps because they like such courses. These last two possibilities make it clear that we can't conclude from this study that taking the argument course was definitely the cause of the students' superior performance. We can only conclude that there is some sort of relationship between the two.

Now, imagine that the observation had been made in an experimental study, that is, a study which involves not only one or more hypotheses to be tested, but deliberate manipulation of the experimental situation and random assignment of participants. Suppose that one year twice as many students signed up to take the argument course as could be accommodated in a single semester. Thus, half of the students would have to take the course in the Fall and the other half, in the Spring. This circumstance meant that at the end of the Fall semester there would be an opportunity to compare the critical reading abilities of the students who had already completed the course with the abilities of those who were waiting to take the course in the Spring. However, allowing the students to decide for themselves whether they would take the course in the Fall or the Spring would create the sorts of problems in interpreting the results that we discussed earlier. For example, the Fall class might attract an inordinate number of "eager beavers," or it might attract few engineers because of a conflict in the Fall schedule with a required science course. To avoid the possibility of such **self-selection biases**, the researcher assigned students at random to the Fall and Spring classes. He then compared the critical reading scores of students who had taken the argument course to those who had not yet taken it, and found, just as the other researchers had, that the students who had taken the course were much more critical readers than those who had not.

The experimental study allows researchers to argue that the course actually *caused* the improvement in student scores. Because students were randomly assigned to conditions, the only systematically imposed difference between the two groups was whether or not they had taken the argument course. Of course, we have to recognize the possibility that the random assignment process might accidentally have placed all, or most, of the smart students in the Fall class. Statistical tests are designed specifically for the purpose of estimating the probability that such accidents might have occurred. If, for example, statistical testing indicated that the results of the experiment above were significant at the 5% level, that would mean either that the course had improved critical reading skills or that the assignment had accidentally been biased in a way that would happen only 5% of the time. The experiment, then, doesn't prove that the course caused the improvement, but it does provide evidence that makes that conclusion much more plausible.

As we indicated in the beginning of this section, the interpretation of an observation depends on the kind of study in which it was made. In the descriptive study, the observation provided only a suggestion that the argument course might be related to students' higher critical thinking scores. In the correlational study, the observation provided evidence that the argument course was related to the students' higher critical reading scores, but it did not provide evidence about what the relation was. In the experimental study, the observation provided evidence that the argument course caused students to score higher in critical reading.

The three types of study clearly differ in the persuasiveness of the evidence they provide. However, the reader should not conclude that one type of study is, without qualification, better than another. Each type of study should be regarded as a tool with a specific purpose. Each type has advantages and disadvantages which depend on the situation. If we are investigating an area new to our experience, it makes good sense to do an descriptive study first in order to get oriented. Doing experiments first might lead us to narrow our focus before we really know what the focus ought to be. Correlational studies can also have an important role to play in an extended investigation of a new area. Some variables, such as age and gender, simply can't be studied experimentally, because they can't be assigned at random. We can't say "Hey, you on the left side of the room! You're going to be the four-year-old girls in this study." For this reason, developmental psychology is built largely on correlational studies. But correlational studies can also play an important role even when the factors being studied can be randomly assigned. In some cases, we may suspect that the process of assignment itself may have an important impact on what is being observed. Assigning students to take the course in the Fall semester might make them feel coerced, or it might make them feel privileged. Either effect could bias the result of the experiment. In such cases, we may get a better understanding of the situation by using both types of study. The experimental study would convince us that the effect wasn't due to extraneous factors such a self-selection bias. The correlational study would convince us that the effect wasn't due to the process of assignment. In many situations, the increased cost involved in using multiple methods to approach the same question is more than offset by the greater confidence we can place in the results.

Table 3 summarizes some of the circumstances relevant in deciding what type of study is most appropriate for approaching a particular research problem.

Table 3

Uses of the Three Major Types of Research

Type	Appropriate Use	Characteristic Outcome
Descriptive	The domain is not yet well explored. The researcher does not have specific hypotheses to test.	Formulate hypotheses
Correlational	The researcher has specific hypotheses to test, but they involve variables which cannot be manipulated, e.g., age, gender.	Establish relations
Experimental	The researcher has specific hypotheses which involve variables which can be manipulated.	Establish causal relations

Table 3. Types of research, appropriate use, and characteristic outcomes

Section C: Modes of Thought and Argument in Empirical Research

Perhaps the most characteristic feature of the empirical research community is its insistence that researchers exercise special care in making and interpreting observations. Researchers are expected to be scrupulous in collecting data. Evidence of carelessness or fraud will seriously tarnish the researcher's reputation. In addition, researchers are expected to describe their procedures carefully enough so that other researchers can repeat them if they want to check the observations for themselves.

Equally important, researchers are expected to be very careful in drawing conclusions from their data. They should draw definite conclusions from their observations only after they have tried to rule out all of the plausible alternative interpretations. For example, suppose that a researcher finds, by conducting a survey, that schools providing their students with computer training have fewer disciplinary problems than other schools, and the researcher then claims on the basis of this observation that computers promote student discipline.

23

Other researchers might question this claim by noting that schools with computers also tend to be the wealthier schools. In this case, the alternate interpretation that the observed difference in disciplinary problems may have to do with economics rather than with computer use is quite plausible.

The researcher in this example would be embarrassed to have overlooked such an obvious alternative interpretation. Researchers are expected to be good at anticipating such rival hypotheses. They are expected either to provide evidence which casts doubt on such alternatives or to hedge their conclusions— that is, to acknowledge the possibility of alternative interpretations explicitly. Researchers who fail to recognize alternative interpretations which readily occur to their colleagues are considered unsophisticated. Indeed, training in recognizing alternative interpretations of results is an essential part of the education of empirical researchers. Texts such as Campbell and Stanley's *Experimental and Quasi-experimental Designs* and Huck and Sandler's *Rival Hypotheses* distill years of experience in the critical analysis of data-based claims by identifying a number of the most common sources of alternative interpretations. In the following section, we list the kinds of alternative interpretations which must most frequently be considered in reading and conducting empirical research in literacy. We have grouped them into five families: Stability, Bias, Reactivity, Confounding Factors, and Faulty Inferences.

Common Sources of Alternative Interpretations

1. **Stability**: Do the observations warrant the conclusion that some stable event or thing has been observed?

   When we look at clouds, we can sometimes see fairly definite patterns such as faces or animals. However, we don't attribute stability to these patterns. We interpret them as accidental arrangements of light and dark patches without permanence or significance. Similar sorts of accidental patterns can arise when we examine data collected in research. If we look long and hard enough at complex data, we are bound to see some patterns. If we do see a pattern in our data, we need to ask if that pattern has stability, in the sense that it can be observed on other occasions and by other people. The next three questions bear on this issue of stability.

   a. **Observer reliability**: Do independent observers agree about the objects or events being observed?

Imagine that a school is planning to institute the following placement policy: all incoming students are to be placed into basic, average, or honors classes on the basis of their performance in writing an impromptu theme. For reasons of fairness, all of the students' essays are to be graded wholistically by the same English instructor, Mr. Brown. At a faculty meeting, another member of the English department, Ms. Jones, voices concern about the placement policy. "Suppose," she says, "that these essays were graded independently by two English instructors and their judgments didn't agree at all. Wouldn't that mean that by the proposed policy we would be assigning students to basic and honors courses pretty much arbitrarily. Why not just draw lots?" Clearly, Ms. Jones has raised the question of **observer reliability**.

The issue here is not Mr. Brown's qualifications. Even if all faculty members were equally qualified as writing critics, they still might not see the same things or value the same things in the students' essays. Thus they may not agree in placing students into basic, average, and honors sections. (See Chapters 12 and 13 of this volume for causes of agreement and disagreement among readers of students' essays.) To estimate how well instructors agree in placing students, it would be appropriate to ask two or more instructors to judge the essays independently. Their judgments could then be compared. The usual way to do this would be to calculate the **correlation** between the judgments of pairs of instructors. A correlation of +0.80 or better is generally taken as indicating a satisfactory level of observer reliability.

b. **Test-retest reliability** and **replication**: Are the observations repeatable?

Suppose that a team of reading researchers report that reading scores for primary school children show a surprising increase in March. They have named this effect "The March Surge" and are giving newspaper and magazine interviews about it all over the country. A critical minded researcher suspects that "The March Surge" may be just another pattern in the clouds, a one-time "glitch" in the data that won't be found in repeated observations. To check out her suspicion, she initiates a replication study. That is, she tries to repeat the original study with a new group of primary school students. To do this, she selects the new group in the same way as those in the original study were chosen and collects data from them by methods as close as possible to those described in the original report. Whether her study confirms or fails to confirm "the March Surge," she will seek to publish it in the same journal that published the original report. This will help to insure that the community that was audience to the original report will consider the new results.

c. **Statistical reliability**: Is the number of observations sufficient to warrant the conclusion?

Imagine that you have designed a new method for teaching paragraph writing. You choose two children at random from a friend's class and teach one by your new method and the other by the standard method. Suppose further that on a subsequent test, the child who was taught by your method writes a better paragraph than the other child. Assuming that your teaching and the test were fair to both methods, is it time for celebration? Of course not! Even if the two teaching methods were equally good, one of the children would likely have done better on the test than the other. The chances that the child who did better would happen to be the child trained by your method would be 50%. You would need to repeat your observations with many children before you could be confident that your method was an improvement over the standard one.

2. **Bias**: Are the observations fair and accurate?

Bias in reporting the facts is something we learn to take into account everyday. We expect salespeople to tell us the good things about their products but not the bad. We know that people often play up their successes and play down their failures. We know that people's judgments are biased by "**halo**" **effects**, e.g., teachers may grade students who have done well in the past more leniently than they grade other students. It is an important part of the tradition in empirical research to try to eliminate or at least control bias in observations. We will talk about three sources of bias: Sampling Bias, Self-reporting Bias, and Researcher Bias.

a. **Sampling Bias**: Is everyone represented equally?

In many cases, considerations of cost and time make it impractical to study all the members of a population we are interested in, e.g., all of the students in a large college or all the children in an urban school system. Instead, we often have to study a **sample** of the population that we hope will represent the whole. How that sample is chosen is important because some ways of choosing samples may systematically bias the results of the study. For example, suppose that a researcher wanted to know what teachers believe about the role of word processing in the teaching of writing. One very natural thing for the researcher to do would be to interview friends who teach since they are easy to access. Unfortunately, one's friends are usually not a representative sample of the population. Friends tend to resemble one another in age, gender, race, and professional specialization. If attitude toward word processing varies with age, as seems likely, or any of the other factors in which friends tend to resemble each other, then samples of friends are likely to provide biased results.

Another procedure would be to post a bulletin asking teachers to volunteer to be interviewed. Unfortunately, samples of volunteers are usually not representative of the population either. Teachers who are hostile to word processing or uninterested in it are less likely to volunteer for interviews than are those who are very enthusiastic about it. Thus, results based on a volunteer sample are likely to be biased.

The best way to pick a sample is through randomization. A **random sample** is one in which every member of the population has an equal chance of being included. Whether a given individual is included in the sample or not depends on a random choice, such as one made by picking a number out of a hat or rolling a die. For example, suppose that we wanted to pick a sample of 20 teachers from the 400 teachers employed at a college. First, we would assign a number from 1 to 400 to each teacher. Then, we could write the numbers on slips of paper, put the slips in a bowl, and stir them up. The sample of teachers would be those corresponding to the first 20 numbers chosen from the bowl. Using a table of random numbers to make the selection or even the last three digits from a page of listings in a phone book might be easier, but the effect would be the same. Choosing samples by randomization is the surest and simplest way to avoid bias.

Sampling bias can apply to materials and contexts as well as to participants. For example, a researcher who was interested in demonstrating that students have trouble understanding their textbooks might be inclined to study the worst of the available textbooks. In fairness, the results of such a study would have to be qualified to indicate how the texts were chosen (e.g., "Students have trouble understanding bad textbooks"). If the results are to be applied to textbooks generally, then the texts studied should be a random sample of those available. Similarly, if we are to draw reasonable conclusions about how students write in college, we should not base that conclusion on observation of students in a single context, for example, English classes. Rather, any such conclusion should be based on observation of students in a random sample of the various and often very different contexts in which college students write, e.g., biology labs, school newspaper offices, philosophy exams, etc.

b. **Self-reporting bias**: Are people reporting about themselves fairly and accurately?

Suppose that a college committee designing a humanities course wants to know what students read on their own outside of class. One way to try to get that information would be to ask students to fill out a questionnaire in which they are asked to report how frequently they read novels, poetry, non-fiction, plays, biography, science fiction, etc. The problem with such self-reporting is that respondents may tend to over-report high prestige reading, e.g., novels and poetry, and under-report low prestige reading, e.g., *Playboy* and *The National Enquirer.* Researchers for the National Assessment of Educational Progress attempted to reduce this kind of bias by asking students to name the books they had read. The assumption here is that students' claims to have read novels are more believable if they are actually able to name some.

Another way to deal with bias in this situation would be to make use of multiple sources of information about student's reading habits. For example, one might get information about what sells at student bookstores, what books are checked out of college libraries, and what reading materials students carry around with them. Using many sorts of measures to investigate the same question from different angles is called **triangulation**. In this case, triangulation can help to control for self-reporting bias because it would allow the researchers to compare survey data which may be biased with bookstore sales which are less likely to be biased.

c. **Researcher bias**: Is the researcher evaluating the results fairly?

Being a researcher doesn't make a person unbiased. Researchers usually care a great deal about how their research comes out. They spend much of their time thinking up clever theories and hypotheses, and they are, quite naturally, eager to see these theories confirmed in their data. The result is that researchers can be quite biased observers. Knowing this, good researchers take special care to reduce and control their own biases in evaluating data.

Suppose that a researcher has designed a new method for teaching argument. He identifies a number of instructors who agree either to teach his method or to act as control teachers. Knowing that he might be tempted to choose the better teachers to teach his method, he decides to assign the teachers at random. To assess the effect of the instruction in argument, all of the students are asked to write an argument on a specified topic. Again, because he is aware of his own bias, he does not grade the essays himself. Rather, he has the essays evaluated by other instructors who are not permitted to know which of the students have received the experimental instruction. This last procedure is called **blind grading** ; like the other tactics just mentioned, it is a common and useful technique in controlling researcher bias.

3. **Reactivity**: Is what is observed changed by the act of observing?

The reactivity of a method of observation is the tendency of that method to change what is being observed. Methods of observation differ in how reactive they are. A method in which a person of one race interviews a person of another race about racial attitudes is likely to be highly reactive. In contrast, an anonymous questionnaire about political attitudes will probably be less reactive. Some observational techniques are not reactive at all. For example, assessing the popularity of various types of reading by examining library circulation records probably has no effect on the public's reading behaviors. Historical studies, of course, are completely non-reactive. There are two major loci of reactivity in empirical studies: researcher effects and participant effects.

a. **Researcher effects**: Is the researcher influencing the outcome?

The potential for researcher effects is especially high in participant observation studies. Participant observers are typically visiting members of the group being studied and are, therefore, not "insiders." Because group members may be uncertain of the goals and loyalties of the observer, especially if the observer is socially or ethnically different, they may not behave naturally in the observer's presence. For example, the presence of a white observer in a black social group might well change the nature of conversation in the group. The more obviously different the observer is from the group being observed, the more one must be concerned with researcher effects.

Researcher effects are important in experimental studies as well. In these studies, researchers often know the condition to which each participant has been assigned. As a result, they may, without intending to, act slightly differently toward participants in the experimental and control conditions. For example, experimental participants might receive somewhat friendlier, more encouraging treatment than controls. Those differences may be conveyed in facial gestures or body language of which the researcher may be completely unaware. It is now well established (Rosenthal, 1976) that researchers can influence a study's outcome through such subtle cues.

Researchers can and should reduce such effects on the outcomes of studies. For example, they can restrict the opportunities they have for treating differently participants in different conditions. Instructions might be scripted or, in some cases, tape recorded or videotaped to insure uniformity of presentation across conditions. Responses to questions might be scripted as well. In many studies, participants' questions are answered simply by referring them to the appropriate section of the instructions. Researchers can try to fade into the background. In a writing study, for example, the researcher might try to stay out of the participant's line of sight and intervene as little as possible during data collection. And some studies can be designed so that the person running the study doesn't know the conditions the participants have been assigned to. Such care in the design of studies can greatly reduce the possibility of researcher effects.

b. **Participant effects**: Is the experience of being observed influencing how people behave?

People who participate in research studies respond in many different ways to being observed. They may feel honored to be singled out for study, they may feel anxious to perform well, or they may feel spied on. In any case, they probably feel and act somewhat differently than they would if they weren't being studied. The probable extent of these differences must be taken into account in interpreting the results of studies. Case studies are especially subject to participant effects because individuals participating in them are singled out for exceptional attention.

Participant effects can be reduced in a number of different ways. For example, it may be possible to design an experimental study so that all of the participants undergo both the experimental and control treatments. In a study of the impact of computers on writing, each participant might write some essays with a computer (the experimental treatment) and other essays with pen and paper (the control treatment). Another strategy is to make it appear that all participants are in the same condition even though they are not. Suppose that a study is to be conducted by distributing packets of experimental and control materials to students in the same classroom. If the researcher does not call attention to the differences in the packets being distributed, the participants may not notice them. Participant effects can often be greatly reduced by incorporating such strategies in the design of the study.

4. **Confounding factors**: Might the effect be due to something else?

When researchers conduct correlational or experimental studies, they naturally focus their attention on certain variables or on certain differences among groups in which they are particularly interested. But this exceptional selectivity of focus may produce a kind of intellectual myopia; the researchers may fail to attend to other variables which change along with the ones they are interested in. For example, a recent article, which one of us reviewed, focused on the relation between writing ability and personality traits. The author had found a strong relation between writing ability and the presence or absence of a particular personality trait. What is relevant for us here is that the personality trait was strongly related to age. Older children had it, and younger children didn't. Thus, what the author of the article had interpreted as a rather surprising effect of personality on writing ability may well have been a not very surprising effect of age. In this study, age was a confounding factor because it varied along with the variable that the researcher was highlighting. As such, it provided opportunities for alternative interpretations of the author's claims about the meaning of the data.

In the following section, we describe five common sources of confounding:

31

a. **Effects of drop-outs**: Has the population changed during the study?

In a study designed to evaluate the effectiveness of a remedial reading course, researchers compared the average score on a reading test achieved by students at the beginning of the course with the average achieved at the end of the course and found a substantial increase. On the basis of this result, the researchers concluded that the course was very effective. In deciding whether or not to accept this conclusion, it is important to ask how many students' scores were involved in each average. If there were many more students at the beginning of the course than at the end, it is possible that drop-outs may contribute heavily to the result. Suppose for example, that the students who dropped out were the ones who had greatest difficulty with the course. These may well also be students with relatively low reading scores. If this were the case, it might be that the reported gains occurred just because these students scores were not included in the end-of-course average.

A good way to protect against drop-out effects would be to base the evaluation only on those students who completed the course, eliminating from consideration the pre-test scores of the students who dropped out. If big gains were found for these students, then we would have evidence that the course actually helped some students.

b. **Maturation**. Could the effect be due simply to the passage of time?

People, especially young ones, get better at a lot of things as they get older. For example, we would expect kindergarten students' vocabularies to increase over the course of time whether we gave them special vocabulary lessons or not. Thus, if a researcher reported that kindergarten students increased their vocabularies by 15% when they were exposed to an enrichment program for a year, we wouldn't know whether to be impressed or not. After all, between ages four and five, children increase their *age* by 25%. Perhaps vocabulary could be expected to increase by a similar amount. To assess the effectiveness of the enrichment program, we would have to compare the reported improvement to the amount students would have improved their vocabulary over the same period of time without the enrichment program. That is, we would need to measure vocabulary gains over the same period in a **control group** of students who *did not* have the enrichment program.

c. **Concurrent events**: What else was going on?

Even though researchers are studying them, people continue their lives in the usual complex way beyond the researcher's view. Sometimes events in the lives of the people being studied are confounded with what the researchers are interested in studying. Such confounding, if unnoticed, can lead researchers to draw unwarranted conclusions from their observations.

Suppose, for example, that researchers interested in the development of writing skills ask students in grade 4, 5, and 6 to write on the topic, "making new friends." They find modest gains in essay quality between grades 4 and 5 but very dramatic gains between grades 5 and 6. One explanation of this result that the researchers consider is that writing development is accelerating during these years. However, one of the researchers notes that there is a possible explanation of the results based on concurrent events in the students' lives. In the school district being studied, students move from primary to middle school between the fifth and sixth grades. For this reason, the sixth grade students have just had a lot of experience in making new friends—experience which may make it especially easy for them to write on the assigned topic. To test whether writing development really does accelerate between grades 4 and 6, the researchers should, at least, have students write on several different topics.

d. **Testing effects**: Could the improvement be due to test practice?

Years of experience in mental testing has turned up a rather odd finding. When individuals are tested twice, they usually do better on the second test than on the first when the two tests are parallel forms, that is, when the tests are on the same topic but with completely different questions. By better, we mean getting higher scores on tests of knowledge or skill or getting more "normal" scores on tests of personality. This effect occurs even when participants are given no feedback or opportunity to study between testings.

The implication of the testing effect for research involving pretests and posttests is clear. A comparison or control group may be necessary if one wants to sort out the effect of the variable being investigated from the effect of testing. For example, suppose that we want to examine the impact of writing on students' topic knowledge. To do this, we give the

33

students a knowledge pretest. We then ask them to write an analytic essay on some aspect of the topic. Finally, we give them a knowledge posttest. Suppose that the students score better on the posttest than on the pretest. What can we conclude? Not much unless we know how big the testing effect is. A good way to assess the testing effect is to use a control group of students who are pretested and posttested but who do not write the analytic essay. A positive effect of writing on knowledge would be indicated by greater **pre-post gains** in the essay group than in the control group.

e. **Order effects**: Could the order of testing have influenced the result?

Suppose that a researcher was interested in determining whether children wrote better on a topic they chose themselves or a topic that the teacher chose. To answer this question, the researcher might have the children write first on the teacher's topic and then on their own topic. If the researcher did this, though, the study would be open to the criticism that any difference found might be due to the order in which the essays were written. Perhaps the second essay would benefit from the students' practice or suffer because of their fatigue or boredom. To deal with this problem, the researcher can require half of the children to write on the teacher's topic first and the other half of the children to write on their own topic first, and then reverse the assignments for the second task. In this way, each topic will, on average, be equally advantaged or disadvantaged by the order in which the essays are written. This process of balancing the testing order is called **counterbalancing**.

5. **Faulty inferences**: Can we really draw that conclusion from the observations?

a. Causation and correlation: One of the most common problems to be found in research studies in literacy is a tendency to draw causal conclusions from correlational data. If two factors are correlated with each other, they may be causally related, but they also may not be; all that we can say for sure is that they vary with each other. Both may be caused by some third factor. For example, writing skill and shoe size are strongly correlated with each other. Why? Not because having big feet makes it easier to write, but rather because both writing skill and foot size are strongly correlated with age. Two year olds' writing skills are weak, *and* they have very small feet.

A frequent form in which this sort of faulty inference appears in the literature is the drawing of pedagogical conclusions from correlational data. For example, if it is observed that writers who plan well produce higher quality essays than those who don't plan well, it is tempting to draw the conclusion that teaching planning would help students improve their writing. However, teacher's time and student's time is too valuable to justify drawing such hasty conclusions. It may be that planning and writing are not directly related but rather are connected through a third factor such as motivation or fluency. Perhaps students who are motivated to do well in school put extra effort both into planning and writing. If the underlying causal factor were really motivation, then teachers might be wasting their time in teaching planning. The simplest and surest way to establish a causal connection is through an experimental study. If we teach planning to one randomly selected group and not to another, and the group taught planning writes better, then we can conclude with much greater confidence that teaching planning skills can improve writing.

b. Drawing inferences from non-independent samples. It is important to know if samples are **independent** or not because most statistical tests are appropriate only for independent samples. If the samples are not independent, the test may be invalid and its results misleading. Before discussing independence and non-independence, though, we need to discuss units of observation and to define the term "sample".

Studies differ from one another in the units of observation they employ. In some studies, the unit of observation is the individual. In others, it may be the classroom, the city block, the school, the county, or any of innumerable other units. If the unit of observation is the individual, then the data of the study will consist of measurements of individuals, e.g., individual's scores or individual's ratings on essays. If the unit of observation is the classroom, then the data of the study will consist of measurements of whole classes, e.g., average achievement scores or average attendance records for the class as a whole.

The samples in an experimental study are the groups of units that are assigned to the various conditions of the study. For example, if the units of observation were students, the samples would be the collections of individual students assigned to the various experimental conditions. If the units are assigned to conditions at random, then the samples are said to be **independent**. They are independent in the sense that the chances that a unit is assigned to a particular condition doesn't depend on which of the other units are assigned to that condition. For example, if children in a kindergarten class are assigned at random to experimental and control conditions, then the chances that a particular child will be assigned to the control group doesn't depend on who the other children in the control group are. The samples would *not* be independent if the researcher tried to create congenial groups by placing best friends in the same group. Such samples are not independent because the chances that a child is included depends on whether that child's friend is included.

The following example shows some of the implications that independence (or non-independence) of samples has for the analysis of study results. Suppose that a high school has 300 ninth grade students in 12 classes of 25 students each. A researcher wants to divide the students into an experimental and a control group of 150 students each and is considering two methods for accomplishing the division. The first method, which might be called "the individual method," involves random assignment of individual students to the experimental and control groups. To do this, students' names would be put into a drum and mixed thoroughly. Then 150 names would be drawn. The students whose names were drawn would constitute the experimental group and the remaining students, the control group. These two groups would be independent samples because each individual was selected for inclusion in the experimental or control group independently of every other individual.

The second method, "the class method," involves random assignment of whole classes to the study conditions. To do this, classes would be assigned numbers from 1 to 12. Six numbers would then be selected at random to identify the classes to be assigned to the experimental group. The remaining six classes would be assigned to the control group. The class method has some practical advantages. Many studies can't be run in classes if members of both experimental and control groups are present. Arranging for times when students can participate in the study out of class may be difficult or impossible. These difficulties can be reduced if whole classes are assigned to conditions. However, the class method also has some serious limitations. If the class is taken as the unit of measurement, then the six classes in the experimental group and the six classes in the control group constitute independent samples. What is important to note here is that, if it is the classes that are selected randomly for assignment to the study conditions, the individuals in the classes cannot be treated as independent units; all the individual students in a single class must be treated as constituents of a larger independent unit, i.e., the class. If one student in a class is in the control group, then *all* the students in the class are in the control group. Statistical tests can appropriately be applied only if the whole class is viewed as the unit of measurement. In this example, appropriate statistical tests would compare *six* experimental measures with *six* control measures — one measure for each *class* in each group. Usually the measure for a class would be the average performance of all of the students in the class. In contrast, if experimental and control groups were selected by the individual method, statistical tests could appropriately compare *150* experimental measures with *150* control measures — one measure for each *student* in each group.

It is not unusual to find studies in which whole classes are assigned to the experimental and control groups but which are never the less analyzed as if students were independent units of measurement. The effect of this error is to make results appear to be more statistically significant than they should. Let's consider an extreme case to emphasize the point. Suppose that a researcher wants to evaluate a new procedure for teaching spelling. To do this, he identifies two classes of 30 students each and randomly assigns one to be the experimental group and the other, the control group. If the researcher analyzes the data as if the student was the unit of measurement and as if there were 30 independent measurements in each group, he might believe he had found a significant advantage (or disadvantage) for the new procedure. However, an appropriate analysis could claim only two independent measurements, one for each group. This more conservative approach to the analysis makes sense because all of the students within a class may be strongly influenced (either positively or negatively) by their teacher. The difference between two classes might simply reflect a difference between two teachers. Two measurements, in any case, are not enough to warrant a claim of statistical significance.

37

Section D: Some Commonly Used Empirical Measures

In this section, we will discuss three sorts of empirical measures:
1. measures of central tendency, 2. measures of variability, and 3. measures of association.

1. **Measures of central tendency**: Measures of central tendency are used to identify a central or representative value for a set of observations. The most familiar of these is the **arithmetic average** or **mean**. The mean age of a class of 25 children is the sum of their ages divided by 25. The mean works well for characterizing factors such as age and reading score, because about as many observations can be expected to be above the mean as below it. However, for some factors, such as the number of books that students read for pleasure, the mean may not produce a representative value. Most children will read fewer than the mean number of books, because the mean is inflated by a few children who read lots of books. In cases such as this, two other measures, the **median** and the **mode**, may yield measures more representative of the group. The value of the median is the value of the middle observation. For example, imagine that the 25 children in a class are arranged in order of age: the median age is the age of the middle or 13th child. The median is representative in the sense that there are as many observations above the median as below it. The mode is the most frequent observation. Imagine now that there are more children who read exactly two books a year for pleasure than any other particular number of books: two is the mode. As the most frequent observation, the mode may be viewed as representative of the group of observations.

2. **Measures of variability**: Groups of observations differ in how variable or "spread out" they are. One measure of variability is the **range** or the difference between the largest and the smallest observation. For example, one class of 30 college freshmen might range in age from 17 years 6 months to 18 years 6 months, and another from 16 years 2 months to 52 years 8 months. The range in ages in the first class is just one year, but in the second class, it is 36 years 6 months.

Another commonly used measure of variability is the **standard deviation** or **S. D.** The standard deviation increases as the variability or spread of the observations increases. Generally, about two-thirds of the observations can be expected to fall in the interval extending from one standard deviation below the mean to one standard deviation above the mean. Standard deviations are included in many data displays so that the reader can judge the degree of precision of the observations being reported (See O'Donnell et al., Tables 1 and 2; Spivey, Tables 3 and 5; and Palmquist and Young, Figures 1, 2 and 3, all this volume.)

3. **Measures of correlation**: measures assess the extent to which two sets of observations vary together. For example, correlations may be used to determine the extent to which reading scores change with age or the extent to which independent raters agree with one another in scoring a set of essays. There are many different measures of correlation. The **Pearson product moment correlation**, which is the one most frequently found in the research literature, is used with interval data. **Spearman's Rho** is used for comparing ranked data, such as judgments of essays ranked by quality. **Cohen's Kappa** is used for comparing categorical data. For example, it could be used to measure the strength of the relation between readers' guesses of the writer's gender and the writer's actual gender. All correlations vary from plus one through zero to minus one. Plus one represents a perfect positive relation, e.g., every paper rated high (or low) by Rater 1 was also rated high (or low) by Rater 2. Minus one represents a perfect negative relation, e.g., every paper rated high (or low) by Rater 1 was rated low (or high) by Rater 2. A zero correlation indicates no systematic relation, e.g., the raters' grades are unrelated to each other.

A Final Word

Reading a research report is a skilled activity. Doing it well requires acquaintance with the conventions of thought and language of the empirical research community. We have tried to introduce you to many of these conventions in this chapter. Further development of your critical skills requires the use of the conventions in the careful analysis and evaluation of representative research studies. We hope that you will be able to read the studies in Section 2 with understanding and enjoyment. In addition, we hope that you will be able to sense some of the excitement of the research enterprise.

References

Campbell, D. T., & Stanley, J. C. (1963). *Experimental and quasi-experimental designs for research*. Boston: Houghton Mifflin.

Huck, S. W., & Sandler, H. M. (1979). *Rival hypotheses*. New York: Harper & Row.

Rosenthal, R. (1976). *Experimenter effects in behavioral research (enlarged ed.)*. New York: Irvington Press.

Swales, J., & Najjar, H. (1987). The writing of research article introductions. *Written Communication, 4* (2), 172-191.

Webb, E.J., Campbell, D.T., Schwartz, R.D., Sechrest, L., & Grove, J.B. (1966). *Nonreactive measures in the social sciences*. Boston, MA: Houghton Mifflin.

Part 2

Chapter 3   Reading Literature

To us, Hunt's research is a wonderful example of an exploratory study that yields the most satisfying result such a study can have: It surprised the socks off the researcher.

> It did not—as far as I can see from the answers I got to this section—lead a single one of my students to understand the point of the story, to savor or even understand the savage irony of the fact that the narrator had had his own sight miraculously restored and had "forgotten" it; that he is so unaffected—certainly unsaved—by the miracle that he not only denies miracles but is apparently going around corrupting people. . . . But they [the students] did not have the sensation, which I had hoped for and planned on at least some of them having, of having the story's meaning explode on their consciousness the way it did on mine the first time I read the story.
>
> I can't quote extensively enough from the responses of my students to the ending of the story to convey how desperately confused they were. . . . (p. 64-65)

Clearly, Hunt loved this story. It had affected him powerfully when he first read it, and he had expected at least some of his students to respond to it as he had. The observation that they were so universally confused was a surprise for Hunt, and with surprise came questions and hypotheses that are of interest to both the teacher and researcher. One can imagine that many teachers might be similarly surprised about the responses of their own students.

One of the engaging features of Hunt's presentation of his study is his understanding of its limitations. For example, on page [46], he warns the reader that because of the small size of his pool of data, his observations are statistically unreliable. On pages [47-49], he cautions the reader about reactivity, about how his method of observation may have influenced what was being observed. For example, he says that "the kind of question you ask or context you create will, of course, strongly affect the kind of answer or response you get. . . " ([p. 48]). On page [49], he expresses concern that researcher bias may have been involved when he selected "typical" data. Since all research methods have their limitations, Hunt quite rightly notes that his method may create difficulties:

> A lot of what I am doing involves ways of putting people in a position to demonstrate that they are engaging in certain cognitive processes without triggering or determining the process by my question, and it is entirely possible that I've outsmarted myself pretty regularly. (p. 47 MS)

What is good to see is Hunt's sensitivity to the possibility and his willingness to acknowledge that the method may not have yielded the information he had hoped for. Although he generously warns the reader to be aware of these potential problems of interpretation, it is clear that he takes his results seriously enough to be genuinely surprised by them.

Generally, exploratory studies can't yield firm conclusions. However, they can, and often do, suggest interesting hypotheses which can be tested in subsequent studies. Among these suggestions in Hunt's study are several ways in which more skilled readers may differ from less skilled ones. For example, Hunt notes that experienced readers are more likely than less experienced ones to respond to the striking image of the caterpillar with which the story opens. He suggests that "a fluent reader is operating on the assumption that divergences from what we might call 'normal' discourse are significant whereas an untrained or naive reader will not only not note such divergences, he will tend to ignore them" ([p. 51]). He also suggests ([p. 51-52]) that, of the two groups of readers, the less experienced ones are more likely to attend to the surface of the story and less to the author's purpose in telling it.

In addition to suggesting hypotheses, exploratory studies can provide striking counter-examples, a point we make in our discussion of case studies (p. 90-91). They can surprise us by showing us instances in which our assumptions are violated. For example, Hunt finds that the readers' predictions about the text "...both among my students and among my colleagues, were too diverse and too different in kind to make any kind of generalization about them easy" ([p. 53]). He remarks that observing the variety of readers' predictions "made me realize, in a way I had not before, just how different my students' readings—and my colleagues' as well—were. . ." (p. 53). Thus, while Hunt quite correctly indicates that firm conclusions should not be drawn from his study, the study is, nonetheless, a rich source of hypotheses for future studies and, therefore, a useful contribution to literacy studies.

Another interesting feature of Hunt's report is its format. Hunt presents us with a dual narrative. While leading us through the Graham Greene story as readers, he also presents us with his participants' responses to that story. By presenting his report this way, Hunt carries us along with both narratives and allows us to make our own comparisons. If he had presented his study in the standard APA format, described in Chapter 2, his results might have been less immediately available to us as readers. Although in many cases the use of the standard format is clearer and more appropriate, this is certainly one case where an unconventional organization conveys the message more forcefully.

44

Russell A. Hunt
St. Thomas University

What Happens When Our Students Read, and What Can We Do About It?

Let me begin with a quick summary of some of the important assumptions that lie behind the exercise which forms the basis for this paper (a fuller exposition can be found in my article in *College English*, April, 1982). Fundamentally, what is involved is my belief that as teachers of introductory literature we need to attend to—and, as well, to teach our students to attend to—the processes which occur as our students read rather than the results of those acts of reading. This is particularly true, I think, today, when our students are no longer largely drawn from the social classes that produce habitual and fluent readers of literature. There are important things one can learn about the skill of reading that the majority of our students haven't learned. I believe many of them can still be learned, and that learning them can make vitally important differences, not only to the ways in which our students relate to language in their other classes and in writing, but to the way they lead their lives.

A secondary assumption which is important to me is that what has been learned about the mechanics of reading in the last decade or so has dramatic implications for the teaching of literature—or, phrasing it a little more accurately, for teaching the students in our freshman and sophomore classes how to read literature. I am beginning with a complex of beliefs: (1) that it is possible to find some things out about the reading processes of our students by techniques like those of protocol analysis, (2) that it will help us to understand the kinds of things we find out if we begin with a notion of some of the basic components of the reading process, or with a simplified model of that process in our minds, and (3) that paying attention to those processes will be useful as a teaching device.

There are three fundamental sources for the kind of model of literary reading I'm trying to develop. One of them is the psycholinguistic work on reading by people like Kenneth and Yetta Goodman and Frank Smith, which offers, among other things, a view of reading as a meaning-driven process, one in which we project forward, construct meanings, and test what is on the page against our expectations. Another is in the work on basic language acquisition by Roger Brown, whose book, *A First Language,* has been very important to me, and which has much to say about the active and exploratory way in which we all acquire language skills. And finally, the increasingly important movement which is usually called reader-response criticism, particularly the work of Stanley Fish, has provided much of the theoretical underpinning for my study. Some of this work has been preoccupied with reading at quite different levels than the ones I am concerned with, but I have not yet seen any convincing evidence that the Goodman-Smith model of the basic reading process does not apply to and illuminate the reading of literature, or that Brown's view of the way infant human beings acquire language skills is not fruitfully analogous to the way our students acquire them. It seems clear, as well, that Fish's view of critical reading is applicable to the activities of the readers at the more basic level typified by our introductory literature students. One way of describing what I am attempting to do, in fact, is to say that I'm testing the hypothesis that it is useful to extend analogically what we know about basic language and language acquisition to more advanced forms of linguistic behavior and language acquisition, and to similarly extend what we know about more advanced ways of reading back down to basic levels.

There is a fundamental caution or two that I ought to offer here. For one thing, because what I'm doing looks at first glance suspiciously empirical, I should make clear that I'm not offering this work as empirical evidence of some general state of affairs, nor would I argue that my results are statistically significant. For one thing, there clearly is not enough data available to me yet; for another, as you will see, I'm still learning to make sense of what I have.

On the other hand, I do believe that examining the actions and utterances of real human beings individually considered remains the best way to understand human beings in general. There is a resonance, a recognition of pattern, that can occur when we watch human beings do things and listen to their discourse, and for the kinds of purposes most of us in the humanities are concerned with, that kind of understanding is more valuable than the results of calculating chi-squares and standard deviations among large groups of subjects.

Finally, before I describe exactly what it is I've been doing, a general caution—or perhaps it ought to be called an admission: windows on cognitive processes, as Kenneth Goodman calls them, are questionable and delicate devices, and I have no real certainty that what I think I'm finding out is what is really happening. The great difficulty with examining the cognitive processes we ourselves, or others, are engaged in, is the delicacy of the processes. In physics, it's only at the subatomic level that it becomes a major consideration that to look at something is to change it: in the kind of thing I'm trying to attend to, it's the very first problem you face. Attending to your own cognitive processes is virtually impossible, of course, because as soon as you're conscious of them they change and vanish; to ask someone else a question about theirs is to interrupt, even annihilate, those processes and to put something else in their place. None of these cautions will be new to anyone who's looked at the work Linda Flower and John Hayes have done on protocol analysis in problem solving and in writing behavior. A lot of what I'm doing involves ways of putting people in a position to demonstrate that they are engaging in certain cognitive processes without triggering or determining the process by my question, and it is entirely possible that I've outsmarted myself pretty regularly.

Its empirical status, however, is not my major concern; I am using the technique not only, or perhaps even primarily, as a research tool. What I have found is that the very act of paying attention to the matters that I am discussing here has been a profoundly useful teaching technique, for me as well as my students. Whether it actually affords us a useful window on the cognitive process of reading literature or not, it seems to me, it offers us a way to turn our students' attention away from the results of their reading and back toward the experience of reading it.

Now let me say some things about the nature of the particular exercise I want to describe here. It worked like this. I divided a short piece of fiction into nine segments, and then presented the segments one at a time, in order, to groups of readers, asking each to write something in response each time. In this particular case, I presented it to two separate groups—my last year's introductory literature class and a group of my colleagues on the St. Thomas faculty who volunteered to participate in the experiment. There were approximately equal numbers in each group (the number varied depending on how many participated in each episode, but tended to remain between ten and twenty). The students were simply all the members of my freshman class. My faculty volunteers comprised five members of the English department, three from history, two each from philosophy, education and Romance languages, and a sociologist, an anthropologist, a psychologist, and a specialist in Eastern religions. Not all of them continued through the whole experiment, and I'm not certain which dropped out because the responses were anonymous.

I decided the length of the segments by purely practical considerations—how much new material I wanted to present readers with at each reading, and how much would fit on a particular duplicated page or overhead projector transparency. The exact points at which I broke the story were determined in large part by the kinds of questions I wanted to ask and by whether I thought certain kinds of expectations or problems would likely be uppermost at that point in the story. For example, if you were to break in the middle of a word, clearly the most conscious process and the one you'd be most likely to tap would be the reader's attempt to predict the rest of that word. Similarly with a sentence or paragraph or narrative episode: there is a hierarchy of expectations operative in reading, and it seems clear that at the more basic or simple levels of text processing, our expectations and predictions operate very powerfully and within a very short time horizon, whereas at higher levels we not only tend to be projecting farther into the future, it is much harder for us to attend to that process of projection or to talk about what it is that we're projecting.

The kind of question you ask or context you create will, of course, strongly affect the kinds of answer or response you get, and thus, the results you get may not tell you much about the natural reading process. What they may do, however, is allow us to make some distinctions between various kinds of readers and readings. In fact, the making of some such distinctions—for instance, between the way the students tended to respond and the way my colleagues tended to respond—turned out to be one of my major purposes in this exercise.

What I'm going to do here now is go through that story, section by section, partly so that you can partake of the attempt to make sense out of it along with my students and my colleagues. I think it's a good idea for you to go through the story with my subjects because it's so difficult for us in the profession to reconstruct, *ex post facto*, the processes of our own reading. For one thing, we hate to admit, even to ourselves, that we've been wrong; we have a professional interest in being "good"—that is, correct—readers. In general, it is central to the reading process to form lots of hypotheses and abandon them as they're disproved; one of the dangers of *ex post facto* discussion—and even of exchanging responses as they occur in class, something I have done—is that people become committed to the defense of their own hypotheses. Part of my aim in focusing all this attention on process is to get rid of the notion of right answers—in fact, to get rid of the notion of "answers" altogether.

As I go through my results, I'm going to try to govern my selection of answers to quote by what I found typical—but, of course, what I found typical

48

may be conditioned by what I expected would be typical (after all, if the skull measurers in Stephen Jay Gould's *The Mismeasure of Man* found it possible to adjust something as concrete as their measurements of cranial capacity according to their preconceptions without knowing it . . .). My point here is that you should test what I quote my students and colleagues as saying and doing against your own experiences in class and against your own reading of the story. I hope that it's illuminating; I hope it doesn't contradict your experience, but rather suggests some things about it you hadn't noticed.

I did not give my class or my colleagues the title of the story. In part that was to avoid or minimize the chance that they would go and find a copy of it—either in order to outsmart me or simply because they got impatient and didn't want to wait to find out what was going to happen. That lack of context may be one of the factors acting to prevent this from being a picture of real reading, because the title of the story is probably a significant factor in the processing the normal reader would do, especially of the first few paragraphs. Even the name of the author might affect the way one reads the opening of this story—but, whatever problems it may cause, I didn't give the title or author to them and I'm not going to give it to you, at least not yet. I think what happens is of interest and value, but, as I have been saying, I would not offer it as a picture of what really happens when real readers read real texts in real living room chairs. Another reason I would hesitate to argue that it represents what readers do is that in most cases there was a significant lapse of time between episodes of the story. In each case, I presented the whole story to any point when I presented a new chunk; even so, I'm sure readers found themselves, as they engaged in this process, doing things they normally would not do as they read.

All these cautions aside, then, let me show you some of what happened during the two versions of this exercise. (I will skip some questions and will not try to summarize all my results, but I will stop after each section of the story.) Here is the first chunk of the story, and the questions I posed about it.

> She found me in the evening under trees that grew outside the village. I had never cared for her and would have hidden myself if I'd seen her coming. She was to blame, I'm certain, for her son's vices. If they were vices, but I'm very far from admitting that they were. At any rate he was generous, never mean, like others in the village I could mention if I chose.
>
> I was staring hard at a leaf or she would never have found me. It was dangling from its twig, its stalk torn across by the wind or else by a stone one of the village children had flung. Only the green tough skin of the stalk held there suspended. I was watching

closely, because a caterpillar was crawling across the surface, making the leaf sway to and fro. The caterpillar was aiming at the twig, and I wondered whether it would reach it in safety or whether the leaf would fall with it into the water. There was a pool underneath the trees, and the water always appeared red, because of the heavy clay in the soil.

I never knew whether the caterpillar reached the twig, for, as I've said, the wretched woman found me. The first I knew of her coming was her voice just behind my car.

1) What do you know about the mother?
2) What do you know about the son?
3) Ask three questions that you think are likely to be answered as you read the rest of the story.

The first two questions are, I think, obviously trick questions, because answering them involves perceiving that the story is being narrated by an unreliable—or at least characterized and thus not necessarily reliable—speaker. Almost all of my students offered, in response to them, paraphrases of what the narrator had told them about the mother and her son. "She was a wretched woman," said another, adding, "She was to blame for her son's vices. She likes to interfere." Part of this response, of course, can be ascribed to the students' inference that this must be one of those "reading comprehension" tests students are always being asked to take (I can't imagine why else they imagined that I was asking questions whose answers must have seemed so obvious and stupid to them). Still, it is clear that virtually none of them were alerted to the narrator's problematic position, either by the caution that it was a short story or by the narrator's own obvious—and questionable—value judgments.

There were confusions which suggested more traditional reading problems as well, of course. For instance, one response, "She was the reason that her son ran away and hid," clearly implies that the student was confusing the narrator and the woman's son (his third-person reference to her son in the first paragraph doesn't seem to have been noticed). A difficulty like this, however, is not only easier to see but is also of a kind that is almost certain to be corrected by further reading. Whether a reader can so easily recover from an inability to perceive the nature of the narrator is a more difficult question.

Almost as important an issue, I think, is the entire lack of concern among my students at this point for what that caterpillar and leaf are doing in the midst of this discourse. The third question I asked was designed, obviously, to allow a reader to raise longer term questions like this one by projecting forward into the story. Almost the first question I myself asked as I read the story for the first time—I can't be sure, of course; we never really know our own reading experience—involved what that strange image with its oddly specified red water was doing there. I won't suggest that I thought it must be symbolic and have something to do with survival and damnation, because I think that would be a lie (the kind we all tell so often about our readings, the kind of *ex post facto* rationalization which makes us all seem so much better readers afterward than we were at the time), but I will say I believe that no sophisticated reader of fiction would pass over that odd juxtaposition without attending to it, whether he consciously noticed it or not.

And indeed, of the nineteen responses to this section I elicited from my colleagues, five directly addressed the problem of the caterpillar's position in the story. For instance, one responded with this question: "Why was the narrator out under the trees ('outside the village') watching a caterpillar crawling across a leaf that dangles from a twig? And what is the connection between the caterpillar and the narrator (and perhaps the mother and the son)????" Three others mentioned the caterpillar, though they did not specifically pose questions about its thematic or artistic function or relevance.

On the other hand, of the seventeen freshman students who were presented with the same question, only four mentioned the caterpillar at all, and three of them posed essentially the same question: does the caterpillar reach the twig? None of them asked directly about the connection between the caterpillar and the rest of the story. One did ask why "the water was always red in its appearance," a question which might have thematic implications; but there is no evidence in the rest of that particular student's paper that he was thinking thematically.

It seems to me that there are important distinctions being suggested here between more fluent or sophisticated readers and the apprentice readers in our introductory literature courses. One of them might be formulated this way: from the beginning, a fluent reader is operating on the assumption that divergences from what we might call "normal" discourse are significant or will be shown to be so later in the narrative, whereas an untrained or naive reader will not only not make note of such divergences, he will tend to ignore them.

A second, perhaps equally important difference has to do with the reader's attention to what Seymour Chatman calls the "story" at the expense of "discourse." (The phrase is his formulation of the Russian formalist distinction between fabula and sjuzhet, between the narrative surface and what it is that is being narrated.) The freshmen who wanted to know whether the caterpillar ever reached the twig were asking a question that sophisticated readers would guess to be irrelevant, because a sophisticated reader would be far more likely to see that the caterpillar and the leaf were part of the discourse, not part of the story.

The next installment of the story was presented as a slightly longer chunk of the story's beginning, and ended in the middle of a sentence. In this case, I asked six questions (it was too many, and I won't do that again).

> "I've been looking in all the pubs for you," she said in her old shrill voice. It was typical of her to say "all the pubs" when there were only two in the place. She always wanted credit for trouble she hadn't really taken.
>
> I was annoyed and I couldn't help speaking a little harshly. "You might have saved yourself the trouble," I said, "you should have known I wouldn't be in a pub on a fine night like this."
>
> The old vixen became quite humble. She was always smooth enough when she wanted anything. "It's for my poor son," she said. That meant that he was ill. When he was well I never heard her say anything better than "that dratted boy." She'd make him be in the house by midnight every day of the week, as if there were any serious mischief a man could get up to in a little village like ours. Of course we soon found a way to cheat her, but it was the principle of the thing I objected to—a grown man of over thirty ordered about by his mother, just because she hadn't a husband to control. But when he was ill, though it might be with only a small/

1) Write the end of the unfinished sentence which ends this excerpt from the story.
2) What do you think is likely to happen in the next 50-100 words of the story? You can either describe, summarize, or explain it, or you can "write" the next 50-100 words as you think they might be coming.
3) What important things have you learned about the mother?
4) What important things have you learned about the son?
5) Do you have an impression of the narrator's personality? What are its main features?
6) Ask three questions which you want to have answered and which you think will probably be answered in the rest of the story.

Question 5 is perhaps the most important, because it tips my hand and directs the reader's attention to the question of the narrator, whether the reader had noticed him before or not. As one might expect, the frequency of responses referring directly to the narrator's reliability increases after this section. On the other hand, it is no clearer than before that the students in general made any operative distinction between the author and the narrator. Question 6, which probably duplicates the second question, in that both ask the reader to project forward, was not answered very often. This may be because six questions are simply too many to expect volunteers to answer.

Asking the students to complete the incomplete sentence is a device whose aim is fairly obvious, and indeed its effect was as I expected. When the students compared their responses with those of others, it dramatized in a way that my telling them could hardly do that texts put complex pressure on expectations. Virtually everyone who answered that question began with a noun or a noun phrase denoting some trivial ailment (nine used the word "cold"; two others used "ailment"; and there were others like "chill," "touch of the flu," "bug," and "fever") and every one continued with a similar syntactic structure saying that the mother showed real concern.

The second question, like many others in this exercise, is far more useful as a teaching than as a research tool. Like the sentence completion, it helped the students to realize the extent to which each of them was bringing his or her own assumptions to the story. One student predicted, for instance, an elaborately developed story which clearly arose out of her own interests.

> I think that the boy, only I guess from the story he is not a boy, but a man, I think that he will probably realize a few good points about his mother. Maybe she pampered him when he was sick. The boy may be grateful for this. He will likely realize just how over protective his mother really is and maybe decide to get out on his own, away from her.

In general, however, the responses to this question, both among the students and among my colleagues, were too diverse and too different in kind to make generalizing about them very easy. On the other hand, reading them myself made me realize, in a way that I had not before, just how different from mine my students' readings—and my colleagues' as well—were, at least at this early point in the story. One colleague, for instance, offered the following prediction of what was going to happen:

> Mother asks the man for money so that her son can get treatment in a hospital in one of the big cities (she can't pay for the trip herself). The man initially refuses to give her the money but finally agrees to loan the money to the son if he works in his store in the evening to pay it back. He also insists that the son will have to live in a rented room rather than with his mother because he will have to work long hours and get home late. Mother doesn't like that idea at all but finally agrees so her son can have the treatment he needs. And they lived happily ever after.

53

There is, of course, some doubt about how seriously to take that—and a number of the other—"predictions" of what will happen in the story. Nonetheless, it is a healthy reminder to everyone concerned of the variety of readers there are out there.

There is an interesting contrast in the responses to question 5. Among the students there was lots of intense but rather generalized hostility toward the narrator. A selection: "I get the impression that he likes to judge people. . . . . [His] main feature is his hatred for the mother and explaining how he feels about the village." "He really likes to find fault with people. He is probably an unhappy person. He seems to have a lot of anger. He has a childish behavior." "The narrator seems to be very opinionated and made rash decisions about the other characters of this story." "His personality dominates in respect to the harsh, opinionated judgments of the son's mother. It is clear that he is bitter against her, doubting her sincerity of treatment to the son."

Among my colleagues, as one might expect, the narrator tended to be the subject of much more sophisticated analysis. For instance: "aware of his limitations, but unable to do anything [but] accept them. . . capable of committing an isolated violent act." They were also less consistently eager to mistrust him: "He is perceptive and competent: he knows what the old woman is up to, and how to handle her, and he is not afraid to act accordingly." They also tended to pay more attention to the specifics of the text. Their skepticism tended to be based on observation of detail: "He describes things to his advantage—the deceit involved in coming home late described as right, etc." And only among the faculty did I find analysis based on emotional impact of physical details: "Emotionally cold—would watch a caterpillar to see if it would make the twig or fall off and drown. He could have helped it." No student tried to describe this kind of connection.

The third section of the story was another short one.

chill, it was "my poor son."

"He's dying," she said, "and God knows what I shall do without him."

"Well, I don't see how I can help you." I said. I was angry, because he'd been dying once before and she'd done everything but actually bury him. I imagined it was the same sort of dying this time, the sort a man gets over. I'd seen him about

the week before on his way up the hill to see the big-breasted girl at the farm. I'd watched him till he was like a little black dot, which stayed suddenly by a square grey box in a field. That was the barn where they used to meet. I've very good eyes and it amuses me to try how far and how clearly they can see. I met him again some time after midnight and helped him get into the house without his mother knowing, and he was well enough then—only a little sleepy and tired.

The old vixen was at it again. "He's been asking for you," she shrilled at me.

"If he's as ill as you make out," I said, "it would be better for him to ask for a doctor."

"Doctor's there, but he can't do anything." That startled me for a moment, I'll admit it, until I thought, "the old devil's malingering. He's got some plan or other." He was quite clever enough to cheat a doctor. I had seen him throw a fit that would have deceived Moses.

"For God's sake come," she said, "he seems frightened." Her voice broke quite genuinely, for I suppose in her way

1) As before, the fragment ends with an incomplete sentence. Finish the sentence.
2) What do you think might happen in the next 50-100 words? Either write the next 50-100 words or summarize what you think is going to happen.
3) Did anything in this new section surprise you?

The incomplete sentence here opened a window on what I suspect may be an important pattern. Among my colleagues, not one produced a completion which suggested anything other than that the mother "cared" or "really did love" her son, and each completion produced a more or less shapely, and certainly coherent, sentence. Among a high proportion of the students, though, something else happened. The hostility toward the mother on the part of the narrator seems to have been so pervasive that they found it impossible to believe anything charitable about her (or, possibly, to believe the narrator would say anything charitable about her)—so impossible that they ignored the clear meaning of the phrase "quite genuinely." They also often ignored the grammatical structure of the sentence. Here are some typical completions:

. . . [in her way] she thought that this might persuade me to come with her.
. . . [in her way] of speaking, there was always some hint of over acting.
. . . [in her way] this was the only method of getting me to come.
. . . [in her way] she never thought of her son trying to escape.
. . . [in her way] it was as close as it ever could be to genuine.

Even when the students were prepared to accept the implications of the word "genuine," they were far more eager than my colleagues to ascribe the woman's concern to less than altruistic motives. In her way, one said, "she was really frightened of the fact that he might die." Or, "[in her way] it took a lot to practically beg me to come." Or "[in her way] of thinking, she might lose her only source of security." Only four of the twenty students who responded were prepared to allow the narrator to say—or to say themselves; it's not always clear that they are speaking with the "narrator's voice"—that the woman, even "in her way," really did love her son.

There was little pattern, again, among the answers to the question about being surprised. It is interesting that three of the students were surprised to see the narrator watching the son and commenting on the excellence of his eyes; only one faculty member remarked on this. Three students, as well, and one of my colleagues, were surprised to find the narrator was not a doctor. I found it interesting to look back over the story and see why it never occurred to me to think of him as a doctor, at least not consciously. The only reason I can find is the phrase, "of course we soon found a way to cheat her," which doesn't sound very doctorly to me.

> she was fond of him. I couldn't help pitying her a little, for I knew that he had never cared a mite for her and had never troubled to disguise the fact. I left the trees and the red pool and the struggling caterpillar, for I knew that she would never leave me alone, now that her "poor boy" was asking for me. Yet, a week ago there was nothing she wouldn't have done to keep us apart. She thought me responsible for his ways, as though any mortal man could have kept him off a likely woman when his appetite was up.
>
> I think it must have been the first time I had entered their cottage by the front door, since I came to the village ten years ago. I threw an amused glance at his window. I thought I could see the marks on the wall of the ladder we'd used the week before.
>
> We'd had a little difficulty in putting it straight, but his mother slept sound. He had brought the ladder down from the barn, and when he'd got safely in, I carried it up there again. But you could never trust his word. He'd lie to his best friend, and when I reached the barn I found the girl had gone.
>
> If he couldn't bribe you with his mother's money, he'd bribe you with other people's promises.
>
> I began to feel uneasy directly I got inside the door. It was natural that the house should be quiet, for the pair of them never had any friends to stay, although the old woman had a sister-in-law living

56

only a few miles away. But I didn't like the sound of the doctor's feet, as he came downstairs to meet us. He'd twisted his face into a pious solemnity for our benefit, as though there was something holy about death, even about the death of my friend.

"He's conscious," he said, "but he's going. There's nothing I can do. If you want him to die in peace, better let his friend go along up. He's frightened about something."

1) Has your impression of the mother been modified since your first introduction to her? In what way?

2) How about your impression of her son?

3) What kinds of things have you learned about the narrator, and what kind of judgment are you forming of him?

4) Ask three questions that (a) you want to have answered; (b) you think are likely to be answered before the story ends; and (c) are about different aspects of the story—are, in other words, different kinds of questions.

In response to the first question here, virtually everyone reported growing sympathy for the mother. She seemed to one student, for instance, "no longer a villainess, but rather a victim of cruel dishonesty. A frightened woman doing what she believes is right, but not clever enough to see the truth." (It may be significant that this student also comments on the narrator as "not as virtuous and innocent as he first seemed. But he is loyal and honest.") Only one reader—a colleague, one of two who were at this point put off by the whole process and apparently bored by the story—said anything negative about the mother, referring to "the self-concern of her own words."

There was much less unanimity about the son. Students tended overwhelmingly to be disapproving of the son, in conventional moral terms. This may, of course, be due to the fact that it's a class—an English class, no less—and those sorts of values often seem to be pushed in English classes. Only one student claimed to feel pity for the son. My colleagues, on the other hand, were much less disapproving, and, as you might predict, more analytical. "A sad case," they said, "insecure." One was surprised to find him bisexual, having concluded that he and the narrator were lovers. Another claimed to be surprised to find me using a masculine pronoun to refer to the narrator, asserting that until then the sex of the narrator couldn't be determined.

Comments on the narrator reflect the pattern of mistrust and hostility that had been building in previous installments, with one exception, a faculty member who said the narrator is "lacking verve, but for all that, a basically good person."

Questions about the story, here as elsewhere, were almost universally questions about the world reported in the story, not about narrative surface or structure. Most inquired about the psychological motivation of character or about matters of fact. The most common questions, of course, were whether the son were really dying and what he was frightened of. Only two questions came close to being concerned with patterns. One colleague asked, "why did the narrator bring the broken leaf-stem into the story?" which may be a question about psychological motivation, or may be intended to be a question about authorial purpose or the place the image has in the text as a whole. Another question involved the story's setting: a student asked, "where is it set in—what country? It sounds eighteenth century European." An interesting question, I think, and one which, when it has been raised, changes the way you attend to the story.

> The doctor was right. I could tell that as soon as I bent under the lintel and entered my friend's room. He was propped up on a pillow, and his eyes were on the door, waiting for me to come. They were very bright and frightened, and his hair lay across his forehead in sticky stripes. I'd never realized before what an ugly fellow he was. He had got sly eyes that looked at you too much out of the corners, but when he was in ordinary health, they held a twinkle that made you forget the slyness. There was something pleasant and brazen in the twinkle, as much as to say "I know I'm sly and ugly. But what does that matter? I've got guts." It was that twinkle, I think, some women found attractive and stimulating. Now when the twinkle was gone, he looked a rogue and nothing else.
>
> I thought it my duty to cheer him up, so I made a small joke out of the fact that he was alone in bed. He didn't seem to relish it, and I was beginning to fear that he, too, was taking a religious view of his death, when he told me to sit down, speaking quite sharply.
>
> "I'm dying," he said, talking very fast, "and I want to ask you something. That doctor's no good—he'd think me delirious. I'm frightened, old man. I want to be reassured," and then after a long pause, "someone with common sense." He slipped a little farther down in his bed.
>
> "I've only once been badly ill before," he said. "That was before you settled here. I wasn't much more than a boy. People tell me that I was even supposed to be dead. They were carrying me out to burial, when a doctor stopped them just in time.

I'd heard plenty of cases like that, and I saw no reason

1) Finish the sentence, and explain what you think is likely to happen in the next couple of paragraphs.

About half the students completed the sentence so as to express the narrator's belief in the situation the son describes; a couple said things like "[I saw no reason] that someone would want to do this to him, he never hurt anyone."

As seems usual, I found no clear pattern among the predictions about what was going to happen—other than that half of them involved the notion that the son is afraid he's going to be buried alive (which, interestingly, is exactly what the narrator thinks). The class included one pollyanna who invariably predicted, a la Melina Mercouri in *Never on Sunday*, that they would all go to the seashore. Here the prediction was: "I think that the boy will recover from his illness and will go somewhere, to start a new life."

why he should want to tell me about it. And then I thought I saw his point. His mother had not been too anxious once before to see if he were properly dead, though I had little doubt that she made a great show of grief. "My poor boy. I don't know what I shall do without him." And I'm certain that she believed herself then, as she believed herself now. She wasn't a murderess. She was only inclined to be premature.

"Look here, old man," I said, and I propped him a little higher on his pillow, "you needn't be frightened. You aren't going to die, and anyway I'd see that the doctor cut a vein or something before they moved you. But that's all morbid stuff. Why, I'd stake my shirt that you've got plenty more years in front of you. And plenty more girls too," I added to make him smile.

"Can't you cut out all that?" he said, and I knew then that he had turned religious. "Why," he said, "if I lived, I wouldn't touch another girl. I wouldn't, not one."

I tried not to smile at that, but it wasn't easy to keep a straight face. There's always something a bit funny about a sick man's morals. "Anyway," I said, "you needn't be frightened."

"It's not that," he said. "Old man, when I came round that other time, I thought that I'd been dead. It wasn't like sleep at all. Or rest in peace. There was someone there, all round me, who knew everything. Every girl I'd ever had. Even that young one who hadn't understood. It was before your time.

59

She lived a mile down the road, where Rachel lives now, but she and her family went away afterwards. Even the money I'd taken from mother, I don't call that stealing. It's in the family, I never had a chance to explain. Even the thoughts I'd had. A man can't help his thoughts."

"A nightmare," I said.

"Yes, it must have been a dream, mustn't it? The sort of dream people do get when they are ill. And I saw what was coming to me too, I can't bear being hurt. It wasn't fair. And I wanted to faint and I couldn't, because I was dead."

"In the dream," I said. His fear made me nervous. "In the dream," I said again.

"Yes, it must have been a dream—mustn't it?—because I woke up. The curious thing was I felt quite well and strong. I got up and stood in the road, and a little farther down, kicking up the dust, was a small crowd, going off with a man—the doctor who had stopped them burying me."

"Well," I said.

"Old man," he said, "suppose it was true. Suppose I had been dead. I believed it then, you know, and so did my mother. But you can't trust her. I went straight for a couple

1) Finish the sentence.
2) In this section, do you learn anything surprising about the characters? Are any suspicions confirmed?
3) At this point, do you have any suspicions as to what's likely to happen in the story as a whole—what the story's going to turn out to be "about"?

A couple of students and one colleague completed this sentence not with a period of time, but with people ("[went straight for a couple] of friends"). This poses an interesting question: would you have made that choice if you hadn't heard me read "went straight" as opposed to "went/straight for"? Knowing how the sentence actually finished, is it possible to reconstruct the first reaction to the phrase?

In a similar confusion about idiom, five students—and one of my colleagues—were surprised when they read "old man" as signifying that the characters were in fact old men. "Maybe it's just an expression they are using," said one.

A continuing phenomenon which surfaces again here is the readers' trust of the narrator. However much they may know that he's biased and merely a character in the story, they keep coming back to his opinions and values as somehow privileged (partly, I suspect, this is related to the penchant, particularly among the students, for calling him "the author"). A couple of students, for instance, were surprised to see the son becoming religious; one of my colleagues accepted the narrator's judgment that the son "apparently cares little for his mother." Hostility toward the narrator, however, has hardly vanished: one faculty member says "the detached attitude of the narrator, his observant/expectant attitudes is beginning to look like voyeurism, touched with sadism."

Perhaps the most extreme view (though not entirely untypical) is this comment, from a student: "all the characters seem to have switched roles. The man seems to be very sincere and realistic. The mother seems to be the one in question. And the narrator seems to be very nice and trustworthy."

All the predictions about what's likely to happen have now become ponderously philosophical. Everyone seems to know that the story's going to have to do with death; many seem to have inferred that it's not going to be a conventional plotted story with a series of events. One faculty member said he was beginning to suspect "that the story is an attack upon religious-grounded fear surrounding death/after-life." Another proposed that "the friend is a minister or clergyman who will offer some type of last rites or spiritual consolation" (how that can be reconciled with snickering about a "sick man's morals" is hard to understand).

Unanimity was still well out of reach, however. One student proposed this scenario: "I think the old lady might be involved in some kind of religious ceremony for example K.K.K. or witchcraft, something weird like that. I think she might even be trying to kill her son."

> of years. I thought it might be a sort of second chance. Then things got fogged and somehow . . . . It didn't seem really possible. It's not possible. Of course it's not possible. You know it isn't, don't you?"
>
> "Why no," I said. "Miracles of that sort don't happen nowadays. And anyway, they aren't likely to happen to you, are they? And here of all places under the sun."
>
> "It would be so dreadful," he said, "if it had been true, and I'd got to go through all that again. You don't know what things were going to happen to me in that dream.
>
> And they'd be worse now." He stopped and then, after a moment,

61

he added as though he were stating a fact: "When one's dead there's no unconsciousness any more forever."

"Of course it was a dream," I said and squeezed his hand. He was frightening me with his fancies. I wished that he'd

1) Complete the sentence this excerpt leaves incomplete.

2) Has your view of what the story's going to turn out to be "about" changed as a result of this section?

Of the students, fifteen said that the narrator wished he'd change the subject. Two wanted him to fall asleep and one completed it this way: "[I wished that he'd] died the first time around." Most of my colleagues answered similarly, but one seemed to ignore the narrator's values altogether: "[I wished that he'd] never forsaken his promise to go straight after that strange recovery." (It's in phrases like this, I think, that you can tell what bases readers are really operating on, as opposed to what they say in answer to direct questions. It seems clear that at least that reader hasn't internalized any real hostility to, or skepticism about, the narrator.) On the other hand, one extremist completed it this way: "[I wished that he'd] died before I arrived."

In answer to the second question, our pollyanna held on to the Melina Mercouri view ("I still feel that he will live and continue his life in a new place"), and another proposes that this time he will "take the warning to heart and remain straight for the rest of his life," but, in general, most readers took the view expressed by one of my colleagues: "Death is the focus of this story, not the relationship between the main characters." Many readers had expected up until this point that the son "had some trick up his sleeve," and now decided that he is genuinely going to die. But, as one reader asked, "what will the story be about after he dies? It had dealt mainly with him up until now."

die quickly, so that I could get away from his sly, bloodshot and terrified eyes and see something cheerful and amusing, like the Rachel he had mentioned, who lived a mile down the road.

"Why," I said, "if there had been a man about working miracles like that, we should have heard of others, you may be sure. Even poked away in this God-forsaken spot," I said.

"There were some others," he said. "But the stories only went round among the poor, and they'll believe anything, won't they? There were lots of diseased and crippled they said he'd cured. And there was a man, who'd been born blind, and he came and just touched his eyelids

62

and sight came to him. Those were all old wives' tales, weren't they?" he asked me, stammering with fear, and then lying suddenly still and bunched up at the side of the bed.

1) React to it in any way that seems appropriate.

2) If I told you that there was only one more paragraph to the story (if you were reading the story in a normal way, you could see that), how would you think it could possibly end? What questions would have to be answered in order for the author to have the story "finish"?

I expected that many readers would react strongly to the narrator's wish that his "friend" would die, and more than half of the students did. The most charitable reading was "perhaps he said that just because he couldn't stand to see his friend the way he is." Of eighteen student responses, only five mentioned any awareness of the religious overtones which were so much more obvious to most of my colleagues. Student awareness of this issue ranges from the general "the story is taking on an interesting spiritual tone" through a couple of specific mentions of Jesus, to this: "I was surprised that the story seems to go back to the days when Jesus was alive and the son may have been saved by Jesus himself when he was a boy."

My favorites, though, were these two: "I think the story is getting very confusing, and that the narrator is beginning to get mysterious also." "This is starting to get very weird, but it does sound familiar."

In general, my colleagues were far more aware of the wider issues, and far less surprised by "die quickly." "I had never imagined as I read that the story could have been set in ancient times," says one. "I assumed that it had to have happened in the last one hundred years. —words like 'pub' and 'doctor' seem out of place." Or: "this changes the whole story again and I don't like it. The miracle man character comes in at the end and trivializes, by an easy explanation, all the mysteries that had cropped up before. BOO!!"

The idea that there was only one more paragraph seemed to startle people and force them to think of outrageous or dramatic endings—or else just give up on the story by saying that the son dies and that's about it. One student proposes that the narrator may reform because of the son's repentant example. But my favorite was this: "it seems like the story will have a strange ending and the question's answers will not be ones I want to know about."

My colleagues mostly speculated on the likely effect of the son's death (they all seemed to assume that the sudden stillness was death; very few of my students seemed sure of that) on the narrator. Only one faculty member still thought the story might end happily: "being an incurable romantic, I imagine 'the man' is going to appear physically/psychically and comfort the poor fellow, who will then die peacefully, and his friend will acquire a new lease on life."

> I began to say, "Of course, they were all lies," but I stopped, because there was no need. All I could do was to go downstairs and tell his mother to come up and close his eyes. I wouldn't have touched them for all the money in the world. It was a long time since I'd thought of that day, ages and ages ago, when I felt a cold touch like spittle on my lids and opening my eyes had seen a man like a tree surrounded by other trees walking away.

> 1) Are there still important questions which you think the story ought to have answered that remain unanswered? (I mean more specific questions than "what does it mean?")
>
> 2) What many readers do when they come to a point in a story where they are surprised (particularly if it's the ending) is to look back through the story for information or ideas which justify the surprise, which make it something other than just a random accident. Do that now; the entire story is reproduced on the back of this sheet. Then, after having looked back, answer the next question.
>
>   What two or three parts of the story seem relevant to this ending? Where did you look in the story for things which might explain or prepare you for the ending?
>
> 3) Did the ending change how you felt about, or what you thought about, anything specific in the story? What?

At this point I have to make a confession. For all practical, pedagogical purposes, at least as they are traditionally conceived, this exercise was a failure. It did not—as far as I can see from the answers I got to this section—lead a single one of my students to understand the point of the story, to savor or even understand the savage irony of the fact that the narrator has had his own sight miraculously restored and has "forgotten" it; that he is so unaffected—certainly unsaved—by the miracle that he not only denies miracles but is apparently going around actively corrupting people.

For more long-term purposes, of course, the exercise was useful—I learned a lot, for instance, and am still learning from it. I think that a lot of my students learned a good deal about being conscious of process as they read. But they did not have the sensation, which I had hoped for and planned on at least some of them having, of having the story's meaning explode on their consciousness the way it did on mine the first time I read the story.

I can't quote extensively enough from the responses of my students to the ending of the story to convey how desperately confused they were, and how defensive about their confusion. Their responses to the first question, for instance, suggested repeatedly that the only question they really wanted to ask was, "What does it mean?" Here are some samples.

> Is this narrator the blind guy that the 'Doctor' let see,
> is he the Doctor, another patient of the Doctor? Does the dead
> son go through the same thing again where they know everything
> he did wrong? What is the significance of the trees
> in the last sentence—anything to do with the first sentence?

> What did he die of? What was his dream about? Did
> the mother in fact have anything to do with it?

> Well, I don't really understand what exactly happened.
> What is he talking about in the last paragraph? What
> exactly had happened a long time ago (ages and ages ago)?

> Yes. (1) Why all the talk and interest at the beginning
> of the story when he was by the trees (2) what exactly did
> the narrator have to do with his mother (3) who was her son?
> (4) what part in time did they live in?

> 1. Who was this Rachel girl? 2. Who was the girl who hadn't
> understood? and why did they move away afterwards?

> 1) Just what exactly did the boy die from? 2) What was he actually
> afraid of? Dying? 3) Why did the mother and son seem to be cast-
> aways?

In some cases you can feel the process beginning that might produce an answer. One wondered, for instance, about the narrator: "The narrator says it was a long time since he'd thought of that day. I wonder what made him think about it now." But in general the more sophisticated the student, the more the prose retreats into generalities. "All the really important questions were answered; like what was on the son's mind, was he really sick . . . Only the unimportant questions are left like what happens to the author? The mother? The story seems to answer most of the questions brought up at the beginning of the story." Or another: "Clearly, none of us were ready or had suspected the outcome. I think that there may have been more important questions to answer like 'What about the mother's animosity,' and that sort of thing but all such questions rapidly fade away when one experiences a small bit of the son's fear and what he spoke of in his final words."

My favorite, however, is this response to the question whether there are still important questions which you think the story ought to have answered: "Only if the caterpillar made it without falling in the puddle. Also how old is the mother if the son is an old man."

Sending the readers back to the text, as the second question attempted to do, solved no problems for them, nor did the information about the author and title of the story they found on the back of the sheet (the story is "The Second Death," by Graham Greene, incidentally). The question about whether the ending changed the readers' reaction to the story didn't help either. Here are some responses to that question.

> I never thought that vices like drinking and womanizing and taking money from your parents really were sins. But they are being punished in this story.

> I was wondering about 3/4 through what was going to happen strangely. Now that I've read the ending I know something strange did happen, but I still don't understand what and how, and who was involved and who wasn't. I don't like surprise endings at all. This story confused me.

> It changed my thoughts about the boy: at the beginning I thought he was pulling another prank. I'm also surprised about the narrator, he seems to be more sympathetic and really care for the boy, whereas he never did at the beginning of the story.

> I guess I felt really sorry for the boy at the end. His friend could have been more understanding. The narrator does not seem quite so harsh at the end as he did in the first of the story.
> The ending changed my view of the story because I thought there would be more between the mother and son, mother and narrator, and narrator and son. The story also seemed to

take a very sharp turn towards religion, which was in direct
contrast to what the narrator had first said about the son.

I was almost as surprised at the number of my colleagues who did not
demonstrate an understanding of the story's irony (they, like some of the
students, may of course have understood more than the kind of question I
asked let them talk about). Some, of course, did markedly better than the
students. Here's one comment: "I feel I would like to have an inkling why the
2 people who were touched by the Miracle did not become saved, rather why
G.G. chose to deviate so far from the accepted surmise. On further thought I
have a possible reason, but nothing in the story to confirm it (so far)—"
Another responded to the question about whether the ending had changed
anything with this:

> Yes—the last couple of episodes made it clear that the
> story could be alluding to the miracles of Jesus Christ
> and what happened to the people on whom he worked his
> miracles. It also indicates or raises the question about
> "The Second Death". Was it a physical death, or the
> seemingly spiritual death of the narrator. He seemed to
> have none of the compassion for the dying man that
> someone else had once had for him. Someone had touched
> his eyes and given him sight; he would not even touch his
> friend's eyes to close them in death. Was the Miracle
> wasted on him? Is he dead spiritually? Or will this be for
> him a spiritual re-awakening?"

This is, of course, not all that's involved. It had not seemed to me at the
outset that it would be necessary to bring in the specific Bible references,
because they did not seem to me to be absolutely necessary in order to "get"
the story's impact. But as a pedagogical device in the class I now did that, and
also distributed them to my colleagues.

Luke 7: 11-17

And it came to pass the day after, that he went into a city
called Cain; and many of his disciples went with him, and much
people. Now when he came nigh to the gate of the city, behold,
there was a dead man carried out, the only son of his mother,
and she was a widow: and much people of the city was with
her. And when the Lord saw her, he had compassion on her,
and said unto her, Keep not. And he came and touched the bier:
and they that bare him stood still. And he said, Young man, I

say unto thee, Arise. And he that was dead sat up, and began to speak. And he delivered him to his mother. And there came a fear on all: and they glorified God, saying, That a great prophet is risen up among us: and, That God hath visited his people. And this rumor of him went forth throughout all Judea, and throughout all the region round about.

Mark 8: 22-26

And he cometh to Bethseda: and they bring a blind man unto him, and besought him to touch him. And he took the blind man by the hand, and led him out of the town; and when he had spit on his eyes, and got his hands upon him, he asked him if he saw ought. And he looked up, and said, I see men as trees, walking. After that he put his hands upon his eyes, and made him look up: and he was restored, and saw every man clearly. And he sent him away to his house, saying, Neither go into the town, nor tell it to any in the town.

Does reading this make any difference to your response to "The Second Death"? What difference? Explain on the back of this sheet.

Although virtually all of my students answered that reading the two passages did make a difference to their response, they were generally not able to tell me specifically what sort of a difference. All of them felt that it "explained" the ending, but I couldn't see that they understood the "explained" ending any better. For instance: "It confirmed my theory that the son had been raised from the dead by Jesus. The 2nd reading helped me understand the ending of the story. The narrator must have been visited by Jesus."

Two respondents admitted that the readings had been no help.

> Well it confused me more . . . uh, I guess the spittle on the narrator's cold lips [sic] has some significance, but what I don't know. Well the only difference all this makes is I now feel that the narrator of "2nd Death" was a religious man, a man once not religious until he got a "2nd chance" at life and became religious.

> Now we can make more sense out of the bizzare ending in the story. To tell you the truth, I still don't know what the heck the ending was about. I think it might have something to do with seeing his friend being taken up to heaven or the author is going blind because he is seeing men like trees. Therefore, he must be regressing in his vision. Or he was having hallucinations because he was upset over the death of his friend or on cheap drugs or something.

> Maybe when he saw men like trees, maybe he just saw trees
> and decided to put a metaphor or simile to it because he
> felt like getting fancy. Or maybe he saw men in trees
> because these men were in costumes that looked like trees.
> Actually, this story made me very frustrated and angry
> because when I don't know the answer to something I get mad!

I share that student's frustration. It seems to me there should be a way to help him, and his peers, learn how to read stories like this one—no, to read literature in general—in more effective ways. What these experiments have taught me over the last few years, more than anything else, is how much there is for students to learn about the way we read, and how little we normally do to help them. Sure, for some of the students in my class, the final discussion and explanation of the story's ending may have helped them to go at the next story they read. They told me it did, of course; and I could tell you that my students came out of this exercise—and all the similar things we did last year—better readers. But I always remember Mina Shaughnessy's caution: somewhere she says that we have made the classroom as private as a bedroom and the triumphs that are reported from there should be given about the same level of credence.

In some ways, this whole exercise has been an attempt to find a way to help someone to "get" the story, like a joke, without having to explain it. For many of my students, for most people generally, I believe, it is with a story as it is with a joke: if it has to be explained it's no longer effective, though it might have some theoretical interest. In general, it's harder for less sophisticated readers to recreate their sense of expectation and doubt and suspense. They already know "how it comes out." A Shakespeare teacher once told me in an undergraduate seminar that every time Macbeth meets the witches, he thought that maybe this time the poor sucker wouldn't fall for their line. It's a skilled reader that recreates the process of assembling the facts and the inferences on a second or third reading. It's worth considering, I think, what might happen if one did this after the subjects had read the story through, or did it with the same story a second time.

There are other ways this device or variations of it can be used. One is to study individual readings through the process of a staged reading like this, in perhaps something like the ways David Bleich and Norman Holland have done, but with attention rather to the ongoing interaction between reader and text, and with more attention to what connects readings and urges them toward similarity than to what makes readers and readings individual. Another is to exchange the comments communally, and thus help the readers form what Stanley Fish calls an interpretive community. However one uses it, it seems to me it is one of the few ways we can get access to an important cognitive process. Even more important, it is a way to remind ourselves how differently people read texts, and that there really are incomplete and inadequate ways to read texts.

One of the important advantages of this technique as a teaching tool, it seems to me, is that it addresses what I think is a central problem of literature teaching. One of the notable differences between the kind of reading a fluent reader of literature performs and that of most of my introductory literature students is that the fluent reader is attending to his experience of the text—his reading is overwhelmingly self-conscious. Indeed, it seems to me one might argue that the most useful way of discriminating between literature and other kinds of discourse is that literature not only invites, but perhaps depends upon, being read in this schizophrenic, self-conscious way. What this technique does is (1) help students to be aware of their own reading as a process, (2) help them to see that it's valuable and enjoyable in itself, regardless of consequences or after effects, (3) perhaps help them to gain some measure of control over the way they read (characteristically, my students treat reading as something that happens to them, rather than something they do). Finally, it might sometimes help them see the point of the sort of text—like, perhaps, "The Second Death"—whose existence as an aesthetic object depends on the participation of an active, synthesizing reader.

Author's Comment—Russell Hunt

In an article about the changes in my own and my colleagues' ideas about reading, teaching and learning over the decade between 1977 and 1987, I said that when you stop being embarrassed by what you used to believe, you've probably died and simply not noticed (Hunt, 1987: 148). So, it's no surprise that much about this study seems misconceived to me now, almost ten years after it was conducted. Most obviously, the ease with which I assumed that I knew what Graham Greene's story was "about" or "did" seems to me a very strikingly questionable assumption. Almost equally important is what I now see as my underestimation of the power of the reading situation, that is, the way the students and my colleagues understood the social situation of my study — their task, and my purposes — to alter the stances readers take toward texts, and thus to affect central and important parts of the reading process.

On the other hand, there's a good deal about the study which I'm still happy with. More than anything else, I'm still pleased with the way in which it tried to address, directly and perhaps naively, a question which many English teachers, it seemed to me, did not want to address; the question of what really was happening when their students read rich and complicated literary texts. My continuing attempts to address that question have led me (and perhaps some others as well) toward a great deal of learning — only some of it about what happens when my students read — that I suspect I might never have come to otherwise.

Another way to describe that basic intention might be to say that the study tries to occupy the territory between research and teaching. I'm no longer so convinced that you can do that this easily, but I continue to think it's worth doing. We need to continue to keep research and theory in touch with practice. That second question — "And what can we do about it?" — may have been an arrogant one, but it highlighted the sense I had that I was at least as much a teacher as a researcher, and that my need to *know* was fueled by an even more immediate need to *do*.

The study also acknowledges the ethical problem I've faced a little more self-consciously since that time: what are our obligations to our research subjects? The problem's not posed here in the dramatic way it is for, say, a medical researcher, some of whose subjects may die in the course of demonstrating that the treatment they didn't get was the efficacious one. But it's

71

nonetheless real: as a teacher, it seemed clear to me that in justice I could only design a study from which I believed my students could learn something. That may, incidentally, be one of the reasons the study may seem engaging to read: it was shaped as much by a desire to share that story and to help the participants in the study grow as readers as by a need to learn about the processes involved. The "data" it yielded were almost a by-product.

As I have continued the process which I was beginning at the time of this study — trying to understand more about why people (especially students) read as they do — I've come to be more and more aware of the limitations, for my purposes, of what Stephen Jay Gould calls "experimental results," and the advantages of what he calls "historical explanation" (Gould, 1989; see Hunt and Vipond, in press, for an account of the research which has pushed me in this direction). Perhaps paradoxically, I now see what I acknowledged in 1982 as the limitations of the study — its ignorance of the methods of statistical inference, its lack of generalizability — as it strong suits. It did push me, and may have pushed some of those who heard it at the conference or read it in manuscript, toward looking hard at what individual readers were doing (as opposed, for instance, to looking for statistical generalizations across readers). Whether we understood any better is probably not as important as the fact that we were trying to understand what those readers were doing, just as Mina Shaughnessy had (1977), a few years earlier, urged us to do with our writers.

The question raised most immediately by a rereading of this study, however, is one that would have surprised me very much in 1982: what is the status of the story as it appears in this text, as you sit and read it as a part of this book? Whose utterance is this story here and now, how is it framed, what points does it afford construction of by its various readers? It seems to me clear that I had not — have not yet — given up on my attempt to frame this story so that someone else would "get it" in something like the way I "got it" when I first read it. I had, the study makes clear, failed with all of my students and virtually all of my colleagues. Like the storyteller who gets to the end and realizes it hasn't worked, that her listeners are desperately resisting the impulse to say, "So what's the point?" (Polanyi, 1979). I eagerly participate in the negotiations that will let us all come to agree on a satisfactory point, and get to some sort of closure on the story. I'm still doing it.

References

Gould, S.J. (1989). *Wonderful life: The Burgell Shale and the nature of history.* New York: W.W. Norton.

Hunt, R.A. (1987). "A decade of change: A correspondence on theory and teaching." *Reading-Canada-Lecture* 5, 3, 148-153.

Hunt, R.A., & Vipond, D. (in press). "First, catch the rabbit: The methodological imperative and the dramatization of dialogic reading." In R. Beach, R. J. Green, M. Kamil, & T. Shanahan (Eds.), *Multidisciplinary perspectives on literacy research*. Urbana, IL: National Conference on Research in English.

Polanyi, L. (1979). "So what's the point?" *Semiotica, 25:* 3/4, 207-241.

Shaughnessy, M.P. (1977). *Errors and expectations: A guide for the teacher of basic writing.* New York: Oxford University Press.

Chapter 4   Archeology of Literacy

Enos's study of rhetorical contests in ancient Greece provides several important contrasts to Hunt's exploration of the reading processes of modern Canadian college students. The obvious contrasts in time and subject matter remind us of the enormous range of topics to which empirical research can usefully be applied.

The two studies also provide a dramatic contrast in their degrees of **reactivity**, that is, the degree to which the act of observation is likely to influence the phenomena being observed. Hunt was acutely and appropriately aware of the potential effects that his method of observation might have on his participants. Asking people to read in an unusual way may well influence how they interpret a story. This is not to say that Hunt's method did influence the readers' interpretations in any important way, but the researcher must keep the possibility in mind, as Hunt clearly does. The Enos study, though, was completely nonreactive. There is no possibility that his observations influenced the people or events he discussed. When Enos and his wife, Jane Helpie traced the epigraphs at Oropos, the contestants had been dead for more than two millennia.

In general, historical studies, such as the one Enos conducted, are nonreactive. However, they are not the only kind of nonreactive study. Webb, Campbell, Schwartz, Sechrest, and Grove (1981) describe a surprisingly wide variety of nonreactive studies for measuring ongoing activities. Our favorite is one that Webb et al. (1981, p. 27) suggested for comparing children's interest in various museum displays in glass cases. Their measure involves cleaning the glass cases each morning and then counting the number of nose prints on each case in the evening.

Enos's paper is intended as a demonstration to his colleagues of the value of empirical research in his field. Indeed, perhaps the most important thing for students to note about this paper is Enos's clear message that such a demonstration is needed. He notes that ". . . many researchers in classical rhetoric . . . have been reluctant to 'dirty their hands'" with empirical data (p. 79). This negative attitude toward certain kinds of data isn't confined to the field of classical rhetoric. Indeed, we find it throughout the various fields which study the use of language. As with many attitudes, the origin of this negative attitude about data isn't clear. However, a view that often accompanies this attitude (Webb et.al.,1981) is that theoretical investigations and empirical research are polar opposites and that one pursues one or the other but not both. In this view, empirical researchers think "small," attend only to detail, and ignore the important high-level ideas. The obvious choice for people who hold such a view, of course, is to avoid empirical research like the plague.

We believe that this view is pernicious. We believe instead that theory building and observation are, or should be, intimately related. In fact, it's difficult to think of scholarly observation that is not guided by some sort of theoretical claims and that does not result in some sort of generalization. Big ideas are important but big ideas can be wrong. The armchair tradition, which Enos alludes to, fails to provide the sort of cleansing and creative criticism of ideas that empirical research can provide. In our view, theory and research together provide us much more than either could alone. We believe that Enos's admonition that the field of classical rhetoric will be impoverished by the omission of empirical work applies with equal force to all fields of language study.

Webb, E. J., Campbell, D. T., Schwartz, R. D., Sechrest, L., & Grove, J. B. (1981). *Nonreactive measures in the social sciences.* Boston, MA: Houghton Mifflin.

Richard Leo Enos
Carnegie-Mellon University

Although the Amphiareion of Oropos is virtually unmentioned by ancient authors, epigraphical evidence reveals that for centuries this sanctuary was a frequent site of rhetorical and literary contests as well as a repository of written communication on these events. Based upon field work in Greece and archaeological reports, inscriptions are examined with other archaeological evidence to reconstruct the nature and duration of these events. This study illustrates that even a relatively small site can yield findings of major importance for the history of rhetoric and emphasizes that scholars should engage in such primary research.

The Art of Rhetoric at the Amphiareion of Oropos: A Study of Epigraphical Evidence as Written Communication

In a real sense, the study of Hellenic rhetoric is confined to one great city—Athens. Such a perspective is understandable, for written communication providing information about the ancient Greek world often originated from, or was written about, this great political and intellectual center. Most of our knowledge of Hellenic civilization comes from literary evidence transmitted by scribes and refined by scholars alike over the centuries. In contrast, much of what we know of antiquity from archaeological evidence has been discovered and systematically studied only for a century, a relatively brief amount of time to fully appreciate the Greek world beyond the obvious remains of such prominent centers as Athens. As a preeminent intellectual center, Athens attracted great scholars who, in turn, recorded in detail the events of this city. Other prominent centers, not enjoying the attention Athens received, did not benefit from enduring records. Thucydides, the prominent historian of classical Athens, was sensitive to the problem that overattention to Athens could distort the accomplishments of other cities. Thucydides cautioned that centuries after the Peloponnesian War—long after Sparta's modest earthen dwellings crumbled while Athens' magnificent marble structures endured—no one would believe that Sparta was a force that rivaled Athens (I. 10. 2).

Thucydides's caution concerning political history is a lesson that applies as well to the history of rhetoric. Even a cursory reading of George Kennedy's research (1963, pp. 3, 26, 27 ff.; 1975, p. 280) reveals that rhetoric was taught

77

and practiced actively throughout the Greek-speaking world. Yet, many of these centers for rhetoric did not enjoy the attention of contemporary writers and, as a result, the literary evidence was not transmitted and their accomplishments faded from recollection as generations passed. These conditions reveal the incompatibility that confronts researchers of the history of rhetoric: an awareness of rhetoric throughout the ancient world but the dependence on "Athenian-oriented" sources for evidence of that history. The resolution to this problem begins by recognizing that standard literary sources need not monopolize evidence and that other types of written communication exist that can both complement traditional philological sources and help resolve the problem of viewing Hellenic rhetoric through Athenian eyes.

Epigraphical sources—written communication inscribed on durable material—are evidence that is recorded contemporaneously with the event and normally remains unaltered since its original composition. In brief, and unlike traditional literary evidence, epigraphical evidence is not subject to the editing and human error of generations of scribes and scholars but speaks directly from antiquity. Many such inscriptions, unearthed only during this century, are now available for research and study. In fact, a preliminary field-work report (Enos, 1979) lists 23 sites throughout Greece where epigraphical evidence relevant to the history of rhetoric has been recorded and preserved for study. Actually, months of study throughout the country and in the Epigraphical Museum at Athens revealed much larger, more diversified evidence than that collection initially recorded. Continued encouragement from the Greek Ministry of Science and Culture and The American School of Classical Studies at Athens promises the opportunity to study systematically such evidence in the hope of providing new knowledge about ancient rhetoric in Greece.

Part of the current problem in researching the history of Hellenic rhetoric is that (for want of a better term) "Victorian" research still persists in our discipline. It was not uncommon, for example, for Homeric scholars of the last century to limit themselves to texts of the *Iliad* and the *Odyssey* in order to determine whether there actually was a Homer or if Troy ever existed. Heinrich Schliemann, the father of modern archaeology, believed that such debates were best resolved by "the test of the spade," and excavated at various sites in Turkey and Greece in order to broaden our view of Homer and the Bronze Age itself beyond the scope of classical texts. Many of Schliemann's contemporaries strongly criticized such an approach to scholarship, frequently advancing disparaging remarks about how scholars need not grovel in the dirt in order to do research (Ceram,1972, pp.55-62; Brackman, 1974, pp.159-174;

see also, Deuel, 1977, pp. 6-7, 13-15, 219-220). Schliemann's innovative, if not sophisticated, methods of research have rewritten much of our knowledge of the Homeric world. Unfortunately, many researchers in classical rhetoric have not learned from Schliemann and have been reluctant to "dirty their hands" in such a manner of research, but rather perpetuate the armchair, traditional methods of analyzing written communication.

As a means of illustrating the value of such evidence, this essay reports on field work done in Greece and reconstructs the history of rhetoric at a sanctuary dedicated to the hero Amphiaraus located near Oropos, a site that had limited attention from ancient authors (e.g., Pausanias 34. 1-5; Strabo 1. 4. 7; 9. 1. 22; 9. 2. 6. Thucydides 7. 28. 1), but was a repository of written communication that provides valuable information about the history of rhetoric. The written evidence available at this one location should establish the point that the potential for significant findings at numerous sites and museums warrants the attention (and effort) of researchers.

For centuries, the remains of the Amphiareion were buried among plane trees, pines, and laurels in the rustic valley where the sanctuary is located. In 1884, the Greek Archaeological Society began systematic excavations under the supervision of Basil Leonardos and continued without interruption until his death in 1929 (Petracos, 1974, p. 29); later research at the Amphiareion was done under Basil Petracos. The recordings of unearthed inscriptions over the last one hundred years, in addition to examination of source material, reveal that the sanctuary at Oropos regularly held contests in honor of Amphiaraus from at least the fifth century B.C. to the first century A.D. (Petracos, 1974, pp. 13, 36); that is, throughout the 500 years in which rhetoric was "invented" to its stabilization as a formal discipline. These inscriptions reveal that rhetorical and literary contests held a prominent place in the games and festivals at the Amphiareion for centuries and provide invaluable evidence of written communication from sources that have been all but totally ignored by historians of rhetoric. This essay synthesizes epigraphical evidence to determine how the Amphiareion of Oropos became a site for rhetorical display, how such rhetorical activities were sustained for centuries, and lastly, the nature of rhetorical displays as revealed by the extant written communication.

The Amphiareion: A Historical Perspective of the Evidence

Oropos is in the coastal district on the northeast frontier between Boeotia and Attica and approximately 31 miles from Athens; the city of Oropos is located on the mainland side of the Euripos between Rhamnous and Delion with Eretria on the opposite side. This location, normally favored by pleasant weather during the warm months, was easily accessible by ship and was an active commercial center. Pausanias (34. 1, 2) indicates that twelve stades (approximately 1 and 1/2 miles) away from Oropos stood the Amphiareion, a site commemorating the divine Amphiaraus, a distinguished warrior and seer from Argos who fought, according to Aeschylus (568-9), as one of the seven against Thebes. A legendary hero from the underworld, Amphiaraus became popular for his abilities as a soothsayer, diviner, and especially a healer (Aeschylus, 568-9; Apollodorus 3. 6. 2-4; Pausanias 34, 1-5). A cult honoring Amphiaraus was adopted by the Oropians in about the fifth century B.C. and established at a spring that became famous for its healing properties. The therapeutic value of this excellent water and the pleasant surroundings soon made the Amphiareion a popular rehabilitation center for Greeks and later for Romans (Strabo 9. 1. 22, 9. 2. 10-11; Pausanias, 34. 3, 4). Various inscriptions, accounts, votive reliefs and even statuary at the Amphiareion, the National Museum at Athens and the British Museum present and describe the activities of this sanctuary in vivid detail (Petracos, 1974, pp. 18-25; AE, 43, 9-10 [no. 127; Hyperides 3, 16 ff.).

As is the case with most sanctuaries, the Amphiareion became an active civic center and several extant inscriptions reveal that important documents were preserved there, including treaties, duties pertaining to the temple, catalogs honoring individuals and (central to this study) public records of rhetorical and literary contests (AE,43 9-10 [no. 127], 11-16 [no. 129],17 [no. 131], 24-25 [no. 139], 43-44 [no. 155]). Specifically, games and festivals were held to honor Amphiaraus, and it is within the written communication of these events that the history of rhetoric at the Amphiareion was recorded. The Amphiareion of Oropos was not an intellectual center such as Athens but rather a center for display and performance; in fact, the remains of its small theatre are preserved at the site. Extant evidence indicates that the games were first held at the Amphiareion in about the fifth century B.C., but the earliest epigraphical sources refer to such games in the mid-fourth century B.C. (Petracos, 1974, p. 36; IG, no. 414). The period from 387 to 338 B.C. was a time of systemization and an extant list of victors, dated to approximately 366 B.C. (IG, no. 414) reveals that major games were regularly held. In this respect, the Amphiareion Games are akin to the larger, more prestigious games of Olympia, Delphi, and Isthmia. Both the "Little Amphiareion," which was held annually, and the "Great Amphiareion," which was held every fourth year, offered events that included rhetorical and literary contests (Petracos, 1974, pp. 9,10, 36).

After the Battle of Chaeronea, Philip gave the Amphiareion to the Athenians; this administrative change reorganized the festivals and games, expanding the contests beyond athletic events to include rhetorical performances (Pausanias 34. 1). A number of inscriptions are available and reveal the expansion and diversity of the Amphiareion games (e.g., IG, nos. 414, 415, 416, 417, 418, 419, 420). In fact, and as Petracos (1974, p. 12) indicates, the period from 287 to 146 B.C. was one of great activity for the Amphiareion games. Even a casual examination of the relevant inscriptions available for examination at the site, and discussed later in this essay, reveals that individuals came from throughout the Greek world for contests in the oral performance of literature, scholarly declamations, dramatic performances, and reading as well as athletic contests.

One reason for the continued popularity, and even the endurance, of these rhetorical contests is Roman patronage. Earlier research has established that Roman patronage was a major force in sustaining the teaching and practice of rhetoric in Athens (Enos, 1977), and it is certainly reasonable to believe that the Amphiareion, under Athenian direction, would also benefit from Roman patronage. An inscription dating back to 156 B.C. shows the Amphiareion games under Roman auspices, and from at least 146 B.C., the games flourished under the direct support of Roman sponsorship, particularly (as a victors' list reveals) during the first century B.C. (AE, 3, 98-101 [no. 2]; IG, nos. 411, 413, 416, 419, 420; AE, 43, 37-38 [no. 151]). Following the donation of the Roman dictator Sulla, for example, the Amphiareion games became increasingly elaborate and, as revealed by one inscription (IG, no. 413, 264), were even renamed the "Amphiareion and Roman" games. The evidence of this Roman participation is available today, for at the site where the stoa was constructed is a series of inscribed statue bases. The first inscription from the East, in a "T" shape, records the list of victors at the "Amphiareion and Roman" games in the first century B.C. (Petracos, 1974, p. 41). Roman patronage of the games is further revealed by an inscription on display at the Amphiareion that records a Roman decree stipulating that taxes collected from the region of Oropos, and its ports Skala and Delphinion, be ceded to the Amphiareion and that such taxes be used to sponsor the games and sacrifices to Amphiaraus (IG, no. 413). This decree, currently on display at the site museum (#8), is endorsed by no less a rhetor than Marcus Tullius Cicero (IG, no. 413, lines 12,13). Such epigraphical evidence clearly reveals that sustained support for these rhetorical and literary contests by influential Romans helped to underwrite the events up to the reign of Augustus in the first century A.D.

Such patronage illustrates also the interdependence between artistic effort and support that existed between Greece and Rome. Roman patronage was a major force in sustaining the Athenian Second Sophistic (Enos, 1977). In fact, Roman sponsorship of chairs of rhetoric and cultural buildings—such as theatres, odeions, and libraries—is well documented from the Republic through the reign of Hadrian, revealing sustained support for rhetoric and literary studies throughout the Empire. In benefiting the arts, Roman support had a direct and pervasive effect on not only the major cities throughout the Empire but even such sanctuaries as the Amphiareion. With the decline of the Roman Empire and the rise of Christianity, sponsorship disappeared and the Amphiareion (similar to other centers) fell into disuse and neglect and eventually was abandoned. For centuries thereafter the ruins of the Amphiareion lay buried and with them the written communication that would provide primary evidence about the practice of rhetoric in the Greek world.

An Analysis of the Epigraphical Evidence

The extant inscriptions of the Amphiareion provide sufficient information to reconstruct the practice of rhetoric for centuries and, in the process, provide invaluable historical evidence. Much of this written communication explains the practice of rhetorical and literary contests and records the victors for posterity. In short, information about procedures and individuals, which would have continued to lie buried in the past—and thus remain unavailable for examination—has literally been brought to light during this century. Epigraphical evidence dated to the time of the Roman Republic reveals that the *agonothetos* had the responsibility of organizing the games (IG, nos. 416, 419, 420, AE, 43, 33, [no.148]). According to legend, Amphiaraus was an athletic champion at the Nemean games, and lists of victors at the Amphiareion from the fourth to the first centuries B.C. emphasize athletic contests for men, young men, and boys in such events as running, wrestling, boxing, the pancrateion, the pentathlon, and hoplite racing (ICG nos. 414, 415, 416, 418, 419, 420; Apollodorus 3. 6. 4). Although athletic contests are evident throughout the inscriptions, the epigraphical sources describing the Amphiareion games also reveal an active and long-standing interest in rhetorical contests. The myth of Amphiaraus had frequently captured the interests of men of letters and was a source of inspiration for several ancient writers and poets. Even an "interpreter" at the Amphiareion named Iophon the Knossian gave responses in hexameter verse (Pausanias 34. 4).

If the customary multipurpose use of theatres around Greece was followed at the Amphiareion, the sanctuary's theatre would have been the location not only for dramatic events but poetic, rhetorical, and musical contests (IG, no. 412, lines 26-28). The diversity of rhetorical events is evident in the inscriptions, and it is likely that the small 300-seat theatre was the site for such recorded contests as sophistic declamations, logical and epic encomia (hortatory speeches of praise and blame), and recitation of rhapsodic verse (IG, nos. 414, 415/417, 418, 420). Along with the athletic contests mentioned above, these rhetorical contests doubtlessly became standard events; in fact, the list of the first events under the new name of the "Amphiareion and Roman" games is extant and shows that contests for rhapsodes and epic encomia were standard aspects of the games (Petracos, 1974, p. 40).

The specific findings of relevant inscriptions provide an even more precise view of the art of rhetoric at the Amphiareion. The earliest preserved list of victors at the Amphiareion games *(IG,* no. 414) dates back to approximately 366 B.C., or between the time of Theban occupation and the return of Athenian control. Contestants participated in 32 known events for men and youth including: the kitheria, flute, sophistic exercises, the long run, the short run, the double run, the pentathalon, equestrian exercises, wrestling, the pancrateion, boxing, heavy-armed exercises, a special charioteer event, and a chariot drawn by a pair of horses. Victors in these contests came from fourteen locations throughout Greece, but the overwhelming number of victors were from Athens, winning 16 of the 32 events. This early inscription clearly indicates that athletic events dominated the contests. In fact, the exercises in sophistic declamations, won by an Athenian named "Pausimaxos," is the sole rhetorical event and appeared with other "artistic" contests.

The next relevant inscription, probably recorded between 195 and 146 B.C., is actually a joining of two known fragments (IG, nos. 415/417), but is housed at the Athens Epigraphical Museum (EM 11969). As is true with the earlier inscription mentioned above, this inscription indicates that athletic contests dominated the Amphiareion games. Yet, the inscription also indicates that rhetorical events increased and included contestants who were victorious in a variety of events. Many of these rhetorical contests include quite specialized skills: the composed encomium, rhapsodic exercises, poetic comedy, rhetorical exercises in the delivery of (usually) dramatic literature by an interpreter-actor (see also: AE, 43, 24-25 [no. 139]; Aristotle, *Rhetorica* 1403B, 1404A), and a declamation on the "glad tidings of Roman conquests." Clearly this written communication of events indicates a diversity and sophistication of rhetorical contests not apparent in the earlier inscription. By their position in the inscription rhetorical events grouped with literary readings, interpretations of dramatic compositions, as well as a contest to permit epideictic praise to Rome. This latter contest was won by a citizen of Oropos.

The evidence of rhapsodic contests in this late inscription is particularly important, for it provides further evidence of the perpetuation of contests for the presentation of oral literature, a tradition rooted in Homeric literature and a well-established practice during the Classical Period (Plato, *Ion* 530B, *Leges* 658B). In addition, one photographed inscription still under study concerns the rhapsodes at the Amphiareion and may fix the duration of their contests well beyond this date.[1] Recorded epigraphical sources at sites other than the Amphiareion (Enos, 1978, p. 142) indicate that rhapsodic contests and training in the preservation, composition, and rendering of oral literature may have continued well into the third century A.D.

As indicated earlier, Romans traditionally were patrons of rhetorical events, and their sponsorship is evident in the inscriptions of the Amphiareion. Inscriptions that record victors during the period of Roman domination show an increasing diversity of rhetorical and literary events. One inscription (IG, no.416) dated to the period of the late Roman Republic includes exercises for heralds; these orators often carried a staff or wand as did Homeric bards, were said to be inviolable, and were considered messengers of Zeus. The events for encomia were expanded to include logical encomia, a sort of "honor roll" encomium, and an epic encomium *(IG,* nos. 416, 420, 418). Poetry readings were expanded also and included readings in heroic verse, satire, rhapsodic declamation, and even new compositions in tragic and comic poetry. Victors in theatrical contests in both old tragedy and comedy were recorded along with victors in the elocution of dramatic literature by a declaimer.

Results and Observations

The list of inscriptions mentioned above indicates a clear tendency for rhetorical, poetic, and theatrical contests to expand to such an extent that they assume increasing emphasis when compared with athletic contests (IG, no. 420). Such an emphasis is in marked contrast to early inscriptions in the fourth century B.C., which had few artistic contests and only a single, broadly termed rhetorical event called "sophistic exercises"—an event that never appears in the later inscriptions of the "Amphiareion and Roman" period (IG, no. 414). The parallel that existed between the active athletic contests and the viable military power of Greece has been well established since the writings of Homer. What is evident in the inscriptions of the Amphiareion, however, is the diachronic transition from an athletic/military emphasis to an artistic/cultural emphasis in the games. For much of its history, rhetoric has been viewed as preparatory training. When rhetoric was a source of political power during the classical period of Athens and the Roman Republic, rhetorical practice reflected training in deliberative and forensic skills that would have a direct, social impact. Poetic composition, with its origins as artistic works, sought to do homage to gods and heroes. During the Roman Empire, the shift in power from a participatory to a centralized political structure deemphasized the social and political advantages of rhetoric. Similarly, poetic displays evolved to be creations not so much to honor others but the artists who composed them. Yet, during the Roman Imperial Period, rhetoric and poetry had already been long-established as synonymous with higher education and cultural refinement. In short, athletic and military contests originally were performed as funeral games and pragmatic exercises for war, where best efforts were initially offered to honor the gods. These contests eventually honored athletes for little beyond the intrinsic merits of their performance. Similarly, rhetorical and literary contests shifted from their pragmatic and religious origins to performance for their own artistic and cultural merits.

The inscriptions at the Amphiareion reflect the transition of power in the Greek world from military to cultural and mirror the findings of those historians of rhetoric who posit that rhetoric survived because it was able to shift emphasis from a political to an educational/cultural source of power during this period of Roman domination. Such an observation is consistent with earlier-mentioned research dealing with Roman sponsorship of rhetoric in Athens, in which a long and sustained patronage of rhetoric was a tradition prominent among influential Romans and Greeks (Enos, 1977, p. 10). Clearly, and particularly during the Athenian domination of the Amphiareion under Roman auspices, this phenomenon is evident in the written communication of the sanctuary.

The results of this research provide a number of observations on the art of rhetoric at the Amphiareion and, in turn, a paradigm for continued research. The earliest inscriptions reveal that rhetoric had a place in the sacred games of the Amphiareion. Moreover, these rhetorical events expanded in number and specialization over the centuries and reached—at least by qualitative degree—increased involvement in the Amphiareion games. Rhetorical events were consistently listed early in the victors' lists and in the same category with poetic, musical, theatrical, and literary contests with participants coming from throughout the Greek world. Roman patronage and support appears only to have encouraged an interest in these forms of epideictic rhetoric, for the latest inscriptions emphasize rhetorical displays as popular artistic events and not preparatory exercises for politics. The composition of these rhetorical events indicates that such displays were seen as literary entertainment and were far removed from the political and forensic rhetoric that was such a dominant social force in fifth-century B.C. Athens.

The nature of such rhetorical displays at the Amphiareion would be unknown to modern historians of rhetoric were it not for the epigraphical evidence that preserved this written communication. Whether the Amphiareion is a microcosm of the sort of rhetoric practiced in similar sanctuaries, or in Greece herself, can only be verified through similar field studies, particularly those in the remote areas of Greece. This study is by no means a definitive statement of the Amphiareion of Oropos. It was not intended to be; indeed, other inscriptions at the sanctuary are available now for continued study. There is no doubt that although the findings here offer evidence to help provide a better understanding of the history of rhetoric, new sources await continued study that will supplement this work (e.g., SEG, no. 427). If such a condition is true at such a relatively small site as the Amphiareion, the implications for continued field work at large sites, where more detailed and complex holdings are centered, is obvious. Yet, if a sensitive understanding of rhetoric in antiquity is to be attained, investigation of those sources that will yield evidence irretrievable by methods other than field work at the location must be done, or historians of rhetoric must be content with an accounting of rhetoric's past that is somewhat less precise than the written communication available would permit it to be.

Note

1. The author discovered this inscription in a sheltered area behind the site museum. Time and resource constraints permitted only a logging of the inscription for future study.

References

Aeschylus. *Septem contra Thebas.*

Apollodorus mythographus. *Bibliotheca.*

Archaeologike ephemeris (1885), 3; (1923), 41; (1925), 43.

Aristotle. *Rhetorica.*

Brackman, A. (1974). *The dream of Troy.* New York: Mason & Lipscomb.

Ceram, C. W. (1972). *Gods, graves, and scholars: The story of archaeology* (2nd ed., E. B. Garside & Sophie Wilkins, Trans.). New York: Bantam Books.

Deuel, L. (1977). *Memoirs of Heinrich Schliemann: A documentary portrait drawn from his autobiographical writings, letters and excavation reports.* New York: Harper & Row.

Enos, R. L. (1977). The effects of imperial patronage on the rhetorical tradition of the Athenian Second Sophistic. *Communication Quarterly, 25,* 3-10.

Enos, R. L. (1978). The hellenic rhapsode. *Western Journal of Speech Communication, 42,* 134-143.

Enos, R. L. (1979). Epigraphical sources for the history of hellenic rhetoric. *Rhetoric Society Quarterly 9,* 169-176.

Hyperides. *Speech in defense of Euxenippus.*

Inscriptiones graecace: Megaridis, Oropiae Boeotiae (1892). 7.

Kennedy, G. (1963). *The art of persuasion in Greece.* Princeton: Princeton University Press.

Kennedy, G. (1975). Review article: The present state of the study of ancient rhetoric. *Classical Philology, 70,* 278-282.

Pausanias. *Description of Greece: Attica.*

Petracos, B. C. (1974). *The Amphiareion of Oropos.* Athens: Esperos Editions.

Plato. *Ion.*

Plato. *Leges.*

Strabo. *Geography.*

Supplementum epigraphicum graecum (1981), 31.

Thucydides. *History of the war between Athens and Sparta.*

Author's Note

The cooperation of the American School of Classical Studies at Athens and the Greek Ministry of Science and Culture is gratefully acknowledged. Without their support this project would not have been possible. This article is dedicated to Dennis S. Gouran, whose unfailing support cannot be adequately acknowledged.

87

Author's Comment—Richard Leo Enos

Readers of "The Art of Rhetoric at the Amphiareion of Oropos," seeing the presentation of data and the general organization of material, may be inclined to infer that this pattern mirrored a sequential process of research. While I would like to claim that this study was the product of systematically calculated deliberation and execution from the start, in actuality the initial efforts were the result of much good fortune. Yet, as the adage goes, good fortune is the result of opportunity meeting preparation, and some initial groping is understandable when one is developing a new procedure for study.

To say that research in classical rhetoric entails a "new procedure" appears to be a contradiction, for the analytical methods are long-established. Yet it is precisely because traditional scholarship in classical rhetoric has a long heritage that its traditional methods have acquired a mystique which poses a constraint on both the discovery of new information and the development of new analytical procedures. The established resources of knowledge of classical rhetoric have been literary artifacts transmitted by generations of scribes and scholars. The bibliographical efforts to assemble and analyze texts became synonymous with philological studies and in turn synonymous with what classical rhetoric meant. Thus to be a classical rhetorician meant to study literary texts in the original Latin or Greek while being familiar with Greek and Roman history. Studying antiquity became synonymous with antiquated methods of study.

While a product of a scholastic tradition of education, I felt resources permitting a more complete knowledge of classical rhetoric were unattended to and that our understanding of ancient rhetoric was thereby limited. Three experiences provided powerful analogies in developing this perspective and, consequentially, my belief in the need for new research procedures. First, I noticed that my colleagues in empirical research did not seem hesitant to oppose traditional views or modes of analysis in their disciplines if they felt that it resulted in a more sensitive understanding of their subject matter. Second, my colleagues in classical archaeology were annually engaged in field studies in Greece to gather new information about the ancient world, and I soon learned that some of their findings included epigraphical sources or writing preserved on such durable material as marble. Third, my work at the American School of Classical Studies at Athens provided me with the opportunity to study under Fordyce W. Mitchel, a well-known expert in epigraphy. Mitchel quickly made it obvious to me that much of the evidence of ancient writing, with work relevant to classical rhetoric included, had been either unexamined for centuries or unearthed only in recent decades. Yet many epigraphists saw as their primary function the recording and presentation of ancient inscriptions but not rhetorical analysis; in fact, many were reluctant to move beyond description.

Over time I synthesized these personal experiences into observations that eventually became the starting points of this study. I felt that developing new methods of analysis through "field work" in classical rhetoric would rival armchair research (characteristic of literary analysis) as a source of primary evidence. Further, the availability of primary evidence, unstudied and uncontaminated by generations of scribes, offered new and valuable sources. Finally, given the above two observations, I was convinced of the need for the systematic assimilation and analysis of data that would provide evidence for rhetorical analysis that was unique to conventional research procedures in the history of rhetoric. In sum, the study of epigraphical evidence for rhetoric was new, and I was convinced that old, venerable methods of research would not provide the most sensitive procedure for assimilating and analyzing evidence. The study thus became a framework for what would be a new research procedure: a synthesis of textual evidence, philological analysis, and on-site data collection through field work at archaeological excavations.

What was necessary for my research, however, was a subject which could be both manageable and yet significant enough to illustrate the importance of the value of such a method of study. In short, I needed a paradigm, and that opportunity came when I first studied in Greece at the American School of Classical Studies at Athens. On one of our many outings in 1974, Mitchel casually—almost off-handed—pointed to a large marble tablet that contained a list of victors of literary and oratorical contests. For Mitchel, the stone was little more than a curiosity at an obscure site, the Amphiareion of Oropos; for me it instantly revealed information unknown to historians of rhetoric and new data about the oratorical and literary practices of Greeks. On my return to America, and for the next two years, I reviewed every inscription I could find recorded that could tell me about rhetoric in ancient Greece. My proposal for field work to examine epigraphical sources for the study of Hellenic rhetoric earned me the Karl R. Wallace Award and with an adjoining grant from the University of Michigan, my wife and I returned to Greece for months of field work under the auspices of the Greek Ministry of Science and Culture and through the American School of Classical Studies at Athens. My travels over Greece confirmed my initial suspicion that ancient inscriptions were indeed an untapped resource. They were dispersed throughout the country, cataloged as well as possible through heroic effort but in varying and frequently imprecise fashion, and, thus, when discovered, they required systematic analysis.

I returned to the Amphiareion of Oropos in 1977 and discovered that it would be suitable for an in-depth study. The sanctuary had long been a site for athletic and literary/oratorical contests. It had been excavated sporadically only in this century, however, and compared to other more prominent sites had received virtually no attention. Yet, the site met my criteria: it was small enough for an in-depth study and large enough to be known by ancient geographers such as Pausanius. In short, I felt that the Amphiareion of Oropos was an excellent "subject" for examination and would not only serve as a resource for new knowledge but, indirectly, an illustration of the benefits of such a procedure of study for other sites. I had hoped that it would serve as a model for continued work and refinement of procedures. From 1977 to 1985 I analyzed all the information I could about the site: the inscriptions my wife, Jane Helppie, and I had photographed and drawn on our field trips, the commentary of ancient sources and the results of archaeological excavations under Basil Petracos.

Since the procedures for analysis of this type of work in classical rhetoric were unique, I had to produce several drafts before I found a way of presenting information that bridged the conventional mode of presentation and still offered no constraint for the presentation of new material and procedures. After years of work, several earlier versions and public presentations, the study was submitted and published by *Written Communication* promptly and with no substantial revision. It should be noted, however, that the speed of acceptance was the result of years of trial and failure. Whether this study will be a prototype remains to be seen. Yet this experience provided me with a valuable lesson about keeping an open mind to new evidence and new procedures and a sensitivity to sources that at first appear unrelated. Most of all, this study was a lesson in disposition. Although I experienced skepticism from conservative scholars in different fields, others saw the merit of not identifying an ancient subject with traditional methods. They saw that trying new methods and examining new resources was not "heresy" but in the best spirit of the best of our earlier scholars. My plans are to visit other larger and better known sites in the hope of providing more extensive information that warrant larger claims. I am sure that as the years go by, I will modify my procedures and methods, but I will always remember the study at the Amphiareion of Oropos as the framework upon which such research procedures were initially built.

Chapter 5   Writing in the Academy: What Really Happens

Case studies are useful when the investigator is trying to answer "how" or "why" questions about events in real-life settings over which he has little control. A case study might involve the careful description of a particular student studying for a literature exam, or an extended account of a reading lesson conducted on a particular afternoon in a particular class. Case studies normally build up detailed answers to the questions by employing several mutually-reinforcing sources of evidence. They can be used to describe or explain a phenomenon, but they have been most commonly used in rhetorical research to explore a particular phenomenon in preparation for developing questions and hypotheses that subsequently become the foci of more sharply focused investigations. Spilka (1988) explored writing in industrial settings by examining carefully what each of a group of writers did as he carried out a writing task at work. Similarly, Sperling and Freedman (1987) explored how students respond to teachers' written comments, examining the interaction between one teacher and one student about the draft of a paper. Nelson's study explored approaches of college students to writing assignments by collecting "detailed writing process logs" from each of 13 students as they worked on papers assigned in their classes, "collecting all notes, drafts, and graded papers the participants produced during the semester, and interviewing both the participants and their teachers" (p. 101).

Any research method can be used for exploration, but case studies have a number of characteristics that make them especially useful for this purpose. First, because they are detailed and try to capture something of the complexity of events, they provide opportunities for discovering unexpected relations. Spilka, for example, discovered to her surprise that most writing in the industry she studied was not intended to convey new information but was used rather to confirm prior oral agreements. Another important characteristic of case studies is that they allow us to recognize the uniqueness of individual people and events. As Nelson's studies show, there is great variety in the way student writers approach assignments: although some take assignments quite seriously, others quite clearly do not. Averaging results from such students would suggest a picture of student writers that would be misleading. No individual writer ever takes an "average" approach to writing just as no family gives birth to the national average of 2.3 children. Psychologists such as Newell and Simon (1972) have long advocated that theories should allow us to understand individual cases rather than group averages. And Russell Hunt makes a similar point when he observes that "examining the actions and utterances of real human beings individually considered remains the best way to understand human beings in general." (p. 46 in MS)

One serious limitation of case studies stems from the same characteristics as their strengths. Because so much information is collected for each case, it is impractical to study very many cases. Indeed, many case studies involve only one instance of the phenomenon being investigated. And in many situations, the small **sample size** imposes a significant constraint on what can be concluded from the study. If we want to generalize from the study, that is, if we want to claim that many or all instances are like the one that has been investigated, then it is important that the sample be fairly large and that it be representative of the whole category of instances—of all the writers in an industry or of all the students in a college. In her study, Nelson was careful to sample a variety of courses and include both more able and less able students. She was also careful to hedge her claims: e.g., "Given the limited number of classroom writing situations examined in this study, it is difficult to speculate about whether certain classroom practices actually encouraged the use of coping strategies to circumvent the demands of writing assignments." (p. 125-126)

However, when a case study is used as a **counter-example** to a categorical claim, sample size is less important. Because a case study can provide an accurate, detailed account of a phenomenon, it can be used to argue against unqualified claims about how or why something happens, following the logical principle that it takes only one counter-example to refute a categorical claim, i.e., a claim that something is always the case or never the case. Janet Emig's highly influential case study, *The Composing Processes of Twelfth Graders* (1971), one of the first of a growing number of case studies in rhetorical research, illustrates the use of the case study both for exploratory purposes and for the refutation of faulty but widely held beliefs about the process of composing. Heath's study of a single case (Chapter 8, this volume) shows us, surprisingly enough, that reading stories to children is not a simple, natural activity that every parent understands. One case is sufficient to make the point that activities that we see as natural may actually be the special product of a particular culture.

Another noteworthy feature of Nelson's study is that, although she is exploring new territory, she knows in some general sense what she is looking for, and this knowledge shapes essential features of the study. We might consider for a moment the metaphor of exploration, since some exploratory studies strike us as excessively unconstrained. Although explorers are likely to be surprised by what they find in their new worlds, competent ones have some expectations beforehand that dictate many of their preliminary choices of what to look for and how to look for it. That is, they aren't wandering innocently hoping that something interesting, anything interesting, would turn up. Robert Yin argues that

> when Columbus went to Queen Isabella to ask for support for his "exploration" of the New World, he had to have some reasons for asking for three ships (why not one? why not five?), and he had some rationale for going westward (why not north? why not south?). He also had some criteria for recognizing the New World when he actually encountered it. In short, his exploration began with some rationale and direction, even if his initial assumptions might later have been proved wrong. This same degree of rationale and direction should underlie even an exploratory case study. (p. 30)

As Nelson notes,

> I wanted to learn more about the kinds of variables that come into play when students set out to define and complete writing assignments in a variety of courses. . . . my aim in conducting this research was to begin to answer three key questions. . . . [p. 121]

References

Emig, J. (1971). *The composing processes of twelfth graders*. Urbana, IL: National Council of Teachers of English.

Newell, A., & Simon, H.A. (1972). *Human problem solving*. Englewood Cliffs, NJ: Prentice Hall.

Sperling, M., & Freedman, S.W. (1987). A good girl writes like a good girl: Written response to student writing. *Written Communication, 4*, 343-369.

Spilka, R. (1988). Adapting discourse to multiple audiences: Invention strategies of seven corporate engineers. Unpublished doctoral dissertation. Pittsburgh, PA: Carnegie Mellon University.

Yin. R.K. (1989). *Case study research: Design and methods*. (rev. ed.) Newbury Park, CA: Sage.

Jennie Nelson
California State University

This Was an Easy Assignment:
Examining How Students Interpret
Academic Writing Tasks

*This study explored academic writing from the students' side of the desk,
examining how different tasks and writing situations influence students'
approaches. The study used interviews and process logs and examined how
13 college freshmen interpreted writing assignments in a variety of courses
and how these interpretations differed from their instructors' intentions.
These case studies revealed that students draw from a range of individual
and situational resources in their efforts to define and complete assignments and that these factors can interact in complex ways to shape students' approaches. Students' responses to assignments depended upon what
they were actually rewarded for producing. In some situations, students
relied on shortcuts to produce papers and failed to engage in the kinds of
learning activities that assignments were designed to promote.*

This research was conducted with the support of a grant from OERI and the
Center for the Study of Writing. Many thanks to John R. Hayes, Dave Kaufer,
Nancy Spivey, Mike Rose, Stephen Simko, and Chris Haas for their encour-
agement and guidance during this project.

> Professor Clark: This assignment should be challenging. I pur-
> posely made it difficult. Students have to boil down the informa-
> tion from the lectures and reading and present a concise argument.
> [Essays could not exceed 200 words.] I believe conciseness forces
> students to take a stand, to weigh the value of every word.
>
> John: This was an easy assignment. All you had to do was reiterate
> what you'd read. I picked lots of names and cited important-
> sounding incidents ... essentially I paraphrased the reports I read. I
> think this assignment was another case of the instructor trying to
> have us learn through reiteration of read[ing] material. In my
> opinion, it didn't work and was a waste of class time.

These excerpts from interviews with Professor Clark and John, a freshman enrolled in his course, provide important insights into students' interpretations of academic writing tasks and how these interpretations can sometimes differ from their teachers' intentions. While Professor Clark intended this assignment to be a challenging exercise in synthesizing and transforming course material into a concise argument, John defined and approached the task quite differently. He essentially ignored the 200 word length restriction, choosing instead to focus on paraphrasing what he had read, and produced a 412 word "reiteration" of the assigned material.

In follow-up interviews, John described the assignment as a waste of time because it "basically called for rewriting what we had been given" [in lectures and assigned readings]. John explained that his teaching assistant's grading practices on previous assignments helped to shape and confirm his assessment of this assignment. The teaching assistant, who was responsible for grading all student homework, wrote very few comments on John's papers. Instead, he wrote checks in the margin next to points which, he explained, corresponded to a list of key points from the readings and lectures that students should have included in their papers. Thus, while Professor Clark, who designed the assignments for the course, stressed the importance of conciseness and taking an argumentative stand in responding to this assignment, the teaching assistant who actually evaluated students' responses stressed the importance of reproducing information from the assigned readings. Hence, while John's approach and assessment of this writing/learning experience differed from what Professor Clark intended, they matched what his teaching assistant was looking for, and as a result, John received full credit for this assignment.

John's story of how he interpreted and responded to this particular writing assignment reveals the central role that tasks and accountability play in shaping students' writing and learning experiences. Recent research suggests that students' writing processes are a function of the task and the context in which writing occurs (Applebee, 1984; Herrington, 1985; McCarthy, 1987; Marshall, 1984; Ruth & Murphy, 1984). As teachers and researchers interested in promoting the effective use of writing in composition courses and across the curriculum, we must learn more about how particular tasks and writing situations influence students' efforts. By examining *when* and *how* students' interpretations of writing assignments converge or diverge from their teachers' intentions, we can increase our understanding of how certain classroom practices and students' assumptions affect student writing. In addition, such research should lead to a richer understanding of the concerns and habits of student writers working on academic tasks in natural settings. This report begins with a discussion of the special nature of school settings and the central role of tasks and accountability in shaping students' learning and writing experiences. Following this discussion, a study is described which examines how various features of specific writing assignments and classroom situations influence students' approaches, and how disjunctions between teachers' and students' task interpretations might occur.

The Special Nature of School Settings

Although student writing processes have been widely studied (Emig, 1971; Flower & Hayes, 1980b; Perl, 1979; Pianko, 1979; Sommers, 1980), many of these studies were conducted in settings in which the subjects were asked to write for the occasion of the research project itself. As a result, much of what we know about the processes and practices of writers during composing comes from this research setting and not from the everyday contexts in which people normally write (Brandt, 1986). Unfortunately, tasks in research or laboratory settings may pose different problems for writers than tasks in everyday settings.

Researchers who have studied "everyday cognition" in natural settings (Odell & Goswami, 1982; Rogoff & Gardner, 1984; Scribner, 1984) stress the importance of social factors in shaping people's approaches to a task. According to Rogoff (1984), "Central to everyday contexts in which cognitive activity occurs is interaction with other people and use of socially provided tools . . . for solving problems . . . People, usually in conjunction with each other and always guided by social norms, set goals, negotiate appropriate means to reach the goals, and assist each other in implementing the means and resetting the goals as activities evolve" (p. 4). These researchers' conclusions suggest that if we want to understand the factors that influence how students interpret and respond to writing tasks, we need to locate our research in the complex social settings of actual schools and classrooms.

Researchers interested in studying writing processes in the classroom must take into account the special nature of school settings. In an extensive review of educational research, Doyle (1983) explains that "academic work is transformed fundamentally when it is placed in the complex social system of a classroom" (p. 185). Doyle describes several important reasons for this transformation. Perhaps most obvious is the fact that academic work is conducted in a social group (the class) where students can rely on their social and interpretive skills to define and negotiate task demands. Hence, Doyle reports, fellow classmates can serve as valuable resources for accomplishing academic work. Peers not only can provide direct assistance on assignments, but can also be used to solicit information from the teacher about the requirements for a particular task. In other words, assignments can be defined and negotiated in the public forum of the classroom.

Another resource that students can rely on for accomplishing academic work is the history of the class itself. Unlike laboratory settings, classes have a history that provides important information about the evolving nature of task demands. Students can use the feedback they receive on early assignments to refine their notions of what "counts" in a particular course. Doyle reports that as "the character of the task system becomes more apparent, students can then selectively attend to information that has consequences for task accomplishment regardless of whether it is explicitly signaled by the teacher" (p. 181). We can see how classroom history served as a valuable resource for John in completing his writing assignment. Because of early feedback he received from his teaching assistant, John selectively attended to information in the writing assignment, ignoring the length restriction and focusing on summarizing course material. In addition, John's comment that "this is another case of the instructor trying to have us learn through reiteration of read[ing] material" suggests that he was drawing from his previous experiences with school writing in general. No doubt, the experience of going to school establishes what Doyle calls "task schemata" (p. 181) which can be used by students like John to interpret similar task situations.

One of the most important features distinguishing academic work from other tasks, according to Doyle, is that it takes place in a highly "evaluative climate" (p. 182) in which grades are exchanged for performance.

As a result, accountability—in the form of the answers and processes students are actually rewarded for—becomes the driving force behind how students respond to school assignments. He explains that "the answers a teacher actually accepts and rewards define the real tasks in the classroom" (p. 182). In other words, students, like John, tend to take seriously only the work for which they actually are held accountable.

The highly evaluative nature of academic work can pose problems for students who not only must struggle to define often ambiguous tasks, but must weigh the risks involved in choosing a particular approach or answer. Many tasks (Doyle cites expository writing tasks in particular) are ambiguous not because teachers fail to explain them clearly but because there is not a single "right" answer or procedure for arriving at an answer available to students in advance. Students must interpret assignments and formulate responses on their own, a complex process that can prove troublesome and sometimes lead to disjunctions between students' approaches and teachers' intentions. Doyle describes several studies (Carter & Doyle, 1982; Dillon & Searle, 1981; MacKay, 1978) which suggest that students invent strategies for managing the ambiguity and risk involved in accomplishing classroom tasks. These strategies include offering provisional or restricted responses to assignments and questions as a way to elicit more information from teachers about the correct response, and requesting that the teacher make task instructions more explicit or provide models to follow closely. Each of these coping strategies provides students with valuable information about what really counts in completing a particular assignment. In addition, these strategies allow students to focus on the *products* they are required to produce instead of on the *processes* they are being asked to engage in. Thus, while these coping strategies may lessen the ambiguity and risk inherent to academic work, they may also provide students with shortcuts for producing acceptable responses—shortcuts that allow them to circumvent the thinking and learning processes their teachers hope to promote.

This brief summary of related research reveals just how important the special nature of school settings can be in shaping students' responses to academic tasks. What emerges from this discussion is a view of academic work from the students' side of the desk. We see students taking advantage of several features of classroom environments in their efforts to define and fulfill their teachers' assignments. They rely on their peers, on their current and long-term experiences with school work, and on various coping strategies to determine what counts in completing a particular assignment for a particular course. Successful students are those, like John, who can determine what constitutes an appropriate response through their interactions with teachers and classmates.

Writing in School Settings

Doyle's well-supported conclusion—that academic work is transformed fundamentally when it is placed in classroom settings—seems especially important for composition researchers. We know that because of the "ill-structured" (Simon, 1973) nature of many writing tasks, writers must actively interpret and define composition tasks for themselves. Studies which have examined how writers represent composition tasks (Berkenkotter, 1981; Flower & Hayes, 1980a; Flower, Hayes, Schriver, Carey, & Haas, 1987) reveal that experienced writers build rich task representations that include goals for dealing with the assigned audience and other rhetorical constraints. Indeed, Flower and Hayes (1980a) suggest that the act of representing one's writing task "may be one of the most critical steps the average writer takes" (p. 23).

Like other rich, naturalistic writing situations, it appears that school settings can influence the critical process of task representation in writing in important ways. Most obviously, students and teachers can openly negotiate and modify writing tasks. In addition, students can rely on their peers and other resources for help in defining and completing assignments. College-level writing assignments typically extend over long periods of time, unlike writing tasks in laboratory settings which normally have fixed time constraints (Marx, Winne, & Walsh, 1985). Consequently, students' task interpretations can change and evolve over time as students receive feedback on their performance and become more attuned to their teachers' requirements. Finally, while laboratory tasks are often designed to be novel (cf. Flower & Hayes, 1980a), classroom tasks are usually very familiar to students (Marx, Winne, & Walsh, 1985). This means that students can draw on their past experiences with school writing (some 12 years by the time they reach college) to help them interpret assignments.

Clearly, each of these features of school settings can shape the way a student approaches a writing assignment. Doyle argues that in order to design effective assignments, teachers "need to think about academic tasks in cognitive terms and become aware of the various paths students invent to get around task demands in accomplishing academic work" (p. 188). In addition, teachers need to understand the importance of accountability, or rewards, in the academic task system and to find effective ways to use it to promote learning. Doyle's advice seems especially relevant for teachers and researchers interested in improving writing instruction in English courses and across the curriculum. The research already cited indicates that students often may invent paths to get around the demands of writing tasks.

Researchers in composition (Brook, 1987; Herrington, 1985; McCarthy, 1987; Marshall, 1984; Sternglass & Pugh, 1986) who have examined student writing processes in classroom settings point out that school settings, with their focus on rewards for products, may limit the way students approach writing tasks. We need to learn more about how particular writing tasks and classroom contexts encourage or discourage students from engaging in the thinking and writing processes we hope to promote.

Case Studies of Naturally Occurring Academic Writing Tasks

The following observational study begins to examine the many factors involved in how students interpret and respond to naturally-occurring academic writing tasks. In particular, it focuses on the following questions:

1. What resources do students rely on to help them interpret and complete writing tasks, and how do specific classroom writing situations influence their approaches?
2. How do students' task interpretations and approaches relate to their teachers' stated goals for assigning writing?
3. Under what conditions do students rely on coping strategies to circumvent the demands of writing assignments?

Participants

Writing assignments, like other academic tasks, are subject to interpretation and negotiation within the complex social system of the classroom and school. For this reason, I have found it useful to approach the study of naturally-occurring writing tasks as a series of case studies. This method has allowed me to examine how particular tasks are conceptualized by teachers and students and how these conceptualizations converge or diverge.

Over the course of a semester (4 months), I examined how 13 freshman students interpreted and responded to the writing assignments they received in a variety of courses. These participants were selected from the class rosters of seven courses (identified through a survey) in the Arts, Sciences, and Humanities at Carnegie Mellon University that required students to write papers. By looking at students working in a range of disciplines, I hoped to get a sample of the kinds of writing situations and tasks students encounter across the curriculum. Students were selected on the basis of their scores on the SAT-verbal exam, the only measure of language ability available for all students. In each course or recitation section, two students were selected as participants, one student with a low score and one student with a high score in comparison to the rest of the members of the course. (During the course of my study, one student withdrew from school and could no longer participate.) This selection process permitted me to examine how students with different scores on this measure responded to features of their writing assignments and situations.

Data Collection

My research methods included collecting of detailed writing process logs in which students described all aspects of the work they completed for papers; collecting of all notes, drafts, and graded papers the participants produced during the semester; and interviewing both the participants and their teachers.

The writing logs kept by the participants included descriptions of all paper-related activities, such as reading, thinking, conducting library research, talking, and writing. Once participants began thinking about or working on a paper, they were required to write daily log entries (even if they did not actually work on papers every day) and were asked to deliver entries and copies of notes or drafts on a regular schedule, at least three times a week.

The findings of other researchers (Faigley, Cherry, Jolliffe, & Skinner, 1985; Sternglass & Pugh, 1986) reveal the benefits of using writing logs as a research tool for examining the concerns and processes of writers working in natural settings over extended periods of time. Sternglass and Pugh (1986) in their semester-long study of the reading and writing processes of graduate students, argue for the value of retrospective accounts. They found that retrospective or concurrent journal accounts "are a rich source of information because they permit consideration of the complex context within which composing occurs" (p. 297). While retrospective reports can reveal—sometimes in remarkable detail—what information writers attend to when they interpret and complete their tasks, the validity of such reports cannot be determined in any definitive way, (see Cooper & Holzman, 1983; Ericsson & Simon, 1980; Morris, 1981; Nisbett & Wilson, 1977; Tomlinson, 1984 for discussions about the value and validity of retrospective accounts of language processes such as those gathered in writing logs.)

The interviews with participants in the current study were open-ended but also included questions about students' initial responses to specific writing assignments, how difficult they thought the paper would be to write, how well they thought they did on assignments, and how they interpreted teachers' comments and grades. In addition to interviews with students, I also interviewed their teachers and asked them to discuss: (1) why they give particular writing assignments, (2) how they structure writing assignments, and (3) how they evaluate papers. This information allowed me to compare teachers' stated goals and purposes for assigning writing with the actual goals and processes students brought to specific writing tasks as revealed in their logs and interviews.

Analyses

The data collected proved to be very rich. It consisted of over 700 pages of material, including writing process logs from the 13 participants, copies of all their assignments, notes, drafts, and graded papers, and transcriptions or notes from interviews with the students and their teachers. My goal in analyzing these extensive materials was to examine, as systematically as possible, (1) how writing tasks were conceived, presented, and evaluated by teachers; (2) how these tasks were interpreted and completed by students; and (3) how various situational and individual resources influenced students' approaches.

To accomplish this goal I identified several factors for analyzing the teacher's and the student's version of individual writing tasks. In order to understand the teacher's conceptualization of a writing task, the analysis focused in particular on the following areas:

1. The teacher's stated goals for assigning writing.
2. The teacher's presentation of the assignment to students, including any resources or procedures students were expected to use to complete their task.
3. The teacher's explanations of the criteria used to evaluate students' papers.

The analysis of the student's conceptualization of a writing task focused on the kinds of resources each student might rely on to interpret and complete assignments. These resources could include:

1. The student's understanding of the purpose of the assignment and the criteria used in awarding grades.
2. The student's understanding of the procedures and resources to be used to complete the assignment.
3. The student's repertoire of "production systems" or strategies for completing certain kinds of school writing tasks.
4. The student's past experiences in the course.
5. The student's past experiences with the subject matter being covered in the course.
6. The student's time and effort allocation.
7. The student's collaborations with peers in the course.

This list of factors for analyzing a teacher's and student's version of class-room tasks is based on a similar analysis scheme developed by Nespor (1987). In her study, Nespor examined how a persuasive essay assignment in a high school English class was defined by the teacher and ten students. Drawing from other examinations of cognitive processes in the classroom (Corno & Mandinach, 1983; Doyle, 1983; Posner, 1982) and her own research, Nespor identified several "heuristics or sensitizing concepts" (p. 210) that proved to be useful for analyzing how classroom tasks are defined. Because Nespor's framework for analyzing academic tasks takes into account the important features of classroom settings that can influence how students define and approach tasks, it proved to be an especially useful analytical tool for the current study.

In order to determine whether students' task interpretations and ap-proaches matched their teachers' intentions for assigning writing for each case study task, I carefully reviewed the teacher's description of the assignment and his or her stated goals and methods for assigning and evaluating writing. I then compared the teacher's conceptualization of the assignment with each student's interpretation and response as revealed in the interviews and process logs. Based upon these comparisons, I made a judgment about whether students and teachers concurred or disagreed in their conceptualizations of the assignment. These judgments were then tested against those of an inde-pendent rater who went through the same process, reviewing information from assignments, logs, and interviews. In every case our judgments matched: 7 out of the 13 students' responses to writing assignments appeared to match their teachers' intentions while 6 did not.

Findings

The following discussion focuses for the most part on the classroom settings where disjunctions occurred between teachers' intentions and students' interpretations. In describing and attempting to account for these disjunctions—and for some instances where teachers and students agreed—my aim is to discover possibly significant factors involved in the complex process of interpreting and responding to naturally occurring academic writing assignments. In particular, by focusing my discussion on the classroom settings where teachers' and students' task interpretations diverged, I hoped to identify the factors that can lead to disjunctions between teachers' intentions for assigning writing and students' responses. Any inferences about causation were made tentatively and, whenever possible, were checked with the participants themselves.

In the following section, the teachers' and students' conceptualizations of three different writing tasks are presented. In order to make the comparison of teachers' and students' conceptualizations of different tasks easier, the findings are presented as case studies of individual tasks: one writing task from a freshman-level sociology course, one task from a freshman-level engineering course, and one task from an undergraduate literature course. First, each case study begins with a brief description of the class in which the writing task was assigned. Then the teacher's conceptualization and presentation of the assignment are described. Next, two students' descriptions of how they interpreted and completed the task and how their papers were evaluated are presented. Finally, each case study ends with a brief summary of the students' interpretations of their task and the resources and coping strategies that appeared to influence their approaches. All of the participants' names in the study are pseudonyms.

Case Study of a Sociology Writing Task: Reports of Field-work

Carnegie Mellon, like many universities, requires entering freshmen to take a series of "core courses" in the Arts, Sciences, and Humanities. Such courses are often large (over 100 students) and taught by lecturers with the help of teaching assistants, who conduct weekly recitation sections and, more often than not, grade students' work. The writing tasks described below were assigned in "Social Influences," a course that all freshmen enrolled in the college of Humanities and Social Sciences are required to take. In Social Influences, writing assignments were designed by the professor and then presented to students and graded by teaching assistants in individual recitation or discussion sections. This practice—while practical and commonplace—complicates our attempt to examine how writing tasks are negotiated and defined in classrooms. In the case of Social Influences, writing assignments can undergo two possible transformations: first, when teaching assistants interpret and translate the professor's assignment for their individual sections; and second, when students interpret and respond to their section leader's assignment. In order to account for the possibility of differences among the professor's, teaching assistant's and student's version of a writing assignment, I chose to examine how writing assignments were presented in two separate recitation sections and how a total of four students (two from each section) defined and completed these tasks. While the following discussion focuses on only two of these four students' approaches, the concluding discussion describes how all four students defined and approached their writing tasks for Social Influences.

During an hour-long interview, Professor Smith explained that the writing assignments for the course consisted of three papers that were designed to "build on each other." Each assignment required that students conduct fieldwork as part of their research and write a 4-page report. The first assignment was intended to help students "to systemize their observations and experiences" by asking them to gather material and use it to present valid conclusions about "socialization" processes at Carnegie Mellon. Dr. Smith explained that for this beginning assignment, it was important "to impress on students the fact that readers don't know what they do" and that they should "learn to write for an uninformed audience." The second paper required students to do fieldwork and examine how power relations are manifested at Carnegie Mellon. Professor Smith described three goals for this assignment: to get students to select and organize data for an argument; to use the theories and concepts discussed in class to frame these arguments; to understand the use of comparative data. The third and final paper, while similar to the others, placed "greater demands" on students. For this paper, students were expected to include "field data, comparative data from the readings, and key concepts from the course." In addition, a "high premium" was to be placed on how the paper was presented.

In response to questions about why she gave writing assignments in her course, Professor Smith explained that "writing is a way of learning, of integrating ideas and experiences. It helps students to go beyond course content, to learn how to systemize what's happening to them." Thus, she believed that writing could play a central role not only in helping students to learn course material, but in allowing them to relate this new material to their own experiences.

Presentation of the Assignment. All three assignments were described briefly in the eleven-page course syllabus. According to the syllabus, each paper was worth 15% of a student's course grade, the same weight as the midterm exam. Thus, grades for all three papers accounted for nearly half (45%) of the student's grade, revealing that writing did indeed play an important role in the course.

Professor Smith provided teaching assistants with a detailed description of the requirements for each assignment, including the kinds of information the paper should include and the criteria for grading. For example, she recommended that papers be graded on a 100-point scale, with 80 points for "content" (data and method; concepts and theories; analysis; conclusions; use of comparative material) and 20 points for "presentation" (description of data; style of the whole paper). In a memo to teaching assistants describing the first paper, she explained that "I realize that the above [description of requirements] gives a bit more than you might want to say to students. Use it as a general framework for instructing students." Several teaching assistants responded by using these descriptions to generate a somewhat shorter list of guidelines which they handed out to students in their sections. These guidelines turned out to play an important role in determining how students approached the assignments.

Two Teaching Assistants' Versions of the Assignment

Sometime during the middle of the semester, two students from different sections of Social Influences were caught plagiarizing. Apparently, one student handed in a paper that a fellow classmate had written and turned in to another section leader. After this event became public knowledge, several students complained to the professor that students in different sections received an unfair advantage on their papers because their teaching assistants handed out explicit guidelines for completing papers while others did not. In answer to these complaints, Professor Smith decided that students in all sections should receive the same detailed guidelines for assignments.

Consequently, both teaching assistants in the sections I studied presented their students with the same seven-point list of steps for completing the second paper. Each of the seven steps students were to follow included advice, examples, or questions to help them focus on key issues. For example, the second step directed students to: "State your assumption; what are you going to test in your study?" (See Appendix for the complete guidelines.)

Even though the two teaching assistants I interviewed presented the same assignment to students, they described different concerns about shaping and responding to student writing. Section leader Stevens explained that the worst advice teachers can give is "to tell students to be clear." He tells students "if you're not confused, you're not learning." Because he believed that students need to struggle to define and express their ideas, Stevens did not like giving students outlines or guidelines to follow for their papers. In fact, on one set of paper guidelines he wrote "Security Blanket Guide—discard as soon as possible." He felt that these guidelines took too much of the "struggle" and, hence, the learning out of the assignments.

When asked how he liked to respond to student papers, Stevens explained that he preferred to respond at different stages in order to "trace their progress, how their thinking is evolving." He liked to ask students questions about their ideas and methods, and to "keep pushing." He also encouraged students to consider rewriting and resubmitting papers.

In contrast, section leader Todd believed in giving students clear advice for producing papers. He spent a large portion of his weekly recitation meeting discussing the second paper with students, telling them to pay particular attention to their "method section." He wanted students to provide more detail about their data-gathering techniques than they had in their first papers, to "be active observers, not passive."

In responding to student papers, Todd explained that it was important to explain his criteria for grading in class and to "talk about where students missed" and "what they could do to improve next time." Todd also encouraged students to share their early drafts with him and told students to call him, at home or at school, if they needed help.

Reports of Fieldwork—Students' Versions of the Assignment

Described below are the responses of two students: Art was enrolled in Stevens' recitation section and Barbara in Todd's recitation section. As stated earlier, both students received the same written instructions for completing their papers, but each student brought different assumptions and past experiences to the tasks.

Art and Barbara—Conceptualizing the Task. When I interviewed Art before he began working on this assignment, he explained that he did not anticipate any "major problems" in writing this second paper. However, he did say "I'll be lucky to get six pages—maybe with wide margins." Art found the first paper easy to write because he could rely on his classnotes and "since it was about my own experiences, all I had to do was BS a little." He explained that while he composed the first paper, friends dropped by to ask how it was going and "I'd say 700 words—950 so far." Art admitted that the conclusion for this first paper could have been expanded but said, "Hey, 1500 words is enough." He was quite satisfied with the B- he received and seemed confident about producing his next paper without much difficulty.

Art's conceptualization of the second paper (a field study of power at Carnegie Mellon) seemed to match his conceptualization of the first paper. He focused on the product requirements (length and format) to define and complete the assignment and failed to engage in many of the processes described by Professor Smith and his recitation leader.

Unlike Art, in preliminary interviews, Barbara described misgivings about writing her paper. These misgivings stemmed from her lack of experience with "long papers" (over 3 pages) and the fact that she was used to producing either "opinionated" papers or research papers where she "could quote a lot from sources and use up space."

She received a B on her first paper for Social Influences, and Todd, her teaching assistant, wrote fairly extensive general comments about how she could improve her paper:

> First, you have not included a section that describes your method-
> ology. How did you collect your data? What kinds of data did you
> collect? This should be made explicit after your introduction. Also,
> additional analysis and interpretation of your observations would
> strengthen your paper considerably.

In a general discussion with the class about how to improve their second paper, Todd once again stressed the importance of describing one's methods in detail. In her reaction to the teacher's comments on the first assignment, Barbara wrote, "I thought they were good points; however, he should have told us before we wrote our paper.... In any case, I was pleased with my grade!" She also explained that "I thought I could work under pressure for my paper. Now I know this kind of paper is not for my usual approach. I think to start my second paper, I'll talk to my recitation teacher for some advice."

Art and Barbara—Planning and Composing the Paper. Two weeks before the paper was due, Art's teaching assistant, Stevens, required students to write one-paragraph openings for their papers and bring them to class for discus-sion. Art wrote about "to what extent professors and teaching assistants can and do use their power." If the goal of this activity was to check how students' work was evolving, it seemed to have failed in Art's case, who reported that he didn't talk about his opening and didn't pay much attention to the discus-sion because he was too worried about the upcoming mid-term exam.

When he returned to the assignment ten days later (just two days before the paper was due), Art reported, "I changed my topic from the power of profes-sors to the power of sports—figured it would be easier since I'm involved with sports." He then reported that he "started writing everything from the top of [his] head, said that [he] had interviewed the coach and interacted with teammates but really didn't." Essentially, Art fabricated his field report. While writing the paper, Art said he watched a basketball game on television, and took several breaks to rest and talk to friends. When he got stuck in his writing, he looked at the paper guidelines for help. He finished his paper in four hours and typed it on the computer the next day, making only minor, word-level changes. As with the first paper, Art reported that "always, throughout the paper, [I] constantly kept track of how many words I had written." In follow-up interviews, Art explained that he used the seven-step assignment guidelines to compose the paper: "I read through each step and tried to answer it." Interestingly enough, Art produced a seven paragraph paper.

Approximately two weeks before her paper on power was due, Barbara wrote:

> I think that I'm gonna write my paper on the power of fraternities because I talked to my roommate and she helped me think of different options for the paper.... Since a guideline was given to help us focus on the issues for our paper, I'll be basically answering the questions given in this guideline and hopefully my answers will stretch to 4-6 pages.

A week later she reported that she had "no new ideas—probably work better under spontaneity."

She did visit her teaching assistant, as planned, but apparently used this visit to get an extension on the paper's due date and not to discuss her work. When she finally sat down to write her paper, her strategy was remarkably similar to Art's. She explained:

> While looking at the guideline that was handed to us earlier, and also the hints given in recitation, I was kinda overwhelmed with all the questions to be included in our papers! I guess I didn't really know how to organize it. However, being the spontaneous person that I am, I finally thought that I should just write the ideas down as they came in mind and try to refer back to the guideline if I wanted to answer more questions.

Like Art, she did no actual planning or field research and relied on the detailed questions in the assignment sheet to generate her paper.

Art and Barbara—Evaluation. Art received 75 out of 100 possible points for this paper. His instructor (Stevens) wrote three questions at the end of his paper: (1) How does the coach regulate the behavior of athletes? (2) Which behaviors are legitimately regulated by the coach? (3) What evidence would you need to back up the claims made? Since Art did not plan to revise the paper, he did not find these comments particularly useful, explaining that his instructor was "a good teacher, but expects too much." Art said he was satisfied with this grade and that his "teacher's comments don't really matter." Apparently Stevens' goal to "keep pushing" students by asking them questions about their research did not always succeed. Art found his feedback largely useless.

Barbara's recitation teacher (Todd) wrote extensive critical comments in the margins of her paper, pointing out that she included irrelevant information in her report, and failed to provide any detail about her methods or observations. In his final comments he wrote, "I think you are capable of much better work, Barbara" and gave her a B-. In follow-up interviews, Barbara revealed that she agreed with her teacher's comments, saying "I knew it was a bad paper when I handed it in—I didn't do any real research." She felt that his criticisms "made sense" and said, "His comments will let me write a better final paper."

However, in spite of these projections, Barbara's system for writing her third and final paper for the course followed the same pattern as before. She composed it at the computer on the day it was due ("right before class"), using the assignment sheet to refer to if she did not have anything to say.

Sociology Writing Task: Students' Interpretations, Resources, and Coping Strategies

Several factors seemed to enter into Art's response to this assignment. Time and effort allocation were kept at a minimum—he stopped writing when he had produced enough words to fulfill the length requirement. The seven-step paper guidelines furnished by his teacher proved to be an especially valuable resource. These guidelines served as a prompt and helped him to produce a "field study" without ever actually collecting any data. Thus, Art's predisposition to expend minimal effort on the writing assignments may actually have been fostered by the resources his teacher provided. Finally, because the teacher's evaluation of his paper and suggestions for further analysis were not tied to any required revision, Art decided that Stevens' comments could be ignored.

Throughout her interviews and log entries, Barbara referred to herself as a "spontaneous" writer whose "usual approach" was to put off assignments and "work under pressure" at the last minute. Early on in the course, after her first paper, she realized that this method for producing papers would not work for the field reports she was being asked to write.

In spite of this realization and promises to change her ways, Barbara continued to put off planning and writing until just before her papers were due. As with Art, it appears that the explicit paper guidelines she received enabled her to continue to rely on this efficient "production system" (Nespor, 1987, p. 214). The guidelines served as a sort of paper generator for both students, allowing them to circumvent the assignment's process requirements and produce fairly acceptable products.

In many ways, these two students' shortcuts for producing acceptable papers are sensible. Rogoff (1984) and other researchers stress the practical and opportunistic nature of cognitive activities in everyday settings. Rogoff (1984) explains that "thinking is a practical activity which is adjusted to meet the demands of the situation. . . Rather than employing formal approaches to solving problems, people devise satisfactory, opportunistic solutions" (p.7). As mentioned earlier, a total of four students (two in each recitation section) were observed in this course, and three out of these four students chose not to use the research methods they had been taught to plan and produce their papers. Instead, they adjusted their approaches to meet the demands of the situation, which they believed called for papers that clearly matched the steps outlined in their detailed assignment guidelines. One student was even astute enough to fabricate her data and conclusions so that they matched the ideas raised in class lectures. However, while these three students found the paper guidelines very helpful, the student who did try to complete the assignment as his teacher intended complained that the explicit guidelines co-opted his own ideas by forcing him to follow a series of steps. He described the paper guidelines as a "narrow constriction" which he felt obliged to follow and explained that "it seems as if we're being graded on how well we can follow directions, not how we think on our own."

It is important to remember that the guidelines for producing papers were provided to students in all sections of the course *only* after they complained to the professor and asked her to make task instructions more explicit. This request is one of the coping strategies outlined by Doyle that students rely on to lessen the ambiguity and risk involved in accomplishing academic work. While Art and Barbara relied on these explicit task instructions to circumvent the research and learning processes their professor hoped to promote, they also brought particular individual "production systems" or writing strategies that influenced their responses.

Time and effort allocation—one of the variables involved in how students define and accomplish academic tasks—seemed to play an important part in students' responses. For the most part, the students I observed in Social Influences seemed unwilling to invest the time and effort necessary to complete the assignments as their teachers intended. Three variables seemed to interact and shape their approaches: the individual "production systems," or set of composing strategies, students brought to the assignments; the explicit task instructions that students received; the nature of the feedback students received—particularly whether it applied to work on later papers. Similar individual and situational variables come into play in the following analysis as well.

111

Case Study of an Engineering Writing Task: Producing a Concise Argument

The following writing task, described briefly at the beginning of this paper, was assigned in a "pilot version" of a new required core course for all freshmen enrolled in the Carnegie Institute of Technology at Carnegie Mellon. This course was developed and taught by a team of four engineering professors, who each designed and presented the assignments for their specific portion of the semester-long course. This particular writing assignment was designed by Professor Clark, and then assigned and graded by teaching assistants in individual recitation sections. As with the previous case study, I will briefly summarize the professor's and teaching assistant's conceptualizations of the assignment, and then present two students' responses.

Professor's Version of the Assignment—Conceptualization of the Task's Goals

As described earlier, Professor Clark explained that he intended this writing task to be a challenging exercise in synthesizing and transforming course material into a concise 200 word argument about the role of "nontechnical issues" in the development of lead regulations. Professor Clark said that when he responded to student writing, he liked to give detailed "constructive feedback," focusing in particular on organization and coherence. He stressed writing in his courses because he believed that writing was "very valuable" and that speaking and writing skills needed to be stressed throughout the engineering curriculum in order to better prepare students for the writing demands they were sure to encounter when they entered the job market.

Presentation of the Assignment. This writing task was presented to students as one of several assignments included in the nine-page syllabus for Professor Clark's section of the course. It was the second task of a two-part assignment worth a total of four points. Specifically, students were told to "write a carefully prepared short statement . . . using information in the assigned articles, in the handout, and presented by all of the speakers throughout this unit." Students were expected to "boil down" all of this material and present a concise argument in 200 words or less.

The Teaching Assistant's Version of the Assignment

In an interview, section-leader Coleman complained that engineering students were not asked to write enough in their other courses and as a result were often "output illiterate." When responding to student writing, he felt that it was important to look for features of "competent writing" such as "complete sentences, spelling, organization, and evidence." He also looked for particular "content features" which consisted of key points from the course readings. (This emphasis on "content features" when evaluating students' performance on the assignment differed from Professor Clark's stated criteria for the assignment.) Coleman said that while he liked to give students "meaningful feedback" and to "tell students ways to improve their writing," he found that there wasn't enough time in the weekly recitation sections to discuss writing.

Producing a Concise Argument—Students' Versions of the Assignment

John and Judy—Conceptualizing the Task. As described earlier, John described this as an easy assignment. He had already completed a very similar writing task for the course, one that likewise had a 200 word limit. He explained that it required the writer to "present an argument based on evidence that was all there" in the assigned material. "I felt like it was BS—basically it called for reiterating what we'd been given."

Judy had a similar response to this assignment, saying it wasn't "motivating" and that the 200 word limit was "utterly ridiculous." She found this constraint especially troubling because it interfered with her "normal approach" to writing school papers. She liked to use the "triangle method" for developing her introductory and concluding paragraphs, a popular technique she had learned in high school. However, because of the length restriction for this task, she had to limit her introduction and conclusion on her first paper to just two sentences, and was very surprised that she received full credit for her paper, which she believed was poorly written. She also said that she would have preferred more freedom in writing these papers because it was nearly impossible to present "enough evidence" in just 200 words.

Like John, Judy understood her teacher's grading criteria to be based on "a list of ideas" from the readings and lectures, and she explained that a check "meant that you'd hit one."

John and Judy-Planning and Composing the Paper. John explained that as he was reading the assigned materials the night before the paper was due, he "formulated the report in [his] head," picking out names and events to mention in his paper. In his last log entry, he said, "Essentially, I paraphrased the reports I read . . . No great insights on this paper—sorry!"

Judy took notes from the assigned readings to prepare for writing the paper, but she limited her reading and notetaking strategies to fit the limits of the assignment, saying, "I just skimmed the assigned articles looking for blurbs about the topic—I don't need a lot of details." Later she reported, "My notes for this assignment are pretty sparse—oh well, the less I have to work with the better, I suppose, since I'm limited to 200 words anyway."

Even with her "sparse" notes, Judy produced a first draft that was 739 words long. She produced two more drafts and kept "looking for shorter ways to say things" until she had cut over 300 words. In a note to her teaching assistant attached to this final version, she said, "Considering the major chop-job I did on my last paper, I absolutely refused to grind this paper up any more. It is simply against my writing principles."

John and Judy-Evaluation. John produced a 412 word paper and received full credit (2 out of 2 points). His teacher's feedback consisted of four checkmarks in the paper's margin and three brief comments, one of which told him that his paper was "a little longer than necessary." John said that he found this writing assignment "a waste of class time."

Judy also received full credit for her paper. Her teacher's feedback consisted of five checks in the margin and two words in the text marked with question marks. Not surprisingly, Judy said that she just looked at the grades she received on these papers and did not bother to look at any other marks or comments.

Engineering Writing Task: Students' Interpretations, Resources, and Coping Strategies

Even though Professor Clark intended this assignment to be challenging, the students I studied found it "unmotivating" or a "waste of time." Unlike John, Judy did struggle to make her paper more concise, but found it impossible to meet the 200 word limit, a constraint that she not only found arbitrary and counter to what she had learned about good writing in past courses, but which seemed to shape her limited reading and note-taking strategies. John seemed to object more to the nature of the assignment itself, which on the surface asked students to take a stand on an issue, but in reality called for "reiterating" what they had read.

Thus two features of the task itself seemed to influence students' responses: the limited purpose for the assignment (i.e., to show that students had read and comprehended course material); and the seemingly arbitrary length restriction. In addition, both students appeared to base their task interpretations and subsequent responses on information about task requirements gained from their interaction with the teaching assistant in the course. In other words, as the nature of their teacher's grading system became more apparent, they were able to "selectively attend to information that [had] consequences

114

for task accomplishment" (Doyle, p.181), namely the production of papers with information that matched the facts on their teacher's list of "content features." It appears in this case that, as Doyle suggests, the "answers a teacher actually accepts and rewards define the real tasks in the classroom" (p. 182).

Both students brought individual experiences which also may have played a role in shaping their negative responses. John alluded to the fact that he had encountered similar assignments in which the teacher used writing to test whether students had learned course material. Apparently he had developed a fairly efficient system for completing such assignments, though he found them a waste of time.

In contrast, Judy had learned a particular method for developing academic essays which did not match the constraints of this specific assignment and may have interfered with her ability to produce a brief 200 word argument. In fact, Judy said that in her previous English class, her major writing problem had been that she presented good ideas but failed to develop them. Ironically, for the engineering assignment, she was expected to condense her ideas, but argued that this requirement went "against her writing principles." It appears that both students' previous experiences interacted with the situational variables discussed above and had an impact on their approaches to this assignment.

In the following section, we will examine the last setting in which a disjunction occurred between the teacher's intentions and one student's interpretation of a writing task.

Case Study of a Literature Writing Task: A Research Paper on the Victorian Era

This final case study examines the teacher's and students' versions of a research paper assignment given in "Reading Texts" a freshman literature course that students (who qualify by scoring above 500 points on the SAT-verbal exam) may elect to take in place of the freshman composition course. Unlike the two previous writing tasks we examined, this assignment was formulated, presented, and graded by the professor of the course.

Professor's Version of the Assignment—Conceptualization of the Task's Goals

The course, "Reading Texts" differs from many traditional introductory literature courses in that it does not present a survey of particular literary genres or periods. Instead, as Professor Green described in his syllabus, the aim of the course was to "study texts as culturally produced and reading as a culturally-acquired process." Throughout the course, students were required to analyze and describe their reactions to different literary texts in several written "response statements." These fairly informal statements were not graded but were commented on by Professor Green, and good response statements were read aloud in class periodically. Professor Green used these short assignments to build up to more formal paper assignments, which consisted of two papers, including the research paper. The response statements made up 30% of the course grade and the two papers were worth 50% of students' final grades. Clearly, student writing played a very important role in the course.

During an interview, Professor Green explained his belief that having to write "changes the way people read literary works [because] it poses problems and changes attitudes toward texts." In structuring paper assignments, he liked to model this process by posing a problem or question and then suggesting a path students could take to solve it. For his course, papers were developed in stages, with students writing informally about paper topics, and then producing drafts and the final version. In responding to student papers, Professor Green said he looked for "argumentative strength" and evidence of "effective reading and interpretive skills."

Presentation of the Assignment. Shortly after the middle of the semester and over a month before papers were due, Professor Green handed out a one-page description of the research paper assignment. The stated goal for the 5-7 page research paper was to "give [students] the opportunity to investigate the repertoire of Victorian texts and to use this information to interpret one or more of them." Students were encouraged to come up with their own topic or issue for the assignment, but Professor Green suggested several possible general approaches in the hand-out and discussed a specific example in class.

In the written instructions he emphasized the kind of paper he wanted students to produce: "Remember that a research paper *is an argument*. It is *NOT* a report of *FACTS*, but a careful marshalling of the judgments, opinions, and ideas of others to support your own position." In addition to these general directions, the written assignment instructions explained that the "audience" for the paper was other members of the class and that a written proposal was due four weeks before the final paper. In this proposal students were expected to indicate the topic of their research, the argument they expected to make, the work or works they would interpret, and to include a bibliography of sources they had used so far.

In presenting this assignment to students, Professor Green tried to make his expectations clear while at the same time leaving room for students to develop their own topics and approaches. In the following description we will see how two students responded to this freedom.

A Research Paper on the Victorian Era—Students' Versions of the Assignment

Described below are two students' responses to this assignment. The first student's response was judged by the independent raters to match her teacher's intentions; however, what is particularly striking is how much this student struggled to understand and define her task.

Helen and Greg—Conceptualizing the Task. When I interviewed Helen before she began working on her research paper, she predicted that this would be a hard paper to write, primarily because she thought students had received very little guidance in choosing topics and formulating their approaches. She wanted more information about what the professor expected. Her insecurity, she explained, was due in part to the fact that she and other students had not received any grades on the work they had turned in so far in the course. Although they had turned in one formal paper, the professor was slow in returning them and as a result, Helen said she had "no idea what the proper approach is or what [the teacher] is looking for on papers." Helen reported that the class had asked for "more feedback" but had not received any yet.

Six weeks before her paper was due Helen borrowed a book on life in Victorian England from her aunt. She planned to use this book to "get some background on the Victorian Period" before she tried to choose a literary text to analyze.

A few days later, the rest of her classmates received their first graded papers back, but she reported, "Mine was lost! So I'm still unclear if I have done anything correctly." After speaking with a classmate about his plans for the research paper assignment, Helen reported, "I realized that I was very confused. He, my classmate, had a totally different idea of the assignment." In class that day, Helen asked her professor to explain the assignment again and wrote in her log entry:

> I think I have a better understanding of the [paper's] goal. We are to propose and support an argument that is somewhat new. This argument must deal with the Victorian era. First, though, I need to choose a topic and create an argument dealing with the topic.

With this clearer conceptualization of the assignment, Helen went to the library two days later and spent five hours looking for information on women in the Victorian era—a topic she had developed by talking to friends. She

117

narrowed her focus to an examination of Thomas Hardy's poem "Ruined Maid" and decided to try to present an argument about the woman he has portrayed. In her proposal she stated her goal even more explicitly: "I have researched the actual lives of prostitutes in the Victorian era and circumstances surrounding their 'fall'. . . Based on my initial research, Thomas Hardy has created a very true portrait of prostitutes and hopefully this paper will show how." Professor Green approved her proposal, and on the same day finally returned her first paper (nearly a month after she had handed it in). She received an A and the professor wrote "This is far and away the best paper I've received for this assignment."

However, in spite of this positive feedback, Helen reported that she continued to struggle to define her professor's expectations more clearly, explaining that she and her classmates spent thirty minutes one day talking about their research topics and "trying to decide what he wanted for these papers." The following excerpt from her log entry suggests one possible reason for her continued confusion:

> I think [the professor] wants us to use others' arguments to develop our own. So, in a sense this isn't a research paper, (i.e., telling what's already been said like in high school) but rather an argument that requires research.

This explicit reference to her previous school experiences suggests that Helen had developed a schema for writing research papers in high school which did not match the requirements for this assignment. Once she realized this, she was able to define her task more clearly.

Unlike Helen, Greg predicted that the research paper for Reading Texts would be easy to write since he was familiar with the material because he had "read lots of Victorian literature and history in high school." He also explained that he had written similar kinds of papers for his high school English classes. In addition, he reported that he was studying Victorian literature in an aesthetics course he was also enrolled in and believed that his work in this course would help him to write the paper for Reading Texts.

On the day that research paper proposals were due, Greg reported in his log that he was still not sure what Professor Green wanted and that he had not yet come up with a topic for his research paper. He was studying Jane Austen's *Pride and Prejudice* in his aesthetics course and finally decided to propose this novel as the focus of his paper. In his written proposal, he explained that his research paper would be "an interpretation of the Victorian best seller, Jane Austen's *Pride and Prejudice*, and the reasons for its popularity in Victorian culture." He admitted that his proposal was a last minute attempt to fulfill a requirement, writing, "My proposal was a conglomeration of pretentious. . .impromptu generalizations and gave me no base for ideas concerning the actual paper." Unfortunately, Greg never bothered to pick up his proposal (which he had failed to write his name on) and as a result did not learn that he had made a serious mistake in assuming that Jane Austen was a Victorian writer. In fact, Professor Green rejected his proposal because Austen wrote her novels several decades before the Victorian era.

Helen and Greg—Planning and Composing the Paper. After Helen had a clearer notion of what her assignment required, she spent several hours in the library doing more research and taking notes. Based on what she learned, she decided to revise her initial claim (described in her proposal) that "Hardy shows reality" about prostitution in his poem.

She reported,"I think [Hardy] may be showing what the public *believes* to be reality." After taking over 20 pages of notes, Helen produced a "rough tree" which laid out the form her paper would take. Then she wrote a detailed three-page outline for her paper. Using this outline and her extensive notes, she wrote a rough draft two days before the final paper was due. She completed and revised her draft the next day, basing some of her revisions on a discussion of Victorian ideals that she and her class had after viewing a film. Helen reported that "I was able to contribute a lot of information to the discussion based on my research. Professor Green seemed pleased with some of the things I mentioned, so I included the ideas he seemed to like into my paper." Clearly, Helen's concern about accountability and meeting her teacher's expectations continued to influence her approach to this assignment.

Greg explained that the rough draft of his research paper was "written entirely from information gleaned from [his] aesthetics class rather than actual research on [his] part." He said that he often wrote research papers for high school this way, doing little, if any actual library research. If he had done some research on the Victorian era, as the assignment required, he might have learned that Jane Austen was not a Victorian author. However, he was confident about his background knowledge of Victorian literature and history, and did not even bother to re-read *Pride and Prejudice*, which he had last read three years earlier. When Greg did decide to go to the library on the night before his final paper was due, he limited his research to books of literacy criticism about Austen's work.

Helen and Greg—Evaluation. Helen received an A on her paper, and Pro fessor Green wrote that it was "a first rate use of history to contextualize and revise one's reading of a literary work." Helen's interpretation and response to this assignment matched her professor's intentions, but it is important to remember how much she struggled to define this task for herself.

Professor Green reported that he was surprised to receive Greg's paper on Jane Austen because he had not approved this paper topic. In fact, after several announcements in class weeks earlier that he had an unclaimed paper proposal with no name on it, he had assumed that the student had decided to withdraw from the course. At the end of Greg's paper, Professor Green wrote, "Jane Austen is not a Victorian writer—this is not an acceptable topic" and gave the paper an F.

Literature Writing Task: Students' Interpretations, Resources, and Coping Strategies

Greg's failure on this assignment can be traced, in part, to his previous experiences with Victorian literature and his mistaken assumption that Austen wrote her novels during the Victorian era. This mistake might have been caught and corrected, but Greg failed to take advantage of the same classroom resources that helped Helen to define and shape her approach. Greg skipped class often and did not ask for feedback from his teacher or classmates on his conceptualization of what the assignment entailed. Unlike Helen, he did not question his initial representation of the task and did not rely on the social-interactional resources available in the classroom to help him test and refine his approach.

While it is difficult to know why Helen worked so hard to clarify her understanding of this assignment, at least two factors may have played a part. First, lack of feedback or grades on previous work appears to have made Helen and her classmates particularly interested in determining what their teacher expected. Without feedback, the ambiguity and risk involved in responding to assignments increases and students must become especially sensitive to any cues that signal accountability (Doyle, 1983). It is not surprising that Helen and her classmates shared and compared their representations of the assignment and asked Professor Green for more explicit information about what he wanted. In this way, students were able to negotiate and refine their task definitions, relying on the social-interactional resources available in the classroom.

Second, Helen's previous experiences with research papers did not seem to match Professor Green's expectations, and after this disjunction became apparent to her, she seemed to find it easier to define her task. In Helen's case, her familiarity with research paper tasks could have been a disadvantage, if she had not realized that what her teacher wanted was "an argument that required research" and not a summary of other authors' ideas.

Helen's story of how she defined her writing task and went on to produce a successful paper illustrates just how important and complex the act of representing one's writing task can be when it occurs in natural classroom settings. She took advantage of the social resources in the classroom and, with her classmates' and teacher's help, was able to clarify and refine her task definition. This process took time, as well. As Helen worked to find a topic and focus for her research paper, she reported that her representation of the assignment continued to evolve.

When juxtaposed in this way, the stories of Greg's failure and Helen's success are interesting because they suggest that successful students, like Helen, may be efficient "resource managers" who make use of several of the resources available for interpreting and completing tasks.

Discussion

These case studies suggest that we can learn a great deal about the concerns and processes of student writers when we locate our research in the complex social settings of actual classrooms. Previous research reveals that classrooms are highly evaluative settings where accountability (that is, the processes and products students are actually rewarded for) often determines how students respond to school assignments. Case studies such as mine are valuable not because they can provide teachers and researchers with clear-cut answers, but rather because they provide opportunities to discover possibly significant factors in students' approaches to writing. By examining when and how students' interpretations differ from their teachers' intentions, we can begin to formulate hypotheses about how features of specific tasks and writing contexts shape students' approaches.

Essentially, I wanted to learn more about the kinds of variables that come into play when students set out to define and complete writing assignments in a variety of courses. As stated earlier, my aim in conducting this research was to begin to answer three key questions:

1) What kinds of resources do students rely on to help them to interpret and complete writing tasks, and how do specific classroom writing situations influence their approaches?
2) How do students' task interpretations and approaches relate to their teachers' stated goals for assigning writing?
3) Under what conditions do students rely on coping strategies to circumvent the demands of writing assignments?

The following discussion of my findings is organized around these three questions. My intention here is not to claim that certain situational or individual variables caused certain kinds of behavior, but rather to use these case studies to speculate about what kinds of variables might play a role in shaping students' responses to academic writing tasks and to suggest areas for further research.

The Kinds of Resources Students Rely on to Help Them Interpret and Complete Writing Tasks and How Specific Writing Situations Influence Their Approaches

Successful student writers are, above all, sensitive decision-makers. They are able to size up a writing situation and adapt their goals and approaches to meet the demands of different classroom contexts. In these case studies, we saw students drawing from several resources in their efforts to define and fulfill their teacher's assignments. These resources included situational, or context-specific, variables and individual, or personal, variables. Specific classroom environments provided students with a range of situational resources to draw from, including feedback from professors and teaching assistants, and the collaborative efforts of classmates who helped each other to negotiate and define their tasks. In addition to these context-specific resources, students also relied on individual resources, such as their past experiences with the subject matter being covered in the course, past experiences with similar kinds of school writing tasks, and individual "production systems" or strategies for completing certain kinds of assignments.

All of the students observed in these case studies relied on some of these situational and individual resources as they struggled to define and complete their writing tasks. However, the students differed in the *extent* to which they drew from these various sources. For example, Helen successfully defined her literature research paper assignment by drawing from several social-interactional resources available in the setting as well as from her own experiences with similar tasks in high school. In addition, Helen refined her task interpretation as her paper evolved. In contrast, Greg relied solely on his past experiences with research papers and Victorian literature to define his task, and he did not question or revise his initial task representation after he had formulated it. Moreover, Greg's teacher provided several chances for students to present their work and receive feedback, but Greg failed to take advantage of these opportunities. Perhaps students like Helen succeed because they are able to rely on a range of available resources and are able to build flexible task representations that evolve as they gain more information about task requirements. Students who fail to determine what counts in responding to different classroom writing assignments may fail, in part, because they rely on a limited number of situational resources to help them and because they do not evaluate and refine their initial task representations. This is certainly a hypothesis worth exploring more fully.

In their extensive study of the contexts in which students learn to write in high school, Applebee (1984) and his colleagues found that students vary their approaches to school writing to meet the demands of particular teachers and assignments. The case study material gathered in my study of college-level writing raises interesting questions about how features of specific tasks and writing contexts shape students' approaches.

The students' responses to the writing tasks in Social Influences provide especially useful examples. Three out of the four students I observed in this course used the detailed assignment guidelines they received to short-circuit their teacher's intentions. These guidelines seemed to allow students to expend minimal time and effort while at the same time enabling them to produce fairly acceptable papers. The only student who did not use the guidelines to circumvent his teacher's process requirements for the assignment complained that the guidelines preempted his own work, saying, "It seems as if we're being graded on how well we can follow directions, not how we think on our own."

These case studies suggest that teachers need to examine the costs and benefits of providing students with such explicit written instructions for producing papers. Students, like those in Social Influences, may pressure teachers to make their task instructions more explicit, but when tasks are tightly defined, students' approaches may be limited as well. In fact, Doyle (1983) and Nespor (1987) argue that by providing overly explicit routines or procedures for accomplishing tasks, teachers may allow students to use only a narrow range of cognitive processes. This appeared to be the case with three out of four students I observed in Social Influences.

Clearly, teachers must also weigh the costs involved in requiring students to deal with complex and unfamiliar tasks on their own. Too often teachers expect students who are newcomers to a field to be able to determine the implicit ways of thinking and presenting evidence required to write successfully in their particular disciplines. Some composition specialists (Bartholomae, 1985; Bizzell, 1982) have argued that we need to identify and teach students the structures, language, and ways of thinking required in different academic discourse communities. It appears, though, that in our efforts to codify the rules of procedure and ways of thinking required in different disciplines, we must be careful not to shortcircuit the learning we are

123

trying to promote. The step-by-step guidelines in Social Influences allowed students to produce a "field study" without ever engaging in the systematic research and thinking processes their teacher intended. Further research is needed in order to find a way to strike an effective balance between providing students with valuable information about the ways of thinking and writing in different disciplines and providing them with "product templates" that pre-empt their own work and allow them to circumvent the learning their teachers hope to promote.

Another feature of classroom writing situations that appears to shape students' approaches is the nature of the feedback they receive. Students rely on teacher feedback, particularly grades, to help them develop and refine their notions of what counts in completing assignments for a particular course. Without such feedback, students find it difficult to evaluate their own perfor-mance. Helen said that she had "no idea what the proper approach" was for writing the research paper in her literature course because her teacher had not returned any graded work. She reported that she and her classmates collabo-rated in their efforts to clarify their teacher's expectations. It is interesting to speculate about whether the absence of feedback and explicit instructions for completing papers might have caused some students to be even more aware of the choices they were making in interpreting their assignment. English teachers who want to encourage students to take responsibility for all phases of their writing—from task interpretation to revision—often put off grading student work. It would be worthwhile to explore this practice further, to learn more about how providing minimal feedback in the highly evaluative climate of the classroom influences students' approaches.

Not surprisingly, the nature of the criteria used to evaluate student writing also appears to have an impact on student responses. Judy and John, the two engineering students, mentioned their teacher's limited grading criteria in their explanations of how they sized-up and completed their assignments. When it became apparent that they were being graded on how many pieces of key information from the readings they included in their papers, both students chose to focus on reproducing what they had read. The teaching assistant's limited grading criteria did not reflect Professor Clark's stated goals for assigning writing, however. Professor Clark stressed the importance of conciseness and taking an argumentative stand (two goals that may have been impossible to meet in this assignment), while his teaching assistant stressed the importance of reproducing information from the assigned readings. Other research (Langer & Applebee, 1987; Swanson-Owens, 1986) has shown that the original goals for writing activities are often transformed when individual teachers adapt assignments to meet their own instructional goals. This suggests that teachers may need to be especially aware of the possible disjunctions that can occur in large college lectures where professors design assignments and teaching assistants grade students' responses.

How Students' Task Interpretations and Approaches Relate to Their Teachers' Stated Goals for Assigning Writing. In my analysis of the case study material, I have focused on the settings where disjunctions occurred between students' interpretations and teachers' stated goals for assigning writing. Out of thirteen case studies, six students' responses did not appear to match their teachers' intentions. Nespor (1987), who found similar results in her study of how high school students interpreted a persuasive essay assignment, argues that such disjunctions are inevitable, given the range of experiences, individual repertoires, and situational resources students draw from to interpret their assignments.

However, while most teachers are probably aware at some level that such disjunctions occur, they may not be aware of the important role that task interpretation plays in shaping students' responses. It seems important for teachers to know that students actively interpret the assignments they receive, and that students often rely on implicit cues to determine what counts in completing tasks. These case studies suggest that students' task interpretations are based, at least in part, on situational factors over which the teacher has some control—namely, the criteria used to evaluate products, the quality and frequency of feedback, and the nature of the instructions and other explicit support materials students receive for completing assignments. If teachers understood the potential impact of these situational factors on student performance, they might be able to make more informed decisions in planning, presenting, and responding to assignments.

In addition to examining how students interpret writing assignments under different conditions, we need to explore the relationship between task interpretation and learning through writing. Research has shown that the kinds of goals students bring to writing tasks and the kinds of processes they use to achieve these goals can shape students' learning in important ways. Further research is needed to examine how particular writing situations shape students' approaches and how these approaches, in turn, influence student learning.

Conditions Underwhich Students Rely on Coping Strategies to Circumvent the Demands of Writing Assignments. Given the limited number of classroom writing situations examined in this study, it is difficult to speculate about whether certain classroom practices actually encouraged the use of coping strategies to circumvent the demands of writing assignments. However, when we combine my findings with those of other researchers (Applebee, 1984; Herrington, 1985; Marshall, 1984) who also have studied student writing in academic settings, we find that certain kinds of task situations may encourage students to rely on shortcuts for producing acceptable papers.

Two task situations in my case studies led to student shortcuts. In the engineering course, students described their assignment as "unmotivating" and a "waste of class time." In the sociology course, three out of four students expended minimal time and effort on their assignments, and used the explicit paper guidelines to fabricate their field reports. Both of these task situations essentially required students to reproduce the content or form the teacher had provided. The engineering students had to paraphrase what they had read, and the sociology students had to follow the step-by-step guidelines for presenting a field report. Applebee (1984) reports that when teachers turn writing assignments into this kind of sophisticated "fill-in-the-blank" exercise, students learn to play the game and also quickly lose interest in the activity.

Still, we must remember that students can turn assignments into trivial exercises when they wait until the last minute and take shortcuts to produce their papers. Clearly, students base their decisions about the amount and kind of effort they will expend on classroom tasks on a range of personal and situational factors. What these case studies reveal is that these factors can interact in complex ways to shape students' approaches. For example, it is difficult to know whether Barbara, the sociology student who saw herself as a spontaneous writer who worked best under pressure, would have changed her methods for writing her Social Influences paper if her teacher had changed the way he presented the assignment. We need to learn more about how students, like Barbara, who have very efficient "production systems" for writing papers, can be encouraged to expand their approaches.

These case studies suggest that the special nature of school settings, with their emphasis on rewards for products, may have an important impact on the way students define and approach writing tasks. In many cases, students focus on the products they are required to produce instead of on the processes they are being asked to engage in. This limited focus can lead students to take shortcuts to produce acceptable papers—shortcuts that may allow them to circumvent the writing and learning processes that assignments are intended to promote. In addition, these studies suggest that certain classroom practices and writing tasks may actually encourage students to take shortcuts and rely on truncated writing strategies. As teachers and researchers we must continue to look critically at the contexts in which students are asked to write, and to examine the practices that may hinder or enhance student writing development and learning.

Appendix: Guidelines for the Second Paper in Social Influences

Paper on Power. The paper is to be a fieldwork study of "power" at CMU.

Power is difficult to study; you will be OPERATIONALIZING a concept that has different meanings and different expressions in various contexts. And you will be doing so without being ETHNOCENTRIC.

Step 1: Determine what "power" means, how you will be using the concept. (cf. Kanter)

Step 2: State your assumption; what are you going to test in your study? (e.g. professors always have power over students; power at CMU is attached to role and not to personality; power belongs to an office and not to an individual, etc.)

Step 3: Figure out the "observable" indicators of power, as you have defined the concept.

Step 4: A) Choose your field site, at CMU, and justify your choice (briefly). You may choose the same site in which you studied socialization processes, and use the information you already have about the group. Data already collected can help you refine methods and theories for this study. B) Outline your methods: how are you going to find out about power; what will you DO? (Make sure your methods fit your choice of a site and allow you to support or refute your assumption.)

Step 5: Collecting the data. Think about the following issues:
1. The significance of emic concepts: do these change your definition of power, the assumptions guiding your study?
2. Immersion/analysis: moving back and forth between "their interpretations" (in words and actions) and "your analytic scheme." Being IN the group without losing your social scientific perspective.
3. When (why) do you have enough data?

Step 6: Interpret your data. Has your initial assumption been supported, or not? Can you generalize your findings to a broader context? Why or why not?

Step 7: Consider the implications and significance of your study for issues of power in society more generally. For example: did power in your group reflect power in the wider setting? Are there aspects of the wider setting that might explain what you have observed in the group you looked at? Or, is this group somehow different, and if so, why?

The paper should be 4-6 pages long, typed or printed. As in the first paper, content and form are both important and grades will reflect this.

Writing-up findings: Your paper should have a clear structure, an organization that takes the reader from beginning to end in an orderly and logical fashion.

1. Introduction: what you are going to do and why
2. Data: how collected; what collected; why those data
3. Results: was your initial assumption born out or not? Explain
4. Conclusions: place your study in a broader framework (to be discussed in section)

Note

This paper must show progress from the first paper, including a better development of methods, a stronger grounding in concepts and terms that have been used in Social Influences, and an understanding of the techniques of interpreting fieldwork data and reaching conclusions on the basis of these data.

References

Applebee, A. N. (1984). *Contexts for learning to write.* Norwood, NJ: Ablex.

Bartholomae, D. (1985). Inventing the university. In M. Rose (Ed.), *When a writer can't write: Studies of writer's block and other composing-process problems* (pp. 134-165). New York: Guilford.

Berkenkotter, C. (1981). Understanding a writer's awareness of audience. *College Composition and Communication, 32,* 388-399.

Bizzell, P. (1982). Cognition, convention, and certainty: What we need to know about writing. *Pretext, 3,* 213—243.

Brandt, D. (1986). Toward an understanding of context in composition. *Written Communication, 3,* 139-157.

Brook, R. (1987). Underlife in writing instruction.*College Composition and Communication, 38,* 141-153.

Carter, K., & Doyle, W. (1982, October). *Variations in academic tasks in high and average ability classes.* Paper presented at the annual meeting of the American Educational Research Association, New York.

Cooper, M., & Holzman, M. (1983). Talking about protocols. *College Composition and Communication, 34,* 284—293.

Corno, L., & Mandinach, E. (1983). The role of cognitive engagement in classroom learning and motivation. *Educational Psychologist, 18,* 88-108.

Dillon, D., & Searle, D. (1981). The role of language in one first grade classroom. *Research in the Teaching of English, 15,* 311-328.

Doyle, W. (1983). Academic work. *Review of Educational Research, 53* (2), 159-199.

Emig, J. A. (1971). *The composing processes of twelfth graders.* (Research Report No. 13). Urbana, IL: National Council of Teachers of English.

Ericsson, K. A., & Simon, H. A. (1980). Verbal reports as data. *Psychological Review, 87,* 215-251.

Faigley, L., Cherry, R., Jolliffe, D., & Skinner, A. (1985). *Assessing writer's knowledge and processes of composing.* Norwood, NJ: Ablex.

Flower, L., & Hayes, J. R. (1980a). The cognition of discovery: Defining a rhetorical problem. *College Composition and Communication, 31,* 21-32.

Flower, L., & Hayes, J. R. (1980b). The dynamics of composing: Making plans and juggling constraints. In L. Gregg & E. Steinberg (Eds.), *Cognitive processes in writing: An interdisciplinary approach* (pp. 31-50). Hillsdale, NJ: Lawrence Erlbaum.

Flower, L., Hayes, J. R., Schriver, K., Carey, L., & Haas, C. (1987). *Planning in writing: A theory of the cognitive process.* (Office of Naval Research Technical Report No. 1.) Pittsburgh, PA: Carnegie Mellon University.

Herrington, A. (1985). Writing in academic settings: A study of the contexts for writing in two college chemical engineering courses. *Research in the Teaching of English, 19,* 331-359.

Langer, J. A., & Applebee, A. N. (1987). *How writing shapes thinking.* Urbana, IL: National Council of Teachers of English.

McCarthy, L. (1987). Stranger in strange lands: A college student writing across the curriculum. *Research in the Teaching of English, 21,* 233-265.

MacKay, R. (1978). How teachers know: A case of epistemological conflict. *Sociology of Education, 51,* 177—187.

Marshall, J. D. (1984). Process and product: Case studies of writing in two content areas. In A. N. Applebee (Ed.), *Contexts for learning to write* (pp. 149-168). Norwood, NJ: Ablex.

Marx, R., Winne, R., & Walsh, J. (1985). Studying cognition during classroom learning. In M. Pressley & C. Brainerd (Eds.), *Cognitive learning and memory in children: Progress in cognitive development research* (pp. 181-203). New York: Springer-Verlag.

Morris, P. E. (1981). Why Evans is wrong in criticizing introspective reports of subject strategies. *British Journal of Psychology, 72,* 465-468.

Nespor, J. (1987). Academic tasks in a high school English class. *Curriculum Inquiry, 17,* 203—228.

Nisbett, R. E., & Wilson, T. D. (1977). Telling more than we can know: Verbal reports on mental processes. *Psychological Review, 84,* 231-259.

Odell, L., & Goswami, D. (1982). Writing in non-academic settings. *Research in the Teaching of English, 16,* 201-223.

Perl, S. (1979). The composing processes of unskilled college writers. *Research in the Teaching of English, 13,* 317-336.

Pianko, S. (1979). A description of the composing processes of college freshmen writers. *Research in the Teaching of English, 13,* 5-22.

Posner, G. A. (1982). A cognitive science conception of curriculum and instruction. *Curriculum Studies, 14,* 343-351.

Rogoff, B. (1984). Introduction: Thinking and learning in social contexts. In B. Rogoff & J. Lave (Eds.), *Everyday cognition: Its development in social context* (pp. 1-8). Cambridge, MA: Harvard University Press.

Rogoff, B., & Gardner, W. (1984). Adult guidance and cognitive development. In B. Rogoff & J. Lave (Eds.), *Everyday cognition: Its development in social context* (pp. 95-116). Cambridge, MA: Harvard University Press.

Ruth, L., & Murphy, S. (1984). Designing topics for writing assessment: Problems of meaning. *College Composition and Communication, 35,* 410-422.

Scribner, S. (1984). Studying working intelligence. In B. Rogoff & J. Lave (Eds.),*Everyday cognition: Its development in social context* (pp. 9-40). Cambridge, MA: Harvard University Press.

Simon, H. A. (1973). The structure of ill-structured problems. *Artificial Intelligence, 4,* 181-202.

Sommers, N. I. (1980). Revision strategies of student writers and experienced adult writers. *College Composition and Communication, 31,* 378-388.

Sternglass, M., & Pugh, S. (1986). Retrospective accounts of language and learning processes. *Written Communication, 3,* 297-323.

Swanson-Owens, D. (1986). Identifying natural sources of resistance: A case study of implementing writing across the curriculum. *Research in the Teaching of English, 20,* 69-97.

Tomlinson, B. (1984). Talking about the composing process: The limitations of retrospective accounts *Written Communication, 1,* 429-445.

Author's Comment—Jennie Nelson

This study grew out of an earlier study I conducted in which I asked a handful of freshman students to tell me the story of how they wrote research papers in a variety of courses. I asked them to keep a daily log or diary of all paper-related activities and to describe in as much detail as possible how their research papers evolved from beginning to end. As the students' log entries began to appear in my mailbox, I was struck by how rich and disturbing these candid views of student writing were.

Students revealed their frustrations in being forced to write papers that they considered "dumb busy work" and described ingenious methods for producing a research paper in just a few hours on the night before it was due, with plenty of recorded breaks for pizza and gripe sessions with friends. In contrast, other students appeared to be deeply engaged with their assignments, spending many days researching, reading, and writing, and discussing what they were learning with anyone who would listen. Much of the research I had read on students' composing processes often depicted freshman writers as novices who relied on a limited repertoire of composing strategies and were unaware of what was expected of them in college writing assignments. This picture of naive, struggling writers did not match the savvy writers I encountered in students' log entries. In an effort to learn more about the factors that shaped students' approaches to writing assignments, I conducted the study described in "This Was an Easy Assignment."

My goal in conducting this research was, once again, to examine academic writing from the students' side of the desk, to provide a behind the scenes view of students' actual attitudes and approaches that I knew teachers would find disturbing. When I shared a draft of this study with two colleagues, their responses were surprisingly similar. One described it as "Nightmare on Elm Street for teachers," and the other said, "you have descended into undergraduate hell and have important tales to tell." These experienced teachers were struck, as I was, by the candid way students described how they sized up their writing assignments and relied on short cuts to produce papers, often failing to engage in the kinds of learning activities that assignments were designed to promote. My ability to descend into undergraduate hell and share these students' important tales depended in large part on the data collection procedure I used, namely the writing process logs, and the role I played as an

131

independent researcher and confidant. However, while the writing process logs proved to be a valuable research tool for this kind of open-ended, exploratory study, I was also aware of what was gained and lost in choosing this particular research method.

Because every student can interpret the task of introspecting and reporting their processes differently, the depth and completeness of such accounts is difficult to assess. Some students who kept process logs included personal information about their feelings, particularly their frustrations, in responding to assignments, while others provided fairly dry, objective accounts of their approaches. In addition, there is some evidence that written accounts are less complete than oral accounts. Thus, while the process logs allowed me to examine students working under natural conditions over more extended periods of time, they did not allow me to capture the more detailed, moment by moment decisions that a think-aloud method would have afforded.

It is difficult to know whether the act of describing composing processes has some effect on the processes a student ends up engaging in. In the case of my own research, however, I found that because I was an independent researcher and assured students that their contributions would be kept confidential, participants seemed comfortable about revealing attitudes and practices that they might not have been willing to reveal to their teachers. Some participants in the earlier study I conducted using process logs de-scribed how they wrote research papers just hours before they were due by lifting large portions of their texts from other sources, while other students revealed that they expended a great deal of effort on papers, turning in notes, outlines, and drafts completed three to four weeks before papers were due. The straightforward nature of these accounts suggests that students did not change their approaches because they were taking part in a study, but any influence is difficult to assess.

Unlike some other research methods, I found that process logs require extensive involvement on the researcher's part. In my earlier study of students writing research papers, I learned that I had to monitor students carefully to be sure that they turned in logs at regular intervals and that they included the kinds of information I needed in their log entries. Once students began thinking about or working on a paper, they were required to write daily log entries (even if they did not actually work on papers every day) and were asked to deliver entries and copies of notes or drafts on a regular schedule, at least three times a week. I often sent brief notes to students, letting them know that I had received their log entries, reminding them to include detailed descriptions of all paper-related activities, and sometimes just thanking them for their punctual contributions. Through these notes, the students and I established a personal relationship that probably contributed to their willingness to share information about the short cuts they took to produce papers. While this information was certainly disturbing, it also provided valuable insights about the classroom conditions that seem to contribute to students' opportunistic short-circuiting of deep engagement with writing.

Chapter 6   Communication in
            Cross Cultural Contexts

This study and the next two explore cultural difference in literacy practices. The Heath and Thomas article describes an **autoethnographic** study of rural black child-raising practices, and the Floriak article discusses the design of documents for low-literate, inner-city parents. The Haas and Funk article presents an exploratory study of communication in two Japanese industrial settings.

Studies of other cultures are of immense importance for our understanding of literate practices. One reason for this is that the study of other cultures teaches us a great deal about our own practices. We tend to believe that our own cultural practices reflect "human nature." For example, we may see the way we raise children, the way we emphasize individual initiative, and the way we communicate with each other as the natural way. This assumption of naturalness is a very conservative one because it carries with it the implication that it is difficult and ultimately counterproductive to try to change what is natural. However, when we see that people in other cultures do things differently, we can see that our practices are not a reflection of immutable human nature but rather of malleable custom. Haas and Funk observe that

> the internationalization of technical communication can involve not
> only sharing common practices and developing needed guidelines
> but also working toward an understanding of communication in
> other cultures. Such cross-cultural encounters may suggest to us
> ways in which our current conceptions of communication issues
> limit us, and can make us more aware of the myriad of ways that
> people communicate with one another. (p. 148)

The Haas and Funk study is a **participant observation** study. Participant observation research is based on the assumption that, as Charles Horton Cooley put it, "the surest way to know men is to have simple and necessary relations with them." (Jacobs, p. v) Participant observers try to establish membership in the group being observed, joining in the group's activities which are to be the subject of inquiry. One of the authors (Funk) played the dual roles of full-time engineer employed by the Japanese companies and of observer of engineers at work. Even as a member of the group, however, the observer is always to one degree or another an outsider, if only because he or she has motives for engaging in the activities of the group that differ from those of other members:

135

he is there to study the activities of a group that he does not fully understand; the members of the group are there simply to engage in the activities, and they understand what they are doing as only insiders can.

The close contact and rich opportunities for observation afforded by group membership do not preclude a host of fundamental and difficult problems associated with data collection. For example, the presence of the observer may change what is being observed in an important way. In the Haas and Funk study, though, it is hard to believe that the presence of one American engineer, working as as an engineer, would have had a major impact on the way work was carried out in a large and busy Japanese office. It seems probable to us that as participant observer, the researcher probably had less impact on the observed activities than he would have had as a tall foreigner standing apart from the group with a clipboard taking notes.

Many of the problems connected with participant observation research center on the **reliability** and **validity** of the researcher's work. "Reliability" here refers to the extent to which the observations are independent of the accidental circumstances of the research situation: for example, one's observations are reliable to the extent that they are consistent (though not identical, which is an impossibility) with those made by other observers, and that they are consistent with other observations of the same phenomenon made at different times. Validity refers to the correctness of the interpretation of the observations: for example, that the observer is looking at what he thinks he is looking at. Imagine a researcher asking "How are you?" of everyone he encounters in a particular social situation, and everyone replying "Fine." The reliability of the observation is likely to be high, for the reply is a well-established social convention. On other similar occasions he would probably get the same response, and other researchers would also probably get the same response to the question. However, if the researcher concluded from his observations that the group of people he was observing was unusually healthy, his interpretation would have little validity, since he was not observing what he assumed he was observing. Reliability and validity can be increased by using a variety of complementary measures and by checking one's observations against the observations of others.

The normal difficulties of conducting participant observation research are compounded in situations where one is working with another language and in another culture. For, as Jose Ortega y Gasset argues,

> the stupendous reality that is language cannot be understood
> unless we begin by observing that speech consists above all in
> silences. A being who could not renounce saying many things

136

would be incapable of speaking. And each language represents
a different equation between manifestations and silences. Each
people leaves some things unsaid in order to be able to say
others. Hence, the immense difficulty of translation: translation is
a matter of saying in a language precisely what that language
tends to pass over in silence... The Englishman leaves unsaid
countless things that Spaniards normally say. And vice versa!
(Man and People, p. 246)

And we might add, what is left unsaid are usually those things that are basic, widely shared and hence, taken for granted in the society — that is, very often just what one needs to know in order to understand what is happening in the group.

Funk speaks Japanese and shares with others in the group being studied an engineering background. Haas notes in her commentary that "his knowledge and ability to speak, to read, and especially to listen were crucial and central to the success of the project." (p. 152) Even so, Funk and Haas seem to have been very much aware of the problems of data collection. They took care to collect a variety of kinds of data: notes on meetings, notes on activities in the office, notes on "everyday" communication outside the office (which "confirmed and sometimes challenged what... [they] were seeing at the office," (p. 151) systematic interviews, and systematic observations of office activities using a rigorous sampling method, written documents produced by others, and so on. We learn from their commentary on the project that they made a sustained effort to corroborate and critique each other's observations. For example:

Matsuda Koji was eager to speak with me to improve his English
and we began to meet every Monday evening at a coffee shop
near the train station. In exchange for the English "lessons," as he
called our conversations, he shared with me his experiences and
opinions about communication at work and his characterizations
of communication in Japanese society generally. I didn't question
or quiz him on communication patterns directly; rather, our
conversations usually centered around his current work projects.
Mr. Matsuda's reports about the activities, goals, procedures, and
problems at the workplace provided another view on the communication situation Jeff and I were studying. (p. 151)

Finally, they checked the findings of this study against those in a more elaborate subsequent study. Haas notes in her commentary that "we wrote 'Shared Communication' early in our stay in Japan: its conclusions are, as we note there, preliminary. However, even after more systematic study, most of the observations still hold...." (p. 150)

References

Jacobs, G. (Ed.) (1970). *The participant observer.* New York: George Braziller.

Ortega y Gasset, J. (1957). *Man and people.* New York: Norton.

Christina Haas
Pennsylvania State University

Jeffrey L. Funk
Westinghouse Corporation

"Shared Information":
Some Observations of Communication in Japanese Technical Settings

An American technical professional who found himself in a comparable job situation in a Japanese company would be struck by profound differences between U.S. and Japanese companies. Organizational structure, professional "mores," corporate goals, even daily schedules and procedures are quite different, reflecting the larger, unique culture of each country (Funk, 1988; Nagao, 1985a; Nagao, 1985b; Ouchi, 1981; & Takkayanagi, 1985).

One of the most obvious differences—and one that is of particular interest to us—is in how technical information is collected, assimilated, and transmitted by and to employees within the company. In short, we are interested in how communication happens in Japanese work settings, and this article is based on our observations as "insiders," working and living in Japan, observing and participating in a variety of communication situations.

Because communication is pervasive in any work situation, we expected that differences would be extreme, and that these differences might help us better to understand Japanese society as a whole and—through comparison—to learn something about our own culture's communication as well.

Our purpose in this article is to sketch out a number of characteristics of communication in a specific Japanese corporate setting. Our goal is not to draw sharp comparisons with similar U.S. situations, although in the course of description we will of course make comparisons to situations more familiar to us, and presumably to our readers. Neither is our goal to provide an exhaustive and comprehensive framework of technical communication in Japan, a task which is clearly beyond the scope of an article and of our own experiences. What we hope to do is to provide a set of observations of facets of a particular Japanese communication situation that we have found especially interesting and thought-provoking. We will conclude by tying our observations to current issues in information design and arguing for the value of cross-cultural studies.

We have defined "technical communication" in an intentionally broad way, as any work-related discourse—written or spoken—occurring at the work site during the course of the work day. We settled on this broad definition in order to capture the full range and scope of communication within the settings we observed. Our focus was on communication *within* the work place, rather than on communication that might be carried on with outside audiences, such as customers, users, or professional associates at other job sites. By looking broadly at communication in these Japanese settings, we sought to understand the shape and scope of the communication situations we observed. Subsequent analyses may focus more narrowly on particular aspects of Japanese technical communication or on explicit comparison with U. S. situations.

Data Collection

Although we sought to be broad in our definitions, the situations in which our observations occurred are quite specific: these observations are drawn from two separate work experiences in Japan, in two Japanese cities, for two major Japanese electronics companies. At each site, the observer was a regular employee for an extended period, from six months to one year, in the mid-1980s. Observation of other employees and their communication activities was made easier by the layout of the offices at each site. As is common in Japanese companies, professionals shared a common workspace—a large room with desks arranged in groups and adjoining open meeting areas.

At the primary job site (from which a greater amount of data was collected) electrical, computer, and mechanical engineers worked to develop equipment for use in manufacturing semi-conductors. Most of the observations were made within a manufacturing design department, consisting of 156 technical professionals, and 9 support staff.

In addition to the proportionately lower ratio of support staff to professionals (approximately one to 17) than one might find in a U.S. corporation, the support staff performed a somewhat broader range of duties than might their U.S. counterparts. The support staff were responsible for office inventory and purchasing, they composed and translated international correspondence in English, and they greeted visitors and served tea; but they also performed such "non-traditional" activities as entering and modifying software code, maintaining databases, and mechanical drafting. As a consequence, they spent only a small proportion of their time performing secretarial duties for the engineers, and as we describe below, this seemed relevant to a number of communication issues.

It was interesting to note that in the entire 1500-employee site within which this department was located, only the facility manager had what might be considered a "personal secretary," a male whose primary job responsibilities included dealing with foreigners, English language issues, and international contacts.

A second job site was also observed, for a shorter period of time. Here the observer was employed in a marketing department, which contained about 80 workers, about half of whom were engineers and the remainder of whom had business backgrounds, such as training in accounting or marketing. The professionals at this job site were responsible for developing domestic and international market analyses and for producing training materials and technical manuals (in both English and Japanese) for use with factory control equipment. Given their job responsibilities, it was interesting to note that only a small proportion of these employees—less than 10%—had formal training in writing, language, or issues of communication, and most of these were foreign language specialists. Four full-time support staff served this department.

Data sources at each site included systematic interviews with other employees, a number of whom were interviewed regularly, on a daily or weekly basis. Some of these interviews were quite formal, while others took place informally. In total, about one-quarter of the members of the department at the primary job site were interviewed, with a smaller proportion interviewed at the other site.

Since the observer also had a specific work assignment at each site, he was a participant in numerous formal and informal meetings at which he made extensive observation notes of both content and procedure. These meetings were primarily in Japanese. Observation notes and sketches were also made of interpersonal exchanges among workers and of office layout and procedures. Translations from Japanese to English were made of numerous departmental memos, procedural instructions, and technical documents.

Our observations of communication in the workplace are supplemented with examples from "everyday" communication—the mundane but pervasive information-sharing situations through which much of the business of daily living is accomplished.

Three Characteristics of Shared Information

"Shared information" is an apt metaphor for the communication situations we observed. In these Japanese technical settings, information seemed not so much exchanged between individuals as shared among them. Rather than individual "experts" exchanging information related to their specialty with other members of a group, information in the situations we observed seemed to be much more a group enterprise. Technical and procedural information was created by, sustained by, and belonged to the group as a whole, whether it be a small work team of three to four people or an entire division. That this shared information is a group enterprise was evident in the public (rather than private) storage of documents; in the frequent (often daily) scheduled meetings of departments, sections, and working groups in which all members took active, participatory roles; in the large visual displays of information that line the walls of labs and offices; and even in the layout of the offices themselves.

In the sections which follow, we outline three characteristics of "shared information": *immediate, consensual,* and *spoken.* While we would not claim that communication within the settings we observed could always be characterized in this way, we were struck by how often these characteristics did apply to the communication we observed. For each characteristic we present examples from our observations in Japanese settings.

Shared information tends to be immediate, rather than delayed.

A great deal of communication we observed was immediate. Information was passed between people very quickly, whether it be a change in procedure or an update on the status of a project. Many of these immediate exchanges occurred face-to-face, but even when the information was passed in a written form, it seemed to change hands very quickly.

The immediacy of the communication—both spoken and written—was facilitated by the arrangement of the office: all workers, from support staff to department managers, shared a common workspace. In a large, open room, employees' desks were arranged in groups, two rows of four or five desks facing one another to form groups of eight to ten. Those who shared common work projects were grouped together, with more senior members of the groups assuming authority by taking desks at the heads of rows.

Because only small desk dividers (about 12 inches tall) separated facing desks and adjoining desks were not separated at all, talk among and between work groups was easy, and it was not uncommon for the noise level in this open office to rise to a much higher level than that in which an American engineer might be comfortable. Interestingly, commentators on Japanese education have noted a similar high level of noise in schools in Japan (White, 1987, p. 114). In any case, the layout of the room made it difficult for individuals to maintain "private information," to know things that were not shared by the group. Similarly, groups of employees usually shared a common telephone, and conversations could be easily overheard by nearby co-workers.

In addition, the immediacy of communication was facilitated by the easy

142

accessibility of employees. Employee "status boards" told not only whether each member of a work team is "in" or "out," but also indicated where in the plant he was at the time (desk, lab, factory floor). Therefore, if a worker received a phone call, or were needed for a meeting, or had information that someone else needed, co-workers could quickly locate him. The engineers themselves, rather than support staff, were responsible for locating the co-workers they needed and setting up meetings, which were often organized within just a few minutes. The employee status boards helped in scheduling the meetings on short notice.

Immediate exchange of information also occurred in these frequent meetings of departments or work groups where workers meet face-to-face to give and receive project-related information. Work groups often met formally as often as twice a day. We found that these meetings were an important source of "shared information" and we discuss them in more detail below. Incidentally, since employees of Japanese firms tend to take the same vacation (during plant or company-wide shutdowns around national holidays) and are often life-long employees of the company, the "links" in the chain of workers giving and receiving information remain fairly unbroken for long periods of time in even very large groups.

Shared information is consensual.

Decision-making tended to be a group activity, with members of the work group or department not only present for the decision-making but participating in it. Consensual information was created by the group in this manner, and responsibility for maintaining, updating, and conveying that information was typically carried by the group rather than by individuals. Record-keeping, document storage, and scheduling of department social events was handled by the engineers themselves, rather than by support staff.

The consensual responsibility for information was evidenced in the status boards which lined the walls of the large office workspace, the labs, and other workrooms. In addition to status boards for employees to show whether they were at their desks, on the factory floor, or on a business trip, there were status boards to show the configuration or workloads of computers or other equipment and ones to show the current status of work projects (expected completion date, personnel, completed and current sub-tasks). These boards were often quite complex: they usually consisted of a magnetic white board with color-coded magnets to reflect various components or states and intricate grids and boxes to reflect the overall design of a project or machine.

Maintenance of some of these status boards was shared across workers, so that the group as a whole—rather than an individual—was responsible for keeping the boards neat and current. Similarly, responsibility for chairing meetings was often rotated so that no one individual assumed complete control. Stored information—in the form of handwritten analysis files or more formal reports—was also public and easily accessible to all. Storage area was somewhat limited, and decisions about what to store were often made by the group, with senior members having greater influence over decisions. Again, the filing and sorting of this stored information was done by the engineers, not by support staff.

At both sites we observed, documentation and manuals were produced, both for internal use and for distribution to customers, and this activity was often shared by the department as a whole. At one job site, documentation was prepared for an international customer who had purchased some complex equipment. Rather than being produced by writing specialists, this documentation was produced collaboratively, with almost every engineer on the project responsible for writing small parts of the manual, verifying facts, checking mechanics, and sometimes even providing a translation. Similarly, much of the editing and revising of a video-tape script about the facility for customers and visitors was done not by writing or public-relations experts, but by the engineers themselves.

Even company or department social events—which occurred as frequently as several times a month—took on a consensual, egalitarian flavor that seems to be common throughout Japanese society (Cummings, 1980). These events, primarily for "insiders," involved long meals with abundant food and drink and took place in restaurants or, during the blossoming of the cherry trees, in parks. At these events, all employees in turn gave a "speech" (sometimes in English, as well as Japanese) about their work, family, and hobbies. There was little, if any, separation at the tables by rank, and responsibility for organizing activities—speeches, group singing—was taken by a different employee for each party. Official and more public functions, particularly those at which outsiders to the company or department were present, might be organized and carried out in a much more formal way.

Shared information is primarily spoken rather than written.

Closely related to the immediacy and the consensuality of communication was our third observation: much information was conveyed primarily in speech rather than writing. A great deal of substantive communication about technical matters was resolved by members of the groups at face-to-face

144

meetings (informal as well as formal), so there was often little need for written documents or memos to convey this information.

Informal collaborative meetings among co-workers seemed almost constant within the large room containing the 156 members of the engineering design department at the primary observation site. These collaborative meetings might consist of two or three employees huddled around a desk sketching a solution to a problem, a half-dozen engineers meeting informally in small alcoves scattered through the room, or a couple of people brainstorming around a computer terminal. During one one-month period in early 1989, we collected data on the proportion of workers working alone. Twenty-five systematic observations were taken and recorded at regular intervals throughout the work day. The proportion of employees working alone ranged from 15% to 49%; the mean was 31.3%. Simply stated, we might expect only about one-third of the workers to be working alone at any given time. An American visitor to the department remarked on how "the Japanese are always talking. When do they get any work done?" It seemed to us, however, that talking *was* one of the ways that work got done at this site.

There were also several types of formal meetings, varying in length, size, and purpose. Departments, consisting of several related work groups, met at least once a week with each member giving a synopsis of his current project goals and accomplishments. Workgroups met as often as twice a day, and the responsibility for conducting the meeting was rotated among group members. Workgroups within the same department met simultaneously and in close proximity, so that, again, keeping information "private" was quite difficult. Presentations in these meetings were highly conventionalized, with the same types of information given in the same order and often with similar phrasing across speakers. This seemed both to aid in the preparation of these oral reports and to make listening for new or important information easier and more efficient. Consequently, the meetings were also quite repetitious, with important goals or upcoming events announced repeatedly several days or even weeks in advance.

Matters of office procedure, upcoming deadlines, even notices of social events which might be conveyed via memos in the U. S., were announced publicly at department meetings. We observed that these Japanese engineers seemed to have much less work-related "mail" to sort through every day than do their American counterparts. Much of this mail was external in origin, coming from outside the company, and those documents which did come from within were often graphs, figures, or other supplements to oral presentations. Even a formal address by one CEO commemorating the beginning of

145

the fiscal year was distributed to various facilities of the corporation on cassette tapes to be played on loudspeaker systems at a specified time—an oral presentation (albeit long-distance and somewhat delayed) rather than a written speech distributed to employees.

We do not wish to suggest that the Japanese offices we observed were without written documents. Of course, written documents were prepared for audiences outside the department: documentation was prepared for customers, formally prepared articles were submitted to internal and external technical journals, and end-of-project corporate reports were prepared.

Analysis papers were also a common type of written document. These were prepared daily by individuals or by small groups and were used as the basis of verbal reports in meetings. Some of these analyses—those for ongoing projects, or those of general interest and usefulness—might be filed together indefinitely in a public storage area. It was not uncommon for these analysis reports to be stored, used, or thrown away—but never make their way to formal, typed status. Most of the people we observed in these technical settings wrote by hand; the word processor, ubiquitous in many U.S. technical settings, seemed to be used much less frequently for daily composing and document production (Haas, 1989). Support staff rarely if ever typed internal documents, and in fact there were no typewriters in the department.

In any case, one result of the reliance on spoken or oral communication was a lower volume of written materials to be created, duplicated, distributed, and stored. This was often advantageous, since the support staffs who would be responsible for duplication and distribution were small, and storage areas tended to be somewhat limited. This suggested to us that cultural differences may sometimes be related to environmental constraints in intriguing ways. Those materials which *did* get prepared as formal written documents, being much less common, may have carried more weight than would similar documents in the U.S.

Everyday Communication

We have used the term shared information to characterize the kind of communication that we observed in Japanese technical settings. However, these qualities were not restricted to technical or work settings but were characteristic of communication within the larger society as we observed it. For instance, personal checks are rarely used in Japan, so much bill-paying seems to go on in face-to-face encounters: a utility representative, after reading the meter, rings the doorbell and asks the consumer to verify the reading and the account is settled immediately, in person and in cash.

146

Similarly, when we registered as "aliens" at local government offices—a procedure required of all foreigners who hold non-tourist visas—we found that our registration was handled not by one individual, but by a group of government workers responsible for alien registration. Each of the four or five persons in this group interacted with us in some way, and the workers "huddled" and conversed among themselves frequently as they helped us fill out forms, asked us for supporting documents, and informed us of proper procedures. A Westerner might find this procedure odd, might be tempted to question the practice of action "by committee," and, if pressed, to suggest that having one worker responsible for one registration would be quicker and less confusing. It is important to remember, however, that cultural procedures, like cultural beliefs and mores, are embedded in a highly complex context, defined in the case of Japan by efficiency, politeness, decorum, and tradition.

Conclusions

To summarize, our goal has been to share our observations of communication within Japanese technical settings and to describe what we saw as some of its distinguishing qualities. We used the metaphor "shared information" to characterize the kinds of communication that we observed and we outlined three qualities of this shared information: it tends to be immediate rather than delayed, consensual in nature, and spoken rather than written. The three qualities of this kind of information are closely related, and often difficult to separate in practice, but we found them useful for describing the communication situations in these Japanese settings.

Observing a different culture and learning something about how communication happens in that culture has been an enlightening experience for us. We were struck by the efficiency, the success, and the egalitarian nature of the technical communication we observed. The currently well-publicized "success" of Japanese corporations may have much to do with how individuals within these corporations communicate with one another.

We were also struck by how "shared information," like document design, is an inherently social process. It involves people in various areas of expertise coming together to form a consensual representation of a task or problem. Participants make use of all forms of communication—oral, written, visual, verbal, nonverbal—to solve common problems. The communication we observed was highly collaborative, probably more collaborative than even advocates of collaborative document design might imagine, and it challenges us to expand our notions of what "collaborative" can mean. In a similar vein, the communication we observed in these Japanese settings seemed to rely less on written texts than we might expect it would in more familiar western settings, and that fact reminds us that our definitions of "technical communication" as primarily written may be somewhat narrow when applied to other, culturally diverse situations.

In fact, one of the primary benefits of this sort of cross-cultural observation is that it helps us learn about our own communication practices by conceptualizing them in comparison to those of other cultures. The internationalization of technical communication can involve not only sharing common practices and developing needed guidelines but also working toward an understanding of communication in other cultural contexts. Such cross-cultural encounters may suggest to us ways in which our current conceptions of communication issues limit us, and can make us more aware of the myriad of ways that people communicate with one another. Increasing our powers of observation and our options for communicating with one another, both within and between cultures, is a worthwhile and important goal.

Note

Throughout this article we have used the masculine personal pronoun because the vast majority of Japanese technical professionals we observed, over 90%, were male.

References

Cummings, W. K. (1980). *Education and equality in Japan*. Princeton, NJ: Princeton University Press, 104-145.

Funk, J. L. (August, 1988). How Does Japan Do It? *Production 100*, (8), 57-62.

Haas, C. (May, 1989). How the writing medium shapes the writing process: Effects of word processing on planning. *Research in the Teaching of English, 23* (2), 181-207.

Nagao, T. (1985a). Japanese Management Philosophy. In Y. Monden et.al. (Eds.), *Innovations in management: The Japanese corporation*, Norcross, GA: Industrial Engineering and Management Press, 6-11.

Nagao, T. (1985b). Japanese Organizational Behavior. In Y. Monden et.al. (Eds.), *Innovations in management: The Japanese corporation*, Norcross, GA: Industrial Engineering and Management Press, 23-40.

Ouchi, W. G. (1981). *Theory Z: How American business can meet the Japanese challenge*. Philippines: Addison Wesley.

Takayanagi, S. (1985). Japanese Participative Management. In Y. Monden et.al. (Eds.), *Innovations in management: The Japanese corporation*, Norcross, GA: Industrial Engineering and Management Press, 67-72.

White, M (1987). *The Japanese educational challenge: A commitment to children*. New York: Free Press, 114.

Authors' Comments

Christine Haas—Pennsylvania State University

After "Shared Information" was published, a number of colleagues commented that the article was somewhat of a departure for me, both in subject matter and in method. I tend to explain it with a cliche: "Well, it's best to bloom where you are planted." (When I recall some of the more difficult days and weeks of living in a new and strange culture, the cliche that sometimes pops to mind is the one about making lemonade with lemons.) Since I had the opportunity to live for a year in Japan, I was determined to do something there that I couldn't do here. The opportunity for this research suggested itself early in our sojourn (more on that below) and turned out to be both personally and intellectually valuable.

Before talking about how this research has been important for me both intellectually and personally, I want to give some idea about how we proceeded, the "nuts and bolts" of the day-to-day data collection. Jeff was much more a participant and I was more the observer in this participant-observer research. Unlike a number of other "Japan watchers" he was not a "guest," but rather an official, contributing member of a group of 12 or so engineers at one of Mitsubishi's design departments in Fukuoka. In many ways, Jeff was one of the group: he had his own, little-too-snug company jacket and a regular work assignment, and he was included in the meetings and social events of his working group and the department as a whole. It is of course true, perhaps especially so in Japan, that someone from another culture can never truly be "one of the group," can never really understand as an insider. Despite this drawback, we felt that we could learn something of value about the communication we were observing and participating in.

Our methods consisted of Jeff keeping detailed notes while he was at work (he filled a half dozen thick notebooks over the course of 11 months). He kept detailed records of the functions and procedures of the department, of the meetings he participated in, and of the frequent interviews he conducted (at least one a day—approximately 8 per week). In many cases, these notes were so detailed that he can even now look back through his notebooks and determine what he was doing at, for instance, 10:30 a.m. on February 7. Some of the interviews Jeff conducted were formal ones but most were short and informal conversations with those with whom he was working most closely. In addition, he collected a great number of documents—memos, procedures, reminders, schedules—most of which were in Japanese. These were translated later, sometimes with the help of our Japanese tutor, Mr. Iwashita.

Each evening, we would discuss what he had seen, heard, and learned during the day. I would ask lots of questions and we would shuffle through his notes looking for new patterns and insights. We discussed our problems and frustrations and those pieces of new information that didn't quite fit. These conversations were then documented in a notebook I kept for the project.

Later, after we had decided to focus on the interaction patterns of the 12 members of the group, I designed data collection forms to make systematic recording of what was going on more efficient and precise. During three separate weeks, at 30-minute intervals, we tallied up the number of people working alone, in pairs or threesomes, and in larger groups. We also noted whether the work—either individual or group—was taking place at or away from the computer. This yielded 2,880 data points (16 observations for each of 12 engineers on 15 separate days), which we subsequently analyzed by drawing flowcharts and looking for patterns.

Another set of data was gathered by noting, at five-minute intervals for three full days, the kinds of group or individual activities each of the 12 engineers was engaged in. Again, we analyzed this data by looking at communication patterns for each individual, for the group as a whole, and for work groups within the larger group. We also looked for differences in communication based on rank or seniority. My contribution during this phase was to think about ways that we could nail down our observations with a systematic look at what was going on over time. (It should be noted that we wrote "Shared Communication" early in our stay in Japan; its conclusions are, as we note there, preliminary. However, even after more systematic study, most of the observations still hold, I believe.)

If Jeff was never truly an "insider" I was at this point very much the outsider, since I was at least two steps removed from the "action." Therefore, one of our biggest frustrations was how to get me into the office and factory. Since the Japanese we worked with seldom encountered professional women (the concept of a professional woman who was the WIFE of a co-worker was particularly strange to them), Jeff's requests to give me a tour of the office and factory were politely acknowledged and then ignored for a long time. Once I did get into the office and factory (Jeff managed to get me included in a two-day tour for some American visitors), I spent a good deal of time casually

150

writing in my notebook. Since I was part of a group of other foreigners who were there, I was pretty much ignored. While a solitary visitor was quite out of the ordinary, groups went through the plant on a regular basis and so I don't think I made the employees as uncomfortable as I had thought I might.

Once we began our more systematic study, we found ways to expand my role as an observer. One of these opportunities was our developing friendship with Jeff's co-workers. In particular, Matsuda Koji[1] was eager to speak with me to improve his English and we began to meet every Monday evening at a coffee shop near the train station. In exchange for the English "lessons," as he called our conversations, he shared with me his experiences and opinions about communication at work and his characterizations of communication in Japanese society generally. I didn't question or quiz him on communication patterns directly; rather, our conversations usually centered around his current work projects. Mr. Matsuda's reports about the activities, goals, procedures, and problems at the workplace provided another view on the communication situation Jeff and I were studying.

In addition, I found opportunities all around me to add to our evolving understanding: the kinds of "shared information" that we had identified in Jeff's workplace were present in other contexts as well. I noticed how the communication at the post office revolved around the "white boards" that lined the walls, how the workers seemed to shift responsibilities—moving from counting and filling stamp machines to sorting mail, to tidying and sweeping, to waiting on customers—within the space of time it took me to finish my daily business there. Similarly, at the bank, at the foreign registration office, at the train station, at small shops and large department stores, I observed what I perceived to be much more group responsibility, many fewer desks or personal, individual workspaces, much more oral communication between employees than I think would be the case in the US. The noise level, for instance was tremendous in most offices and places of business, a reflection of the amount of oral communication and group interaction that takes place in the workplace. These day-to-day experiences sometimes confirmed and sometimes challenged what we were seeing at the office, but they were an invaluable part of the entire experience.

The language barrier was paradoxically something of an asset, as far as it let me to attend to the "how," rather than the "what," of the communication situations I observed. That is, because I typically wasn't able to follow all of the content of the conversations around me, I could focus on what people were "doing" as they talked and worked together, rather than on what they were "saying." Of course, this was a luxury only afforded by Jeff's facility with the language, since his knowledge and ability to speak, to read, and especially to listen were crucial and central to the success of the project.

The "Shared Information" article was based on our early, initial observations and we have continued to refine our thinking in light of more substantial data we collected as the year progressed. (See Funk & Haas, "The Elements of Japan's Corporate Culture" in J. Funk, *Teamwork Japanese Style: How Japan's Corporate Culture Leads to Manufacturing Success,*" in preparation, for more details.) Looking back, I realize how personally and intellectually valuable this work has been for me. The collaborative nature of the work created a dynamic in which we both learned, and taught, a great deal. The research was highly collaborative even in its inception, as early encouragement was provided by Karen Schriver (who also worked with us through several iterations of the piece) and by the participants of a Research Network small group session (chaired by Pat Sullivan of the University of New Hampshire) at the 1989 CCCC.

This was also important work for me because, in the midst of the confusion and frustration of living in another culture, this research allowed me to begin to perceive or to compose an order on the very new and strange world outside my door. Through this work, I learned something of the paradox of "control"—I was at once trying to gain some "control" over the experience and at the same time acutely aware of how little "control" this method of research—especially in this setting—afforded me.

Finally, my experiences living and learning in Japan enabled me to gain a new perspective on my own ways of looking at the world. Dichotomies such as oral vs. written or public vs. private and concepts, such as "technologically advanced," were problematized as we learned something about how communication and culture are realized in a society very different from our own.

Jeffrey Funk—Westinghouse Corporation

I will center my reflections on the "Shared Information" article around collaboration and the skills and knowledge that we each brought to the research. The larger goal of my research in Japan was to understand how Japanese firms are able to achieve certain objectives (e.g., few delays, faster development to design to marketing cycles) much better than U. S. firms typically can. For example, several researchers have found that Japanese manufacturing firms are able to introduce new products much more quickly and smoothly into production and marketing. This kind of smooth transition requires a great deal of "teamwork," and communication obviously plays an important role in any form of teamwork.

However, since communication occurs much differently in Japanese and U.S. firms, one of the early challenges was redefining "technical communication" to include not only technical texts but the kinds of group communication I was seeing. Chris had a couple of early conversations—most notably with Karen Schriver — which convinced her of something I hadn't been able to: that what I was seeing, what we were daily trying to make sense of, was actually a valid issue for Chris to look at. I wanted to convince her of the legitimacy of the research because I knew I needed her expertise at examining the communication events.

Some of the observations we made were in a sense rather obvious, even pedestrian (that Japanese work together in groups, for instance) but the significance of this only became important because of 1) Chris's experience and training in focusing on particular communication events, and 2) my knowledge of how a manufacturing firm needs to work. Our complementary background knowledge allowed us first to carefully and systematically examine a subset of the communication in the office and second to relate our conclusions to the larger context of the corporate culture.

---

[1] The Japanese convention of family name first is used here.

Chapter 7   Communicating with Low-literate Adults

Our attention was attracted to the Floreak article because of its sensible use of empirical methods to approach a practically significant but daunting communication problem. Floreak and his colleagues had undertaken the task of providing printed materials, that is, visuals and text, to help social workers convey parenting information to low-literate adults. This task posed the problem of bridging the communication gap between the low-literate, lower class, and largely black audience and the high-literate, middle class, and largely white writers and designers.

Floreak worked with an interdisciplinary design team including writers, graphic designers, social workers, and psychologists. Because he and his colleagues recognized that they knew little about their audience, they began their project (Project First Steps) with a series of explorations. They surveyed the literature and carried out descriptive studies including open-ended interviews with members of the audience and visits to audience members' homes to see something of their daily lives. In addition, the design team asked more focussed questions to identify audience preferences for information source, content, and sequence, and for illustration style. The result of these investigations was the selection of a poster format with features especially designed to meet the needs of the audience.

Was Project First Steps a success? Toward the end of the article, in the section labeled "Effectiveness Testing," Floreak reports the results of observations of two groups of families, nine who had counseling with the project posters and nine who had counseling without the posters. Comparison of pre- and post- counseling observations did not reveal an advantage for either group. By focusing on these results, readers might conclude that the project was not a success. Before drawing this conclusion, though, readers should ask two questions: "When is it appropriate to draw negative conclusions from negative results?" and "What is the most appropriate way to evaluate the success of the project?" We raise the first question because we believe that drawing a negative conclusion from the "effectiveness testing" comparison is risky. The problem is that this comparison might not have been capable of revealing a difference even if one were present. If this were true, a negative result would provide no information about whether there was a difference or not.

The ability of a comparison to reveal a difference is called its **statistical power**. The statistical power of a comparison depends on the size of the difference the researchers are trying to find, the number of observations included in the comparison, and the variability of those observations. We have two reasons to suspect that the statistical power of the "effectiveness testing" comparison may be low. First, the sample size of nine per group is relatively small. A sample of 40 per group would have approximately doubled the power of the comparison. In addition, the measures of parenting behavior were probably quite variable because they were made in a complex setting, the parent's home, where visiting adults and children, bill collectors, telephone calls, etc may intrude. Further, judgments of the parent's behavior may have depended on how well their child happened to behave on the day of the observation and on how well the parents related to the observer. Because the power of the comparison may be low, we should be cautious in concluding that the posters had no impact on parenting behavior.

In addressing the question of how best to evaluate the success of the project, the reader might note that the project can be viewed as consisting of two phases. In the first phase, the researchers designed materials to communicate parenting information to low-literate parents. Success in the first phase could be measured by the extent to which these materials made it easier for the parents to understand the information. In the second phase, the parents applied or failed to apply the information presented in the project posters. Success in the second phase could be measured by changes in parenting behavior—changes such as those examined in the "effectiveness testing" comparison. Since the focus of the article was on the use of audience feedback in the design of effective communication, it seems reasonable to evaluate the project on the basis of the success of the first phase rather than the success of the second.

The Floreak article was written for an audience of technical writers rather an audience of researchers. For this reason, the results were reported with less technical detail than would be appropriate in a research journal. Issues involved in reporting research to various audiences are discussed in more detail in Chapter 13.

Notes on Technical Issues:

Many readers may not know what **readability tests** are based on or how they should be interpreted. There are several different readability tests, e.g., the Fry index, the Gunning Fog index, etc., but all are based on tabulating a few simple properties of text such as average word length and average sentence length. The readability score computed from these tabulations is often expressed as a grade level. If a text is assigned a grade level of 4, that means that, in certain simple properties such as average sentence length, the text resembles texts that fourth-graders read. However, it doesn't mean that fourth-graders can in fact read it, because readability scores leave out most of the factors that influence the reader's ability to comprehend, such as how familiar the topic is or how well the text is written. To realize how much readability scores leave out, consider this: if you were to scramble the order of all the words in this text, you would make it impossible to understand but you wouldn't change its readability score at all!

In discussing the measures used in the studies, Floreak mentions one that the reader may not be familiar with, at least not by name — the **Likert scale**. Likert scales, which are commonly used in surveys and public opinion polls, work like this: Respondents are shown a statement such as "The President is handling domestic policy well." and asked to indicate whether they "strongly agree," "agree," "disagree," "strongly disagree," or are "undecided."

Michael J. Floreak

DESIGNING FOR THE REAL WORLD:
Using Research to Turn a "Target Audience" into Real People

This article describes *Project First Steps,* a research-based communication design project to develop parenting education materials for low-literate adults. Members of the target audience were involved throughout the design process, providing input that directed the way the communication pieces were conceived, organized, designed, written and revised. In pre-design stages, interviews with members of the audience in their homes yielded information about preferences for content, illustration style and information ordering that guided the rhetorical approach to the pieces. This opportunity for interaction also helped turn the design team's assumptions about a "target audience" into experiences and knowledge about real people. In later stages of the program, the design team and audience met again for preference and usability testing that suggested the format, organization and style that would be most communicative and appealing for the audience. The article also discusses the integration of other forms of evaluation into the design process.

One of the writing fallacies I try to convince myself of, from time to time, is that I'm the one in control of what I communicate. I also try to convince myself that I always understand exactly how a particular audience thinks and processes information. Sometimes I can picture people out there thinking and processing. It's a group who prefers lists to sentences, who scans and skips in all the "right" ways, who reads the headings and demands to get information in chunks. It's a group that believes what I believe and reads the way I write.

Sometimes, I'm successful when I make these kinds of assumptions. I've learned, however, that I can be more successful—and make exciting discoveries—when I admit that I'm not completely in control and that I need to find out more about what my real audience believes and thinks.

This paper describes such a process of discovery. It describes *Project First Steps,* a two-year project to develop materials to educate functionally illiterate parents about caring for their children (See Figure 1). In *First Steps,* the audience became an integral part of the Information Design process — a partner along the way involved from initial information gathering through final evaluation, providing input that affected how the communication pieces were conceived, designed, written and edited. The project team included a writer, a graphic designer, a cognitive psychologist, an expert in learning disabilities, an expert in child development and research volunteers — all contributing in unique and important ways to the communication we produced as a group.

The project, as the writer and project manager, reinforced my belief that many different perspectives demand attention in thoughtfully designed communication. And it taught me that what we don't know is more interesting—and sometimes more important—than what we do know.

The Rhetorical Context

The idea for First Steps originated with the Diocesan Child Guidance Center, a social service agency in Columbus, Ohio, that provides mental health services to children. To serve the interests of children, the counselors and development experts at the Child Guidance Center often work with parents—providing in-home training, family counseling and parenting classes for people who are at high risk for neglecting or abusing their children. The goal of the program is to develop a positive relationship between parents and children by helping parents understand and become involved in their children's development.

By educating parents about their children's abilities, growth and needs, the Child Guidance Center helps change abusive behavior that results from parents' unreasonable expectations. However, reaching and motivating this audience is often a difficult task. Many of the people in the program have emotional or learning difficulties that stand in the way of becoming better parents. In most cases, only the legal threat of having their children taken away motivates parents to participate in a program like the one offered by the Child Guidance Center. By successfully completing the Child Guidance Center program, parents can demonstrate to the courts that they can responsibly take care of their children.

From years of working with parents who have motivational and learning problems, the counselors at the Child Guidance Center recognized a need to communicate their parenting information as completely as possible. They especially recognized a need for printed materials that would reiterate the messages of their one-on-one counselling.

A survey of materials uncovered a great deal of information on developmental milestones and activities for infants, babies, and toddlers. However,

Figure 1 on Page 160 should appear as follows:

Figure 1

Project First Steps is a series of nine posters designed to educate functionally illiterate parents about caring for their children. Developed with significant input from the audience, the large colorful posters feature simple words and a combination of visual styles that the audience found appealing and communicative. The front of each poster focuses on a specific developmental stage. The back features a chart showing the entire developmental progression from birth to two years.

most of the materials were developed for a very general audience and relied heavily on written information that might not be readable by low-literate parents. Recognizing that there are as many as 90,000 functionally illiterate adults in Franklin County (Ohio), the Child Guidance Center was committed to using materials developed especially for the needs of low-literate adults. Because no such pieces were readily available, the Child Guidance Center initiated a project to produce its own pieces.

The Center required that the pieces communicate information clearly through a combination of visuals and text and that the pieces be readable by low-literate audiences. While this task may be difficult enough, the information pieces also had to be motivating for parents who can be resistant or indifferent to learning about child care.

To develop their concept of low-literate educational materials, the Center knew that they needed to combine their expertise in child care with outside expertise in writing and design. They approached us at Fitch RichardsonSmith, a design consultancy whose U.S. headquarters are located in Worthington, Ohio, near Columbus.

Evolution of Complete Design Team

The combination of the Child Guidance Center and Fitch RichardsonSmith's Information Design Group proved to be a good one for this project. The Information Design Group at Fitch RichardsonSmith includes people with backgrounds in writing, graphic design and research. We emphasize the merging of different perspectives to design visual and verbal information that communicates as simply as possible.

Our usual process for solving communication problems involves working closely with our clients and finding out as much as we can about our audience. With First Steps, both the client and the audience became completely integrated in the design team, each providing an important perspective on the problem.

Upon bringing together our project team, we discovered that each member entered the project with very specific understandings of our target audience. We each approached the project as a writer, a designer, a psychologist, a child development expert, a marketing expert, or a teacher. And we brought with us the unique assumptions, sympathies, prejudices and understanding derived from our particular communication projects, academic course work or day-to-day interaction with clients. Individually, we assumed that the audience might be unsophisticated in their tastes, indifferent or uncooperative toward the project, consistently confrontational toward the counselors or completely neglectful of their children. But despite these uncertainties, we all also brought enthusiasm to the project. However, none of us brought explicit experience producing communication for low -literate audiences. Our lack of experience and our need to learn more about our audience benefitted the project more than we could have first anticipated.

Armchair Assumptions and a Research Plan

Before ever starting the project, we talked through some of our armchair assumptions about the audience and their needs. We assumed we would have to keep our communication simple and we discussed some of the ways we might do that. Mostly, we threw out a lot of questions that demonstrated our naivete about the audience and the project. We wondered what kind of learning problems might they have. Would they be able to read at all? What things are important to them? Who do they identify with? What do people who abuse their children expect from their children? How detached would they be from their children? How do they see their children? What do they respond to on TV? How do they find out the simple things about caring for their children?

From our discussion, we recognized that the things we didn't know made the project interesting. And we realized that knowing the answers to these questions would make us able to communicate to the parents the Child Guidance Center serves in a way that no one else has seemed to be able to do.

The answers to our questions lay within our reach—with our audience. Unlike the amorphous group I sometimes talk myself into writing for, this audience existed and was available for me to get to know. According to the Ohio Children's Trust Fund Grant that funded this project, our audience was "parents served by child-service agencies in Central Ohio." We felt that the project would benefit from as much interaction as possible with the audience. Therefore, we created a research plan that included a number of different methods for getting at both general questions about the audience and specific ones about our project. The research plan put us in contact with the audience through the whole design process. Our research began with a literature review in which we took another look at existing parent education materials to find good and bad examples of information presentation techniques. From there, we used a number of different evaluation methods which I describe below, highlighting (1) "timing" issues, that is, when the evaluation took place in the document design process; (2) our purposes in using the method; and (3) the method itself.

Pre-design Audience Analysis

Timing: Pre-design.

Purpose: To determine the audience's information needs, reading abilities, lifestyles, preferences, and interests specifically relative to this project. To give us a personal interaction with the audience. To shape the overall rhetorical approach to the pieces.

Method: Interviewed approximately 25 parents who would receive the final communication pieces. Included the use of open-ended questions, a Likert scale, and an observation checklist to find out about the parents' preferences for illustration style, sequencing methods, and information content. Recorded verbatim responses to questions and also described the attitude, environment and interaction.

162

Usability and Preference Testing

Timing :   After first conceptual design.

Purpose: To evaluate the potential usability and appeal of various media
            and communication approaches and select the most appropriate
            method for final design. To clarify specific problem areas antici-
            pated in the design.
Method: Interviewed approximately 25 parents who would receive the final
            pieces. Included the use of simple preference questions and open
            ended questions in which the parents selected among various
            communication pieces, including designs created specifically for
            this project. Also used a series of open-ended questions and
            paraphrase tests to determine the parents' understanding of
            various communication techniques.

Effectiveness Testing

Timing: After final design and first distribution to families
Purpose: To understand the effect of using the parenting education pieces
            on the home environment and on parent-child interaction.
Method: Professional counselors observed 18 families before and after
            receiving parenting education training. The families were ob-
            served in their home environment, and notes were made on the
            interactions between parents and children. A comparison was
            made between nine families receiving the communication pieces
            and one-on-one counseling and nine families who received only
            the one–on-one counseling.

We also built in several other research methods that helped us evaluate the
success of the project from other perspectives. These methods didn't directly
involve the end users and, therefore, had a less direct impact on our design.

Readability Testing

The final text was tested with a software package of standard readability
tests. This testing was used only as one minor indicator in the success of the
communication. Because readability is affected by discourse-level issues such
as organization, sentence structure, layout, typography, and other factors not
easily measured in readability testing, readability testing was used only as a
cross check with the usability and effectiveness testing done directly with the
audience.

Professional Evaluation

The pieces were reviewed by child care professionals. Their responses helped us understand the effectiveness and shortcomings of the pieces and guided our revisions of the pieces as the project continued.

While our research plan seemed rather ambitious given the constraints of a very limited budget, we were actually able to complete it rather efficiently and very inexpensively. Often, user research gets left out of the communication design process because it is perceived as a drawn out and expensive process. With this project, funded by state money, we discovered that by carefully planning the kinds of research we did, we were able to yield a lot of useful information and make very efficient use of our time.

A "Target Audience" Becomes Real People

With the beginning of pre-design audience interviews, our ill-defined image of a "target audience" became real people. For the audience interviews, members of the Fitch RichardsonSmith team paired up with the Child Guidance Center's child development expert to visit parents served by the Center's program. The experience of visiting families in their homes, asking questions and seeing the ways that they interact with each other helped provide the answers we needed. And it made a lasting impression that affected the way we wrote and designed our pieces.

As mentioned above, we visited about 25 families in the pre-design stage. We met most families in their homes where we had the opportunity to see parents and children interact in their regular day-to-day setting. We also had the chance to better understand the context in which the counseling took place and the environment in which our communication pieces would be used.

When visiting the homes, we asked a consistent set of open-ended questions and close-ended questions, using a Likert scale, to find out about the parent's abilities, opinions, preferences, and interests relative to this communication situation. As we visited the homes, we sat with the parents and showed them a set of stimulus materials consisting of existing child care information pieces that we thought might be appealing to them. Specifically, we asked the parents for their understanding of and feelings about the following:

- *Illustrations.* We showed several different illustration styles (photographs, black-and-white line drawings, cartoon style drawings, and colored drawings) and asked them to tell us which ones they liked and which ones they didn't like.

- *Information Sequencing.* We showed the parents several pieces that sequenced information in different ways (left to right, circular, numbered, un-numbered) and then asked questions about which method was the most communicative and the most appealing.
- *Content to Include.* Although the content of the pieces was already established as the basic developmental issues the Child Guidance Center covers in its counseling services, we wanted to know what subjects parents were interested in. We felt that highlighting information that parents were most interested in could help make the pieces more relevant and appealing.
- *Information Sources.* We asked parents questions about how they usually get information about child care and other subjects. Because television seemed likely to be the most consistent information source, we also asked specific questions about the kinds of television programs and advertisements they liked. We hoped to gain a better understanding of what kinds of information sources were appealing to people who don't read at all or at a very basic level.

While we recorded parents' responses to our questions, we also wrote down observations about the environment, the children, and the parents' attitudes. Some of the observations were very important to the way we approached our writing and design. For example, we noticed that very few of the homes had any kinds of books, magazines, or newspapers. However, we found the television on in almost every home we visited. Through the discussions, we found out that television was an extremely important source of contact with the outside world — one of the only such contacts for people who often don't have other support systems of friends or extended family.

We found that most parents were very anxious to please us in the interviews. But we also encountered some difficulties working with them. Some of the parents had a difficult time making decisions about things or understanding some of our questions. For example, when we asked one mother whether she liked to look at a color photograph or a black and white drawing, she responded "I like this one, it has a happy baby. I don't like that one, it's about changing diapers. I'm sick of changing diapers." A few other parents responded with "They're all nice. I like them all." The experience of asking these questions (and, at times, re-asking them in different ways) helped us understand some of the inherent problems in finding a common ground for communicating with the parents in terms that they understood and responded to. We recognized that we needed to keep our questions focused and ask them in very clear terms. We found the audience to be very literal, suggesting

165

that we needed to be very explicit and clear in the communication we designed.

Here are some other general characteristics of the audience that we discovered:

- Most of the parents were very cordial about talking to us, but we didn't see a great motivation to learn about parenting. For example, some people responded that everything we showed them was very nice and they would use them all. Those responses often contradicted other responses about how they get parenting information. Some parents might have felt that they couldn't be critical because we were working with the Child Guidance Center.
- Information and attitudes about parenting were deeply ingrained. Several parents found items in the stimulus material that didn't match their own beliefs or understanding. They actively pointed out the things that were "wrong." For example, several parents pointed to a poster about bathing a baby and said that "Everyone knows you're never supposed to clean the inside of a baby's nose with a cotton swab."
- The parents were used to receiving information in a very passive way. Most of the people got most of their information from television. From our discussions, the set seemed to stay on most of the time. People are used to tuning in and tuning out as things of interest come and go. Other sources of information included doctors or social workers who filled something of a parent role — a more experienced, knowledgeable person who gives them advice.
- The parents were very literal in the way they read information. For example, a number of people didn't understand the point of a cartoon in which a parent praises a child who attempts to dress himself but doesn't do it right. They didn't see the point in praising a child for doing something "wrong" even if the child gave a good try (see Figure 2).

Turning Research Conclusions Into Specific Design Criteria

Based on our review and analysis of the information gathered during our visits, we were able to develop very specific communication objectives and design criteria that would guide our first concepts of the communication pieces.

The objectives and criteria listed below are particular to our project . They've come from specific research with a specific audience, so they may not be appropriate for other projects or other audiences. However, for our project, these criteria set an important foundation for the approach we took to our communication design.

- *Make sequencing of information apparent.* The sequencing needed to follow a clear left-right progression. Almost all the parents seemed to prefer a left-to-right sequencing that also included numbers.
- *Make steps in a sequence very clear.* In illustration, limit the number of details, focusing on the ones that are important for communicating the key points. For example, one mother commented on "all those babies" in a sequencing sample that was illustrated with seven different steps; she seemed to ignore the steps.
- *Use both expressive and instructional images.* Many of the parents had very positive reactions to images of happy mothers and babies together. Yet they seemed to get more specific information from simple drawings. We decided to combine expressive images that establish the context of a positive parent-child interaction and simple, uncluttered instructional images to communicate steps in a process.
- *Segment information into small, manageable chunks.* Because a number of parents, like the mother who commented on "all those babies," seemed overwhelmed by large numbers of steps, we decided to simplify procedures as much as possible and limit the number of steps to no more than four or five.
- *Be specific, concrete, and literal.* Our experience interviewing the parents helped us understand how literal the audience could be. The subjects covered, words used, and images shown needed to relate directly to the experiences and interests of parents. We couldn't count on the audience necessarily responding to generalizations, metaphors, or flowery description.
- *Tell a complete story with visuals and supplement with words.* Even people who read at the lowest levels seemed to look for words in their communication. However, to be most effective, we needed to tell as complete a story as possible with pictures, using words to add detail and specifics for people who can read.
- *Make any verbal information as simple as possible.* To reach the largest possible audience, the text needed to read at a very basic level.
- *Make the pieces exciting and attention-getting.* The people who were to receive the pieces are not motivated to want to read or to take the time to learn about child care. We could improve the chances for usability by

167

designing pieces that caught the attention of the audience and invited them in for more.

With these design criteria in hand and the impressions of our visits in mind, we began developing concepts for the communication pieces (see Figure 2). Up to this point, we had not defined what the "communication pieces" would really be. We knew that the form the communication took would be important to making the pieces easy to use and motivating parents to use them. We considered game, poster, and brochure formats. Games and posters were less traditional communication formats and would, perhaps, be more motivating or approachable for someone who didn't read. Brochures were the more expected format and easier for counselors to use, but might be intimidating for non-readers.

Figure 2 on page 168 should appear as follows:

Figure 2

The developmental activities covered in each poster are limited to four steps. A black-and-white photograph helps establish the context. The steps of the activities are explained with basic illustrations and simple written information.

Taking Our Concept to the Audience

To determine the appropriate communication format, we created concepts for both posters and brochures. We selected the poster format because it could be instructional but also large, colorful, and highly visual. As a large text it could be less likely to be thrown away or ignored. A social worker could work through the information with the parent, hang the poster in the child's room, and ask the parent to keep the poster up and refer to it until the next visit. We also decided to test a brochure format because it was the most traditional format, most like the other kinds of education pieces parents were likely to receive.

We took our completed, full-color concepts back to the audience to test for both preference and understanding. We randomly inserted our concepts in with other existing parenting education materials that ranged from high-quality pieces produced by a baby products company to some low-cost photocopied materials developed by other social service agencies. We asked parents to examine each piece and select the one they liked best. We then used a series of open-ended questions to help determine what parents liked about their choice. We also asked for their second favorite and finally for their least favorite. We followed each with a series of open-ended questions. We recorded each response verbatim.

While the parents were examining the pieces, we also observed their behavior. We tried to observe whether they seemed to be reading information or just looking at the images, and we also noted whether they spent an especially long or short amount of time on any one piece.

After finding out about their preferences, we then focused in on information about our concepts. We asked parents for their opinions about the ways that illustrations, sequencing, and color were used in the two different concepts. We then tested for comprehension by asking the parents to explain in their own words what was happening in several specific sequences covered in the concepts. We also looked for opinions and comprehension of three specific communication elements: the way we represented a dialog between parent and child in the samples, the size and readability of type, and the use of written text .

While not specifically asking about it, we also looked for overall comments about the racial and gender depictions in the pieces. For the project, we very consciously used a mixture of boys and girls and various racial groups representative of our audience. In the concepts tested, however, the children we used for our photos and drawings happened to be white boys. None of the people interviewed made any comments about racial or sexual bias.

In the concepts we also attempted to address the problem of sexist language. Because we knew our audience was very literal in the way they read things, we wanted to avoid the use of the generic "he." The text of the posters described activities and milestones that apply generally to children of a specific age. However, these issues are illustrated with a specific example of a parent and child interacting. The purpose and use of the pieces made the use of "he" inappropriate for several reasons. Most importantly, in half the posters, the parent-child interaction would be demonstrated with a girl. But also, we wondered whether parents who are very literal would understand that the same things apply to their child even if their child is not of the same sex as the child shown in the picture.

After considering alternatives ranging from the contrived (avoiding any pronouns at all) to the simple (using "he" if the poster featured a boy and "she" if it featured a girl), we settled on a solution that is used commonly in conversation, but less frequently used in print. Instead of using "he" or "she," we used "they." In this case, "they" often referred to the singular noun "your baby." One poster, for example, included the following statement: "Your baby is making big changes. They are starting to be more like a big kid." While this construction may seem awkward in agreement, it represents a conversational technique that is used by many people — and is especially familiar to the parents we were writing for. While some of our design team had hesitations about using something that was non-standard on the posters, our work with the audience led them to understand that making the communication work was more important than using schoolbook English.

When we showed the concepts to the parents, we found that none of the parents made any notice of our grammatical liberties. And we made other interesting observations that guided our final design. Importantly, we discovered that parents preferred our poster format over any of the other communication pieces they saw. The comments ranged from "I could sit and look at them all day." to "I like this. It's for my kids. This is how my kids eat." Many of the parents specifically mentioned that they liked the large photographs, happy kids, and bright colors.

The parents also helped us recognize a need for some modifications. We had conceived of the posters as a series of nine pieces, each covering a specific age group between the ages of birth and two years. We discovered that we were correct in assuming that parents only wanted to see information about their child's specific age. Parents with children in the age groups covered by the concepts responded well and related the information to their own children. One mother related to a sequence explaining that older toddlers like to dress themselves, even though they may not be very success-ful at it. "He's so rough. He likes to take his own clothes off." Another mother related to a sequence explaining that playing with spoons and sand helps children learn the motor skills needed to feed themselves. "The sand helps them get ready for using the spoon. My Cory gets so that she wants to feed herself. That's good."

The parent's favorable reaction to another poster, produced by an infant products company, helped us discover a missing element in our posters. The infant products poster used a stair-step chart to show child development. This technique helped provide some context for where a child was in the overall development process. Parents found it a valuable information tool. Positive reactions to this piece included "This shows how your baby grows. I have something like this from my (parenting) class. I kept it with all my papers." and "I like this because it tells stages your baby goes through." These responses helped us recognize that our posters gave a very isolated picture of the ages and skills we were covering. Because parents would only receive one poster at a time, they wouldn't necessary have a point of comparison for how their child has grown developmentally or where they are going. We decided, therefore, to incorporate a developmental chart that would appear on the back of each poster showing developmental stages from birth to age two. This addition helped our posters focus on specific age segments on the front of the poster and provide an overall child development context on the back.

From this input, we decided that our poster format was the type of commu-nication that most appealed to our audience. With the addition of content on the back and other minor modifications, we were able to proceed with developing communication pieces that seemed most likely to meet the needs of our audience.

Other Research Findings

Most of the input that guided our design and writing came directly from the audience. However, as mentioned above, we did build several other research methods into the process to help us evaluate the effectiveness of the pieces.

Readability Testing

After writing the concepts and taking them to the target audience, we also looked at the readability of the pieces. As our interaction with the audience suggested, the pieces scored well on readability tests: at grade level 2.5 on Spache, at grade level 3.7 on Gunning Fog, at grade level 1.0 on Fry, and at or below grade level 3.0 on Raygor. The fact that the pieces scored somewhat unevenly could probably be attributed to the use of vocabulary like "cooing," "toddler," or "Cheerios" that were not part of the word lists used in the formulas, but were familiar spoken vocabulary for parents of small children.

We used the readability tests simply as a way of confirming our efforts in a minimal way. The formulas could not factor in the contributions made by the visuals in the pieces. Nor could they consider the discourse-level issues of using simple sentences or using "they." Therefore, we considered the readability scores primarily as objective support of the methods we had undertaken to make the posters easy-to-use. We did not use the readability evaluation as a criterion for refining the posters. Our audience analysis provided much clearer and more specific indications of potential usability problems that went well beyond the word and sentence level.

Evaluation by Professionals

As the final pieces were printed, professionals who would be using the posters received copies and were asked to evaluate their effectiveness with clients. The comments from professionals told us a great deal about the social and political contexts in which the posters were used. The comments were strongly positive, ranging from "Easy for parents to comprehend and relate to. Parents love them." to "I like the steps that demonstrate how the child develops." to "I think we should use these posters with all parents, not just low-literate parents." However, several professionals commented on the importance of maintaining a racial and sexual balance in the posters. Comments included, "I have problems with the all white/male format." and "Leaves me with the impression you are only concentrating on white male children." Even before these strong comments, we had planned that the nine posters would included a balance of boys and girls and would represent an ethnic mix representative of the audience. Several professionals also commented on the "lamentable grammar" demonstrated with our non-standard use of "they."

Effectiveness Testing

As the final method of gaining input from the target audience, professionals who work with the audience evaluated the effect of using the posters on producing changes in parenting behavior. In the evaluation, 18 families served by the Child Guidance Center were given a pre- and post-test: "Home

172

Observation Measurement of Environment." Areas observed included: the emotional and verbal responsiveness of the parent, the avoidance of punishment, the organization of the child's environment, the appropriateness of play materials, the involvement of the parent with the child, and the indication of appropriate daily developmental stimulation. Half the families received only one-on-one parenting counseling. The other half received the same counseling plus the First Steps posters. After 60 days, both groups showed improvement. In her evaluation, the Child Guidance Center's development expert said, "The addition of low-literate materials augments and reinforces the home-based instruction. The materials meet the needs they were designed to fulfill — encouraging parents to become involved in their child's development and enhancing their child's environment."

The effectiveness testing was based on subjective evaluations of family situations. Therefore, its value was largely in demonstrating that the posters are being used positively in counseling situations. The testing was not designed to be statistical, but it did provide a look at the use of our communication pieces once in the hands of the audience.

Conclusion

Almost two years after our first armchair evaluation of the audience, we have completed the entire series of nine Project First Steps posters that are now being used by thousands of families in Central Ohio.

The discoveries I've made during this process are quite a bit more complex than what I might have assumed at the start. Most importantly, I've discovered that there is a difference between "knowing about my audience" and "knowing my audience." At the beginning of the project, I had a rather vague picture of what the people I was writing for might be like. And I assumed that most of my blanks could be filled in by reading what the "experts" had to say about child development and communicating with low-literate audiences. After visiting parents in their homes, seeing their children, asking questions, listening, observing, talking and testing, I now have quite a richer picture of the real needs and attitudes of my audience. I can now attach specific names, faces, incidents, comments, and anecdotes to my assumptions about who this audience is and what they need. I also now recognize that my audience is made up of individuals, each of whom will interact personally with the material I write. Such individuals understand things very literally, read pictures more carefully than words, and prefer communication that talks to them in their own terms. I've also discovered that research can be an exciting process of discovery that has its place *throughout* the information design process, not just at the beginning or at the end.

Mostly I've been reminded that communication design is a process in which information needs to flow both from the writer to the audience and from the audience to the writer.

Acknowledgements

This project represents a two-year team effort. It succeeded through the combined effort of the following people who contributed their talents and time to the project and their experiences to this article: Liz Sanders, Jaimie Alexander, Keith Kresge, Dave Smith, and most of the rest of Fitch RichardsonSmith, Mary Kay MacLean, Ruthann Jepsen, Victoria Lucas, and the dedicated volunteers from the Diocesan Child Guidance Center, Lori Reder and George Anderson.

References

Duffy, T. M., & Kabance, P. (1982). Testing a Readable Writing Approach to Text Revision. *Journal of Educational Psychology, 74,* (5) 733-748.

Huckin, T. N. (1983). A Cognitive Approach to Readability. In P.V. Anderson, R.J.Brockman. & C.R. Miller (Eds.), *New Essays in Scientific and Technical Communication.* New York: Baywood Press.

Holland, V. M. (March, 1981). Psycholinguistic Alternatives to *Readability Formulas.*Washington: American Institutes for Research.

Leach, P. (1978). *Your Baby and Child from Birth to Age Five.* New York: A.A. Knopf.

Rubin, R.,Fisher, J.J. III, & Doering., S.G. (1980). *Your Toddler Ages One and Two.* New York: Johnson & Johnson Child Development Publications.

Schriver, K.A. (in press). *Evaluating Text Quality: The Continuum from Text Focused to Reader Focused Methods.* IEEE Transactions in Professional Communication,.

Zimmerman , M.L. & Perkin, G.W. (1982). *Print Materials for Nonreaders: Experiences in Family Planning and Health* Seattle, WA: PIACT Paper Eight, PIACT.

Author's Comments—Michael J. Floreak

Arm chair assumptions about what an audience needs and rules of thumb
for good communication often guide much of the communication design
process. While these kinds of internalized knowledge are important to
communication designers, they can never take the place of actually meeting
the audience face-to-face—finding out who they really are, asking what they
really need. In business contexts, user research is often viewed as complicated, involved and expensive with limited uses beyond market testing.
However, this isn't necessarily true. Especially when dealing with definable
and specialized audiences, research doesn't need to be elaborate or involved.
The experience of meeting, observing and engaging in a dialogue with
members of a target audience can give communication designers a rich and
thorough understanding of the needs of the audience—an understanding that
only comes from real hands-on experience. The key to this kind of research is
the recognition that users can provide valuable input throughout the design
process. The only other necessities are setting objectives for what information
you need from users and the ability to observe and evaluate. The resulting
process of discovery makes communication designers better able to assess
and meet the real needs of a real audience.

Chapter 8   Bedtime Stories in the Piedmont

We selected this study not only because of the intrinsic interest of its content — its surprise value — but also because it illustrates well some of the special features of **ethnographic research**. There are two features the reader should pay particular attention to. First, the reader should notice that the researcher has not treated the people being studied simply as a *source* of data. Rather, they have been included in a significant way in the *interpretation* of the data. Charlene Thomas, the co-author, is the mother in the family that was observed. This makes good research sense, especially in exploratory studies and in cross-cultural studies. After all, the people being studied know a lot about themselves and their environments and can, therefore, help the researcher understand the meaning of the events observed. We saw Funk and Haas doing something similar, though not in such a thorough-going way, in their work with Haas' Japanese tutor. As Haas remarks,

> Matsuda Koji was eager to speak with me to improve his English and we began to meet every Monday evening at a coffee shop near the train station. In exchange for the English "lessons," as he called our conversations, he shared with me his experiences and opinions about communication at work and his characterizations of communication in Japanese society generally. (p. 151)

As Heath points out in her personal statement, this kind of study, which is something of an ethnographic and something of an **autoethnographic study**, illustrates the richness of the data that can be gathered in an environment when one approaches it with a well-focused question, but allows the subjects to participate in the data collection and interpretation. In addition, this study suggests that rather than allowing one "off-the-rack" method to drive the design of a study, methods can be tailored to fit the peculiarities of the situation.

Second, the reader should note the detail with which human interactions are being analyzed in this study. The study explored the effect of introducing a "literacy artifact" (children's books) and a "literacy event" (reading those books to a preschooler) into the home of a rural black family. The study focuses not on gross features of the situation, such as how much time the mother spends in reading to the child, but rather on exactly what happens in particular interactions involving the mother, the child, and a book. The surprising results of this study are to be found in the fine grain of that interaction, revealed in details such as whether the mother says "Say cat!" rather than "What's that?" while pointing at the picture of a cat. The fact that interesting and useful information can be found in this kind of detailed account indicates that ethnographic analysis has an important role to play in our society's efforts to solve problems of literacy.

Heath and Thomas lay out a basis for studying literacy development in the Thomas household by introducing the results of Heath's long-term ethnographic research in Trackton (Heath, 1983). By identifying features of literacy development typical of families in Trackton and then contrasting them with features linked to such literacy artifacts as children's books and such literacy events as bedtime stories, they establish a basis for understanding how these artifacts and events might be expected to impact the immediate environment.

In what was apparently a happy oversight, no directions were given to T on how to use the artifact once it had been introduced into the environment. This was fortunate for the purposes of the study, since it allowed Heath and Thomas to observe what appears to be a natural, i.e., untutored, process of change. Other than introducing children's books and the act of reading into the environment, no other effort was made to be intrusive or instructive. It is true that T (Charlene Thomas) was given the directives not to use force to make De sit to read and to leave the books out for him at times other than those officially set aside to read, but neither of these were suggestive of ways in which she should use the books to interact with De or how De should be made to interact with the books.

In laying out the field notes and observations, a pattern of behavior with the literate artifact seems to emerge. Initially, T uses the books as a "launching pad" to name the objects and people in the book and then in the immediate environment. Starting with directives such as "Say cat," she "reads" to De by focusing on naming things in the book and then switches her attention to people immediately available: "Say mama, say daddy." Rather than using questions such as "What color is the dog?" to explore the fictitious characters in the stories, she equates reading with the act of naming. Heath and Thomas comment that they are not certain as to the sources of this interpretation of reading—but suggest that it is in keeping with the behavior that Heath noted in other adults in Trackton who did not attempt to expand upon or interpret their children's utterances.

As Heath and Thomas point out, introducing an artifact into an environment is no trivial thing. They use the example of the introduction of the fork in

Europe in the fourteenth century to make their point that such artifacts can have both immediate and long-range effects. This study is a good example of the kind of "immediate resonance" that such an artifact might have. In addition, as Winograd and Flores (*Computers and Cognition* ,1986) point out in their discussion of the computer as an artifact in literacy and human communication, it is important to detail the process by which the artifact or tool for accomplishing a task becomes subsumed in the act of accomplishment. They argue that the tool will, by virtue of its characteristics, change the nature of the act (and a lot more, in the case of both computers and forks!). Once an artifact has been adopted, it can have an impact on behavior without the user's being consciously aware of it. That being the case, methods such as introspection and protocol analysis cannot reveal how the artifact changes the behavior.

Finally, we should note the care with which Heath and Thomas call attention to the limits of the study and its implications for the focus and methodology of future work:

> T may be a unique individual, and the behaviors that occurred simultaneously with book-reading for her may not follow for other individuals in the same cultural conditions. Other fine-grained analyses of different individuals in the same cultural conditions are needed to allow generalizations about the interdependence of patterns of oral and written language use under this innovation. . . . (p. 204)

> To accomplish these goals, we need new and different research strategies. Cooperative work between teachers and researchers has here been extended to a student-parent. The productivity of this research method, as shown by the present study, suggests that it could be added to the present inventory of parent education techniques. . . .(p. 204)

Such statements locate the study in larger contexts that help to give it significance and to shape future research agendas.

References

Winograd, T., & Flores, F. (1986) *Understanding Computers and Cognition.* Morwood, NJ: Ablex.

Shirley Brice Heath with Charlene Thomas

The Achievement of Preschool Literacy
for Mother and Child

Since the second decade of the twentieth century, parent education has become a common phenomenon in those nations that provide 10 to 12 years of schooling for the majority of the national youth. Initially, the major emphasis was on the physical health and development of the child. In the 1960s, the focus shifted to the parent-child interaction and its effects on the social and cognitive development of the child (Brocher, 1980). Professionals in child welfare began to assert that parents needed to be "socialized" in child-rearing skills and "developed" in their abilities to smooth children's entrance to school and transition into secure and capable adults. Subsequently, parent socialization has focused on specific types of interactions to increase the "effectiveness" of parents and enable them to "improve" the quality of their relations with their children (Fantini, 1980).

Parent-Child Book-Reading

Book-reading with preschoolers or "reading before school" (Smethurst, 1975) is a popular form of interaction highlighted in parent education programs. Numerous parent-academicians have written accounts of their personal experiences with early readers and writers. Almost all these studies report the early reading of mainstream middle-class children, and their focus is on what the child learns about the uses of literacy and gains from being an early reader. The caregiver's interactions with the young child and the artifacts of literacy (children's books, crayons, pencils, and paper) in the literacy event[1] of book-reading receive little attention, but instead seem to be considered givens or somehow "natural" to parenthood.

By the mid-1970s, however, psychologists, linguists, and anthropologists began to detail the negotiated social construction of such parent-child interactions. Ninio and Bruner (1978) describe one middle-class mother and her preschooler reading a book, with the mother focusing the child's attention, requesting labels, and providing opportunities for the child to move forward in knowledge about the contents and uses of the book. Scollon and Scollon (1981) describe mother and child engaged in book-reading as exhibitor-questioner and spectator-respondent. The mother displays the book, points to, and names items upon which the child is to focus attention; she then asks questions about the names of items, their features and location in the book; the child watches, listens, waits, and responds. In many ways, these book-reading episodes are similar to descriptions of mainstream middle-class caregivers talking to their children (Snow & Ferguson, 1977; Gleason & Weintraub, 1978; Snow, 1979). Scollon and Scollon (1981) and Heath (1982b, 1983) call attention to the intricate ways in which oral language learning patterns are related to literacy habits that focus on naming, retelling, and paying close attention to features of the environment chosen for emphasis by the adult.

These accounts of book-reading illustrate the bundle of collectively sustained symbolic structures that embody overlapping and reinforcing ideas of what it means to acquire literacy skills and to become literate in mainstream school-oriented society. In the classroom, students encounter similar literacy activities in reading circles, social studies lessons, and language arts classes. There, as in mainstream homes, adults select the story or book, focus the child's attention on particular objects, and expect the child to respond as spectator and respondent (see Chap. 1 for an account of book-reading in a school setting). Studies of mainstream middle class children at home and of literacy activities in classrooms have shown that what is being transmitted in preschool book-reading is much more than how to read and write. The children learn a set of master patterns of language use, which serves as a basis for the subsequent acquisition of other patterns of language and thought. Heath (1983) details the multiple ways in which mainstream parents immerse their children in an environment of repetitive, redundant, and internally consistent habits which enable their children not only to read and write but also to use book knowledge in other contexts. These children learn to link items in one setting to items in their books, to name their points of similarity and their attributes, uses, and functions. Moreover, as these children enter school, their parents continue to stress the early pattern of individual display and achievement lessoned first in bedtime story-like events (Heath, 1982b). All these studies provide support for Bourdieu's (1967, 1973) notion that the transmission of cultural capital by the middle class involves much more than the provision of books and leisure time for book-reading; it implies also a host of sustained institutional and routine mechanisms that work together harmoniously to integrate children from such homes into learning with literacy.

What set of associated habits and multiple minute adjustments of verbal and nonverbal behavior accompany book-reading with a preschooler? If, into a home in which parent-child book-reading has not been a habit, we intro-

181

duce children's books as literacy artifacts and provide minimal guidance in the literacy event of a caregiver reading with a preschooler, what behavioral changes, if any, will occur along with this innovation? For the anthropologist, this question is no different in principle from that which asks about the behavioral changes that followed the introduction of the fork in Europe in the fourteenth century. The possibility of spearing chunks of meat rather than gnawing flesh from the bone brought changes in menus, requirements for foodstuffs, and types of utensils for cooking and serving food (Kroeber, 1948). Many of these changes seemed unrelated to the fork itself; moreover, many could not have been predicted, for they seemed to occur spontaneously and in patterns linking habits not consciously related to eating as it is understood by humans.

In this chapter, we trace the behaviors that occurred simultaneously with the innovation of book-reading for an unemployed, high school dropout, black mother of two preschool children. Aside from the financial difficulties caused by the unemployment of the mother and several members of her family (in a period of widespread joblessness), the mother seemed to have ways of living similar to those of the residents of Trackton, a black Piedmont community of the Carolinas described in Heath (1983).

A Review of Trackton

All adults in Trackton could read and write, but they did not consciously model, demonstrate, or tutor reading and writing for their children. There were no special children's books, and the only materials written especially for children were Sunday school pamphlets or leaflets brought home from church. There were no special times for reading and no routine reading activities such as bedtime stories. At an early age, Trackton children began to tell stories modeled on oral tales they heard adults exchange in their everyday banter, in which a good story was the best way to win an argument, smooth over a disagreement, or prove a point. Adults did not question children about bits and pieces of the stories the children told. In addition, in their interactions with young children, they did not pick out sounds the youngsters made and respond to them as though they were labels of items in the environment. They also did not ask preschoolers the common teaching questions, such as "What is this?" or "What color is this?" Instead, adults talked about items and events in the environment without simplified speech or special types of questions addressed to young children. Questions asked of young children with the greatest frequency were of the type "What's that like?" "Where'd you get that?" In short, Trackton parents did not exhibit the routines and patterns of talking,

182

reading, and writing with their young children that were described in the research literature on mainstream school-oriented families. Nonetheless, their children did learn to talk, and they went to school with certain expectations of print and were able to recognize such reading materials in their environment as the names of cars and motorcycles, brand names of products, and T-shirt slogans.

In Trackton, I collected these details of the forms and functions of written and spoken language through my participation as an ethnographer in the community for nearly a decade. I did not attempt to introduce any artifacts or events that were not native to the community. However, some years later in another community, in my work with the mother described here, both her ninth-grade English teacher and I did make efforts, though minimal, to introduce into this mother's ways of living a new literacy artifact (children's books) and a new literacy event (reading those books with her preschool child). Furthermore, throughout the year described here, her English teacher and I encouraged this mother to keep a record of her own activities and her 2-year-old's uses of language. As the full record began to develop, the mother agreed to be a research associate and to work with me to provide a published report of her achievement of preschool literacy with her son.

The Story Behind This Story

The conditions and goals of the work which led to the description given here are unusual and merit explanation. The mother described here is Charlene Thomas, (T), a 16-year-old who dropped out of the ninth grade early in the 1981 school term. She was repeating the ninth grade because she missed most of the previous school year when her mother had an extensive illness and died. She had a son born in September of 1980, and another was born in 1982. In September of 1981, T was enrolled in a ninth-grade basic English class in a high school in a town of 30,000 in the deep South of the United States. The school provided two academic tracks: a general track for students who planned to attend college or technical school, and a "basic" track for those who scored below the fifth-grade level in reading and language arts skills.

The teacher of T's English class was Amanda Branscombe, (B), with whom I worked in a teacher-researcher relationship during 1981 and 1982.[2] B's emphasis in her classes was on writing and reading. As a teaching strategy, she set up letter-writing teams, each composed of one student in her basic English class and one student in her eleventh-grade general English class. The school was large enough and sufficiently socially segregated by the two-track system that it was highly unlikely that students in the two classes would meet. The eleventh graders studied English only in the first semester (from September through December). Therefore, to ensure that the ninth graders had an audience and a reason for writing beyond December, I began corresponding with them as a class in the fall and continued throughout the spring.

In addition, I asked the ninth graders to become associates with me in my interests as an anthropologist in oral language and reading and writing in communities around the world. They began taking field notes on topics such as the types of questions used in their homes and communities. They interviewed family members about recollections of themselves learning to read and write and memories of their children's early language development. To the students, my goal was explained as the comparison of these habits with the research I had conducted in the Southeastern part of the United States, which was being prepared for publication as a book (Heath, 1983). The teacher read portions of the book's manuscript to the class so the students would have some idea of the final product created from field notes. Approximately every 2 weeks during the fall term, B sent me copies of the ninth-grade class's writings and her own field notes describing what she did in class and how the students were responding to their reading and writing. In turn, I provided feedback on developments I saw in the individual students' writing, and B and I discussed research in writing and its implications for classroom teaching in bi-monthly phone conversations.

In late November, B told me that T had missed 15 days of school, which, according to school policy, exceeded the number of absences allowed to a student in one semester. She would have to repeat the grade. I suggested that we encourage T to continue writing letters to the eleventh grader, and B and I also agreed to write to T. I suggested that I ask T to take field notes of her toddler's activities, especially his talking, and I would send some books and ask her to read to her toddler. B agreed and suggested she visit T and take her books, audiotapes, and a tape recorder. The purpose of the tape recorder was to give T an "easy" way to stay in touch with us and to tell us what she was doing with Davaris (nicknamed De), her preschooler, in case she did not continue writing.

The dual goals of this "project" were then to create what might perhaps be some motivation for a school dropout to read and write with her preschool child, and to continue her membership in the community of writers and researchers B had created in her ninth-grade class. The field notes and audiotapes the students had made on their reading, writing, and talking habits and those of their families had legitimated this activity for the ninth graders; moreover, the class had accepted the fact that I was exceptionally curious about how, when, where, and with whom they talked, wrote, and read. The description reported in this chapter, then, does not come from a preplanned "research project" but is an accidental by-product of a pedagogic activity initiated for a high school dropout mother by a teacher and a researcher.

Some background on T's writing in the months between September and November will provide an idea of the literacy skills and habits T had when she quit school. At the beginning of the academic term, B paired the ninth-grade and eleventh-grade students on the basis of their interests as indicated in brief self-introductory letters written by each student. One class period each week was used for the letter exchange: students read the letters they received and answered them. T entered B's class 10 days late and was paired for the letter-writing with a senior girl (L) who was a serious student, walked with a limp, rode horses, and was the daughter of a teacher-minister. The teacher paired the two girls because they both said in their introductory letters that they were interested in riding, although the girls' letters soon revealed that L meant horseback riding whereas T meant riding in a car. To T's first letter (Fig. 4-1), L responded with sympathy for the difficulties of entering school 10 days late and answered the questions T had raised in her letter. In her second letter, T included a salutation and closing and had begun to develop a dialogue with L. By the fifth letter, she told L that she had few friends at school, was the mother of a son, and had lost her own mother the previous year. L responded by telling T about her limp and her own frequent absences from school because of sickness.

In early November, after only eight letter exchanges, the teacher asked the students to write a brief paragraph about what the letter exchange had meant to them . T's note (Fig. 4-2) indicates that prior to the ninth grade, she had not written a letter.

By mid November, T had missed 16 days, and she quit school. I wrote to her within the week expressing dismay that her own nightmare of missing 16 days in 1 year had become a reality for her friend. Two weeks later, T wrote a letter to L in which she explained: "Well, as you know, I have quit school. I didn't really want to quit. But it just came to point I know I had to do." She asked L to keep writing to her and closed her letter with this postscript: "I wished I could have know who you was." One week later, she wrote to her teacher, explaining that she had quit school because she was expecting another baby in April and she did not believe she should be another girl making "blacks look bad" by "walking around the school with a stomach."

Figure 4-1. Charlene's letter of introduction to L., September 11, 1981.

My name is — Charlene I just started school Tuesday . I seem to like some of my classes and one class i like is math and I think that I'm going to like english. I like to go riding on Sunday. Maybe you would like to go. I like doing alot of fun thing's just when it come down to play space and soft ball,

Figure 4-2. Charlene's essay on the meaning of the letter exchange, November 6, 1981.

I enjoyen writting L———. Because she help me with promble and i help her. And I love to write letter sometime. But this is the only time I really have sit down and wrote a letter. So i guess this why I enjoyen writting. Sometime it good to write to someone to get a promble off of your mind. But the most inportant thing you dont have to write S.

By Charlene Thomas

Achieving Literacy

Both B and I wrote T, and B visited, encouraging her to try to obtain her high school diploma through night school. In a letter to T, I asked if she would be willing, now that she was at home all the time, to take field notes on her son's language learning and his daily activities. She responded in late February with three pages of field notes (printed here as they appeared in the original).

Fieldnote   *Feb 27, 82*

Kid's in my community is in school. And I don't be around many of them that's not in school. But I have a 17 months old son. And his name is Davaris. He is walking and talking a little bit. Well when he started talking it was baby talk. But now I have got that I can understand him. I sit an teach him different thing's. As who people is. And what not to do. And what to do. Kid that he do be around they teach him things. Such as Know' no, and try to teach him what thing's is. Like Dog & cat's. And now he can tell me pot pot. And he mean's he got to use the bathroom. And like when he want something to drink he go and get his cup. And I open up the refrigerator and he point to what he want. But mostly I believe that they learn more from beening around grow up. They watch everything that goes on. And they try it.The way he tell me he wont to go somewhere. He say come go. And he get my hand and take me where he wont to go. It just amazing how kid learn to talk. Because when we came up we didnt know different thing. As these kid's now day is faster than we is. He do talking to himself but

186

mostly is baby talk. And some is when he here me say to him. Like get and what. no' no. Mama, Dada. He does read the only thing he do is look at picture. And say what they are. I teach him how to count. He say one, two, five, six. He cant say the rest of the number yet. But he is learning. I think the more him be around me and other adult He will be smart. He sit A watch TV. Cut it off. Stand up in chair's pick up the phone. And do baby talk sometime he say what. Somebody knot on the door he use to say who. But now he don't say nothing. He will come an get me or somebody. He go outside by hisself when the door is open. Put his cup in the sink. Pull the chair up to the sink and try to wash dish. pull it up to the table. It just so much that he do. So I'm going to let this be it. He stay busy all the time. I hope that this can be a help.

Your friend Charlene

In these field notes, T terms De's early language "baby talk," and she emphasizes her own priorities for his learning: that he should know who people are, respond to commands, be independent, and learn by watching others and trying. She notes that the children around teach him commands and "what thing's is."

The new baby was due in April 1982. T was the sole housekeeper in a household in which she, the new baby, De, the children's father, her teenage brother Mike, her father, and two other adult males lived. Realizing she had limited time for writing field notes and anxious to give her a specific task, I wrote asking her to read to De for 10 minutes each day and to tape-record (on a recorder borrowed from B) the reading sessions with him and the time when he played alone in his room immediately following the reading. In early May, B reinforced my request by taking children's books, audiotapes, and a new tape recorder as a gift for T. Within the week, T recorded an oral account of what she could remember of De's language development. She reported that De weighed 8 Ib. 2 oz. at birth, and within the first week he was holding up his head. By 9 months, he "walked and talked." Her account continues:[3]

> Then, really, when he started to talking, he was about 7 months old; that's when he start doing kinda like with baby talk. I really couldn't understand 'im. Then when he was 9 months old, he got two teeth; then he was talkin' and walkin', and then he start to saying things like "dada" and "mama" and "bye bye." Mostly that was all he could say then, 'cause the rest of it was baby talk. Then when he got older, he started to pick up things, like when I would say "no," he would learn that word, that when I was saying "no," he know what it mean. And then when I would tell him, I would say "don't do that," he would say "don't" but he couldn't say "do." and then when

187

I would tell him, I would say "stop" and he would say "stop. " Now
when I tell him things, like I'll say "juice," he'll say "juice," and things
like that. And then he started to, he get to know to where he say
"Mike." He can call mostly all of my sisters' and brothers' names.
Mostly he can say things now like, he can say "baby," he say "ball,"
he say [unintelligible]. And sometime like when he wants to go
outdoors, he say "door," else when he want something to drink, he
say "juice," and then like when he get ready to eat, he will tell you, he
will say "eat." And then, like, when something in the refrigerator he
want, he got where he could go and open up refrigerator 'n' get
whatever he want out of it. You tell him, like when his little cousin
come down here you tell him to play, they don't like to play together,
but they fight most all the time when they play and things, so they
fuss and carry on and tell each other "shut up" and "no," and don't do
things, like "don't do that." And then he's get where he run around
outdoors and go up the road [unintelligible]. I tell him to get outta
road, 'cause he don't know how to get outta road when the cars
come, and he'll say "no, no." Now he's beginning to try to potty train,
I tell him to go to his pot, and I say "sit on the pot," and then like
when he got to pot, he be saying "water, water," he be telling me he
gotta use his pot.... But mostly, my little brother, he sit down and
teach him, he say "one," and he say "one," and he'll tell him to call
"daddy," and he say "daddy," and you tell 'im to say "mama," he say
"mama," and you tell him to go get something, he'll go get it. And
then like when you're trying to get him to count, he'll say "one," and
"two," and "three." Then I'll say, "Davaris, how old are you?" and he'll
show you one finger; he be saying "one."

In this record, made 3 months after T's written field notes, she included
specific details of both De's speech and that of others around him. She pointed
out that he was independent, obeyed some commands, repeated words after
adults, called household members, and was tutored by adults to call family
members and to respond to a range of situational circumstances in the busy
household in which many people regularly came and went. The remainder of
this tape was a recording of T's efforts "just to get De to talk." In several sessions, T said she held one of the children's books in her lap, but on the tape she
cannot be heard talking about the book; instead she asked De to name objects
in the room and to call members of the family. She named body parts for him,
and during this naming, she put her face very close to his. For this and all other
labeling, she neither held up nor pointed to the objects or people being named.

On May 28, B returned to T's house and they listened to the tape together as
the teacher wrote an account of T's talk about the nonverbal details and general
context at the time of the taping. This procedure was followed on each subsequent visit. On this visit, B took with her several books, including an "alphabet
book," (groups of items beginning with the same letter on each page), and *The*

Gingerbread Man. Proudly, T said she had ordered a set of Walt Disney books for De and had put them away on a high shelf in the bedroom. She did not report having read to him from them. During the visit, T opened the alphabet book, pointed to an item, and told De "say cat." She sat on the sofa; De stood in front of her looking into the book momentarily, but he focused his attention on only the tape recorder. B left, discouraged, reminding T to try to read to De 10 minutes daily.

On June 2, the teacher returned and listened to the tapes made since May 28. T reported that during these sessions, she sat on the sofa, while De stood in front of her and looked into the book or continued to play. In each of the five sessions recorded on the tape, T began the reading by focusing on the objects in the alphabet book and saying, "Say ___." After only several such directives, the requests shifted to people and objects: "Say mama, say daddy." After each request, she waited for De to repeat. Often he made no response; on other occasions he repeated the name, and at other times, his repetitions were indistinct in pronunciation but clearly imitative in rhythm and intonation. T reported that she had not "started reading" to De because she could not get him to sit still long enough. B suggested bedtime, and T replied "He be sleep before I go to bed." The teacher proposed that T read to De at *his* bedtime or whenever he seemed sleepy, tired, and willing to settle down on the bed or sofa sitting close to his mother and looking at the book with her.

During this visit, T, in an effort to get De to read with B, forcefully made him sit down, after which the teacher asked her to follow only two rules when reading with De: never to hit him or force him to read or write with her, and to leave the books available for him to play with whenever he wished. While the tape was being replayed and B and T were visiting, the television was on, and often as many as a dozen people passed through the living room from outside or other parts of the house.

Tape recordings made between May 24 and June 2 indicated that T tried to "read" with De, but in these attempts, she usually told De to "say," and she often focused for less than 1 minute on the items pictured in the book. She then moved on to tell him to repeat after her the names of objects and persons in his immediate environment. At one time or another, all members of the household could be heard on the tape, instructing De to "say ___" and repeat after them commands to others (for example, "open it"). Several people tried to get De to call members of the family or to call the dog. In one period, when T left the recorder on while De was playing alone, the child repeated names he had just been asked to say in a session with his mother. He used a sharp staccato tone in the repeating exercise: "cat (pause) dog...."

In T's field notes and oral account of De's language development, she did not mention that she asked him questions such as "what is this?" or interpreted any of his self-initiated utterances as labels of objects. Neither on the tapes nor in person did B hear an adult address such talk to the new baby or to other preschoolers who were visiting. Thus until June, T and others around De seemed to follow many of the patterns of interaction with young children that were described for Trackton residents (Heath, 1983). In Trackton, adults did not talk to infants or young children as though they expected them to be communicative partners, although they talked about children in their presences and surrounded them with verbal and nonverbal communication. The cooing and babbling sounds of children were referred to as *noise* (or in T's terms *baby talk*). The focus in Tracton and in T's account of De's language development was not on the children's language productions but primarily on their exhibitions of how they come to know—that is, how they respond to the language of others.

In her account of De's language development, T indicated how De learned to make language work for him in a variety of functions (see Halliday, 1975). He moved from interactional language, engaging those around him ("dada," "mama"), to instrumental language which, when combined with nonverbal cues (such as standing by the refrigerator), met his desires for juice or food or attention to his toilet needs. Once he began to try to control the actions of those around him, De used language for both regulatory and personal functions. By 8 to 9 months of age, he used pointing as a way of referring to or identifying objects, and he had some utterances that apparently were isolable and bounded by pauses, since T reported that he referred to objects in the environment with sounds she could not understand.

In her account, T placed almost no emphasis on her role or that of other adults in teaching De to talk, and she indicated no special efforts on the part of adults to try to interpret, expand, or repeat De's utterances. Once again, this behavior parallels that of Trackton adults who did not speak of *teaching* children to talk. Nonetheless, during the initial weeks of trying to read with De, T and other family members seemed to equate reading with saying the names of things. At this stage, the adults extended this practice from repeating names of objects to requesting that De call people or the dog, say "no" to others, and repeat specific commands to others. Neither B nor I suggested this approach, and the source of this behavior is not clear. The format of the alphabet book may have been a factor. An even more important source may have been T's sister, a high school graduate who visited T often and "read" with her daughter Eureka, who is 6 months older than De, by saying words and waiting for her to repeat them. Once the project had begun, she spent several hours weekly at T's home. Early tape recordings contain sessions in which she asked her daughter to repeat all the letters of the alphabet, each one after her mother, and to say names of items and people in the room.

Between June 2 and 24, T began what she called *reading* with De, for she was able to get him to sit still beside her while they both focused on the book. She tape-recorded a total of 3 hours in these weeks, but most of the taping was done between June 21 and June 24, the day of B's visit. T estimated that she or another member of the family had read to De approximately a dozen times, but she had not recorded all these sessions. Therefore, we do not know whether all sessions were focused on books or on requests for repetitions of words unrelated to the book but seemingly prompted by an initial session with a book.

Figure 4-3 is a transcript of what T regarded as her first successful reading session with De.[4] It was T's first attempt to read to De by holding him beside her on the bed at his bedtime. She began with the alphabet book, reading and occasionally asking De to look when she pointed to items in the book.

De began his participation by offering a repetition of her pronunciation of the letter A after she had moved on to B. When T shifted from the names of letters to object names, De vigorously repeated after her "cow" and "cake" for several repetitions. The time between T's offering of the stimulus and De's repetition decreased significantly once T switched to names of objects. When De fastened on "cake," T shifted to the letter G (for reasons which she could not explain, except that she kept turning pages in the book, trying to keep De's interest). At this point, after only three object names, De focused his attention on the pictures of the boy with a hat and did not repeat but instead labeled the object "hat." Following this, he tried to take over the task of attention-focusing from T, saying repeatedly, "Look," but his mother reasserted her central role in choosing the focus of attention (line 9, Fig. 4-3) and introduced *The Gingerbread Man*. While she read for 40 seconds, De repeated "look." T stopped after the fifth utterance of "look" to point out an object in the book. When De repeated after her, she offered no confirmation until he said "bread" for gingerbread man, to which she responded "yeah" and resumed reading. De once again repeated "look" during the reading and later pointed out a pig ("See that pig.") and then a cow (a term noted in the alphabet book several minutes earlier). T then responded to him and offered another word for repetition. However, De had already focused on the duck in the water and he labeled the duck. In trying to focus attention on the cow, T offered the first topic comment on the book's pictures or content (lines 19 and

191

Figure 4-3. Transcript of a taped reading session, recorded between June 21 and 24,1982.

T reading from text of alphabet book	T talking about text	De's responses
1 this book right here? say A,A.		
2 look		
A (pause) B//		//A
B, C, C, C,	(2 sec.) C (softly)	
cow		(7 sec.) cow
cake		(3 sec.) *cake*
cook		(3 sec.) cake
cook		(2 sec.) cake
3	say G	
4 G, G	say G	(l sec.) hat
5 (De's attention here seems	look, say *boy*	hat
6 to be focused on a picture	boy, say *boy*	look, look,
7 of a boy with a hat on the	boy	look
8 page illustrating the	say girl	look
9 letter G)	look, lemme read this book	
(De tries to get down)		
10 (T picks up *The Ginger-*	wanna read the gingerbread	
bread Man)	man?	
11	look	
Once upon a time. . .		look (repeated four
(continual reading for		times during reading)
40 sec.)		
12	look at the pig, see that pig?	(2 sec.) pig
13	the gingerbread man	(1 sec.) bread
14	yeah	
(resumes reading for 25 sec.)		look (repeated three times)
		see that pig
		cow, cow
15	look at that cow, cow	cow
16 (book pictures cow beside	*water*	duck
17 pond with ducks)	cow=	=duck
18	the cow ran	cow, cow
19	look, look at this cow	
20	sittin' down, she tired	sh (unintelligible)
But she couldn't catch the		
21 gingerbread man	see the house	(4 sec. unintelligible)
22	gingerbread man	(2 sec.) gingerbread

23 (resumes reading for 20 sec.) (book pictures two bears		
24 having a picnic)	look at the bear	(2 sec. two unintelligible squeals)
25	say bear, look at the bear, say bear	hat
26	yeah, hat, see that hat on that bear head	
27	hat	(1 sec.) hat
28	yeah, hat	(1 sec) hat
29	yeah, you see the bear=	=hat
30	yeah, but they can't catch the gingerbread man	
31 (turning pages to end of	look, De, look at this fox	
32 book) (resumes reading for 25 sec.)	say fox	(3 sec., unintelligible utterance repeated four times)
33	look at dat fox, say fox	
34	fox, look, De	
(resumes reading for 23 sec.)		(two unintelligible utterances repeated one after the other)
35	see the fox	
36 (resumes reading for 25 sec.) (resumes reading for 10 sec., in which fox snaps up	look	
37 gingerbread man) (reads final statement) and that was the end of the	look	
38 gingerbread man.	look, see that fox	(2 sec.) um?
39	fox=	=fox, fox
40	yeah, fox, look	
41	look at my alphabet	
(session with alphabet book continues for 1 min. more, until baby cries; just as baby cries, De asks:)		what that?

20, Fig. 4-3). She resumed reading only briefly and then pointed out other objects, but she did not do so with question intonation or a direct request for repetition. When T reached the pictures of two bears having a picnic, she broke away from the text (lines 25 through 30, Fig. 4-3), asking for labels, but once again De had focused on the hat of one of the bears, and his mother expanded his response into a well-formed sentence and commented on the picture and the relation of what was happening in the picture to the book's purpose. She then flipped to the end of the book and focused De's attention on the fox. Here, her tone was heightened, and she said "look" more insistently than earlier, as she urged De to focus his attention on the fox. The child listened and watched the book, saying nothing until his mother had finished the story. She repeated her request that he look at the fox, and he immediately repeated "fox" so that his repetition was connected without pause to her second request. T returned to the alphabet book but the baby cried. At the sound of the baby's cry, De tried to engage his mother's attention, using language heuristically to ask "What that?" while pointing to something in the book.

Between this session and the next recorded session, transcribed in Figure 4-4, T or her brother Mike read *The Little Red Hen* to De once or twice, but T did not record those readings. The sessions transcribed in Figures 4-3 and 4-4 probably took place within 24 hours of each other. The reading of *The Little Red Hen* that took place during the Figure 4-4 session, then, was either the second or third time De had heard this story. T began with a request for him to focus on the hen. De interrupted her with "hen" and then said "red" when she was saying "hen." T's reading segments throughout this session lasted less than 10 seconds each and she stopped often to focus on objects in the pictures, to ask for repetitions, or to make topic comments. De readily said "chick" when she offered "chicken," and later (line 6, Fig. 4-4), he anticipated what the text said just before his mother read "cluck cluck." He emphasized the second syllable, and his timing clearly indicates that he was following the text so closely that he knew the sentence "then she said to her baby chicks . . ." would end with "cluck cluck." T offered no confirmation or reinforcement of this participation until De interrupted again with "chick." Later in the session, when he focused on the duck in the picture, she again offered no confirmation. At line 15 (Fig. 4-4), T wanted her son to focus on a picture of the hen with many baby chickens, but instead De fixed on the hat in the pictures, and T expanded his word into a well-formed sentence and added a tag question. Her talk about the book continued (lines 15 through 33) until she decided to have De read by repeating the exact words of the text: "They walked. . . . " He repeated "they"

194

and she then asked him to say "walk" and "cluck cluck," but De said only the latter. At this point, he tried to get off the bed and move away. T then commented on the story-reading episode as a "nightnight story." De repeated this entire phrase after her with clear imitation of the rhythm and intonation. They tried to continue with the alphabet book, but the baby cried and T left the room, leaving the tape recorder on.

T reported, in her account to B on later hearing this portion of the tape, that when she walked by the room, De was holding and throwing the books, talking to himself. During this period, much of his talk was unintelligible, but on three occasions on the tape, he said something that clearly related to the books. The first time he said, in rapid succession in sharp, stacatto style, "Look, look, look." On the second occasion, he began by saying "lemme look," and he named "cat, dog." In the third segment, he apparently was "reading" *The Little Red Hen,* and he said "chick chick" several times through a series of utterances that were imitative in rhythm and voice quality of his mother's reading of the text.

In T's next session of reading with De, she began with the alphabet book. Many people were in the living room, where the recording took place, and there were many distractions. She began with the letter A and moved through B, C, and D. When she reached D, she said several times, "Say D, "and then asked, "Where's D?" Because De did not respond she repeated, and he said, "Um?" She said "De, say D, where's D?" shifting the meaning of the sound from the name of an alphabet letter to his nickname. He softly offered an unintelligible reply and she shifted to asking, "Where Mike?" and naming other members of the family who were present. This was the only evidence on the tapes of a phenomenon Scollon and Scollon (1981) emphasize in their characterization of "incipient literacy," a focus on playing with language and its similarities and differences in written and oral uses.

In a session taped on June 24 and described to B when she came to pick up the tapes, De and Eureka (his female cousin) were playing together in the living room, where several adults were visiting. The books were scattered about on the floor, and Eureka wanted to play with them. De screamed in protest, captured a book, and climbed into a chair with his legs straight in front of him, holding the book on his lap. Eureka retook the book, and T asked De to let the cousin read, but De pulled the book away from her and said, "Where chick, chick, chick?" He repeated this question several times, each time more shrilly. Adults finally intervened and started the children on the routine of counting. Adults said the number, and one or both of the children repeated immediately afterward. During this episode, they soon

Figure 4-4. Transcript of a taped reading session, recorded between June 21 and 24,1982.

T reading from *The Little Red Hen*	T talking about text	De's responses
1 the little red hen	you see that little red	//hen
2	//hen?//	//red
Once upon a time there		
3 lived a mother hen	see that hen?	(2 sec.) um?
4	chicken	(1 sec.) chick
(resumes reading for 7 sec.)		chick
5	see that chickchick	(1 sec.) um chick
6	chickchick	(1 sec.) chickchick
(resumes reading for 4 sec.)		
. . . then she said to her		
baby//		//cluck*cluck*
chicks, cluckcluckcluckcluck,		
we will take a walk=(pause)		=chick
		chick
7	yeah, chicken	(3 sec.) chick
(resumes reading for 10 sec.)		look
8	look, *look,* look	
(resumes reading for 7 sec.)		chick
9	look at the chick=	=pig
10	look at the pig, pig=	=pig
11	duck	(2 sec.) duck
12	chicken	(1 sec.) chicken
13	bird, biddy, say biddy	(2 sec.) duck
14 (Mike, T's brother, may	say Mike	(2 sec.) Mike, ike
have entered the room, or		
she may have understood		
duck as *Mike* in De's		
15 previous utterance)	look, look at that picture,	
	whoeeee	
16	look at that picture, see	
	that chicken 'n' them biddies	(2 sec.) chickchick
17	yeah, that chicken 'n' them	(1 sec.) chick
	biddies	
18	yeah, chick (pause) hat	(1 sec.) hat
19	yeah, that hat on that chicken	
	ain't it?=	=hat
20	yeah	
21	lets see what else in here	
22	um see, lookahere, look at	
	that man	(2 sec.) wh

23		whoeee, look at that man, you see	(2 sec.) man
24 (turning pages of book)	yeah, that man'n'that chicken look	
25	you look at that, De, say bread	(3 sec.) yeah, chick
26	chicken eat bread	
27	you see them chicken at the table?	
28	look, say chicken	
29	you see hat chair, lookahere	
30	chair, see that chair, look here, look	
31	look at the pig 'n' the duck	
32	see that pig 'n' the duck?	
33	read the book	
34	let's see can you read?	
35	say they, De, say they	(2 sec.)
36	walk=	=they (with a shout)
37	say walk, say cluckcluck	(1 sec.) cluckcluck (softly)
38	say cluckcluck, cluckcluck, cluckcluck=	(3 sec.) cluckcluck=
39 (De seems to want to take	say pig	
40 the book and move away)	you ain't gonna let me finish reading?	
41	let mama read you a story	
42	let read you a nightnight story	
43	wanna read nightnight story?	(5 sec.) nightnight story um?
44		
45	yeah	(3 sec.) um

(Charlene tries to continue with the alphabet book for approximately 30 sec. more, then she leaves De alone in the room for 16 min. He plays with the books she has just read: the alphabet book first, and then *The Little Red Hen*) turned to the alphabet. At the letter D, De repeated 'D" first with the intonation he usually gave it in the alphabet repetition game but then shouting "De, De," with a different intonation, he danced around the room seemingly recognizing his own language play.

During the month of July, T and her children moved out of the house to live with another relative, and T began temporary work. By mid-August, she was back in her earlier household, and she made two tape recordings, one summarizing De's language progress over the past 2 months and another including readings and a session in which she introduced De to writing. She gave De crayons and paper at the kitchen table and offered no instructions other than for him to use the crayons rather than the pencil he wanted. Near the end of the writing episode, she asked, "You gonna write your name?" His writing fits Platt's (1977) description of the first level of writing—scribbling that has no isolable parts or recognizable repeated designs, or which are not identified by the child as writing which represents something else. After De's scribbling, T wrote at the top left corner of his paper "Davaris Thomas as Dede."

In late August, B noticed that De held his baby brother (now 4 months old) and read to him. The baby was able to follow when De pointed to objects in the book. B suggested to T that, whenever possible, she read with the baby in her left arm and De on her right, letting De hold the book. De also had a new friend who was a few months younger than he and he read to his friend as she sat by him and tried to imitate his pointing to and naming of objects in the book. T reported that De sometimes did not want her to read to him, but instead he wanted to take the book, turn pages, and read to himself by labeling the items in the book's pictures.

On September 8, T recorded another update on De's activities. She reported that he was completely toilet-trained, could give the baby his bottle, went to bed upon direction, got his own water from the kitchen sink, and enjoyed playing with Mike's electronic games. She also reported:

> He calls hisself readin'—tryin' to read, but the only thing he's done is readin' the picture book. After a while, he can soon learn how. And now he gets where he had learned to count a little bit, but he can't put 'em in order. He will just say the numbers just out of order. But then you sit down and teach him how to say hisABCs, he'll mock you 'n' stuff like that.

She reported that De talked to the baby:

> And then he'll get to talkin' to him, he'll say "hey, babe." You know how the way little kids talk to another baby, the way is mighty strange; they just learn each 'n' every day from their parents. You

know when they parents teachin' 'em how to talk to a child and now he just beginnin' to learn how to talk to the baby like he should.

On a tape made on September 19, 2 days before De's second birthday, T told him, "Talk to baby. Tell baby, 'Hey, babe' " (with exaggerated intonation). On this tape, she sang "The Little Drummer Boy" to De while showing him the pictures in the book. The first time through he listened without a sound, but in later sessions recorded on this tape, he picked up the song at the ends of the bars and hummed the tune after his mother. Also, a story-reading episode on this tape was interrupted by T's pointing to a sore on De and saying, "Sore, say 'sore,' 'hurt,' and 'sore hurt.'" She said this several times, and each time De repeated her words. After a long pause, T stopped repeating, followed by De's saying 'sore hurt' several times. This was the only tape-recorded occasion in which T built a proposition with De about objects that were not pictured in books. She did not, however, expand the proposition into a well-formed sentence, such as "your sore hurts." However, later on this tape, in a long exchange with De's cousin Eureka, T picked up an utterance made by Eureka and then built propositions with her and expanded the child's statements into well-formed statements. This conversation was one of the rare occasions when T and a child were alone together and dialogue occurred without the stimulus of a book. Mike had gone to bed, and Eureka spontaneously said, "Gotta go to school Mike." T responded, "Yea, Mike gotta go to bed 'n' go to school." She then asked Eureka a series of real questions, beginning with "you wanna go to school?" This conversation follows the pattern of those described for mainstream adults who build from the utterances of the child a set of intentions and restate the child's utterances into well-formed sentences. T did not simplify her talk to Eureka, and the two acted as conversational equals building cooperative propositions in response to utterances initiated by the child.

Retaining Literacy

T's progress in her own literacy skills in the year between September 1981 and September 1982 was considerable. Outside stimulation was minimal. I wrote her six brief letters but never saw her; our communication has been entirely through letters, audiotapes, and B's field notes of her ten visits to T's home. We had provided T with books, tapes, and a tape recorder. She was never given any direction other than to read with her child, record the reading and his play immediately following the reading, and to listen to the tapes with B during her visits and summarize the activities that had surrounded the recording.

A comparison of T's first letter to L. (Fig. 4-1) and her later letters and field notes written in February indicates her increased confidence in expressing herself, some improvement in her command of the mechanics of writing, and development of an ability to write a well-formed friendly letter and to summarize facts in a narrative style. Following the first history of De's early language development, made at my request, T decided when to provide summary updates of his language progress, and she initiated the recording of each of the five subsequent summaries over the year. Her reading had not been restricted to De's books; she has read my letters and drafts of this chapter. In reviewing the latter with B, she clarified facts, discussed interpretations, and added assessment of her own and De's achievements. T's keen observational skills (demonstrated in her first tape about De's language development) have improved with each recounting of the details surrounding tape-recorded events and De's subsequent language progress.

With regard to the specific reading and writing sessions with De, T has found her own way to numerous literacy socialization strategies. She has learned when and where to read with him, how to hold him and the book, and how to focus his attention on the book. She makes some use of attentional vocatives; she waits and lets De make his contribution to the reading. She tends to use vocatives primarily at those points in the reading when De is restless, and she then also moves from a strict reading of the text to topic-comment structures and attention-focusing commands. She has mastered the basic components of a dialogue with De about a book's content. De repeats her entire utterance, selects segments for repetition, or offers topic comments. T has provided him with crayons, pencils, and paper, and she supervises his drawing and writes his name on his drawings. In short, she has achieved preschool literacy with De.

What cannot now be known is whether T will retain and extend these skills with De and his younger brother. During the past year, T has initiated activities and talk that call attention to language itself. However, the tape recordings do not indicate that, as yet, she engages in the common mainstream ways of extending the functions and uses of literacy—providing narratives on items and events in books and real life, asking De a wide range of teaching questions, and carrying on extended dyadic conversations with him. T does not yet link objects or events in books to their real-world counterparts. Neither she nor other adults in the household do more than minimal reading and writing, and these activities consist primarily of reading the daily newspaper and filling out job applications. In the final months of the summer of 1982, Mike began to buy and read sports magazines. Either the television or the radio is on at all times, and as many as a dozen people often are in the busy, noisy household. In T's busy schedule of caring for an infant and maintaining a large household, she has little time to be alone with De. The reading and writing events are almost the only times in which her involvement with him is not focused on physical caregiving or disciplining. However, the motivation for reading and writing with De is high, since both T and the father of her children remember they were not successful in Head Start and had to repeat their year. Both are now high school dropouts, and they believe that failing Head Start was the beginning of their academic downfall. Both compare De to themselves before Head Start; they say of themselves, "We were fast, but Head Start slowed us down." De's parents want him to "pass" Head Start "so he can finish high school." As a dropout, T sometimes expresses despair over her lack of choices, points to her daily routine, and asks, " Do you realize I be doing this the rest of my life?" (recorded August 16, 1982).

Historical and cross-national studies of literacy have reexamined traditional claims that for both the society and the individual, literacy brings certain changes: e. g., benevolence (Lockridge, 1974), improved socioeconomic status (Graff, 1979), increased reasoning abilities (Creesy, 1980) (for a comprehensive review of these studies see Graff, 1983). In spite of all the claims about consequences of literacy, recent research has shown that the changes which have come with literacy across societies and historical periods have been neither consistent nor predictable. We cannot yet make generalizations about literacy as a causal factor, nor indeed as a necessary accompaniment of specific features of a society. The prior conditions and co-occurring contexts of literacy in each society determine its forms, values, and functions.

A recent survey of societies into which literacy had recently been introduced suggests that certain specific factors are critical to the *maintenance* of literacy by any group that achieves basic literacy (Heath, forthcoming). What is needed are certain ways of talking about language and repeated occasions for using talk in institutions. The extension of literacy within a society depends on opportunities for new literates to participate in redundant, multiple, and reinforcing occasions for oral construction of the shared background needed to interpret written materials. Some societies seem to carry within their habits of talking about language and using talk in institutions the precursors of the development of extended literacy, whereas other groups seem to have to acquire, along with literacy, new ways of viewing language and new occasions for interpreting written materials.

We suggest here that the two conditions necessary for the maintenance of literacy by a group are also essential to an individual's retention of literacy.

Thus, for T to sustain her newly achieved preschool literacy habits with De and his younger brother, she will continue to need occasions for talking about what she and De have learned from their jointly achieved literacy, and she will need opportunities to see that this literacy can extend to institutions outside her home. At present, she has acquired some aspects of the first condition for literacy retention, new ways of talking about language as such.

The case of T's development of preschool literacy gives overwhelming evidence that an individual's ways of using talk about language are highly interdependent with patterns of acquiring literacy. In her home, before she began reading with De, T did not exhibit the patterns of talking to children that were described in the mainstream literature. She did not simplify her talk, adapt situations to the child, and structure times and places for dyadic interactions with him. Rather, she seemed to expect De to adapt to the multiple visitors and shifting situations of his everyday environment.

Ochs and Schieffelin (in press) compare their fieldwork in Western Samoa and Papua New Guinea with reports of mainstream language development and suggest two orientations of caregivers toward children and two corresponding patterns of talking to children. They point out that mainstream parents adapt situations to children, simplify their talk, and negotiate meaning through expansions and paraphrase. These adults build propositions cooperatively with young children, and they respond to topics children initiate. In contrast, caregivers in Western Samoa and Papua New Guinea adapt the children to the situation, engage children in a wide variety of multiparty speech acts that are not simplified, and continually direct children to notice others. Talk arises from a wide range of situations to which the caregivers want the children to respond. Heath (1983) details other orientations toward children and corresponding caregiver speech patterns and suggests that certain relationships obtain between sociocultural characteristics of the society and the types of language addressed to children.

All indications from T's reports and from the recordings in the early weeks of the project suggest that the adults in T's household did not focus De's attention in redundant and multiple nonverbal and verbal ways on objects. They did not provide labels or talk to De in short sentences with simplified verb forms. Instead, they directed him to notice others, to call them by name, to greet them, and to give them orders (for example, "go home"). Adults modeled these and other unsimplified utterances for De to repeat to third parties, asking De to "Say ____" or tell [someone else]_____."

The introduction of literacy artifacts and the literacy event of book-reading seemed to bring with it simplified language input focusing on labels of objects and requests for repetition. Book-reading provided opportunities for dyadic interactions between mother and child outside nurturing occasions. During these literacy-focused sessions, T spontaneously began using some teaching questions and topic-comment structures. T's evaluations of De also appear to have changed as the reading and writing continued. In the early tapes, T spoke positively of both De's independence and his willingness to fight and be boisterous with other children. In tapes recorded in September 1982, she described De as "wise," and she talked to both De and Eureka about their going to school in the future. When De carried his books under his arm, she asked: "De, are you going to school?"

In this household, mother-child book-reading was the first occasion of extensive labeling, and the link between reading and labeling was made not only by T, but also by other members of the household. The act of book-reading shifted the family's orientation toward the child from enabling him to learn to needing to teach him, at least in some circumstances. Adults (and De) now point to objects in the environment and name them and talk about them for De's younger brother. This behavior contrasts with earlier non-focused requests for De to repeat a given term. Both T and others in the household are now heard talking to the infant and attempting to engage him as a participant in pointing out and labeling activities.

Sutton-Smith (1979) has pointed out the powerful orientation of middle-class parents to objects in their interactions with young children. Snow (1979) has emphasized the link between object orientation and the semantic content of speech addressed to young children—a focus on the present tense, concrete nouns, and events in the here and now. Heath (1983) demonstrates, however, how mainstream caregivers shift from a focus on present items and events to the future in interactions as the toddler grows older. Actions of the present are repeatedly linked to the future .

More than a decade ago, Geertz characterized the culture of a people as an "ensemble of texts, themselves ensembles, which the anthropologist strains to read over the shoulders of those to whom they properly belong" (1972, 129). In this chapter, we have looked over T's shoulder to discover what happened when she initiated, with minimal guidance, a new form of parent-child interaction (book reading) with De, her preschool child. Introduced with almost no direction from B, the on-the-spot intermediary, this innovative behavior gave rise to other new forms of behavior. Book-reading seemed to bring with it new ways of talking to the toddler, changed perceptions of the child and of caregiver roles, an increased consciousness of the child's language development, and altered patterns of talking about language.

T may be a unique individual, and the behaviors that occurred simultaneously with book-reading for her may not follow for other individuals in the same cultural conditions. Other fine-grained analyses of different individuals in the same cultural conditions are needed to allow generalizations about the interdependence of patterns of oral and written language use under this innovation. In addition, we need to know what caregivers in other social and cultural contexts do with their children when new literacy artifacts and events are adopted. The majority of writings on the consequences of literacy speak only of very general behavior shifts, such as increased socio-economic mobility. It is extremely difficult to speak of literacy as a causal condition for the host of behavioral changes which may come with such an abstract shift. The case of T suggests that we must more closely examine fine details of behaviors which are concomitant with specific literacy events. Only with more of such "close readings" (Geertz, 1972) of human behaviors will we be able to speak with confidence about ways in which uses of oral and written language are related and to identify prior conditions and consequences of literacy. Moreover, this type of research may enable us to recognize the sociocultural conditions under which literacy may not only be achieved but also sustained and extended. In short, we need more and different kinds of literacy research before we can identify the habits of perception and conceptualization which are the unconscious supports behind the collectively sustained symbolic structures of literacy in varied societal contexts.

To accomplish these goals, we may also need new and different research strategies. Cooperative work between teachers and researchers has here been extended to a student-parent. The productivity of this research method, as shown by the present study, suggests that it could be added to the present inventory of parent education techniques. Professionals in parent education help parents to care for their children and to provide them with access to information and skills necessary in order for them to take their places as adults in the community. Traditionally, parent educators have focused on issues of physical and mental health and school achievement. With respect to the latter, the goal of parent educators' programs has been to help parents prepare their children for reading and writing tasks as performed in schools. It is common to sponsor "books for tots" programs and to encourage parents to read to their children at home; often such programs contain explicit attempts by professionals to help parents teach, discipline, and interact with their children in ways which will help prepare them for school. Despite a growing awareness on the part of parent educators of cultural differences in parenting, they often have no answer to the question of how to enable parents, in settings rarely experienced or even imagined by teachers, to act as partners with teachers to improve their children's academic achievement (Hess, 1980). At present, many parent educators acknowledge that their programs have been planned without parent input and without evidence from child language or psycholinguistic research, and many have had as a common base the presumed incompetence of parents. Presented in this chapter is a possible new model of parent education, a model based on the parent as researcher. In this study, the parent identified a problem she considered important and relevant to her concerns, and she plans to continue as a partner with a teacher and professional researcher.[5] The power of decision-making has rested primarily with the parent, and the teacher and researcher have supported her in the collection, analysis, and interpretation of data. Thus, in this project, the parent has been playing an active role as a researcher of literacy socialization, while at the same time she has been acquiring and transmitting some of the skills of reading and writing involved in the achievement of preschool literacy for herself and her children.

Notes

[1] A *literacy event* is any occasion in which a piece of writing is integral to the nature of participants' interactions and their interpretive processes (Heath, 1982a). See also Chapter 2 and Anderson et al. (1980) for illustrations of literacy events. Following Hymes (1972), these researchers contend that there are rules for the occurrence and internal construction of literacy events, just as there are for speech events.

[2] See Goswami (forthcoming) for case studies of teachers as researchers. Branscombe (forthcoming) describes her activities as a teacher working with Heath in a cooperative search for answers to questions raised by Branscombe about what was happening in her classroom. This relationship and the participation of Branscombe and Heath as "real researchers" legitimated for students in Branscombe's class numerous extended reading and writing activities.

[3] T is a speaker of Black English, who shifts toward some standard English features in some registers. No attempt is made to represent the exact sounds of her speech. The modified spellings are used here to represent the natural flow of her speech and in full awareness that all natural English speech differs from what the standard orthography seems to indicate.

[4] The following conventions are used in Figures 4-3 and 4-4: underlining represents heightening of primary stress by vowel-lengthening and raising of pitch; double virgules (| |) represent interruption and overlap; a question mark represents rising intonation and pause; a period indicates end-of-sentence falling intonation and a full pause; and an equals sign (=) indicates continuous utterances.

[5] The identification of the subjects of this research has been done with the full written consent of Charlene Thomas and her father. We expect to continue to work together to follow the progress of De and his brother through 1983. Throughout this year, Charlene has played a

role similar to that of graduate students who compile data, provide summary reports, discuss and interpret their professors' write-up of the material, and provide suggestions for revision and additions to drafts of the article. With the students in Branscombe's ninth-grade class, I made an agreement that they were to be acknowledged research associates to the fullest extent possible. I also frequently reminded them that with this role came responsibilities for gathering and reporting data carefully, discussing on tape or in person my questions and challenges of their data, and allowing their writing and their oral discussions of the research to be reported in any publication that resulted. The goal of this policy was to make research, reading, and writing as meaningful as possible to the ninth graders and to motivate them to see themselves as becoming writer-researchers. Several other articles are currently being prepared with students who were in Branscombe's ninth-grade class in 1981 through 1982.

References

Anderson, A.B., Teale, W. B., & Estrada, E. (1980). Low-income children'spreschool literacy experiences: Some naturalistic observations. *The Quarterly Newsletter of the Laboratory of Comparative Human Cognition, 2*, 59-65.

Bourdieu, P. (1967). Systems of education and systems of thought. *International Social Science Journal, 19*, 338-358.

Bourdieu, P. (1973). Cultural reproduction and social reproduction. In R. Brown (Ed.), *Knowledge, education, and cultural change: Papers in the sociology of education.* London: Tavistock.

Branscombe, A. (in press). Giving away my classroom: Teacher as researcher. In D. Goswami & L. Odell (Eds.), *Teacher as researcher.* Sharon, CT: Boynton-Cook Publishers.

Brocher, T.H. (1980). Toward new methods in parent education. In M.D. Fantini & R. Cardenas (Eds.), *Parenting in a multicultural society.* New York: Longman.

Creesy, D. (1980). *Literacy and the social order: Reading and writing in Tudor and Stuart England.* Cambridge: Cambridge University Press.

Fantini, M.D. (1980). The parent as educator: A home-school model of socialization. In M. D. Fantini & R. Cardenas (Eds.), *Parenting in a multicultural society.* New York: Longman.

Geertz, C. (1972). Deep play: Notes on the Balinese cockfight. *Daedelus 101* (1), 1-38.

Gleason, J., & Weintraub, S. (1978). Input language and the acquisition of communicative competence. In K. Nelson (Ed.), *Children's language*, Vol. 1. New York: Gardner Press.

Goswami, D. (Ed.). (in press). *Teacher as researcher.* Sharon, CT: Boynton-Cook Publishers.

Graff, H. (1979). *The literacy myth: Literacy and social structure in the nineteenth-century city.* New York: Academic Press.

Graff, H. (1983). *The legacies of literacy: Continuities and contradictions in Western society and culture.* New York: Academic Press.

Halliday, M.A.K. (1975). *Learning how to mean: Explorations in the development of language.* New York: Elsevier North-Holland.

Heath, S.B. (1982a). What no bedtime story means: Narrative skills at home and school. *Language in Society, 11*, 49-76.

Heath, S.B. (1982b). Protean shapes in literacy events: Ever-shifting oral and literate traditions. In D. Tannen (Ed.), *Spoken and written language*. Norwood, NJ: Ablex.

Heath, S.B. (1983). *Ways with words: Ethnography of communication, communities, and classrooms*. Cambridge: Cambridge University Press.

Heath, S.B. (in press). Taking language apart and building institutional talk: Critical factors in literacy development. In S. de Castell, K. Egan, and A. Luke (Eds.), *Literacy: What is to be done?*

Hess, R. (1980). Experts and amateurs: Some unintended consequences of parent education. In M. Fantini & R. Cardenas (Eds.), *Parenting in a multicultural society*. London: Longman.

Hymes, D. (1972). Models of the interaction of language and social life. In J.J. Gumperz & D. Hymes (Eds.), *Directions in sociolinguistics*. New York: Holt, Rinehart, and Winston.

Kroeber, A. (1948). *Anthropology*. New York: Harcourt-Brace.

Lockridge, K. (1974). *Literacy in colonial New England*. New York: Norton.

Ninio, A., & Bruner, J.S. (1978). The achievement and antecedents of labelling. *Journal of Child Language, 5*, 5-15.

Ochs, E., & Schieffelin, B.B. (in press). Language acquisition and socialization: Three developmental stories and their implications. In R. Shweder & R. Levins (Eds.), *Culture and its acquisition*. Chicago: University of Chicago Press.

Platt, P. (1977). Grapho-linguistics: Children's drawings in relation to reading and writing skills. *The Reading Teacher, 17*, 241-245.

Scollon, R., & Scollon, S.B.K. (1981). *Narrative, literacy and face in interethnic communication*. Norwood, NJ: Ablex.

Smethurst, W. (1975). *Teaching young children to read at home*. New York: McGraw-Hill.

Snow, C. (1979). Conversations with children. In P. Fletcher & M. Garman (Eds.), *Language acquisition: Studies in first language development*. Cambridge: Cambridge University Press.

Snow, C., & Ferguson, C. (Eds.). (1977). *Talking to children*. Cambridge: Cambridge University Press.

Sutton-Smith, M. H. (1979). *Play and learning*. New York: Gardner Press.

207

Author's Comment—Shirley Brice Heath

Ethnographers take it as a matter of course within their publications to say something about how their work came about; the context of research extends in anthropology to prior assumptions as well as to paths of access and entry into the field. This approach differs from that of other disciplines and areas, including research in education, where researchers are particularly anxious to avoid being pulled into "involvement" with the "subjects" of their studies. The general view is that those being studied should not know the questions that drive the inquiry and cannot be partners in the collection, analysis, and reporting of the data.

For anthropologists, such strictures effectively cut off the possibility of ethnography and most certainly of "autoethnography." For decades, ethnographers attempting to understand cultures other than their own have become participant observers, speakers of the languages of those under study, and partners with those being studied to consider how events happen and what their various meanings might be. Ethnographers, often miles away from home, have been dependent on their "subjects" as hosts, and they have had to become collaborators with those they study in everything from gardening to surviving harsh weather changes and invasions from hostile neighbors. Inevitably, ethnographers have joined with those they study in the selection and collection of data.

Yet, in spite of such joint efforts in the field site, ethnographers, once home, have rarely allowed those they studied to participate in the final analysis and reporting of data. It is the rare scholarly paper, book, or article in anthropology that includes more than a smattering of words from those whose lifeways are being reported. Almost never do those who were studied have a chance to speak out at length about what they saw in the data or how they felt about being "subjects," objectified and frozen in the fallacy of the "ethnographic present."

Autoethnography, a form of ethnography that began to gain widespread attention among anthropologists in the 1980s, provides data and analysis directly from those being studied. Groups, such as racial minorities, indigenous populations of former colonies, and members of lower classes, give voice to their collective memories and direct experiences under conditions of contact between powers of differential strength. Subjects offer counter analyses regarding the interpretation of data collected by anthropologists about their lives. Those who speak for themselves are far less likely than anthropologists to be influenced by theoretical constructs, the desire to make explanations consistent, and the urge to ignore anomalies.

The collaboration between Heath and Thomas around the acquisition of literacy by Thomas' children does not fall neatly into either ethnography or autoethnography. Heath and Thomas have never met face-to-face, but they have corresponded about data in much the same way that academic colleagues who may never meet write to each other about a shared area of inquiry. The goals of the inquiry were to answer questions that both Thomas and Heath had about what happens during reading with young children and to help relieve Thomas' boredom at home with her toddler when she dropped out of school to await the birth of her second child. Footnote 5 of the article as well as the section "The story behind this story" explain the basis of the relationship. Thomas and Heath had the advantage of a local broker in Amanda Branscombe, Thomas' ninth grade teacher when the research began in 1981. Once Thomas dropped out of school, Branscombe and Thomas met in Thomas' home to go over the tapes of the readings and to talk about responses to books. In the preparation of this article and another (Heath and Branscombe, with Thomas, 1986), Thomas and Branscombe jointly reviewed the data's contexts and meanings and selected portions for inclusion in the articles. Thomas read and responded to various drafts of the articles and reflected on the effects of the process on her own views of what she and her children were doing in their reading. She knew that her classmates in Branscombe's class at school were involved in the same process with their particular areas of research (see Heath and Branscombe, 1985).

In 1990, Thomas is an educational leader in her community, helping shape early education programs for children and working with parents of young children. After some initial problems in school because of their "imaginative" ways of responding to stories, De and Tutti are in classes for the gifted and talented. De announced in the spring of 1990 that he wanted to be a writer of stories. Branscombe and Thomas collaborate often in planning local policy initiatives in education.

The article does not claim that the behaviors that came simultaneously with book-reading for Thomas will necessarily follow for other individuals in the same cultural conditions. Similarly, there is no claim that becoming a research partner will change the course of a life or lead to educational leadership. However, the distance gained from moving outside the immediate display of experience carries over into the ability to take a comparative view of institutions—from family to school to bureaucracy. Such a view can give an individual a sense of control, power, and adaptability otherwise unavailable. After all—"We all have very much more of the stuff [experience] than we know what to do with, and if we fail to put it into some graspable form, the fault must lie in a lack of means, not of substance" (Geertz 1986:373). Researchers collaborating with "subjects" can help provide the means.

References

Geertz, C. (1986). Making Experiences, Authoring Selves. In V.W. Turner & E.M Bruner (Eds.), *The Anthropology of Experience*. Urbana: University of Illinois Press. pp. 373-380.

Heath, S.B., & Branscombe, A. (1985). Intelligent writing in an audience community: Teacher, students, and researcher. In S.W. Freedman (Ed.), *The Acquisition of Written Language: Revision and Response*. Norwood, NJ: Ablex. pp. 3-32.

Heath, S.B., Branscombe, A., & Thomas, C. (1986). The book as narrative prop in language acquisition. In B.B. Schieffelin & P. Gilmore (Eds.), *The Acquisition of Literacy: Ethnoqraphic Perspectives*. Norwood, NJ: Ablex. pp. 16-34.

Chapter 9   The Elusive Topic Sentence

Braddock's study, "The Frequency and Placement of Topic Sentences in Expository Prose," is a classic in research on literacy. It is widely cited, widely replicated, and still very influential. We include it here because it clearly exemplifies many of the features that good studies should have. The first requisite for any successful research is a good question to be answered. It must be researchable, that is, capable of being answered persuasively, and it must be significant, that is, it must be worth answering. Braddock's question, "Do skilled expository writers use topic sentences in the way handbook writers say they do?" was an easily researchable question because the texts of skilled writers were readily available for examination. Braddock needed only to devise a systematic way of examining their use of topic sentences to arrive at a satisfactory answer. Braddock's question was significant because it concerned the **validity** of recommendations given to millions of student writers. From a broader perspective, it was also significant because it repre-sents an important, on-going tradition in rhetorical research in which inherited handbook conventions—that is, norms of mechanics, usage, and style—have been subjected to close analysis and verification. This research tradition has helped to create an increasingly sophisticated and defensible pedagogy of writing.

Another feature of the Braddock study that we admire is the careful way in which he drew conclusions from his data. For example, he noted that his results for the type of writing he studied, that is, magazine writing, may not apply to scientific or technical writing. Here, he was being appropriately cautious in not generalizing beyond the genre of the texts he studied. Further, he pointed out quite specifically that he was not recommending that "teachers stop showing their students how to develop paragraphs from clear topic sentences" [p. 301]. This disclaimer is quite appropriate to the conventional argument Braddock is examining, which may be diagramed as follows;

Claim 1: Students should write paragraphs with initial topic sentences

because

Claim 2: Professional writers typically write paragraphs with initial topic sentences.

In this argument, Claim 2 serves as support for Claim 1. But Braddock's result suggests that Claim 2 is false and, therefore, can't provide support for Claim 1. However, that result does not suggest that Claim 1 is false. Indeed, Braddock denies any such implication and limits his conclusion to Claim 2 saying simply ". . . students should not be told that professional writers usually begin their paragraphs with topic sentences" [p. 301].

The practice of limiting one's claims, as Braddock does, is called "**hedging**" and is an important characteristic of research writing. Appropriate hedging warns the reader of the limitations of the study and cautions against generalizing the results too far or drawing implications that are not justified. Failure to hedge appropriately may lead readers to misunderstand or, if the failure to hedge is noticed by readers, may lead them to question the writer's critical abilities.

Braddock's study is also a dramatic illustration that research results can do more than confirm the obvious. In fact, what Braddock's study did was to demonstrate that a widely held belief was actually false. This is an important point to remember because a number of critics have suggested that empirical research doesn't really tell us anything new — that it simply confirms what was already apparent to any reasonably intelligent adult. Irmscher (1987), for example, voices this complaint about reading research articles in literacy: "After one struggles through the prose and the statistics and the diagrams, one discovers that the investigator has complicated the familiar and obfuscated the obvious." (p. 83) Clearly, in Irmscher's view, empirical research is just a waste of time. However, the view that research results are obvious is an illusion of about the same magnitude as the 40-year-old's belief that life as a teenager was just wonderful. It is as easy to forget the painful side of adolescence as it is to forget what we would have predicted before we heard a research result.

Recently, Gage (1991) reviewed studies on judgments of the obviousness of research results and found that people not only tend to regard research results as obvious but also tend to regard the opposites of those results as obvious. For example, Gage reported results by Baratz (1983) in which college students were shown either actual social science research results or the opposite of the actual results. The actual results were judged obvious by 80% of the students but the opposites of the actual results were viewed as obvious by 66% of the students. Gage also reported a study by Wong (1987) in which college students and teachers were asked to decide which of 12 pairs of statements was correct. One member of each pair stated an actual research result and the other stated the exact opposite of that result. For four of the pairs, the students and teachers identified the actual result as correct more frequently than its opposite. However, for the remaining eight pairs, they chose the opposite more frequently. The criticism that research results are obvious, then, appears to depend at least in part on illusion — the illusion that when we hear that something is true, we believe we already knew that it was true.

References

Baratz, D. (1983). How justified is the "obvious" reaction? *Dissertation Abstracts International,* 44/02B, 644B. (University Microfilms No. DA 8314435.)

Gage, N. L. (1991). The obviousness of social and educational research results. *Educational Researcher, 20,* 10-16.

Irmscher, W. F. (1987). Finding a comfortable identity. *College Composition and Communication, 38,* 81-87.

Wong, L. (1987). Reaction to research findings: Is the feeling of obviousness warranted? *Dissertation Abstracts International,* 48/12, 3709B. (University Microfilms No. DA 8801059.)

Using a newly established data source and a combination of techniques, this essay sheds new light on a topic in composition that has long been shrouded in the mystery of tradition. Both researchers and teachers of writing must rethink their usual set of beliefs about the nature and placement of the topic sentence in expository prose.

Richard Braddock
The University of Iowa

The Frequency and Placement of Topic Sentences in Expository Prose

Most textbooks on English composition have presented some concerted treatment of topic sentences, long hailed as means of organizing a writer's ideas and clarifying them for the reader. In the most popular composition textbook of the nineteenth century, for example, Alexander Bain recognized that topic sentences may come at the end of a descriptive or introductory paragraph, but he emphasized that expository paragraphs have topic sentences and that they usually come at the beginnings of paragraphs:

> 19. The opening sentence, unless obviously preparatory, is expected to indicate the scope of the paragraph...This rule is most directly applicable to expository style, where, indeed, it is almost essential. (Bain, 1890, p. 108)

In one of the more popular composition textbooks of the present, Gorrell and Laird present a similar statement about topic sentences—a statement which is paralleled in many other textbooks these days:

> Topic sentences may appear anywhere, or even be omitted. . . .
> but most modern, carefully constructed prose rests on standard paragraphs, most of which have topic sentences to open them.

And of 15 items on "Paragraph Patterns" in a commercial test of "writing," three involve the identification of topic sentences in brief paragraphs. In each of the three, the correct answer is the first sentence in the paragraph (*Basic Skills,* 1970).

How much basis is there for us to make such statements to students or to base testing on the truth of them? To clarify the matter, I studied the paragraphs in representative contemporary professional writing, seeking the answers to these two questions:

1. What proportion of the paragraphs contain topic sentences?
2. Where in the paragraphs do the topic sentences occur?

Procedure

As a body of expository material representing contemporary professional writing, I used the corpus of 25 complete essays in American English selected by Margaret Ashida, using random procedures, from 420 articles published, from January, 1964, through March, 1965, in *The Atlantic, Harper's, The New Yorker, The Reporter,* and *The Saturday Review.* Ashida indicated possible uses of the corpus:

> . . . this corpus could be used for a wealth of investigations by students, teachers, and research scholars—for anything from a relatively superficial examination of controversial matters of usage, to the exploration of the deep (and equally controversial) questions being raised by theoreticians of the new rhetorics. Because the sample has its own built-in validity, it represents a *common* corpus for use by many different scholars—something we desperately need in rhetorical research . . . (Ashida, 1968, pp. 14-23).

Paragraphs

Working one-by-one with xerographic copies of the 25 articles,[1] I numbered each paragraph from the first paragraph of the essay to the last. For this study, a paragraph was what we normally take to be one in printed material—a portion of discourse consisting of one or more sentences, the first line of type of which is preceded by more interlinear space than is otherwise found between lines in the text and the first sentence of which begins either with an indentation or with an unindented large initial capital.

Headnotes and footnotes were not counted as parts of the text for this study and hence were not numbered and analyzed. A problem appeared when one article included an insert, consisting of a diagram and some ten sentences of explanation, which was crucial to an understanding of the text proper.[2]

This insert arbitrarily was not counted as a paragraph in the article. In those few essays in which dialogue was quoted, each separately indented paragraph was counted as a paragraph, even though it consisted in one case merely of one four-word sentence (Taper, p. 138).

215

After numbering the paragraphs in an essay, I proceeded to insert a pencilled slash mark after each T-unit in each paragraph and to write the total number of T-units at the end of each paragraph.

The T-unit, or "minimal terminable unit," is a term devised by Kellogg Hunt to describe the "shortest grammatically allowable sentences into which . . . writing can be segmented" (Hunt, 1965, pp. 2-21). In other words, consideration of the T-units of writing permits the researcher to use a rather standard conception of a sentence, setting aside the differences occurring between writers when they use different styles of punctuation. A T-unit, then, "includes one main clause plus all the subordinate clauses attached to or embedded within it...." (Hunt, p. 141). Hunt wrote that an independent clause beginning with "and" or "but" is a T-unit, but I also included "or," "for," and "so" to complete what I take to be the coordinating conjunctions in modern usage.

Although in the vast majority of cases, there was no difficulty knowing where to indicate the end of a T-unit, several problems did arise. Take, for instance, the following sentence:

> The Depression destroyed the coalfield's prosperity, but the
> Second World War revived it, and for a few years the boom
> returned and the miner was again a useful and honored citizen
> (Caudill, p. 49).

Obviously, one T-unit ends with "prosperity" and another with "revived it," but is what follows "revived it" one T-unit or two? I made the judgment that "for a few years" was an integral part of both clauses following it and that "and for a few years the boom returned and the miner was again a useful and honored citizen" was one T-unit. Similarly, I counted the following sentence as one T-unit, not two, judging the intent of the first clause in the speech of the Protocol man to be subordinate, as if he had said "If you put an ambassador in prison":

> For another, as a Protocol man said recently, "You put an ambassa-
> dor in prison and you can't negotiate with him, which is what he's
> supposed to be here for" (Kahn, p. 75) .

In marking off T-units, a person must be prepared for occasional embedding. Sometimes a writer uses parentheses to help accomplish the embedding:

> Gibbs & Cox (Daniel H. Cox was a famous yacht designer who
> joined the firm in 1929, retired in 1943, and subsequently died) is the
> largest private ship-designing firm in the world (Sargeant, p. 49).

That sentence, of course, has one T-unit embedded within one other. In the following example, dashes enclose two T-units embedded within another, and the entire sentence consists of four T-units:

> "They're condescending, supercilious bastards, but when the 'United States' broke all the transatlantic records—it still holds them, and it went into service in 1952—they had to come down a peg" (Sargeant, p. 50).

But embedding does not prove to be a problem in determining what is and what is not a T-unit. With the exception of perhaps a dozen other problems in the thousands of sentences considered in the 25 essays, marking off and counting the Tunits was a fairly mechanical operation.

Topic Sentences

The next problem was to decide which T-unit, if any, constituted a topic sentence in each paragraph. After several frustrating attempts merely to underline the appropriate T-unit where it occurred, I realized that the notion of what a topic sentence is, is not at all clear.

Consultation of composition textbooks provided no simple solution of the problem. Gorrell and Laird, for example, offered this definition of a topic sentence:

> Most paragraphs focus on a central idea or unifying device expressed in topical material. Occasionally this topical material is complex, involving more than one sentence and some subtopics; sometimes it carries over from a previous paragraph and is assumed to be understood or is referred to briefly; but usually it simply takes the form of a sentence, sometimes amplified or made more specific in a sentence or two following it. This topic sentence may appear at the end of the paragraph as a kind of summary or somewhere within the paragraph, but most frequently it opens the paragraph or follows an opening introduction or transition (Gorrell and Laird, p. 25).

The authors further clarify their definition (pp. 25-26) by stating that a topic sentence has three main functions: (1) to provide transition, (2) to suggest the organization of the paragraph, (3) to present a topic, either by naming or introducing a subject, or by presenting a proposition or thesis for discussion. In the next several pages, the authors consider various types of "topic sentences as propositions" (or theses) and the problems in writing them with precision.

From my preliminary attempts to identify topic sentences in paragraphs, I could see the truth of a complex definition like Gorrell and Laird's. But such a comprehensive definition presents problems. Sometimes a paragraph opens with a sentence which we could all agree is transitional but which does not reveal much about the content of the paragraph. The second sentence may name the topic of the paragraph but not make a statement about it. The actual thesis of the paragraph may be stated explicitly in a succeeding sentence or in several sentences, or it may merely be inferred from what follows, even though it is never stated explicitly. In such a paragraph, which is the topic sentence—the first, second, a succeeding sentence, perhaps even all of them? Many of the sentences seem to fit the definition. An all-embracing definition does not seem helpful to me in deciding which sentence can be named the topic sentence.

Furthermore, as Paul Rodgers demonstrated (1966), paragraphing does not always correspond to a reader's perceived organization of ideas. Sometimes a paragraph presents an illustration of the thesis of the preceding paragraph. The second paragraph thus extends the previous paragraph, and the paragraph indentation seems quite arbitrary. Or sometimes a thesis is stated in a one-sentence paragraph and the following paragraph explains that thesis without restating it. In such situations, one cannot simply identify a topic sentence in each paragraph.

It seemed to me that the best test of topic sentences is the test a careful reader might make—the test offered when one constructs a sentence outline of the major points of an essay, drawing the sentences insofar as possible from the sentences the author has written. In constructing a sentence outline, one usually omits transitional and illustrative statements and concentrates on the theses themselves. Consequently, I decided to prepare a sentence outline of each of the 25 essays and *then* determine which paragraphs had topic sentences and where in the paragraphs they occurred.

Outlines

From the beginning of the first one, I was aware of the serious problems in constructing a sentence outline to study the organization of another person's writing. To what degree would I tend to impose on an essay my own interpretation of what was written? Does it do violence to discursive writing to cast it into the form of a sentence outline, trying to make the outline understandable by itself when the essay includes details of thought and qualities of style omitted in the process? Would the paragraphing and other typographical features of the edited essay distract me from the ideas and structure of the written essay? Of course I would try to preserve the author's intent in all of these matters, but what I actually did would be so much a matter of judgment that I should expose my outlines for the criticism of others, permitting comparison to the original articles. Moreover, the outlines might be helpful to other investigators who would like to use them without going to the extensive effort of preparing their own. Although it is impractical to include the outlines here, I will make them available to others for the cost of the copying.

In outlining an article, I read it through in sections of a number of paragraphs which seemed to be related, underlining topic sentences where I could find them and constructing topic sentences where they were not explicit in the article. In constructing a topic sentence, I tried to include phrases from the original text as much as possible. Whatever sentences, phrases, or key words I did use from the original I was careful to enclose in quotation marks, indicating by ellipsis marks all omissions and by brackets all of my own insertions. Opposite each entry in the outline I indicated the number of the paragraph and T-unit of each quotation used. Thus the notation 20:2,3 and 4 indicates that quoted portions of the outline entry were taken from the second, third, and fourth T-units of the twentieth paragraph in the essay. On a few occasions where I took an idea from a paragraph but it did not seem possible to cast it in the author's original words at all, I put the paragraph number in parentheses to indicate that. But I tried to use the author's words as much as I could, even, in some cases, where it yielded a somewhat unwieldy entry in the outline.

To illustrate the approach, let me offer in Figure 1 the opening paragraphs from the first article in the corpus, indicating the corresponding entries in the outline.

Notice the different types of outline entries necessitated by the various kinds of paragraphs the author writes. Topic Sentence B is an example of what I would call a *simple topic sentence,* one which is quoted entirely or almost entirely from one T-unit in the passage, wherever that T-unit occurs. (Incidentally, the last sentence in Paragraph 2 is not reflected in Topic Sentence B because that last sentence is an early foreshadowing of the main idea of the entire article.)

Topic Sentence C is a fairly common type, one in which the topic sentence seems to begin in one T-unit but is completed in a later T-unit. In Paragraph 3, the first sentence does not make a specific enough statement about the two existing statutes to serve as a complete topic sentence, even though it reveals the subject of the paragraph. One must go to the third sentence to find the predicate for the topic sentence. Let us term this type a *delayed-completion topic sentence.* Not all delayed-completion topic sentences stem from separated subjects and predicates, though. Sometimes the two sentences present a question and then an answer (Fischer, 18:1,2), a negative followed by a positive (Fischer, 38: 1,2), or metaphoric language subsequently explained by straight language (Drucker, 8:1,2). The T-units from which a delayed-completion topic sentence is drawn are not always adjoining. In one instance, I discovered them separated by three T-units (Collado, 29: 1,2,6); in another, in adjoining paragraphs (Caudill, 17: 2 and 18: 1); in still another, nine paragraphs apart (Lear, 1:1 ,2 and 10:1) .

Notice that Topic Sentence A is an example of a statement assembled by

Figure 1

Sample Paragraphs and Outline Entries

Opening Paragraphs from Drew, P. 33	Excerpt from Outline	
Among the news items given out to a shocked nation following the assassination of President Kennedy was the fact that Lee Harvey Oswald had purchased his weapons, a 6.5 mm Italian carbine, from a Chicago mail-order house under an assumed name. The rifle was sent, no questions asked, to one "A. Hidell," in care of a post-office box in Dallas. The transaction was routine in the mail-order trade; about one million guns are sold the same way each year.	I. By the ordinary rules of the game, the events in Dallas should have ensured prompt enactment . . ." of gun control legislation by Congress. A. "President Kennedy had recently been shot with one of the "one million guns . . .sold . . .each year" through "the mail-order business in guns."	2:2 1:1,3,4
At the same time, a bill was pending in Congress to tighten regulation of the rapidly expanding mail-order business in guns. By the ordinary rules of the game, the events in Dallas should have ensured prompt enactment, just as the news of Thalidomide-deformed babies had provided the long-needed impetus for passage of stricter drug regulations in 1962. But congress did not act-a testimonial to the daily aim of the shooting lobby.	B. "At the same time, a bill was pending in Congress to tighten regulation of the rapidly expanding mail-order business in guns."	2:1
Two existing statures presumably deal with the gun traffic. Both were passed in reaction to the gangterism of the prohibition era. But because of limited coverage, problems of proof, and various other quirks, they have had a negligible impact on the increasing gun traffic.	C. "Two existing statures . . .[had] a negligible impact on the increasing gun traffic."	3:1,3
The investigation of the mail-order traffic in guns began in 1961 under the auspices of the Juvenile Delinquency subcommittee.		

quotations from throughout the paragraph. The first sentence in Paragraph 1 cannot properly be considered the topic sentence: it includes such phrases as "the news item" and "a shocked nation" and such details as the name of the assassin, the size and make of the carbine, and the location of the mail order house—such matters as are not essential to the topic sentence; and it omits such a detail as the scope of the problem—"one million guns . . . sold . . . each year"—which helps convey the idea in Statement I. To ease later reference to this type of topic sentence, let us call it an *assembled topic* sentence.

Finally, there is what we might call an *inferred topic sentence,* one which the reader thinks the writer has implied even though the reader cannot construct it by quoting phrases from the original passage. Though the paragraph in Figure 2 comes out of context—from an article on cutting the costs of medical care—it may still be clear why the corresponding topic sentence had to be inferred.

As I was determining what were the topic sentences of an article, I was also keeping an eye out for what we might call the *major topic sentences* of the larger stadia of discourses. That is, a series of topic sentences all added up to a major topic sentence; a group of paragraphs all added up to what William Irmscher (1972) calls a "paragraph bloc" within the entire article. A major topic sentence (designated with a Roman numeral) might head as few as two topic sentences (designated with capital letters) in the outline or as many as 12 topic sentences (in the Kahn outline) or 15 (the most, in the Mumford outline) . On the other hand, it was frequently apparent that the main idea of a paragraph was really a subpoint of the main idea of another paragraph. Let us call these *subtopic sentences*. As few as two and as many as seven subtopic sentences

Figure 2
Sample of Paragraph Yielding Inferred Topic Sentence

Paragraph from Sanders, p. 24	Excerpt from Outline
Fortunately most ailments do not require such elaborate treatment. Pills cost a good deal less but even they are no small item in the medical bill. From 1929 to 1956 prescription sales climbed from $140 million to $1,466 million a year, and the average price per prescription rose from 85 cents to $2.62. Citing the findings of the Kefauver Committee, Professor Harris makes a strong case for more—and more stringent— regulation of the pharmaceutical industry by the govenment.	Prescription drug costs have risen.

(in the Taper outline) were headed by a topic sentence. Sometimes a major topic sentence or a subtopic sentence was simply stated in a single T-unit, but sometimes it had to be assembled, sometimes inferred. Some occurred as delayed-completion topic sentences.

After completing the rest of the outline, I arrived at the main idea (the thesis) or, in the case of the Kahn and Sargeant articles (both *New Yorker* "Profiles"), the purpose. And as with the various types of topic sentences, I drew quoted phrases from the article to construct the statement of the main idea whenever possible, but with one exception— if a term or phrase occurred frequently in the article, I would not enclose it in quotations and note its location unless it seemed to me to have been put by the author in a particular place or signalled in a particular way to suggest that he was at that time intentionally indicating to readers the nature of his main idea.

After all of the outlines were completed, I went back through each one, classifying each topic sentence as one of the four types and checking the outline against the text of the original essay.

Findings

A tabulation of the frequency of each type of topic sentence for each of the 25 essays is presented in Table 1. It should not escape the reader that the number of topic sentences in an outline does not correspond directly to the number of paragraphs in its essay. Sometimes a major topic sentence and a topic sentence occurred in the same paragraph, and sometimes several paragraphs seemed devoted to the presentation of one topic sentence. (The total number of topic sentences—including the main idea or purpose, major topic sentences, topic sentences, and subtopic sentences, if any— and the total number of paragraphs are given in the two columns at the right of the table.)

One conclusion from Table I is that the use made of the different types of topic sentences varies greatly from one writer to the next. Another is that the four articles taken from the *New Yorker* (each one a "Profile") tend to have yielded a higher proportion of assembled topic sentences than most of the other essays.

Frequency of Types of Topic Sentences

Table 2 combines the data for the 25 essays, indicating the distribution of topic sentences of each type. It is clear that less than half of all the topic sentences (45%) are simple topic sentences and almost as many (39%) are assembled. It is also apparent that—except for the statements of the main idea

222

Table 1

Freqency of Types of Topic Sentences in Each of the 25 Essays

Essay No.	Author	Magazine	Main Idea	Simple			Del-comp			Assembled			Inferred			Total TS's	Total Pars.
				MTS	TS	STS	MTS	TS	STS	MTS	TS	STS	MTS	TS	STS		
1	Drew	Reporter	Inf.	3	8	2	0	2	0	2	2	2	0	0	0	22	20
2	Tebbel	Sat. Rev.	D-C	1	5	2	1	2	2	0	5	2	1	0	1	23	25
3	Collado	Sat. Rev.	Sim.	3	8	3	1	2	2	0	4	9	0	1	0	33	50
4	Sargeant	New York.	Inf.	1	3	0	0	0	0	1	13	6	3	3	1	32	26
5	Chamberlain	Atlantic	Inf.	3	5	2	0	2	0	1	7	3	0	0	0	24	24
6	Daniels	Sat. Rev.	Sim.	3	8	0	0	0	0	0	6	0	0	0	0	18	27
7	E. Taylor	Reporter	Ass.	2	8	0	0	2	0	1	2	0	0	1	0	17	19
8	Kaufman	Atlantic	Ass.	0	13	5	0	2	7	1	0	2	0	5	0	35	41
9	Kahn	New York.	Inf.	4	7	0	0	1	0	1	25	0	4	0	0	44	45
10	Handlin	Atlantic	Sim.	2	11	0	0	7	0	1	4	0	0	1	0	28	35
11	Francois	Reporter	Ass.	2	5	0	0	1	0	0	3	0	0	3	0	13	13
12	Sanders	Harper's	Sim.	3	12	0	0	4	0	1	6	0	2	1	0	32	35
13	Lear	Sat. Rev.	Sim.	0	7	0	2	2	0	2	15	0	2	2	0	32	67
14	Lyons	Atlantic	Sim.	4	8	0	0	1	0	1	13	0	1	0	0	31	53
15	Ribman	Harper's	Inf.	5	20	0	1	4	0	1	13	0	1	2	0	44	56
16	Taper	New York.	Inf.	4	14	1	0	3	0	3	16	11	0	1	0	53	53
17	Fischer	Harper's	Inf.	4	11	9	1	1	0	1	9	3	1	0	0	41	42
18	Mumford	New York.	Inf.	2	17	0	0	2	1	3	27	0	0	0	0	54	49
19	Drucker	Harper's	Sim.	5	15	1	0	5	1	0	16	1	0	0	0	45	53
20	Caudill	Atlantic	Sim.	2	10	3	0	7	0	2	6	3	0	0	0	31	39
21	C. Taylor	Atlantic	Sim.	1	11	0	0	1	0	2	7	3	1	1	0	29	29
22	Cousins	Sat. Rev.	Sim.	1	2	0	1	2	0	2	3	0	0	0	0	11	13
23	Clark	Harper's	Sim.	4	8	0	0	1	0	0	4	1	0	0	0	21	26
24	Durrell	Atlantic	Sim.	1	5	0	1	0	0	1	6	0	0	0	0	15	13
25	Rule	Atlantic	Ass.	3	15	0	1	3	0	1	9	0	0	0	0	33	36
Totals			25	64	236	28	10	56	13	27	220	43	16	21	2	761	889

MTS = major topic sentence   TS = topic sentence   STS = subtopic sentence

223

or purpose—the more of the text that the topic sentence covers, the more likely it is to be a simple topic sentence. That is, of the 117 major topic sentences, 55% were simple; of the 533 topic sentences, 44% were simple; of the 80 subtopic sentences, 33% were simple.

One might well maintain that simple and delayed-completion topic sentences are relatively explicit, that assembled and inferred topic sentences are relatively implicit. Pairing the types of topic sentences in that fashion, Table 2 reveals no great changes in the tendencies of the percentages. Slightly more than half of all the topic sentences (55%) are explicit, slightly less than half (45%) implicit. Again, with the exception of statements of main idea and purpose, the more of the text which the topic sentence covers, the more likely it is to be explicit.

If what the composition textbooks refer to as "the topic sentence" is the same thing as this study terms the simple topic sentence, it is apparent that claims about its frequency should be more cautious. It just is not true that most expository paragraphs have topic sentences in that sense. Even when simple and delayed-completion topic sentences are combined into the category "explicit topic sentences"—a broader conception than many textbook writers seem to have in mind—the frequency reaches only 55% of all the entries in a sentence outline. And when one remembers that only 761 outline topic sentences represent the 889 paragraphs in all 25 essays, he realizes that considerably fewer than half of all the paragraphs in the essays have even explicit topic sentences, to say nothing of simple topic sentences.

Placement of Simple Topic Sentences

How true is the claim that most expository paragraphs open with topic sentences? To find out, I studied the paragraph location of the 264 topic sentences and subtopic sentences in the outline. Gorrell and Laird, like others,

Table 2
Percentages of Topic Sentences of Various Types

Types of Topic Sentences	No.	Sim.	D-C	Explicit	Ass.	Inf.	Implicit
Idea or purpose	25	48	4	52	16	32	48
Major topic sentences	117	55	9	63	23	14	37
Topic sentences	533	44	11	55	41	4	45
Subtopic sentences	86	33	15	48	50	2	52
All types together	761	45	11	55	39	6	45

Table 3

Location of Simple Topic Sentences and Simple Subtopic Sentences

Location	1	2	3	4	5	6	7	8	9	10	11	12	13	14	15	16	17	18	19	20	21	22	23	24	25	Tot	%
Paragraph (Shorter than 4 T-units)	1	1	4	0	3	2	6	5	0	4	1	7	4	0	9	0	6	1	4	2	0	1	6	1	6	74	(28)
First T-unit	6	2	2	3	3	2	0	2	6	4	2	2	1	2	7	5	7	3	6	5	8	1	0	3	7	89	47
Second T-unit	1	4	2	0	0	1	1	2	0	1	0	1	0	1	1	0	4	5	0	2	2	0	1	0	0	29	15
Last T-unit	0	0	1	0	0	1	0	4	0	0	0	0	2	0	0	1	1	4	3	2	1	0	1	0	1	22	12
Elsewhere	2	0	2	0	1	2	1	5	1	2	2	2	0	5	3	9	2	4	3	2	0	0	0	1	1	50	26
Total no. of TS's and STS's in essay	10	7	11	3	7	8	8	18	7	11	5	12	7	8	20	15	20	17	16	13	11	2	8	5	15	264	
Total no. of paragraphs in essay	20	25	50	26	24	27	19	41	45	35	13	35	67	53	56	53	42	49	53	39	29	13	26	13	36	889	

had written that the "topic sentence may appear at the end of the paragraph as a kind of summary or somewhere within the paragraph, but most frequently it opens the paragraph or follows an opening introduction or transition" (p. 25). Thus I decided to tabulate the occurrence of each simple topic sentence as it appeared in each of four positions: the first T-unit in the paragraph, the second T-unit, the last, or a T-unit between the second and last. To do that, of course, I could consider only paragraphs of four or more T-units. Consequently, I excluded from consideration paragraphs with three or fewer T-units. The results are presented in Table 3.

More than a fourth (28%) of all those paragraphs presenting simple topic sentences or simple subtopic sentences contained fewer than four T-units. Of the rest, 47% presented a simple topic sentence or simple subtopic sentence in the first T-unit, 15% in the second T-unit, 12% in the last T-unit, and 26% elsewhere. But these figures are based on the 190 paragraphs of four or more T-units which contain simple topic sentences or simple subtopic sentences. There were 355 paragraphs from which other topic sentences or subtopic sentences were drawn—delayed-completion, assembled, and inferred. One cannot say that they "have topic sentences to open them." Consequently, it is obvious that much smaller percentages than the above pertain to expository paragraphs in general. Furthermore, there were at least 128 paragraphs from which no topic sentences at all were drawn. If one adds the 190, 355, and 128, he has a total of 673 from which percentages may be computed, if he wishes to estimate what percentage of *all* of the paragraphs in the 25 essays open with a topic sentence. Using those figures, I estimate that only 13% of the expository paragraphs of contemporary professional writers begin with a topic sentence, that only 3% end with a topic sentence.

Implications for Teaching

Teachers and textbook writers should exercise caution in making statements about the frequency with which contemporary professional writers use simple or even explicit topic sentences in expository paragraphs. It is abundantly clear that students should not be told that professional writers usually begin their paragraphs with topic sentences. Certainly teachers of reading, devisers of reading tests, and authors of reading textbooks should assist students in identifying the kinds of delayed-completion and implicit topic statements which outnumber simple topic sentences in expository paragraphs.

This sample of contemporary professional writing did not support the claims of textbook writers about the frequency and location of topic sentences in professional writing. That does not, of course, necessarily mean the same findings would hold for scientific and technical writing or other types of exposition. Moreover, it does not at all mean that composition teachers should stop showing their students how to develop paragraphs from clear topic sentences. Far from it. In my opinion, often the writing in the 25 essays would have been clearer and more comfortable to read if the paragraphs had presented more explicit topic sentences. But what this study does suggest is this: While helping students use clear topic sentences in their writing and identify variously presented topical ideas in their reading, the teacher should not pretend that professional writers largely follow the practices he is advocating.

References

Ashida, M.E. (1968). Something for everyone: A standard corpus of contemporary American expository essays. *Research in the Teaching of English, 2,* 14-23.

Bain, A. (1890). *English composition and rhetoric,* enl. ed. London: Longmans, Green. *Basic skills system: Writing test.* (1970).Form A. New York: McGraw Hill.

Gorrell, R.M., & Laird, C. (1967). *Modern English handbook,* 4th ed. Englewood Cliffs, NJ: Prentice Hall.

Hunt, K.W. (1965). *Grammatical structures written at three grade levels.* Research Report No. 3. Urbana, IL: NCTE.

Irmscher, W.F. (1972). *The Holt guide to English.* New York: Holt, Rinehart, & Winston.

Rodgers, P. Jr. (1966). A discourse-centered rhetoric of the paragraph. *College Composition and Communication, 17,* 2-11.

[1] The copies were supplied through the generosity of the Department of English, University of Iowa.

[2] Here and hereafter, reference to specific articles in the corpus will be made simply by using the author's last name—or, in the cases of the two articles by individuals of the same last name, bu using the first initial and last name (see Table 1)—The paragraph referred to here is in Lear, p. 89.

Chapter 10 Replicating Braddock

As its title indicates, Baumann and Serra's study is a "modified replication" of Braddock's study. A **modified replication** is a study which is similar to the original study in most ways but differs from it in certain important features. For example, the Baumann and Serra study employs children's social science texts rather than magazine texts. In contrast, a **strict replication** is a study which matches the original study as closely as possible. Often researchers will do a strict replication when they don't believe the results of the original study. They want to put themselves in a position to say, "Look, I did exactly the same study and the results came out differently." On the other hand, researchers will do a modified replication when they believe the results of the original study but want to extend them. Baumann and Serra believed Braddock's result and wanted to see if they could extend it to children's social science texts.

The Baumann and Serra study illustrates some of the important advantages to be gained when one study builds on another. First, as we have already indicated, a modified replication can extend the generality of the original result. Baumann and Serra showed that Braddock's result, which Braddock was appropriately reluctant to generalize beyond the sorts of magazine writing represented by his texts, in fact, applied equally well to social science texts written for elementary school children.

Second, replication studies often suggest improvements in the procedures used in the original study. In the case of the Baumann and Serra study, although they followed Braddock's procedure fairly closely, they also modified and improved it in several ways. For example, they provided an explicit definition of the concept "main idea" which had been defined only implicitly in the Braddock article, and they combined two of Braddock's four topic sentence types when they found that they could not consistently differentiate between them. More important, though, they introduced the reliability measures which Braddock had not used. Braddock clearly recognized that observer reliability was a problem. He knew that he needed to convince his readers that his judgments about the locations of the main points of paragraphs were ones that others could agree to. The credibility of all of his subsequent analyses hinged on the readers' confidence in these judgments.

However, although he recognized the need to establish the reliability of his observations, he did not have command of modern procedures for measuring reliability. Currently, in such situations, researchers ask an independent rater to make the same judgment that they have made and then they assess the agreement between the two sets of judgments. The measure of agreement may be a percent of identical judgments, or a **correlation** between the judgments such as **Pearson's product-moment correlation** or **Cohen's Kappa**. Lacking these procedures, he did something which was nearly as persuasive. He offered to provide a list of his judgments about the texts to anyone who cared to see them.

Baumann and Serra's replication, then, led to a number of improvements in Braddock's original research design. Unfortunately, replications are relatively uncommon in the research literature on literacy. As a result, there are many reported results that have never been challenged and never been followed up. Further, the research designs which produced the results have not been honed by repeated use into increasingly effective instruments for investigation. We believe that if replication were more common, our field could have achieved more than it has.

Braddock and Baumann and Serra brought very different perspectives to the study of topic sentences. Braddock focused on the problems of teaching college students to write paragraphs and Baumann and Serra focused the problems of teaching primary school students to read them. When we (the editors) first read Baumann and Serra's article after having read Braddock's, we felt an expansion in our understanding of Braddock's study. We saw it from a new perspective and were reminded of the strong interconnectedness of reading and writing.

The Baumann study shows how communication among researchers can reveal greater breadth and utility in a finding than might have been apparent to a researcher working in isolation. Although biographical accounts often emphasize the individual nature of the researcher's work, we should recognize the very important influence that the research community typically has on the researcher, through published articles, conference presentations, teaching, and even casual conversation. Many of the authors of the articles in this volume report such influences in the "Author's Comment" sections.

230

James F. Baumann
Department of Education,
Purdue University

Judith K. Serra
Cleveland School of Science

The Frequency and Placement of Main Ideas in Children's Social Studies Textbooks: A Modified Replication of Braddock's Research on Topic Sentences

Braddock (1974) evaluated adult, expository reading materials for the frequency and placement of topic sentences (main ideas). Results indicated that relatively infrequently were main ideas directly stated in expository prose, and that paragraphs opened with a simple topic sentence only 13% of the time. This study was a modified replication of Braddock's research in which second-, fourth-, sixth-, and eighth-grade social textbooks were examined for the presence of explicit and implicit main ideas in paragraphs and short passages. Results were generally consistent with Braddock's findings on topic sentences: only 27% of all short passages that were examined in the social studies textbooks contained explicit main ideas; only 44% of all paragraphs contained explicit main ideas; and only 27% of all paragraphs opened with a directly-stated main idea. Implications for teachers, publishers, and reading researchers are discussed.

Research indicates that children have considerable difficulty comprehending main ideas in expository prose (Baumann, 1981, 1982, 1983a; Dunn, Matthews, & Bieger, 1979; Taylor, 1980; Tierney, Bridge, & Cera, 1978-1979; Winograd, in press). Given all the interest in main idea comprehension (Baker & Stein, 1981; Cunningham, 1983), it is somewhat surprising that no researcher has asked the question, "How pervasive is the phenomenon of explicit main idea in expository reading materials for children?" When one considers that explicitly stated main ideas have been shown to be more comprehensible than implicit main ideas (Aulls, 1975; Baumann, in press; Kieras, 1978), and that the initial placement of main ideas also aids main idea comprehension (Kieras, 1980), one would hope the exposition for children would contain a relatively high proportion of explicit main ideas, especially placed at the beginning of paragraphs and selections.

Braddock (1974) examined adult, expository reading materials (essays from periodicals such as *The Atlantic Harper's* and *The New Yorker*) for the frequency and placement of topic sentences. His analysis revealed that only 30% of all paragraphs presented a simple topic sentence. When he examined the location of topic sentences, he found that only 13% of all the paragraphs in the essays opened with a topic sentence. As Braddock concluded, "It just is not true that most expository paragraphs have topic sentences" (p. 298) and "It is abundantly clear that students should not be told that professional writers usually begin their paragraphs with topic sentences" (p. 301). Because teachers and instructional materials for children regularly state that most paragraphs have topic sentences, and because subsequent instruction focuses on teaching children how to identify topic sentences (explicit main ideas), it is important to evaluate how frequently children encounter explicit main ideas in exposition. It was the purpose of this study, therefore, to determine the frequency and placement of main ideas in expository materials written for children (social studies textbooks).

Modifications of Braddock's Methods

The present study was an attempt to replicate Braddock's (1974) analysis of adult exposition for the frequency and placement of topic sentences using expository materials intended for children. Whenever possible, Braddock's methods were replicated, although in several instances modifications were necessary.

Braddock selected 25 essays and segmented each into T-units (Hunt, 1965). Hunt defined T-unit, or "minimal terminable unit," as that which "includes one main clause plus all the subordinate clauses attached to or embedded within it" (Hunt, 1965, p. 141). Therefore, each T-unit consists of an independent clause and all accompanying subordinate clauses. Next, Braddock subjectively constructed a sentence outline of the major ideas in each essay, "drawing the sentences insofar as possible from the sentences the author has written [omitting] transitional and illustrative statements" (p. 292). These outlines were then examined for the presence of four types of topic sentences: (a) *simple topic sentence:* "one which is quoted entirely or almost entirely from one T-unit in the passage" (p. 292); (b) *delayed-completion topic sentence:* "one in which the topic sentence seems to begin in one T-unit but is completed in a later T-unit" (p. 293); (c) *assembled topic sentence:* "a statement assembled by quotations from throughout the paragraph" (p. 295); and (d) *inferred topic sentence:* "one which the reader thinks the writer has implied even through the reader cannot construct it by quoting phrases from the original passage" (p. 295).

In the present study, the term *main idea* was used rather than topic sentence, since we wished to use the more generic concept and colloquial term. Main idea has a multiplicity of definitions (Aulls, 1978; Moore, 1983; Pearson, 1981; Pearson & Johnson, 1978; Winograd & Brennan, 1982). To develop operational definitions for identifying main idea types in social studies textbooks, Aulls (1978) definition was used:

> The *main idea* of a paragraph signals to the reader the most
> important statement the writer has presented to explain the topic.
> [Topic previously being defined as that which "signals to the reader
> the subject of the discourse."] This statement characterizes the
> major idea to which the majority of sentences refer. This statement
> is *usually* developed in a single sentence. . . . An implied main idea
> may be inferred from postulating the dominant relationship
> between the superordinate and subordinate topics of a paragraph.
> (p. 92)

In pilot analyses, we attempted to translate Braddock's four types of topic sentences into four parallel categories of main ideas at two different levels; main ideas for short sections in the social studies textbooks and main ideas for individual paragraphs within these sections. We had difficulty, however, distinguishing between the assembled and inferred types and subsequently abandoned the assembled category. This was done because the process of "assembling" a main idea from various statements within a text was considered to be functionally no different from inferring a main idea. Reducing the categories to three and relying on Aulls' definition, we constructed the following definitions of main ideas for text sections and individual paragraphs: (a) *simple main idea* — found in a section/paragraph which possesses a topic sentence identifiable in a single T-unit; (b) *delayed-completion main idea* — found in a section/paragraph which contains no simple main idea but one in which no more than two complete or partial T-units are used to construct the main idea; and (c) *inferred main idea* — a section/paragraph which contains no simple nor delayed-completion main idea but one in which there is a "dominant relationship" that can be readily inferred from the "subordinate topics."

Conducting the analyses according to the above modification, we posed two specific research questions: (a) With what frequency do the three types of section and paragraph main ideas occur in social studies textbooks?, and (b) How frequently do simple main ideas reside at the beginning of paragraphs in social studies textbooks?

233

Method

Materials

Social studies textbooks at grades 2, 4, 6, and 8 of five major publishers were selected. The second-, fourth-, and sixth-grade textbooks were taken from the most recent elementary social studies series: Follett (Buggey, 1983), Ginn (Tiegs, 1983), Holt (Cangemi, 1983), Houghton Mifflin (Anderson, 1980), and Laidlaw (King, Rudman, & Leavell, 1981). Each elementary series conformed to the standard social studies curriculum: second grade—neighborhood/communities; fourth grade—regional geography; sixth grade—contemporary or historical world geography. Since the elementary series concluded with the sixth-grade text, the most recent eighth-grade social studies textbook (which in every case was an American history text) was selected for the same five publishers: Follett (VerSteeg, 1982), Ginn (Branson, 1982), Holt (Bauer, 1979), Houghton Mifflin (Bartlett, Keller, & Carey, 1979), and Laidlaw (Sobel, LaRaus, DeLeon, & Morris, 1982).

Five passages from the texts at each grade level for all five series were selected, a total of 100 passages (25 from each of the four grade levels, 20 from each of the five publishers). Criteria for passage selection consisted of the following: (a) The passages were written in an expository style, as opposed to fictional accounts (or pseudo-narratives, Pearson, Gallagher, & Goudvis, 1981). (b) The passages were self-contained, coherent selections, beginning and ending with a heading or subheading; that is, they were comprehensible taken out of context. (c) Comprehension of the text was not dependent upon graphic or pictorial information. The mean length of all passages was 171 words, the mean number of T-units per passage was 15.6, and the mean number of paragraphs per passage was 3.9. It should be noted that because the second-grade textbooks were not consistently written in paragraph format, this latter value is based only on the fourth-, sixth-, and eighth-grade texts.

Procedure

The procedure for identifying main idea types was modeled after Braddock's (1974) technique. The first step involved numbering the paragraphs in each passage. Next, each passage was segmented into T-units.[1] Segmenting texts into T-units was quite mechanical and proved to be very reliable. Each experimenter independently segmented 12 passages into T-units, resulting in 100% agreement in T-unit boundaries. Table I presents one of the fourth-grade texts. Each paragraph is numbered, and T-unit boundaries are identified by virgules. T-units within each paragraph are numbered consecutively. This enabled any T-unit in a passage to be easily identified by paragraph and T-unit number. For example, 2:3 identifies T-unit 3 in paragraph 2.

After paragraphs and T-units were identified, each text was read several times to determine what type of section main idea and corresponding paragraph main ideas were present. In the example in Table 1, the overall section main idea is inferred, since no simple nor delayed-completion main idea is present. Similarly, the main idea for the first paragraph is inferred. Paragraph two contains a simple main idea located in the first T-unit, and paragraph four's simple main idea is located in T-unit 4. The main idea in paragraph three is a delayed-completion type, and T-units 3 and 4 are the source of the quoted information. These procedures were also quite reliable. Of the 12 passages that each experimenter evaluated independently, there was 92% agreement (11/12) on the section main idea type and 92% agreement (42/44) on individual paragraph main idea types. The few differences were resolved in conference. Simple main ideas within paragraphs were labeled *beginning* if

Table 1

Sample Fourth-Grade Text and Corresponding Main Idea Analysis

---

THE IRON SWORD OF THE HITTITES

1 [1]The metal that people depend on most today is iron./ [2]It is not as beautiful as copper or bronze,/ [3]but it is much stronger./ However, iron is harder to take from the rocks./ [4]And it must be hammered at very high temperatures./

2 [1]The Hittites were probably the first people to use iron./ [2]The Hittites lived in the mountains near the Black Sea, in what is now Turkey./ [3]At first, the Hittites worked with silver and bronze./ [4]They knew about the metal called iron,/ [5]but they had not yet found a way to work with it./

3 [1]Finally the Hittite metalworkers found a way to hammer iron/ [2]so that it would make a sword blade sharper and stronger than bronze./ [3]Soon only the Hittite soldiers had swords made of the new metal./ [4]Iron weapons made the Hittites powerful./ [5]They fought many wars and won many battles./

4 [1]When peace came, the Hittites began to trade their iron weapons./ [2]Other people learned how to make iron./ [3]The knowledge of working with iron spread to people in Asia, North Africa, and southern Europe./ [4]Iron tools and weapons became common all over the ancient world./

Section Main Idea:
Inferred: The Hittites developed the iron sword, which made them powerful and influential.

Paragraph Main Ideas:
Paragraph 1: Inferred: The use of iron has advantages and disadvantages.
Paragraph 2: Simple (T-unit 1): "The Hittites were probably the first people to use iron."
Paragraph 3: Delayed-Completion (T-units 3,4): "Soon only the Hittite soldiers had swords made of the new metal" ... [which] made the Hittites powerful."
Paragraph 4: Simple (T-unit 4): "Iron tools and weapons became common all over the ancient world."

235

the main idea was contained in the first T-unit, were labeled *end* if it resided in the last T-unit, and were labeled *middle* if it was found in neither the first nor the last T-unit.

Results

Section Main Ideas

Table 2 presents percentages for the three types of section main ideas by grade level of textbook for the 100 passages that were examined. Overall, 27% of section main ideas were simple (i.e., explicit), 6% were delayed-completion, and 67% were inferred.[2] Braddock reported that 48% of the essays he examined contained simple topic sentences that captured the gist of the entire essay. Therefore, compared to adult, expository reading materials, children's social studies textbooks appear to contain even fewer explicit main ideas for multiparagraph sections of text. The analysis also revealed considerable variance across publishers. For example, the Laidlaw series contained 50% simple and 50% inferred section main ideas, whereas the Ginn program contained only 5% simple but 90% inferred section main ideas.

Paragraph Main Ideas

Table 2 presents percentages for the three types of paragraph main ideas. Of the 75 fourth-, sixth-, and eighth-grade passages that were examined, 44%

Table 2

Percentages of Section and Paragraph Main Idea Types by Grade Level of Textbook

Main idea type	Second[a] grade	Fourth grade	Sixth grade	Eighth grade	Across grades
		Section main ideas			
Simple	52	16	20	20	27
Delayed-completion	24	0	0	0	6
Inferred	24	84	80	80	67
		Paragraph main ideas			
Simple		41	38	52	44
Delayed-completion		38	36	18	30
Inferred		21	26	30	26

Note: Calculations based on five selections each from textbooks at each grade level for five series.

[a]Because the second-grade texts were not written consistently in paragraph form, no second-grade values appear for paragraph main ideas.

236

of the paragraphs contained simple (explicit) main ideas, 30% contained delayed-completion main ideas, and 26% contained inferred main ideas. Braddock reported that 45% of all topic sentences were simple. However, since many of the topic sentences he identified did not correspond directly to paragraphs (e.g., topic sentences for entire essays), his data were reanalyzed. This revealed that only 30% of all the paragraphs in the essays presented a simple topic sentence. The frequency with which simple paragraph main ideas occur in the social studies textbooks examined is somewhat higher than that which Braddock reported. Nevertheless, results suggest that students would encounter explicit paragraph main ideas less than half of the time in their social studies textbooks.

Placement of Simple Paragraph Main Ideas

Table 3 presents the percentage of simple paragraph main ideas occurring at the beginning, middle, and end of paragraphs. Overall, 62% of the simple paragraph main ideas were stated in the first sentence, 25% appeared somewhere in the middle of the paragraph, and 13% were found in the last sentence of the paragraph. These percentages, however, reflect only the placement of main ideas in paragraphs that actually contained simple main ideas. To obtain a clearer picture of the frequency with which simple paragraph main ideas appear at various locations, it is necessary to consider *all* the paragraphs in the selections. Of the 294 paragraphs that were examined in the fourth-, sixth-, and eighth-grade textbooks, only 80 paragraphs, or 27%, had simple main ideas stated in the first T-unit. Although this percentage is somewhat greater than the 13% Braddock reported, it appears, nevertheless, that children would encounter an explicitly stated main idea at the beginning of only one out of every four paragraphs in their social studies textbooks.

Table 3

Percentage of Simple Main Ideas Occurring at the Beginning, Middle, and End of Paragraphs

Location in paragraph	Fourth grade	Sixth grade	Eighth grade	Across grades
Beginning	64	49	70	62
Middle	19	40	18	25
End	17	11	12	13

Note. Because the second-grade texts were not written consistently in paragraph form, percentages for grades 4, 6, and 8 only are reported.

Discussion

Results of the study essentially replicate Braddock's (1974) findings. Specifically, only about one fourth (27%) of all the passages examined in the social studies textbooks contained explicit (simple) section main ideas; less than half (44%) of all paragraphs contained explicit (simple) main ideas; and only about one fourth (27%) of all paragraphs began with an explicit (simple) main idea statement. Taken collectively, the results indicate that readers of these social studies textbooks will need to rely quite heavily on their inferential comprehension ability to identify main ideas.

These findings are in agreement with other research on children's content area textbooks (Anderson, Armbruster, & Kantor, 1980; Armbruster, 1982; Armbruster & Anderson, 1981) in which it was found that difficulty with the structure, unity, coherence, and audience appropriateness resulted in "inconsiderate" text; that is, passages that simply were not clearly written. It might be argued that since adult, fluent readers are reasonably skillful at comprehending main ideas (Duchastel, 1979; Johnson, 1970; Kintsch & Keenan, 1973; Kintsch, Kozminsky, Streby, McKoon, & Keenan, 1975; Meyer, 1975), they are capable of detecting a high proportion of inferred main ideas. However, children, unlike adults, have not fully developed their ability to comprehend main ideas in expository prose (Baumann, 1982), especially to infer implicit main ideas (Aulls, 1975; Baumann, in press; Kieras, 1978), and hence they presumably will have considerable difficulty identifying the important concepts in textbooks that present explicit main ideas far less than half the time.

What are the implications of these findings? First, for teachers, it is clear that students need to develop skill in identifying both explicit and implicit main ideas in content reading materials. Skill in the latter area is particularly important since the majority of section and paragraph main ideas do not appear to be directly stated in the text. Therefore, teachers need to provide adequate *instruction* in main idea comprehension, since children do not have great inherent skill at comprehending main ideas, particularly in expository prose (Baumann, 1982). In light of the paucity of direct instruction in reading comprehension skills that occurs in elementary classrooms (Durkin, 1978-1979) and the limited amount of guidance basal readers provide teachers in teaching comprehension skills (Durkin, 1981), teachers will need to supplement or augment existing lessons on main idea comprehension. Baumann (in press) reported that an intensive, direct instruction strategy for teaching sixth-grade students to comprehend implicit and explicit main ideas at both the passage and paragraph level was more effective than traditional basal reader

238

instruction in main ideas. The application of this or other direct instruction models (Baumann, 1983b; Carnine & Silbert, 1979; Hansen, 1981; Hansen & Pearson, 1983; Pearson, 1984; Pearson & Gallagher, 1983) may be critical if students are to acquire this set of complex reading comprehension skills. In addition, teachers need to be informed about how relatively infrequently explicit main ideas occur in social studies textbooks, and perhaps in expository prose written for children in general, so that they do not focus instruction primarily on the comprehension of explicit main ideas.

A reasonable recommendation for publishers of content textbooks would be to have them encourage or require authors to more frequently include explicit main idea statements for both paragraphs and larger units of text, since it is clear that readers are more adept at identifying and comprehending main ideas when they are directly stated (Aulls, 1975; Baumann, in press; Kieras, 1978). It is also critical that basal reader publishers not only include more direct instruction on main idea comprehension but also include substantial amounts of instruction on implicit main ideas, since the majority of main ideas children encounter, at least in social studies textbooks, appear to be implicit.

Winograd and Brennan (1983) suggest that varying the placement and density of clues necessary to find main ideas (after Jenkins & Pany, 1980) or perhaps using Beck's (in press) two-track system of "easy" passages rich in clues and "hard" passages less rich in clues are sensible approaches to main idea instruction. Essentially, these techniques provide systematic, sequenced instruction in which students are first presented with samples of text which contain obvious, simple examples of the targeted skill, followed by progressively more complex and sophisticated texts. Baumann (in press) applied these principles when designing direct instruction lessons on main ideas and found them to be very effective. This and other strategies for main idea instruction (Alexander, 1976; Aulls, 1978; Axelrod, 1975; Dishner & Readence, 1977; Donlan, 1980; Jolly, 1967; Moore & Readence, 1980; Putnam, 1974; Taylor, 78) need to be evaluated further and, if proven to be effective, included in basal reader skill instruction.

In conclusion, on the basis of this study, Braddock's (1974) statement that "it is abundantly clear that students should not be told that professional writers usually begin their paragraphs with topic sentences" (p. 301) could be easily rewritten as "it is abundantly clear that elementary and middle school students should not be told that social studies textbook writers usually begin their paragraphs with topic sentences." The challenge remains for publishers of content textbooks to write textbooks such that main ideas are more often clearly and explicitly stated—especially at lower grade levels—and for reading researchers and publishers of instructional materials to provide teachers with valid, sensible strategies for teaching children to be more skillful at comprehending implicit main ideas.

References

Alexander, C. F. (1976). Strategies for finding the main idea. *Journal of Reading 19(4)*, 299-301.

Anderson, L. F. (1980). *Houghton Mifflin windows of our world social studies program.* Boston: Houghton Mifflin.

Anderson, T. H., Armbruster, B. B., & Kantor, R. N. (1980). *How clearly written are children's textbooks? Or, of bladderworts and alfa* (Reading Education Report No. 16). Champaign, IL: University of Illinois, Center for the Study of Reading.

Armbruster, B. B. (1982, March). *Learning from content area textbooks: The problem of "inconsiderate text."* Paper presented at the Conference on Research Foundations for a Literate America, Racine, WI.

Armbruster, B. B., & Anderson, T. H. (1981). *Content area textbooks* (Reading Education Report No. 23). Champaign, IL: University of Illinois, Center for the Study of Reading.

Aulls, M. W. (1975). Expository paragraph properties that influence literal recall. *Journal of Reading Behavior, 7*, 391-400.

Aulls, M. W. (1978). *Developmental and remedial reading in the middle grades.* Boston: Allyn & Bacon.

Axelrod, J. (1975). Getting the main idea is still the main idea. *Journal of Reading. 18(5)*, 383-387.

Baker, L., & Stein, N. (1981). The development of prose comprehension skills. In C. M. Santa & B. L. Hayes (Eds.), *Children's prose comprehension: Research and practice* (pp. 7-43). Newark, DE: International Reading Association.

Bartlett, R. A., Keller, C. W., & Carey, H. H. (1979). *Freedom's trail.* Boston: Houghton Mifflin.

Bauer N. W. (1979). *The American way.* New York: Holt, Rinehart and Winston.

Baumann, J. F. (1981). Effect of ideational prominence on children's reading comprehension of expository prose. *Journal of Reading Behavior, 13(1)* 49-56.

Baumann, J. F. (1982). Research on children's main idea comprehension: A problem of ecological validity. *Reading Psychology, 3(2), 167-177.*

Baumann, J. F. (1983a). Children's ability to comprehend main ideas in content textbooks. *Reading World, 22,* 322-331.

Baumann J. F. (1983b). A generic comprehension instructional strategy. *Reading World, 22,* 284-294.

Baumann, J. F. (in press). The effectiveness of a direct instruction paradigm for teaching main idea comprehension. *Reading Research Quarterly.*

Beck, I. L. (in press). Developing comprehension: The impact of the directed reading lesson. In R. C. Anderson, J. Osborn, & R. J. Tierney (Eds.), *Learning to read in American schools*. Hillsdale, NJ: Erlbaum.

Braddock, R. (1974). The frequency and placement of topic sentences in expository prose. *Research in the Teaching of English, 8*, 287-302.

Branson, M. S. (1982). *America's heritage*. Lexington, MA: Ginn & Company.

Buggey, J. (1983). *Follett social studies program*. Chicago: Follett.

Cangemi, J. (1983). *Holt social studies program*. New York: Holt, Rinehart, and Winston.

Carnine, D., & Silbert, J. (1979). *Direct instruction reading*. Columbus, OH: Merrill.

Cunningham, J. W. (1983, December). *Getting the main idea*. Symposium conducted at the Thirty-Third Annual Meeting of the National Reading Conference, Austin, TX.

Dishner, E. K., & Readence, J. E. (1977). A systematic procedure for teaching main idea. *Reading World, 16(4)*, 292-298.

Donlan, D. (1980). Locating main ideas in history textbooks. *Journal of Reading, 24(2)*, 135-140.

Duchastel, P. (1979). Learning objectives and the organization of prose. *Journal of Educational Psychology, 71, 100-106*.

Dunn, B. R., Matthews, S. R., & Bieger, G. (1979). *Individual differences in the recall of lower-level textual information* (Tech. Rep. No.150). Champaign,IL: Center for the Study of Reading, University of Illinois. (ERIC Document Reproduction Service No. ED 181-448)

Durkin, D. D. (1978-1979). What classroom observations reveal about reading comprehension instruction. *Reading Research Quarterly, 14*, 481-533.

Durkin, D. D. (1981). Reading comprehension instruction in five basal reader series. *Reading Research Quarterly, 16*, 515-544.

Frederiksen, C. H. (1975). Representing logical and semantic structure of knowledge acquired from discourse. *Cognitive Psychology, 7*, 371-458.

Hansen, J. (1981). The effects of inference training and practice on young children's reading comprehension. *Reading Research Quarterly, 16*, 391-417.

Hansen, J., & Pearson, P. D. (1983). An instructional study: Improving the inferential comprehension of good and poor fourth-grade readers. *Journal of Educational Psychology, 79*, 821-829.

Hunt, K. W. (1965). *Grammatical structures written at three grade levels* (Research Report No. 3). Urbana, IL: National Council of Teachers of English.

Jenkins, J. R., & Pany, D. (1980). Teaching reading comprehension in the middle grades. In R. J. Spiro, P. C. Bruce, & W, F. Brewer (Eds.), *Theoretical issues in reading comprehension* (pp. 555-574). Hillsdale, NJ: Erlbaum.

Johnson, R. E. (1970). Recall of prose as a function of structural importance of the linguistic units. *Journal of Verbal Learning and Verbal Behavior, 9, 12-20*.

241

Jolly, H. B. (1967). Determining main ideas: A basic study skill. In L. E. Hafner (Ed.), *Improving reading in secondary schools: Selected readings* (pp.81-109). New York: Macmillan.

Kieras, D. E. (1978). Good and bad structure in simple paragraphs: Effects on apparent theme, reading time, and recall. *Journal of Verbal Learning and Verbal Behavior, 17,* 13-28.

Kieras, D. E. (1980). Initial mention as a signal to thematic content in technical passages. *Memory and Cognition, 8,* 345-353.

King, F. M., Rudman, H. C., & Leavell, L. R. (1981). Laidlaw understand the social science's program. River Forest IL: Laidlaw.

Kintsch, W. (1974). *The representation of meaning In memory.* Hillsdale, NJ: Erlbaum.

Kintsch, W., & Keenan, J. M. (1973). Reading rate and retention as a function of the number of propositions in the base structure of sentences. *Cognitive Psychology, 5,* 257-274.

Kintsch, W., Kozminsky, E., Streby, W. J., McKoon, G., & Keenan, J. M. (1975). Comprehension and recall of text as a function of content variables. *Journal of Verbal Learning and Verbal Behavior, 14,* 196-214.

Meyer, B. J. F. (1975). *The organization of prose and Its effects on memory.* Amsterdam: North-Holland Publishing Company.

Moore, D. W. (1983, December). *Mapping the domain of main idea instruction: A literature review.* In J. W. Cunningham (Chair), *Getting the main idea.* Symposium conducted at the Thirty-Third Annual Meeting of the National Reading Conference, Austin, TX.

Moore, D. W., & Readance, J. E. (1980). Processing main ideas through parallel lesson transfer. *Journal of Reading, 23(7),* 589-593.

Pearson, P. D. (1981). Comprehension: An idea whose time has come. In C. M. Santa & B. L. Hayes (Eds.), *Children's prose comprehension: Research and practice* (pp. 2-3). Newark, DE: International Reading Association.

Pearson, P. D. (1982). *A context for instructional research on reading comprehension* (Tech. Rep. No. 230) Champaign, IL: University of Illinois, Center for the Study of Reading.

Pearson, P. D. (1984). Direct explicit teaching of reading comprehension. In G. G. Duffy, L. R. Roehler, & J. Mason (Eds.), *Comprehension instruction: Perspectives and suggestions* (pp. 222-233). New York: Longman.

Pearson, P. D., & Gallagher, M. C. (1983). The instruction of reading comprehension. *Contemporary Educational Psychology, 8,* 317-344.

Pearson, P. D., Gallagher, M., & Goudvis, A. (1981, December). *What kinds of expository materials are occurring in elementary school children's textbooks?* Paper presented at the Thirty-First annual meeting of the National Reading Conference, Dallas.

Pearson, P. D., & Johnson, D. D. (1978). *Teaching reading comprehension.* New York: Holt, Rinehart, & Winston.

Putnam, L. R. (1974). Don't tell them to do it . . . Show them how. *Journal of Reading, 18(1),* 41-43.

Sobel, R., LaRaus, R., DeLeon, L. A., & Morris, H. P. (1982). *The challenge of freedom.* River Forest, IL: Laidlaw.

Taylor, B. M. (1980). Children's memory for expository text after reading. *Reading Research Quarterly, 15,* 399-411.

Taylor, M. J. (1978). Using photos to teach comprehension skills. *Journal of Reading, 21* (6) 514-517.

Tiegs, E. W. (1983). Ginn people and their heritage social studies series. Lexington, MA: Ginn and Company.

Tierney, R., Bridge, C., & Cera, M. (1978-1979). The discourse processing operations of children. *Reading Research Quarterly 14,* 539-597.

VerSteeg, C. L. (1982). *American Spirit.* Chicago: Follett.

Winograd, P. N. (in press). Strategic difficulties in summarizing texts. *Reading Research Quarterly.*

Winograd, P. N., & Brennan, S. (1983). Main idea instruction in the basal readers. In J. A. Niles & L. A. Harris (Eds.), *Searches for meaning in reading/language processing and instruction.* Thirty-second yearbook of the National Reading Conference (pp. 80-86). Rochester, NY: National Reading Conference.

Author Notes

A paper reporting the results of this investigation was presented at the Thirty-Third Annual Meeting of the National Reading Conference held in Austin, Texas, December 1983.

The authors thank Patrick Shannon, Edward Kameenui, and Peter Winograd for responding to earlier drafts of this paper. The assistance of Barbara Taylor and the members of the Editorial Advisory Board who reviewed this manuscript is also greatly appreciated.

[1] Although other, more sophisticated linguistic and psycholinguistic procedures (Frederiksen, 1975; Johnson, 1970; Kintsch, 1974; Meyer, 1975) are available to parse text and identify hierarchical elements, Hunt's (1965) T-units were used in the present study for several reasons: (1) This enabled the researchers to replicate Braddock's technique for identifying topic sentences (main ideas), and (2) T-units, as opposed to case grammar based linguistic elements (agent, object, cause, goal, etc.), provided a level of specificity sufficient to designate main ideas, especially for large numbers of texts.

[2] Parametric tests on the data were not conducted since the research questions were not answerable through tests of statistical significance. For example, if it were determined that 33% of the paragraph main ideas were simple, 30% delayed-completion, and 37% inferred, inferential statistics would probably indicate no significant differences. In terms of *practical* significance, however, such values may be educationally significant, when one considers that only one third of all paragraphs provide children with an explicitly-stated main idea.

Author's Comment—James F. Baumann

The context for this experiment is purely pedagogical. I am a former elementary classroom teacher, hold graduate degrees in curriculum and instruction and reading education, and have held appointments in colleges of education at several universities. As such, my research has always involved inquiries into ways to enhance the teaching and learning of children's literacy abilities. The particular aspect of literacy teaching and learning that captured my attention in the early 1980's was children's ability to identify and extract an author's main points in expository, nonfiction prose, that is, children's main idea comprehension.

In several descriptive experiments (Baumann, 1981, 1983), I explored the impact the hierarchical nature of expository text had on children's reading comprehension. Contrary to experiments with adults which indicated that they were facile at comprehending hierarchically-prominent ideas (e.g., Meyer, 1975), my experiments with children demonstrated otherwise: The 3rd, 4th, and 6th graders in my studies were just as likely to recall low level ideas as hierarchically important "main ideas." Although this was seemingly contradictory with the adult research, and some research with children, it came as no surprise to me, for my teaching experience suggested that children were drawn to the saliency of information (e.g., the gory details) as much as they were to the hierarchical level of those ideas. Further, I argued that it was inappropriate to draw educational implications from much of the main idea research with children due to low levels of external or ecological validity (Baumann, 1982).

Given this work, the teacher in me said, "Okay, it's no surprise that kids cannot comprehend main ideas very well, so let's experiment with methods for *teaching* them how to comprehend main ideas." Therefore, I did a pedagogical experiment with 6th graders (Baumann, 1984) and found that systematic, explicit instruction enhanced significantly their main idea comprehension abilities. This prompted me a bit later to invite various writers of theoretical, empirical, and pragmatic works on the topic of main idea comprehension to contribute chapters to an edited volume I simply titled *Teaching Main Idea Comprehension* (Baumann, 1986).

In the spring of 1984 as I was writing the review portion of the paper reporting the results of my instructional experiment with 6th graders, I went off on a tangent of sorts and began to read what educators were saying about the teaching of main idea comprehension to children (most all of which was not empirically based). This review revealed that part of the conventional wisdom was the assumption that most nonfiction texts have explicit main ideas—usually found in a topic sentence—and that these topic sentences were typically found at the beginnings of paragraphs. The skeptic in me said, "Wait a minute, if this were true, then why do kids have such difficulty comprehending main ideas?" Further, my experience with instructional expository materials written for children suggested that the initial placement of topic sentences assumption was a bit of an overgeneralization. Hence, the researcher voice in me said, "Hey, guy, go out and test this."

As I was discussing the possibility of an experimental analysis of instructional materials for children, one of my colleagues said, "You're talking about doing an experiment similar to what Braddock did quite a while ago examining sophisticated materials for adults." After reading Braddock's (1974) work, I abandoned my plans to employ a more sophisticated text analysis system to address my research questions and instead chose to use a modified version of Braddock's simple, but elegant, techniques. I was fortunate to receive a 1984 summer research grant to do the text analyses, and I was also fortunate that Judy Serra, a top-notch Master's advisee of mine, had indicated an interest in getting some experience with educational research. So, Judy and I collaborated on the analyses during the summer of 1984. Hence, the background to the modified replication study.

Modified replications are both simple and difficult. They are simple in that you, as researchers, already possess the basic research methods you will employ. They are difficult in that invariably one needs to adapt methodologies to fit a new experimental context and different research questions. Our modifications of Braddock's (1974) methods were necessary because we operated with a somewhat different set of definitions (main idea versus topic sentence), the types of texts we examined were different (instructional materials for children versus sophisticated adult essays), and because our purpose was exclusively pedagogical. Thus, replications are challenging, but they are fun to do. Most importantly, replications provide a means to explore the generalizability of a research finding across experimental contexts.

References

Baumann, J. F. (1981). Effect of ideational prominence on children's reading comprehension of expository prose. *Journal of Reading Behavior, 13,* 49-56.

Baumann, J. F. (1982). Research on children's main idea comprehension: A problem of ecological validity. *Reading Psychology, 3,* 167-177.

Baumann, J. F. (1983). Children's ability to comprehend main ideas in content textbooks. *Reading World, 22,* 322-331.

Baumann, J. F. (1984). The effectiveness of a direct instruction paradigm for teaching main idea comprehension. *Reading Research Quarterly, 20,* 95-115.

Baumann, J. F. (1986). (Ed.). *Teaching main idea comprehension.* Newark, DE: International Reading Association.

Braddock, R. (1974). The frequency and placement of topic sentences in expository prose. *Research in the Teaching of English, 8,* 287-302.

Meyer, B. J. F. (1975). *The organization or prose and its effects on memory.* Amsterdam: North-Holland.

Chapter 11 Reporting on Journalists

The Schumacher et al. study serves two very important functions in this volume. First, it explores the effects of expert knowledge in a very interesting genre, journalistic writing, and second, it provides an excellent example of the use of "think aloud" **protocols** in exploratory research.

The study of journalistic writing seems especially important now when the most popular models of writing (Hayes & Flower, 1980; Bereiter & Scardamalia, 1987) are based largely on observations of expository writing done in school. As Schumacher, Scott, Klare, Cronin, & Lambert (1989) have pointed out, journalistic writing makes very different demands on writers than does exposition. Expanding the scope of research to include journalistic writing as well as other genres appears to be a very good research strategy at this time.

In the think aloud protocol technique, the participant's primary responsibility is to perform some task such as writing an essay or trying to understand a computer manual. The participant's second responsibility is to say anything that occurs to him or her while work on the task is progressing. The order of priorities is important here. The participant should concentrate primarily on doing the task and only secondarily on talking. Further, the instructions to the participant should not specify what is to be talked about. Instructions such as these are typical:

> Say anything you read, anything you write, or anything you think.
> Say whatever comes into your head even if it is only swearing.

It is important not to limit or direct what the participant talks about. Any suggested limitation or emphasis might distort the process being observed by suggesting that certain things are more important than others.

It is important to notice that a protocol is a **concurrent measure**, that is, it provides information while the task is being carried out. It should be contrasted to **retrospective measures**, that is, to accounts given after the task has been completed.

The use of think aloud protocols is now widespread in psychological research and fairly widespread in literature on writing and reading. At one time, though, protocol research was quite controversial (see for example, Nisbett & Wilson, 1977, and Cooper & Holzman, 1983). The concerns that people had about protocols were quite reasonable ones. For example, Nisbett and Wilson (1977) were concerned about the unreliability of self reports. They pointed out that when people are asked to explain why they did something, they will often make things up. For example, they report a study (p. 237) which found that male participants volunteered to take much more severe electric shocks when the researcher was female than when the researcher was male. When asked to account for their willingness to take severe shocks, the participants showed no awareness of the influence of the researcher's gender. Instead, they accounted for their behavior on such grounds as prior experience with electricity. Nisbett and Wilson, by providing a number of such examples, made a convincing case that people can be quite unreliable when they are asked to give reasons for their actions.

Cooper and Holzman's critique (1983) was focused on issues of reactivity. That is, they felt that the act of talking while writing was very likely to cause serious distortions of the writing process. In an extensive review of the research literature, Ericsson and Simon (1984) have considered critiques such as those of Nisbett and Wilson and Cooper and Holzman and have provided some useful observations concerning the use of think aloud protocols in research. First, they found that think aloud protocols, if they are carried out with the cautions suggested above, do not distort the processes being observed in any serious way. Second, they found that retrospective reports also give generally accurate information about the participant's processes although they may be more subject to forgetting than concurrent processes. Finally, they found that if participants were asked about things that they were not attending to while performing a task, as they typically were in the studies reported by Nisbett and Wilson, they often gave inadequate or inaccurate answers.

Bereiter, C., & Scardamalia, M. (1987). *The psychology of written composition.* Hillsdale, NJ: Erlbaum.

Cooper, M., & Holzman, M. (1983). Talking about protocols. *College Composition and Communication, 34*, 284-293.

Ericsson, K. A., & Simon, H. A. (1984). *Protocol analysis: Verbal reports as data.* Cambridge, MA: MIT Press, Bradford Books.

Hayes, J. R., & Flower, L. S. (1980). Identifying the organization of writing processes. In L. Gregg and E. Steinberg (Eds.), *Cognitive processes in writing: An interdisciplinary approach.* Hillsdale, NJ: Erlbaum.

Nisbett, R. E., & Wilson, T. D. (1977). Telling more than we can know: Verbal reports on mental processes. *Psychological Review, 84*, 231-259.

Schumacher, G. M., Scott, B. T., Klare, G. R., Cronin, C. F., & Lambert, D. A. (1989). Cognitive processes in journalistic genres: Extending writing models. *Written Communication, 8*, 390-407.

Gary Schumacher
Ohio University

Jane Gradwohl Nash
Ohio University

Byron T. Scott
University of Missouri

Mary K. Brezin
Ohio University

Donald A. Lambert
Ohio University

Sharon E. Stein
Ohio University

Expertise in News Writing

The objective of this study was to investigate the nature of expertise in news story writing. Individuals from four levels of journalistic experience (those who had no journalistic training, had one news writing course, were journalism seniors or graduate students, were reporters for newspapers) were asked to gather information from 20 different sources on a developing story and write a news story by a deadline. They produced a protocol as they did the task. Results showed that performance generally increased with experience on all measures of writing product and process with the major changes occurring between the first two and last two levels of experience. Some changes also occurred between the last two levels. Expertise in news story writing was found to involve knowledge differences of several types (journalistic, strategic, world, and linguistic), processing differences, and metacognitive differences. The results are compared to expertise findings in other writing and non-writing domains.

The Nature of Expertise in News Writing

Over the last decade researchers have become increasingly interested in understanding the nature of expertise in various cognitive domains. Researchers, for example, have investigated expertise in computer programming (Anderson, Farrell, & Sauers, 1984), physics (Larkin, 1985), mathematics (Anderson, 1982; Schoenfeld & Herrmann, 1982), medical diagnosis (Lesgold et al., 1988); chess (Chase & Simon, 1973); and bridge (Charness, 1989). This work has led to a detailed understanding of the nature of expertise and to the realization that expertise in different domains shows a number of consistent patterns (Anderson, 1990; Glaser, 1986).

Some of the early research on expertise investigated relatively simple task domains and suggested that experts were more proficient than novices in carrying out certain processes crucial for successfully performing these tasks. In more recent years as researchers have explored expert performance in more complex domains, it has become increasingly clear that an understand-

249

ing of expertise necessitates a detailed understanding of the nature and types of knowledge structures which individuals bring to a given task, and how these knowledge structures interact with processing abilities. Glaser (1986) captured this change in emphasis when he noted, ". . .the problem-solving 'difficulties' of novices can be attributed largely to the nature of their knowledge bases, and much less to the limitations of their processing capabilities" (p. 921).

Thus, it has been found that experts and novices differ in how they represent problems to be solved. Novice representations tend to be organized around the surface or literal aspects of a problem (e.g., whether a physics problem involves an inclined plane or a pulley system) while experts organize their representations around deeper principles crucial to problem solution (e.g., whether a problem involves Newton's second law). Novices and experts have also been found to differ in how proceduralized their knowledge is. The knowledge of novices is more static or declarative in nature and novices may be unclear under what conditions or situations their knowledge applies. The knowledge of experts on the other hand is tightly linked to the conditions under which that knowledge can be applied. Thus, experts in geometry will not only know the various theorems that exist in geometry, but they will know the conditions under which these theorems apply, allowing them to draw more quickly on their knowledge in solving a problem.

The detailed knowledge of experts closely intertwines with solution or search processes in effective ways. Because experts recognize complex patterns existing in a problem situation, they become able to draw upon particular problem tactics that can be applied effectively in a part of a larger problem. On a broader level, the detailed knowledge of experts also influences the overall strategic moves they take. Novices, for example, frequently employ a general working-backwards-heuristic to solve problems. Experts, however, are likely to recognize a specific problem type and employ a specific problem-solving strategy applied in a forward manner.

Finally, experts differ from novices in what is called metacognitive or self-regulatory abilities. Thus, experts understand better than novices what they know or don't know; they are better planners, make more efficient use of their time and resources, and more effectively monitor how their problem-solving efforts are proceeding (Glaser, 1986).

It is clear, therefore, that there are large and systematic differences in the characteristics of experts and novices in how they understand and solve problems. Because of the explicitness of the knowledge which experts show, researchers have found that expertise develops over long periods of time.

Hayes (1989), for example, notes that in many domains, time periods up to ten years are involved in achieving high levels of expertise. It has also been found that expertise tends to be very specific in character and consequently that expertise in one area is no guarantee that an individual will show expertise in another area.

In summary, the extensive work on expertise in a number of problem-solving domains has led to a detailed understanding of what is involved in expertise. At the same time that this work has been underway, there has been a growing body of evidence on the nature of what might be called expertise in writing, although the term expertise has not been used uniformly to describe this work. The work on expertise in writing has taken on several different emphases, some quite different from the work on expertise in other domains. We follow Geisler's (1990) structure in describing these different emphases.

First, there are studies that have emphasized cognitive differences among writers of varying levels of sophistication (Bereiter & Scardamalia, 1987; Berkenkotter, 1983; Flower & Hayes, 1981; Jolliffe & Brier, 1988; Rymer, 1988; Schumacher, Klare, Cronin, & Moses, 1984). Bereiter and Scardamalia (1987), for example, compared adult writers to fifth- and tenth-grade writers and found they differed in a number of ways. The adult writers were likely to take more time before beginning to write, to create notes that helped structure a text rather than to immediately begin producing final text, and to show extensive revision activities as compared to the children. Bereiter and Scardamalia interpreted these differences in writing activities to demonstrate that writers move from a less complex knowledge telling model of writing to a more sophisticated knowledge transformation model. Flower and Hayes (1981) investigated the nature of the plans that college writers employed in writing; these included plans for generating ideas and plans for producing the paper. They noted that poor writers often lacked plans or had plans which were not well articulated while good writers made effective use of detailed plans at several levels in the writing process. Schumacher et al. (1984) compared the cognitive processes of beginning and advanced college student writers as they composed essays. They found evidence of an increased level of automaticity in writing in the advanced students as indicated by shorter pauses during writing while carrying out more activities per pause. Finally, Jolliffe and Brier (1988) investigated the impact of subject matter knowledge on the writing of nursing and political science students. They found that their more successful writers had effectively internalized knowledge of subject matter and investigative strategies, and knowledge of text organization and format. In summary, this first category of work on expertise in writing has emphasized the cognitive characteristics of expert in contrast to novice writers. The large majority of these investigations have dealt with the broad category of academic writing. Relatively little work has been done in other areas of writing such as technical writing, journalism, and creative writing.

The second type of research on expertise in writing has emphasized the social aspects of expertise and has examined the uses of writing in demarcating various groups (Doheny-Farina, 1986; Myers, 1985; Winsor, 1989,1990). Doheny-Farina (1986), for example, investigated how the writing of a business plan shaped and reflected the organizational context of a small company. He studied nine individuals who either worked for or were consultants for the company and showed how the writing process was both shaped by this social context and helped modify the organizational interaction among the individuals. Winsor (1989, 1990) investigated the impact of the social milieu on the writing of engineers in a manufacturing firm. She noted that the reports prepared by these engineers depended heavily on both previously written documents in the firm and communal interactions among firm members.

The type of findings noted in the research by both Doheny-Farina and Winsor emphasizes the strong social impact on expertise and is consistent with extensive research in several other task domains, suggesting that expertise should not be placed solely in the individual but viewed in a broader fashion as being located in a particular contextual setting (Belmont, 1989; Saxe, Guberman, & Gearhart, 1987).

Some researchers who have emphasized the social aspects of expertise have been primarily concerned with how expertise is acquired (Anson & Forsberg, 1990; Berkenkotter, Huckin, & Ackerman, 1988; Herrington, 1985). Anson and Forsberg (1990), for example, investigated how six individuals made the transition from academic to professional writing. They noted three stages through which the individuals passed as they developed competence in their professional writing settings, expectation, disorientation, and transition and resolution. The authors viewed this transitional process as one of "adapting to a new social setting, involving not only idiosyncratic textual features of a discourse community but a shifting array of political, managerial, and social influences as well" (p 225). In a similar manner, Herrington (1985) investigated how chemical engineering students learned to write in two different chemical engineering forums, and Berkenkotter et al. (1988) traced how a rhetoric student acquired literacy within his discipline. These studies again emphasize the crucial social aspects of the acquisition of expertise within a writing domain.

252

A third line of research on expertise in writing comes from a very different tradition and raises the issue of the function of expertise (Geisler, 1990). Specifically, this research has looked at how the acquisition of expertise in writing serves to control individuals and maintain a certain status quo (Chase, 1988; Rose, 1988; Killingsworth & Steffens, 1989). Chase (1988), for example, discussed how students accommodate to and resist accepted forms of writing in given disciplines. Killingsworth and Steffens (1989) illustrated how the accepted form of environmental impact statements has both a controlling impact on its authors and an intended role in environmental decisions. Rose (1988) debated the issues involved in whether the acquisition of expertise in writing has a significant effect on individuals as to how they conceptualize and operate within their cognitive worlds.

From this brief review it is evident that there has been extensive interest in the concept of expertise in writing over the last decade. There are some general conclusions about writing expertise which can be drawn from all the research which has been conducted. First, it is clear that knowledge plays a fundamental role in expertise. Individuals who are expert writers bring a variety of kinds of knowledge to any given writing task (Jolliffe & Brier, 1988; Geisler, 1990; Bazerman, 1990; Hayes, 1990). Expert writers draw on extensive content or subject matter knowledge and bring elaborate and detailed content schemas to the writing task. They also bring a detailed knowledge of the organization and arrangement of text. They understand the nuances of a specific writing form and genre. Experts demonstrate extensive and subtle sophistication about linguistic factors. They show an in-depth understanding of syntax and word meaning. A number of recent articles suggest that writing expertise involves an ability to create and manipulate knowledge representations and make transformations from representations in one problem space to representations in another (Bereiter & Scardamalia, 1987; Dyson, 1988; Flower & Hayes, 1984; Geisler, 1990).

Second, because writing expertise is so knowledge dependent, expertise in writing is very domain specific. As Bazerman (1990) noted:

> people who are identifiably experts in writing frequently are only remarkably competent within one limited domain of writing or other. They are novelists, or poets, or journalists, or technical writers. Competence in one domain does not particularly indicate competence in another (p. 2).

Third, expertise involves an ability to quickly and accurately identify patterns which indicate potential problems or demarcate "good" writing (Flower, Hayes, Carey, Schriver, & Stratman, 1986; Hayes, 1990). This allows them to detect difficulties during revision and increases the likelihood of correcting mistakes and misinterpretations. Fourth, expert writers appear to have automated a number of lower level tasks which allow them to attend to larger and more encompassing issues (Schumacher et al., 1984).

These conclusions about expertise in writing, however, must be treated cautiously because they are based almost exclusively on investigations of academic writing. There have been relatively few studies which have tapped various types of professional writing (e.g., technical writing, journalism, or business writing) or creative writing (e.g., poems, short stories, novels). Such a restriction in our knowledge base about expertise in writing is particularly important because writing expertise seems to be so specific. We may wonder, for example, what role content knowledge plays in areas such as journalism and technical writing where writers may be asked to write about topics in which they have relatively little background. Writing in professional areas also draws upon a different set of genres and information-gathering procedures. How do such differences influence our understanding of writing expertise?

The purpose of the study reported here is to provide an initial and exploratory look at the nature of expertise in one professional area of writing-news story journalism. In contrast to most expository and narrative writing genres, the news story is a highly constrained genre which shows extensive internal structure (Schumacher et al., 1989; van Dijk, 1985, 1986). Van Dijk (1985, 1986), for example, described three types of structures involved in the conventional news story–thematic structure, schematic structure, and relevance structure. These three types of structure intertwine with each other with the first two being strongly related to the aspects of semantic and syntax in linguistic discourse.

Thematic structure represents the global content of a news story. According to van Dijk (1985), "The thematic structure represents a formal or subjective collection of topics, which each organize part of the meaning of the text" (p 79). Thus, within a given news story one or more main episodes may be treated with reasons, causes and/or consequences of the episode communicated. This underlying thematic structure is subject to a certain amount of subjective interpretation by both the writer and the reader and thus it is not possible to conclude that there is one, objective underlying thematic structure.

As in linguistics, where a complete understanding of semantics depends on syntax, so in the news story a complete understanding of the thematic structure depends on understanding the schematic structure. News stories show a detailed and highly constrained schematic structure or form. At a simple level this form is captured by the "inverted pyramid." This notion suggests that the first lines of a story contain a summary lead including the most important information followed by paragraphs dealing with less and less important information (Izard, Culbertson, & Lambert, 1990). van Dijk (1985, 1986) elaborates this structure showing its rich hierarchical structure. Figure 1 demonstrates this elaborate structure. Here, we see that news discourse shows two major categorical breaks-a summary and the news story.

The summary includes any relevant headlines and the lead to the story which captures the significant events. There is a strong relation at this summary level between the thematic structure of the text and its schematic structure. The major themes are expressed in the headlines and lead, whereas, lesser aspects of the story will occur in the following paragraphs of the news story. The news story itself also shows a rich internal structure involving a series of episodes composed of events with their consequences or reactions. The events may include background information regarding the circumstances or history surrounding the story. According to van Dijk (1986) the last item in

Figure 1
Schematic Structure of News Discourse. Adapted from van Dijk (1985)

the news story will usually include comments involving conclusions, expectations, or evaluations made by the journalists or others regarding the story. There are strong ordering relationships which go with these various categories. The summary, of course, always comes first and comments last. Usually the main event follows immediately after the summary. This is usually followed by various background information such as history or context. Some of these ordering rules are more strict than others, but they do appear to play key roles in news story production. In particular, Schumacher et al. (1989) found that journalists writing news stories paused more frequently than did journalists writing editorials, apparently to check whether the various conventions and rules of the news story structure were being followed.

The last form of structure apparent in news stories is the relevance structure. This refers to an ordering of news story information within the constraints of the schematic structure by importance or relevance. Some of the major characteristics determining relevance or importance include the recency of the information, the frequency of occurrence, the meaningfulness, the unexpectedness, and the reference to elite persons or groups (Galtung & Ruge, 1973). Schumacher et al. (1989) found that issues of relevance showed up prominently in the protocols of student journalists as they decided how to structure a news story they were producing.

Although there is quite extensive information about the structure of news stories, there is relatively little information available regarding how the expert journalist produces such stories (van Dijk, 1985). Pitts (1982) described the role of the lead in news story writing. Conn (1968) presented a model of the news writing process although it was not strongly empirically based. van Dijk (1985) speculated about how the process might be related to or governed by aspects of the news story structure. Schumacher et al. (1989) used protocol and pausal data to investigate the cognitive process differences in producing editorials and news stories.

The purpose of the present study was to provide direct evidence regarding how individuals of varying levels of journalistic expertise proceed in the production of a news story. This provides an initiation point in exploring the nature of expertise in one area of professional writing. Since understanding news story expertise necessitates not only an understanding of the actual writing of the news story, but also the processes of gathering the relevant information for the story, a methodology was employed that required subjects to gather information on a developing story and write a news story by an impending deadline. Efforts were made to make the circumstances of the story as realistic as possible while maintaining a degree of experimental control. It was hoped this would improve both the internal and external validity of the study. The primary data sources for the study were verbal protocols done as the subjects gathered the information and wrote the story and the final story produced by the subjects.

Method

Subjects

Nine individuals from four levels of experience in news story writing served as subjects. At the first and lowest level of experience were two individuals (one female, one male) who were students who had been accepted into a journalism school but had not yet taken any news writing classes. The female was in her second quarter of undergraduate school, had taken no courses in journalism, and had a grade point average (GPA) of approximately 3.1. The male was in his ninth quarter of undergraduate school, had taken one journalism course in graphics, and had a GPA of approximately 2.4. At the second level of experience were two individuals (one female, one male) who were completing the basic news writing course. The female was in her fifth quarter of undergraduate school, had taken one journalism course in graphics, and had a GPA of approximately 3.5. The male was in his eleventh quarter of undergraduate school, had take three non-news-writing courses in journalism, and had a GPA of approximately 2.7. At the third level of experience were two individuals (both female) who were graduate or advanced undergraduate students in journalism. One of the individuals had completed 12 quarters of undergraduate school, had completed 12 journalism courses including both writing and non-writing courses, and had a GPA of approximately 2.8. The other individual was a second year graduate student with a speciality in magazine journalism. She had taken 52 quarter hours in the master's program and had a GPA of approximately 3.7. At the fourth and highest level of experience were three individuals (one female, two male) who were general assignment reporters for two small daily newspapers. The female was completing her master's degree in journalism with an emphasis in news story writing. She had worked for one year as a general assignment reporter. One of the males was a reporter who had worked eleven years for a daily newspaper as a general assignment reporter covering education, police, and city hall issues. The other male was a reporter who had worked for one and one-half years for a daily newspaper as a general assignment reporter. All nine subjects were volunteers and were not paid for participating in the study.

Stimulus Materials

The stimulus material for the study was a computer program (Apple 11) called *Super Scoop* (Owens, 1984a) which presents a news tip about a death in a hospital surgery room and then provides the subjects with 20 potential sources who may be contacted through simulated phone calls via the computer. The phone calls take the form of a conversation between the subject and the source, although the questions asked the source are provided in the program and are not under the control of the subject. Each source provides information about the story and may be called more than once with each call providing new information about the story. Occasionally, a source's phone line is busy, but a recall at a later time may find the source available. Each call uses up a certain amount of simulated time and when the simulated time reaches six hours, no further calls are allowed. On average it takes individuals about 40 - 50 minutes to reach the simulated time of six hours.

Apparatus

An Apple 11 computer was used to present the Super Scoop program to the subjects. Subjects were provided with an electric typewriter with which they could write their story. A Panasonic videotape system with a small microphone which could be attached to the shirt or blouse of the subjects was used to record the subjects' developing papers, the computer screen which the subjects were viewing, and the verbal statements the subjects made while producing their protocols. A small digital clock was placed in the room so that subjects could monitor the time left before the imposed time deadline.

Procedure

Each individual was brought to a small, quiet room, shown the various pieces of equipment (including the videotape camera), and given instructions regarding the experimental task. The subjects were given a brief practice period to become familiar with producing a verbal protocol. After the practice period was completed, the subjects were asked to gather information on a breaking news story and write a story for an upcoming edition of a paper due to go to press in two hours (real time). They were asked to say aloud everything that they read, wrote, or thought as they decided on sources, contacted those sources, took notes, and prepared their story. After the instructions were completed and any questions answered, the experimenter left the room. Subjects were videotaped throughout the experimental session.

Data coding and scoring

The audio portions of the videotapes were transcribed and prepared for coding by underlining all reading, writing, and thought comments in different color inks. Because of the relative paucity of evidence regarding the character of expertise in news story journalism and because of the limitation in sample size, we approached the analyses of the protocols and final papers in an exploratory fashion. The protocols were analyzed in several different fashions including rating scales, analyses of idea units, and other measures. First, based on the prior research on writing expertise in general, interviews with journalists, and an initial reading of the protocols, six dimensions were chosen for analysis of the protocols. For these six dimensions the unit of analysis was the entire protocol. The intent of these analyses was to determine whether judgments of the protocols on these six dimensions would systematically vary depending on the level of expertise. The six dimensions used in this analysis were journalistic knowledge, knowledge about strategies, world knowledge, linguistic knowledge, systematic interview strategy, and goal orientation. These dimensions were not thought to be independent, but rather to tap identifiable aspects of the kinds of knowledge and strategies which might play important roles in journalistic expertise.

Journalistic knowledge refers to rather specific knowledge about the journalistic enterprise itself; it includes such topics as how the news story is structured, when it is appropriate to use certain kinds of story knowledge, what types of information should be quoted directly in a story, how newspapers differ in style and format, and what role an editor plays in developing a story. Knowledge about strategies involves knowledge about the importance of keeping sources from becoming defensive, of how to use indirect procedures to develop a story, of what approach is likely to be effective in obtaining information, and when it is appropriate to approach a source. World knowledge includes an understanding of the duties of various public officials, what various terms mean such as "smoking gun," what information is normally provided by certain public offices, or how people react under stress. Linguistic knowledge involves an understanding of how language can color the interpretation of an event, how certain terms can be inflammatory, how certain expressions might lead readers to make unintended inferences and generally, how linguistic factors function to make writing clear or unclear. Systematic interview strategy involves an assessment of how systematic the subject was in gathering information for the story. It involves determining whether the subject used a haphazard strategy in contrast to a coherent and systematic

259

strategy aimed at gathering key information needed for the story. Finally, goal orientation assesses whether the protocol emphasizes general and unfocused issues such as "who" was involved in the action or "where" the action took place instead of specific concerns involved in the story. Two judges independently scored the protocols on these six dimensions using five-point rating scales. The two judges initially rated the protocols and then rerated any judgment on which their scores differed by two or more points. The final interrater reliabilities for the six categories were as follows: journalistic knowledge — .89; knowledge about strategies — .88; world knowledge — .85; linguistic knowledge — .90; systematic interview strategy — .80; and goal orientation — .96. A third judge recorded specific events in the protocols related to these six areas.

Second, the protocols were divided into idea units using the criteria described in Swarts, Flower, and Hayes (1984) and scored for the number of idea units dealing with concerns about libel. Third, the number of phone calls made throughout the experimental session was recorded. Fourth, the number of key events on which information was obtained by the subjects was determined. The latter measure was based on a list of key events which are thought to occur in the story episode according to the author of the Super Scoop program (Owens, 1984b).

The final products were analyzed along seven different dimensions based on suggestions made by journalists, the author of the Super Scoop program (Owens, 1984b), and consideration of various articles on news story writing (Schumacher et al., 1989; van Dijk, 1985, 1986). These various analyses provided insight into the final products and the processes subjects used in constructing their news stories (Witte & Cherry, 1986).

The seven dimensions used in the analyses were prototypical news story, appropriateness of news story, organization, language, balance and fairness, accuracy, and content of lead. These dimensions were scored on rating scales on which judges were asked to rate the final product as a whole. The first dimension, prototypical news story, involved a judgment of whether the story produced was a good or bad exemplar of a standard news story, that is, whether it had the important and significant features of the standard news story (see the schematic structure described in van Dijk, 1985). The second dimension, appropriateness of the news story, involved whether the story produced dealt with the information that should be covered regarding this particular story. This dimension is related to the relevance structure described by van Dijk (1985) and involves judgments of the newsworthiness of information included in the story. The third dimension, organization, deals with whether the information is presented in a logical and coherent fashion, includes good transitions, and is easy for the reader to follow. This goes beyond the structural information in the prototypicality dimension to take into account issues of the quality of transitions and coherence. The language dimension involves issues of grammatical accuracy, spelling, word choice, and punctuation. Generally, it deals with the appropriateness of stylistic conventions. The dimension of balance and fairness involves whether the story presents a balanced view of the various viewpoints of the story and whether it is free of editorial comments, value judgments, or unsubstantiated charges or generalizations. The accuracy dimension involves consideration of the accuracy of quotes or facts, or the accurate identification of sources of information. The dimension of content of lead involves whether the lead appropriately captured the significant fact in the story about a rare, drastic error being responsible for the death of an individual—an important point related to the issue of thematic structure. This is the fact judged crucial for the lead by the author of the Super Scoop program and other journalistic sources. The final stories were scored by a journalism faculty member and an advanced journalism graduate student on the seven five-point scales. The two judges initially rated the products and then rerated any judgment on which their scores differed by two or more points. The final interrater reliabilities for the seven product scales were as follows: prototypic news story — .88; appropriateness of news story — .73; organization — .97; language — .85; balance and fairness — .95; accuracy — .57; and content of lead — .80.

Results and Discussion

Our analysis of the nature of expertise in news story journalism is based on quantitative and qualitative evidence drawn from both the protocols and the final products. We present first an overview of the quantitative data and then integrate these data with qualitative analyses of the protocols and products.

In Table 1 are displayed the average ratings of the protocols made by the judges on the six five-point Likert ratings for each of the four levels of subject experience. Because of the small samples, no statistical tests were run on these data; thus, all conclusions based on these quantitative measures should be treated with caution.

A review of the overall means across the six rating scales indicates that the largest change in the row means occurred between the students who had taken the first course in news writing and the advanced undergraduate and graduate students (1.38 to 3.38 respectively). This difference was uniform

Table 1
Average Protocol Ratings

	Journalistic Knowledge	Knowledge about Strategies	World Knowledge	Linguistic Knowledge	Systematic Interview Strategy	Goal Orientation	Row Means	Number Of Libel Units	Number Of Calls Made	Number Of Key Events
PJ	1.75	2.25	2.00	2.50	2.00	1.75	2.04	0	20.0	6.50
J1	1.75	1.75	1.25	1.00	1.50	1.00	1.38	0	19.5	6.75
JS	3.75		3.50	3.00	3.50	3.50	3.38	.5	16.0	5.50
JR	4.33	4.17	3.83	4.00	4.50	4.17	4.17	9.7	17.7	7.33

PJ Jounalism students who have not taken a news writing course
J1 Jounalism students who were completing the basic news writing course
JS Advanced undergraduate and graduate students
JR General assignment reporters for newspapers

Table 2
Average Product Ratings

	Prototypic News Story	Appropriateness News Story	Organization	Language	Balance and Fairness	Accuracy	Content of Lead	Row Means
PJ	1.00	2.00	1.75	2.00	1.25	2.50	1.75	1.75
J1	2.25	2.00	2.00	1.75	2.25	3.00	2.25	2.21
JS	3.00	2.75	4.00	4.00	3.75	3.50	4.25	3.61
JR	3.83	4.00	4.17	3.50	4.17	3.33	3.50	3.79

PJ Jounalism students who have not taken a news writing course
J1 Jounalism students who were completing the basic news writing course
JS Advanced undergraduate and graduate students
JR General assignment reporters for newspapers

across all six rating categories with the smallest difference being 1.25 rating units (in the category of knowledge about strategies). Thus, the students are showing important changes throughout the period of their undergraduate journalism training.

Also displayed in Table 1 are the number of idea units in which the writers deal with the issue of libel, the number of phone calls individuals made in finding out information for their stories, and the number of key events about which information was obtained through these phone calls. More detailed comments about these categories are made later in the article.

In Table 2 are displayed the average ratings on the final products made by the judges on the seven five-point scales for each of the four levels of subject experience. A review of the row means across the seven categories indicates that the scores increased with each successive level of journalistic experience. This increase was not completely uniform across the seven product categories but did generally hold. From the row means it is clear that the largest change in performance occurred between the students who had taken the first course in journalism and the advanced undergraduate and graduate students (2.21 to 3.61 respectively). This increase in performance was uniform across all seven categories with the minimum increase being .50 (in the category of accuracy).

Finally, in Table 3 are presented the correlations among the various product and process measures. Since there are a large number of correlations reported in this table and this increases the chance of some of these correlations reaching significance by chance, only those correlations which are significant at the .01 level are marked. The correlations reported in Table 3 allow us to see interrelationships within the process measures and within the product

Table 3
Intercorrelations Among Measures

	Journ	Strat	World	Ling	Systm	Goal	Libel	Calls	Key	Proto	Apprp	Organ	Lang	Bal	Accur	Lead
Strat	.90*															
World	.93*	.87*														
Ling	.83*	.88*	.83*													
Systm	.95*	93*	.93*	.95*												
Goal	.96*	.93*	.97*	.89*	.97*											
Libel	.61	.60	.52	.64	.60	.54										
Calls	-.31	.05	-.41	-.05	-.18	-.26	-.17									
Key	.27	.37	.38	.47	.45	.39	.40	-.10								
Proto	.75*	.62	.69	.47	.65	.74	.43	-.45	.27							
Apprp	.73	.70	.73	.76*	.77*	.81*	.63	-.31	.51	.84*						
Organ	.84*	.69	.80*	.65	.77*	.84*	.46	-.46	.10	.91*	.85*					
Lang	.69	.52	.72	.28	.66	.74	.23	-.51	.01	.77*	.75*	.94*				
Bal	.83*	.72	.74	.60	.75*	.81*	.46	-.33	.13	.95*	.83*	.97*	.86*			
Accur	.18	.07	.29	.22	.29	.32	-.19	-.42	.52	.48	.52	.41	.54	.39		
Lead	.77*	.48	.80*	.46	.67	.72	.22	-.75	.19	.71	.53	.77*	.76*	.71	.50	

Journ	Journalitic knowledge	Key	Number of key events
Strat	Knowledge about strategies	Proto	Prototype news story
World	World knowledge	Apprp	Appropriateness of news story
Ling	Linguistic knowledge	Lang	Language
Systm	Systematic interview strategy	Accur	Accuracy
Goal	Goal orientation	Bal	Balance and Accuracy
Libel	Number of libel idea units	Organ	Organization
Calls	Number of calls made	Lead	Content of lead

measures as well as across these types of measures. We will refer to this table frequently as we consider the characteristics of expertise in news story journalism.

The Character of Expertise in News Story Journalism

The extensive work on expertise in general and expertise in writing in particular has suggested some major dimensions along which experts and novices differ; in particular, knowledge differences, processing differences, and metacognitive differences. These differences serve as useful organizing categories for discussing the results of this study on expertise in news story writing. At the outset it is important to note that the results here need to be treated cautiously since the study used a relatively small sample of subjects, and was carried out in a laboratory setting which might influence subject response patterns.

Knowledge and Journalistic Expertise

Expertise in the area of news story journalism appears to involve sophistication in a number of different kinds of knowledge. In each of the four areas of knowledge rated by the judges from the subject protocols — journalistic knowledge, knowledge about strategies, world knowledge, and linguistic knowledge, there was a large increase from the first two levels of journalistic experience to the last two levels (for the remainder of the paper we refer to subjects in the first two levels of experience as novices and subjects at the second two levels of experience as experts). The average for the novices across the four knowledge categories was 1.78 while for the experts it was 3.77 (see Table 1). A more detailed understanding of the kind of knowledge the experts demonstrated is seen by looking in more detail at each of the knowledge types. We again emphasize that these knowledge categories are not separate and distinct as is indicated by the high and significant correlations among the four knowledge measures (see Table 3). These high correlations may indicate that the four measures of knowledge are all assessing the same thing or that individuals who are high in one kind of knowledge are also high on the others. We think that the latter conclusion is more appropriate as detailed analyses of the protocols seems to indicate.

Journalistic Knowledge. On the journalistic knowledge rating scale (see Table 1) the expert writers were found to rate a full two points higher than the novices (4.1 versus 1.75). Detailed analyses of the protocols showed that this higher rating seemed dependent on a more sophisticated understanding of several aspects of the journalistic enterprise. The experts showed understanding of all three aspects of journalistic structure outlined by van Dijk (1985)—thematic structure, schematic structure, and relevance structure. Regarding thematic structure, the experts showed concern for ensuring that the story contained the key information, that it held together well and had substance. The higher ratings on the content of lead rating of the final product (see Table 2) supports the belief that the experts were better able to judge which information needs to be included in the lead to make the story coherent (3.8 versus 2.0). This concern for content is also evident in the following two protocol statements. One expert, apparently concerned about the coherence of her story, noted:

> Now what I would like to put in there is some information,
> specifically about what was going on in surgery at the time.

In another instance an expert is concerned with ensuring that the reader understand and accept some crucial content:

> Okay, I'm going to use Insley's um, own words. Kind of according
> to, okay, according to hospital spokesman, Dr. Dan Insley. The
> reason I'm going to do that is because it'll lend a little more
> substance and credibility to the lead.

Novices seemed less specific and confident regarding such issues as suggested in the following two statements:

> Okay, I think maybe I've misplaced emphasis on this story.

> We'll leave out the other stuff because it may not pertain to this
> story.

Experts and novices also differed on aspects of schematic structure of the news story. This is evident from the rating on the prototypical news story scale of the final product (see Table 2). This scale which assessed whether the story produced was a good or bad exemplar of a standard news story showed ratings by the experts that were twice as high as those produced by the novices (3.5 versus 1.63). Comments in the protocols also indicated that the experts were very aware of schematic or structural issues, for example, where certain information should be placed in the story. Note the following comment from an expert:

> Okay, so it's under investigation. That always goes at the end of
> the story.

They were also aware that certain information needed to be attributed to someone:

Now I obviously have to attribute that to someone.

This schematic structure information also went beyond the bounds of a single story. Experts were aware that a given news story did not stand alone, but could be viewed in a broader context of related or follow-up stories. As one expert noted:

> Tomorrow's follow-up will be another story, with more of the details and more talking to employees and finding out what the atmosphere was like and stuff.

Or yet another expert who saw the story as part of a larger structure, each part of which played a different role:

> Since I did not obtain complete information about quotes from credible sources, I would print a small story as I have written to relay the facts thus far to the public . . . and be prepared to do a follow-up article concerning the medical facts and risks of this happening to prevent a panic and create public awareness.

The third aspect of news story structure, relevance structure, also showed differences between experts and novices. The rating on the final product of the appropriateness of the news story (see Table 2) is relevant to this aspect and the experts rated over one point higher on this scale (3.5 versus 2.0). One manner in which this issue of relevance structure appeared in the protocols involved judgments of what information was newsworthy. Experts were quick to make judgments based on some internalized criteria of what was relevant and what wasn't. For example, at one point in an interview an expert found out a new piece of information about a doctor and responded in the following fashion:

> Lost daughter to drunken driving crash last spring. Not news, drop it.

A second expert coming on the same information noted:

> What's that got to do with anything?

Novices, on the other hand, were more likely to note this information as a possible justification for the poor performance of the doctor in surgery. These findings on relevance structure are consistent with those of Schumacher et al. (1989) in which they reported that journalists used some type of criterion list in making judgments about the relevance and importance of certain story information.

Two other differences in journalistic knowledge between experts and novices were also apparent in the protocols and final papers. The first concerns the broad issue of fairness and how this is documented in the story. On the final product rating scale labeled balance and fairness (see Table 2), the experts rated substantially higher than did the novices (4.0 versus 1.75). This concern with balance was evident throughout the protocols. Sometimes it took the form of questioning the goals of a source as the following two statements from different experts suggested:

> Okay, now I want to talk to somebody official again now that I found out who this Rob Porter is which I didn't know going into it that he might have an axe to grind.

> It's good. I wonder who this guy is though? Who is Rob Porter?

Other times it took the form of making judgments of when to use information:

> Okay, these are just rumors, so I'm not going to use that actually.

Or concerns about credibility:

> But this story has no credibility unless you can say you've covered all your bases.

Sometimes it involved a judgment regarding an approach to the whole story:

> I won't want to sensationalize this. My editor may want to after he reads what I write, but I would prefer to go more with just the facts as they are given.

Novices did show some concern about sources being biased and showed rudimentary understanding about how to deal with sources who have asked to be off the record.

The final way in which the expert journalists demonstrated more journalistic knowledge involved the day-to-day process of putting out a newspaper. The experts realized, for example, that each particular newspaper has a particular style that it follows. This may involve a style of wording, how a paper documents its sources, or what role the editor plays in putting together a story. For example, some papers choose to use the word Ms. for all women while others use no titles. One expert noted this dilemma:

> . . . so I'm going to put the woman's name over here. I don't know about this paper's style, but we don't use the word 'Mrs.' so I'm going to call her Courtney.

Similarly, experts were closely attuned to the role that editors play in producing a story. They understand issues that will need the approval of the editor and realize that the editor will set the overall tone and direction that a story may take. The function of editors is demonstrated by one expert:

> I'm going to discuss this with my editor.... it's her decision whether

267

> we would use an anonymous source, in other words, for such an
> important piece of information.

In contrast, the novices were less knowledgeable about the editors and their roles. They seemed rarely to think about them and when they did they described them in a relatively low-level fashion. As one novice noted:

> It's the editor's job anyway, isn't it, to correct the spelling?

In summary, expert news story journalists have developed an extensive knowledge of the characteristics of the news story which guides them in selecting content and generating the typical structure of the news story. But this journalistic knowledge goes beyond narrow content and structural issues into more value laden aspects such as the importance of balance and fairness in the final story produced. Finally, experts also have developed a detailed understanding of how newspapers work, including what are the appropriate roles for writers and editors.

Now we turn to another kind of knowledge that differentiates the expert and novice news story journalist—strategic knowledge. While this could be included under journalistic knowledge, we treat it here as a separate focus, for it emphasizes more what the journalist must know about how to gather information for the story.

Strategic Knowledge. A second kind of knowledge which differentiates expert and novice journalists involves knowledge of effective strategies for gathering information and writing the story. We need to make a distinction at this point between knowledge of the strategies and the actual use of the strategies in carrying out the task. These are two close but separable aspects of expertise. It is possible for one to have detailed knowledge about effective strategies but still fail to employ these processes in the carrying out of a task. In this section we deal with the knowledge of the strategies; in a later section we will deal with the processes employed.

The expert writers were given higher scores on the judged ratings of the knowledge about strategies scale (see Table 1) than were novices (3.7 versus 2.0). This knowledge took different forms and was often quite subtle and sophisticated. We deal with three different aspects of this knowledge that appeared clearly in the protocols. The first deals with the understanding that the types of questions one asks can have a significant impact on the success of an interview. Experts were sensitive to the fact that the wrong type of question would anger sources and make them less likely to respond with useful information. This concern was clearly demonstrated in several cases. For example, at one point in one of the simulated interviews, the computer program asked a source the following question for the writer:

268

I've been told that one of your doctors killed a patient by administering the wrong blood type. Can you confirm that for me?

At this point one expert worried that this might be too aggressive and noted:

Oh God, I'm not quite sure I would've asked that question. . . I would say to the guy, instead, I was wondering if you could tell me more about the cause of death of this person.

In a similar situation in another interview a different expert noted:

One thing, I wouldn't call someone up and say, um, this guy killed your mother, so these aren't the answers I'd get.

In yet a third case one expert noted:

"Why don't I call [the] Medical Examiner. He can give me official information, and then, oh God . . . it's okay, it's okay, I'm going to try . . . see you don't want to get everybody on the defensive about something like this so I'm going to call my friend, Nurse Liz Palmer.

Comments such as these were not found in the novice subjects. It appears the experts carefully judged the impact of their questions, realizing that the questions they asked could markedly influence the answers they received. Novices occasionally showed some sensitivity to this issue but usually in less elaborated ways. For example, after the program asked a source whether he was denying the story, one novice noted:

Good question.

A second aspect of strategic knowledge deals with the order in which one approaches sources. Experts were aware that certain ways of approaching a story were more likely to bear fruit than others. Sometimes this was the case because these approaches would allow the experts to obtain certain key information first before interviewing tougher or more crucial sources. One example of this showed up in the following expert protocol:

I don't really want to go to the top of the heap until I can talk to somebody else who might tell me something I can confront them with.

Finally, experts were also cognizant about the underlying motives of their sources and that this had to be taken into account in obtaining information for a story. This might be the case because the source had certain interests they must protect or that they had certain positions which they would like put forward. One expert, for example, expressed this latter concern in reflecting on a potential interview source:

> State Health Administrator, okay, he's probably a good bet because
> he doesn't have anything to hide.

Thus, experts had a wealth of strategic knowledge that was drawn on in deciding overall interview strategy, selecting sources for interviewing, and even in framing individual questions for their sources. This detailed and sophisticated strategic knowledge was notably absent in the novice journalists.

World Knowledge. A third form of knowledge which appeared prominent among the expert journalists is best described as world knowledge. The expert writers were judged to have higher scores on the world knowledge scale (see Table 1) than were novices (3.7 versus 1.63). This kind of knowledge again took several forms. One form of this world knowledge involved a general understanding of people and how they interact with one another. Sometimes this involved making judgments of people from their comments and behavior. In one telephone interview a source is very caustic about another person, but provides what appears to be very interesting information. Even before completing the interview one expert noted:

> Well, obviously I can't take this guy's word for granted.

In other cases, experts were noted to make detailed judgments about individuals and their behaviors. Three examples are instructive. In the first case an expert judged his source's intentions and noted a subtle manipulative intent:

> Otts' comment . . . you just can't inject A-negative into O-positive
> and expect a picnic. He didn't actually say that's what happened is
> the problem. He sort of tried to steer me in that direction, but he
> didn't actually say that's what occurred.

In the next two cases two different experts make judgments about psychological properties of potential sources:

> ...he's going to be angry, so he might be willing to talk based on
> anger.

> I would probably call my friend Liz just to see if she has anything
> to say about that, um. As a friend [ought to be] willing to talk to me
> a little bit and while that may be using a friendship, she's got her
> finger on what's going on, the pulse over there and she's under no
> obligation to tell me anything, but then again if she feels strongly
> enough about it she may.

Such analyses were notably absent in the novice journalists. In fact, in some cases the novices showed considerable naivete. For example, one novice decided to call the State Police Sergeant:

. . . because he might be able to tell the truth. He might have to legally.

A different form of world knowledge involved an understanding (or lack thereof) of what certain terms mean, and how various public offices function, and what information can be normally obtained from them. Some experts, for example, noted that some of the potential interview sources did not exist in their own county or that the offices functioned differently than the ones in the program. As one expert noted:

I'm not quite sure how this county [referring to the county mentioned in the program] works. I mean in [my] county, I would know. I would have a better idea of who to call.

In contrast, novices were occasionally puzzled by certain offices and even concepts as the following two protocol statements indicated:

Public Records. What is that?

...damage control plan. What's that?

Thus, experts appeared to have developed a broad-based background of knowledge about people, offices, and even concepts. It is unlikely that this kind of knowledge is overtly taught in early journalism classes, but rather is acquired through a variety of experiences. In some ways it should probably not be considered as part of news story expertise but rather part of a wider, more general expertise acquired with worldly experience. It is interesting, however, that it does correlate highly with other kinds of knowledge (see Table 3).

Linguistic Knowledge. The final form of knowledge notable in the expert journalists is linguistic knowledge. This involves a concern with the subtlety of language—a concern that how something is said could be very important in a story. As with the other knowledge types, the experts' protocols were again judged to be higher on this measure (see Table 1) than were the novices' (3.6 versus 1.75). A higher level performance for the experts than the novices on the final product for the language rating (see Table 2) was also found (3.7 versus 1.88). While all subjects showed some concern with linguistic factors such as word choice, the experts were sometimes found to be very specific in their concerns. They were more cognizant that word choice might confuse readers or lead them to make unwarranted inferences or attributions. Three different examples from experts capture the flavor and subtlety of these concerns. The first deals with problems involved in working with technical terms:

271

> You have got to be really careful when you start talking to the
> doctors and stuff, because sometimes they might not say things
> clearly, because, you, um, are a layman, they don't think about that
> and you can't make assumptions being a layman. You have to be
> very careful if you call an I.V. a transfusion, or whatever.

The second statement demonstrates how careful one must be with wording
so that improper attributions are not made. In the first sentence, the expert
described a system for ensuring the proper blood is given to a patient. He then
analyzed this statement and reworded it to make it a safer statement:

> This two person system eliminates careless errors and mistakes are
> witnessed. Okay, there's something about this, because it's not
> attributed to anyone, um, rather say something like this, two
> person system is designed to eliminate careless errors and mis-
> takes, and is designed to eliminate careless errors and something
> about witnessing mistakes, *so that it is less of a statement. It's more
> of a description, um, of what the system does.* [our emphasis]

Finally, the third protocol statement captures the subtle meaning of key
terms which may lead readers to make unintended inferences:

> I'm not going to put the 'but' because 'but' can be inflammatory
> because I'm suggesting, I might be inadvertently suggesting that
> there's some connection between the two, so I'm going to change
> that into two separate sentences. I'm just reporting on two separate
> people's recollections.

These concerns of the expert journalists over subtle meanings and implications of words is consistent with the findings of Myers (1985) in his work with
expert biologists in writing proposals for research funding. He found that his
experts would carefully screen words so that the committees reviewing the
research proposals would not draw incorrect inferences about the proposed
research.

In contrast to the experts, the linguistic concerns of novices more often
dealt solely with issues of word choice. These situations frequently dealt with
standard linguistic constraints such as repeating words too often or failing to
have the correct meaning for an intended idea (Flower and Hayes, 1980). For
example, protocol statements such as the following were typical of novices:

> . . .would have been accountable. I like that word better.

> . . . he hadn't even been informed of the tragic, tragic miscalcula-
> tion. No, I already used that once. Tragic, uh, mistake. . .

The lack of journalistic experience and training in particular linguistic
patterns in the novices would occasionally be expressed directly:

> I'm not sure whether I could say, whether I should say, I say 'this
> reporter' or 'this paper' or whatever. I don't know. I've never had a
> class I've had to do this in.

Experts thus showed detailed and sophisticated linguistic knowledge that allowed them to carefully and concisely communicate their intended meaning. This careful use of the language seemed closely linked with concerns that the reader draw the correct conclusions from the article. It is as if the expert journalists see the linguistic factors as tools that must be precisely used to convey a correct representation of an event.

In summary, the expert journalists investigated here, in contrast to their novice counterparts, demonstrated a wide range of detailed, sophisticated, and often subtle kinds of knowledge. This knowledge included a very refined understanding of the news story genre, including its structure and content restrictions; a sophisticated understanding of the strategies for obtaining knowledge from sources including the kinds of questions and interview approaches which might prove effective; an elaborate knowledge of people and governmental and private offices and how they function; and a subtle and refined understanding of language and how it must be used carefully to convey an accurate rendition of an event. The range of knowledge shown by these expert journalists is as impressively diversified as the kinds of knowledge shown by expert academic writers as described by Jolliffe and Brier (1988). It is important to note that the specific kinds of knowledge appear to differ between academic and journalistic writing (e.g., in the knowledge about the respective genres, in the knowledge of specific subject matter). These differences provide further support for Bazerman's (1990) contention that expertise in writing is specific to subdomains of writing. The data reported here would suggest that the kinds of knowledge found among our expert news story journalists would not necessarily allow them to be expert academic writers. Now we turn to another aspect of writing that also appears to differ between expert and novice journalists, the processes used in producing the news story.

Process and Journalistic Expertise

The expert journalists differed from the novices not only in knowledge, but also in the processes and procedures used in gathering information and writing the story. Geisler (1990) and Voss and Post (1988) have suggested that an important element involved in expertise is the construction and use of mental models. Williams, Hollen, and Stevens (1983) describe a mental model as a system of objects each responding to changes in the others which can be decomposed, and which can be made to function by putting information through the system. By employing such models, a person can observe and predict changes in the domain covered by the model. Geisler (1990) suggests that expert academic writers run such models in the area in which they are writing to aid them in constructing a written argument. Such models allow them to see the strength of their argument and to determine what kind of evidence or data they will need to make their argument stronger.

Expert news story journalists also appear to employ mental models in constructing news stories and these models play an important role in the processes they do throughout the entire news story writing process—from information gathering to writing the story. A good understanding of the role of these models and the processes involved in writing the story necessitates a consideration of two major process-related components of news story writing—the generation of models of the story events and the testing of these models. We look at each of these in turn.

The Generation of Models. An important difference between the expert and novice journalists involved how they went about gathering information from the potential sources. The expert journalists seemed highly focused in their evidence gathering and often seemed to be generating potential models (or hypotheses) that could both account for the information already in hand and guide the further collection of evidence. This model building would frequently appear very early, sometimes even while the expert was being given the initial tip about the news event. One expert, for example, within the first minutes after getting the tip on the story from a person named Rob Porter, noted:

> I'd want to know why the guy's dangerous and, um, who is
> covering it up and what Porter means by the real people. Who is
> he referring to? Um, and, are there other, have there been other
> situations because he says they've been covering up their own
> incompetence and I'd be interested in finding out if there have
> been other situations that have occurred.

Sometimes these models were openly articulated. For example, one expert in emotionally graphic form noted:

> See the reason I'm still searching is because nobody has told me
> that it's [the information about a doctor's actions resulting in the
> death of a patient] not true. In fact, they're intimating that these
> people are being extremely protective for some reason and they're
> intimating that the problem is not that he didn't do anything
> wrong, that is, that his daughter died in a car crash. Well, I'm
> really sorry about that but *if he's screwing up at the County
> Hospital* [our emphasis], that's what our job is and obviously I can't
> just stop...

The italicized segment indicates one hypothesis that might explain what happened. Such hypotheses appeared to play a key role in guiding the sequence in which the experts interviewed their potential sources. Experts typically interviewed their sources according to what information was needed to complete a portion of one of their models. Thus, one expert attempted to determine through one portion of his interviews what the blood type was of the patient who died. He noted:

> I wonder whether, why, why the anesthesiologist didn't match blood type.

At another point he commented:

> What I'm trying to do is pin this to somebody.

Thus, experts appeared to be creating mental models of the events in the story to see if they fit the data, and then used these models to gather additional information to fill in gaps in the model.

In contrast, the novices' approach to the task seemed less tightly focused and usually emphasized relatively unguided fact gathering. The sequence of calls by the novices was not random, but was only occasionally focused on finding out some specific missing piece of information. For example, one novice noted:

> Well, I'm not sure in the first place that this guy is telling the truth so I have to interview some people.

Later this novice commented:

> Let's go back to my source and see why he really wants . . . I want to go back to him and see what this union stuff is.

More commonly, the novice protocols showed general fact-gathering strategies as shown in comments such as the following:

> Let's talk to another doctor.

> Let's see what the police are up to.

> Let's go to Pathology Nurse. Whatever it is, let's go there.

Thus, in contrast to the experts, the novices' procedure for gathering evidence was general in character and not aimed at obtaining information related to a model of the event. The lack of specific and systematic strategies actually ended up with the novice subjects making more phone calls (20) as compared to the expert subjects (17). This pattern of results is consistent with that reported by Johnson (1988) in his work on how physicians (experts) and undergraduate students (novices) made decisions about applicants for internship and residence positions. He found that the experts made fewer searches of the applicant files than did the novices. It is also interesting to note that the five expert subjects in our study did not obtain any more of the key facts through their interviews than the four novice subjects (6.60 versus 6.63, respectively—see Table 2). The fact that the experts produced the overall better stories, however, suggests that they knew better how to employ that information which they obtained.

The models employed by the experts also played an important role in their writing. The models they developed for the story clearly helped articulate and structure the story. In fact, at times it appeared the experts were filling slots in the news story genre. For example, one expert noted:

> Now I can say definitely that the surgeon involved here was Dr. Adams. Not because he said it, but, um, because several nurses confirmed to me off the record that he was indeed the doctor.

It also appeared that if the experts' model was not as articulated as they liked they would adjust the story accordingly. As one expert noted:

> It's all just too tentative, too vague, so I think that all I can say is that the records were impounded.

In contrast to this strong role of the model in composing the story, the novices lacking such an operating model were left floundering. This sometimes frustrating situation is seen from the perspective of one novice:

> I don't know if I should write this or not. I have to tell them something. If I state that his daughter died, that would be like leading the reader, but I shouldn't do that, but I don't have anything else to say.

In summary, the experts appeared to generate mental models of the developing story as part of their news writing process. These mental models not only served as a means to organize the incoming information, but also appeared to guide both the interviewing process and the story writing process.

Model Testing and Confirmation A second procedural aspect which differentiates expert and novice journalists deals with the extensive effort experts put into confirming their model of the story. Schumacher et al. (1989) noted that journalists were quite concerned about issues of accuracy in their reporting. Such concerns also arose with our experts and were translated into actions both in evidence gathering and story writing. During evidence gathering, for example, experts would sometimes consider contacting sources solely to provide confirmation. In debating her next interview, one expert noted:

I don't have anybody who can say, confirm, that the doctor was responsible. . .

Another expert noted:

Try Otts and see if he'll go on the record.

This concern with confirmation also carried over into actual story production. Depending on the degree of confirmation, experts were likely to modify their story to match their degree of confirmation. One expert, for example, noted:

The thing here is that most of the information here is extremely sketchy, so I think I'm going to stick. . . I'm going to leave out the anesthesiologist's name.

Another expert noted:

You might be asking at this point why I haven't put the doctor's name near the front. And there's a very good reason, because I don't want to make allegations about this man, or what's going on at this point. What if it really was an accident? What if it was mislabeled or something? What if a nurse called in the, uh, call for O-blood? I mean I don't know that, so I'm not going to make any wild allegations about this doctor.

Novices only occasionally wrestled with the issue of confirmation, but their lack of knowledge sometimes led to severe vacillation. For example, one novice noted:

I'm not going to state the doctor's name. I don't think I can. I might be able to. . . I don't know if I want to.

The concern of experts over carefully testing and confirming their model often appeared motivated by concerns over libel. Novices, however, seemed to show little concern about this issue. For example, there was not a single idea unit in the protocols of the novices which involved concerns about libel. In contrast, three of the five experts wrestled with concerns about libel with an average of six idea units per protocol concerned with this issue. Some experts were emphatic in their concern:

I want to take this down. In a case like this I want to get this absolutely the same as it is here, because somebody could contest this later. It's just such a touchy issue, I want to list, even though this is kind of a dry quote, I want to list it just so people have no questions that I'm turning words around.

Other experts were less specific but still to the point:

". . . can't use Porter because I don't even know what his credibility is, so that's not good at all. Could land me right in a libel suit."

Some were even more graphic:

> I want to cover my ass.

In summary, expert news story journalists exhibited extensive process differences from novice journalists. Their information gathering and story production processes seemed linked to the generation and confirmation of models of the events in the developing story. This focused model testing seems similar to that demonstrated in academic writers (Geisler, 1990). Such model testing might prove to be an integral part of expertise in many different domains of writing. There is one remaining area in which differences between expert and novice journalists appeared. It involves issues of what psychologists call metacognition.

Metacognition and Journalistic Expertise

As we noted in the introduction, one dimension along which experts and novices differ in many fields involves metacognition (Glaser, 1986). Experts were found to be better planners, to be more efficient in their processing, and generally to better understand how their cognitive systems operated. The expert journalists investigated here also showed evidence of metacognitive sophistication in contrast to the novices. This is seen on two rating scales over the protocols—the scales on systematic interview strategy and goal orientation (see Table 1). The scale on systematic interview strategy involved a rating of how systematic and coherent the writer was in selecting sources and obtaining information. The expert journalists scored systematically higher on this scale than the novices (3.9 versus 1.75). The scale on goal orientation assessed whether the subjects appeared specific and goal oriented in their activities, such as gathering evidence and constructing the story, in contrast to being unfocused and general. Again experts scored higher on this scale than did novices (4.1 versus 1.38). These two scales are highly intercorrelated ($r = .97$) and appear to be tapping very similar issues.

Generally, it appears that the experts were planful, focused, and systematic in their approach to gathering information and producing the story. They would often articulate this planfulness in describing their activities. One expert, for example, noted:

> What I'm basically trying to do is get some sources outside the hospital and find out if they know what is going on.

Another expert suggested that he had set up his interviews in an order which would more likely guarantee success. Finally at one point he noted:

> I think it's time; it's almost time to speak to the anesthesiologist himself.

This goal-oriented, evidence-gathering process is very similar to that reported by Johnson (1988) in his work on expert physicians making decisions about internship and residence applications, and Lawrence (1988) in her work on expert magistrates making judicial decisions.

Although novices would occasionally show signs of planful behavior, they were more likely to be less goal oriented during interviewing as indicated by the following novice's justification for a phone call:

> Let's get back to him, just for kicks.

This lack of focus and goal orientation is also seen in the production of the final story. This is captured most poignantly in the following almost pleading comment by one novice:

> I've got an hour and a half. Okay, oh my, my, my. I don't even know the date of the death. Oh, yes I do. Where is it? Okay, deceased 8/21/84. October. Wait. September. October, 10, no 8, good grief. January, February, March, April, May, June, July, August. August 21, 1984. Oh, my goodness. I don't know what to write. I don't know how to start it all. Who, what, when, where, why. Who what, when, where, why. Do I know any of these questions?

In summary, as in other domains of expertise, expert news story journalists showed a more planful, organized, and systematic approach to the news writing task. This shows up both in the process of gathering evidence for the story and in producing the story once the evidence is collected.

Summary and Conclusion

The data presented here, although exploratory in nature, demonstrate that expertise in news story writing is similar to expertise in other domains of human functioning. This is the case because expertise in news story writing depends on the acquisition of a number of detailed kinds of knowledge, processes, and metacognitive skills much as expertise in other domains necessitates similar kinds of development.

However, the particular kinds of knowledge, cognitive processes, and metacognitive skills are very specific, making the expert news story journalist different from the expert academic writer, novelist, or perhaps even magazine journalist. The expert news story journalists are ones who have detailed knowledge about the news story genre, how newspapers operate, and what strategies are effective in gathering data. They also have extensive knowledge about the world of which they are writing and how language can modify and influence people. These journalists also tend to generate specific models of the story they are writing and try to confirm both for themselves and in writing whether their interpretation is correct. They are very planful, focused, and specific in orchestrating their activities. This particular set of knowledge and skills is highly specific to news story journalism alone. Thus, as Bazerman (1990) suggested, expertise in writing is a specific kind of expertise unlikely to be easily transferred to some other domain of writing.

We have said little in this paper about the factors which lead to expertise in news story writing. Partially this is the case because this study was better designed to point out differences than to suggest causes. The fact that the largest differences appeared to occur between the beginning groups of subjects (the prejournalists and the students who are just completing the first news writing course) and the last two groups (advanced students and general assignment reporters) suggests that the training that students receive during journalism school plays an important role in the development of expertise. However, the fact that there are some changes occurring between the highest two groups (see Tables 1 and 2) suggests that experience in the field also plays an important role in developing the expert news story writer. Further research aimed at carefully investigating these causative factors would be worthwhile. It is also important that even more experienced journalists than our highest level be investigated. There may well be important and significant changes that occur in news writing expertise with extremely high levels of experience.

These data also suggest that a significant portion of the news story writing process is being carried out during the evidence collecting phase of developing a news story. Training procedures for journalists should take this factor into account in designing coursework and practicum experiences for journalism students. Training that solely relies on such procedures as fact sheets to provide information for stories does not provide the range of experience necessary to develop good news writing skills.

In summary, the development of expertise in news story writing involves the acquisition of a complex set of knowledge and processes. In this sense, becoming an expert news story journalist is similar to becoming an expert academic, scientific, or creative writer. However, the fact that the kinds of knowledge and processes acquired are very specific to a domain of writing suggests that while all expert writers share much that is general, they differ in much that is specific.

References

Anderson, J. R. (1982). Acquisition of cognitive skill. *Psychological Review, 89*, 369-406.

Anderson, J. R. (1990). *Cognitive psychology and its implications* (3rd ed.). New York: W. H. Freeman.

Anderson, J. R., Farrell, R., & Sauers, R. (1984). Learning to program in LISP. *Cognitive Science, 8,* 87-129.

Anson, C. M., & Forsberg, L. L. (1990). Moving beyond the academic community: Transitional stages in professional writing. *Written Communication, 7,* 200-231.

Bazerman, C. (1990, April). Expertise does not always come in packages. In A. J. Herrington (Chair), *The nature of expertise in writing.* Symposium conducted at the meeting of the American Educational Research Association, Boston.

Belmont, J.M. (1989). Cognitive strategies and strategic learning. *American Psychologist, 44,* 142-148.

Bereiter, C., & Scardamalia, M. (1987). *The psychology of written composition.* Hillsdale, NJ: Erlbaum.

Berkenkotter, C. (1983). Decisions and revisions: The planning strategies of a publishing writer. *College Composition and Communication, 34,* 156-169.

Berkenkotter, C., Huckin, T. N., & Ackerman, J. (1988). Conventions, conversation, and the writer: Case study of a student in a rhetoric Ph.D. program. *Research in the Teaching of English, 22* 9-44.

Charness, N. (1989). Expertise in chess and bridge. In D. Klahr & K. Kotovsky (Eds.), *Complex information processing: The impact of Herbert A. Simon* (pp. 183-208). Hillsdale, NJ: Erlbaum.

Chase, G. (1988). Accomodation, resistance and the politics of student writing. *College Composition and Communication, 39,*13-22.

Chase, W. G., & Simon, H. A. (1973). Perception in chess. *Cognitive Psychology, 4,* 55-81.

Conn, E. (1968). Tentative conceptualization of the newswriting process. *Journalism Quarterly, 45,* 344-345.

Doheny-Farina, S. (1986). Writing in an emergent organization: An ethnographic study. *Written Communication., 3,* 158-185.

Dyson, A. H. (1988). Negotiating among multiple worlds: The space/time dimensions of young children's composing. *Research in the Teaching of English, 22,* 355-390.

Flower, L., & Hayes, J. R. (1980). The dynamics of composing: Making plans and juggling constraints. In L. W. Gregg & E. R. Steinberg (Eds.), *Cognitive processes in writing* (pp. 31-50). Hillsdale, NJ: Erlbaum.

Flower, L., & Hayes, J. R. (1981). Plans that guide the composing process. In C. H. Frederiksen & J. F. Dominic (Eds.), *Writing: The nature, development, and teaching of written communication* (pp. 39-58). Hillsdale, NJ: Erlbaum.

Flower, L., & Hayes, J. R. (1984). Images, plans, and prose: The representations of meaning in writing. *Written Communication, 1,*120-160.

Flower, L., Hayes, J. R., Carey, L., Schriver, K., & Stratman, J. (1986). Detection, diagnosis, and the strategies of revision. *College Composition and Communication, 37,* 16-55.

Galtung, J., & Ruge, M. (1973). Structuring and selecting news. In S. Cohen & J. Young (Eds.), *The manufacture of news: Social problems, deviance, and the mass media* (pp. 62 -72). London: Constable.

Geisler, C. (1990, April). The nature of expertise. In A. J. Herrington (Chair), *The nature of expertise in writing.* Symposium conducted at the meeting of the American Educational Research Association, Boston.

Glaser, R. (1986). On the nature of expertise. In F. Klix & H. Hagendorf (Eds.), *Human memory and cognitive capabilities: Mechanisms and performances* (pp. 915-928). Amsterdam: Elsevier.

Hayes, J. R. (1989). *The complete problem solver* (2nd ed.). Hillsdale, NJ: Erlbaum .

Hayes, J. R. (1990, April). The role of perceptual knowledge in writing skill. In A. J. Herrington (Chair), *The nature of expertise in writing.* Symposium conducted at the meeting of the American Educational Research Association, Boston.

Herrington, A. J. (1985). Writing in academic settings: A study of the contexts for writing in two college chemical engineering courses. *Research in the Teaching of English, 19,* 331-361.

Izard, R. S., Culbertson, H. M., & Lambert, D. A. (1990). *Fundamentals of news reporting* (5th ed.). Dubuque, Iowa: Kendall/Hunt.

Johnson, E. J. (1988). Expertise and decision making under uncertainty: Performance and process. In M. T. H. Chi, R. Glaser, & M. J. Farr (Eds.), *The nature of expertise* (pp. 209-228). Hillsdale, NJ: Erlbaum.

Jolliffe, D. A., & Brier, E. M. (1988). Studying writers' knowledge in academic disciplines. In D. A. Jolliffe (Ed.), *Advances in writing research. Volume 2: Writing in academic disciplines* (pp. 35-87). Norwood, NJ: Ablex.

Killingsworth, M. J., & Steffens, D. (1989). Effectiveness in the environmental impact statement: A study in public rhetoric. *Written Communication, 6,* 155-180.

Larkin, J. H. (1985). Understanding, problem representations, and skill in physics. In S. F. Chipman, J. W. Segal, & R. Glaser (Eds.), *Thinking and learning skills. Vol. 2: Research and open questions* (pp. 141-159). Hillsdale, NJ: Erlbaum.

Lawrence, J. A. (1988). Expertise on the bench: Modeling magistrates' judicial decision making. In M. T. H. Chi, R. Glaser, & M. J. Farr (Eds.), *The nature of expertise* (pp. 229-259). Hillsdale, NJ: Erlbaum.

Lesgold, A., Robinson, H., Feltovich, P., Glaser, R., Klopfer, D., & Wang, Y.(1988). Expertise in a complex skill: Diagnosing X-ray pictures. In M.   T. H. Chi, R. Glaser, & M. J. Farr (Eds.), *The nature of expertise* (pp. 311-342). Hillsdale, NJ: Erlbaum.

Myers, G. (1985). The social construction of two biologists' proposals. *Written Communication, 2,* 219-245.

Owens, P. (1984a). *Super Scoop.* Wentworth, NH: COMPress.

Owens, P. (1984b). *Super Scoop Teacher's Manual.* Wentworth, NH: COMPress.

Pitts, B. J. (1982). Protocol analysis of the newswriting process. *Newspaper Research Journal*, *4*, 12-21.

Rose, M. (1988). Narrowing the mind and page: Remedial writers and cognitive reductionism. *College Composition and Communication, 39,* 267-302.

Rymer, J. (1988). Scientific composing processes: How eminent scientists write journal articles. In D. A. Jolliffe (Ed.), *Advances in writing research. Volume 2: Writing in academic disciplines* (pp. 211-250). Norwood, NJ: Ablex.

Saxe, G. B., Guberman, S. R., & Gearhart, M. (1987). Social processes in early number development. With Commentary by R. Gelman and by C. M. Massey and B. Rogoff; with Reply by G. B. Saxe, S. R. Guberman, & M. Gearhart. *Monographs of the Society for Research in Child Development, 52* (2, Serial No. 216).

Schoenfeld, A. H., & Herrmann, D. J. (1982). Problem perception and knowledge structure in expert and novice mathematical problem solvers. *Journal of Experimental Psychology: Learning, Memory, and Cognition, 8,* 484-494.

Schumacher, G. M., Klare, G. R., Cronin, F. C., & Moses, J. D. (1984). Cognitive activities of beginning and advanced college writers: A pausal analysis. *Research in the Teaching of English, 18,* 169-187.

Schumacher, G. M., Scott, B. T., Klare, G. R., Cronin, F. C., & Lambert, D. A. (1989). Cognitive processes in journalistic genres: Extending writing models. *Written Communication, 6*, 390-407.

Swarts, H., Flower, L., & Hayes, J. R. (1984). Designing protocol studies of the writing process: An introduction. In R. Beach & L. S. Bridwell (Eds.), *New directions in composition research* (pp. 53-71). New York: Guilford.

van Dijk, T. A. (1985). Structures of news in the press. In T. A. van Dijk (Ed.), *Discourse and communication: New approaches to the analysis of mass media discourse and communication* (pp. 69-93). Berlin: Walter de Gruyter.

van Dijk, T. A. (1986). News schemata. In C. R. Cooper & S. Greenbaum (Eds.) *Studying writing: Linguistic approaches* (pp. 155-185). Beverly Hills, CA: Sage.

Voss, J. F., & Post, T. A. (1988). On the solving of ill-structured problems. In M. T. H. Chi, R. Glaser, & M. J. Farr (Eds.), *The nature of expertise* (pp 261-285). Hillsdale, NJ: Erlbaum.

Williams, M. D., Hollen, J. D., & Stevens, A. L. (1983). Human reasoning about a simple physical system. In D. Gentner & A. L. Stevens (Eds.), *Mental models* (pp. 131-153). Hillsdale, NJ: Erlbaum.

Winsor, D. A. (1989). An engineer's writing and the corporate construction of knowledge. *Written Communication, 6,* 270-285.

Winsor, D. A. (1990). Engineering writing/writing engineering. *College Composition and Communication, 41,* 58-70.

Witte, S. P., & Cherry, R. D. (1986). Writing processes and written products in composition research. In C. R. Cooper & S. Greenbaum (Eds.), *Studying writing: Linguistic approaches* (pp.112-153). Beverly Hills, CA: Sage.

Author's Comment—Gary Schumacher

In the course of interviewing creative writers over several years, we have found it surprising how many times these writers mention how small events play a significant role in the development of a story. For example, Daniel Keyes, author of *Flowers for Algernon* (from which the movie "Charlie" was taken), noted in an interview with a writing class that he had been struggling with this story because he couldn't envision the lead character. He commented that one day while teaching an English class, a young man came to his desk and asked him if this class was the "slow" class. While Keyes struggled to answer the question, he suddenly realized that this individual was Charlie; the short story from which the full novel was drawn was completed a week later. In a similar vein, David Martin (1990) described how the name ESMERALDA festooned across the rear window of a passing Nova on a car trip to the South served as a focal point for the short story, "Sunday Morning."

In many ways science is not unlike this process of creative writing. Of course, science involves well-conceived designs, careful data collection, and systematic data analyses. But it also involves periods of doubt, stages of limited progress, and flashes of insight sometimes triggered by seemingly trivial events or observations. Certain settings or combinations of individuals may increase the likelihood of such insights, but there is no guarantee that they will happen. The conduct of the study which is reported in "The Nature of Expertise in News Writing" has its share of such events; a look at one of these helps capture this discovery side of research.

The initial idea for this study occurred several years prior to its eventual conclusion in an offhand remark made while returning from a cafeteria after lunch. Several of us had been visiting Dick Hayes and his colleagues at Carnegie Mellon University. In one of the sessions we had described some of our work on journalistic writing which had made use of fact sheets to control the content of the news story writing. We had been impressed with the degree of automaticity involved in this kind of writing and, thus, how the writing appeared substantially different from more academic kinds of writing that had been studied in most previous investigations. On the way back from lunch Linda Flower wondered whether much of the planning of the news stories might be going on in the process of gathering data for the story. If this was the case, of course, the methodology we had been using in our prior studies would have been missing this important stage.

We were in the midst of finishing some other projects so this question was left on a back burner, reappearing on occasion during research team meetings. It was during one of these exchanges that Byron Scott noted that he had seen an interesting demonstration of a computer based reporting simulation at a journalism conference. The simulation, titled Super Scoop (Owens, 1984), provided the lead to a story and then gave 20 potential sources one might contact to obtain information about the story. We quickly realized this might be the solution to our problem. By using this simulation as stimulus material for our subjects, we could get access to what journalists did during the initial data gathering phase of writing a story and still control content.

We worried, of course, whether the simulation would seem sufficiently natural so that it would elicit responses from our subjects which would be similar to those which they would show in real-life settings. We had a suspicion that it would be okay when Byron reported that at the conference at which he'd first seen Super Scoop, a number of journalists were crowded around the computer during a demonstration of the program. These individuals were so involved in the program that they were shouting out which of the sources should be contacted next. Our suspicions were confirmed both during pilot phases of our project and throughout data collection. Subjects were found to curse at sources who evaded hard questions or who appeared to be providing useless or misleading information. Comments as to the origins of the parents of certain sources were heard to be made even if their phone lines were busy. Follow-up reports from subjects indicated how they rapidly became enmeshed in the nuances of the situation.

This anecdote emphasizes how important it is that researchers have access to a wide variety of experience and background knowledge in carrying out research. This diversity may arise from working with an interdisciplinary team of researchers as was the case in this study. Each brought his or her own range of experience which provided not only different perspectives on a problem, but different resources which were useful. The diversity of experience does not have to be interdisciplinary, however, but may involve drawing on a wide set of readings and experience. In this idea generation aspect of research, key insights can and often do arise from the most unlikely sources.

In his fascinating little book, *The Modularity of Mind,* Jerry Fodor elaborates a distinction that those who train researchers sometimes fail to emphasize (or even explain) to the scientific novice—the distinction between scientific "confirmation" and scientific "discovery." Much of what is described in our scientific articles deals with confirmation and it seems so rational, controlled, and often statistical in character. Much of what doesn't get written about is where key ideas for the study come from, the discovery process. It is in this phase, Fodor argues, that literally any knowledge one may have may be relevant to a key insight that initiates a study. In this sense, then, the off-hand comment made on a walk, the observance of a reporting simulation at a conference, or any number of other seemingly unrelated experiences can provide the key to unlock an important study.

References

Fodor, J.A. (1983). *The modularity of mind.* Cambridge, MA: MIT Press.

Keyes, D. (1966). *Flowers for Algernon.* New York: Harcourt, Brace, & World.

Martin, D. (1990). "Sunday morning": A commotion of memory and place. In E. Shelnutt (Ed.), *Writing: The translation of memory.* New York: Macmillan.

Owens, P. (1984). *Super Scoop.* Wentworth, NH: COM Press.

Chapter 12—Teaching Experience and Placement Skill

Smith's paper is an especially interesting one because it illustrates some important concerns about the nature of measurement scales and in particular about the sorts of scales we use to evaluate writers. In the article presented here, Smith was following up earlier observations on the evaluation of placement essays. These observations suggested that accuracy in placing students into writing courses depended on the judges experience in teaching those courses. His observations led him to ask two fundamental questions about the nature of the judgments that his raters were making. The first was "What sort of measurement scale do these judgments represent?" and the second was "Are the judgment categories exhaustive?"

The scales of measurement most often found in literacy studies are of three sorts: **interval**, **ordinal**, and **nominal**. Interval scales are the ones that are most likely to come to mind when we think of measurement. They are called interval because they consist of an ordered set of equal intervals or units. The most familiar example of an interval scale is the common foot-ruler marked off in 12 equal units of one inch. The critical feature of the interval scale is the equality of its units. Perhaps the best way to think about the significance of the equality of intervals would be to think about a world in which rulers had inches of variable size. In such a world, two students might start out a foot different in height, each grow six inches, and then no longer be a foot different in height because the inches they grew were different in size. Clearly, there are advantages in being able to use equal interval scales. Factors which are measured on interval scales include students' ages, the lengths of their essays, the number of days they attend school, etc.

An ordinal scale is one that allows us to identify an order in what we have measured, e.g., this is better than that but not as good as something else. However, it does not allow us to identify equal intervals between observations. Our familiar academic grading scale A, B, C, D, and E is an example of an ordinal scale. The student who get an A is doing better than the student who gets a B, and a student who gets a B is doing better than the student who gets a C. However, there is no reason to believe that the difference between the A and the B student is equivalent to the difference between the B and the C student. The units in an ordinal scale are not necessarily comparable in size. Another example of an ordinal scale is the **Likert** scale with its categories "strongly agree", "agree", "disagree", and "strongly disagree." All ranking scales are ordinal in character.

A nominal (or categorical) scale is one that assigns individuals to categories without implying that the categories have any order among themselves. Race, gender, academic major, and country of birth are common examples of nominal scales. The various races are not ordered with respect to each other. They are just different.

Measurement scales can have "holes" in them, that is, they may not exhaust all of the judgments we want to make. For example, when we grade our students, we often find that the available grading scales are inadequate to capture our judgment of particular individuals. We may be required to give "A"s, "B"s, and "C"s when our judgment is that some students are clearly "B+" or "A-". In other cases a student may be entirely off the scale. We may have to grade him "C" when we really want to grade him "Good effort."

In his article, Smith addresses the question of whether his raters' judgments in placing students in classes are nominal or ordinal in character. Do the raters treat class B as if it were between class A and class C, suggesting ordinal judgments, or do they just treat the three classes as different from each other, suggesting nominal judgments? Further, he wants to know if there are holes in the placement scale. Are there students who really don't fit in any of the available categories? The exciting thing to observe in Smith's paper is how he compares his data to alternative models in order to answer these questions.

William L. Smith
University of Pittsburgh

The Importance of Teacher Knowledge in College Composition Placement Testing

Direct assessment of student writing has, over the past decade, become the dominant method for evaluating students' writing performance and abilities. This method requires students to write an essay which is then read and evaluated using what is generically called "holistic" reading, i.e., a relatively fast reading resulting in a single score based on the reader's gestalt impression. However, the generic term masks some very specific differences in the purposes of the assessment and the methods used, and it is, therefore, highly probable that research on one purpose/method may not be applicable to other purposes/methods.

There are two very different purposes for direct assessment. The first, the one almost exclusively reported in the literature, is to assess the quality of written compositions with no direct impact on the writer. That is, regardless of the results, the writers are not affected in grade-in-course, progress in curriculum, or placement into or out of a course. Quite commonly, the results of such assessment are used to draw conclusions about writing ability (e.g., research on instructional methods or large-scale descriptive studies such as the National Assessment of Educational Progress studies), but these conclusions apply only to groups of writers, not individuals. Such assessment would more precisely be called "assessment of writer-groups through direct assessment of text".

The second purpose is to assess the essays with a direct impact on the writer. That is, the real purpose is not to assess the text but to assess the writer in order to make a decision about that writer. This purpose underlies all placement testing, either into courses (e.g., pre-enrollment placement into diversified college composition courses) or out of courses (commonly called "exit exams"). This purpose would more precisely be called "assessment of individual writers/students through direct assessment".

Within this purpose, the scale and technique used to derive the final score will depend upon the constituency being served. If that constituency is broad, for example several schools or colleges, each with different curricula and/or pedagogy, the scale may have any number of points and can be derived in at least three ways: 1) it may be the sum of raters' ratings, 2) it may be the

289

average of the raters' ratings, or 3) it may be the modal, or more frequent, rating. Each school or college would then establish local cut-off points for each course placement.

However, when the constituency is one school or college, the scale can be tailored to local needs. The scale can be curriculum derived, each scale point (or set of scale points) representing a specific course. The real purpose of the assessment is to use the student's text as a window into that student so as to place the student into the course which best matches her needs and abilities. The technique used must produce a final score which refers to a course. Summing or averaging raters' scores is sometimes used, but the most common procedure is to use modal scores. When the primary raters (usually two) agree, that is the modal score. If these raters disagree and the split-resolver agrees with one rater, then that is the modal score. When the primary raters disagree by more than one scale point, quite commonly the split-resolver's score becomes the final score. (From discussions with colleagues at other universities, we have found that none use more than three readers to determine a modal final score.)

Although there is a considerable body of literature on direct assessment, little is devoted to placement testing (e.g., Smith et al., 1980; Alexander and Swartz, 1982). Even the best works on testing in composition (e.g., White, 1985) devote little space to this type of testing. Furthermore, no research has been done on the relationships between the two purposes of direct assessment. No one has compared, using the same texts, how the two purposes affect final ratings or the distribution of ratings. Therefore, I will limit my interpretations to only placement testing within a local constituency, the University of Pittsburgh. And, thus, some information about the University of Pittsburgh composition program and courses must be presented to frame my discussion.

The University of Pittsburgh Composition Program and Courses

The composition program is based on four concepts (or dimensions): that writing is an effort to make meaning, that writing is closely related to reading, that to make meaning a writer must develop a sense of authority, and that students gradually come to that sense of authority. Consequently, in all of our courses, the students respond to a sequence of assignments on a central topic (see Coles, 1981, Bartholomae, 1983, and Bartholomae and Petrosky, 1987 for more detailed exposition of the bases of the program). It is also important to note that we do not consider composition courses to be "service" courses. That is, they are not intended, specifically, to train students to write for other courses. Consequently, we, for example, do not have students write research papers, nor are they required to write papers in the various modes (narrative, exposition, etc.).

Because our students have varied abilities along these dimensions, the composition program consists of three courses, each addressing a particular range of ability. Course A is designed for students who have serious writing problems which indicate problems with reading and appropriating a text they have read. These students' essays lack development of ideas, lack coherence, are not well organized, and do not address the issue. Commonly, these students either inadequately summarize the given passage or make general statements about the issue. But they do not interrelate the passage and their own ideas. These students also typically have patterns of surface level errors caused by their inability to read and proofread. However, error alone is not a good predictor of placement in Course A.

Course B is designed for students who have significant problems with writing (e.g., development of ideas, coherence, and organization), but these problems are not related to their ability to read the given passage. Instead, they indicate a lack of a sense of text and a lack of authority. Surface level error commonly exists in their texts also, error and error patterns caused by their lack of a sense of text. If asked whether they read their own texts as they read other texts, they will say they don't, and if pressed for reasons, will say that their own writing doesn't merit such reading.

Course C is designed for students who have the ability to read and make meaning but need more experience in developing their abilities, particularly in dealing with problematic texts and in using writing as a means for working their way through complex problems. Our research has shown that the students placed into Course C actually make more surface-level errors than the students placed in the other courses, but these errors are not caused by a lack of sense of text. Rather, they are either "typos" or result from risk-taking.

Some students are exempted from composition courses because the writing ability they demonstrate on the placement test suggests that these courses would not be of significant value. Thus, when we conduct our placement ratings, we use a four point nominal scale: Course A, Course B, Course C, and Exempt.

One might assume that these four alternatives might be treated as points of an ordinal scale, with Exempt representing the best outcome, followed by Course C, Course B, and Course A in that order. However, this assumption is not necessarily correct because the students placed into Course A do not subsequently take Course B. Instead, they move to Course C. In effect, then, Courses A and B are parallel but serve different student needs (see Figure 1).

291

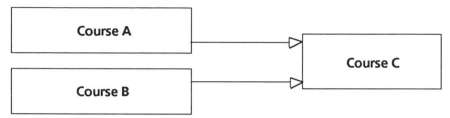

Figure 1

Pattern of Movement from Course to Course

Problems in Placement Testing

It is generally agreed that in all direct assessment, including local constituency placement testing, raters must be highly reliable, i.e., give the same ratings to the same essays. There are two common methods for increasing reliability. The first, and most common, is to train or "calibrate" the raters in practice sessions so that they come to agreement prior to rating the essays (see Myers, 1980 and White, 1985 for methods). It is generally agreed that the minimum acceptable level of agreement is .70 (Cooper, 1977). The other method, one particular to local constituency placement testing, is to use raters who have taught the range of courses and thus are perceptive to the kinds of students typical of each course. This creates what might be called a local discourse community calibration (cf. Follman and Anderson, 1967) concerning homogeneity versus heterogeneity of raters [academic experiential backgrounds] as sources of reliability and unreliability). To increase that reliability, the raters participate in practice sessions, typically before each rating session.

Practical experience tells us that even two highly trained readers commonly disagree about the relative quality of a text. This is especially true if we believe that students' texts are a form of literature–that is, if the purpose of writing is to make meaning (cf. Bartholomae, 1983 and many others). This is a crucial point in the research presented below, for the curriculum and the pedagogy driving each of our composition courses are built on this belief. However, disagreements about <u>quality</u> do not necessarily mean disagreements about placement because the raters focus on the writer, not the quality, per se, of the text. Disagreements about placement, then, may be quite different than disagreements about quality.

Because errors do happen in the placement rating, double-checks are commonly used. For example, during the first week of each term, classroom teachers have their students write an essay which is evaluated to determine whether any students should be moved to a different course. But even with elaborate double-checks, schools must find methods to determine the reliability of their own raters for two reasons: 1) to determine whether the raters need additional or better or different training, and 2) to provide public evidence that students are not subject to capricious placement. The obvious, and most common, method to assess the reliability of raters is to compare the raters' ratings. However, this method does not adequately determine reliability in local constituency testing because there is one factor that makes such testing different from other forms of direct assessment: each scale point is specifically related to the local curriculum, i.e., there is one scale point for each course, and the purpose of testing is to place each student into the course which best fits his or her needs. Thus, the scale used cannot be considered interval because the intervals between scale points, the courses, are unknown (and may be unknowable). It is really either a nominal (or an ordinal) scale. Further, even if the curriculum is based on careful analysis of the needs and abilities of the local population, not all students will fit neatly into the courses. Invariably, some will be "between courses."

The Study

In earlier research on rater reliability (Smith, forthcoming), I found evidence that when one pair of raters disagreed about the placement of a student, a second pair of raters was likely to disagree in the same way. I had thought it reasonable that some students could show characteristics of two distinct courses, but that might not be the real reason for the judgment split. The split might be related to the raters, not the writer. Therefore, I reanalyzed the data, looking at the raters' backgrounds. I discovered that one other possible reason might be the course that the rater had most recently taught. It is important to remember here that all of the raters in the pool are teachers of composition courses and that they are placing students, not just rating essays. Furthermore, in order to teach Course B, one must have successfully taught Course C, and to teach Course A, one must have successfully taught Course B. Thus, the Course B raters would have knowledge of courses B and C, and the Course A teacher would have knowledge of all three courses, but that knowledge might be several years old. My reanalysis of the data showed that almost all of the disagreements between the raters happened when the raters had most recently taught different courses. One of the most striking features of these differences was that most of them involved two raters, each of whom judged that the student didn't belong in the course that he or she was most familiar with. For example, a rater most familiar with Course A judged that the student belonged in Course B while a rater most familiar with Course B judged

293

that the same student belonged in Course A.

While I was conducting the first study, I also collected some Think-Aloud Protocols (TAPs) on raters while they were rating, and those data led me to a new perspective. The TAP data showed that when raters were reading an essay which they would place into the course they had most recently taught, their comments were not just about the essay. They also made specific comments about the writer as a student. They would say such things as "This student is one of those who never talks in class." or "This student will make significant progress in the first few weeks." When reading an essay they would place into some other course, there were no statements about the writer as student, only comments about the text or the writer as writer. The writer-as-student comments indicated that the raters had a privileged sense of the students in the course they had most recently taught, and this might alter their placement decisions.

Thus, it seemed that I might have missed the real point. The raters' expertise, the expertise which comes from working with their students, might be more powerful than any training session in which they are told about the various courses and read essays prototypic of those courses. I call this expertise "Most Recent Course Taught" expertise. In effect, I was speculating that a rater's expertise is linked to the course that rater has most recently taught because those are the students most recently encountered. This is not unlikely. If, for example, fourth grade teachers were asked to grade-rate essays written by students from a wide range of grades, they would make the most errors on the grades farthest from their own grade. Their expert-vision would be greatest when the students were near the fourth grade. Thus, it might be the case that raters are less able to make expert judgments when reading essays written by students who don't belong in their course. Therefore, I conducted the following experiment to test the theory that agreement among rater-sets differs according to the course-taught expertise of the raters. Specifically, I was testing the hypothesis that raters who have most recently taught the same course will agree with each other, whereas there would be lower agreement when the raters have most recently taught different courses.

Procedure

For this experiment, I selected essays from a previous placement rating session (a month previous) which had been rated by rater sets composed of specific combinations of raters with particular Most Recent Course Taught (hereafter "RCT") experience (see Figure 2). I could not use all possible combinations of rater-sets and their decisions because that would have overloaded the placement session and, thus, might adversely affect placement decisions. I excluded all "D" (Exempt) ratings because D is not a course and thus there could be no "course-taught expertise." I randomly selected eight essays from within the six high frequency combinations (see Figure 2). These high frequency combinations included cases in which both raters accepted students into the course they were most familiar with, e.g., AA in Figure 2 indicates that the student was assigned to Course A by two raters most familiar with Course A, and cases in which both raters were rejecting students from the course they were most familiar with, e.g., AB in Figure 2 indicates that the student was assigned to Course B by the rater most familiar with Course A and to Course A by the rater most familiar with Course B. Other combinations than those shown in Figure 2 were possible but relatively infrequent. Figure 2, then, defines the categories of the essays used in the study.

The raters for this study were randomly selected from the raters working in the placement session, with the constraint that four had most recently taught Course A; four, Course B; and four, Course C. I will refer to the original rater as R1 and the rater in this study as R2. Each rater set read a total of 48 essays, 8 from each of the six categories of ratings (e.g., AA, AB, etc.). Thus, each R2 read eight essays previously rated by an R1 set of raters with the same RCT patterns and forty essays previously rated by R1 raters with different RCT patterns. The target essays were randomly placed into the stacks of essays the raters were to read. Original versions were used so that the raters would not know that these essays had been previously rated.

Results and Discussion

When given essays which the two Course A raters in R1 had rated AA (i.e., accepted), only the Course C R2 raters disagreed (See Table 1). In seven cases, a Course C rater produced a B rating. When given essays which the two Course B raters in R1 had rated BB (i.e., accepted), only the Course A and the Course C R2 raters disagreed. Course A raters produced seven C decisions, and Course C raters produced two A ratings. When given essays which the two Course C raters in R1 had rated CC (i.e., accepted), only the Course A R2 raters disagreed, producing three B ratings and five D ratings. These data indicate that the Course B raters never disagreed with R1 on any non-split and that when Course A and Course C raters disagreed with R1, they never placed the student into their own course. Although we have been careful not to assume apriori that the courses are ordered with Course A on the bottom, Course C on the top, and Course B between them (see Figure 1), the pattern of rater judgments suggests that the raters were treating the courses as if this

295

ordering assumption were true. In the following discussion, we will show how the rater's judgments are consistent with the ordering assumption. If the raters do treat the courses as ordered, then, when Course B raters "reject" students, they must either place them above or below, and this creates agreement with the R1 raters. Thus, it would be expected that they would disagree less on prototypic essays (although they might give a Course C student a D rating). When Course A or Course C raters "reject" students, there is more "room" for placement. Course A raters select from three ratings above their course. When Course A raters disagreed on a student rated B by R1, they couldn't select A because they had already rejected the student from their course. Thus they had to select C. (Selecting D would be unlikely because the essay would not have the right characteristics for exemption.) When they disagreed on a student rated C by RS1, they could, and did, produce B, C, and D ratings. The pattern here is that a disagreement will be "one course off", i.e., a course contiguous to the course determined by R1. Similarly, when Course C raters "reject," they have two courses below theirs, and all of their disagreements were also one course off. It should be noted, however, that disagreements were far less common than agreements. Twelve raters read each of the twenty-four non-split essays, yet there were only 24 disagreements. Thus, they agreed on 91.6% of the cases.

Figure 2
Essays Selected for the Second Study
(8 essays per study)

Rating	RS1, by Course Taught
AA	Both ratings given by Course A rater (i.e., accept into course")
AB	"A" rating given by Course B rater "B" rating given by Course A rater (i.e., both "reject from course)
BB	Both ratings given by Course B rater (i.e., "accept into course")
BC	"B" rating given by Course C rater "C" rating given by Course B rater (i.e., both "reject from course")
CC	Both ratings given by Course C rater (i.e., "accept into course")
AC	"A" rating given by Course C rater "C" rating given by Course A rater (i.e., both "reject from course)

Split decisions offer a more taxing test of the course-taught expertise theory. If the theory is right, then when two R1 raters disagree (i.e., produce a split vote), the matched R2 raters should agree with that decision. All split-vote essays selected for this study share one commonality: the raters never "accepted" the students into their own courses (see Figure 2). Thus, for the R1 AB split, the A was given by a Course B rater and the B by a Course A rater. The theory would predict that R2 Course A raters would not "accept."

When given an AB split, the R2 Course A raters always rejected as did the Course C raters. The Course B raters rejected in 93.75% of the cases. When Course A raters rejected a student, they always placed the student in Course B. Thus, since A was not possible, B is the only remaining possibility because their prior experience teaching Course C allowed them to deduce that the student didn't belong in C. The Course C raters had more "room" for a decision. A rejected student could be placed into either A or B, and these raters were clearly not in accord with each other on which placement to select. Nineteen of the thirty-two decisions (59.38%) were for A, thirteen (40.62%) were for B. Thus, it seems that the Course C raters, when given an

Table 1
Ratings Given By Individual RS2 Raters

Essay Rating (RS1 rating)	RS2 Rater (by RCT)	Rating Given by RS2 Raters			
		A	B	C	D
AA	A	32	0	0	0
	B	32	0	0	0
	C	25	7	0	0
BB	A	0	25	7	0
	B	0	32	0	0
	C	2	30	0	0
CC	A	0	3	24	5
	B	0	0	32	0
	C	0	0	32	0
AB	A	0	32	0	0
	B	30	2	0	0
	C	19	13	0	0
BC	A	0	12	20	0
	B	0	1	31	0
	C	1	31	0	0
AC	A	0	15	17	0
	B	5	21	6	0
	C	17	15	0	0

essay which has characteristics of both Course A and Course B, very nearly flip a coin. This confirms the course-taught-expertise theory, for since Course C raters had not taught Course A or Course B, they did not have expert vision when making their decisions.

When given a BC split, the same phenomenon occurs. The raters from all three courses always reject the students. Course B raters always give a C because that is the only alternative for a student who isn't B but is higher. (They could have given a D, but the students apparently didn't have the right characteristics for exemption, or the raters were being conservative. Whatever the reason, none of the raters gave these students a D rating.) The Course C raters always rejected, and since the student were not at the C level, they would have to be either A or B. B is the more probable choice (R1 had already determined that) and thus the Course C raters produced a B rating in all but one case. The Course A raters rejected the students, and thus had to select between B and C as ratings. They favored the C rating, giving this rating in twenty of the thirty-two cases (62.50%). Thus, the data from the BC split are almost exactly the same as the data from the AB split. This confirms that the original split decision was probably well deserved.

The one macro-split tested in this study, AC split, the split that provoked this experiment, provides a somewhat different picture. The most notable difference is that it elicited every possible combination of votes (assuming D was not a possibility).

The AC split data, like the AB and BC split data, reveal that Course A and Course C raters never accepted a student. However, these raters had equal dispersion in their decisions. The Course A raters gave 15 Bs and 17 Cs; the Course C raters gave 17 As and 15 Bs. If Courses A, B, and C really were un-ordered, one might expect the AC split data to look like the AB and BC split data, but it did not. The AB students and the BS students were "rejected" by all three rater groups. In contrast, in nearly two-thirds of the cases, the Course B raters *accepted* these students. What is clear about the AC students is that they are neither A nor C. Not once did a Course A or Course C rater accept an AC student. One might suspect that the AC students were really BB students who had been misclassified by the R1 raters. However, this does not appear to be the case. Table 1 shows that although Course B raters accepted AC students in nearly two-thirds of the cases, they accepted BB students in all cases. Further, Table 1 also shows that although Course A and Course C raters classified AC students as B in 30 out of 64 cases, they classified BB students as B in 55 out of 64 cases. Thus, although the AC students resemble the BB students more than they resemble any other group, they do not appear to be fully typical of that group. To confirm this observation, I had an additional rater-set, composed of two Course B raters, rate the eight A-C essays. These raters rated B in 10 out of 16 cases, or just under two-thirds of the time, confirming the earlier observation.

Perhaps the most compelling result in this study is the exceptionally high "accept/reject" agreement (99%) among the raters with common RCTs (see Table 2). This led me to reconsider the standard method used for placement rating. The standard method specifies that the essays be randomly assigned to raters, regardless of the course they have most recently taught or ever taught, and that those raters place students into the appropriate course (i.e., make full-scale decisions). The new method I devised specified that raters determine only whether a student should be accepted into or rejected from the course they have most recently taught. The new method relies, therefore, on the "expert" opinion of each rater, that rater's expertise having been gained by teaching the students. Furthermore, the method does not require raters to make judgements based on the full scale, a scale which includes courses they have not taught. They are only concerned with "accepting" into their course or "rejecting" from it.

The "expert" rating model predicts that acceptance implies rejection, i.e., that acceptance into course X by a rater whose RCT is course X implies rejection from course Z by a rater whose RCT is Z. To test this assumption, I selected twelve essays which had been accepted by raters in each of the three courses, Courses A, B and C, and had those essays re-rated by raters from the other courses. Not one of the 36 essays was accepted. Thus, I could conclude that the raters were highly reliable. They knew whether an essay fit into their course, and, as these data show, they knew when it didn't.

However, the expert model does not predict that rejection implies acceptance, for it is possible that a student doesn't belong in any extant course. To test this aspect of the model, I selected 63 essays which had been rejected by raters of contiguous courses and had them rated by two other raters of those courses. Of these, only one was accepted by another rater. Thus, out of 126 ratings, there was a 99.2% agreement rate. One essay, an essay which a Course B rater had rejected-high and a Course C rater had rejected-low (thus, by inference, that student could not belong in A or D), was put through 13 iterations. That is, it was read by 13 Course B raters and by 13 Course C raters. That essay was never accepted. Although they never agreed on the final placement (and thus would seem unreliable using standard reliability measures), in fact, they always agreed and were perfectly reliable. We just don't have a placement slot for such students; they are reliably between scale points.

Thus, it appears to me that our standard methods of examining reliability—of determining reliability by asking how often raters agree on a scale-point—misses the point. The scales we use are made up by us. In the case of placement, the scale is often determined by the number of course placements. In other types of testing, that scale, whether it has 4 or 12 points, is still concocted by us. To assume that there are only 4 or 12 categories of students or texts seems untenable. Some students (or essays), regardless of the number of points on the scale, will not fit neatly into that scale.

Conclusions and Implications

The results from this study, especially when combined with the results from the previous study, permit two conclusions. First, the method we use to determine reliability is inappropriate, certainly in placement testing and probably in all direct assessment ("holistic") testing. To assume that only agreement (giving the same score) between raters indicates reliability does not take into account either the artificial nature of the scales we use or that good raters can legitimately disagree. Second, the role of expertise—in the case of placement testing, course-taught expertise—has not been adequately utilized. Raters can, with high reliability, determine who belongs in their courses and

Table 2

Acceptance and Rejection from Rater's Own Course:
A Comparison of RS1 Raters and RS2 Raters

		RS2 RCT = A	
		Accept	Reject
RS1 RCT = A	Accept	32	0
	Reject	0	64
		RS2 RCT = B	
		Accept	Reject
RS1 RCT = B	Accept	32	0
	Reject	2	62
		RS2 RCT = C	
		Accept	Reject
RS1 RCT =C	Accept	32	0
	Reject	0	64
		RS2 ALL	
		Accept	Reject
RS1ALL	Accept	96	0
	Reject	2	190

who does not belong (i.e., "accept" and "reject"), but they do not appear to be as reliable when making decisions about who belongs in other courses.

The results from the studies have three immediate implications. The first is that what might be considered a lack of rater reliability may, in reality, be high reliability. We simply use the wrong approach when determining reliability and thus assume that the raters are not reliable. This research implies that disagreement among raters, which is normal, is not something which must be avoided if we are to be credible. However, this research doesn't tell us whether this is true in all types of direct assessment. I would not generalize to non-local placement testing because that constituency is much broader and the scale points cannot be defined in terms of specific courses. Furthermore, the raters involved in such testing probably do not have the same sense of the immediate impact their decisions will have on students. Thus, when an essay is problematic, these raters would not be swayed toward a particular decision just because, for instance, they think that, when in doubt, it is better to require one course than to exempt from all courses.

The second implication concerns local placement and exit-exam testing where the scale points refer to courses and, thus, there can be no between-point placement. If a student fits into neither course, some additional measure (e.g., a second piece of writing, a portfolio, or an indirect measure of writing ability) may be necessary because split-resolving seems to be problematic. Additional research on these students is necessary, examining both their performance in the course and the teachers' perceptions of the adequacy of the placement (See Smith, forthcoming, for some preliminary evidence about teacher perception).

In particular, two lines of research seem appropriate. The macro-split texts contain symptoms of quite diverse needs and abilities, and the split-resolvers (who consistently place such students in the course between the primary ratings) seem to sense this dissonance and resolve it by a default to the middle. Since it appears the Rater-Set method allows us to locate such students, it is possible to track these students to determine how they perform and the degree to which the "default to the middle" puts them "at risk". These essays could also be analyzed to determine whether there are common causes for the diverse ratings. If such causes are found, they might provide insights into how raters read. Furthermore, the essays could be rewritten (much like Freedman, 1979, rewrote essays) and re-rated to determine whether, and how, particular changes evoke different ratings.

The third implication concerns the use of split-resolvers. Since split-resolution by a third rater can be problematic, it might be worthwhile to investigate the use of rater-conferencing to come to agreement. For local placement testing, the key issues would be whether conferencing requires significantly more time (cost being the underlying issue) and whether the conference method produces better results. Determining the latter would require several years of research, for students would have to be tracked at least through the sequence of composition courses.

There is another implication which concerns the courses offered to meet the needs of the population. By using the rater-set method for determining reliability, one gains considerable new information about the fit of the curriculum to the students. If, for instance, a large number of the students are reliably "between courses", then there is clear justification for either creating new courses to fit those students' needs or revamping existing courses. This method seems more useful for department heads or writing program administrators who want to make an empirically motivated claim for altering the courses or the structure of the sequence of courses, or for adding or deleting courses.

The results may also have implications for a commonly used scaling method in all types of direct assessment where essays are rated by two raters on a 1 to N scale, but the ratings are summed so that the scale is actually 2 to 2N. One consequence of this method is that essays which have quite different ratings become the same when summed. For example, an essay given ratings of 2 and 4 would be considered the same as an essay given ratings of 3 and 3. The raters in this research denied this equation.

At one level, this research shows that highly trained, well qualified raters can disagree reliably. That, in itself, is of considerable importance. At another level, this research indicates how little we know about placement testing (and about how much we are willing to believe without hard evidence), about the way readers make decisions about students (not about texts, but about the writers of those texts), about the fit between our testing procedures and the courses into which we place students, and about our methods for evaluating how well our courses match and meet the needs of the populations we serve. Clearly, we need to know much more about the effects of placement, especially about the students who receive micro- and macro-split votes, before we can make any legitimate public statements about the reliability or validity of our placement testing.

While the expert-rater method may not transfer to all testing situations, the theory behind it should. Basically, that theory has three points:
1) Rating scales are limited and, thus, not all essays or writers can fit neatly into them. There are bound to be essays which fall between the scale

points. I call this the "space-between points" hypothesis. This, by necessity, leads to lower inter-rater reliability, unless the raters have a protocol which tells them what to do with those essays (e.g., when in doubt, select the higher rating). But that seems like artificial reliability.

2) The more points on the rating scale, the more likely that the essays will fit within a point. Conversely, if a scale has only two points (e.g., pass/fail), it is also likely that most of the essays will fit within a point. The problem, therefore, is determining the number of points. This decision cannot be just statistically motivated, especially when the decision has a direct impact on the writer. And this leads to the third point.

3) The greater the number of scale-points, the greater the difficulty for the raters, and the greater the number of scale-points, the greater the likelihood of error and low inter-rater reliability. It is very difficult to keep 6 scale points in mind while reading. But it's much easier to keep just one in mind, especially when one has expertise on that point. Thus, it is possible that we could increase the reliability and the validity of our rating by revising the standard rating method so that each rater is responsible for only one scale point.

Models of Scales and Decision-Making

The two types of holistic assessment discussed in the introduction, the No-Direct-Impact on writers (NDI) and the Direct-Impact on writers (DI), share an important feature: For both types, the raters create their range for each scale-point (i.e., the range of essays which would fall within a scale point) on the basis of their experience with a set of essays. For NDI raters, the data-base would be the calibration essays (the "range-finders"). For the DI raters, the data-base would be the essays/students the teacher/rater has encountered in her course.

The theory underlying NDI testing is that the scale-points are contiguous, that the scale is either interval or ordinal, and that all raters have the same scale-point ranges. (This theory also seems prevalent in DI ratings.) Schematically, this theory looks like this:

Rater 1	Scale-point A	Scale-point B	Scale-point C	Scale-point D
Rater 2	Scale-point A	Scale-point B	Scale-point C	Scale-point D

If this were the case, then there would be no disagreements. Every essay would have to fall within a scale-point and every rater would make the same decision. But disagreements do exist. I have not seen one piece of research

303

where rater agreement was perfect. Thus, it must be the case that either the raters do not have exactly the same scale-point ranges or that the scale-points are not contiguous and the distance between the scale-points is not known.

Contiguous	Scale-point A	Scale-point B	Scale-point C	Scale-point D

Non-Contiguous	Scale-point A	Scale-point B	Scale-point C	Scale-point D

The "between points" would be the grey areas in which raters are pressed to make a fuzzy decision. And it would be the essays in these grey areas that would produce low intra-rater reliability.

It seems reasonable to assume that neither any group of NDI raters nor any group of DI raters would have exactly the same ranges. Thus, two raters, of either type, might have scale-point ranges which look this:

Rater 1	Scale-point A	Scale-point B	Scale-point C	Scale-point D

Rater 2	Scale-point A	Scale-point B	Scale-point C	Scale-point D

Consequently, given five essays (E1 through E5) near scale-point B on the continuum, the two raters would agree on only three, E1 (both would say "A"), E3 (both would say "B"), and E5 (both would say "C").

```
          E1   E2   E3   E4   E5
           |    |    |    |    |
```

Rater 1	Scale-point A	Scale-point B	Scale-point C	Scale-point D

Rater 2	Scale-point A	Scale-point B	Scale-point C	Scale-point D

However, on E2, Rater 1 would say "B" whereas Rater 2 would say "A", and on E4, Rater 1 would say "C" whereas Rater 2 would say "B". And this is for only one scale-point. The number of disagreements would be compounded by the number of scale-points.

The problem is compounded when the raters' scale-point ranges are non-contiguous and are of different sizes. In the example below, only E3 would produce two B ratings. For Rater 1, E1 and E5 would be clear decisions (A and C), but for Rater 2, those essays would require fuzzy decisions. Conversely, for Rater 2, E2 and E6 are clear decisions, but they are fuzzy for Rater 1. E4 requires a fuzzy decision by both raters. Thus, for these six essays, agreement could range from 17% (agree on one essay) to 100% (agree on all six). Clearly, the problem of inter-rater reliability is compounded when the raters' scale-point ranges are both non-contiguous and of different sizes.

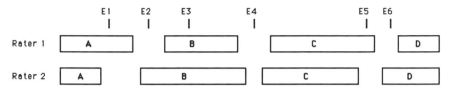

In all of these models, there is an assumption that the scale points are ordinal. If we alter that assumption, the models change. All assessment is based on someone making a decision about "where to place" (or "what grade to give"). The decision is proscribed by the scale (e.g., A to F grades) as well as the assumption that the scale is linear, ordinal, or nominal. There are also assumptions about the discreteness of the scale points (whether the boundaries are sharp or fuzzy).

Schematically, the three courses in Pitt's composition program (A, B, and C) can be portrayed as follows, assuming that they are not ordinal.

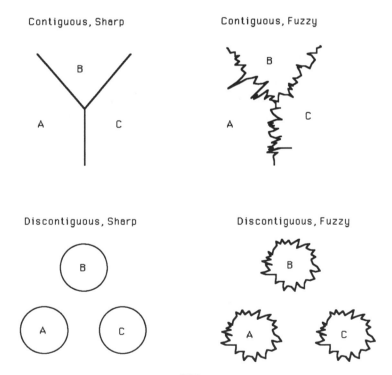

These four models can be tested using the placement data. The Non-Contiguous, Sharp model accounts for all of the non-split data and for the micro splits. The AB and BC splits would be as shown below.

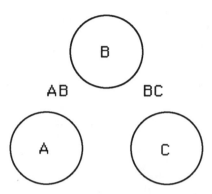

However, the macro-split (AC) data does not fit this model, for while those essays were always rejected by both Course A and Course C raters, they were often accepted by Course B raters. In effect, the Course A and C raters said "Definitely not in my course" while the Course B raters said "Maybe in my course."

If the model is revised to accommodate the sharp and fuzzy boundaries, all of the data fit, and the resulting diagram (below) becomes more ordinal, thus closer to what we assume about our students and our courses, i.e., that Course A students are less well prepared than Course B students, who are less well prepared than Course C students.

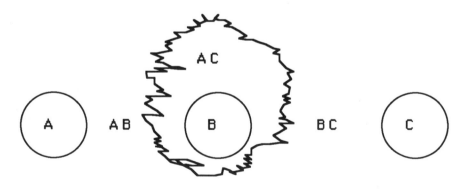

A Decision Model

If the data concerning the decisions raters made are combined with the TAP data, a process decision model emerges.

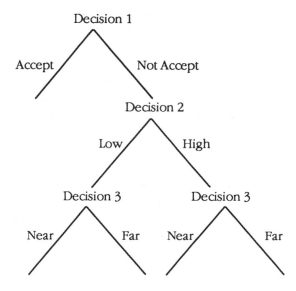

The TAP data showed that the first decision was whether or not to "accept" the student into the rater's own course. If "not" accept", the second decision was "High" or "Low" and the third was "how high or low". The data from the research shows that the raters have 100% accuracy on both Decision 1 and Decision 2, but they become "fuzzy" on Decision 3. They can't always tell "near" from "far".

The fuzziness of the near-far decision, in our placement system, can be partially explained by the course-taught expertise of the raters. Those Course C raters who have not taught Courses A and B would not have the privileged knowledge needed for making the distinction between A and B, except, perhaps, when it is a very clear call , i.e., the student is prototypic of the course. The Course A raters have taught Courses B and C, but not recently. Thus, they must rely on remote memory of those students. Even the Course B raters, whose only near-far decision would be Course C/Exempt, had trouble making that distinction.

This explanation, of course, begs a question: How do raters who are teaching two of the courses respond? Our composition program, in nearly all cases, prevents studying this question because our policy is to have teachers teach only one course, i.e., to have only one preparation. Thus, this research must be done elsewhere.

The decision-making model was based, in part, on the TAP data on our raters. I know of no similar data on placement raters at other universities, but if we assume that placement raters at other universities have taught the relevant courses, those raters would provide the best test of the tree, especially if they are required to make full-scale placement decisions. If their tree is similar, then their decisions become fuzzier as they move away from their most recent course(s) taught.

In large scale, no-direct impact assessments, where the raters are "calibrated" to all scale points and must make full-scale decisions, the assumption is that the raters are equally adept (expert) in making decisions on all scale points. Here again, there is no research to provide information concerning this assumption, but it does seem possible that when given more than five scale points, raters might not be "equally adept", for memory limitations might make decisions fuzzy (cf Miller's (1956) 7±2 hypothesis). It is also possible that raters who do not have the analog to course taught expertise might be most adept in making decisions on one scale point and, thus, become fuzzier at distant points. Testing this hypothesis would not be difficult, and it might help explain the disagreements which are common in all testing.

The Expert Model

The advantage of the expert rater method, where raters only "accept" or "reject" (or "reject high" and "reject low") is that disagreement is altered because agreement is not basesded on whether the raters agree on specific courses. Thus, the problem of "between-points" disappears. Furthermore, the data indicate that the scale points surrounding the "accept" space are sharp. For example, for "A", "B", "C", and "D" raters, the spaces would look like this:

Expert on "A"	Accept	Reject-High	
Expert on "B"	Reject-Low	Accept	Reject-High
Expert on "C"	Reject-Low		Accept	Reject-High
Expert on "D"	Reject-Low			Accept

However, the problem of raters not having the same ranges within their "accept" space still exists. As the figure below illustrates, even if two "B" raters did not have the same exact scale-point ranges, the potential for agreement is increased. (The black areas indicate areas of agreement; the cross-hashed areas indicate areas of disagreement.) But even the areas of disagreement between two raters with the same RCT can be resolved by agreement because the expert-rater model specifies that any essay Rejected-Low must be read by a rater whose RCT is that "lower" area and any essay Rejected-High must be read by a rater whose RCT is that "higher" area. Thus, an essay which Rater 1 had Accepted and Rater 2 had Rejected-Low would be then read by a Course A rater. It is highly probable that this rater would Reject-High, for in order to Accept that rater would have to have a very high top end on her range, an unlikely possibility. Thus, even in cases where there is disagreement between two raters with the same RCT, there will be appropriate final resolution.

Rater 1	Reject-Low	Accept	Reject-High

Rater 2	Reject-Low	Accept	Reject-High

Since the data from the second study showed that raters had the greatest trouble when the student was not from the raters' own course or from a contiguous course, the expert method radically alters the number of times the raters agreed with the R1 raters and with the other R2 raters. For the non-split essays, there was total agreement. On the essays rated AA by R1 (that is, "accept-accept" by the R1 Course A raters), the R2 Course A raters also always accepted them and the Course B and Course C raters always rejected them. (Compare to Course B raters: 32 A ratings; Course C raters: 25 A and 7 B ratings.) On the essays rated BB by the R1 Course B raters (i.e, "accept-accept"), the R2 Course A raters always rejected-high, the Course B raters always accepted, and the Course C raters always rejected-low. (Compare to Course A raters: 25 B and 7 C ratings; Course B raters: 32 B ratings; Course C raters: 2 A ratings and 30 B ratings.) On the essays rated CC by R1 Course C raters ("accept-accept"), The R1 Course A and B raters always rejected-high, and the Course C raters always accepted. (Compare to Course A raters: 3 B, 24 C, and 5 D ratings; Course B raters: 32 C ratings; Course C: 32 C ratings.)

309

The splits provide even stronger evidence. On the essays rated AB by R1 (i.e., "reject low" by the Course B rater and "reject-high" by the Course A rater), Course A R2 raters always rejected-high, and Course C raters always rejected-low. All but two of the Course B raters also rejected-low (two accepted). Thus, there was 97.9% agreement. (Compare to Course A raters: 32 B ratings; Course B raters: 30 A and 2 B ratings; Course C raters: 19 A and 13 B ratings.) On the essays rated BC by R1 ("reject-low" by Course C raters and "reject-high" by Course B raters), Course A and Course B raters in R2 always rejected-high, and the Course C raters always rejected-low. Thus, there was 100% agreement. (Compare to Course A raters: 12 B ratings and 20 C ratings; Course B raters: 32 C ratings; Course C raters: 1 A and 31 B ratings.) On the essays rated AC by R1 ("reject-low" by Course C raters; "reject-high" by Course A raters), Course C raters in R2 always rejected-low and the Course A raters always rejected-high. The Course B raters spread their ratings over all three categories, but most (65.6%) returned a B rating. (Compare to Course A raters: 15 B and 17 C ratings; Course B raters: 5 A and 21 B, and 6 C ratings; Course C raters: 17 A and 15 B ratings.)

Thus, what would be considerable disagreement if the raters had to determine which course the students belonged in became very high agreement when the raters made only the "Accept-Reject" decision.

The "space-between" hypothesis is testable, and it may even be possible to measure the space. For example, if no essay is ever rejected-low by a "B" rater and also never rejected-high by an "A" rater, then there would be no space between scale-points A and B. But if some essays are rejected-low and rejected-high, then that space would exist, and the space size could be calculated.

The data from the two experiments clearly shows that such space exists. If that space is real, i.e., if it is not just caused by raters' having different scale-point ranges, then other measures, such as final grades, should corroborate it. We have found that the final grades of students who are "B/C" (in the space between Course B and Course C) are different from those who are either "B/B" or "C/C". Since we have no "B/C" course, all such students must be placed into either Course B and Course C. If placed into Course B, they received higher grades than the B/B students, and if placed into Course C, they received lower grades than the C/C students.

Obviously, my research on expert placement method is not sufficient to draw firm conclusions. It has to be tested at other institutions to determine whether the results are just an artifact of the training and courses at Pitt. And we need to test the method in other types of testing. We need to know, for instance, whether this method is too expensive to be feasible. My data shows that it actually is cheaper because the raters can work at higher speeds. The method has cut rating time by about thirty to forty percent, but this may be an artifact of the training (seminars and teaching the courses) of our raters. We also need to know the optimal number of scale points a reader can handle. I have seen no research on that.

The "comfort" raters feel in their decisions is also an issue that has not been addressed. Anyone who has done holistic rating has had the feeling of being under the gun to conform to the group, has had to make "coin flip" decisions (raters often put a "+" or "-" next to such decisions), and, in the case of placement testing, has worried about the effect of the decision on the student. It stands to reason that when raters are comfortable, they will perform better, more efficiently and more effectively. Although I have no large data set on rater comfort, my conversations with raters who have worked with both our old and new methods indicate that they much prefer the new. They have stated that 1) they felt less pressure when rejecting because they knew that other raters, with different course expertise, would read the essay, 2) they felt they were making more defensible decisions, and 3) they had greater freedom in the way they read the essays. This diversity in the way of reading is confirmed by the TAP data. When raters made an initial, tentative decision to accept (i.e., to place into their course), their subsequent way of reading varied more than when the initial decision was to reject. They were more likely to skip to the last paragraph or sample-read through the essay. When the initial decision was to reject, they usually read the essay linearly.

A Potential Problem with the Expert Model

Since my experience with raters suggests that "having taught" training is more powerful than "calibration" training (the TAP data most clearly showed this), the potential problem is that there could be a shift in the "having taught" training because we place the between-course student (I call them Tweeners) in the higher course. Thus, the teachers of the higher course might develop a "lower threshold" for decision making. In effect, we would have a shift in the scale point range. Students who are currently rejected because they are Tweeners would be accepted into the higher course and a new set of Tweeners would evolve. It will take several years of research to determine whether this problem exists, but it can be done.

For the past several years, I have included previously rated essays (from previous years and for previous rating sessions within the year) in the stacks of essays the raters read. The data have shown that, using the old placement procedure—where the raters were required to make a four-way decision— a very small percentage of the non-split essays (i.e., the two primary raters agreed) were placed into a different course on that second reading, but a somewhat larger percentage of the split-vote essays were placed differently. However, I have no idea whether these "good reliability" results were facts or artifacts. Given what I found in the two studies, the raters during the second year/session may have just repeated the errors made the previous year/ session. Thus, my conclusion back then, that "between year/session" reliability was adequate, may be quite inappropriate or even dead wrong. This is, of course, extremely important, for placement must not depend on the session or year. I have always assumed that if the reliability were high, I could claim that our placement procedure is valid. Yet if that reliability is just a compounded error—an error which may be caused by the methods used to determine who rates each essay and to determine the kinds of decisions raters may make— then validity cannot exist.

References

Alexander, J. & Swartz, F. (1982). The dynamics of computer assisted writing sample measurements at Ferris State College. Paper presented at the annual meeting of the Michigan Council of Teachers of English, East Lansing, MI, October 29-31. (ERIC Document Reproduction Services No. ED 233 344).Bartholomae, D. (1983). Writing assignments: where writing begins. In P.L. Stock (Ed), *Fforum: Essays on Theory and Practice in the Teaching of Writing*, Upper Montclair, NJ: Boynton/Cook, Pp. 300-312.

Bartholomae, D. & Petrosky, A. (1987). *Ways of Reading: An Anthology for Writers*. New York: Bedford/St. Martin's Press.

Cohen, A. M. (1973). Assessing college students' ability to write compositions, *Research in the Teaching of English*, 7, 356-371.

Coles, W. E., Jr. (1981). *Composing II: Writing as a Self-Creating Process*. Rochelle Park, NJ: Hayden Book Company.

Cooper, C. R. (1977). Holistic evaluation in writing. In Cooper & Odell (Eds), *Evaluating Writing: Describing, Measuring, Judging*. Urbana: National Council of Teachers of English.

Follman, J. C. & .Anderson, J.A. (1967). An investigation of the reliability of five procedures for grading english themes, *Research in the Teaching of English*, 1, 190-200.

Freedman, S. W. (1979). How characteristics of student essays influence teachers' evaluation, *Journal of Educational Psychology*, 71, 328-338.

Hillocks, G. (1986). *Research on Written Composition*. Urbana: ERIC Clearinghouse on Reading and Communication Skills.

Hughes, D. C., Kelling, B., & Tuck, B.F. (1980). Essay marking and the context problems. *Educational Research*, 22, 147-148.

Miller, G. A. (1956). The magic number seven, plus or minus two. *Psychological Review, 69*, 81-97.

Myers, M. (1980) A Procedure for Writing Assessment and Holistic Scoring. Urbana: National Council of Teachers of English.

Smith, L. S., Winters, L., Quellmalz, E. S., & Baker, E. L. (1980). Characteristics of student writing competence: an investigation of alternative scoring systems. (Research Report No. 134). Los Angeles: Center for the Study of Evaluation. (ERIC Document Reproduction Services No. ED 217 074).

Smith, W. L. (forthcoming). Determining the adequacy of using holistically rated essays as a writing course placement technique: a case study. In M. Williamson (Ed), *Advances in Writing Research, Vol 4: Holistic Scoring: New Theoretical Foundations and Validation Research*. Ablex.

Smith, W. L., Hull, G. A., Land, R. E., Moore, M. T., Ball, C., Dunham, D. E., Hickey, L. S., & Ruzich, C. W. (1985). Some effects of varying the structure of a topic on college students' writing. *Written Communication, 2,* 73-89.

White, E. M. (1975-81). *Comparison and Contrast: The California State University and College Freshman English Equivalency Examination*. Long Beach: English Council of the California State Universities & Colleges. (ERIC Document Reproduction Services No. ED 227 510).

White, E. M. (1985). *Teaching and Assessing Writing*. San Francisco: Jossey Bass.

Author's Comment—William L. Smith

All composition teachers and researchers constantly confront two problems: Our willingness to believe our lore rather than to seriously question it, and our tendency to adopt rather than adapt methods and premises from other disciplines. These two problems have plagued me for many years.

When I became the Director of Testing for the University of Pittsburgh's Composition Program, I inherited a method for placing students. That method was a standard method, one used in many universities. It seemed to work, so there had been no impetus to examine it, let alone change it. The incoming students were placed into our courses efficiently and with what appeared to be a tolerable numbers of errors. Perhaps this alone explains that there is almost no literature on placement testing.

But something about the system nagged the backburners of my brain. So, I began what has become a long series of research projects, most focusing on why students are misplaced, then later on how they are placed, that is, on how raters make decisions. My article in this chapter presents a small series of studies, but these studies are the culmination of many previous studies, the product of years of wandering down blind alleys as well as into light.

In order to understand how I came to the present research (or, as a dear colleague said, how I came to the painfully obvious), let me trace some history.

If error exists in placement, that error must be caused by something or a combination of somethings. The most obvious choices are 1) the writing prompts, 2) the conditions under which students write, 3) the writers not writing essays which adequately represent them, 4) the raters not making good decisions, 5) an inadequate rating scale, and 6) me. I include "me" because I make decisions such as whom to hire as raters, because I design the rating procedure, and because I design the studies and analyze the data.

Our first study focused on the writing prompts. We found that, given what we teach in our composition courses, those prompts were the most effective, so the prompts, by themselves weren't the cause of errors.

The second study looked at the conditions, e.g., whether writing the essay in a large group produced different results than writing in a small group, whether the two-hour time limit was a factor, whether "warm-up" exercises

314

alter students' writing, and whether a difference resulted when there was a real teacher in the room—one who made preliminary comments about how we teach, how we read, and what we expect. The results showed that group size and time were not factors, and "warm-ups" and teacher presence made only slight differences—primarily with students who are weaker writers. But the differences were not consistently positive. Thus, the conditions might be a factor, but not a very powerful one.

The research on the writers indicated that they were a factor, but not one that I could control. For example, we found that some writers, especially males, were often distracted. For many, the trip to campus to take the placement tests (in math, foreign language, and composition) and to sit through "orientation" sessions was the first trip to our campus. Thus, encountering the new setting and new people was a distraction. More than one student has come to the composition test quite drunk—they had discovered that beer is readily available and their parents and high school peers were no longer restraining forces.

The "error rate" in placement has always been measured by the number of students we move to new courses during the first week of class. (This is the case at most universities.) During that first week, the instructors in all composition courses have their students write an essay which is read as a check on placement. If a teacher thinks a student is clearly misplaced, the essay is read by senior faculty and we make any appropriate adjustments. Of course, this double check itself introduces more than one variable. Students who don't like where they are placed may try harder on the first-week essay, but students who like their placement may not. Teachers may not identify many students as potential misplacements because they don't want to have many students transferring out because that would mean others would be transferred in— and that creates extra work. Furthermore, a few students don't even bother to attend the first few classes. I presume they are extending their vacations. Thus, the first-week essay provides only marginal evidence about how many students we misplace. I have long suspected that this measure seriously under-estimates the error rate.

Because I didn't, and still don't, trust this measure of error, I had to find a different measure. That research cost me three years, but I found that—to no teacher's surprise—the best measure is the teacher's perception of the goodness of placement. However, we also found that this perception must be obtained within a rather narrow band of time. If the teacher is asked too early (before the third week of class), she doesn't have sufficient evidence to make the decision. If she is asked too late (after mid-term), the response correlates

315

almost exactly with the final grade and, thus, is not a perception of placement. As is often the case with research, what you looked at reveals unexpected, and often more interesting information.

Since the errors in placement could not, with any consistency, be attributed to the prompts, to the conditions, or to the students, that left the raters, the scale, and me. And these are the foci of the research for this chapter.

What I really found is that the raters are extremely good, but the rating system didn't allow them to be that good. Since I chose the rating system, the problem was me because I adopted straight from the literature without questioning it. There was nothing wrong with the scale; it is dictated by our curriculum. But my ways of interpreting the rater's ratings—i.e., their use of the scale—were also adopted straight from measurement and evaluation paradigms. For example, I accepted the standard methods for "inter-rater reliability." I did not adapt them to the very special conditions of writing.

The bottom line, then, of my research up to now is quite simple. 1) Don't accept anything until you've tested it for several years, don't "believe" before testing. 2) Don't adopt methods or paradigms until they are tested in two ways. First, test them with whatever common sense you have. As a teacher, I knew that writers do not fit into a bell curve, but that is the assumption underlying some of the statistical methods I used. Second, test them with discipline-relevant assumptions and research. Rating essays is more than a bit like grading: the more evidence one has the more likely one is to make an appropriate decision. It should not shock anyone that teachers—who know the student, the human, as well as they know student's writing—do not give the same "grades" as raters who don't know the student.

And 3) I have hardly begun to tap into the more interesting problems, such as the social construction of teachers (e.g., all that affects how they teach and grade and rate essays), the cognitive process involved in making what seems to be simple decisions, or the ways we can use what we know about readers/raters to make our teaching more effective and our students better writers.

Chapter 13 Writing for Different Professional Audiences: Telling Teachers and Researchers about Text Evaluation

In this chapter, we present two articles by Sarah Warshauer Freedman on the same topic, one written for *College Composition and Communication* and the other for the *Journal of Educational Psychology*. In these articles, Freedman describes a study of factors which influence teachers' judgments of student papers. Although the two articles describe the same study and have the same general organization, they have different audiences and different purposes. The *CCC* article was written in an informal style accessible to a general audience of teachers many of whom do not read the research journals and are unfamiliar with concepts in statistics and experimental design. Its primary purpose is to convey the major conclusions of the study to teachers who might want to make use of them in the classroom. The second article was written to convince a potentially critical audience of researchers, familiar with the literature and knowledgeable about research techniques, that the conclusions of the study are valid. Unlike the *CCC* article, it is an elaborate argument for the validity of the conclusions rather than a description of an inquiry.

The differences in rhetorical stance between these two papers — describing conclusions to practitioners versus arguing for their validity to empirical researchers—are reflected in important structural differences between the papers. The differences are apparent even in the first paragraphs of the articles. The *CCC* article frames the problem to be addressed in terms of familiar teacher experiences ("We all know the student who says. . . ." p. 341). In contrast, the *JEP* article frames the central question in the context of the research literature with no reference to teacher experience ("Very little is known about the process of evaluating students' writing. Most past research. ." p. 322).

Another difference between the articles can be seen in the detail with which the data collection methods are described. In the *CCC* article, the methods are covered in six paragraphs. The same methods are described in the *JEP* in eleven paragraphs of small type together with a full-page table. Providing such extensive detail serves two important rhetorical purpose for a research-oriented audience. First, it serves a persuasive purpose. A powerful argument for a critical audience is to say, "Here is exactly what I did. If you

317

don't believe my results, go and try it yourself." In fact, studies which are not described in sufficient detail to be replicated by other researchers may not be believed. The expectations of the audience and the conventions of research reporting are so well established and so well defined that the absence of this kind of detail is likely to immediately arouse suspicions. Second, the detail may serve a clarifying purpose. For example, the *JEP* article notes, as the *CCC* article does not, that the essays used in the study were written by students from colleges which "ranged in type from highly select, private schools to open-admissions, public schools" (p. 324). Without this information, a critical reader might wonder if the essays had been collected from a special population and suspect that the results of the study might not be generalizable to other populations.

A number of differences between the articles reflect differences in the technical knowledge that the author can assume in the reader. For example, the **analysis of variance** tables that appear in the *JEP* article are omitted from the *CCC* article, and the technical term **"interaction"** is neatly sidestepped in the discussion in paragraph 12 of the *CCC* article. The discussion of **rater reliability** and **Cronbach's alpha** in paragraph 23 of the *JEP* article is replaced by the assertion in paragraph 5 of the *CCC* article that "The teachers proved to be the good judges I thought they would be" (p. 342). The discussion in the introduction of the *JEP* article contrasting the merits of **experimental** and **correlational studies** is entirely omitted from the *CCC* article.

Some of the omissions of technical materials from the *CCC* article appear to make little difference, at least to the trained researcher. A research-oriented reader of the *CCC* article could easily infer that paragraph 12 is about interactions. However, some of the omissions do have an important impact on the persuasive power of the article for such an audience. For example, by omitting the analysis of variance table, the author has removed the only source of information about the significance of the interaction terms. Critical readers of the *CCC* article would want know the significance levels of these terms before they would be convinced that they are real. Similarly, the omission of quantitative measures of reliability such as Cronbach's alpha may lead critical readers to wonder if perhaps the reliability of the quality judgments was embarrassingly low. Finally, the discussion contrasting experimental and correlational studies in the *JEP* article points out that since the study being described is experimental, it therefore provides much more convincing evidence about causal relations than do previous studies which were primarily correlational. Because this discussion is omitted in the *CCC* article, the reader

318

may fail to appreciate the persuasive power of this study compared to previous ones.

The final difference to which we will call the reader's attention is the use of **hedging**, that is, pointing out the limitations of one's own study. For example, in paragraph 37 of the *JEP* article, Freedman hedges when she says that "One limitation of this study is the difficulty in interpreting the exact results of rewriting," and again in the following paragraph when she says, "A second limitation is the homogeneity of the raters in this study." She does not hedge in the *CCC* article. Hedging is an important way for researchers to create and maintain ethos, that is, their credibility in the minds of their readers. Researchers who admit the weaknesses of their own studies, who do not try to claim more than the evidence will support, are more likely to be seen as honest and careful and are, thus, more likely to be persuasive.

We want to emphasize that we are not criticizing either of these articles at the expense of the other. We think that they are both well done, each serving a different purpose. The *CCC* article is readily accessible and well adapted to its audience, many of whom are unlikely to have read the *JEP* article. The *JEP* article is much less accessible, but it has special features which are critically important for convincing an audience of researchers. These special features are closely tied to the developing rhetorical tradition in literacy studies.

Notes on Technical Issues

Three statistical procedures mentioned in Freedman's *JEP* article occur so often in the literature that they should be noted here. The first is **Cronbach's alpha**, which Freedman uses to measure the reliability of the ratings of groups of judges. The reader can think of this measure as a kind of average correlation among the judges' ratings. In measuring the reliability of ratings, a correlation among judges of .70 or better is considered desirable.

The second statistical procedure Freedman uses is **analysis of variance**. Extended discussions of analysis of variance may be found in several of the introductions to research and statistics listed in the "Reference" section of this book. The following discussion is intended simply as emergency aid which the reader can use until more substantial help arrives. The purpose of analysis of variance is to help in drawing conclusions in situations such as this: Suppose that you have conducted a study on the vocabulary size of ninth through twelfth grade male and female students. A vocabulary test was given to 20 students in each grade, 10 males and 10 females. The average results are shown here:

Score on Vocabulary Test

		Grade			Row Average
	9	10	11	12	
Male	22.7	30.8	33.1	40.6	31.8
Female	27.1	30.4	37.3	45.2	35.0
Column Average	24.9	30.6	35.2	42.9	33.4

Analysis of variance can provide help with three questions in this situation: First, "Over all, is gender related to vocabulary scores?" or, in other words, "Are the row averages for males and females significantly different from each other?" If the analysis of variance shows a significant difference, then we would conclude that on average, in the populations sampled, females had larger vocabularies than males. Such a difference is called a **main effect**—in this case, a main effect for gender.

The second question: "Over all, is grade level related to vocabulary scores?" or in other words, "Are there significant differences among the column **averages**?" If analysis of variance shows a significant difference, then we can conclude that there are significant differences among the column **means**, i.e., that there is a main effect for grade. However, we could not specify which of the particular differences among grades was significant. Although we could be confident that the vocabularies of ninth and twelfth graders were significantly different (since they showed the largest mean difference), we could not be sure whether or not any of the other differences (e.g., ninth vs. tenth graders) was significant. Deciding which of these differences was significant is a job for post hoc tests, which will be discussed in a later chapter.

The first two questions concerned main effects. The third question has to do with what are called **interactions**. Two variables are said to interact if the effect that one of them has on the dependent variable depends on the value of the other. For example, if girls had bigger vocabularies in the early grades but not in the later grades, then we would say that there was an interaction between gender and grade level.

Freedman used analysis of variance to assess the impact of four independent variables (content, organization, sentence structure, and mechanics) on the dependent variable (essay quality). Table 2 of the Freedman *JEP* article shows the results of this analysis. The top four rows of the table are for main effects. These are labeled by the name of the variable, e.g., "content" in the left-hand column. The lower rows are for interactions which are labeled by

320

the initials of the variables connected by "x". For example, "CxSS" represents the interaction of content (C) and sentence structure (SS). The right-hand column, labeled "F", specifies values of the **F-statistic**. In general, large values of F correspond to significant effects of the independent variable on the dependent variable. In this article, the significance levels are indicated by asterisks in the right-hand column. Thus, the main effects for content and organization are significant at the .001 level, the main effect for mechanics is significant at the .01 level, and the interaction between organization and mechanics (OxM) is significant at the .001 level. (In some articles, significance levels are indicated in a final column labeled "p".)

The third statistical procedure Freedman uses is **chi-square**, which measures the strength of relation between pairs of variables. To illustrate how this works, imagine a survey in which 50 men and 50 women have been asked two questions: "Do you enjoy broccoli?" and "Do you enjoy a good cry?" The results of the survey are shown below:

	"Do you enjoy broccoli?"			"Do you enjoy a good cry?"	
	Yes	No		Yes	No
Male	30	20		5	45
Female	30	20		45	5

Clearly, answers to the first question are not related to gender, but answers to the second question are. The proportion of "Yes" and "No" answers to this question are very different for males and females. The chi-square statistic is sensitive to these differences in proportion. As the difference in proportion increases, so does the value of chi-square. The bigger the difference in proportion, the bigger chi-square will be. For 2x2 tables such as this one, chi-square values of four or more are significant at the .05 level. The value of chi-square for the first question is much smaller than four and for the second question, much larger. Freedman used the chi-square statistic to evaluate the significance of the relations shown in Table 7 of her *JEP* article.

Sarah Warshauer Freedman
San Francisco State University

How Characteristics of Student Essays
Influence Teachers' Evaluations

This article explores the question of why competent evaluators award the ratings they do to college students' expository essays. Essays were rewritten to be stronger or weaker in four categories: content, organization, sentence structure, and mechanics. Twelve evaluators first used a 4-point holistic rating scale to judge the essays' quality. Then they rated whether each of the four rewriting categories in each rewritten essay was strong or weak (perceptions). Analyses of variance revealed content and organization to affect ratings most ($p < .001$). Mechanics and sentence structure had smaller effects, which differed when measured by the actual rewriting versus by the perceptions. Mechanics and sentence structure were significant in their interaction with organization ($p < .001$ and $p < .01$, respectively).

Very little is known about the process of evaluating students' writing. Most past research on composition evaluation has been correlational rather than experimental. In the usual correlational study in this area, students write papers and teacher-judges rate the quality of the papers. The researcher then examines the paper or the judges for traits associated with high and low ratings. One type of past correlational study (e.g., Hiller, Marcotte, & Martin, 1969; Nold & Freedman, 1977; Page, 1968; Slotnick & Knapp, 1971; Thompson, Note l) attempted to predict ratings with measures of characteristics in the student papers, such as the number of spelling errors or the length of the essay. Another type (e.g., Diederich, French, & Carlton, 1961, and Meyers, McConville, & Coffman, 1966) sought to account for ratings with characteristics of the judges, such as their personal biases or their degree of leniency. The past studies show that characteristics of papers and of judges are associated with or correlated with ratings.

One study (Harris, 1977), which was published while this study was in progress, used a quasi-experimental design to discover what qualities within student papers most influenced high school teachers' responses. Harris had teachers rank order 12 student papers that were fixed so that the rank order would come out one way if the teachers based their judgments mostly on the category, content and organization, and another way if they cared more about a second category, sentence structure and mechanics. For the most part, the papers were chosen because of their natural strengths and weaknesses, but in some cases errors were introduced into the papers. Harris found a definite but statistically insignificant tendency for teachers to give the most weight to the content and organization category when assigning the rankings. In a questionnaire, the teachers reaffirmed the priority they gave to content and organization; however, in their comments to students they paradoxically emphasized mechanics.

To determine what within the paper influences the judge, I manipulated characteristics in student essays in a more systematic and more refined way than Harris (1977) did. Hiller et al. (1969), after completing their correlational study of student essays, first articulated the general question motivating the following experiment and then called for experimental research to provide a satisfactory answer:

> If a given characteristic is present in an essay, does that characteristic affect the essay's quality as reflected in the grade assigned by expert graders? To answer this question we should have to manipulate the quality and quantity of relevant category items under an experimental procedure. (Hiller et al. 1969, p. 274)

I decided to manipulate four characteristics in essays: *content, organization, sentence structure and mechanics.* In effect, I created four categories, whereas the Harris (1977) study had two. More precise features, which fall under these still general categories, such as the number of spelling errors or length of essay, had been the focus of many of the correlational studies in the first type cited earlier. However, for this first completely experimental study, I thought it wise to manipulate general yet pedagogically interesting characteristics so that in future studies on the influence of characteristics in papers on ratings, the features of the influential general categories could be investigated.

I next rewrote essays of moderate quality to be either stronger or weaker in the four categories of content, organization, sentence structure, and mechanics. Exactly how to perform the rewriting proved to be a very complex problem, which I discuss in detail in a separate section. In almost every correlational study some aspect of content or a marker of content (e.g., essay length) predicted ratings. Based on this finding I posited one hypothesis about the effects of the rewriting: *Essays rewritten to be strong in content would be rated significantly higher than those rewritten to be weak in content.* The findings of past studies about the relationship between judges' ratings and the quality of the organization, sentence structure, and mechanics were not so consistent, making it difficult to predict the potential effect of rewriting in these three categories. Nevertheless, my experiment would allow me to determine the effects of these pedagogically interesting characteristics on ratings too.

Selection of Essays to be Rewritten

College students in two different required writing sections at each of four Bay Area colleges wrote essays for the study. According to Cass and Birnbaum's (1972) most recent descriptions of admissions criteria, the colleges ranged in type from highly select, private schools to open-admissions, public schools, providing writers representing a wide range of abilities.

Students wrote the essays in class on one of eight topics designed to elicit essays in the argumentative mode of discourse. The topics asked students either to compare and contrast two quotations or to argue their opinion on a current, controversial issue. A sample of each type of topic follows:

1. A Founding Father said: "Get what you can, and what you get hold; 'Tis the Stone that will turn all your Lead into Gold." A contemporary writer said: "If it feels good, do it." What do these two statements say? Explain how they are alike and how they are different.
2. President Ford gave Nixon an "unconditional pardon." Do you agree or disagree with Ford's decision? Give reasons for taking your position.[1]

The papers of eight students from each class, one on each of the eight topics, were used as the basis for the rewriting in this study. In all, there were eight student essays on each of eight topics, a total of 64 papers. In an earlier study, four judges had rated each essay holistically (Freedman, 1977). Of the eight student essays on each topic, the four rated to be most average in quality in the earlier study were selected for experimental rewriting in this study. The other four, which were not rewritten, were the two that had been rated highest and the two that had been rated lowest on each topic in the earlier study. These non-rewritten essays served as anchors for studying the reliability of the ratings in this study.

---

[1]Topic 1 was first developed by the California State Universities and College System for their Freshman English Equivalency Examination. Both of these topics as well as two more of the eight topics were also used in the Nold and Freedman (1977) study.

Method

Rewriting

Because of the dearth of operational definitions for strength and weakness of content, organization, sentence structure, and mechanics, I pondered, at first, how to undertake the rewriting task. Based on both a study of actual student papers and on guidelines in rhetoric texts, I decided on the set of procedures in Table 1. To validate the rewriting procedures, I trained two different students to rewrite. If the two students and I as independent rewriters produced no significantly different results in essay ratings, I then could obtain a measure of the effects of rewriting the four categories to be weak or strong on the ratings of the essays. Furthermore, the fact that it would be possible to train others to follow the rewriting procedures consistently indicates that the rewriting could be replicated.

Rewriting the content category to be weak brought one major constraint. When the content was made weak. the organization could never be made strong. It would have been an exercise in absurdity to attempt to order illogical ideas logically or to order and provide appropriate transitions for a group of inherently unrelated ideas. Thus, there were 12 possible rewriting combinations (C = content; 0 = organization; SS = sentence structure; M = mechanics; + = strong; - = weak), as follows:

1. +C, +0, +SS, +M.
2. +C, +0, +SS, -M.
3. +C, +0, -SS, +M.
4. +C, +0, -SS, -M.
5. +C, -0, +SS, +M.
6. +C, -0, +SS, -M.
7. +C, -0, -SS, +M.
8. +C, -0, -SS, -M.
9. -C, -0, +SS, +M.
10 -C, -0, +SS, -M.
11. -C, -0, -SS, +M.
12. -C, -0, -SS, -M.

As rewriters we had a commitment to create a revised paper that retained, insofar as possible, the sense of the original essay. We attempted to highlight the strengths and weaknesses in each category in each paper. Nevertheless, the act of highlighting often produced a new paper substantially unlike the original. In spite of how unlike the original rewritten version became, we

Table 1

Rewriting Rules

Strong	Weak
Content	
1. Delete all misinterpretations of quotations; add sound reinterpretations.	1. Retain all misinterpretations of quotations; add one misinterpretation if none are present.
2. Delete ideas not relevant to the topic unless they can be made relevant. If no ideas in the paper are relevant, either justify their inclusion or pull together possible relationships.	2. Retain all ideas not relevant to the topic. Do not add extra irrelevant ideas.
3. Delete repetition of entire arguments.	3. Include repetition of entire arguments. [a]
4. Take remaining ideas and: develop, resolve logical contradictions within ideas, clarify (this involves changes in word choice).	4. Take remaining ideas and: delete development, include contradictions within ideas, make ideas unclear and ambiguous (this involves changes in word choice).
Organization	
1. Paragraph appropriately.	1. Include three misparagraphings per 250 word page.
2. Order ideas logically. Respect rules of "given-new" information. Keep main ideas together.	2. Violate logical order by separating development of a main idea (three times per two pages). Violate "given-new" strategies.
3. Include appropriate inter- and intraparagraph transition: repeat key words and use transition words and phrases appropriately.	3. Delete inter-and intraparagraph transitions: vary the lexical items chosen for key words and avoid using transition words and phrases appropriately.
Sentence Structure	
1. Combine and balance sentences to achieve a mature syntactic style: reduce number of compound sentences, untangle awkward and unclear sentences, include final free modifiers and graceful parallel structures.	1. Achieve an immature syntactic style; include simple, primer sentences (include much compounding) or include long, rambling, uncontrolled, awkward sentences, delete graceful parallelism, include verboseness on the sentence level.
2. Vary sentence structure.	2. Include sentence fragments and run-together sentences.
3. Include at least one advanced punctuation mark: semicolon or colon.	3. Delete advanced punctuation marks: semicolon or colon.
4. Use appropriate tense and reference between and within sentences.	4. Use inappropriate tense and reference between and within sentences.
5. Change any misused words. Do not alter overall vocabulary level.	5. Include misused words.

326

Table 1

Rewriting Rules (Continued)

Strong	Weak
Mechanics	
1. Follow conventions of standard edited English.	1. Commas. Violate at least three of the following rules: comma before conjunction in compound sentence; comma after introductory adverbial clause; comma within quotation marks; commas between words and phrases in series.
	2. Quotation marks. Overuse and use inconsistently; use to emphasize words; forget either to open or close quotations.
	3. Possessives. Misuse 's; omit when needed; use structures like their's.
	4. Capitalization. Omit for proper names; forget to capitalize first word of sentence; add inappropriately for emphasis.
	5. Underlining. Overuse and use inappropriately for emphasis.
	6. Spelling. Include four or five errors per page.

Note: The operational definitions—the general rules followed for rewriting all four categories to be weak and strong—were adapted from descritptions on analytic rating scales (Adler, 1971; Diederich, 1974; Freedman, 1977) were based on definitions used in past correlational research on readers' responses (Thompson, 1976); and also were based on critical analyses of the strengths and weaknesses within the student papers written for this study.

aThroughout the table, "include" is used to mean retain and/or add.

remained committed to rewrite papers to be like the papers students actually produced. Still, the rewriting aimed to reproduce only the reasonable extremes of strength and weaknesses for each category. Papers were never rewritten to be average in any category.

The rewriting was performed in layers: content first, then organization, then sentence structure, and finally mechanics. When an earlier layer was rewritten as strong and a later one was rewritten as weak, the rewriters had to be extremely careful not to obscure the strength of the earlier category with the weakness of the latter. When rewriting content to be strong, weaknesses in organization, sentence structure, or mechanics were not allowed to obscure the ideas and the development of those ideas. Similarly, when rewriting sentence structure to be strong, weaknesses in mechanics were not allowed to obscure the strength of the sentences.

Finally, the four broad rewriting categories were defined to include all possible specific features in an essay that relate to its quality. Thus, if a composition was rewritten to be strong in every broad rewriting category, then it would have no residual weaknesses. Likewise, if a composition was rewritten to be weak in every category, it would have no residual strengths. Because I used only four category headings, some features related to essay quality did not fit under any particular category. For example, the feature *word choice* seemed to fit under none of the category headings. In fact, word choice fit under both the content and the sentence structure headings. Some changes in word choice affected the clarity of presentation of an idea: they were included under content. Other changes affected the parallel structure of a sentence; they were included under sentence structure. Other changes, which were purely matters of diction, arbitrarily were placed under sentence structure.

Design. This section discusses the plan for rewriting the four student papers on each of the eight topics. First, each of the papers was rewritten in three different versions. Each original essay was keyed to 3 of the 12 possible rewriting combinations listed earlier. The 4 essays, each rewritten in 3 versions, made 12 versions on each topic. The 12 rewritten versions on each topic represented the 12 possible rewritten versions. Across the 8 topics, with 12 rewritten versions per topic, there were 96 rewritten papers. In the end, because of the constraint against combining weak content and strong organization, two thirds of the 96 rewritten papers were strong in content; one third were strong in organization. Half were strong in sentence structure, and half were strong in mechanics. Of course, the remainder for each category were weak in that category.

Procedure. All rewriters practiced applying the operational definitions for strength and weakness in the four categories (Table 1) to training essays, in order to establish and define common ground as readers and writers. During practice all rewriters independently rewrote the same essay according to the same rewriting combinations and then exchanged rewrites and discussed points of agreement and disagreement. During the actual rewriting, one rewriter always wrote all three versions of an essay. A second rewriter checked the rewriting, and the third remained uninvolved.

Evaluating

Design. Twelve evaluators were chosen according to the following criteria: (a) strength of professional recommendations, (b) quantity of teaching experience, and (c) educational background. All were highly recommended teachers on the staff of Stanford University's freshman English program. I placed the evaluators into three types from most (Type 1) to least (Type 3) teaching experience and education. Evaluators were divided into four reading groups of three judges each. Each group rated essays on two of the eight topics. The different types of evaluators were balanced across the groups in order to avoid placing a group of less experienced evaluators together.

Training and reading packets were compiled for each rater for each topic. The training packets contained holistic scoring forms and two training essays typical of those in the experimental set. In the reading packets two supplemental training essays were followed by eight experimental student essays. Of the eight experimental essays all three evaluators in each group received the four essays that had not been rewritten. The four remaining essays in the experimental set were selected for each judge from those that had been rewritten. Each of the three evaluators received one of the three versions of each of the four rewritten essays. The rewritten versions were assigned to evaluators according to a balanced plan. The order of the eight experimental essays was randomized for each evaluator.

Procedure. The evaluations took place on four consecutive days. One group of three evaluators rated essays on two of the eight topics on the first day; a second group of three evaluators rated essays on another two of the eight topics on the second day; and so on. Each group of evaluators was informed that college students had produced the essays. The fact that some essays had been rewritten was concealed from the evaluators. All essays were typed.

Before rating any essays, the group of evaluators rated two training essays on the first topic in order to practice using the 4-point holistic scale and to practice rating essays on the topic. Then the evaluators received their reading packet on the first topic and began the holistic ratings. If the judges disagreed with one another on scores for the supplemental training essays in the reading packet, the reading was interrupted to continue training with these optional training essays. This same procedure was repeated for the second topic.

The group of judges first gave holistic evaluations to all essays on both topics. After completing both holistic evaluation sessions, the judges were asked to provide a more detailed evaluation for the rewritten essays on each topic. For these essays, the judges had to determine whether the content, organization, sentence structure, and mechanics were weak or strong. The fact that these essays had been rewritten to be weak or strong in these four categories was still concealed from the judges.[2]

Reliability

To assess the reliability of the judges' ratings, I used the Cronbach alpha (Cronbach, 1970, p. 159; Calfee & Drum, in press). The reliability for the ratings given by each group of judges was determined by comparing the ratings the different judges in a group assigned to the four papers on each topic that had not been rewritten. All ratings proved highly reliable. The reliability scores within each group of raters ranged from .86 to .96. These reliabilities are quite high but may represent the upper bounds of the reliability because they are based on papers taken from the extremes of the original distribution.

Results of Rewriting

An analysis of variance (Table 2) supports the hypothesis that essays rewritten to be strong in content would be rated significantly higher than those rewritten to be weak in content. The largest main effect of the rewriting was for the content variable. The organization variable also proved to have a highly significant effect on the judges' scores. Mechanics too had its effect. Additionally, there were significant interactions between organization and mechanics and between organization and sentence structure.

Table 3 helps explain these main results. It reveals that the difference between the average score given papers weak in content and the average score given papers strong in content was 1.06 points, a difference quite large in relation to the 4-point scale. Strong versus weak rewriting in organization also led to a difference of about 1 point. The effects of mechanics and sentence structure rewriting were about 1/2 and 1/4 point, respectively.

The interactions between organization and mechanics and organization and sentence structure in these main results show that only if the essay had

330

Table 2
Analysis of Variance for Holistic Scores:
Rewriting Effects

Source	df	MS	F
Reader (R)	11	.488	
Content (C)	1	9.860	37.78**
Organization	1	5.195	29.68**
Sentence structure (SS)	1	1.5	2.54
Mechanics	1	5.042	9.77*
C x SS	1	1.960	6.30
C x M	1	.990	3.18
O x SS	1	3.767	12.11*
SS x M	1	.001	0

Note: F for main effects is based on R by source (df = 11): F for interactions is based on residual error variance (df = 31).

*p < .01 **p < .001

Table 3
Mean Holistic Judgments

	Strong		Weak		
Variable	Judgement	n	Judgement	n	Difference
Content	2.375	64	1.313	32	1.062
Organization	2.656	32	1.703	64	.953
Sentence structure	2.146	48	1.896	48	.250
Mechanics	2.250	48	1.792	48	.458

Note: Scale: 4 = highest; 1 = lowest. Total N = 96 rewritten essays.

Table 4
Effects of Interaction Between Organization and Mechanics and
Sentence Structure on Holistic Scores

	Strong		Weak	
Variable	M	SD	M	SD
Mechanics				
Strong	3.124	.957	1.183	.592
Weak	2.188	.834	1.594	.615
Difference	.936		-.411	
Sentence structure				
Strong	3.000	1.03	1.719	.581
Weak	2.313	.873	1.688	.644
Difference	.687		.031	

Note: Scale: 4 = highest; 1 = lowest. For Organization x Mechanics, p < .001; for Organization x Sentence structure, p < .01

strong organization did the strength or weakness of the mechanics and sentence structure matter (Table 4). If the organization was strong, the mechanics rewriting caused almost an entire point difference between the strong and weak essays' average scores. In the same situation, sentence structure rewriting caused about a 1/2-point difference. The relation between organization and mechanics was more significant than that between organization and sentence structure.

In summary, the main results of the rewriting showed that the most significant influence on raters' scores was the strength of the content of the essay. The second most important influence proved to be the strength of the organization of that content. The third significant influence was the strength of the mechanics. Furthermore, the strength of the mechanics was most important when the organization was strong, and because the sentence structure alone was insignificant, the strength of the sentence structure was important only when the organization was strong.

Evaluators' Perceptions and Rewriters' Intentions

I next prepared to examine a secondary set of main results. Instead of using the actual rewriting as the independent variable, I wished to examine the holistic ratings according to the raters' perceptions of the strength or weakness of each of the rewritten categories. The raters' perceptions were determined by their indication of their judgment of the strength or weakness of the rewritten categories of the rewritten essays. However, before I could examine the results using the raters' perceptions, it was first necessary to measure how well the raters' perceptions of the strength or weakness of the rewritten categories matched with the way the rewriters intended to rewrite them. If the match was exact, there would be no reason to seek these secondary results. Since the categories were rewritten to be extremely strong or weak, I expected the raters to perceive the rewriting accurately for the most part even though they were not given the criteria for the rewriting.

Table 5 specifies the overall percentage of match and mismatch for each category. Raters usually judged the strength and weakness of the categories accurately, although they did not always. The content category proved most difficult for the raters to assess; organization was next in difficulty, followed by sentence structure and then mechanics. This order seems quite logical; the evaluators' overall perceptions of the different categories matched with the rewriters' intentions a lower percentage of the time for the more difficult to define, abstract categories than for the more objective, concrete categories.

Table 5

Reader-Rewriter Match/Mismatch

Variable	% match	%mismatch
Content	80.2	19.8
Organization	83.3	16.7
Sentence structure	84.4	15.6
Mechanics	90.6	9.4

Evaluators' Perceptions and Their Holistic Evaluations

Since the evaluators' perceptions of the quality of the content, organization, sentence structure, and mechanics of the essay did not match the rewriters' intentions exactly, I next examined the secondary set of major results, the relationship between raters' perceptions and their holistic scores. The evaluators' perceptions of the strength or weakness of the content, organization, sentence structure, and mechanics became the independent variables in the analysis of variance rather than the actual rewriting of the categories. Table 6 shows that the results for content and organization were similar to those found in the main results detailed earlier. The findings for mechanics and sentence structure, this time, appear to be different. However, all of the results based on the perception data are inconclusive because some of the pairs of variables are correlated with one another (Table 7).

The chi-square analysis reveals significant correlations between the following pairs of main effects: perceived content with organization and perceived sentence structure with mechanics. The original rewriting design built in the content/organization correlation by not including strong organization with weak content; however, sentence structure and mechanics were originally independent variables. The raters, not being privy to the rewriting definitions, confounded these categories when giving their perceptions. When they perceived sentence structure as strong, they perceived mechanics as strong too; likewise, when they perceived sentence structure as weak, they perceived mechanics as weak. Finally, raters' perceptions of organization and mechanics were correlated to a lesser extent; raters tended to perceive mechanics to be weak when they perceived organization as weak, but mechanics was perceived as strong independent of organization. Because some of the main effects are correlated, it is not possible to assess how the interactions between them contribute to the variance in the holistic score.

Table 8 shows a comparison of the average difference between ratings on the perceived strong and weak level of each category across the rewritten essays. Notice that the average difference between scores for strong versus weak sentence structure is almost identical to that between strong versus weak mechanics. The significance of perceived sentence structure and lack of significance of perceived mechanics in contributing to the holistic score is most likely an artifact of the nonorthogonal, correlated design.

Table 6
Analysis of Variance for Holistic Scores:
Perceived Rewriting Effects

Source	df	MS	F
Reader	11	.377	
Content perceived	1	12.537	41.65**
Organization perceived	1	5.566	19.81**
Sentence structure perceived	1	3.501	7.34*
Mechanics perceived	1	1.132	3.48

Table 7
Chi-Square Pairwise Correlations:
Perceived Rewriting Frequencies

Variable	Content perceived Strong	Weak	X^2
Organization perceived			
Strong	24	7	15.97*
Weak	22	43	

Variable	Sentence structure perceived Strong	Weak	X^2
Mechanics perceived			
Strong	31	14	13.47*
Weak	16	35	

Note: N = 96 rewritten essays
*p < .001

Table 8
Mean Holistic Judgments: Perceived Rewriting

Variable	Judgment	n	Judgment	n	Difference
Content perceived	2.565	46	1.520	50	1.045
Organization perceived	2.742	31	1.677	65	1.065
Sentence structure perceived	2.340	47	1.714	49	.626
Mechanics perceived	2.356	45	1.725	51	.631

Note: Scale: 4 = highest; 1 = lowest. total N = 96 rewritten essays

Discussion

In the interpretation of the results, several areas deserve mention. First, for these argumentative essays all methods of analysis show that the most important influences on the raters' scores were the content and then the organization of the essay. These two aspects of the argumentative text merit the special attention of the writing student, teacher, and researcher. Sentence structure and mechanics proved much less significant influences on holistic judgments.

Because the influences of sentence structure and mechanics are neither as strong nor as consistent as the influences of content and organization, raters are probably less conscious of the effects of these less important influences. The correlation between the judges' perceptions of the categories *sentence structure* and *mechanics* suggests that the raters either could not consistently distinguish between these two categories or could not correctly perceive one category as weak and the other as strong. It would be interesting to see whether raters could be trained to apply a set of definitions to the two categories and then perceive them discretely. The analysis according to the actual rewriting showed mechanics to contribute more significantly than sentence structure to the holistic score: it is unknown whether or not this finding would hold according to the raters' perceptions.

Two raters were disqualified from the research because the frequency of their mismatch was more than 2 standard deviations above the mean. These raters also exhibited a different pattern of mismatch from the others. They mismatched on all categories, and they mismatched more than the others on the more objective categories, mechanics and sentence structure. The raters who did not show frequent mismatch tended to cluster their mismatches on content or organization, mismatching mostly on only one category. Perhaps raters' abilities to perceive the quality of rewritten categories within essays could be used to test their competence before choosing them to participate in evaluation projects. The raters, both in their mismatch patterns and with their holistic scores, showed a significant tendency to evaluate students' writing negatively. In all categories, when their perceptions did not match the rewriters' intentions, they judged strong rewriting as weak more of the time than not. Also, the distribution of the holistic scores was skewed toward the lower end of the scoring range. Conlan (1976), at Educational Testing Service, corroborated this tendency of readers to rate negatively: "Unfortunately, no reader—experienced or inexperienced— seems to need assurance about giving out 2's and 1's [lowest scores on 4-point holistic scale]; what all readers seem to need from time to time is the reminder that not all the papers are '2' papers or '1' papers" (p. 4). Perhaps evaluators should be less reluctant to compliment student writing.

One limitation of this study is the difficulty in interpreting the exact results of the rewriting. When each category was rewritten, several aspects of the category were rewritten at once. The exact aspects of the category that influenced raters' reactions to that particular category remain unknown and are a topic for further study. It is possible that the raters reacted to the rewriting of all the aspects for each category. It is equally possible that they reacted to some part or combination of parts of the rewriting. For example, perhaps order but not transitions was what influenced raters in the organization rewrite. Broad areas of influence on raters' judgments have been identified; the more precise influences need to be examined.

A second limitation is the homogeneity of the raters in this study. They were carefully defined as a select, homogeneous group of college writing teachers from a major university. It would be interesting to learn how other raters would react. Joseph Williams (Note 2), rewriting essays in nominal and verbal styles, compared the responses of several types of evaluators who thought they were evaluating for different reasons. His judges included new graduate students in a Master of Arts in Teaching program, experienced college English professors, and evaluators who regularly read essays for a state proficiency examination. Some evaluators thought they were helping a fellow graduate student with a research project, others thought they were determining the reliability of a college writing examination. He found that different types of raters preferred different types of essays. Some groups preferred a nominal style; others preferred a verbal style.

Pedagogical Significance

If society values content and organization as much as the raters in this project and many of the earlier studies apparently did, then according to the definitions of content and organization used in this study, a pedagogy for teaching writing should aim first to help students develop their ideas logically, being sensitive to the appropriate amount of explanation necessary for the audience. Then it should focus on teaching students to organize the developed ideas so that they will be easily understood and favorably evaluated. The interactions between organization and mechanics and between organization and sentence structure, showing that the quality of the mechanics and sentence structure matter most when the organization is strong, point even more

336

strongly to a pedagogy aimed at teaching the skills of organization before or at least alongside those of mechanics and sentence structure. At the very least, teachers should not value content and organization while commenting to students mostly on mechanics as those in the Harris (1977) study did. It seems today that many college level curricula begin with a focus on helping students correct mechanical and syntactic problems rather than with the more fundamental aspects of the discourse. It is important to supplement these curricula with carefully planned curricula for teaching content and organization. Certainly, because of the excellent research in the area of written sentence structure (Christensen, 1967; Hunt, 1965; Mellon, 1969; O'Hare, 1971) and because of the objective nature of the mechanical rules for standard edited English, sentence structure and mechanics have become easier to teach than content and organization. The English profession knows more about teaching, evaluating, and doing research on sentence structure and mechanics than on the less objective areas of content and organization. Conceivably, instruction in strengthening sentence structure or mechanics could result in strong content or organization. But such a hypothesis has not been tested.

Scholars like Donald Murray (1968), Ken Macrorie (1970), and Peter Elbow (1973) have advocated college writing curricula centered around the larger levels of the discourse. However, although Murray, Macrorie, and Elbow offer pedagogical suggestions for encouraging students to find and expand their ideas, they do not offer as complete or as well-defined a pedagogy as, say, Christensen does for syntax in *The Christensen Rhetoric Program* (1968). Other scholars, like Kenneth Burke (1945), D. Gordon Rohman (1965), and Young, Becker, and Pike (1970) have contributed to developing a modern theory of invention. Young, Becker and Pike, in particular, have developed heuristic procedures for helping students retrieve, analyze, and order their ideas for a particular audience. Besides such work in invention, with pedagogies focused primarily on idea generation, more research focusing on how to analyze, teach, and evaluate the logical development of the already generated ideas (content) and the techniques used for ordering and making transitions between those ideas (organization) is badly needed before more concrete pedagogies can evolve.

Conclusions

The methodology employed in this experiment provides a framework for studying the evaluation of student writing in many other contexts. Certainly the following aspects of the evaluation process deserve attention:

1. The more exact effects of the rewriting (what within the categories influences the evaluators, does the influence work in a continuum—if so, where are the critical spots on the continuum?).
2. Evaluations given by different kinds of evaluators (e.g., peers, classroom teachers with varying amounts of experience who teach different subjects to different ages, teachers from non-mainstream cultural groups, teacher trainers).
3. The evaluation of papers written by students from other age groups (elementary through senior high school).
4. The evaluation of papers written in other modes of discourse (at least narrative or some expressive modes of writing).

I believe a more in-depth and more precise investigation of the aspects within the two most influential rewriting categories, content, and organization, is the most important and the most promising area for future research. In this study, much of the rewriting in these categories was done intuitively. Now that some aspects of content and organization have been proven powerful influences on evaluators' judgments, the precise aspects of content and organization that influence evaluators must be explored more carefully. Schemes for the linguistic analyses of texts (e.g., Kintsch, 1974) might provide a foundation for more careful experimentation in these aspects of writing. Out of such explorations a sound basis for developing curricula focused on teaching the skills of content and organization can evolve.

By using experimental research to learn more about the evaluation process, educators will be able to develop more efficient and fairer means of evaluation. Teachers as well as researchers need to know how to evaluate the quality of student writing. Discoveries of the bases of evaluators' responses will contribute to a set of definitions of what evaluators see as good writing. These definitions then can be examined critically, and those criteria of good writing that seem sound can be incorporated into pedagogy and into training evaluators of student writing. One of the first steps in improving the evaluation and teaching of student writing is understanding how evaluators evaluate as they do.

Reference Notes

1. Thompson. R. *Predicting writing quality, writing weaknesses that dependably predict holistic evaluations of freshman compositions.* English Studies Collections, Series 1, No. 7, 1976. (Available from Scholarly Publishers, 172 Vincent Drive, East Meadow, New York 11554).

2. Williams, J. *Nominal and verbal styles: Some affective consequences.* Chicago: University of Chicago, 1977. (Mimeograph)

References

Adler, R. (1971). *An investigation of the factors which affect the quality of essays by advanced placement students.* Unpublished doctoral dissertation, Urbana-Champaign: University of Illinois.

Burke, K. (1945). *A grammar of motives.* New York: Prentice-Hall.

Calfee, R., & Drum. P. (in press). How the researcher can help the reading teacher with classroom assessment. In L. Resnick & P. Weaver (Eds.) *Theory and practice of early reading.* Hillsdale, NJ: Erlbaum.

Cass, J., & Birnbaum, M. (1972). *Comparative guide to American colleges.* (5th ed.). New York: Harper & Row.

Christensen, F. (1967). *Notes toward a new rhetoric: Six essays for teachers.* New York: Harper & Row.

Christensen, F. (1968). *The Christensen rhetoric program.* New York: Harper& Row.

Conlan, G. (1976). *How the essay in the CEEB English composition test is scored: An introduction to the reading for readers.* Princeton, NJ: Educational Testing Service.

Cronbach, L. (1970). *Essentials of psychological testing* (3rd ed.). New York: Harper & Row.

Diederich, P. (1974). *Measuring growth in English.* Urbana, IL: National Council of Teachers of English.

Diederich, P., French, S., & Carlton, S. (1961). *Factors in judgment of writing ability. (Research Bulletin 61-15).* Princeton, NJ: Educational Testing Service.

Elbow, P. (1973). *Writing without teachers.* New York: Oxford University Press.

Freedman, S. (1977). *Influences on the evaluators of student writing .* Unpublished doctoral dissertation, Stanford University.

Harris, W. (1977). Teacher response to student writing: A study of the response pattern of high school English teachers to determine the basis for teacher judgment of student writing. *Research in the Teaching of English, 11,* 175-185.

Hiller, J., Marcotte, D., & Martin, T. (1969). Opinionation, vagueness, and specificity distinctions: Essay traits measured by computer. *American Educational Research Journal, 6,* 271-286.

Hunt, K. (1965). *Grammatical structures written at three grade levels.* Urbana, IL: National Council of Teachers of English.

Kintsch, W. (1974). *The representation of meaning in memory.* Hillsdale, NJ: Erlbaum.

Macrorie, K. (1970). *Uptaught.* New York: Hayden.

Mellon, J. (1969). *Transformational sentence-combining: A method for enhancing the development of syntactic fluency in English composition.* Urbana, IL: National Council of Teachers of English.

Meyers, A., McConville, C., & Coffman, W. (1966). Simplex structure in the grading of essay tests. *Educational and Psychological Measurement, 26,* 41-54.

Murray, D. (1968). *A writer teaches writing.* Boston: Houghton Mifflin.

Nold, E., & Freedman, S. (1977) An analysis of readers' responses to essays. *Research in the Teaching of English, 11,* 164-174.

O'Hare, F. (1971). *Sentence combining: Improving student writing without formal grammar instruction.* Urbana, IL: National Council of Teachers of English.

Page, E. (1968). Analyzing student essays by computer. *International Review of Education, 14,* 210-225.

Rohman, D. G. (1965). Pre-writing: The stage of discovery in the writing process. *College Composition and Communication, 16,* 106-112.

Slotnick, H., & Knapp, J. (1971). Essay grading by computer. A laboratory phenomenon? *Educational Measurement, 9,* 253-263.

Young, R., Becker, A., & Pike, K. (1970). *Rhetoric: Discovery and change.* New York: Harcourt, Brace, & World.

Sarah Warshauer Freedman
San Francisco State University

Why Do Teachers Give the Grades They Do?

We all know the student who says, "I turned in this very same paper last year and got an A on it. Now you're going to give me a D?" Luckily, this student is a relatively rare one. First, most students rightfully fear the consequences of handing in a paper twice or at least feel too guilty to confront the teacher with such discrepancies. But, as Don Hirsch noted in his keynote address at the 1978 CCCC's meeting in Denver, more times than not, two or more teachers would give the same paper a different grade. But the good teacher does not grade purely on the basis of whimsy or idiosyncratic values either. In this article, I shall discuss composition evaluation from the point of view of that "good teacher." I shall report the results of a study[1] in which I asked the questions: (1) why do teachers give the grades they do? (2) are there any specific, definable parts of student papers that influence teachers? (3) and if there are, which of the parts influence teachers most?

To find answers to these questions, I rewrote student papers to be weak or strong in four broad, but pedagogically interesting, areas: content, organization, sentence structure, and mechanics. Then teachers judged the overall quality of the rewritten papers. The teachers did not know I had tampered with the papers. I found that specific, definable parts of the student paper did influence these teachers. They valued content first and then organization. They also valued mechanics, but not as much as they did content and organization. Interestingly, they cared more about mechanics, proper punctuation, and the like than about the quality of the structure of the sentences. They valued mechanics most, though, when the organization was strong, and they valued sentence structure only when the organization was strong. The effect of weak content was so powerful that it made nothing else matter.

Now, for all of these results to be meaningful, I must go back and explain a bit about how I got them. First, what specifically do I mean by these broad areas: content, organization, sentence structure, and mechanics? Rhetoric texts certainly conflict in their definitions, and we all know that mechanics play a big part in sentence structure. I will briefly summarize the definitions for the categories, the definitions which formed the basis for the rules for rewriting the student papers. Briefly, content was the development of, and logical consistency between, the ideas. It had nothing to do with the absolute quality

341

of the ideas. To rewrite content to be strong, I took the core ideas the student had and tried to develop them into something that seemed logical. So when I say good teachers valued content most of all, I mean that they valued the development and the logical presentation of the ideas, not necessarily the ideas themselves.

Organization had three main parts: order, transitioning, and paragraphing. Sentence structure focused on matters of form particular to the sentence level; mechanics focused on the pickiest items of usage and punctuation. I tried to define each of the areas in a way that would make it discrete from, or independent of, every other area.

I chose the papers that I would rewrite from a set of papers I collected for another, earlier study.[2] For that study I collected papers from a varied population of college students, papers the students wrote in class on eight different topics in the argumentative mode of discourse. Two Stanford students and I rewrote four of the papers on each topic, 32 papers in all. We selected for the rewriting the four essays that had already been judged in the earlier study to be in the middle of the quality range. We wanted papers that we could make better and worse, so we needed mid-range papers. When I had the teachers judge the rewritten papers, I stuck in four non-rewritten papers on each topic to test their reliability. The teachers proved to be the good judges I thought they would be.

After I trained the two student rewriters to follow my set of rewriting guides, I divided up the rewriting task between the three of us in as balanced a way as I could. We rewrote each of the 32 papers in three different versions each. In all, there were 12 possible ways a given paper could be rewritten, and each of the ways or versions was represented once on each topic. The 12 possible rewriting versions were these:

1. +C,	+0,	+SS,	+M.
2. +C,	+0,	+SS,	-M.
3. +C,	+0,	-SS,	+M.
4. +C,	+0,	-SS,	-M.
5. +C,	-0,	+SS,	+M.
6. +C,	-0,	+SS,	-M.
7. +C,	-0,	-SS,	+M.
8. +C,	-0,	-SS,	-M.
9. -C,	-0,	+SS,	+M.
10 -C,	-0,	+SS,	-M.
11. -C,	-0,	-SS,	+M.
12. -C,	-0,	-SS,	-M.

C = Content
O = Organization
SS = Sentence Structure
M = Mechanics
+ = Strong
- = Weak

In the end, we had 96 rewritten papers. We simultaneously rewrote all four areas—content, organization, sentence structure, and mechanics—on every paper. The rewriting task posed one major restriction: we never combined weak content and strong organization. It would have been an exercise in absurdity to try to order illogical ideas logically or to order and transition appropriately a group of inherently unrelated ideas.

When we rewrote, we were committed to creating a revised paper that retained, insofar as possible, the sense of the original student essay, the one that was the base from which we rewrote. We attempted to highlight the strengths and weaknesses in each of the four areas in each paper. Nevertheless, the act of highlighting often produced a new paper that was substantially unlike the original. Still the rewritten papers were like the papers real students actually produced. We rewrote papers to be very strong or very weak in each of the four areas, but these extremes were meant to reflect the extremes of the papers students produce.

After we finished all of the rewriting, I chose twelve teachers who were good evaluators. I used three main criteria to insure that they would indeed be good evaluators: strong professional recommendations, successful college-level teaching experience, and strong academic preparation. I divided the teachers into four reading groups of three teachers each. Each group rated essays on two of the eight topics. I trained the groups of teachers to judge essays on both topics the group would judge with training essays that I had used in the earlier study. I chose the training essays because they represented the quality of the essays students actually wrote for the earlier study.

The evaluations took place on four consecutive days. One group of three teachers rated essays on two of the eight topics on the first day; a second group of three teachers rated essays on another two of the eight topics on the second day, and so on. I informed each group of evaluators that college students had produced the essays, concealing from them the fact that some essays had been rewritten. All essays were typed. The teachers rated the essays using a four-point holistic scale.

I used an analysis of variance to measure whether the rewriting characteristics contributed significantly to the difference in the scores the raters gave to

343

the different papers. As I revealed earlier, content proved to have the greatest influence on the scores the raters gave. If the content was strong, the score was high; if it was weak, the score was low. Content was significant at the .001 level of confidence. The quality of the organization likewise affected the scores; it too was significant at the .001 level. Mechanics proved significant only at the .01 level.

The difference between the average score given papers strong in content versus the average score given papers weak in content was 1.06 points. The maximum possible difference between a score was 3 points since 4 was the highest score, and 1 was the lowest score a paper could receive on the 1-to-4 holistic scale. Thus, an average difference of over 1 point is quite large. Strong versus weak rewriting in organization also led to an average score difference of about 1 point. The effect of mechanics and sentence structure rewriting was about 1/2 and 1/4 point, respectively.

Remember also that mechanics and sentence structure affected teachers mostly after the teachers assessed that the organization was strong. If the organization was strong, the mechanics rewriting caused almost an entire point difference between the average score of a paper with strong mechanics versus one with weak mechanics. In the same situation, sentence structure rewriting caused about a 1/2 point difference. But if the organization was weak, the quality of the mechanics and of the sentence structure didn't matter to the teacher. Remember from the rewriting combinations that when the content was weak, so was the organization. In such cases, mechanics and sentence structure had little effect. But when the content was strong, the organization too had to be strong in order for the strength or weakness of the mechanics and of the sentence structure to affect these teachers.

In summary, the rewriting showed that parts of the paper did influence the grade that the teachers gave. The most significant influence proved to be the strength of the content of the essay. The second most important influence proved to be the strength of the organization of that content. The third significant influence was the strength of the mechanics. Furthermore, the influence of the mechanics was most important when the organization was strong, and because the sentence structure alone was insignificant, the influence of the sentence structure was important only when the organization was strong.

What are the implications of these findings? Most important, if society values content and organization as much as the teachers in this project did, then according to the definitions of content and organization I used in this study, a pedagogy for teaching writing should aim first to help students develop their ideas logically, being sensitive to the appropriate amounts of explanation necessary for the audience. Then it should focus on teaching students to organize the developed ideas so that they would be easily understood and favorably evaluated. The interaction between organization and mechanics and organization and sentence structure, showing that the quality of the mechanics and sentence structure matter most when the organization is strong, points even more strongly to a pedagogy aimed at teaching the skills of organization before, or at least alongside, those of mechanics and sentence structure.

It seems today that many college-level curricula begin with a focus on helping students correct mechanical and syntactic problems rather than with the more fundamental aspects of the discourse. It is important to supplement these curricula for teaching content and organization. Certainly, because of the excellent research in the area of written sentence structure, on sentence-combining, and on the cumulative sentence and because of the objective nature of the mechanical rules for standard edited English, sentence structure and mechanics have become easier to teach than content and organization. The English profession knows more about teaching, evaluating, and doing research on sentence structure and mechanics than on the less objective areas of content and organization. Conceivably, instruction in strengthening sentence structure or mechanics could result in strong content or organization. But such a hypothesis has not been tested.

Discoveries about why teachers evaluate papers as they do can contribute to a set of definitions of what influences teachers as they evaluate student writing. These definitions, then, can be examined critically, and those criteria of good writing that seem sound can be incorporated into pedagogy and into training evaluators of student writing. One of the first steps in improving the evaluation and teaching of student writing is understanding why teachers evaluate as they do.

Footnotes

1. This paper is based on part of my doctoral dissertation, *Influences on the evaluators of student writing*, Stanford University, 1977.

2. The results of the earlier study are also contained in my dissertation.

3. See my forthcoming article "How Characteristics of Student Essays Influence Evaluators." *Journal of Educational Psychology*, 71 (June, 1979) .

Author's Comment—Sarah Warshauer Freedman

This study comes from my dissertation on the evaluation of student writing. I think I cared and still care about that topic because when I reached a stage where I consciously wanted to write better (I think not until I was an M.A. student in English literature at The University of Chicago), I realized that what was stopping me and what had always stopped me from being able to improve my writing was my inability to articulate what made some pieces I wrote better than others. And my teachers' comments never seemed to help me very much. By studying texts and teachers' judgments, I thought, I would be able to find some clues to what good writing was.

Before doing my proposal for my dissertation, I had begun studying teachers' judgments with my then colleague Ellen Nold. We had worked out a design for an earlier correlational study (see "An Analysis of Readers' Responses to Essays," *Research in the Teaching of English*, pp. 164-174, 1977). I thought I would continue just as we had begun, with another correlational study. I planned to broaden the kinds of writing the raters were evaluating and look for new features that might correlate highly with their judgments.

I must admit that part of me was looking for a quick and easy way out of Stanford's Ph.D. program. My advisor had retired the year before, and so I had no thesis director; the article Ellen and I wrote got published in a pretty reputable journal, and so I thought we were on a good enough track; I knew how to do a follow-up study without help. I had talked to a few professors who seemed supportive of my plans and even had one who agreed to direct my dissertation.

Although I thought I could take the quick and easy route out of Stanford, a complication arose—as often happens for Ph.D. students. In my case, a new professor entered the arena, Bob Calfee, who had been assigned the job of reviewing my proposal. A committed experimental psychologist and a specialist in experimental design, Bob liked my basic research question but thought that the last thing needed was another correlational study. He challenged me to rethink my design, told me I could do a mediocre thesis if I didn't want to accept his challenge, but that he would work with me if I wanted to take the route he was suggesting. Fearing mediocrity, I accepted the challenge, and that's how I came to do an experimental study. With Bob's help and encouragement, I rethought the way I was looking at the issue of

346

reader response and tried to come up with a theoretical understanding of all the factors that might influence readers to respond as they do. Then I figured out how systematically to vary or control those factors. Since I was most interested in text-based factors, those became the main variables in my design, and instead of looking at a laundry list of mechanical, word-level, or sentence level variables that would be easily countable, I began to think about a set of categories that would cover all levels of the text and to think about how I could see how they interacted with one another when raters scored students' essays. So that's how I decided on development, organization, sentence structure, and mechanics. Basically, with an experimental design, I gave myself freedom to revise essays in specifiable but not in countable ways, and then I was able to examine the messy text-level variables of content development and organization, as well as sentence structure and mechanics

I ended up doing a much more complex study than I had originally planned, but I learned a lot more than I would have, and it was well worth the effort. I've always been grateful to Bob Calfee for challenging me to push my thinking and for providing me with the support I needed along the way. It's a role he still plays for me and one I try to play for my students and hope they will play for theirs.

Chapter 14 Defining Writing Tasks for Students

One of the most striking things about this study is how carefully the question that drives it was drafted. The researchers began by discriminating potential sources of difficulty in carrying out the revision process:

1. detection: students can't see the problems in their texts,
2. application: students lack the skills needed to improve their texts, or
3. task definition: students don't understand what the task of revision entails.

Using the results of previous studies, Wallace and Hayes were able to home in on the question to be investigated: If students are in fact able to detect problems in their texts, but are unable to improve them, then either they lack the skills necessary to remedy the problems or they have the skills but do not understand the task of revision, which may require global as well as sentence-level reworking of the text. Thus Wallace and Hayes were led to ask, "Can freshmen carry out global revision successfully if they are instructed to do so?" To answer the question positively, they must demonstrate, "first, that students instructed to revise globally do more global revision than students simply asked to revise, and second, that students instructed to revise globally produce better revisions than students simply asked to revise." (p. 355)

Their question allows them to address both the issue of whether these students lack necessary revision skills and the issue of whether they lack an understanding of the task of revision. A positive answer adds substantially to our understanding of revision and the ability of students to carry out the process effectively; it also has immediate **practical significance** in that it suggests a way of improving student writing performance quickly and at small cost in time and effort, since all that is required is instruction in the nature of global revision.

Not only is the study driven by a really "neat" question, it is also so carefully designed and executed that it allows little room for **rival hypotheses**. As Wallace mentions, he and Hayes went to great pains in designing this study to assure **internal validity**. The simple design using random assignment of the test and control groups and only one treatment and one day to carry it out enabled them to control for such sources of confounding as **concurrent events** and **maturation** (it would be hard to argue that the subjects changed

349

much due to historical or physical developments over a period of 8 minutes!), **testing effects** (the test was administered only once), **sampling bias** (the students were randomly assigned to treatment groups), and **drop outs** (no students were lost in the 8 minute instruction period or the revision task). In other words, if the students in the test group were able to do more global revision and produce qualitatively better texts after the treatment, it was almost assuredly because of the 8 minutes of instruction they received on how to revise globally.

The researchers' account of how their thinking changed after the original research design had been completed reveals two processes which are quite common in the evolution of research projects. First, as it became more evident that the study would have a reportable outcome, the researchers became more active in considering how the audience might evaluate the study. As Wallace remarks,

> before collecting the data, we had planned to compare the texts for the quality of the revisions . . .. However, we didn't see the need for the global revision analysis until we had completed the quality analysis. Anticipating the possible criticism that the quality measure was incomplete, we added the global revision measure to insure that the task definition cue produced *both* better quality and more global revision. (pp. 367-368)

Thus, one of the two major analyses in the study (the analysis of global revision) was conceived only after the first analysis (the analysis of quality) had been completed and the authors began to consider how critics might respond to that analysis. This anticipation by the researchers of the critical response of the audience illustrates the importance of a critical research community for stimulating researchers to think carefully about the interpretation of their data.

Second, when the researchers collected their data, it didn't look quite as they had expected. Indeed, the major differences that had been anticipated between the experimental and the control group were there. However, without reflecting about it carefully, the researchers had also anticipated that writers who did well at the revision task would differ among themselves about as much as writers who did poorly. This assumption lead them to believe that the appropriate way to assess coder reliability would be to use the familiar **Spearman rank order correlation**. What they observed, however, was that it was easy to rank the revisions of writers who did well but that the revisions of writers who did poorly were almost indistinguishable. Given this configuration of data, the researchers realized that **Diedrich's top-quarter**

tetrachoric correlation was more appropriate for their analysis. Thus, seeing the data may force one to reevaluate the appropriateness of the anticipated data analysis.

Notice that Wallace and Hayes **hedge** their conclusions carefully (p. 363). They warn readers not to overgeneralize the results of the study by pointing out 1) that the students were revising somebody else's writing, so no claim can be made about how the technique would affect revision of their own work; 2) that their findings may not apply to students in the primary grades, who may lack fundamental revision skills and the ability to manage them; and 3) that they have not shown that the effect that was produced by the 8 minutes of instruction persists, a qualification that is especially important to any teacher. What they have shown, however, is that there is a potential for helping students do better, and that is a matter of considerable practical significance.

Notes on Technical Issues

Wallace and Hayes used the **Mann-Whitney test** to test for differences in revision quality between treatment and control groups. To perform the Mann-Whitney test, they ranked all of the revisions for quality, assigning "1" to the best revision, "2" to the second best, and so on. The ranks were then summed for the treatment group and for the control group. If the treatment had no effect on revision quality, we would expect that the sum of ranks for the two groups would be about the same. On the other hand, if the treatment helped students to write better revisions, then we would expect that the sum of ranks for the treatment group would be smaller than for the control group, since the treatment group would receive more low (good) ranks than the control group. The Mann-Whitney test provides a way to assess whether an observed difference in the sum of ranks is statistically significant.

David L. Wallace
Department of English
Carnegie Mellon Unviersity

John R. Hayes
Department of Psychology
Carnegie Mellon University

Redefining Revision for Freshmen

This study investigates the impact of task definition on students' revising strategies. Our primary aim was to determine if freshmen students could revise globally if instructed to do so and if those global revisions would result in improved texts. We asked two groups of freshmen to revise a text provided by the experimenters; one group was given eight minutes of instruction on how to revise globally, and the other was simply asked to make the text better. The texts written by students who received the instruction were judged both to be of significantly better quality and to have included significantly more global revision. Further, the improvement appears to affect the treated population generally rather than just a small part of that population.

Redefining Revision for Freshmen

When students have trouble revising, teachers must consider several possible sources of difficulty. First, students may have trouble because they are missing essential revision skills. In a protocol study, Hayes, Flower, Schriver, Stratman, and Carey (1987) found that college freshmen often lacked the skills necessary for them to detect problems in their texts. For example, students often read the following sentence several times: "In sports like fencing for a long time many of our varsity team members had no previous experience anyway." One of these students not only failed to find any fault but actually commented favorably on it saying, "Freshmen would like that." Further, Scardamalia and Bereiter (1983) working with fourth, sixth, and eighth grade students and Bartlett (1981) working with seventh and eighth grade students report that even when students do detect problems in text, they may lack the skills necessary to fix them. For example, Bartlett (1981) found that students attempting to fix one type of ambiguity succeeded in less than 60% of cases. Lack of skills needed to detect and fix both local and global problems is perhaps the greatest difficulty the student faces. Overcoming this difficulty typically requires students to engage in extended training and practice.

A second potential source of revision difficulty has been discussed most extensively by Scardamalia and Bereiter (1983). They suggest that even if students have all of the necessary low-level skills required for revision, they may not have the executive procedures required to coordinate those skills. Thus, although students may have the skills to deal one at a time with issues of syntax, diction, or audience, they may not be able to handle them simultaneously. For example, students might fail to attend to the interests of their audience because they are completely absorbed in dealing with problems of grammar or word choice. Scardamalia and Bereiter (1983) applied a method they developed called "procedural facilitation" to help students coordinate revision skills. To facilitate the revision process, the researchers provided 30 fourth grade, 30 sixth grade, and 30 eighth grade students with cards that reminded students of evaluations they might make or tactics they might employ. The cards contained statements such as "People may not believe this," "I think this could be said more clearly," and "I'd better give an example." As students revised sentence by sentence, the cards helped them to remember to address both local and global issues. For each sentence, they were first to choose the most relevant cards, and, then, where appropriate, to revise.

Scardamalia and Bereiter (1983) reported that these elementary and middle school students had little trouble in mastering the procedure and generally reported that the cards helped them to think about their writing; however, their revisions were not better in overall quality than their original texts. Thus, it seemed that procedural facilitation did help them to coordinate their revision skills, but, as Scardamalia and Bereiter (1983) observe, when the students found problems, they lacked the skills required to fix them. Thus, the advantages provided by procedural facilitation in recognizing problems were not translated into improved text. Procedural facilitation, then, appears to be a promising way to help coordinate revision skills. However, unless all of the requisite skills are in place, it may not result in improved texts.

A third source of difficulty in revision, and this difficulty will be the focus of this paper, is inappropriate task definition. By task definition we mean the writer's understanding of what he or she is supposed to do when facing a writing task such as revision. When teachers assign revision tasks, they typically hope that the students will define revision in the same way they do, that is, that their students will set the same goals, make use of the same procedures, and apply the same criteria for success. However, considerable evidence suggests that many freshmen students define revision very differently from their teachers.

A number of studies indicate that more skillful writers approach the task of revision differently than do less skillful writers. Many researchers have found that inexperienced writers typically treat revision as a *local task,* that is, a task of changing words and sentences rather than of modifying the goals or organization of the text to meet criteria of the rhetorical situation. Stallard (1974) found that only 2.5% of twelfth grade students' revisions were focused above the word and sentence level. Bridwell (1980) also found that relatively few of twelfth grade students' revisions were above the sentence level. In contrast, more skillful writers treat revision as a *global task,* that is, one concerned with the purpose, the audience, and the overall organization of the text. This contrast is also seen in Sommers's (1980) study in which she found that freshmen college students "understand the revision process as a rewording activity . . . they concentrate on particular words apart from their role in the text" (p. 381). Again, as in Bridwell's study, experienced writers (e.g., journalists, editors, and academics) focused on global issues. Sommers (1980) notes that they "describe their primary objectives when revising as finding the form or shape of their argument" (p. 384). That is, she found that experienced writers have a second objective, "a concern for their readership," that went beyond making local changes. Faigley and Witte (1981) supported Sommers's conclusions by finding that expert writers were more likely to make global revisions and revisions that changed meaning than were either advanced students or inexperienced students. Most recently, Hayes, Flower, Schriver, Stratman, and Carey (1987) provided further confirmation for these observations in a protocol study of college freshmen and of experienced writers (writing instructors and writer-editors). They found that during revision the experienced writers were much more likely than freshmen to adjust the text globally to the audience's needs and the author's overall purpose. The freshmen, in contrast, tended to focus on changing individual words and sentences within the text.

Although it is clear that most freshmen approach the task of revision at a more local level than do more experienced writers, it isn't clear why they do so. One possibility is that freshmen have not yet acquired the skills necessary for handling global text problems and that they revise locally because they can't do otherwise. Another possibility is that freshmen have the requisite skills to revise globally but that they have an inappropriate task definition, that is, they have not defined revision as a task that requires attention to global problems. Results obtained by Matsuhashi and Gordon (1985) with basic

354

college writers provide some support for this possibility. These authors found that students who were asked to "Add five things to your essay to improve it" did make more additions to their texts than students who were asked to "Revise your essay to improve it." Thus, these students had the ability to add to their text even though they normally did not do so during revision. The authors argue that for basic writers, any additions very likely constituted improvements to their typically spare texts. However, since Matsuhashi and Gordon (1985) did not evaluate the quality of the texts before and after revision, it is not clear that the additions actually improved the texts.

The present study was designed to answer the question, "Can freshmen carry out global revision successfully if they are instructed to do so?" To give a positive answer to this question we must demonstrate, first, that students instructed to revise globally *do more global revision* than students simply asked to revise, and second, that students instructed to revise globally *produce better revisions* than students simply asked to revise.

The pedagogical attractiveness of modifying students' task definitions is that, if it works, it can presumably yield improvement quickly and cost-effectively; that is, it may cue students to use abilities that they already possess. However, if it is to work, the students must have both the underlying revision skills as well as the ability to coordinate those skills. Whether or not typical college freshmen meet these two conditions for a given writing task is by no means obvious.

Briefly, we designed this study as a test case to assess the impact of changing students' task definition on their performance in a revision task. Specifically, we asked the freshmen writers in this study to revise a text that describes a procedure (purifying water at a treatment plant) for a particular audience. Half of the students were given eight minutes of instruction on how to revise globally, and the other half were simply asked to make the text better. Our primary aim was to determine if freshmen students could revise globally if instructed to do so and if those global revisions would result in improved texts.

Method

Participants

The participants in this study were 38 students enrolled in two entry-level college writing courses at Carnegie Mellon University. The students were enrolled in the colleges of Fine Arts, Engineering, and Humanities and Social Sciences.

Materials

The text to be revised was a 437-word description of the procedure by which river water is processed at a treatment plant (see Appendix A). We chose a text that described a process because such texts and writing tasks are common in school and because procedural texts require global coherence. In addition, the variety of local and global problems in the text allowed for a wide range of revision behaviors. For example, the text had both a number of local problems such as errors in spelling, punctuation, diction, and agreement, and a number of global problems such as poor organization and poor adaptation to audience concerns; the text was intended to be used as a handout for high school students who tour a water treatment plant. To facilitate revision, the text was presented in 2 1/2 typewritten triple-spaced pages.

Procedure

The study was conducted in two writing classes during the ninth week of a sixteen-week semester. Half of the students in each class were randomly assigned to the treatment group; the other half served as the control group. The mean SAT verbal score for the control group (532.2) was slightly higher than that for the treatment group (514.4); however, a t-test revealed that the difference between these means was not significant.

After giving brief instructions about the nature of the study, an experimenter (not the instructor for the course) asked the students in the control group to go with another experimenter to a nearby room to complete the experiment. The experimenters read the same brief task instructions to both the treatment and control groups. These task instructions (see Appendix B) informed students that they would have 30 minutes to revise a short text about the operation of a water treatment plant so that it could be used as a handout for high school students who tour the plant. The instructions specifically cued students to revise so that the handout would be "clear, organized, easy to read, and free of errors." The instructions also directed students to mark deletions, additions, changes, and movements of text in standard ways such that a typist could easily retype their revised texts.

After reading these instructions and asking for questions, the experimenters reminded the students that they had 30 minutes to complete their revisions and instructed them to begin. The students were informed when they had 15 minutes and 5 minutes remaining. For each of the treatment and control groups, the procedure was completed within the 50-minute class period.

Procedures for the two groups were identical except that an experimenter presented eight additional minutes of instruction to the treatment group. The eight minutes taken by the special instruction of the experimental group was approximately equal to the time it took to change rooms for the control group.

The purpose of this instruction was to cue students to revise globally by illustrating how an expert writer and a novice writer revised a similar text. The experimenter illustrated differences between the revision activities of the expert and the novice writers using overhead transparencies. First, he explained the differences in basic approach and procedure—the expert writer read through the entire text to identify major problems and then focused on improving the whole text. In contrast, the novice writer began making changes immediately and proceeded to search through the text for local errors.

After this overview, the experimenter illustrated differences in the amount and types of changes that the two writers made using transparencies of the two writers' actual revisions of the sample text. The transparencies illustrated that the expert writer not only made more revisions but made different kinds of revisions. The effect was rather dramatic; while the novice writer limited himself to eliminating spelling, wordiness, and grammar errors, the expert writer also addressed global issues, adding an initial purpose statement, selecting and deleting information for the specified audience, reorganizing the text, and providing explicit cues to the new overall organization.

Results

Three separate analyses were conducted: a global revision analysis, a text quality analysis, and an error correction analysis. In all of these, the experimental treatment under which the revisions were produced was hidden from the judges.

The global revision analysis was conducted to determine if the 8 minutes of experimental instruction had, in fact, led students to do more global revision. To make the revised texts easier for the raters to read, each text was retyped making all changes indicated by the writers. The retyped texts were spell-checked and proofread for accuracy against the writers' handwritten revisions. Two raters independently rank-ordered all 38 revised texts for the extent to which they incorporated global revisions of the original text.

This analysis focused most directly on the number of changes made and the extent to which text changes altered the sample text. To illustrate, nearly all of the students made some attempt to clean up egregious spelling and punctuation errors, to explain difficult vocabulary, to smooth out awkward sentences, and to add temporal signals (e.g. *first, next, the next step*) making the water treatment process clear. However, some of the students limited themselves to these types of changes, not making any changes beyond the sentence-level. In contrast, the revised texts that were judged more successful also made global changes in addition to such local changes.

In general, students whose texts succeeded in making global revisions added or revised sections of text to make global purpose statements, reordered sections of text to make the water treatment process more clear, and added specific transitions between parts of the treatment process. To illustrate, in Figure 1 below, a student recasts the information in the first paragraph and last two paragraphs of the original text to make a new opening paragraph which highlights the purpose of the plant and briefly previews the water treatment process. The same student also clarifies the water treatment process by rearranging the information in the second and third paragraphs of the original text and adding transition words and phrases to make the process

Figure 1
Global Revisions to Highlight Purpose

Original text
The following is a description of the process by which water from the Merrimack River is made potable at the Lowell Water Treatment Facility.

The entire process takes about 31 hours: 1/2 hour in the intake station and static mixer; two-and-a-half hours in the flocculation basin; 4 hours in the sedimentation basin, 24 hours in the filters and clear well.

As the major water treatment plant in the region, the average daily production is 14 million gallons (MG), of which 12 MG is for consumption and 2 MG is for storage. The plant supplies water not only to Lowell but to neighboring communities like Chelmsford, Tewksbury, and Dracut.

Revised Text:
The Lowell Water Treatment Facility is the major water treatment plant in the region, supplying water not only to Lowell but to neighboring communities like Chelmsford, Tewksbury, and Dracut. On the average the plant produces 14 million gallons (MG) of water every day—12 MG for consumption and 2 MG for storage. The process by which raw, unusable water from the Merrimack River is transformed into water that may be used for drinking and cooling is long and complicated, requiring about 31 hours for completion.

358

clear (see Figure 2). Notice particularly that in addition to adding transition signals such as *first* and *next*, this writer has reorganized information and rewritten sentences to make the treatment process more clear. Also, she adds summary clauses (e.g. *all this is done to incite flocculation*) that indicate the nature of the relationship between steps in the water treatment process.

The reliability of the raters for the extent of global revisions was evaluated in two ways. The Spearman rank order correlation between raters was .60, and Diederich's (1974) top-quarter tetrachoric correlation yielded an adjusted agreement rate of .92. We used the Diederich measure in addition to the Spearman rank order correlation because of the peculiar distribution of

Figure 2
Global Revisions to Reorganize and Signal Organization

Original Text:
The Merrimack River water pumped by an intake station contains various particals. Chlorine is added to the water to kill all pathogenic (disease-causing) organisms before the water is conveyed to the static mixer, which blends the consitutents to a specific degree of uniformity, In addition, chemicals like NaOH and Al(OH)$_3$ are added; the former adjust the water pH to a satisfactory level, which is needed for the treatment process; the latter acts as a coagulant. Coagulation is reduction of net electrical repulsive forces at particle surfaces. This process is required to facilitate flocculation in the next step.

Flocculation is when particals are aggregated by chemical bridging between particals in order to increase there weight and size, and makes the next state—sedimentation—possible.

Revised Text:
First, the water is pumped by an intake station into the plant. Chlorine is added to the water to kill all pathogenic (disease-causing) organisms, and chemicals like NaOH and Al(OH)$_3$ are added. NaOH adjusts the water to a satisfactory pH level for the treatment process, and Al(OH)$_3$ acts as a coagulant, reducing the net electrical repulsive forces at particle surfaces, which is required to facilitate latter steps in the process.

Next, the water is conveyed to the static mixer, which blends the consitutents to a specific degree of uniformity. All this is done to incite flocculation, a process in which particals are aggregated by chemical bridging between particals in order to increase their weight and size. Without this step the water could not progress to the next state—sedimentation.

359

revision activities across participants. Some revisors changed the original text extensively whereas others changed it very little. Differences among the more extensive revisors are larger and easier to agree on than differences among the less extensive revisors. Thus, measures such as Diederich's, that focus on the more extensive revisors, will typically yield higher and, we hope, more informative indexes of reliability than will measures, such as the Spearman correlation, which do not.

The global revision rankings averaged across the two judges were significantly higher for students in the experimental group than for students in the control group at the .008 level by Mann-Whitney test [U=90]. In fact, the seven highest ranks were all obtained by students in the treatment group.

To compare the quality of the revised texts, the second analysis compared the treatment and control groups for the overall quality of the revised texts. In this rating, the judges were primarily concerned with the quality rather than the quantity of revisions. Although we expected similarity between the global revision analysis and the quality analysis, we anticipated that extensive revisions might not necessarily be effective revisions. Two additional judges independently rank ordered the texts. The reliability of the raters was again evaluated in two ways. The Spearman rank order correlation between raters was .53, and Diederich's (1974) top-quarter tetrachoric correlation yielded an adjusted agreement rate of .86.

Similar to the results for global revision, the quality rankings, averaged across the two judges, were significantly higher for students in the experimental group than for students in the control group at the .012 level by Mann-Whitney test [U=94]. The six highest ranks were all obtained by students in the treatment group. In addition, the two dependent measures, global revision and overall quality, are strongly related. The Spearman rank correlation between the average global revision rankings and the average quality rankings was .805.

It is possible that the effect of the special instructions depended entirely on 6 or 8 participants who "get the message" while the rest are unaffected; that is, the performance of a few students in the treatment group could account for the significant difference between the two groups of writers. If this were the case, we would expect the treatment group to dominate the top rankings but to be relatively evenly distributed over the remainder of the rankings. To explore this possibility, we divided the 38 quality rankings into five groups: ranks 1-8, 9-16, 17-24, 25-32, and 33-38. Figure 3 shows that for quality rating, the proportion of participants in the treatment group declines steadily across the five ranks while the opposite is true for the control group. For example, in

Figure 3
Experimental and Control Conditions

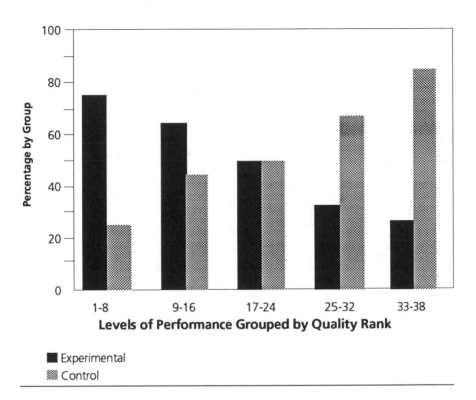

Levels of Performance Grouped by Quality Rank

■ Experimental
▓ Control

the highest-rated group (ranks 1 through 8) 75 percent of the participants were in the treatment group. Moving to the right, the proportion of treatment group participants declines steadily and nearly linearly as quality decreases. Figure 4 indicates the same general trend for the global revision rating although the rate of decline across ranks for the experimental group is not as linear. While not conclusive, these results suggest that the instruction helped most of the participants in the treatment group to improve their performance rather than just a few.

The error correction analysis compared treatment and control groups for the numbers of word and sentence-level errors in the original texts that were not included in the revised texts. To conduct this analysis, a rater compared each of the revised texts (the participants' original texts, not the retyped versions) against the set of errors identified in the original text and judged whether each error had been either corrected or eliminated. To establish

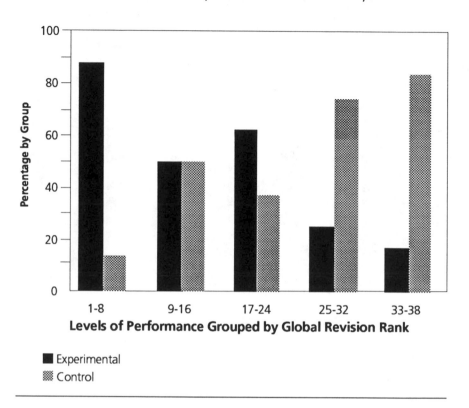

Figure 4
Gobal Revision for Experimental and Control Groups

Levels of Performance Grouped by Global Revision Rank

■ Experimental
▦ Control

reliability, a second rater followed the same procedure for a 20 percent sample of the data. With approximately 15 minutes training, the raters reached a direct match agreement rate of .99. On the average, writers in the treatment group eliminated 10.3 errors and writers in the control group, 8.8 errors; however, the difference was not significant by a one-way analysis of variance. Thus, although we might have expected the treatment group to focus more on global problems than on local ones, neither group eliminated significantly more of the sentence-level errors from the text.

Discussion

The most striking result of this study is that we were able to produce a significant increase in global revision and in revision quality with just eight minutes of instruction. Further, the improvement appears to affect the treated population generally rather than just a small part of that population. What effect did the eight minutes of instruction have? Did participants learn how to make global revisions during the instruction or were they simply cued to make use of what they already knew? Given the complexity of the revision activities elicited in the treatment group and the brevity of the instruction, we believe that most of the skills exhibited must have been present before instruction and that the effect of instruction was simply to recruit these skills for application to the immediate revision task. It is not certain, though, whether something was also learned. We would be pleased if the students generalized their experience to other writing situations but we don't know that they did. Thus, as a test case, we have been able to show that a very brief instructional prompt resulted in more global revision behaviors and improved revision quality in a substantial proportion of the treatment group.

Although this is good news, the results must be qualified in several ways. First, we have observed students revising texts written by others. Whether our instruction would help people revising their own texts remains to be seen. Second, we believe that instruction to change task definition can be effective only if the participants already have certain fundamental revision skills and the ability to manage those skills. Since the results of Scardamalia and Bereiter (1983) and Bartlett (1981) suggest that these conditions may not be met in primary school students, it would be unwise to assume that results similar to ours could be obtained in the primary grades. Third, we have not shown that the results of our instruction persist. That is, we have not shown that the next time students in the treatment group revise, they will do it any better than the control group. We have shown, though, that the potential for doing better is there. And, even if a single presentation of the instruction has only transitory effect, that is not reason to be discouraged. Because the instruction is extremely inexpensive in instructional effort, students can be reminded frequently about global revision without great cost.

Authors' Note: The authors would like to thank Rebecca E. Burnett, Karen Schnakenberg, Ann Blakeslee, Lorraine Higgins, and Linda Flower for their help with various aspects of this study.

References

Bartlett, E. J. (1981). *Learning to write: Some cognitive and linguistic components*. Washington, D.C.: Center for Applied Linguistics.

Bridwell, L. S. (1980). Revising strategies in twelfth grade students' transactional writing. *Research in the Teaching of English, 14,* 197-222.

Diederich, P.B. (1974). *Measuring growth in English*. Urbana, IL: National Council of Teachers of English.

Faigley, L., & Witte, S. (1981). Analyzing revision. *College Composition and Communication, 32,* 400-414.

Hayes, J. R., Flower, L. S., Schriver, K. A., Stratman, J., & Carey, L. (1987). Cognitive processes in revision. In S. Rosenberg (Ed.), *Advances in psycholinguistics, volume II: Reading, writing, and language processing* (pp. 176-240). Cambridge, England: Cambridge University Press.

Matsuhashi, A., & Gordon, E. (1985). Revision, addition, and the power of the unseen text. In S. W. Freedman (Ed.), *The acquisition of written language: Response and revision* (pp. 126-249). Norwood, NJ: Ablex.

Scardamalia, M., & Bereiter, C. (1983). The development of evaluative, diagnostic and remedial capabilities in children's composing. In M. Martlew (Ed.), *The pychology of written language: Developmental and educational perspectives* (pp. 67-95). New York: Wiley.

Sommers, N. (1980). Revision strategies of student writers and experienced adult writers. *College Composition and Communication, 31,* 78-88.

Stallard, C. (1974). An analysis of the writing behavior of good student writers. *Research in the Teaching of English, 8,* 206-218.

364

Appendix A: Original Text (Lowell Water Treatment Facility)

The following is a description of the process by which water from the Merrimack River is made potable at the Lowell Water Treatment Facility.

The Merrimack River water pumped by an intake station contains various particals. Chlorine is added to the water to kill all pathogenic (disease-causing) organisms before the water is conveyed to the static mixer, which blends the consitutents to a specific degree of uniformity. In addition, chemicals like NaOH and Al(OH)$_3$ are added; the former adjust the water pH to a satisfactory level, which is needed for the treatment process; the latter acts as a coagulant. Coagulation is reduction of net electrical repulsive forces at particle surfaces. This process is required to facilitate flocculation in the next step.

Flocculation is when particals are aggregated by chemical bridging between particals in order to increase their weight and size, and makes the next state—sedimentation—possible.

Sedimentation is the removal of solid particles from a suspension through gravity settling. The liquid that has not been flocculated is run out to sludge lagoons and stored there. The Merrimack's water is brown because of various particals; the method used to clear it is sedimentation. The settling particals in sedimentation are the ones that sink down due to their weight. Nonsettleable particals and other impurities are removed by rapid sand filters, which are extremely complicated. Their action can be described as consisting of a combination of straining, flocculation, and sedimentation together.

The next step takes place in the activated charcoal filter where odor is removed from the water by a vegetable carbon that has been heated in a special atmosphere consisting of the components of CO_2 and steam.

The fluoridation and post chlorination are done in the clear well. The amounts of fluoride added is one unit of fluoride per 1,000,000 units of water; it is required for dental care. Chlorine is re-added to the water after treatment has been completed to kill any remaining surplus pathogenic organisms. After this stage, water is potable and is transported and conveyed to pipelines.

The entire process takes about 31 hours: 1/2 hour in the intake station and static mixer; two-and-a-half hours in the flocculation basin; 4 hours in the sedimentation basin, 24 hours in the filters and clear well.

As the major water treatment plant in the region, the average daily production is 14 million gallons (MG), of which 12 MG is for consumption and 2 MG is for storage. The plant supplies water not only to Lowell but to neighboring communities like Chelmsford, Tewksbury, and Dracut.

Appendix B: Directions

Your task for the next 30 minutes is to revise a short text about the Lowell Water Treatment Plant so that it can be used as a handout for the high school science students who tour the plant. When you've finished, the text should be clear, organized, easy to read, and free of errors. Keep in mind that it will be used as a handout for high school students.

Any changes that you make in the text should be clearly marked so that a typist could easily retype the text making your changes. The text that you will revise has been triple-spaced to give you room to make changes; you will also find blank paper in your packet should you need it. Please use the following system for marking changes:

Deletions: To delete something from the original text, place an X through it.

Additions: To add something to the original text, write it in close to its position in the text and mark the exact position with an arrow. Should you wish to insert something that you have written on the blank paper into the original text, please place it in brackets (i.e. [ ]) and number it (i.e. #1). Then simply place [#1] at the appropriate place in the original text.

Changes: To change wording, spelling, punctuation, or capitalization mark out the appropriate word(s) or punctuation with an X and add the new word(s) or punctuation near the change.

Moves: To move something in the original text, place brackets [ ] around it and use an arrow to indicate where you wish it to be placed.

Please do not turn this page until instructed to do so.

Author's Comment—David L. Wallace

This study began as a conversation. As we tossed around some ideas for doing a study together, Dick (John Richard Hayes) and I found a mutual interest in task definition. The effect of task definition on revision was one of the items on Dick's list of research issues waiting to be investigated. Dick's interest had been piqued by an earlier study that had been abandoned and some previous work on revision (Hayes, Flower, Schriver, Stratman, & Carey, 1987) that had called attention to substantial differences between the basic approaches and strategies that expert and novice writers brought to revision. For me, the question was largely one of application. Given the differences between experts' and novices' basic understanding of revision, what should the reseacher do about it? We decided that we wanted to try to nail down the impact of task definition on teaching revision; over the course of a couple meetings we set up a simple experiment.

Much of the design of the study was dictated by our desire for a clean, simple comparison and by pragmatics. We needed about 40 participants to have sufficient power to insure a possible significant result of our comparison. To get them, we "borrowed" two sections of a freshmen composition class. Cognizant of Hillocks's (1979) concern for eliminating teacher effects, we decided to split each class randomly into treatment and control groups; this meant shuffling students around and some extra work finding free classrooms for the control group in each class.

As a writing teacher, my guess was that an effective cue would depend on a dramatic comparison of the differences between a strictly local approach to revision and one that addresses global issues, differences which were also suggested by previous studies. We drew the instructional material from a previous study which had compared expert and novice revisions of a text. The instructional intervention was limited to 8 minutes largely because we wanted to complete the data collection within a single class period. However, the idea of a short instructional cue also appealed to us because it would be easy for teachers to adapt for classroom use.

Although the design of the study and the data collection were carefully planned, we made many of the decisions about how to analyze this data after it was collected. Before collecting the data, we had planned to compare the texts for the quality of the revisions and randomly assigned numbers to each revised text to hide the experimental condition. However, we didn't see the need for the global revision analysis until after we had completed the quality analysis. Anticipating the possible criticism that the quality measure was incomplete, we added the global revision measure to insure that the task definition cue produced *both* better quality and more extensive global revision.

A second analysis decision concerned the best way to score the data and report reliability. We decided first to rank order the texts instead of using some type of primary trait or holistic scoring scale because we wanted to maximize the possible distribution. However, by choosing to rank order we created a problem for reporting reliability. The Spearman correlation, which is typically used for rank ordered data, yielded low scores, but also scores which, upon reflection, we did not believe accurately reported the agreement which our judges reached. When we looked at the spread of the disagreements, we discovered that the judges were very accurate for texts at the top of the scale, texts which had many changes from the original, and less accurate for texts at the bottom of the scale, those with few changes. Thus, our measure of reliability was influenced by a floor effect; not surprisingly the judges had more difficulty accurately rating texts when they had less information (changes from the original texts) on which to base their assessment. We needed, then, some means of estimating reliability that focused on the top end of the scale. Fortunately, I had recently read about Diederich's top quarter tetrachoric while reviewing some literature on holistic scoring and essay rating. Given the extensive research and practical experience that Diederich reported in the 1974 NCTE monograph, we felt comfortable using this as another means of estimating reliability. However, we hedged our bets and reported both scores.

About six months after we had finished the study, we sent off a version of the present article to *Research in the Teaching of English*, reporting and carefully delimiting the results. While the manuscript was out for review, we began to see that delimiting the results was not sufficient for teachers and researchers to completely understand how and why the cuing worked. I took the results on the road, presenting them to groups of teachers and at a conference panel. Although the response was positive, the questions that people asked help us to see that we needed to frame the study as a test case showing the potential impact of task definition. We had never considered shrink wrapping the eight minutes of instruction in cellophane and marketing them as a composition cure-all. However, we also had not seen that simply delineating the limitations was not sufficient for teachers and researchers to understand what our results meant. They needed more information about the writing task and how the instruction enabled students to do that task, if they were to begin to figure out how to develop cues to change their own students' task definition of revision. While we knew we had good news to tell, it took us a while to figure out an effective way to tell it.

Finally, the feedback from colleagues has also convinced us to take the next step, to try to develop reliable methods for assessing the impact of task definition on students' revisions of their own texts.

References

Diederich, P.B. (1974). *Measuring growth in English*. Urbana, IL: National Council of Teachers of English.

Hayes, J.R., Flower, L.S., Schriver, K.A., Stratman, J., & Carey, L. (1987). Cognitive processes in revision. In S. Rosenberg (Ed.), *Advances in psycholinguistics, volume II: Reading, witing, and language processing*. (pp. 176-240) Cambridge, England: Cambridge University Press.

Hillocks, G. (1979). The effects of observational activities on student writing. *Research in the Teaching of English, 13*, 161-164.

Chapter 15 The Impact of Cooperative Writing

First and foremost, a good study must ask a good question — a question that has either practical or theoretical significance. The study by O'Donnell and her colleagues is exempary because it addresses questions of both practical and theoretical significance. It also addresses a question of considerably less significance and, thus, provides a contrast useful for highlighting issues involved in the selection of research questions.

The O'Donnell et al. study addresses three questions:

1. Do pairs of college students who cooperate on writing assignments produce better texts than individuals who complete assignments alone?
2. Does the experience with cooperative writing lead to the improvement of later individual writing, that is, does the experience of cooperative writing **transfer** positively to later writing?
3. In what ways is later writing influenced by the cooperative writing experience?

We believe that question 2 has considerable practical significance. If experience with cooperative writing does improve later writing, then it could be a valuable tool for teaching writing. However, if there is no evidence that the experience of cooperative writing transfers to later writing, it may well be a waste of time to introduce it into the writing classroom. In either case, the consequences are clearly practical. Further, we believe that question 3 is of theoretical significance. Learning what it is about later writing that is facilitated by the cooperative writing experience could help researchers understand what sorts of skills and sensitivities contribute to writing ability.

In contrast to questions 2 and 3, question 1 has relatively little practical or theoretical significance. To see that this is so, consider a question that is analogous in many ways to question 1: Do pairs of students who cooperate in digging holes, dig bigger holes than students who dig holes alone? The expected answer, of course, is "yes" and it is less than exciting theoretically. An answer of "no" would indicate a disasterous situation in which working together had reduced the diggers' efficiency by 50% or more. Indeed, if one were really interested in the efficiency of cooperative hole digging, one would want to know that two people working cooperatively for one hour accomplished as much or more than one of them working alone for two hours. And, similarly, if a teacher or employer were really interested in cooperative writing as an efficient method for producing text, then one would want to know if two people writing cooperatively for one hour would produce a better text than a writer working alone for two hours. Generally, though, teachers are not interested in increasing the efficiency with which students produce writing assignments. Rather, they are interested in improving students' writing abilities. Thus, question 2 would be of far more interest to them than question 1.

We should emphasize here that we are not criticizing O'Donnell and her colleagues for having asked and answered question 1. They did so in passing, on the way to answering questions 2 and 3. However, studies which have addressed only question 1, are, we believe, of little value.

In selecting a research question, it is good practice to consider carefully the practical and theoretical implications of each of the possible answers to the question. If none of the answers has interesting implications, it is time to look for a better question.

A second reason for liking the study is that it does such a good job of explaining just what the significance of the study is. Note how carefully and methodically the context for this study is developed. Much of the research related to student interaction and learning, they say, "has investigated whether group performance of a task is superior to that of individual efforts" (p. 374). Past research has focused on brainstorming and on cooperative learning. The brainstorming research has compared individual generation of ideas and group generation, with the relative efficacy of group generation being called into question. In contrast, research has shown that cooperative learning not only facilitates academic achievement but has the potential for improving individual learning as well. However, the research has focused on the acquisition of information and not on writing skills, which, they hypothesize, may also "be enhanced by the same processes" (p. 375).

Of course, they point out, the suggestion is not new in composition studies, but the evidence in support of it has been informal and unsystematic. Hence, their experimental study.

Notes on Technical Issues

An important feature of the O'Donnell study is its use of **covariates**. Although the researchers were primarily interested in the relation between cooperative writing and writing performance, they recognized that other

372

differences among participants were likely to influence performance as well. Covariate analysis is a method for taking some of these differences into account.

The basic idea behind covariate analysis is this: Suppose that the researchers know that some variable of interest, say, writing quality, tends to increase as the the writer's SAT-Verbal score increases. Let's say that for every 10 points increase in SAT-Verbal score, the quality of students' essays increase on the average by a quarter of a grade point. Knowledge of this relation allows the researcher to use SAT-Verbal to adjust the quality scores for students or groups of students. Thus, the researchers can calculate how well each student did in comparison to how well that student would have been *expected* to do on the basis of his or her SAT-Verbal score.

There are two advantages to be gained by using covariates. First, they can be used to adjust for accidental differences among treatment groups. For example, suppose that the control group happened to have greater SAT-Verbal scores than the experimental group. If unaccounted for, this difference could lead researchers to underestimate the effect of the experimental treatment. Covariates can be used to estimate what the difference in performance between the two groups would have been if they had had equal SAT-Verbal scores. The second advantage is that covariates can be used to account for some of the variability of the observations. For example, some of the variability within each group may be due to differences among participants in a covariate such as SAT-Verbal score. Accounting for the variability due to differences in the covariate, in effect, makes the measurements more precise (e.g., less "noisy") and, therefore, allows for the identification of smaller differences than would otherwise have been possible. An analysis of variance (ANOVA) that makes use of covariates is called an **analysis of covariance (ANCOVA).**

Angela M. O'Donnell
Donald F. Dansereau
Thomas Rocklin
Judith G. Lambiotte
Velma I. Hythecker
Celia O. Larson
Texas Christian University

Cooperative Writing: Direct Effects and Transfer

This study compared the performance of students who cooperated on an instruction writing task with students who worked alone. The effects of transfer from a cooperative experience to an individual writing task was also assessed. A total of 36 students were recruited from introductory psychology classes and were randomly assigned to a cooperative or individual condition. The results of the study showed that students in the cooperative condition significantly out-performed the individual group on a measure of the communicative quality of the writing on both the initial task and on the transfer task (ps<.01). No differences between the groups were found on a measure of the completeness of the written instruction on either task (ps>.05). It appears that cooperating dyads can improve the communicative quality of their instruction writing.

In recent years, there has been a growing interest in the potential of students interacting with one another to improve their acquisition and application of knowledge and skills. Much of the research has investigated whether group performance of a task is superior to that of individual efforts. One task that has received much attention is "brain-storming." Research using this task has typically contrasted individual generation of ideas with group generation of ideas. In a comprehensive review of the brainstorming literature, Jablin and Seibold (1978) concluded that brainstorming in short-lived, noncohesive groups is ill-advised. Groups do not perform as well as the summated efforts of individuals working alone. Hill (1982) also suggests that groups are likely to suffer from process loss in the performance of a task (i.e., the members of a group do not perform as well as they would if working alone).

In contrast to the group problem-solving literature, prior research has consistently demonstrated that cooperative learning facilitates academic achievement (Dansereau et al., 1979; Sharan, 1980; Slavin, 1980). Furthermore, cooperative learning appears to have the potential to facilitate transfer to individual learning (McDonald, Larson, Dansereau, & Spurlin, in press).

374

The tasks typically used in cooperative learning experiments have focused almost exclusively on the acquisition of information (Sharan, 1980). It is hypothesized that cooperative learning is effective in this domain because the cooperative situation provides an opportunity for observational learning (i.e., cross-modeling of skills and strategies) and for immediate peer feedback. It seems likely that the learning of writing skills would be enhanced by these same processes. As a consequence, the present experiment has been designed to explore the potential of improving writing via cooperative dyads.

The potential of cooperative learning as an instructional tool in the teaching of writing has been proposed previously (e.g., Gebhardt, 1980; Jacko, 1978). The National Council of Teachers of English (cited by Jacko, 1978) recommended that instruction in writing should include having students read and edit each other's papers. Informal evaluations of the effectiveness of peer editing and training on writing effectiveness have led to positive results (Bissland, 1980; Gebhardt, 1980; Jacko, 1978).

However, although the potential of cooperation among students has been acknowledged, the research on this topic has typically been unsystematic and uncontrolled. Also, there have been no systematic attempts at identifying the aspects of the writing sample that are affected by cooperative interactions.

In order to correct the above shortcomings, this study was designed to (1) compare the performances of college students who cooperate on a writing assignment with those of individuals who complete the assignment alone, (2) assess the effects of transfer from a cooperative experience to an individual writing task, and (3) to identify what aspects of the writing (i.e., completeness and communicativeness) were influenced by the cooperative experience.

The writing of concrete instructions (e.g., starting a car) was chosen as the task to be analyzed because of its pervasiveness in everyday activities (almost everyone has to write instructions at one time or another) and because the goals of the task can be clearly established. This latter characteristic allows for the establishment of more objective scoring procedures than can be employed with other forms of writing. In particular, the communicative effectiveness and adequacy of the responses to the writing assignment can be more adequately evaluated when the writing task has been clearly delineated. Both of these aspects of written productions have been viewed by prior researchers and editors as the critical components of good writing (Diederich, 1974; Flower & Hayes, 1980; Hirsch & Harrington, 1981). Because there is a scarcity of adequate measures of these components, a secondary purpose of this research was to develop a scoring system for written instructions.

Method

Participants

A total of 36 students were recruited from introductory psychology classes at Texas Christian University. The students received course credit in return for their participation.

Materials

Two instruction writing tasks were selected. These tasks (operating a tape recorder and starting a car) were chosen because of their familiarity and level of complexity. In both tasks the students were told that the target audience consisted of English-speaking people unfamiliar with the equipment and the procedures to be described.

The Delta Reading Vocabulary Test (Deignan, 1973) and the Group Embedded Figures Test (GEFT; Oltman, Raskin, & Witkin, 1971) were administered and used as covariates in subsequent analyses. The Delta, a 46-item multiple-choice test, was used as a measure of verbal ability. Prior research has shown this test to be moderately correlated with other measures of verbal ability such as the Scholastic Aptitude Test (Dansereau, 1978).

The GEFT provides a measure of field dependence/independence and requires individuals to detect single shapes within complex figures. This measure has been shown to be related to text processing in a number of studies (Brooks & Dansereau, 1983; Brooks, Dansereau, Spurlin, & Holley, 1983).

Procedure

The experiment was conducted in two sessions of approximately 2 hours each. During the first session, all participants completed the Delta Reading Vocabulary Test. The participants were then randomly assigned to either the "cooperative" condition or the "individual" condition. Students in the cooperative condition were randomly assigned to same-sex dyads. The dyads were asked to cooperate in producing a set of instructions for starting a car and driving it away from the curb. They had 50 minutes in which to complete the task. They were not given any guidelines about how to interact or about what form their cooperations should take. The individuals were instructed to perform the same task on their own. The participants were also informed that the target audience was totally unfamiliar with a car.

During the second session that took place the following day, each of the participants, working alone, wrote a second set of instructions. Again, the participants had 50 minutes in which to complete the task. The second assignment required the participants to write instructions for using a tape recorder to record and play back a conversation. Again, the audience to be addressed was described as being completely unfamiliar with the task. The participants then completed the GEFT.

Results

The dependent measures were scores that assessed the communicativeness and the completeness of the instructions. The communication score assessed the ease with which the instructions could be followed. The attributes of the instructions that were included in the communication score were as follows:

(1) inclusion of the purpose of the task
(2) the use of illustrations
(3) reference to the illustration in text
(4) ratings of the helpfulness of the illustrations
(5) use of steps in the procedure
(6) enumeration of steps
(7) correct ordering of steps

Each of these features has been shown to aid the comprehension of technical text (Frase,1981; Gross,1983; Wright,1977). Each set of instructions was scored for the presence or absence of these features and the scores were summed to form an overall communicativeness score.

The completeness score was derived from a checklist of the equipment and procedures necessary to follow the instructions. The checklists of required equipment and activities for both tasks were compiled from detailed and exhaustive descriptions of the tasks provided by colleagues. A total completeness score provided an assessment of the number of pieces of equipment or required actions that were included in a set of instructions.

The sets of instructions were scored without knowledge of group affiliation by two raters. Interrater reliability was established by having the raters exchange a randomly selected subset of the sets of instructions. Correlations between raters ranged from .73 to .98 on the dependent measures. Because the total available scores for the two tasks differed, the participants' scores were standardized within task in order to facilitate direct comparison of the results for both tasks.

Because of the possible dependence between pair partners' scores, a conservative approach to the analysis of the data was taken. The mean of each dyad's score on all of the dependent measures was computed and the mean

377

scores were then used in subsequent analyses.

Preliminary analyses of the covariates indicated that the assumptions of homogeneity for the regression slopes for the dependent measures were not violated. Two 2 X 2 repeated measures ANCOVAs (groups as the between subjects factor and task, cooperative versus individual, as the repeated measure) were performed. The participants' scores on the Delta and GEFT served as covariates (mean covariate scores were computed for partners) and the communicativeness and completeness scores were the dependent measures.

The results of the "communicative" ANCOVA showed a significant effect of the group factor, $F(1,23) = 17.80$, $p < .01$. The means and standard deviations are presented in Table 1. The dyads outperformed the individuals on both tasks. No other effects were significant. The results of the "completeness" ANCOVA were not significant (see Table 2 for means and standard deviations).

A series of X^2 analyses were conducted in order to identify the attributes of the communication score, described earlier, which contributed to significant differences between the groups. Significant results on the first assignment were found for the inclusion of steps ($X^2 = 13.6$, $p < .0002$), the numbering of steps ($X^2 = 9.4$, $p = .002$) and the correct ordering of steps ($X^2 = 11.4$, $p = .0007$). The pattern of results for the X^2 for the second assignment was identical. The inclusion of steps, the numbering of steps, and the correct ordering of steps were again significant ($X^2 = 14.14$, $p < .0001$; $X^2 = 12.04$, $p < .0005$, $X^2 = 12.04$, $p < .005$, respectively).

Table 1

Means* and Standard Deviations on Communicativeness Scores for the Cooperative and Transfer Tasks

	COOPERATIVE				TRANSFER			
			Adjusted				Adjusted	
	$\overline{X}$	SD	$\overline{X}$	SD	$\overline{X}$	SD	$\overline{X}$	SD
Pairs (n = 9)	.56	.94	.72	.99	.61	.87	.87	1.03
Individuals (n = 18)	-.56	.61	-.36	.60	-.61	.51	-.44	.54

*Standard scores.

378

Discussion

The results of this study indicate that students who worked in cooperative dyads wrote instructions that are more communicative than did students working as individuals. Further, compared to students who had not had the cooperative experience, students who had worked in cooperative dyads, when subsequently working alone, wrote instructions that are more communicative. Because an equal amount of time was allowed for the production of both sets of instructions, these results cannot be attributed to time-on-task differences. Also, we should note that the students who worked together did not differ significantly from the individuals on measures of completeness for either task.

In the absence of specific instructions or experimenter-induced instructional set, cooperating dyads write instructions that are as complete as those produced by individuals but that have a higher communicative quality. Although a detailed protocol of the dyadic interactions is desirable, we decided not to attempt to obtain such protocols during this study. This decision was made because of the preliminary nature of the study. Previous research has demonstrated that the performance of individuals on a task can be affected by the presence of an observer or recording equipment (Geen, 1980; Scheier & Carver, 1980). Because of this potential disruption, we decided to delay detailed observations until future experimentation.

Informal observations of the students in the "cooperative" condition suggested that the dyads alternated between oral discussions and writing. It is likely that the dyads' discussions were concerned with planning, and that they

Table 2

Means* and Standard Deviations of Completeness Scores on the Cooperative and Transfer Tasks

	COOPERATIVE				TRANSFER			
			Adjusted				Adjusted	
	X̄	SD	X̄	SD	X̄	SD	X̄	SD
Pairs (n = 9)	-.05	1.01	-.09	1.05	.26	.82	.35	.74
Individuals (n = 18)	.05	.93	.05	.99	.40	1.05	.17	1.01

• Standard scores

subsequently wrote instructions according to these agreed-upon plans.

The analyses of the communicative aspect of the instructions indicate that dyads divide the instructions they write into steps, number the steps, and place them in the correct order more frequently than do individuals. Students who participate in a cooperative situation subsequently engage in these activities when writing alone.

It appears that cooperating dyads can spontaneously improve the communicative quality of their writing. The cooperative situation differs from peer editing situations by providing an opportunity for modeling as well as feedback. The improved communicative quality of instructions written in a cooperative setting and in a subsequent individual setting may be a consequence of these processes. Further research is necessary to identify the type of interactions engaged in by the dyads and the impact of these interactions on the processes involved in writing.

References

Bissland, J. H. (1980). Peer evaluation method promotes sharper writing. *Journalism Educator, 34* (4), 17-19.

Brooks, L. W., & Dansereau, D. F. (1983). Effects of structural schema training and text organization on expository prose processing. *Journal of Educational Psychology, 75* (6), 811-820.

Brooks, L. W., Dansereau, D. F., Spurlin, J. E., & Holley, C. D. (1983). Effects of headings on text processing. *Journal of Educational Psychology, 75* (2), 292-302.

Dansereau, D. F. (1978). The development of a learning strategy curriculum. In H. F. O'Neil, Jr. (Ed.), *Learning strategies.* New York: Academic Press.

Dansereau, D. F., Collins, K. W., McDonald, B. A., Holley, C. D., Garland, J., Diekhoff, G., & Evans, S. H. (1979). Development and evaluation of a learning strategies training program. *Journal of Educational Psychology, 71* (1), 64-73.

Deignan, G. M. (1973). *The Delta reading vocabulary test.* Lowry Air Force Base, CO: Air Force Human Resources Laboratory.

Diederich, P. B. (1974). *Measuring growth in English.* Urbana, IL: National Council of Teachers of English.

Flower, L., & Hayes, J.R. (1980). The cognition of discovery: Defining a rhetorical problem. *College Composition and Communication, 31* (1), 21-32.

Frase, L. T. (1981). Writing text and the reader. In C. H. Fredericksen & J. Dominic (Eds.), *Writing: process, development, and communication.* Hillsdale, NJ: Erlbaum.

Gebhardt, R. (1980). Teamwork and feedback: Broadening the base of collaborative writing. *College English ,42* (1), 69-74.

Geen, R. G. (1980). The effects of being observed on performance. In P.B. Paulus (Ed.), *Psychology of group influence*. Hillsdale, NJ: Erlbaum.

Gross,A. G.(1983). A primer of tables and figures. *Journal of Technical Writing and Communication, 13* (1), 33-55.

Hill, G. W. (1982). Group versus individual performance: Are N+1 heads better than one? *Psychological Bulletin, 91* (3), 517-539.

Hirsch, E. D., & Harrington, D. P. (1981). Measuring the communicative effectiveness of prose. In C. H. Fredericksen & J. F. Dominic (Eds.), *Writing: Process, development, and communication*. Hillsdale, NJ: Erlbaum.

Jablin, F. M., & Seibold, D. K. (1978). Implications for problem-solving groups of empirical research and "Brainstorming": A critical review of the literature. *Southern Speech Communication Journal, 43* (Summer), 327-356.

Jacko, C. M. (1978). Small group triad: An instructional mode for the teaching of writing. *College Composition and Communication, 29* (3), 290-292.

McDonald, B. A., Larson, C. O., Dansereau, D. F., & Spurlin, J. E. (in press). Cooperative dyads: Impact on text learning and transfer. *Contemporary Educational Psychology*.

Oltman, P. K., Raskin, E., & Witkin, H. A. (1971). *Group embedded figures test*. Palo Alto, CA: Consulting Psychologists Press.

Scheier, M. F., & Carver,C. S. (1980). Private and public self-attention, resistance to change, and dissonance reduction. *Journal of Personality and Social Psychology, 39* (3), 390-405.

Sharan, S. (1980). Cooperative learning in small groups: Recent methods and effects on achievement, attitudes, and ethnic relations. *Review of Educational Research, 50* (2), 247-271.

Slavin, R. E. (1980). Cooperative learning. *Review of Educational Research, 50* (2), 315-342.

Wright, P. (1977). Presenting technical information: A survey of research findings. *Instructional Science, 6*, 93-134.

Author's Comment—Angela M. O'Donnell

Overview

The study described in *Cooperative Writing: Direct Effects and Transfer* compared the performance of students who cooperated on an instruction writing task with the performance of students who wrote alone. All of the students then engaged in a second writing task alone. The results of the study showed that cooperation among students improved the communicative quality of the instructions written. When the cooperating students subsequently engaged in an individual writing task, they continued to write more communicative instructions than students who did not have a cooperative experience.

Selection of Research Topic

I think that the selection of a research topic often combines a broad intellectual interest in objectively framed questions with a more personal interest. My selection of "cooperative writing" as a research topic certainly stemmed from a combination of sources. Two primary reasons sparked my interest in the topic. The first of these related to the kind of work I had been doing. I had been conducting research on the effects of dyadic interaction on the acquisition of technical information. A second set of tasks that I chose to study involved production tasks. These differed from the acquisition tasks in that they required students to utilize the knowledge they had in complex ways. "Writing" was a clear example of such a task and one that students must frequently perform. I chose to use "instruction writing" as a task because of its fit with my other research.

A second reason for becoming interested in the topic, particularly of technical writing, was the difficulties I had experienced with technical writing. My undergraduate degree included an emphasis on English literature and I found that writing about poetry and drama was radically different from the kinds of writing required in a graduate program in experimental psychology. I became very interested in the idea of "knowing one's audience" as a result of my own difficulties in writing within different disciplines. I think this duality of reasons for becoming interested in the topic helped with the methodology and conceptualization of the study.

382

Writing Tasks

There are a number of aspects of the methodology upon which I would like to comment. The first of these relates to the selection of the writing task. "Instruction writing" is a very complex task and often falls prey to the consequences of proceduralized knowledge of the expert. People who are expert at what they do often fail to give good instructions because much of their skill is automated or they make assumptions about what the novice actually knows or understands. Asking for basic instruction in computer use from an accomplished computer user is often frustrating for these reasons because the expert often loses sight of the things that pose difficulties to the learner. Cooperation among peers when writing seemed to have a lot of potential to improve the quality of instruction writing. A writer generally writes for an invisible audience. Requiring students to cooperate provides the student writer with an immediate visible audience. Assumptions about pre-existing knowledge can be readily tested.

An important aspect of the selection of the writing task was to remove the component of differential knowledge on the part of the participants as far as possible. A poorly written set of instructions can result from a variety of causes. For example, I might write an inadequate set of instructions because (a) I didn't know enough about the topic (a problem of knowledge); (b) I couldn't retrieve the appropriate information (a problem of memory), (c) I had an inadequate grasp of the mechanics of the language; or (d) I did not consider the audience appropriately. In the study described above, I wanted to limit the range of possible explanations for the quality of the instructions produced. Minimizing the difficulties associated with differential knowledge or retrieval of information was accomplished by selecting tasks with which all the participants were expected to be familiar. Participants were asked to write instructions for driving a car and for operating a tape-recorder. The tasks were also expected to be so familiar that people were not expected to experience difficulty in remembering appropriate information to include in their instructions. Instead, participants were expected to have difficulty in selecting an appropriate level of detail. They were also expected to experience difficulty in monitoring the assumptions they would make with respect to anticipating what was known about the task by the target audience.

Selecting Outcome Measures

The selection of outcome measures is always a thorny issue in any research. The outcome measures must be appropriate to the task and must also be sensitive to change brought about through experimental manipulation.

Two different indices of the quality of the instructions were used: completeness and communicativeness. The second measure was expected to be more influenced by dyadic interaction than the former as participants in dyads essentially have a trial run in their communications. An individual working alone is attempting to communicate to an unseen audience without feedback about how successful their communications are.

The communicative quality of instruction writing can be very easily assessed by having someone attempt to follow the instructions. I rather liked the possibility of trying this manner of assessment in this study. I did not know how to drive and was very willing to try to follow the instructions that people wrote. However, I could not get any of my co-authors to agree to this type of assessment as it would have involved lending me their cars! Apparently they had little faith in our participants' instruction-writing capability or in my instruction-following capability.

Having excluded the most obvious test of the communicative quality of the instruction, we used the available literature on technical writing to derive a checklist of attributes of technical writing that enhance communication and comprehension. The specification of "completeness" was a much simpler task as I collected exhaustive descriptions of the tasks from colleagues who were acquainted with the need to be as complete as possible.

In reconsidering the article for the purposes of writing this commentary, I was reminded that the conduct of research is never as objective as it appears to be. At all stages of the research process (from conceptualization to discussing the implications of the research), the personal histories of the researchers can influence important decisions. I was also reminded that the research was also great fun. The discussions we had as a research group about the advisability of having me drive my colleagues' cars to test the communicative quality of the instructions provided us with a great deal of insight into the desired characteristics of a well-written instructions.

Chapter 16 Development of Literary Awareness

The question that Beach and Wendler asked ("How do students' responses to literature develop?") led them across the boundaries of diverse fields. In designing their study, they have borrowed from literary theory, child development, education, and social and cognitive psychology. However, some see dangers in such borrowing (e.g., Ede, Irmscher). And indeed, there may well be dangers, since people sometimes borrow without adequate understanding. For example, we have seen claims in the technical writing literature that no more than seven bullets should be used on a slide and no more than seven subheads on a two-page spread, because literature on information processing indicates that immediate memory capacity is limited to about seven chunks of information. However, there are many reasons to question such inferences, the most evident of which is that immediate memory limitations apply to situations in which one does not have an external text available to aid memory. The argument that we should not borrow because we sometimes get it wrong seems to us untenable. If we were to avoid doing things because others have done them badly, we would find ourselves with little to do.

Richard Weaver is probably the foremost spokesman for another, more fundamental argument against borrowing from other disciplines, one that goes considerably beyond the observation that people may borrow without sufficient understanding. His argument concerns **scientism**, "the application of scientific assumptions to subjects that are not wholly comprised of naturalistic phenomena" (p. 203), such as the humanities. Weaver's notion appears to grow out of an excessive preoccupation with disciplinary boundaries and a tendency to see them as rigid and impermeable. Our own position is more pragmatic. If a method is useful in helping the inquirer solve his problems, we would argue, then he has every right to make use of it. Abraham Kaplan, a philosopher of science, put our position well when he remarked in *The Conduct of Inquiry: Methodology for Behavioral Science* that " . . . the domain of truth has no fixed boundaries within it. In the one world of ideas there are no barriers to trade or to travel. Each discipline may take from others techniques, concepts, laws, data, models, theories, or explanations—in short, whatever it finds useful in its own inquiries" (4). We are inclined to go still further and say that if it helps researchers solve the problems better than they could solve them with a more traditional approach, they have an obligation to make use of it. To do otherwise is to prefer disciplinary purity to effective inquiry. We believe, then, that the arguments in favor of the sort of borrowing illustrated by Beach and Wendler's study are compelling. It would be surprising if how one thought about characters in a story had nothing to do with how one thought about people more generally. It would be equally surprising if the development of children's responses to literature had nothing to do with their development in other areas of life. Although there may be dangers in borrowing from scholars who may have different perspectives and different training than ours, we believe that the dangers are small in comparison to the potential benefits. Indeed, it is one of our objectives in this text to help the reader read empirical literature with a critical understanding that will reduce the danger of misinterpretation and increase the availability of diverse perspectives.

Notes on Technical Issues

Although some studies examine only a single dependent variable, such as essay quality or vocabulary size, others examine several dependent variables simultaneously. In the Beach and Wendler study, three dependent variables were examined simultaneously: the reader's conceptions of acts of characters, perceptions of characters, and goals of characters. The researchers might have analyzed their data using three separate analyses of variance, one for each dependent variable. (Analysis of variance can handle only one dependent variable at a time.) Instead, they analyzed all three at once using a **multiple analysis of variance (MANOVA),** which can handle an unlimited number of dependent variables. MANOVA looks for main effects and interactions of the independent variables on the dependent variables as a group. Beach and Wendler found that grade level (the one independent variable) "had a significant overall effect" on the dependent variables and summarized the results of the analysis in this compact expression: "$(F[9,456] = 6.9, p<.001)$." To interpret this expression notice first that we are dealing with the F-statistic — the same one used in analysis of variance — and that its value is 6.9. For present purposes, the reader need not be concerned with the numbers in the square brackets, which are called "**degrees of freedom**" and are related to the numbers of conditions and the numbers of observations in the study. (The topic of degrees of freedom is beyond the scope of this text but is discussed in several of the texts listed in the reference section at the end of the book.) Notice also that the significance level of the result is expressed as "$p<.001$," which may be read as "probability less than .001."

When a MANOVA produces a significant result, the researchers can conclude that the independent variables have influenced the dependent variables in some way. It might be that all of them are influenced, or some of them, or just one of them. Further analysis is required to determine exactly what the pattern of influence is. The usual next step is a univariate (ordinary) analysis of variance for each of the dependent variables. When Beach and Wendler did this, they found that grade level had a significant effect on each of the three dependent variables.

But finding a significant main effect of grade level on readers' conceptions of acts, perceptions and goals doesn't indicate what the differences are among the grades. It might be that each grade is significantly different from each of the other three grades, or that three grades are equal to each other but different from the fourth. To determine what the differences were among the grade levels, Beach and Wendler used a **post hoc test**. Two commonly used post hoc tests are the **Duncan** test and the **Newman-Keuls** test. Applying the Duncan test, Beach and Wendler found a significant difference in "act inferences" between eighth and eleventh graders, and between both eighth and eleventh graders and college students, but they found no difference between college freshmen and college juniors.

References

Ede, L. (1984). Is Rogerian rhetoric really Rogerian? *Rhetoric Review, 3,* 40-48.

Irmscher, W. (987). Finding a comfortable identity. *College Composition and Communication, 38,* 81-87.

Kaplan, A. (1964). *The conduct of inquiry: Methodology for behavioral science.* San Francisco: Chandler.

Weaver, R.M. (1970). Language is sermonic. In R. L. Johannesen, R. Strickland, and R. T. Eubanks (Eds.), *Language is sermonic: Richard M. Weaver on the nature of rhetoric* (pp. 201-225). Baton Rouge: Louisiana State Univesity Press.

Richard Beach, University of Minnesota
Linda Wendler, Northwestern College

Developmental Differences in Response to a Story

*This study compared eighth graders', 11 th graders', college freshmen's,
and college senior's inferences about characters' acts, perceptions, and goals
in one short story. Readers' inferences about acts, perceptions, and goals for
six story incidents were clustered into composite categories. Inferences about
characters' acts were then rated according to degree of focus on social/
psychological meanings. Inferences about characters' perceptions were rated
according to the degree of focus on beliefs; and goal inferences were rated
according to the degree of focus on long-range goals*

*The results suggest that from early adolescence to young adulthood,
readers shift from a "describer orientation"—conceiving of characters in
terms of immediate surface feelings or physical behaviors—to conceptions of
characters in terms of long-range social or psychological beliefs and goals.*

Readers' ability to make inferences about characters' acts, perceptions, and
goals affects their overall understanding of a story (Bruce, 1981; Schank &
Abelson, 1977). Readers differ in their act, belief, or goal inferences because
they apply different social constructs (Kelly, 1955, 1970) to a story (Black &
Seifert, 1985; DeVries, 1973; Hynds, 1985). For example, some readers may
conceive of a character's act in terms of physical behaviors ("raising his
hand"), while others may conceive of that act in terms of social or psychological motives ("impressing the teacher"). Some readers may conceive of a
character's perception of other characters in terms of a character's own
emotions ("she liked him"), while others may conceive of a character's
perceptions in terms of their beliefs about other characters' needs ("she
believed that he cared about her"). And, some readers may conceive of a
character's goal in terms of *immediate* needs or plans ("he wants to hit a
home run"), while others may conceive of the goal in terms of *long-range*
social or psychological needs or plans ("he wants to impress his parents").

The differences in these social constructs reflect differences in readers' level
of cognitive development (Fusco, 1983; Hynds, 1985; Parnell, 1984; Petrosky,
1977). Previous cognitive developmental research has analyzed the differ-

ences in literary inferences in terms of levels of generalization or abstraction (Fusco, 1983; Parnell, 1984), indicating that older readers are more likely to abstract about texts than are younger readers.

Much of the developmental research on literary response charts an overall increase during adolescence in the ability to generalize (Applebee, 1978; Hillocks & Ludlow, 1984) or interpret (Education Commission of the States, 1981; Purves, 1981). An analysis of 11-, 14-, and 18-year-olds' responses to the question, "What is this poem about?"— indicated that 18-year-olds were significantly more likely to infer the thematic points of poems than were 11 and 14-year-olds (Svensson, 1985). The 18-year-olds were more likely than the younger readers to justify their interpretations by noting that poems have significant meanings or messages, reflecting an increased knowledge of literary conventions.

However, little of this research has focused on developmental differences in readers' specific act, belief, or goal inferences. Analysis of inferences about dialogue acts in a one-act play indicates that college juniors made significantly more long-range goal inferences regarding social consequences than did eleventh graders, suggesting that college students conceive of acts more in terms of long-range social or psychological goals than do secondary students (Beach, 1985).

Assuming that secondary and college literature teachers are concerned about developmental differences reflected in their students' responses, it would be useful to know more about how differences in the content of readers' inferences reflect cognitive and social developmental differences from early adolescence to young adulthood.

Cognitive and Social Developmental Research: Implications for Differences in Inferences

Early Adolescence

Cognitive development research indicates that early adolescents reasoning at the initial formal operations stage are more likely to think in terms of surface aspects of phenomena (Dulit, 1972; Elkind, 1967; Flavell, 1977). Early adolescents also tend to conceive of themselves in terms of physical behaviors (Bernstein, 1980; Damon & Hart, 1982). When asked to define "who they are," early adolescents often talk about what they do —"I mow the lawn; I play baseball." Peel (1971) characterized this as "describer thinking"— conceiving of experience in terms of underlying beliefs, motives, or goals.

389

Given this developmental orientation, early adolescents may therefore conceive of characters' acts in terms of surface physical behaviors or conceive of characters' perceptions in terms of immediate emotional reactions.

They may also be more likely to conceive of goals in terms of immediate short-term needs rather than long-range consequences of actions (Lewis, 1981; Peevers & Secord, 1973).

Early to Late Adolescence and Young Adulthood

As they move into the final formal operations stage, late adolescents are more likely to conceive of phenomena in terms of larger social or psychological needs or consequences (Inhelder & Piaget, 1958; Flavell, 1977). Lewis (1981) found a steady increase from ages 13 to 18 in adolescents' ability to infer the social consequences of actions. In his research on moral development, which parallels Piagetian stage models, Kohlberg (1969) found an increase in adolescents' ability to reason about moral dilemmas in terms of social or community norms.

Late adolescents are also more likely to conceive of self in terms of social relationships with others (Dusek & Flaherty, 1981; Ellis, Gehman, & Katzenmeyer, 1980; Kegan, 1982). As they become less egocentric, middle and late adolescents become more adapt at inferring or adopting other persons' thoughts or perspectives (Gollin, 1958; Montemayor & Eisen, 1977; Selman, 1980), resulting in the ability to engage in "recursive thinking," adopting another's perspective in order to impute perceptions (Barenboim, 1978).

Young adults continue to demonstrate an increased ability to adopt different perspectives in thinking about a situation (Perry, 1970). They also improve in their ability to define the social or psychological consequences of actions (Kegan, 1982; Peevers & Secord, 1973; Schlossberg, 1981) or long-range social or professional goals relative to specific contexts.

Late adolescents and young adults may therefore conceive acts more in terms of underlying or long-range social or psychological phenomena.

In summary, this research suggests the following trends from early adolescence to young adulthood in readers' conceptions of characters' acts, perceptions, and goals:

- *characters' acts*—from conceiving of acts as autonomous physical behaviors to conceptions of acts as embedded within socially or psychologically defined contexts.
- *characters' perceptions*—from conceiving of perceptions in terms of characters' own immediate feelings to conceiving of them in terms of characters' social or psychological beliefs.

- *characters' goals*—from conceiving of goals in terms of characters' immediate or short-term needs to conceptions of long-range plans or strategies.

The purpose of the present study was to examine differences between eighth graders', eleventh graders', college freshmen's, and college juniors' act, perception, and goal inferences.

Method

Participants

Forty students were randomly selected from each of four grade levels, for a total of 160 participants. The eighth-grade participants, with a mean age of 14.3 *(SD.7)*, and the eleventh-grade participants, with a mean age of 17.2 *(SD .8)*, were students in English classes in a suburban school district with a high percentage of students attending post-secondary institutions. The college freshmen, with a mean age of 19.4 *(SD .9)*, were students in freshman composition courses at a large midwestern urban university. The college juniors, with a mean age of 22.3 *(SD 1.2)*, were education majors at the same university.

Methods and Procedure

The story used in this study, "Goodnight, Irene," by Robert Weesner, portrays an adolescent boy's attempts to develop a relationship with a girl who has just moved to town. Because Felix is shy and insecure, he has difficulty communicating with Irene and with his father, an alcoholic single parent. Felix is also a good basketball player who is on the varsity team but quits when another player, the son of his father's boss, is favored by the coach.

For each of six story incidents, students answered questions such as:

> "What is [character A or B] doing?" (characters' acts)

> "What does [character A or B] think about [character A or B]?" (characters' perceptions)

> "What is [character A or B] trying to accomplish?" (characters' goals)

Students answered eleven questions about characters' acts, sixteen questions about characters' perceptions, and eleven questions about characters' goals, for a total of thirty-eight answers.

As part of their regular literature instruction, students in these classes were asked to read the story without interruption. The next day, they were asked to re-read the story and to answer the above questions.

Analysis

The analysis of the inferences involved three stages. The first stage involved determinihg composite answer types by grouping the act, perception, and goal inferences according to similarity of content.

For each of the 38 questions, three raters, all English teachers with extensive experience teaching literature, clustered the answers according to the similarity of content (Beach, 1983, 1985) producing a set of three to five composite categories for each answer. The raters met periodically to compare their groupings and, based on inter-rater agreements, further refinements were made in the categories. The raters then titled each of these groupings with a statement summarizing the content. Answers were also categorized according to a "no answer" category and a "dust bin" category, for answers that could not be included in any of the composite categories (no more than 8 percent of the answers). For example, in response to the question, "What is Felix doing?" in reference to his making a swish shot during a basketball practice, the raters defined four composite categories, "playing basketball," "trying to make the team," "showing off his ability," and "proving himself in order to gain confidence."

The three judges' interrater reliability was determined according to agreement on categorizing inferences for each of the 38 questions (Cronbach's alpha). The reliability scores for act inferences were all above .85; for the perception inferences, .82; and, for the goal inferences, .83.

The second stage of the analysis involved rating each of these composite answer types (as opposed to each individual subject's answers) using three 3-point scales.

Act inferences: Focus on social/psychological meanings. Composite inference categories for each of 11 questions requiring inferences about acts were rated according to the degree of focus on social meanings as opposed to physical actions ("1" = less focus on social/psychological meanings, "3" = more focus on social/psychological meanings). Inference types that involved conceptions of the acts in terms of the characters' physical behaviors were rated lower on this scale. Inference types that involved a conception of the acts in terms of social or psychological phenomena were rated higher on the scale. Interrater reliability (Cronbach's alpha) across raters and answers was .85.

The composite inference categories that received a "1" rating for degree of focus on social/psychological meanings (with most focus on physical behaviors) included "talking to Irene," "riding her bike," "talking with Felix," "getting to know Irene," "shooting the ball," "praising Felix," "speaking to Irene," "trying to get a date," "bragging," "giving up," "telling him she can't go."

Inference categories that received a "3" rating for this scale include "trying to support Felix," "getting confidence back," "having a positive effect on Felix," "establishing a boy/girl relationship," "using Felix as an example," "being friendly but aloof" "proving himself/gaining confidence," "expressing negative perceptions about self," "trying not to get hurt," "reassuring Felix."

Inference categories receiving a "2" rating fell between these two extremes.

Perception inferences: Focus on beliefs. The composite inferences categories for each of 16 questions requiring perception inferences were rated according to the degree of focus on characters' beliefs as opposed to characters' feelings ("1" = less focus on characters' beliefs, "3" = more focus on characters' beliefs). Inference types that were rated low on the scale involved conceptions of characters' perceptions in terms of the characters' feelings or emotional relationships. Inference types rated high on the scale involved conceptions in terms of the characters' beliefs about their own or other characters' social or psychological status. Interrater reliability (Cronbach's alpha) across raters and answers was .82.

Inference categories that received a "1" rating for degree of focus on characters' beliefs included: "she likes him," "she doesn't like him," "he feels confident," "he feels good," "he has confidence," "likes Felix," "that he's good."

Inference categories that received a "3" rating included: "she is attempting to determine his perceptions," "that he has to be more independent," "that practicing hard pays off," "that Felix is a good model of potential," "that his father doesn't understand him," "that she has more confidence than he does," "that he lacks confidence," "that others have treated him unfairly."

Inference categories that received a "2" rating fell between these two policies.

Goal inferences: Focus on long-range goals. The composite inferences for 11 questions requiring goal inferences were rated according to the degree of focus on long-range social or psychological needs as opposed to short-term physical actions ("1" = less focus on long-range goals, "3" = more focus on long-range goals). Inference types rated low on this scale involved concep-

393

tions of goals in terms of immediate, short-range needs or desires, while types rated high on the scale involved conceptions of goals in terms of characters long-range social or psychological needs or desires. Interrater reliability (Cronbach's alpha) across raters and answers was .84.

Inference categories that received a "1" rating for degree of focus on long-range goals included: "wants to go out with Irene," "wants to get a date," "wants to be friends with Irene," "wants to quit the team."

Inference categories that received a "3" rating included: "wants to be accepted by his father," "wants to keep his self-esteem," "wants to be more stable," "wants to be independent."

Inference categories receiving a "2" rating fell between these two poles.

In case of disagreement in using these three scales, the score on which two of the three raters agreed was used as the rating for the composite inference.

The third stage of the analysis involved assigning these ratings to each readers' answers. Based on the judges' rating of the composite answers, each reader then received a rating score for each of their 38 inferences. The mean ratings across the act answers, perception answers, and goal answers for each reader were then determined.

Because they gave more than two "no answers," five of the 160 readers were eliminated from the analysis, leaving a total of 155 participants.

MANOVA was used to determine the effect of grade level (eighth graders vs. eleventh graders vs. college freshmen vs. college juniors) on mean ratings for the three scales: Focus on Social/Psychological Meanings, Focus on Beliefs, and Focus on Long-range Goals. Univariate analysis of variance was then used to examine the effects of grade level for each of the three scales separately. Post hoc tests (Duncan, $p < .01$) were used to determine significant differences between grade-level means.

Results

The mean ratings for act, perception, and goal inferences for each of the four grade levels are presented in Table 1.

The MANOVA results indicated that grade had a significant overall effect on the ratings for act, perception, and goal inferences combined ($F[9, 456] = 6.9$, $p < .001$).

Act Inferences.

Grade level had a significant univariate effect on mean Focus on Social/ Psychological Meanings ratings for characters' acts ($F[3, 152] = 20.1$, $p < .001$). A post hoc Duncan test ($p < .01$) indicated that the eighth graders focused

394

significantly less on social/psychological phenomena than did the eleventh graders. And, both the eighth and eleventh graders focused significantly less on social/psychological phenomena than did the college freshmen and the college juniors.

Perception Inferences

Grade level had a significant univariate effect on mean Focus on Beliefs ratings of characters' perceptions ($F[3, 152] = 10.1$, $p < .001$). The eighth graders and eleventh graders focused significantly less on the characters' beliefs than did the college freshmen or the college juniors.

Goal Inferences

Grade level had a significant univariate effect on mean Focus on Long-range Goals ratings of characters' goals ($F [3, 152] = 5.7$, $p < .001$). The eighth graders and eleventh graders focused significantly less on long-range goals than did the college freshmen or college juniors.

In summary, grade level had significant effects on ratings of Focus on Social/Psychological Meanings, Focus on Beliefs, and Focus on Long-range Goals goal ratings. Post hoc tests indicated that eighth and eleventh graders differed significantly from the college freshmen and juniors on all three scales. The eighth graders also differed significantly from the eleventh graders on Focus on Social/Psychological Meanings ratings for act inferences.

Table 1

Mean Ratings (and Standard Deviations) for Act, Perception, and Goal Inferences for Each of Four Grade Levels

	Inference Type		
	Acts	Perceptions	Goals
Grade Level			
Eighth graders	1.4 (.5)	1.2 (.3)	1.3 (.4)
Eleventh graders	1.8 (.4)	1.4 (.3)	1.3 (.4)
College freshman	2.0 (.3)	1.6 (.3)	1.6 (.4)
College juniors	2.1 (.2)	1.6 (.3)	1.6 (.4)

Note. Grade level had a significant effect on each of the three inference types (p < .001). Results of Duncan post hoc tests (p < .01) are noted below.
a. Eighth graders < eleventh graders < college freshman and juniors
b. Eighth and eleventh graders < college freshman and juniors

Discussion

The fact that the college freshmen and juniors focused significantly more on social/psychological phenomena as opposed to physical actions, on characters' beliefs as opposed to feelings, and on long-term as opposed to short-term goals than did the eighth and eleventh graders is consistent with the expected grade-level differences suggested by the cognitive and social developmental research.

Focus on Social/Psychological Meanings Ratings for Act Inferences

The fact that eighth graders differed significantly from eleventh graders in mean ratings for Focus on Social/Psychological Meanings may reflect a cognitive shift from the initial to the later formal operations stages that typically occurs between eighth and eleventh grade (Applebee, 1978; Fusco, 1983; Parnell, 1984; Petrosky, 1977). The act inferences with "1" ratings on the Focus on Social/Psychological Meanings scale, (e.g., "'talking to Irene," "riding her bike," "shooting the ball") reflect a focus on surface behaviors or immediate physical contexts more characteristic of thinking at the initial formal operations stage. In contrast, act inferences with "3" ratings, (e.g., "establishing a boy/girl relationship," "getting confidence back," "having a positive effect on Felix," "being friendly but aloof," "proving himself/gaining confidence," "expressing negative perceptions about self") involve a conception of acts in terms of larger psychological or social contexts more characteristic of thinking at the formal operations stage (Applebee, 1978; Fusco, 1983; Parnell, 1984; Petrosky, 1977).

However, it is difficult to explain why these social/psychological inferences necessarily reflect characteristic formal-operations stage thinking. It may be the case that these inferences reflect developmental differences in readers' conception of self. In conceiving of characters' acts, a reader may attempt to relate those acts to certain personality attributes consistent with their own self-concept. Given early adolescents' propensity to define self in terms of actions or physical behaviors (Bernstein, 1980; Crowther, 1983; Peel, 1971), the eighth graders may have been more likely to conceive of characters' acts in terms of physical behaviors. In contrast, the fact that the eleventh graders and, to a greater degree, the college freshmen and juniors focused significantly less on physical behaviors may reflect their conception of self defined more in terms of social and psychological relationships with others (Crowther, 1983; Kegan, 1982).

The grade-level differences may also reflect differences in readers' ability to conceive of acts as related to larger themes in a text, for example, Felix's lack of confidence. Many of the higher-rated inference types ("getting confidence back," "having a positive effect on Felix," "proving himself/gaining confidence," "expressing negative perceptions about self") consistently refer to the theme of Felix's lack of confidence. Hunt and Vipond (1985) find that readers who are able to read a story in terms of its point (a "point-driven" orientation) are better able to define how certain aspects of a story contribute to that point than are readers who simply read for the enjoyment of a story (a "story-driven" orientation). This ability to conceive of a text in terms of larger symbolic or thematic meanings is related to amount of previous reading of literature and to literature instruction (Svensson, 1985). The fact that the college students may have acquired more of a point-driven orientation from reading of and instruction in literature may provide another possible explanation of their ability to conceive of acts in terms of a theme.

Facts on Beliefs Ratings for Perception Inferences

The fact that college freshmen and juniors were significantly more likely to conceive of characters' perceptions in terms of beliefs than were the eighth and eleventh graders may be related to their ability to infer social/psychological meanings for characters' acts. Hillocks and Ludlow (1984) found that being able to abstract about characters' acts was a prerequisite for abstracting about characters' perceptions and relationships. The older readers may have used their social/psychological inferences about acts to infer related character beliefs. When asked, for example, to describe the coach's comment about Felix's swish shot, the college freshmen and adults were more likely to infer that the coach was "using Felix as an example." They then were more likely to infer the coach's perception: "that Felix is a good model of potential." The older readers' initial act inference—"using Felix as an example," imputing underlying psychological motives—may have prepared them to infer the related logical explanation—the coach would use Felix as an example because he was a "good model of potential."

In contrast, the eighth and eleventh graders' conceptions of acts in terms of physical actions may not have so readily implied beliefs, but rather, characters' feelings—"she likes him," "she doesn't like him," "he feels good."

The older readers were more likely to conceive of perceptions in terms of conflicting perceptions between characters (for example, "that his father doesn't understand him," "that she has more confidence than he does," "that others have treated him unfairly") inferences implying conflicts between Felix and Irene, his father and the "others." In contrast, the eighth and eleventh graders' orientation toward characters' feelings makes little reference to conflict. As readers acquire knowledge of narrative conventions, they may then recognize an author's development of conflict by portraying characters with conflicting beliefs (Bruce, 1981).

Focus on Long-range Goals Ratings for Goal Inferences

The significant difference in Focus on Long-range Goals between the secondary and college level groups confirm a previous finding that college level students are better able to infer long-range goals than secondary students (Beach, 1985). The fact that the secondary participants were more likely to conceive of goals in terms of characters' short-term goals ("wants to get a date," "wants to get rid of Felix") may again reflect their conception of self in terms of actions or physical behaviors (Bernstein, 1980; Crowther, 1983; Peel, 1971). In contrast, the college level participants long-term goal inferences may reflect an increased ability to infer long-range social motives for actions (Lewis, 1981).

The ability to abstract about acts and perceptions may also have been related to the college students' long-range goal inferences. In Schank's model of story inference (1982), the ability to abstract about characters' acts and perceptions helps to evoke prior knowledge of prototypical long-range goals associated with these acts and perceptions. Conceiving of Felix's acts and perceptions in terms of Felix's psychological need to establish a relationship with Irene, may have helped the older readers evoke goal inferences associated with Felix's needs.

Summary

This study assumed that readers' cognitive development, social cognition, and self-concepts influence their inferences (Beach & Brunetti, 1976; Holland, 1975; Hynds, 1985; Peters & Blues, 1978; Petrosky, 1977; Thompson, 1973). Results indicate that college students had significantly higher mean ratings for degree of focus on all three of these scales than did secondary students; on the degree of focus on social/psychological meanings for act inferences, 11th graders also differed significantly from 8th graders. The older readers' ability to conceive of characters' acts in terms of social or psychological implications may reflect not only their social cognitive development but also their ability to conceive of acts in terms of their thematic meanings. Determining the relationship between measures of cognitive development, social cognition, or self-concept and their inferences would enhance explanations of these grade-level differences.

References

Applebee, A. (1978). *The child 's concept of story*. Chicago: University of Chicago Press.

Barenboim, C. (1978), Development of recursive and nonrecursive thinking about persons. *Developmental Psychology, 14,* 419-420.

Beach, R. (1983). Attitudes, social conventions, and response to literature. *Journal of Research and Development in Education, 16,* 47-54.

Beach, R. (1985). Discourse conventions and researching response to literary dialogue. In C. Cooper (Ed.), *Researching response to literature and the teaching of literature (* pp. 10-127). Norwood, NJ: Ablex.

Beach, R., & Brunetti, C. (1976). Differences between high school and university students in their conceptions of literary characters. *Research in the Teaching of English, 10,* 259-268.

Bernstein, R. (1980). The developmental of the self-system during adolescence. *Journal of Genetic Psychology, 136,* 231-245.

Black, J., & Seifert, C. (1985). The psychological study of story understanding. In C. Cooper (Ed.), *Researching response to literature and the teaching of literature* (pp. 190- 211). Norwood, NJ: Ablex.

Bruce, B. (1981). A social interaction model of reading. *DiscourseProcesses, 4,* 273-311.

Crowther, E. (1983). The sensitivity of adolescents to the process of change when viewed in relation to their own lives. *Educational Review, 35,* 15-23.

Damon, W., & Hart, D. (1982). The development of self-understanding from infancy through adolescence. *Child Development, 53,* 841-864.

deVries, J. (1973). A statistical analysis of undergraduate readers' responses to selected characters in Shakespeare's The Tempest. (Doctoral dissertation, University of Illinois). *Dissertation Abstracts International, 34,* 5906A.

Dulit, E. (1972). Adolescent thinking: The formal stage. *Journal of Youth & Adolescence, 1,* 68-79.

Dusek, J., & Flaherty, J. (1981). The development of the self-concept during the adolescent years. *Monographs of the Society for Research in Child Development, 46,* Serial No. 191.

Education Commission of the States. (1981). *Reading, thinking, and writing.* Denver: National Assessment of Educational Progress.

Elkind, D. (1967). Egocentricism in adolescence. *Child Development, 38,* 1025-1034.

Ellis, D., Gehman, W., & Katzenmeyer, W. (1980). The boundary organization of self-concept across the 13 through 18 year age span. *Educational and Psychological Measurement, 40,* 38-44.

Flavell, J. (1977). *Cognitive development.* Englewood Cliffs, NJ: Prentice-Hall.

Fusco, E. (1983). The relationship between children's cognitive level of development and their response to literature. *Dissertation Abstracts International, 45,* 5A (University Microfilms No. 84-10, 959).

Gollin, E. (1958). Organizational characteristics of social judgment: A developmental investigation. *Journal of Personality, 26,* 139-154.

Hillocks, G., & Ludlow, L. (1984). A taxonomy of skills in reading and interpreting fiction. *American Educational Research Journal, 21,* 7-24.

Holland, N. (1975). *Five readers reading.* New Haven: Yale University Press.

Hunt, R., & Vipond, D. (1985). Crash-testing a transactional model of literary learning. *Reader, 14,* 23-29.

Hynds, S. (1985). Interpersonal cognitive complexity and the literary response processes of adolescent readers. *Research in the Teaching of English, 19,* 386-402.

Inhelder, B., & Piaget, J. (1958). *The growth of logical thinking from childhood to adolescence.* New York: Basic Books.

Kegan, R. (1982). *The evolving self.* Cambridge: Harvard University Press.

Kelly, G. (1955). *A theory of personality* (2 vols.). New York: Norton.

Kelly, G. (1970). A brief introduction to personal construct psychology. In D. Bannister (Ed.), *Perspectives in personal construct theory* (pp.145-172). London: Academic Press.

Kohlberg, L. (1969). Stage and sequence: The cognitive-developmental approach to socialization. In D. Goslin (Ed.), *Handbook of socialization theory and research.* (pp. 347-480) Chicago: Rand McNally.

Lewis, C. (1981). How adolescents approach decisions: Changes over grades seven to twelve and policy implications. *Child Development, 52,* 538-544.

Montemayor, R., & Eisen, J. (1977). The development of self-conceptions from childhood to adolescence. *Developmental Psychology, 13,* 314-319.

Parnell, G. (1984). Levels of aesthetic experience with literature. *Dissertation Abstracts International, 45,* 1681A. (University Microfilms No. 84-18,725)

Peel, E. (1971). *The nature of adolescent judgment.* London: Staples Press.

Peevers, B., & Secord P. (1973). Developmental changes in attribution of descriptive concepts to persons. *Journal of Personality and Social Psychology, 27,* 120-128.

Perry, W. (1970). *Forms of intellectual and ethical development during the college years.* New York: Holt, Rinehart, & Winston.

Peters, W., & Blues, A. (1978). Teacher intellectual disposition as relates to student openness in written response to literature. *Research in the Teaching of English, 12,* 127-136.

Petrosky, A. (1977). Genetic epistemology and psychoanalytic ego psychology: Clinical support for the study of response to literature. *Research in the Teaching of English, 11,* 28-38.

Purves, A. (1981) *Reading and literature: American achievement in international perspective*. Urbana, IL: National Council of Teachers of English.

Selman, R. (1980). *The growth of interpersonal understanding*. New York: Academic Press.

Schank, R. (1982). *Dynamic memory: A theory of learning in computers and people*. Cambridge: Cambridge University Press.

Schank, R., & Abelson, P. (1977). *Scripts, plans, goals, and understanding*. Hillsdale, NJ: Erlbaum.

Schlossberg, N. (1981). A model of analyzing human adaptation to transition. *Counseling Psychologist, 9*, 125-146.

Svensson, C. (1985). *The construction of poetic meaning*. Uppsala, Sweden: Liber Press.

Thompson, S. (1973). Response of students in grades 7-12 to selected short stories and the relationship between those responses and certain reader characteristics. *Dissertation Abstracts International, 34*, 7114A. (University Microfilms No. 74-10,183)

Author's Comment—Richard Beach

As the developmental research reviewed in our report indicates, during the years of ages 13 to 17, adolescents experience some profound changes in the ways in which they think about the world. They become better able to see "the big picture." They learn to play with alternative ideas and psychological theories. They begin to consider others' perspectives as distinct from their own. And, they are continually acquiring discourse practices in ways of making sense of texts.

In planning this study, we assumed that these developmental changes would influence their responses to literature. Unfortunately, preservice or inexperienced teachers often do not appreciate these differences. Fresh from a heady series of literary analysis courses, a student teacher may walk into an eighth grade class and expect students to infer symbolic or psychological meanings. They assume that students will respond as they do, failing to recognize the enormous gulf between their own and their students' ways of responding, differences due to years of studying literature and living life.

Given this pedagogical problem, we believed that it would be useful to examine the differences between secondary and college students' responses to literature, differences that reflect differences in acquired "procedural" knowledge of social and literary conventions necessary for making sense of social events or texts (Beach & Brown, 1987). However, it is difficult if not impossible to directly "test" for differences in "procedural" knowledge. We can only intuit that differences in knowledge are shaping readers' responses from examining their actual responses.

We then turned to cognitive and social developmental theory to generate some possible hunches as to how secondary students would differ from college students. That theory suggests that not only do college students differ from secondary students, but also junior high students may differ from high school students. This meant that we needed to use two different secondary groups. The theory also suggested that from early to late adolescence, students shift in their thinking from describing "immediate" or "physical" phenomena to interpreting underlying psychological motives, beliefs, or goals. This review suggested that these orientations would result in differences in the nature of inferences about character's acts, beliefs, and goals. The developmental theory therefore drove the ways in which we set up the study to elicit and to analyze

402

students' responses. Beginning researchers need to recognize the important role of initially defining and clarifying their theoretical assumptions in framing their research.

In designing the study in a manner consistent with a developmental perspective, it is important to recognize the influence of what are defined as "**confounds**" — factors other than age or grade level that might influence the results. For example, in this study, we compared students in a "large midwestern urban university" to those in a "suburban school district." This itself could create a "confound" in that the differences between the university and secondary students may be due to the fact that the university students represent a more selective population than those in a secondary school. (Conversely, if we had compared students in a highly selective secondary school with "college" students in an "open-admissions" community college, we may have had to contend with another "confound" working in favor of the secondary students.) We, therefore, used students in a school district "with a high percentage of students attending post-secondary institutions." Had we used a district with a small percentage of students going on to post-secondary institutions, we would have been open to the charge that the differences were due to differences in the students' knowledge of literature or their writing ability rather than to differences in grade level.

Note also that we selected university students in freshmen composition classes and education majors. Had we selected English majors, we would have been open to the charge that the differences were due to the specialized training in responding to or writing about literature unique to English majors.

Category Analysis of the Content of Responses.

While recognizing the importance of their own theoretical perspectives, researchers also need to continually challenge previous research methods. Much of previous developmental research on literary response has analyzed responses according to "types" of responses, for example, "engagement," "autobiographical," "description," "interpretation," and "evaluation" (Purves & Beach, 1972; see Beach & Hynds, 1990, for a review of research on literary response). Thus, studies would find that older students are more likely to interpret, while younger students were more likely to employ "engagement" or "description," a finding that, as does a lot of research, confirms the obvious.

Rather than focus simply on the "types" of responses, we therefore wanted to study the content of responses—what it is that students actually said about a literary text. We wanted to examine the content of responses because we assumed that college students' inferences would differ in content from those of secondary students. For example, in a previous study (Beach, 1985), I had compared college and high school students' inferences about the dialogue in a comic one-act play by Dorothy Parker about a newly-wed couple. In the play, the couple, headed off to New York for the wedding night, are continually bickering about inconsequential matters. The college students, as a group, were consistently more likely to recognize the humor in the play, humor that eluded the secondary students. Understanding the humor required some insight into the couple's underlying psychological needs and long-range goals. By comparing the content of the students' goal inferences for specific dialogue acts, I found that the college students were consistently more likely to infer "long-range" goals than the high school students, whose inferences reflected more immediate goals. For example, when the bride became upset with the groom for not recalling the color of her hat in order to locate the hat, the high school students would infer that the bride's goal was to get the groom to find her hat. In contrast, the college students were more likely to infer that she was testing out the groom's concern about or allegiance to her. The college students may have been more likely to infer these "long-range" goals than the high school students because they may know more about marital relationships, as well as the literary conventions of comic drama.

However, this study compared only two groups—the high school and college students. In order to examine developmental differences, it is important to have at least three groups in order to determine a consistent pattern or trend. In order to compare not only the junior high and the high school students, as well as college freshmen with older college students, who may have been exposed to some college literature instruction, we ended up using four groups: 8th graders, 11th graders, college freshmen, and college juniors.

In order to compare grade level differences in the *content* of responses, we extended the "cluster-analysis" technique employed in the 1985 study (not to be confused with the statistical method) to devise a set of composite categories (see the study for a description of this technique; see also Beach & Brown, 1987). While we appreciated the fact that each reader has his or her own unique response to literature, we also recognized that readers also make relatively similar inferences about the same specific text episodes. In order to generate a set of composite inference types, we asked a set of judges to cluster each of the answers to the act, belief, and goal questions according to similarity of content. And, drawing on **"factor analysis"** statistical analysis, we asked them to name these composite groupings. While individual judges didn't have too much difficulty doing this, each judge may have derived totally different sets of categories representing their own unique perceptions of the responses. This is why we had to achieve a reasonably high degree of inter-judge **reliability** (.85 for act inferences, .82 for perception inferences, and .83 for goal inferences) in order to demonstrate that the judges were agreeing in their judgments.

However, once we had completed this analysis, we were left with a mountain of category data for each of the 38 questions. In order to compare grade-level differences across these inferences, we had to devise some way of combining the data. Using **chi-square** analyses to determine the relationship between grade level and the category results would have required us to further collapse the response categories so that we could for example, run four by two chi-squares. We were reluctant to further reduce the variety of different types of category responses. And, we would still be left with answers to each question. We therefore developed a rating system for analyzing each of the inference categories, a rating system derived from the developmental theory. Once we had rated each of the categories, we could then assign scores to each of the reader's answers.

Using ratings meant that we could combine mean ratings across the different act, belief, and goal answers. And, in order to determine between-group differences for four groups, we could then use an **analysis of variance** with **post-hoc tests** to determine significant differences both between and among groups. This ended up being important for determining differences for the act inferences. For the ratings of the degree to which students focused on "social/psychological meanings," post hoc tests indicated the eighth graders differed significantly from the 11th graders, who, in turn, differed from the both of the college groups. The fact that the 8th and 11th graders differed on this scale is particularly telling because the "describer orientation" refers particularly to the ways in which early adolescents such as the eighth graders in this study process their experience.

In all of this, we attempted to avoid value judgments that inferences involving social or psychological meanings and/or "long-range" goals were somehow "better" than those involving a "describer orientation." We hoped to convey the important developmental idea that these ratings entailed *differences* in ways of responding. However, much of developmental research on the "levels" of research (see Beach & Hynds, 1990) cannot escape the value assumption that some responses are more "sophisticated" or "fuller" than other responses. At the same time, I believe that we can judge a student's response as more probing, insightful, and well-developed than other students' responses. However, we need to realize that these differences reflect and

405

privilege differences in experiences and instruction often not available to many students.

Subsequent Research Studies.

Since conducting this study, I conducted two other studies that examined developmental differences in writing, studies that yielded somewhat similar results. In one study (Beach, 1987), I compared seventh graders', college freshmen, and graduate students/teachers' autobiographical essays. The seventh graders' descriptions of past events reflected the "describer thinking" (Peel, 1971) found in the response study. Their essays consisted primarily of bare-bones descriptions of events, with few reactions or commentary. And, the graduate students/teachers were more likely to perceive their past event in terms of a set of attitudes than did the younger two groups. In the second study (Beach & Anson, 1988), we compared ninth graders', twelfth graders', college juniors', and adult graduate students' writing of memos in a role play situation. The college and graduate students were more likely than the secondary students to begin their memos with references to their relationship with their audience, a rhetorical ploy that reflects their knowledge of social discourse practices. In contrast, the younger students were much more "action-oriented," often simply demanding results with fewer references to background social relationships. The older students in the memo study may have developed a strategic awareness of the need to build a political network in order to achieve their long-range social goals, an awareness that reflected the same awareness of long-range goals found in the current study and in the one-act play study. What has been most satisfying about these subsequent studies is that they point to a similar developmental pattern suggested in the initial 1985 one-act play study.

Limitations of this Study

In hindsight, one always recognizes limitations, limitations that we didn't discuss in the study report:

* *the nature of the prompts.* In order to compare readers' inferences to the same episodes, we had to ask specific questions about the same acts. These questions and the required focus on specific acts may have limited the degree to which students could explore their responses. It may be the case that secondary students, if given the opportunity through more informal writing and/or "think-alouds" to explore their related experiences and/or prior knowledge, could ultimately infer responses that equaled those of older students (Beach, 1990). Older students may simply be able

to more readily or quickly access their knowledge than younger students. And, responding to more impersonal questions, may discourage students from applying their own personal experiences or attitudes. Simply changing the wording of questions to a more personal prompt can result in significantly higher levels of interpretation (Newell, Suszynski, & Wingart, 1989).

- *the number of texts.* We used only one story in this study. It would have been useful to have included another story in order to compare the results for the two stories. Had we gotten similar results for two or more stories, we would have been able to make a stronger case for the validity of our results. Had we gotten different results, we might have explored the differences in the kinds of knowledge necessary for understanding the two stories, differences that themselves may be related to developmental differences.
- *within-group differences.* Using mean ratings served to mask the within-group differences in responses. Had we more space to report additional results, we might have gone back to the category data and discussed the within-group differences for individual questions. For example, for certain questions, the differences within the ninth grade group may have been just as pronounced as the between-group differences.
- *examining reasons for development.* Much of recent developmental research has shifted away from simply identifying phenomena as representing certain cognitive or social stages to examining the nature and reasons for shifts between these stages. For example, rather than simply identifying students as "dualists" or "relativists," adult development research has been considering reasons for shifts in these ways of thinking. It would, therefore, be interesting to examine reasons for the shifts found in the study. On the one hand, these shifts may be due to differences in basic cognitive ability. Or, they could be due to increased background knowledge of social or literary conventions (Beach & Brown, 1987). Or, they could be due to the accumulative experience or practice of articulating responses to literature.

Similarly, it would be interesting to examine moments of disequilibrium in which students perceive the inadequacy of their current way of thinking relative to their transaction with the text. It is those moments of disequilibrium that may foster growth in an awareness of and knowledge about the act/belief/goal schemas operating in a variety of social and literary contextual worlds.

At the same time, in trying to explain developmental differences, I remain intrigued by poststructuralist notions of social reproduction of discursive practices. I wonder if the students in this study had not simply been socialized to respond according to prevailing cultural "discourses" operating in academia. This suggests the need to go beyond cognitive or social models of development to examine response to literature as part of larger institutional or cultural contexts.

Having to grapple with such alternative theoretical perspectives itself say something about my own development—that development requires a continually rethinking and occasional debunking of previous ideas. Thus, through studying development, one develops.

References

Beach, R. (1985). Discourse conventions and researching response to literary dialogue. In C. Cooper (Ed.), *Researching response to literature and the teaching of literature.* Norwood, NJ: Ablex. Beach, R. (1987). Differences in autobiographical narratives of English teachers, college freshmen, and seventh graders. *College Composition and Communication, 38,* 56-69.

Beach, R. (1990). The creative development of meaning: Using autobiographical experience to interpret literature. In D. Bogdan &S. Straw (Eds.), *Beyond communication.* Portsmouth, NH.: Boynton Cook.

Beach, R. & Anson, C. (1988). The pragmatics of memo writing: Developmental difference in the use of rhetorical strategies. *Written Communication, 5,* 157-183.

Beach, R. & Brown, R. (1987). Discourse conventions and literary inferences. In R. Tierney, P. Anders, & J. Mitchell. *Understanding readers' understanding.* Hillsdale, NJ: Erlbaum.

Beach, R. & Hynds, S. (1990). Research on response to literature. In P.D. Pearson, R. Barr, M. Kamil, & P. Mosenthall (Eds.), *The handbook on reading research.* White Plains, NY: Longman.

Newell, G., Suszynski, K, & Wingart, R. (1989). The effects of writing in a reader-based and a text-based mode on students' understanding of two short stories. *Journal of Reading Behaviors, 21,* 37-57.

Peel, E. (1971). *The nature of adolescent judgment.* London: Staples Press.

Purves, A., & Beach, R. (1972). *Literature and the Reader.* Urbana, IL: National Council of Teachers of English.

Chapter 17 Experimenting in Schools

One reason we like this study is that Hillocks' approach to an apparently simple though chronic problem in student writing has such practical significance. "Most teachers of composition," he says, "recognize lack of specificity in student writing as a continuing problem from junior high school to college" (p. 412). He hypothesizes that a series of observational exercises not only will effectively address the problem of specificity but will do so in a relatively short time, that the students' subsequent writing will be judged more creative, and that the organization of their writing will also improve. The results of the study support all of the hypotheses. The study does well what it sets out to do, but in the process it also raises a number of other issues that are extremely important for both the teacher and researcher in composition. Of course, any method that can achieve such significant gains with such a small commitment of time and energy has to be considered carefully, since such methods are rare in writing pedagogy. But beyond that the study contributes to the art of rhetorical invention: one of the difficult problems the art addresses is not so much how to help students to write something, but how to help them to write something that is accurate, original, and to the point, rather than a series of clichés strung together like beads. It also has implications for both our definition of creativity and for a pedagogy designed to enhance creativity through direct instruction, an approach that traditionally has been considered unpromising. And it raises questions about the usefulness of the study of models in teaching writing and of a structuralist approach in the teaching of organization and develpment. Such issues are bread and butter for the composition teacher and researcher.

Teaching experiments carried out in school settings, as was the case with Hillocks' project, offer researchers far more than their usual share of difficulties. The classroom is a chaotic environment for doing studies, at least, in comparison to the laboratory. Attendance varies. Announcements and fire drills interrupt ongoing activities. Student's interests are drawn to many things more important to them than the researchers' concerns: sports, friendships, romance, pressures from home. In addition, practical requirements of classroom management may seriously restrict the time that is available for research or force the researcher to present one treatment to a whole class rather than randomly assigning students within classes to treatments.

This last constraint is perhaps the most serious one that the school environment may impose on the researcher. As we discussed in Chapter 2, observations of individuals in the same class cannot be considered independent of one another. As a consequence, the researcher must use the class rather than the student as the **unit of analysis**. This is what Hillocks very appropriately did. However, it meant that although he tested more than 200 students, he could claim no more than ten independent measurements — one for each of the ten classes. Any method that can be shown to be useful in the chaos of the classroom, then, must be robust. That is, it must make enough difference to enough students to be detected through the confusion imposed by the practical world.

Yet, despite their difficulties, classroom teaching experiments are extremely valuable for research in literacy because they provide a degree of real-world validity that laboratory experiments typically can't provide. Procedures that may work well in the laboratory under controlled circumstances may not work at all in the much less controlled classroom environment. The best evidence that we can have that a teaching procedure is useful is a clear demonstration that it works in the classroom.

Hillocks' study is a model of how to manage a teaching experiment in a complex school environment. Although he had only ten independent observations, his methods of design and analysis allowed him to make very effective use of them. For example, Hillocks had each teacher teach both an experimental and a control class. By comparing each teacher's performance in the experimental condition to that same teacher's performance in the control condition, Hillocks was able to obtain data which was relatively free of variability due to differences among teachers. Further, by using pretest scores as a covariate in his analysis, Hillocks was able to account for some of the variability among classes due to individual differences and thus was able to increase the sensitivity of his study. These design features helped to make the study a success despite the difficult circumstances under which it was conducted.

Another point worth noting about the design of the study is that the control groups in Hillocks' study were doing something that could reasonably contribute to their writing skill. This is an important point. We could compare students who engage in the experimental training to students who do nothing. But this isn't an appropriate comparison. School time is valuable and alternative instructional activities are in competition for the available time. If schools adopt the experimental training, they will have to drop something else which might be equally valuable. The question, then, should not be "Is the experi-

410

mental training better than no training?" but "Is the experimental training better than what the students would otherwise be doing?"

Notes on Technical Issues

Hillocks study makes use of the **t-test**, a statistical procedure that has not been mentioned in this text. A t-test, however, is not actually new to the reader. It is exactly the same thing as an analysis of variance for one variable with just two values. For example, if we had conducted a study comparing reading in second and third graders, we could analyze the data using either a t-test or analysis of variance. The significance levels that we would get from the two procedures would always be identical. However, if we were to extend the study to include an additional grade level or an additional variable, then the t-test would no longer be an appropriate alternative to the analysis of variance.

George Hillocks, Jr.
University of Chicago

The Effects of Observational Activities on Student Writing

Most teachers of composition recognize lack of specificity in student writing as a continuing problem from junior high school to college. They frequently find college freshmen writing the same kind of vacuous, unsupported generalizations as seventh graders. Even when students are confronted with actual, concrete situations to observe and write about, their writing omits details that might enable them to capture the timbre and quality of the given situation. Either they believe that their prose does convey their own specific perceptions, or they are, for some reason, oblivious to the particular details which give any subject its peculiar qualities.

Talks with students about what they have just observed (a seashell, a painting, a dispute between two students, etc.) seem to indicate that the latter is the case. They simply do not examine experiences very carefully. Although greater power in observing seems to be the primary requirement, it seems clear, also, that student writers need opportunities in which they can gauge the effect of their reports on an audience. Accordingly, an extensive set of exercises has been developed. They begin with close observation, move to the recording of those observations, and end with sharing reports of the experience with other students. These exercises have been described in detail elsewhere (Hillocks, 1974).

Hypotheses

During their development the exercises were piloted with a wide variety of students: students in an advanced writing course at a state university, a group ranging in age from 11 to 16 years, a class of seventh graders at a private university school, ninth and tenth graders in an inner-city school, etc. Subjective examination of the students' writing indicated that they were writing more specifically, that their writing had what might be called greater creativity, and that the focus of the writing was stronger. The pilot studies suggested the following hypotheses as appropriate for research.

412

Hypothesis 1: that students involved in observational activities would show greater gains in the specificity of their writing than students involved in a more traditional sequence of instruction, even one such as the traditional approach to paragraph development which emphasizes the support of generalizations with specific details and examples.

Hypothesis 2: that the gains hypothesized above could be achieved in a relatively short sequence of instruction.

In addition to the major hypotheses above, the pilot studies seemed to indicate that the following hypotheses were also appropriate.

Hypothesis 3: that students whose writing showed gains in specificity would also be judged to be more creative.

Hypothesis 4: that the gains in measures of organization would be greater for students involved in observational activities than for those studying the traditional paragraph structure of topic sentence supported by details and examples.

Procedures

In order to test these hypotheses, three studies were conducted in three schools, utilizing five teachers and ten classes. The cooperation of the school personnel was secured through the offices of a teacher who had indicated interest in participating in research. Once the cooperating teachers were identified, a table of random numbers was used to select the particular classes which would be involved and to assign them to treatments, either control or experimental. Each teacher taught two classes, one experimental and one control.

From School A, a parochial school for girls in a blue collar neighborhood on the west side of Chicago, four classes of ninth grade girls were selected. School B, a middle-class suburban public school on the northwest side of Chicago, provided two classes of eleventh graders, and school C, a middle-class suburban school on the west side of Chicago, four classes of ninth graders.

Students in the experimental classes spent their time almost exclusively in observational activities, recording visual, tactile, auditory, olfactory, and internal sensory perceptions. Each activity involved responding aloud, taking

413

notes, or writing brief compositions—usually not more than a few sentences in length. For example, in one activity, students, working in groups of four to five, put on blindfolds and examined a plate of objects including such material as sandpaper, carpeting, an elastic bandage, a piece of onion, a slice of potato, etc. Students first tried to identify the objects and then, still wearing the blindfolds, tried to think of words and phrases which best described the texture of each item. After removing the blindfold, students examined the several "rough" objects on the plate: the backing, the carpet, a piece of unfinished plywood, a piece of sandstone, and a piece of sandpaper. As a group, they developed a list of words and phrases which discriminated among the kinds of roughness they observed. Later they reported these lists to the class as a whole. Another activity involved physical exertion through dynamic tension exercises. As students performed the exercises, they observed what-ever changes in bodily sensations occurred. After each exercise, they wrote a brief description of those sensations. A follow-up assignment asked students to imagine they had been chased by a mysterious looking person to a hiding place where they remained as silent as possible. The assignment was to describe the sensations they experienced as a result of their exertion and fear. Two lessons were designed to help students select details to create a particular impression. The specific sequence of activities designed for use in school A and used subsequently as the basis for the experiment in schools B and C has been described in detail by Sjostrom (1976).

Although the instruction on paragraphs varied somewhat from school to school, because of differences in books and audiovisual materials available, students studied the same topics and in much the same way. Typically, the lessons included work with topic sentence; supporting details, concluding sentences; identification of purpose, word choice, unity, and emphasis; the difference between general and specific words, and so forth. One lesson focused on using concrete words to describe emotions, feelings, and abstract reactions concerning something or someone the person likes very much. A lesson on selecting necessary and appropriate details included an assignment which asked students to compose a newspaper account of the episodes concerning the father's theft and trial in the novel, *Sounder,* which had been read by the students in school A. The lessons made use of a substantial number of models written by professional writers. In addition, students were given a number of opportunities to read and comment on what their class-mates had written. The lessons used in the school A control groups have been described in detail by Sjostrom (1976). The teachers in schools B and C used similar plans which they believed would be more effective than those used in school A.

Although the experimental treatment was essentially new to each teacher involved, no extensive training program was undertaken. The purposes and procedures of the experimental lessons were explained briefly to the cooperating teachers. They were supplied with detailed lesson plans, but they collected their own materials for use in the observational activities. In contrast, the work with paragraph structure was an established part of each curriculum. Cooperating teachers not only provided instruction on paragraph structure, but believed in the necessity for and efficacy of such instruction.

Certain key elements of instruction which might have influenced the outcome were held constant in control and experimental groups: the number of models examined for the use of sensory detail; the number of small group meetings in which students read and responded to each other's writing; the number of small group work sessions; the number of notetaking activities; and most important, the number of compositions written. The key difference between the experimental and control groups was simply that the experimental groups spent well over half their class time in actual observation while the control groups spent approximately the same amount of time engaged in the direct study of paragraph structure through textbooks and slide presentations. The control group did not engage in any special observing activities in the classroom. The experimental group did not study the structure of paragraphs.

The time allotted to instruction for control and experimental groups did not vary within an individual school. The initial study for school A was planned with ten days of instruction in both experimental and control groups. However, since the custom of that school was to spend two days a week on writing and grammar and the remainder of the week on literature, the ten days of instruction were spread out over five weeks. In school B the cooperating teacher preferred to teach the ten days in two weeks. In school C the cooperating teachers extended the instructional time to fifteen days because they felt they needed that long to complete the instruction. Although the time allotment varied among the three schools, time, as well as other elements of instruction, was held constant within each school.

Prior to instruction two compositions (pre-tests) were collected from all students in the experimental and control groups. Following the instruction, another two compositions were collected from all students (post-tests). One pretest and one post-test were written in class. The second pre-test and the second post-test were written outside class and turned in to the teacher. The topics were very much the same. The directions for pre-test 1 read as follows:

415

"Write about a person or place (real or imaginary) that interests you in some way. Be as specific as you can in describing the person or place. Try to write so that the reader of your composition will see what you saw and feel what you felt." The second pre-test and post-test assignment directed students to "write about an event (real or imaginary) and its consequences, that concerned you or someone you know. Be as specific as you can in describing the event and its consequences. Try to write so that a reader of your composition will see what you saw and feel what you felt." Unfortunately, not all students wrote all of the assignments. Students who did not complete all papers were excluded from the study. About equal numbers of students in the control and experimental groups were lost in this way.

Analysis

What English teachers mean by specificity in writing is not easy to define. If it were, conscientious students would be able to "be specific." It seemed necessary to settle for an operational definition that would permit judging student papers in terms of levels of specificity. The researchers began by isolating words and phrases in student writing that they agreed were specific. At first they attempted to count details. For a given phrase, however, they frequently could not decide whether they were confronting one, two, or even three details. However, it was possible to isolate sentences and phrases which contained specific details. Because they had no method for the analysis of details that was reliable and efficient (strategies which were attempted proved far too time-consuming), they decided to use a scale extending across the range of specificity found in student papers written during the pilot studies. Using the examples of specific details isolated initially, the researchers identified some very vague papers and some highly specific papers from the pilot study to be used as bench marks. After discussions of the nature of specific detail and the sample papers, a group of four experienced teachers examined a set of forty randomly selected papers from the present study. They found no papers that were more vague than those in the pilot studies and none that were more specific. They proceeded to divide all forty papers into five piles, each representing a level of specificity. Next, they read through all the papers in each pile to determine whether or not all papers in a particular pile displayed a comparable level of specificity. Papers which did not were moved to an appropriate stack. Model papers were then selected to serve as representative of each scale score from 1-5. In addition, operational definitions of each level were developed.

416

The specificity (detailedness) of any particular phrase must be judged in context, a situation which necessarily involves a degree of subjectivity and ambiguity. The word *detail* implies both subordination to some larger focus and a belonging to that focus. That is, any detail is necessarily a detail of something else. If a writer deals with a highly abstract subject or develops a grossly panoramic view of something, the details are likely to be rather abstract. For example, in the sentence "The city of Chicago is dotted with neighborhood parks," the phrase "dotted with neighborhood parks" may be regarded as a detail. It is subordinate to the larger subject "the city of Chicago" and belongs to that subject. However, the concern here was with details at a much lower level of abstraction. In this study, *detail* was defined as a phrase or sentence which conveyed a mental image of particular sensory impressions. For example, the following sentence uses such details in a post predicate position: "The city of Chicago is dotted with neighborhood parks, many with their own playground facilities: concrete sewer pipes set at strange angles for climbing, tall slides whose shiny steel beds slip children over two or three waves to the ground, as well as the more mundane swings, teeter-totters, and monkey bars." The phrase "concrete sewer pipes set at strange angles for climbing," is an example of what was designated a detail. A catalogue of items (swings, teeter-totters, and monkey bars) was also considered to be a detail. In addition, statistics (60%, four out of five, etc.) and direct quotations were considered to be details. The most specific papers also contained elaborated details, such as the phrase about the slides in the sentence above.

Ultimately, although an analytical approach could not be used in scoring the papers, the analysis of detail outlined above was invaluable in enabling raters to focus on detail rather than on other qualities in the writing. Thus, a paper containing a great many details would receive a high score regardless of serious flaws in organization, sentence structure, or mechanics. Scores were assigned to papers if the density of their detail matched that of the model in the scale. Analysis was used only when a decision was difficult. When ambiguity remained, the ground rule was to assign the lower score.

> Score 1: These papers included no, or possibly one, detail. They were composed largely of generalizations and cliches without any attempt to deal with the topic in concrete ways.

> Score 2: These papers were likely to include one or two details and/or to convey a fairly clear, though not particularly detailed, account of some person, place, or event. Cliches were fairly frequent at this level.

417

Score 3: These papers were likely to include two or three details with some elaboration and a clear account of the subject. Details and generalizations irrelevant to the central focus might be included. Some cliches are apparent

Score 4: These papers have a relatively high density of detail, four, five, or more with considerable elaboration. Few cliches appear. However, the central focus is not clearly defined. The impact of the piece is marred by tangential material.

Score 5: These papers are characterized by a high density of detail with considerable elaboration. Cliches are almost nonexistent at this level. The focus is sharp, tangential material has been excluded, and the impact is strong.

Although there was a tendency for papers which scored 4 and 5 to be longer, some 4's and 5's were very short and concise. At the same time, some papers which were scored 1 and 2 were very, very long. Raters made every attempt to exclude problems of usage, mechanics, and bad hand-writing from consideration.

In preparation for scoring the compositions, assistants removed names and dates from all papers after assigning them random code numbers. Graders were unable to determine which classes, teachers, methods, or test periods a given paper represented. Four reliability checks yielded Pearson product moment correlations of .85, .86, .89, and .93.

Results

For the following analyses, the two pre-test scores for each student as well as the two post-test scores were summed. For one part of the statistical analysis, these sums (or combined scores) were treated as single measures on a scale of 2 to 10. The summary statistics for the combined scores appear in Table 1. A glance at that table prompts a number of observations. First, very few students in the sample wrote specifically prior to the instruction. A given student's score must be at least 2. A class mean of 3.2 for two papers, for example, indicates that nearly half the students received a combined score of 3 or 2. Second, the means of pre-test scores for the two groups of eleventh graders (school B) are not much higher than those for three of the ninth grade classes. Third, the gains for the experimental groups (observing and writing) are clearly greater than the gains for the control groups (paragraph study).

Table 1

Summary of the Effects of "Observing and Writing" Activities Compared to the Effects of Paragraph Study on Specificity in Student Writing

| | | Mean Scores | | | |
		Combined Pre-Tests	Combined Post-Tests	Gain or Loss	Difference in Mean Gains
School A	Teacher 1: Paragraph Study n = 18	4.16	4.61	0.45	
	Observing and Writing n = 12	4.42	6.91	2.49	+2.04
	Teacher 2: Paragraph Study n = 17	2.70	3.23	0.53	
	Observing and Writing n = 21	4.70	6.40	1.70	+1.56
School B	Teacher 3: Paragraph Study n = 25	4.39	5.00	0.61	
	Observing and Writing n = 23	4.70	6.40	1.70	+1.09
School C	Teacher 4: Paragraph Study n = 14	3.21	4.07	0.86	
	Observing and Writing n = 23	3.96	5.96	2.00	+1.14
	Teacher 5: Paragraph Study n = 20	4.10	3.35	0.75	
	Observing and Writing n = 18	3.67	4.61	0.94	+1.69

The combined pre-test scores and the combined post-test scores were subjected to a two-way analysis of covariance. The results appear in Table 2. Although some significant differences between teachers exist, no significant interaction between teacher and method appears. That is, the success of the method does not depend upon the teacher using it. At the same time the difference between methods, with an F value of *54.45* is significant with a probability of less than .0001. Clearly, the method of using observational activities results in significantly greater specificity, as assessed by the scale described above, than the method of paragraph study.

419

Table 2

*Results of Two-Way Analysis of Covariance by Teacher and
Method of Specialty Scores*

Source of variation	DF	Mean Square	F	Significance of F
Pre-test scores	1	90.707	34.329	.0001
Main Effects	5	40.510	12.331	.0001
Teacher	4	15.549	5.884	.0001
Method	1	143.890	54.456	.0001
2-Way Interactions Teacher: Method	4	1.994	.775	.556

Bock (1975) argues that because the mean gains for students within a particular class are correlated by virtue of their having the same teacher or method, the teacher or method should be the unit of analysis. In a second statistical analysis, then, the mean gains of each class constituted the independent observations. A t-test was run using the mean gain scores recorded in Table 1. The difference between the experimental (observing and writing) group's mean and the control (paragraph) group's mean is 1.5, a difference which yields a t-value of—3.936, which is significant at .005.

Samples of the pre-test and post-test compositions underwent further analyses —one attempting to judge creativity and one to judge organization and support of generalizations.

The judgment of creativity was limited to 40 compositions: the papers of 10 students who showed a gain on the specificity scale of two or more points from pre-test A to post-test A and the papers of another 10 who showed a gain of two or more points from pre-test B to post-test B. The sample included 20 students with two compositions each. These 40 compositions were duplicated in the original handwriting and distributed to five graduate students in English who rated them for creativity. They were asked to use a five-point scale for which they could develop their own criteria, sort the papers into five stacks, each representing one point on the scale, and review each stack for consistency of judgment, reordering papers when that seemed appropriate.

When raters had completed the reordering of the compositions, they wrote descriptions of the qualities of the papers in each of the five piles. Informal analysis of those notes reveals that the raters agreed that those compositions which they had rated 1 (least creative) were characterized by "simple statement of event" and lack of "specific" or "effective" imagery. Judgment terms

420

used by raters in describing compositions at this level included the following: monotonous, cliched, stagnant, perfunctory, flattened effect, simple, obvious, bland, and general. All five raters suggested at least one of the following: that the writers were uninvolved, bored, made no effort, lacked motivation, did not like writing the compositions, or did not want to write them. Such inferences were *not* requested in the directions.

At the opposite extreme, compositions which had been rated 5 (most creative), all of the raters commented on the "excellent," "ingenious," "astute and interesting," "effective," or "selective" use of imagery or specific detail. Four commented on the complexity and/or sophistication of the *perceptions* expressed. Apparently, effective or specific imagery was an important criterion in rating the papers for creativity.

Each paper received five scores, one from each rater. The means of these scores were then correlated (using the Pearson product moment formula) with the specificity scores assigned earlier. The correlation was .83, indicating a very close relationship between specificity and what the judges regarded as creativity. Although technically no causality can be inferred, it seems reasonable to assume that more specific writing will be judged more original and creative.

Because the control groups had concentrated on paragraph structure and the support of generalization with specific detail, examples, etc., it was decided to rate a sample of the papers for organization. One pre/post-test assignment, the request that students write about a person or place, seemed to be more conducive to the use of traditionally defined paragraph structure. Writing about an event or experience would not be so likely to produce a generalization supported by details. All pre- and post-tests related to writing about a person or place for school A were submitted to three experienced high school English teachers for judgment. The three judged the papers in terms of organization and the support of generalization, sorting the papers into five ranked stacks and reading through the stacks to insure consistency, shifting papers when that seemed appropriate. The raters were asked to write descriptions of the papers in each stack. All raters agreed that papers they had scored 1 were highly generalized, lacked a clearly stated or implied topic, and failed to present supportive detail. Two commented on the inclusion of extraneous material and two on repetitiousness of the papers. Papers which they had rated 5, in contrast, were characterized, they felt, by a clear sense of direction, clearly stated or implied topics, and generalizations which were carefully supported by appropriate detail and metaphor. Other criteria which raters commented upon included the presence or absence of cliche, and weak or strong sentence structure. The important point here is that, once again, specificity appears to be an important dimension of the ratings.

The mean scores for these ratings were correlated with the previously assigned specificity scores, again using the Pearson product moment formula. The resulting correlation was .85. In addition, the mean gain scores for organization were submitted to a t-test. A summary of those data appears in Table 3. The two control groups (n = 35) show no gain in organization. The slight loss is not statistically significant. The two experimental groups (n = 33) show a gain of nearly one point on a five point scale. The test of t indicates a difference between the control and experimental groups which is significant at .001.

The results of the research support all four hypotheses. Students who were involved in observational activities did increase the level of specificity in their writing. They outstripped students who studied the structure of paragraphs. They achieved those gains in a relatively short period of time. Further, the gains in specificity were closely paralleled by judgments of creativity. If students wrote more specifically, their papers were judged to be more creative. Finally, writing for specificity resulted also in the judgment that papers were better organized and supported. Students in the experimental groups showed far greater gains than did those who had specifically studied organization.

Discussion

Perhaps the most interesting finding of the study is that the changes in writing took place after only 10 days of instruction in three classes and after only 15 days in two. A great many experimental studies of the effects of instruction on student writing show no or only trivial gains. Those that do show changes tend to be conducted over fairly long periods of time, a semester or a full year. The problem is one of explaining the results. Why should observational activities result in marked changes while the traditional

---

Table 3

Difference in Mean Gains on Ratings for Organization between Control and Experimental Groups

	n	Mean Gain	Difference	df	t-score	P
Control	35	0.103	1.08	66	10.28	.001
Experimental	33	+0.979				

study of models results in little or no change? At least three explanations are possible:

1) The observation activities permit students to receive sensory stimuli different from those they were able to receive prior to the activities. More colloquially, the activities enable them to "see" new things.

2) The observation activities somehow condition/persuade students to verbalize consciously entertained perceptions which they had not verbalized before. That is, student writers always "know" what they perceived; they just do not say it.

3) The activities prompt students to reorganize the sensory stimuli which they receive and, therefore, to verbalize different perceptions. That is, the activities enable writers to "see" the old things in new ways.

The first explanation is almost a cliche in some educational literature which demands that a teacher teach students "to see." Such literature, however, does not define the word *see* with any care. It is intuitively obvious that classroom experience cannot improve the functioning of a child's sensory organs. Beyond that, the testing situations in this research call upon students to present not what is immediately before them, but what they can recall or assemble from past experience, sensory stimuli which has been received through the sense organs at the time of the experience. Therefore, the problem is clearly not one of teaching students to receive different sensory stimuli.

The second explanation is equally suspect. In both the control and experimental groups of this study, students were urged "to be as specific as possible." Teachers' comments and grades reward specificity. In both groups *specificity* was defined operationally through examples. One is almost forced to conclude that had students consciously entertained the necessary details, they would have verbalized them in their writing simply as a result of being urged to do so. But even after considerable exhortation and example, students in the control groups, with a few exceptions, proved as reluctant as ever to provide detail.

That, of course, leaves us with the third explanation: that the observation activities prompt students to reorganize stimuli which they had received and, therefore, to verbalize different perceptions or different propositions. The most convincing argument for this explanation lies in gestalt psychology. Kohler (1959) examines the problem of why we perceive the "shapes" we do in visual and other experience. For simplicity, the following discussion is limited to visual perception. He argues that "the retinal stimuli constitutes a mere mosaic, in which no particular areas are functionally segregated and shaped. When the nervous system reacts to this mosaic, and when organization develops, various circumscribed entities may originate, and be shaped . . ." (p. 107). Everyone is familiar with the pictures and diagrams which seem to change shape as we look at them. In one example, we see a white vase in a black area. As we stare at it, we suddenly see two symmetrical faces looking at each other across a white area. The vase has disappeared. In another example, we see a picture of a beautiful young woman wearing a large hat. As we stare at the picture, it switches to the portrait of an old hag. The young woman's delicate cheek and neck become part of the hag's ugly face. The elegant hat becomes the hag's shawl. Obviously, the stimuli alone cannot account for such changes. As the nervous system imposes different organizations on what we perceive, we "see" different things.

Further, Kohler points out that "visual shapes are given only so long as the lines or areas in question are set apart in the fields" (p. 110). That is, we tend not to notice shapes which are a part of some larger whole. One of Kohler's examples is a figure 4, the vertical and horizontal lines of which are extended into new designs of which the figure 4 remains a part. The result is nearly total obfuscation of the numeral. It is on this phenomenon that the art of camouflage depends: if shape A occurs as a part of shape B, shape A is likely to lose its identity to the viewer.

Comparison of student writing completed before and after instruction suggests that the observing activities did prompt students first, in gestalt terms, to examine the parts of larger segregated shapes (and thus, find new ones) and second, to reorganize to find new relationships. The most common shift is that of focusing down on parts of larger wholes. In pre-test compositions, students tend to record the larger shapes of what they have seen. In the post-test compositions, they tend to focus on the parts of the larger experience so that those detailed shapes become significant.

The sets of excerpts which follow were written by two students under similar conditions. In each set the first is a pre-test and the second is a post-test. The first set of examples strikingly reveals shift in focus from the larger whole in the pre-test to the parts of the whole in the post-test.

Student A, The first time I went into a forest, I was amazed at all the living
Pre-Test things around me. The tall green trees with bright green leaves, the beautiful wild flowers, and the free and wild animals.

I was surprised at how the animals weren't being hunted for or caged. I loved how the clean air softly blew, and how the morning sun had shined through the trees. I could feel the soft, dewy grass between my toes. It was cold, and felt refreshing.

I always did like the outdoors, but I never really looked at it this way.

The forest is a wide and vast area, full of living things, and unseen features. Some animals are becoming extinct, yet they still exist in the forest without being bothered by man.

The forest could be considered a mother. She gives birth to new and living things. She also protects them from man and some of his destructive ways. A forest is a beautiful creation and should be respected by man for without plants or animals we would not be alive. Just think, *man extinct*. Humans should protect their beautiful forests, which give us so much.

Student A,
Post-test
The old man, wearing torn and tattered clothes, with worn patches, sat on the warped, wooden, green park bench, reading a two day old newspaper.

The man's face was rugged and full of prickly whiskers. His face and hands were dirty. As he read the newspaper, he swung his foot slowly and very steadily. He seemed to be enjoying himself.

As the man was reading, he pulled out a pack of cigarettes, took one out and lit it. The matches looked old, and he was very careful putting the pack back into his pocket. He slowly puffed on the cigarette, enjoying every bit of it. I couldn't help but wonder where he got the money from. The heavy smell of the smoke filled the surrounding air. The smoke rose to the sky in little clouds, puffy and gray. They would soon disappear with the gentle, passing wind.

Studying the old man's face, I noticed a small hoop earring on his left ear, giving me the feeling that he may have once been a sailor or pirate. His eyes were shiny, not quite glassey, but bright with contentness. His teeth were yellow or brown, full of cavities.

The man seemed to be a person full of old story tales or folk lores. As more people came close to where he was sitting, he got up and left. The old, ragged man walked slowly, but with a slight limp or bounce—I'm not sure. He very closely examined the area around him, taking in as much air and sunshine as he could.

His eyes seemed to dance with contentness, or happiness with his inner self.

425

Two of the above writer's sentences provided fascinating clues to the organization of her perceptions: "I always did like the outdoors, but I never really looked at it this way. The forest is a wide and vast area full of living things and *unseen features.*" (italics added.) The forest she describes is certainly "wide and vast," wide enough and vast enough to be any forest or no forest at all. The important observation for this writer which provides the unity as well as the didactic tone of the paper is that the forest is full of beautiful living things. Some might argue that the student is simply trying to provide "what the teacher wants." That argument seems specious in view of the directions to ". . . be as specific as you can in describing the person or place. Try to write so that a reader of your composition will see what you saw and feel what you felt." It seems more reasonable to assume that the writer really does see the significance of the forest to lie in its vastness, its beauty, and its abundant life. Against the "shape" of the forest, seen on that scale, the "unseen features" must remain insignificant.

In the second composition, the student displays a dramatic shift in perspective. The significant shapes are no longer global generalizations. On the contrary, although generalizations have not disappeared, each rests on one or more details.

Not only did the observation activities result in a shift of attention from the broad outlines of larger shapes to the details within them, but they also appear to have resulted in reorganization of perceptions that emerge as metaphoric expression and shifts in perspective. The following set of examples indicates both.

Student B, The clouds were high and fluffy and sweet smelling. They
Pre-test looked like marshmallows in a cup of hot chocolate. This place has wide green meadows with flowers scattered allover. Animals all around you were ever you walked. You could go to this place and just think for awhile. There were places for sports allover the place and easle painting on. The arts there were magnificent in colors of many. The fresh smell of summer would always be near, if you listen closely so many things you hear such as animals and chirping coming from the birds crickets, and flowers blooming. The pools and ponds were warmed by the sun, were fish swam and ducks float one by one. I like this place, its plain like me, not covered up with pretty faces and fakeouters because thats not me. I like to be known for the way that I am not for the way people want me to be and this place I can sit and just be me. I wish that this place could be real, but maybe some day there will be. So now the smells dullen to dark tones and yellow, the sounds are fading away. Time to leave, good night.

426

Student B, My two wishes were gone and I had one left, my
Post-test last wish was to be a inch tall for 5 minutes. Bang!! The world
was giant, the grass was as tall as a jungle and the blades hurt
when you grasped them. My dog was just standing there
looking at me. I climbed on her foot and then on to her nose
as she bent down. The sound of everything was so loud and I
couldn't hear anything but blasting. Everything was so giant I
walked into my house and all of a sudden I saw I big black
shadow over me. I jumped away and I saw it clamp down. It
could have been me down there. I ran into my room and just
stood there looking at my room in the giant shag carpet. The
smell of my mothers spagetti cooking was tempting but I
thought I better stay out her way. I looked at my watch 3
minutes left. I couldn't imagine the things I could hear, like a
pin drop and people tying there shoes. And the best part was
walking on my dog. Oh, no! My dog just sat down, I'm sliding
and then bang I'm on the floor. I woke up and I was down on
the floor just having a dream.

Both the pre-test and the post-test deal with imaginary content. The first
line of each attempts to put the reader into the scene immediately, the first
through description of the scene, the second through identification with the
first person narrator. Both close with rather cliched escapes: "Time to leave,
good night." and "just having a dream." However, the content and perspective
of the two pieces differ considerably. The first is an attempt to represent
directly a kind of sylvan paradise through glittering generalities that catalogue
the main features. Cliches predominate. Even the only simile draws on cliche,
and unfortunately, the writer has not considered the extension of the
simile,with care. "Marshmallows in a cup of hot chocolate" suggests that the
sky is milky brown, not, one suspects, the impression the writer wished. The
rhyming patterns (near/hear, sun/one) only intensify the cliched quality.

In the second composition, the writer makes a dramatic shift in perspective
and includes details which are both convincing and powerful. The shift allows
him to reorganize the details of experience. Gordon (1961) argues that such
shifts are important to creative problem solving because they permit the
reorganization of sensory data to permit the appearance of new relationships.

If these explanations of the research results are valid, the almost singular,
traditional emphasis on the study of verbal models as a means of learning to
write appears to be inappropriate. The close examination of experience from
a variety of perspectives may yield far more important results in improving
student writing. At the very least, the research holds promise for getting
students beyond vacuous generalities, no mean accomplishment in itself.

References

Bock, R. D. (1975). *Multivariate statistical methods in behavioral research*. New York: McGraw-Hill.

Gordon, W. J. J. (1961). *Synectics*. New York: Harper and Row.

Hillocks, George, Jr. (1974). *Observing and writing*. Urbana, IL: National Council of Teachers of English.

Kohler, W. (1959). *Gestalt psychology*. New York: New American Library.

Sjostrom, N. (1976). *Observation activities as a means of teaching specificity in writing*. Unpublished master's thesis, University of Chicago.

428

Author's Comment—George Hillocks Jr.

The story of "The Effects of Observational Activities ..." is a very long one, one that for me, at least, is not over. Thinking about it now, I realize that that story has many, many episodes. These fall into three major segments: the generation of the ideas for instruction, the impetus for and development of the study, and the impact of the study on my later thinking about the teaching of writing.

As a teacher of freshman English and later as Director of Freshman English at Bowling Green State University (Ohio), I was constantly amazed at the lack of specificity in the writing of my students. It seemed that I was always writing out the advice, "Try to be more specific about this." A rather avant garde freshman text that we used in 1970-71 included an essay under the title "A Pencil is One of the Best Eyes" by Samuel H. Scudder. (Yes, the same essay derogated by Robert Scholes in *Textual Power*.) The essay was impressive, my students read it, and I tried very hard to persuade them to observe things before writing about them. The result was greater specificity on the part of many students, but far from all. In the summer of 1971, I taught an advanced composition class populated by juniors and seniors whose writing was every bit as vacuous as that of my freshmen. As with the freshmen, my exhortations to be more specific had little effect. In frustration I took into class some natural objects for my students to examine and write about—specifically: large pine cones, interesting chunks of rose quartz, and other rocks and minerals. I remember starting with the large sugar pine cones and asking students, "How would you describe the color here?" We passed the cones around for the students to examine closely. (It was a small class of 12 to 15.) "Brown," they said as though I were silly. "Is that really brown? What other colors do you see in there?" I urged them to examine the cones. After a few moments of close examination, they began to note the grayish-silver tips of the petals, the dull yellow, almost orange at the base of the petals, and so forth. As they looked and handled the pine cones, they began to notice many other details: the ways in which the petals were arranged, the sharp needlelike points at the ends of the tips, and so forth. Then class discussion seemed to illustrate what I meant by specificity, and appeared to provide some impetus for specificity in the writing that I saw immediately thereafter. However, I could not think, at the time, of other activities and the writing began to drift back toward vague generalities. Over a year later, I began to develop a wide variety of observational activities which were eventually used with students at many different grade levels and schools in a variety of neighborhoods. Not only did the activities have an impact on student writing, but students clearly enjoyed their engagement in them. Many of these activities were eventually published in *Observing and Writing* (1974). Unfortunately, I had no money to conduct an appropriate study of their effects on writing.

That brings us to the second segment—the impetus for the study. The impetus for the study was Nancy Sjostrom, a master's degree student at the University of Chicago, who was in search of a thesis topic. I suggested the possibility of a quasi-experimental study examining the effects of these observational activities on student writing. She received the idea with considerable enthusiasm and we began to develop a design for a study that would last a month. She proposed that two acquaintances of hers would be willing to do the instructional programs for both experimental and control classes and, further, that two other acquaintances would help with the scoring of the compositions. With the design worked out, she went to the school's principal to ask permission to run the study for the period of a month using four different classes, two of which would serve as experimental groups and two of which would serve as the controls. The principal and department chair, however, were unwilling to take students away from the regular grammar studies for that long a period. They would allow Nancy to work with the classes for only ten days, two days a week for five weeks. When I learned of this proposal, I discouraged Nancy from pursuing the study. I was quite positive that we could have no impact in a mere two weeks, especially spread out over two days a week for five weeks. However, Nancy wanted to persist, and to my great surprise, the results were positive. I remained skeptical, thinking of the small sample and special circumstances, but nevertheless sought out the cooperation of teachers in schools B and C. (Doing the study in pieces, however, entailed rescoring all of the papers from school A along with those from B and C.)

This happy result brings us to the third segment of the story. I had already begun to think about what other strategies writers might learn best through the examination and discussion of concrete data. These results were very encouraging and led to my publication of "Inquiry and Composing" in 1982, an idea which I have continued to work on, and the development of various materials for enabling students to discover and support generalizations about sets of data, generate criteria for discriminating complex concepts, and developing complex arguments. In addition, my work on this study was in part responsible for my identification of a category which I labeled "inquiry" in a synthesis of research on the teaching of writing (Hillocks, 1986).

Though the story is a long one, it seems not to have ended even yet. Every year, I use observing-and-writing activities with my students who wish to become English teachers and require that they develop comparable activities of their own and test them in classrooms. My work on the idea of inquiry for composition continues in two relatively large projects which I hope will come to fruition soon. I suspect that this study has had very little impact on the practice in schools, at a time when teachers who are concerned about writing focus their students' attention on what might be called the general process of writing. Probably the booklet of activities, *Observing and Writing,* has had more impact than the study, but the study has had a profound impact on me, on my thinking, and on the way I conduct my work.

Clearly, the study has helped me, at least, to answer some questions and to find many new directions for exploration. There is one question that I may never answer to my own satisfaction. In the second paragraph of the study I state quite confidently, "They simply do not examine experiences very carefully." I ask, "What colors do you see in this pine cone?" The students respond, "Brown." I say, "Look again. What colors do you see besides brown?" They look again, carefully, and begin to indicate other colors that come to their attention. It seems as though they simply don't look closely. But maybe not. Perhaps they simply see no need to be specific. Perhaps they have been encouraged to look beyond the specific details to generalizations. Maybe our schools do that. Perhaps they simply don't realize the impact that specific details can have on readers. Perhaps there are other reasons. Perhaps it's a combination of all these factors and others I haven't begun to consider. I'd like to know. But that's another study for some other day.

References

Hillocks, G. (1974). *Observing and writing.* Champaign, IL: National Council of Teachers of English and ERIC.

Hillocks, G. (1982, November). Inquiry and Composing: Theory and Research. *College English*.

Hillocks, G. (1986). *Review of research on written composition.* Champaign, IL: National Conference on Research in English and ERIC.

Chapter 18 Metacognition in Writing

The Bracewell article is not an "easy read." Readers will have to pay careful attention to follow some of the arguments. The effort, though, will be very well rewarded because the article is an excellent example of the researcher's craft. In particular, it shows the progression from the generation of a scientific concept to the invention of empirical methods to anchor the concept in observation.

The article is about **metacognition**, that is, it discusses people's abilities to think about their own mental activities. Much of the research on metacognition has focused on **metacognitive knowledge.** People demonstrate metacognitive knowledge when they can accurately describe their own cognitive processes, e.g., "I can remember a list of about eight numbers" or "I have trouble writing thank-you notes." Bracewell argues on the basis of his analysis of the literature that to understand metacognition fully, we also need to attend to what he calls **metacognitive skill**, that is, to people's ability to exercise deliberate control over their own cognitive activities.

Having proposed the concept of metacognitive skill, Bracewell then looked for concrete situations in which to demonstrate the relevance of the concept in practice. He created the desired situations by designing two very clever experiments. Both are studies of the sort that make other researchers say, "I wish I had thought of that." For example, the experimental manipulation in the first study is both very unexpected and very appropriate. Asking children to write as badly as they can is not something that readily occurs to one. It is clear, though, that the contrast between what children do when they are asked to write well and what they do when they are asked to write badly is a very sensible and appropriate measure of deliberate metacognitive control of writing skills. And Bracewell uses that measure with great effect. His observation that second graders write about the same whether they are asked well or badly and that fourth and sixth graders fail to write either as well or as badly as they would like to is clear evidence that metacognitive skill develops with age but that it continues to be an important problem for sixth graders even in simple tasks.

The idea of metacognitive skill that Bracewell poses is, we feel, a very important one, not just in the primary grades but for adult writers as well. We agree with Bracewell's position that the deliberate control of writing skills is hallmark of the expert. In the late '70's, the plain speech movement operated on the assumption that good writing is writing that conveys its message as simply as possible. However, efforts to introduce plain language into business and government immediately ran into difficulties. Organizations had their preferred writing styles. Individuals who wrote plain language in business or government organizations often found themselves seriously out of step with the rest of the organization. Plain language made them less rather than more effective. The experience of the plain language movement illustrates a more general point. In teaching writing, we will probably serve our students better if we avoid teaching them that there is one best way to write and teach them instead so that they obtain deliberate control over their writing so that they can modify it to suit the situation. In other words, we should teach them metacognitive skill.

Bracewell's article was first published in *Research on writing: Principles and methods.*, edited by Mosenthal, Tamor, & Walmsley. The opening remarks in his article refer to that volume rather than this one.

Notes on Technical Issues

Bracewell decided that it was not appropriate to use the chi-square test to analyze the data shown in his Table 6.5. His reason was that some participants were represented more than once in the table. Since there are 31 observations reported in Table 6.5 and only 16 participants, on the average, each participant contributed about two observations. This fact causes two sorts of problems. First, as was discussed in Chapter 2, two observations of the same participant are not necessarily independent of each other. Since the chi-square test requires independent observations, it could not validly be applied to this data. Second, although the participants contributed an average of about two observations each, some contributed more observations than others, and, thus, had more influence on the results than others. The problem that this inequality can create is illustrated in the following example. Suppose we asked 25 college freshmen to list the books that they had read for pleasure over the past year and found that the total number of non-fiction books outnumbered fiction by a ratio of about 2:1 (let us say 72 to 35). Does this result indicate a strong preference for non-fiction among freshmen, one that might lead us to consider redesigning freshmen reading assignments? The answer depends on whether the preference is characteristic of most of the 25 freshmen or just a few. If we found that most had read about 3 non-fiction and 1 or 2 fiction books, then the preference would be a general one. But if we found that high counts for non-fiction came from only two students (let us say that each had read 20 non-fiction books and 1 fiction book), then the preference would not be general; and no change in reading assignments would be warranted.

To provide a valid statistical test for his data, Bracewell calculated a single score for each participant indicating whether that participant's data tended more to confirm or to disconfirm Bracewell's hypothesis. A positive score indicated a tendency toward confirmation and a negative one, a tendency toward disconfirmation. To evaluate his data statistically, Bracewell used a **binomial test** which is also known as a **sign test**. The binomial test is a very simple test which is based on the assumption that positive scores are just as likely as negative scores if the hypothesis is not true. This is comparable to saying that a coin is just as likely to come down heads as tails, if it is fair. In fact, the scores were positive for 13 of the 16 participants. If the hypothesis were not true, this result would be just as unlikely as tossing a fair coin 16 times and getting 13 heads, an event that would happen less than one time in a hundred.

References

Mosenthal, P., Tamor, L., & Walmsey, S. (Eds.) (1983) *Research on writing: Principles and methods.* New York: Longman.

Robert J. Bracewell
McGill University

Investigating the Control of Writing Skills

The Control of Writing Processes

By control of writing processes, I mean the deliberate manipulation by the writer of whatever mental and physical activities that lead to the production of text. Of course the production of text does not require deliberate control of writing activities for either the skilled or unskilled writer; but I shall present the position that the ability to do so, when necessary, is the hallmark of the expert.

Before we begin one may ask, "Is it worthwhile writing a chapter on such a topic when just about everybody would acknowledge that such control is indeed a good thing for a writer to have?" Those with some knowledge about writing and its development would grant this, but would advance as more worthy of consideration such issues as the possible developmental constraints on learning to write and the overcoming of writing blocks and apprehension. After all, children simply do not do very much writing (Applebee, 1981; Fillion, 1979; Graves, 1978), and any methods or principles for increasing their output should take precedence over issues of secondary importance, such as how to control writing once one is able or willing to do it. But those with more knowledge still would bring together some facts that implicate control as a crucial issue in the development of writing skills. It is true that children (and most adults) do not do much writing; moreover, when they do, they display few of the activities of expert writers, such as planning, note taking, and so on. Curiously however, when asked to do things that experts do, such as planning, what unskilled writers do is to compose text in complete sentences (Bereiter, Scardamalia, Anderson, & Smart, 1980). So, infrequent writing is not due to an inability to produce text; it must be due to something else. As the facts briefly touched on above suggest, the causes of infrequent writing are complex. But two things are clear. First, children can express themselves in writing; somewhat surprisingly (because children are usually very fond of expressing themselves), they do not do very much writing. Perhaps part of the reason for this puzzling juxtaposition lies in an ability to write that is paired with an inability to exercise a great deal of control over the processes of writing.

The issue of control of writing processes addresses for a specific area a general issue that is of increasing importance in education, namely, the control

436

by the student of various mental activities and strategies that increase learning. Within education, this issue is often talked about in terms of study skills, awareness of comprehension failure, and learning how to learn. Within cognitive psychology, it is talked about under the rubric of metacognition, a buzzword that has begotten many little metas — metalinguistics, metamemory, metacomprehension, and so on. Such terms, even though they seem to proliferate and have little more than descriptive status, do point to an important generalization (dare one say principle?) about learning. Generally, the better grasp students have of their abilities and strategies for learning, the quicker they are able to acquire new knowledge and skills.

It is worthwhile to elaborate on what is meant by grasp of learning abilities and strategies to resolve part of the considerable confusion at the theoretical level and in the interpretation of data in this area. This confusion is well represented in the field of metacognition, and the discussion presented here focuses on this area and its terminology; but similar problems exist in the related areas of educational research. For example, how can we adequately characterize learning-how-to-learn abilities? What methods can we devise to identify their use by the learner?

Metacognition is a term used to refer to two different types of behavior (Brown, 1978; Brown & Campione, 1980; Flavell & Wellman, 1977). The first is the learner's ability to take stock of his or her own cognitive resources and task demands. A typical example would be a learner's knowledge that a list of facts grouped by categories is easier to learn than an ungrouped list. Of course, such metacognitive knowledge might not be used by a learner. This brings us to the second aspect of metacognition, the use of these abilities and strategies in a learning situation. For example, in learning a list of facts, the student would try to impose some classification on them to aid acquisition.

The criterion for the first kind of behavior, labeled metacognitive knowledge, is quite straightforward, that is, the possessor of such knowledge should be able to *state verbally* characteristics of learning, knowing, or task structure that influence performance on the task (Brown & Campione, 1980). The reason verbalization is used as a criterion is that saying what is metacognitive about a task requires deliberate choice from among all the things that might be said about a given task. In other words, the assumption is made that the learner must exercise control over the selection of knowledge relevant to the task. Certainly, it seems unlikely that such knowledge can be faked, for example, by rote memorization. In addition, the verbalization criterion permits a reasonable separation between metacognitive knowledge and cognitive knowledge because tests of invariant aspects of metacognition may be operationalized by examining stability of metacognitive responses across different tasks that vary in cognitive content.

This straightforward method for assessing metacognitive knowledge contrasts with criteria for assessing the other type of metacognitive behavior. This second type is concerned with the use of metacognitive knowledge in carrying out cognitive tasks, which, for ease of reference, I shall call metacognitive skill to differentiate it from metacognitive knowledge. As criteria for the presence of metacognitive skill, various activities have been proposed, such as checking, planning, selecting, monitoring, and inferring (Brown & Campione, 1980); self-interrogation and introspection (Brown, 1978); and monitoring and interpretation of ongoing experience (Flavell & Wellman, 1977). Although adequate operationalizations for most of these activities can be specified, one runs into considerable difficulty in deciding whether they are adequate criteria for distinguishing metacognitive from cognitive activity. All the above activities are certainly candidates for indices of metacognitive skill, especially planning, self-interrogation, monitoring, and checking, but others occur also in the course of cognitive activity. For example, the use of language (and all metacognitive tasks are language tasks) requires inferring, selecting, and interpretation of ongoing experience. How are we to separate the metacognitive use of these skills from the simply cognitive use?

The chameleonlike quality of metacognitive skill is illustrated in statements about its characteristics. In earlier characterizations, the conscious regulation of cognitive activity was emphasized:

> Metacognition refers, among other things, to the active monitoring and consequent regulation and orchestration of these processes in relation to the cognitive objects on which they bear, usually in the service of some concrete goal or objective. (Flavell, 1976, p. 252)

> The processes described as metacognitive are the important aspects of knowledge. . . in the domain of deliberate learning and problem solving situations, conscious executive control of the routines available to the system is the essence of intelligent activity. (Brown, 1978, p. 79)

More recently, metacognitive skills have been characterized as including nonconscious regulation of cognitive activity as well:

> They (metacognitive skills) are also not necessarily statable as a great deal of selecting, monitoring, inferring, etc. must go on at a level below conscious awareness. (Brown & Campione, 1980, p. 13)

438

In part, this extension of the domain of metacognitive skill to include nonconscious regulation represents acknowledgment of the complex nature of the phenomena of intelligent behavior. Flavell and Wellman (1977) succinctly summarized this complexity in considering the possible relationship between memory and metamemory behavior:

> Paradoxically, metamemory in the sense of present, conscious monitoring of mnemonic means, goals, and variables may actually diminish as effective storage and retrieval behaviors become progressively automatized and quasi-reflexive through repeated use and overlearning. The metamemory-memory behavior link of the older child is not thereby extinguished, of course. However, the need for it to become clearly conscious may well diminish as the behaviors it once mediated become more self-starting. (pp. 28-29)

It is probably true that the need for conscious monitoring declines with experience on a task; nevertheless, this extension of metacognitive skill does vitiate the theoretical usefulness of the term because it considerably obscures whatever it is we mean by the learner's use of abilities and strategies for learning. Consider as a concrete example the results of a comprehension study by Brown and Smiley (1977). In this study, primary-grade children did two tasks with short stories that they read. The first was simply to retell the story in their own words. Analysis of the retellings demonstrated that children included important information and deleted nonessential information. The second task was an editing task in which children were to underline important information in a story. That is, the children were asked to use deliberately the knowledge of what was important in a story that they had displayed on the retelling task. Their performance on this latter task was substantially inferior to that on the former, with consistent differentiation of important and unimportant information only beginning to emerge with older children. A reasonable speculation on these results is that children tacitly used their knowledge of story structure on the retelling task but were unable to access this knowledge deliberately for the editing task. With respect to metacognition, should we say that the children displayed metacognitive skill on the retelling task but not on the editing task? If so, does it make sense to maintain a distinction between metacognitive and cognitive skill when tacit use of knowledge in the absence of its deliberate use can be demonstrated in many skill areas? With such a definition, would metacognitive skill serve to differentiate the novice from the expert or the intelligent from the unintelligent?

My own preference is to reserve the term metacognitive skill for those behaviors that reveal the deliberate and conscious manipulation of cognitive skills. For those phenomena where there is a discrepancy in the use of cognitive skills on similar tasks, as in the Brown and Smiley study (1977), we should turn to other constructs, such as accessibility to knowledge and strategies (Brown, 1980) and automaticity of cognitive processes, both to account for the data and to endow the term metacognitive skill with more than merely descriptive status.

The reason that constructs such as accessibility and automaticity emerge as important in this area has to do with our increasing knowledge of learner characteristics, task demands, and the acquisition of skill. On the one hand, because of capacity limitations in working memory, certain subskills of more complex cognitive skills are not simply acquired but, in the course of acquisition and practice, are also automated in the sense that the subskill may be used without demanding attentional capacity. The nature and significance of such automated acquisition is being examined for reading (e.g., Kolers, 1975; LaBerge & Samuels, 1974) and for arithmetic (e.g., Groen & Parkman, 1972; Groen & Resnick, 1977). On the other hand, especially for complex cognitive tasks, such as reasoning and writing, that depend on the development of a strategy for effective performance, the deliberate control of certain subskills is required. Although the acquisition of such control has received less attention from researchers, primarily because study of strategy-dependent skills is fairly recent, the importance of control is recognized in mathematical problem solving (Greeno, 1976) and in writing (Bereiter & Scardamalia, 1982; Bracewell, 1980).

In writing, the ability to control deliberately certain subskills is particularly important for two reasons. First, writing is a language skill that is acquired on the basis of a well-developed skill, namely oral language, that has many already automated subskills. Much of the acquisition of writing skill requires not the learning of novel subskills but the assuming of control by the writer over already automatized language subskills. Second, writing is a type of problem solving—a skill that requires the construction of a solution that in its particulars is unique for a given task. One definition of a problem is a task that does not yield to routinized procedures for its resolution. In constructing solutions to writing problems, the writer must have conscious access to writing subskills that range from vocabulary to genre levels.

Given that control ability is essential for writing skill, one is still left with the problem of identifying whether a writer has it. This is essentially a problem of identifying metacognitive skill, which has been characterized above as the deliberate and conscious manipulation of cognitive skills. What we need is a criterion comparable to the verbalization criterion for metacognitive knowledge; that is, a type of behavior whose presence would make it reasonable to

440

infer that deliberate, as opposed to tacit, use was being made of a cognitive process. The criterion proposed as an index of metacognitive skill is the production of both optimal and nonoptimal outcomes for a given task. When the task is writing, this means that the metacognitively skilled writer should be able to produce both good and bad versions of text on the same topic. In a close parallel to the assumption made for the verbalization criterion, the assumption for the optimal/nonoptimal criterion is that the production of such outcomes requires deliberate[2] manipulation of writing processes from among all the possible processes that could produce text on a given topic. For logical reasons outlined below, particular attention is paid to the structure of nonoptimal productions in analyzing the texts. To date, the method has been used to examine writing skills, primarily at the sentence level; however, the method should be readily extendable to examination of writing skills at discourse levels.

Studies on the Control of Writing Processes

Study 1: Children's Manipulation of Simple Sentences

Every child who writes displays a variety of syntactic and language forms, as indicated by variability in number of words per sentence; use of different syntactic structures, such as coordinate and dependent clauses; and so on. We have carried out a number of studies on children's ability to manipulate syntactic form and to use conjunctions appropriately when writing (Bracewell, 1980; Bracewell & Scardamalia, 1979). The writing skills we were interested in were rather elementary, of the kind that would lead to the following different surface structures for the same content:

> Ernie has a dog. Grover has a cat. Grover has a canary. Grover has a dog.

and

> Ernie has a dog; but Grover has a cat, a canary, and a dog.

In keeping with the elementary nature of the task materials, the children who participated were at the beginning stages of learning to compose, being in grades 2, 4, and 6 (approximately ages seven, nine, and ten respectively).

The variability of language form seen in children's writing is in some sense controlled because children by and large do write grammatical sentences. But the production of a variety of grammatical and other language forms does not by itself indicate *deliberate* control over the cognitive processes that lead to these forms. Many of the factors that govern these processes appear to operate at an intuitive level. Sometimes, as is the case with oral language, these factors

441

can be isolated (e.g., rules of conversation, Grice, 1975, and linguistic and extralinguistic cues from other speakers); but often, as is the case with children's writing, these factors must be inferred (e.g., Bereiter et al.'s 1980 "associative strategy" in producing text). At the same time, the achievement of deliberate control over language form is an important objective for the writer because it is only with such control that one is able to communicate reliably the full range of one's ideas and intentions to different readerships. The deliberate fitting of form to meaning is closely related to what Hirsch (1977) labels semantic integration—the coordination of meaning that forms the basis of readable prose.

In writing, the burden of making decisions about appropriate ways to express ideas falls on the writer. To make such decisions, writers must possess metalinguistic skill. That is, they must be able to generate and to analyze at will different ways of relating content and to select the best language form for achieving these relationships. But the fact that variability of language form in writing is often produced non-deliberately brings us face to face with a methodological problem. By what methods can we differentiate intentional variation in children's writing from variation produced by non-intentional factors? Of course, this is a particular case of the problem of differentiating metacognitive from cognitive skill. In Study 1, the method used in assessing children's deliberate control of language form was based on the criterion proposed earlier for assessing metacognitive skill, namely, the production of optimal and nonoptimal outcomes for a given task. Specifically, each child was asked to write up the same information in ways that the child considered to be both good and bad.

Tasks and Materials. Asking children to produce optimal and nonoptimal (in this case, "best" and "worst") write-ups is a decidedly odd request that leads to a number of problems. Apart from the fact that few, if any, children ever do something where an important goal is to perform *poorly,* there are issues of task definition. The first concerns how to tell children that what we are interested in is deliberate manipulation of syntax rather than all the other aspects of writing that can be optimal or nonoptimal, like handwriting, spelling, grammar, semantic content, and so on. Obviously, simply telling children to manipulate syntax is not sufficiently informative. Showing children examples of the various ways that the same ideas can be put together in sentences would appear more adequate. But this leads to a second issue that is concerned with not restricting the task definition so much that it becomes simply a memory task rather than metalinguistic. If the experimenter, in attempting to orient children toward syntax, simply told them a good and a bad way to put together ideas in sentences, then the subsequent writing task could become merely a memory task where the goal was to recall the surface structure of the examples.

In an attempt to navigate between Scylla and Charybdis, we had the children carry out a "read-and-choose" task before they did the writing task. In this prior task, children read different ways of writing up the same information, thereby (we hoped) orienting themselves toward syntactic aspects of writing. But instead of the experimenter designating which sentence write-ups were "good" or "bad," the children chose those write-ups they themselves thought were good or bad. One of the reasons for having children do this was to engage their own abilities to evaluate ways of expressing information and to attempt to avoid strategies in which memory for a particular sentence surface structure was used. This read-and-choose procedure was carried out as follows. First, children were presented with a matrix of content words and four different ways of writing up the matrix content in sentences. An example of these matrix and sentence materials is presented in Table 6.1. The matrix consists of content words and a title that serves to organize the words into four simple propositions (e.g., Ernie has a dog. Grover has a cat.) The different ways of writing up the matrix content were not selected randomly but were ordered by an increasing degree of coordination among the propositions achieved by the use of syntactical rules, conjunctions, and cohesive relations. In the sentence items of Table 6.1, the degree of coordination increases from top to bottom. Sentence item (1) contains four propositions expressed as simple sentences. Because no relationships are expressed among the propositions, this item was assigned a coordination level of 0. Sentence item (2), in which the use of *and*, signals a coordination of the related set of propositions about Grover, was assigned a coordination level of 1. Sentence item (3), which contains, in addition, a coordination signalled by *but*, the word, between the first proposition and the latter three, was assigned a coordination level of 2. Sentence item (4), which contains these coordinations plus the relationship to the superordinate term, *pets* was assigned a coordination level of 3. Matrices and associated sentences were designed for four different topics. Each topic used vocabulary familiar to grade-school children.

To do the read-and-choose task, the child first read the title and words of the matrix. The sentence items, typed on individual slips of paper, were placed in front of the child in random order. The child then read these items pointing out the similarities and differences in wording and structure among them. This analysis included counting the number of sentences in each sentence item. The child then chose which items he or she considered the best

443

and the worst written. The order of selecting best and worst was counterbal-
anced across children. Specific instructions were, "Point out for me the one
that you think is the best (worst) written one. Which one sounds the best
(worst) to you when you read it? In which one are the words put together in
the best (worst) way?" The child read aloud each item after choosing and then
was asked to justify the choice.

The use of this task prior to writing accomplished a number of purposes.
First, it oriented the children to the syntactic aspect of writing that was the
focus of the task. Second, the use of an ordered set of sentence items provided
a metric for assessing the child's sensitivity to syntactic coordination of
content. Third, the choice of well and poorly written sentences together with
the child's justification for each choice provided an assessment of
metalinguistic knowledge against which metalinguistic skill in manipulation-
language form could be compared.

Immediately following the read-and-choose task, each child wrote "best"
and "worst" sentences, using a matrix on the same topic as that used on the
reading task but with different content words. An example of such a matrix is
presented in the bottom section of Table 6.1. After reading the title and words
of the matrix, the child wrote a sentence item using the content. Instruction
order conformed to that used on the reading task; that is, students who had
chosen best and worst written items wrote a best sentence item and then a
worst sentence item. Those who had chosen in the worst-best order wrote a
worst item and then a best item. Verbal instructions that paralleled those used
on the reading task were, "Put together the words of the matrix in a sentence
or sentences so that what you write sounds like the best (worst) one you
picked out before. Coordination levels for the possible selections on the read-
and-choose task are presented in Table 6.2. The assignment of coordination
levels for written productions followed a procedure like that outlined above
for the sentence items of the read-and-choose task. That is, assignment of a
level was determined by the maximum number of relationships expressed for
any one of the four basic propositions. For example, the production "Ernie has
a dog. Grover has a cat. Grover has a canary. Also Grover has a dog." was
assigned a coordination level of 1 because the last proposition is signalled by
the conjunction, "also," as being related to previous propositions.

Results and Discussion.

Before examining the results, let us speculate on what one might expect if
the student had full metacognitive control over language skills. First, on the
read-and-choose task, one would probably find a difference in coordination

level between sentence items selected as best and worst. One might expect, in addition, that the coordination level of best sentence items would be higher on the average than the coordination level of worst-sentence items, although this might not be the case for all students' selections—certainly one can think of contexts in which a lower degree of coordination would be more appropriate than a higher degree. Second, on the writing task, one would find that the degree of coordination achieved in the student's own productions would be the same as those selected on the read-and-choose task. That is, the coordination level of the best-written item would be the same as that coordination level of the item chosen as best and the coordination level of the worst-written item would be the same as that chosen as worst.

The coordination levels of children's selections and productions did not, of course, show such a straightforward pattern. The pattern that was found was a much more intriguing one that throws some light on the control of syntax in writing, has important implications for how we evaluate children's writing, and raises many more researchable questions about how children acquire control over their writing skills.

Table 6.1

Language Materials Used for Syntax Manipulation Study

Example of matrix materials, read-and-choose task:		
Title: Who has what pet?	Who	Pet
	Ernie	dog
	Grover	cat
	Grover	canary
	Grover	dog

Example of sentence materials, read-and-choose task:

1. Ernie has a dog. Grover has a cat. Grover has a canary. Grover has a dog.

2. Ernie has a dog. Grover has a cat, a canary, and a dog.

3. Ernie has a dog; but Grover has a cat, a canary, and a dog.

4. Ernie has a dog; but Grover has three different pets, a cat, a canary, and a dog.

Example of sentence materials, writing task:		
Title: Who has what pet?	Who	Pet
	Bert	hamster
	Kermit	goldfish
	Kermit	turtle
	Kermit	hamster

From Bracewell and Scardamalia, 1979

Let us deal with the data from grade 2 children first.[3] The average coordination levels for these children are presented in the top half of Table 6.2. Here we see that the average coordination levels of different tasks and instructions hovered around Level 1. In fact, there were no statistically significant differences among the means. This uniformity of coordination levels together with a comparatively high degree of unsystematic variability in selections and productions, both within and across second-grade children, suggests that these children were not able to exercise metalinguistic skills on either the read-and-choose or the writing tasks. Now let us turn to the data from grade 4 and grade 6 children. The average coordination levels for these children, which did not differ across grades, are presented in the bottom half of Table 6.2. The principal finding for these children was an interaction effect of tasks and instructions. For both the read-and-choose and the writing task, coordination levels for best instructions exceeded those for worst instructions, but this difference between best and worst was attenuated for the writing task. Coordination level for best writing was less than that for best choices; coordination level for worst writing was *greater* than that for worst choices. This pattern for grade 4 and grade 6 children, when considered together with other data from this study, suggests a number of things about children's control of syntactic form in writing.

First, the clear differentiation in coordination levels between best and worst sentences on both reading and writing tasks together with children's comments on their choices and productions, implies metalinguistic skill and metalinguistic knowledge. This is most evident for data from the read-and-choose task. At the same time, the differences in coordination levels between the reading and writing tasks raise questions about the relationship between the metalinguistic knowledge and skill for these data. On the read-and-choose task, metalinguistic skill was implied not only by the differentiation in coordination levels but also by the finding that coordination level for best choices was not at ceiling. The children were not selecting best sentences in an unreflective manner based on some global impression of sentence complexity. Most children thought that the Level 1 or Level 2 sentence items were the best write-ups. As one child put it in rejecting the Level 3 sentence item. "You don't have to say they're different pets, everybody already knows that." The making of deliberate choices is also implied by the rational justifications the children offered for their choices. Children who chose the O Level item (four-sentence) as worst cited the use of four sentences as being poor, saying further that they did not like the repetition of the subject noun (i.e., Grover). When choosing a more coordinated sentence item as best, they said that they liked the use of such words as "and" and "but" as well as the way the words were "put

446

together in one (or two) sentences." Children's ability to comment in this way on their choices also implies metalinguistic knowledge (albeit of a fairly rudimentary kind) about how words can be put together to make effective sentences; however, the role that this knowledge played in helping children to make choices is unclear. It is possible that the knowledge implied by the justifications determined sentence-item choice; on the other hand, such knowledge may have been adjunctive, an epiphenomenon of the metalinguistic skills used in making choices. Evidence that the latter possibility more accurately describes the status of these justifications is provided by the intermediate coordination levels found on the writing task, particularly by the higher coordination levels found for worst productions compared with worst selections. Those children who were attempting to write four simple sentences for a worst version were aware that this was their goal and, having written, were quite confident that they had produced four sentences. When asked to count the actual number of sentences in their write-up, those children who had produced less than four sentences (for example by coordinating Grover propositions) showed considerable surprise that their production had not met their stated objective. This disassociation between goals and actual performance, of which the children became aware only after examining their productions, makes it unlikely that overt knowledge about sentence structure was governing their productions. It appears that these children

Table 6.2

Mean Coordination Levels for Tasks and Instructions

	Task	
	Read	Write
Grade 2 students[a]		
Instruction		
Best	1.25	0.94
Worst	1.15	0.82
Grade 4 and 6 students[b]		
Instruction		
Best	2.04	1.41
Worst	0.15	0.46

[a]Square root of (MSe/n) = .17 (for subjects as error term).
[b]Square root of (MSe/n) = .06 (for subjects as errot term).
From Bracewell and Scardamalia, 1979.

were in something of a transition period with respect to metalinguistic knowledge about sentence structure—one in which the ability to talk about sentences requires the perceptual support of already-written sentences. Of course the emancipation of such knowledge and the development of the ability to apply it in the course of sentence production emerges as an important educational issue.

Second, the attenuation of coordination levels for best and worst write-ups compared with those found on the read-and-choose task indicates that the children could not exercise full control over syntactic production processes. The most important results are those found for worst write-ups as compared with worst selections. The children's worst write-ups, which by and large were to be simple uncoordinated sentences, contained a significant degree of coordination. This finding rules out a simple explanation of writing and reading differences based on capacity limitations in working memory and differential task difficulty. Such an explanation can account for the pattern of data for best write-ups—writing is a more capacity-demanding task than reading. In attempting to compose sentences, children hit a capacity limitation for coordinating information; hence, the coordination level achieved for writing was less than that for reading. But the pattern of the data was reversed for worst write-ups. The simplest strategy for producing worst write-ups would have been to write a series of single simple sentences. But this is not what a significant proportion of the children did. In coordinating propositions when attempting to write worst sentences, grade 4 and grade 6 children used what appears to be a logically more, not less, capacity-demanding strategy.

Third, the differences between what was intended and what was produced on the writing task suggests that the cognitive processes of sentence production were largely automatic, in the sense that they operated within (and sometimes despite) conscious attention. Of course the observation that we can do things without having to attend to them, especially in domain of language, has been noted and discussed by many investigators. Given a limited capacity-processing system for attention, the results could scarcely be otherwise. But the nature of automaticity implied by these results is stronger—namely, that children were *unable* to pay attention to their production processes. The strength of these automatic processes is illustrated by results of a variant of the matrix task carried out with grade 4 children (Bracewell, 1980). This variation emphasized memory for surface structure. Children simply were asked to find the four sentence write-ups from among a group of sentence items, like those in Table 6.1, and then were asked to write up information from a different matrix in four simple sentences. All children were able to identify the four sentence items easily (that is, the item with O level coordination), and the request to write such an item frequently led to astonishment that adults could be interesting in such a simple and mundane task. Nevertheless, the degree of coordination found in children's productions was the same as that found for worst productions on the above task.

It is one thing not to have to pay attention to carry out a task, it is quite another not to be able to do so. The writing difficulties children experienced on these matrix tasks were not related to writing activity per se but to the purposeful control of writing activity. Of course, the data inferred on these simple tasks essentially amount to a demonstration of automaticity of syntactic production processes, although they are perhaps all the more striking because of the simplicity of the tasks and materials. In further research, two important directions to pursue are (1) the investigation of such a phenomenon on true composing tasks, where children select a topic and provide content themselves and (2) the investigation of how children learn to pay attention to, monitor, and eventually control such automatic processes. For both directions, the use of optimal/nonoptimal production strategies is likely to be an important aspect of the research methodology.

Study 2: Recognition and Production Or Grammatical Errors

Difficulties in the manipulation of syntax that suggest automatic-writing processes are not limited to beginning writers. We have found evidence for such processes with older writers when investigating the control that secondary-school students were able to exercise over syntactic structures that are considered to be grammatical errors (Bracewell & Kress 1979; Kress & Bracewell 1981). A list of the errors examined together with an example of each (the erroneous structure is underlined) is presented in Table 6.3.

Such errors although distressingly familiar to most English educators are noteworthy in a number of ways. First, these are errors primarily because of convention. Which is the correct form and which is the incorrect form is arbitrary and not derived from rational analyses. Certainly, it is the rare instance, especially when embedded in text that such errors lead to a problem in understanding. Second, for some students such errors are very difficult to overcome. Nor is this afflicted group of an insignificant size in the secondary schools—the appearance and reappearance year by year in English curricula of instructional units on "major grammatical errors" testifies to the extent of the difficulty of mastering such conventions, as well as to the intransigence of their associated errors. Third, in spite of the fact that failures to follow such conventions interfere little, if at all, with communication, much of the hue and cry over writing skills raised by the public and by higher education authorities focuses on such errors. This focus, whether one agrees with it or not, makes the teaching of these writing conventions of practical importance to English educators. The fact that errors on these conventions are difficult to overcome, despite (in most cases) a quite regular surface structure, makes them of theoretical interest to those of us who study writing processes.

A common workbook exercise on grammatical errors at the secondary-school level is one that presents a list of sentences and requires students to find and correct the errors contained in the sentences. Students often achieve a considerable measure of success doing such tasks, yet continue to produce erroneous grammatical structures in their own compositions. This transfer failure from the workbook to composing suggests a problem of control of writing processes. It is not that such students lack knowledge of grammatical errors, it is that they lack sufficient control over their writing activity to be able to apply it when it is appropriate. Specifically, they lack the ability to control those syntactic production processes that lead to the production of grammatical errors.

The lack-of-control explanation for grammatical errors can be tested by using the optimal/nonoptimal strategy. In an optimal task the objective would be to write the conventionally correct structure and avoid making an error. In a nonoptimal task the objective would be to write the incorrect structure, thereby deliberately making an error. If the lack-of-control explanation is correct, then the following hypothesis can be made about the data pattern from these two tasks. On the optimal task, because they have difficulty controlling syntactic processes, students should make at least some grammatical errors. On the nonoptimal task, again because of difficulties controlling syntactic processes, students should be unable to make deliberately those errors that they produce on the optimal task.

Tasks and Materials.

Public opinion to the contrary, the occurrence of grammatical errors in the writing of secondary-school students is an infrequent event. The majority of sentences that students write are grammatically correct, and it is the troubled student, indeed, who on the average, commits more than one syntactic faux pas for every ten sentences written. Moreover, students do not habitually make a large number of different types of error; an individual student's problems usually are limited to one or two conventions. In carrying out

450

research of this kind, such infrequency of errors leads to problems of amassing a data base sufficiently large to test a hypothesis. To increase the amount of data available for analysis two special features were incorporated into the research design. The first had to do with selection of the students who contributed data. These were sixteen grade 11 students (aged fifteen to seventeen years) who had voluntarily enrolled in a remedial writing class because of difficulties they were having with writing, which included making grammatical errors. Although such a selection restricts the potential generality of our results, we thought it worthwhile at the beginning to cast our control hypothesis on what was likely to be fertile ground. In the course of their studies, the students were taught to recognize and correct most major grammatical errors, including those listed in Table 6.3.

The second feature had to do with the operationalization of the optimal production strategy. For grammatical conventions, the optimal strategy consists of producing the correct syntactic structure and avoiding an error. The most naturalistic method of gathering data on students' error patterns when the objective is to produce conventionally correct syntactic structures would be to search their prior compositions. To gather sufficient data, a search of

---

Table 6.3
Common Grammatical Errors

Error Name	Example
1. "Be" plus adverbial clause	A hangover is <u>when</u> someone has had too much to drink.
2. "Sense" verb plus adverbial clause	I see <u>how</u> Tom Lewis has been expelled from school.
3. Reason plus "because" clause	John is unable to sit still. The reason is <u>because</u> he wants to leave.
4. Fragment sentence	The C.N. Tower, <u>which is the world's largest free-standing structure</u>.
5. Fused sentence and comma splice	<u>You can still go almost everywhere by subway there are many stops</u>.
6. Redundant preposition	Valley Hill is the town in which we used to live <u>in</u>.
7. Pronoun case	Don't tell anyone our secret; this is strictly between you and <u>I</u>.
8. Pronoun number agreement	Everyone has to listen to <u>their</u> own conscience.
9. Past modal plus "of"	Couldn't you <u>of</u> told me he was having trouble?
10. Faulty pronoun reference	All through the rock concert <u>it</u> was really fantastic.
11. Faulty parallelism	He was not only stubborn, <u>but he was also</u> shy.
12. Dangling participle	<u>Being</u> just six years old, my mother took me with her when she plowed the field.

From Bracewell and Kress, 1979.

compositions written over many months would have had to be made, a lengthy time period that raises its own problems about stability of processes that lead to errors, possible learning effects, and so on. To avoid these problems, we decided to test students' production of syntactic conventions by using a paper-and-pencil test called *The Diagnostic Writing Test* (Kress, 1978). The test consists of sentence items that the student must complete either by adding or rearranging words to make a grammatically correct sentence. The items have been derived from examples of errors that previous students have made in their writing. For example, one of the items designed to test for the error of the redundant preposition is:

Valley Hill is a town in which_____

A correct completion for the item would be:

Valley Hill is a town in which we used to live.

An incorrect completion, in which a redundant preposition is used, would be:

Valley Hill is a town in which we used to live in.

The errors tested were those listed in Table 6.3; an example of one test item for each error is presented in Table 6.4. On the diagnostic test, there were three different sentence items for each error. The items were presented in a fixed random order.

For nonoptimal productions, students were asked to produce sentences containing syntactic errors. An assessment of students' ability to produce deliberately the errors about which they had been taught was made by having the students carry out the Competitive Proofreading exercise from the Scardamalia and Bereiter writing exercise handbook (1979). In this exercise, students write a composition in which they purposely bury some of the errors that they have learned. They make two copies of the error-filled composition. On the one that they keep, they underline the errors; the other copy is given to another student, whose task it is to proofread the composition, locating and correcting as many of the inserted errors as he can. The task is competitive in that the author receives points for the number of errors that the proofreader is unable to find and correct. Thus, from this exercise, it is possible to obtain a record of which language structures that author thinks are grammatical errors. The Competitive Proofreading exercise allows the student to select which errors to bury in his or her composition. This selection procedure, as opposed to a procedure in which students would be told which errors to try to make, was used because we were interested in assessing the grammatical errors that students themselves felt capable of making. To avoid possible contamination, the diagnostic test was administered one week after the proofreading task. It is possible that certain of the items of the diagnostic test are memorable enough that they could have been copied from memory on the proofreading task rather than generated by the student .

Results and Discussion.

The terminology we use to refer to the possible outcomes on the two tasks is based on the intentions of the students for each task. On the diagnostic test, students attempted to avoid grammatical errors. Hence, a properly completed item is referred to as *correct*, an item in which the grammatical error is made is referred to as *incorrect*. On the proofreading task, students attempted to place grammatical errors in their texts. Hence, an error properly made on this task is referred to as a *success*. A word or string of words marked on the proofreading task that was not, in fact, an error is referred to as a *failure*. Thus, *correct* and *incorrect* refer to the diagnostic test; *success* and *failure* refer to the proofreading task.

Table 6.4

Grammatical Errors and Sample Items from The Diagnostic Writing Test

Error Name	Example
1. "Be" plus adverbial clause	A hangover _____ when someone has had too much to drink.
2. "Sense" verb plus adverbial clause	I see _____ Tom Lewis has been expelled from school.
3. Reason plus "because" clause	John is unable to sit still. The reason is _____ he wants to leave.
4. Fragment sentence	The C.N. Tower, which is the world's largest free-standing _____.
5. Fused sentence and comma splice	You can still go almost everywhere by subway _____ (many, there are, stops)
6. Redundant preposition	Valley Hill is the town in which_____.
7. Pronoun case	Don't tell anyone our secret; this is strictly between you and_____.
8. Pronoun number agreement	Everyone has to listen to _____ conscience.
9. Past modal plus "of"	Couldn't you _____ told me he was having trouble?
10. Faulty pronoun reference	All through the rock concert _____ was really fantastic.
11. Faulty parallelism	He was not only stubborn, but _____ shy.
12. Dangling participle	_____ just six years old, my mother took me with her when she plowed the field.

From Kress, 1978.

453

Our hypothesis was that, because of lack of control of the syntactic production processes, those grammatical errors that a student made on the diagnostic test should have been the ones that he or she failed to make on the proofreading task. A corollary of this hypothesis is that those grammatical errors that the student succeeded in making on the proofreading task should have been the ones completed correctly on the diagnostic test. Errors successfully made on the proofreading task indicate control over those syntactic production processes responsible for the particular error. Hence, on the diagnostic test, the student should have been able to control the processes and avoid making that error. In brief, incorrect completions on the diagnostic test should have been paired with failures on the proofreading task; correct completions on the diagnostic test should have been paired with successes on the proofreading task.

The extent of this pairing can be evaluated by constructing a cross classification table of the outcomes on the two tasks. This cross classification is presented in Table 6.5. The rows of the table present the outcomes for the Diagnostic test; the columns present the outcomes for the proofreading task. The entries within the cells of the table are totals of outcomes taken across students and across error types. For example, if a student was successful in making a particular error on the proofreading task and then completed items for that error correctly on the diagnostic test, a score of 1 was entered in the top left-hand cell of Table 6.5.

Generally, the pattern of results presented in Table 6.5 confirmed the hypothesis. When students completed items of an error set correctly on the

Table 6.5

Outcomes for Optimal and Nonoptimal Writing of Grammatical Conventions

	Proofreading Task (Nonoptimal Operationalization)	
	Success	Failure
Diagnostic Text (Optimal Operationalization)		
Correct	19	3
Incorrect	1	8

From Bracewell and Kress, 1979.

diagnostic test, they tended to bury successfully that particular error on the proofreading task (19 versus 3 outcomes); when students completed items of an error on the diagnostic test incorrectly, they tended to fail to make that error on the proofreading task (8 versus 1 outcomes)[4]. A direct statistical evaluation of this pattern cannot be made because each count for the outcomes in Table 6.5 does not necessarily come from a separate student. Thus, the assumption of independence of events for chi-square tests of association is questionable. A related relationship can be evaluated statistically, however—namely, whether individual students showed greater response pairing than nonpairing on the two tasks. That is, for individual students, did the number of outcomes in which incorrects were paired with failures and corrects paired with successes exceed the number in which corrects were paired with failures and incorrects with successes? The answer to this question is yes; for thirteen of the sixteen students, the number of pairing responses exceeded the number of nonpairing responses (by a binomial test $p < .01$, $p = q = 0.5$). Of seven students who failed to make errors on the proofreading task, the number of failure-incorrect pairs exceeded the number of failure-correct pairs for six of the seven. Of twelve students who successfully made errors on the proofreading task, the number of success-correct pairs exceeded the number of success-incorrect pairs for ten of the twelve. An additional factor that is useful in evaluating the data pattern of Table 6.5 concerns the number of different types of errors for which a pairing tendency was observed. Pairing outcomes were found for eight of the twelve error types: "sense" verb plus adverbial clause, reason plus "because" clause, redundant preposition, pronoun case, pronoun number agreement, past modal plus "of," faulty pronoun reference, and faulty parallelism. To summarize, the pairing effect was a general one, obtained from a majority of students on a number of different grammatical conventions.

One of the major results of this study is rather remarkable: Students demonstrated that they were capable of making a given grammatical error (e.g., faulty pronoun reference) by inadvertently making the error on the diagnostic test; however, when attempting to make the error deliberately on the proofreading task, they were unable to make the error. In most cases, students were able to produce an error deliberately only when they also avoided making that error on the diagnostic test. The pattern of results is one that would be expected if students possessed metalinguistic skill only over some grammatical production processes, whereas other processes operated in an automatic way that is not subject to metalinguistic skill.

Of course, an automaticity interpretation is not the only one that can account for the pairing effect. An alternative explanation can be based on the possibility that what students think is an error and what is usually scored as an error do not correspond. For some types of error, students may overgeneralize the language structures considered to be erroneous; for others, they may undergeneralize. By making some reasonable assumptions about the frequency of such noncorrespondence, it is possible to generate a pairing pattern very much like that found in Table 6.5 (Bracewell, unpublished research note, January, 1981). One problem with such an explanation is that it does not account for the difficulty that many students experience in learning these conventions, which have a quite regular and seemingly salient surface structure in many cases. In other words, one would still have to account for how the overgeneralizations and undergeneralizalions arose in the first place. Evidence that would discriminate between the two interpretations and that would considerably strengthen the automaticity interpretation would be to demonstrate that students could recognize and correct errors on workbook exercises but that on production tasks, they would continue to make the same error when composing and also be unable to produce an example of it deliberately. Such a test has not yet been carried out.

Research and Educational Implications

The information yielded by the technique of asking students to produce both optimal and nonoptimal kinds of writing has important educational implications for language and writing research and instruction, of which I shall mention three.

The first concerns the definition of metalinguistic awareness and its measurement. A major focus of metalinguistic research has been on the relationship between reading ability and knowledge of words, syllables, and phonemes. This area is too large to review in detail, and in any case quite competent reviews already exist (Ehri, 1979). But even a cursory glance at the recent literature makes one wonder whether our insights into the development of metalinguistic awareness and its relationship to reading have progressed much beyond the seminal formulations of the Russian psychologists (Elkonin, 1971; Vygotsky, 1962). It appears that there is a positive relationship between metalinguistic awareness and reading skill, but the exact nature of the relationship remains a mystery. In part, this mystery is to be expected because of the complex cognitive nature of reading; but in part, our difficulties lie in an inadequate specification of what we mean by metalinguistic awareness. We do not possess the conceptual foundation to tell us why, for example, having a child tap for each word of a sentence is an adequate test of

456

word awareness, or why counting phonemes of a syllable is an adequate test of phoneme awareness. One can sense the unease with this lack of definition in the various alternative explanations advanced for successful or partially successful performance on such tasks—prosodic cues in the case of word identification and articulatory movements, in the case of phoneme counting. But such alternatives do not resolve the problem of inexplicitness.

The critique of metacognitive awareness presented in the introductory section applies equally to metalinguistic awareness at word, syllable, and phoneme levels. Questions about metalinguistic knowledge as assessed by stability criteria are obviously inappropriate given the verbal skills of children this age. In any case, what one is interested in is how metalinguistic knowledge is used by the child. The question then is how to assess metalinguistic skill. It is here that the optimal/nonoptimal criterion provides a standard. Performance requiring metalinguistic skill is one in which the child can achieve both optimal and nonoptimal outcomes with the same materials. For example, can the child segment a sentence into words in two different ways? At first glance, such a task may seem odd or pointless; but performance in which a child always segments a sentence into conventional word segments does not reveal whether performance is linguistically or metalinguistically based, in the same way that application of categorization skills in a metamemory task is equivocal concerning meta versus memory skills. Because of the conventionality of English word segmentation, successful performance on such a task is certainly suggestive of metalinguistically based performance, but other linguistic knowledge may also serve as a basis. The issue is how to differentiate the two.

Generally, tasks intended to tap metalinguistic skill do not permit examination of a broad enough range of behavior from the child to allow such a differentiation. In particular, the tasks are too recognitory, requiring the child to respond to presented language sequences. This restriction of methodology to receptive tasks is curious given the fascinating results reported for about a decade concerning invented spellings by children (Chomsky, 1971, 1979; Read, 1971, 1975). The very nature of the phenomenon reported, namely that orthography progresses naturally from highly variable and idiosyncratic to regular and conventionalized, would appear to make it an obvious candidate for accounts based on an emerging rational analysis by the child of problems involved in recording language, and the need for systematic as opposed to unsystematic variation in language representation. It seems likely that in these manipulatory—indeed, essentially play-like—activities (Cazden, 1974), the child begins to experience and to master the variations possible for representing language. Awareness of such possible variation provides a basis for selecting or at least appreciating principles of language representation, such as separating words with a space, which are correlated with reading skill. As the two studies reported in this paper indicate, a better picture of children's metalinguistic skills is obtained from tasks that examine the variation children are able to achieve in their own productions. It seems likely that more progress will be made in this area when the methodologies used capitalize on the promising results found for invented spellings and are expanded to include assessments of variability in children's productions.

A second implication may be called substantive in that it provides a rationale for the meager amount of writing done by students in many North American schools (Applebee, 1981; Fillion, 1979; Graves, 1978). Both the matrix and the syntactic error studies suggest that the students themselves are aware of this gap (although this latter finding is more evident in the matrix studies). If such results are borne out in further studies, then one reason for low writing output may be simply that students find composing self-defeating (Bracewell, 1980). It is a punishing situation when you wish to do certain things in writing—things that you are given ample evidence can be attained in the materials you read—yet fail to achieve them in your own composing. And everybody tends to avoid punishing situations. In fact, a number of studies have indicated that the production of text is not a problem for beginning writers once the perceptual motor components of composing have been overcome. When the writing situation is properly developed (i.e., children select a topic with which they feel comfortable and they write for a trusted adult who values their output) children have little difficulty producing text (Bereiter & Scardamalia, 1980; Scardamalia & Bracewell, 1979). The problem for beginning writers is one of controlling and manipulating this output to achieve a satisfying product. Such findings suggest that simply encouraging children to do more writing in schools is more likely to exacerbate than to ameliorate any anxiety children feel about their writing unless instructional means are found for helping children manipulate their texts.

The third implication of these results concerns instructional methodology. At present, many instructional methods for writing can be characterized as discrimination training (Bracewell & Kress, 1979). Following the common model-analyze-write procedure, teachers usually begin by presenting an example of text (e.g., a common grammatical error) to students. Teachers and students then analyze the text in order to determine and give verbal labels to distinguishing features of the language form. Having determined these features, the students are usually set to a writing task that requires use of the language form. The rationale for this procedure is quite straightforward. By learning to recognize distinguishing language features, students should be able to apply them (or avoid them in the case of errors) in the production of their own texts. The problem with this method is that it seems not to be very effective. The automaticity interpretation offered in this paper suggests why this should be so. The model-analyze-write procedure addresses and seeks to foster knowledge about writing. But what needs to be cultivated is not just knowledge but the mental processes that underlie the activity of writing. Instruction on writing should be oriented toward the doing, not the facts, of writing.

To make this maxim more concrete, let me give an example of an instructional task that focuses on writing activity rather than on writing knowledge. The task is presented in Table 6.6; dubbed the "Uh-oh Prediction Exercise," it is intended to foster awareness of cognitive processes involved in a worrisome point of punctuation, that of the use and misuse of commas. In the course of playing this game, students develop a feeling for the types of sentence structures that lead inevitably to a comma.

The ability to predict a comma is a far more useful skill than the ability to explain where a comma ought to be used, because the prediction task has a better chance of leading to the actual *use* of a comma while the student is writing.

Table 6.6
"Uh-oh" Prediction Exercise for Comma Use

---

1. Students are taught some point of grammar or punctuation. Henceforth, commas will be used to illustrate.
2. Students are divided into teams of four.
3. The teacher begins writing a sentence on the board. He or she may write one word or several.
4. Each group, in turn, is asked to supply, within five seconds of being asked, a next word for the sentence. Any team that cannot produce a word to continue the sentence loses 2 points.
5. The moment a comma is perceived to be inevitable—because of the way in which the sentence is developing—the person who notices yells, "Uh-oh!"
6. The group, one of whose members has said, "Uh-oh!", must finish the sentence, putting in the comma(s) and explaining the applicable rule. The team gets 2 points for a successful completion; it loses 2 points for an unsuccessful completion.
7. Any other team in the class may then gain 2 or more points by showing that there is a way to complete the sentence without using any commas.
8. The teacher begins a new sentence.

From Kress and Bracewell, 1981.

Prediction tasks need not be so complicated nor is their use limited to instruction or writing conventions. Many exercises that are presently in use could be made into prediction tasks with only minor alterations. Sentence-combining techniques (O'Hare, 1975), for example, lend themselves very well to this sort of adaptation (e.g., "What will I have to be careful about if I try to combine 'George arrived late' and 'George is thankful the class has not yet begun' and 'because' into one sentence?"). Another good prediction task is one in which students must complete correctly a sentence begun by the teacher. The dangling participle, famous in song and story, might very well be examined by asking students to finish a sentence beginning, "Having replaced three of the wheels during a fifteen-second pit stop, _____."

Generally, the objective of such prediction tasks is to recruit automatic language processes by requiring a sequence of activities over time that parallels the time sequence of the language production process. Conducted as a group exercise, a prediction task would provide feedback to the students on their predictions, and because the predictions derive from the language process, on the language process itself. Note how the prediction task differs from the analysis of a model. In the latter, all the language is given to the student. Although the student must read the model, this reading may not involve the language production processes that produce the error in the student's writing.

This is not to say that perceptual discrimination methods should be abandoned in teaching writing. But what is required is some additional procedure, such as prediction tasks, that will permit the hookup between knowledge of language structures and the processes that produce them. It seems likely that it is only process-based instructional methods that will lead (in the jargon of cognitive psychologists) to student writers with metalinguistic skills or, in more straightforward terms, to student writers who are able to control their composing skills.

Notes

1. The research reported in this paper was supported by grants from the Alfred P. Sloan Foundation, the Ontario Institute for Studies in Education, and the Social Sciences and Humanities Research Council of Canada. Preparation of the paper was supported by grants from the Faculty of Graduate Studies, McGill University and Le Programme de Formation de Chercheurs et d'Action Concertee, Quebec. I thank Mark Aulls and Carl Frederiksen for their critical comments on an earlier draft of the chapter.

2. It is important to note that what is being proposed is an index of deliberate and conscious decision making, not a definition. Definitions in this area would involve us in philosophical issues concerning the concept of intention that certainly will not be resolved in the near future, if ever. In proposing the optimal/nonoptimal criterion, I assume only that it is unlikely, not impossible, for successful performance to be achieved in the absence of deliberate manipulation of cognitive skills .

3. Coordination level results were assessed by a series of analyses of variance. All effects reported were significant ($< .05$) by minimum quasi-F statistics that used child and matrix topic as random variables. Each child in grades 4 and 6 completed reading and writing tasks for three different topics. There were no differences between grade 4 and grade 6 performance. Pilot testing revealed this to be too lengthy a procedure for grade 2 children. Consequently, these children completed reading and writing tasks for only two topics—hence, the separation between analyses and results of grade 2 and those of grades 4 and 6.

4. Table 6.5 presents data relevant to an evaluation of the lack-of-control hypothesis. Additional data obtained from these tasks suggest that information processing demands resulting from the syntactic complexity of the particular sentence that a student was attempting to write also affected error production. Complete results are presented and discussed in Bracewell and Kress (1979).

References

Applebee, A. N. (1981, April). *A study of writing in the secondary schools*. Paper presented at the annual meeting of the American Educational Research Association, Los Angeles. Bereiter. C. (1980). Development in writing. In L. W. Gregg & E. R. Steinberg (Eds.), *Cognitive processes in writing*. Hillsdale, NJ: Erlbaum.

Bereiter, C., & Scardamalia, M. (1982). From conversation to composition: The role or instruction in a developmental process. In R. Glaser (Ed.), *Advances in instructional psychology* (Vol. 2). Hillsdale, NJ: Erlbaum.

Bereiter, C., Scardamalia. M., Anderson, V., & Smart, D. (1980, April). *An experiment in teaching abstract planning in writing*. Paper presented at the annual meeting of the American Educational Research Association, Boston.

Bracewell, R. J. (1981). The *ability of primary school children to manipulate language form when writing*. Paper presented at the annual meeting of the American Educational Research Association, Boston.

Bracewell, R. 1. (1981). Writing as a cognitive activity. *Visible Language, 14,* 400-422.

Bracewell, R. J., & Kress, F. (1979, May). *Taught but not learned: Some reasons why students have difficulty correcting their grammatical errors.* Council of Teachers of English, Ottawa.

Bracewell, R. J., & Scardamalia, M. (1979). *Children's ability to integrate information when they write.* Paper presented at the annual meeting of the American Educational Research Association, San Francisco.

Brown, A. L. (1978). Knowing when, where, and how to remember: A problem of metacognition. In R. Glaser (Ed.), *Advances in instructional psychology* (Vol. 1). Hillsdale, NJ: Erlbaum.

Brown, A. L., & Campione, J. C. (1980, January). Inducing *flexible thinking: A problem of access* (Technical Report No. 189). Urbana-Champaign: Center for the Study of Reading, University of Illinois.

Brown, A. L., & Smiley, S. S. (1977). Rating the importance of structural units of prose passages: A problem of metacognitive development. *Child Development, 48,* 1-8.

Cazden, C. (1974). Play with language and metalinguistic awareness: One dimension of language experience. *International Journal of Early Childhood, 6,* 12-24.

Chomsky, C. (1979). Approaching reading through invented spelling. In L. B. Resnick &P. A. Weaver (Eds.), *Theory and practice of early reading* (Vol 2), Hillsdale, NJ: Erlbaum.

Chomsky, C. (1971). Write first, read later. *Childhood Education, 47,* 296-299.

Ehri, L. C. (1979). Linguistic insight: Threshold of reading acquisition. *Reading Research: Advances in Theory and Practice, 1,* 63 -114 .

Elkonin, D. B. (1971). Development of speech. In A. V. Zaporozhets & D. B. Elkonin (Eds.), *The psychology of preschool children.* Cambridge, MA: The MIT Press.

Fillion, B. (1979). Language across the curriculum: Examining the place of language in our schools. *McGill Journal of Education, 14,* 47-60.

Flavell. J. H. (1976). Metacognitive aspects of problem solving. In L. B. Resnick (Ed.). *The nature of intelligence.* Hillsdale, NJ: Erlbaum.

Flavell, J. H., &Wellman, H. M. (1977). Metamemory. In R. V. Kail, Jr. & J. W. Hagen (Eds.). *Perspectives on the development of memory and cognition.* Hillsdale, NJ: Erlbaum.

Graves, D. (1978). Balance *the basics: Let them write.* New York: Ford Foundation.

Greeno, J. G. (1976). Cognitive objectives of instruction: Theory of knowledge for solving problems and answering questions. In D. Klahr (Ed.), *Cognition and instruction.* Hillsdale, NJ: Erlbaum.

Grice, H. P. (1975). Logic and conversation. In P. Cole & J. J. Morgan (Eds.), *Syntax and semantics* (Vol. 3): *Speech acts.* New York: Academic Press.

Groen, G., & Parkman, J. M. (1972). A chronometric analysis of simple addition. *Psychological Review, 79,* 329-343.

Groen, G. & Resnick, L. B. (1977). Can preschool children invent addition algorithms? *Journal of Educational Psychology*, *69*, 645-652.

Hirsch, E. D. (1977). *The philosophy of composition*. Chicago University of Chicago Press.

Kolers, P. A. (1975). Memorial consequences of automatized encoding. *Journal of Experimental Psychology: Human Learning and Memory*, *1*, 689-701.

Kress, F. (1978, June). The *diagnostic writing test*. Unpublished manuscript. North York Board of Education, Toronto.

Kress. F., & Bracewell, R. J. (1981). Taught but not learned: Reasons for grammatical errors and implications for instruction. In I. Pringle & A. Freedman (Eds.), *Teaching writing learning*. Ottawa: Canadian Council of Teachers of English.

LaBerge, D., & Samuels, S. J. (1974). Toward a theory of automatic information processing in reading. *Cognitive Psychology*, *7*, 293-323.

O'Hare, F. (1975). *Sentencecraft*. Lexington, MA: Gage.

Read, C. (1971). Pre-school children's knowledge of English phonology. *Harvard Educational Review*, *41*, 1-34.

Read, C. (1975). Lessons to be learned from the preschool orthographer. In E. H. Lenneberg & E. Lenneberg (Eds.), *Foundations of language development*. New York: Academic.

Scardamalia, M. & Bracewell, R. J. (1979, April). *Local planning in writing*. Paper presented at the annual meeting of the American Educational Research Association, San Francisco

Vygotsky, L. S. (1963). *Thought and language*. Cambridge MA: The MIT Press.

Author's Comment—Robert J. Bracewell

Two related studies on the control of writing processes are presented in the paper. They were conducted concurrently, but the initiating event concerned the second one on grammatical errors and was serendipitous—as is the case more often than is admitted, although to paraphrase Pasteur serendipity favors the prepared mind. In the paper the theoretical analysis of metacognition and metacognitive skill is presented as motivating the empirical studies. This is not quite how it occurred. Rather, the data were collected before the *detailed* analysis was constructed, largely because I and my colleagues recognized the significance of the potential results given our background knowledge of the metacognitive and metalinguistic literature. I had every confidence that if the pattern of results turned out as anticipated then the elaboration of the theoretical basis for the patterns would be straightforward.

With respect to the initiating event, my colleague and collaborator on the study, Flemming Kress, had been lamenting that the Competitive Proofreading exercise from the Cognitively Based Writing Activities (Scardamalia & Bereiter, 1978) would have to be extensively revised since his field testing had shown that the students could not do it reliably. When we examined the field data, we found that students would indicate that they were going to place a particular error in their composition for their partner to find, but would then fail to produce the erroneous structure. This contrast between intent and performance immediately seized my attention, especially since the exercise provided the proofreading partner with bonus points if he or she found an "error" that was, in fact, correct. The explanation for the finding and a way of testing it formed in my mind in about a minute: A discrepancy between intent and performance indicated sentence production processes that were not under deliberate control. If this was correct, then students who failed to produce the error on the Proofreading exercise, should, in fact, make the error in their compositions. Conversely, students who could plant the error on the Proofreading exercise should not make the error in their compositions. Thus, was born the optimal/nonoptimal method of evaluating control over writing processes (although we did not call it that for many months). In the actual study, our search through the students' compositions yielded too few grammatical errors to test the explanation, so Flemming modified his Diagnostic Writing Test (Kress, 1978) to allow us to gather a larger base of optimal data.

The pattern of results supporting the control explanation can be found in Table 6.5 of the paper.

The first study presented, on the manipulation of simple sentences, arose from doubts about cognitive capacity limitations as a satisfactory explanation for difficulties in writing. With Carl Bereiter and Marlene Scardamalia, I had been working on ways to measure cognitive load in writing using word lists and matrices of different lengths and sizes which we asked students to turn into sentences.

The general idea was that omissions of information would provide a metric of cognitive load. This work looked promising, but all of us sensed it was simplistic: Cognitive capacity explanations readily apply to tasks like learning to drive a car in which many new procedures and much new knowledge must be mastered. But learning to write takes place on a well-developed base of oral discourse production skills, a circumstance that should have the effect of reducing cognitive load as a source of difficulty in writing. What other factors might also contribute to problems in learning to write? An obvious one was the very skill in oral discourse, which could lead to highly automatized language production processes not readily controllable by the beginning writer. The optimal/nonoptimal approach provided a way to test this control hypothesis, although the operationalizations of the optimal and nonoptimal tasks gave me many headaches. It is a very odd task to ask a child to perform nonoptimally in a specific way. The key prediction of the hypothesis was that writers with control difficulties should coordinate information even when their intent is to write separate sentences. The results supporting this prediction are presented in Table 6.2 of the paper.

Of course these studies are essentially demonstrations showing that control of processing is a factor in mastering writing. Going beyond the demonstration stage is a harder task. I have spent much of my scholarly effort since in pursuing (and sometimes even contributing to) the knowledge of discourse linguistics, semantic representation, and pragmatics required to assess and train control on realistic writing tasks.

465

Chapter 19 Writing from Sources

Spivey's study is an example of reading research in the **constructivist** tradition, a tradition that emphasizes the active role of readers in constructing meaning from text and of writers in constructing text for readers. This tradition has deep roots in the field of reading research (Bartlett, 1932) and, more generally, in psychological research (Koffka, 1935). Spivey's constructivist orientation is clearly reflected in her focus on three processes by which readers and writers construct meaning—selecting, organizing, and connecting. The constructivist view, which emphasizes the activity of the individual in rendering his environment meaningful, should be carefully distinguished from the **social constructionist** view (Bruffee, 1986), which emphasizes the role of the social environment in shaping individual behavior.

The task that Spivey has chosen to study, discourse synthesis (sometimes called "writing from sources"), is especially useful if one wants to explore the relationships that exist between reading and writing. By asking two groups of students with different reading ability to perform a discourse synthesis task, Spivey was able to carry out a detailed analysis of how participants selected content items from source texts, grouped them by theme, and connected them to create consecutive text. Two results of Spivey's study strike us as especially interesting: First, the observation that the participants who were selected as more able readers also turned out to be the more able writers. Reading and writing are often treated as sharply separable activities; in some cases, one has been valued and the other devalued. However, Spivey's work on making text from texts affirms close connections between reading and writing, which may well have important implications for how the abilities associated with literacy are to be taught. The second feature of her work that we find especially interesting is her success in tying the superior writing performance of the more able readers to the processes of selecting, organizing, and connecting text. Despite the importance of the processes Spivey is investigating and their ubiquity in the classroom, surprisingly little is known about them. Her extended discussion of the need for further research is a particularly appropriate way to end the study.

Spivey's study includes both **process measures** and **product measures** as dependent variables. A process measure is one that reflects the properties of the process or procedure by which the participant carries out a task, e.g., the amount of planning involved in the task or the length of time the task requires. In contrast, a product measure is one which reflects the properties of the final product (e.g., the quality or the length of the text that the participant wrote). In Spivey's study, it happens that most of the interesting results are to be seen in the product measures rather than in the process measures. See, for example, her Table 4. However, a survey of the studies in this volume indicates that although some rely most heavily on product measures (e.g., Freedman, Wallace & Hayes, and O'Donnell et al.), others rely most heavily on process measures (e.g., Nelson, Haas & Funk, and Heath).

This difference in the measures used is important to note. Because of the current emphasis on process in rhetorical theory and writing pedagogy, which has led to a partial eclipse of product-oriented pedagogy, some readers might assume that process measures are to be preferred to product measures. But to assume this would be a serious mistake. The best test for selecting appropriate measures in research is pragmatic: any measure that helps to answer the question the researcher is asking is appropriate. It is worth noting that even studies which are concerned entirely with process may make use of product measures. For example, protocol studies of writing, which are designed to identify writing processes, make extensive use of the written product in interpreting the writer's behavior. Whether an idea expressed during a think-aloud protocol was just a fleeting possibility or a definite decision is usually ascertained by looking to see if the idea appears in the finished essay. Similarly, although Spivey was interested in tracking down the processes by which writers create meaning, she included product measures in her study. It was a good decision on her part, since the best indicators of process in her study happened to be product measures.

References

Bartlett, F.C. (1932). *Remembering*. Cambridge: Cambridge University Press.

Bruffee, K. A. (1986). Social construction, language, and the authority of knowledge: A bibliographical essay. *College English, 48*, 773-90.

Koffka, K. (1935). *Principles of gestalt psychology*. New York: Harcourt, Brace.

Nancy Nelson Spivey
Department of English
Carnegie Mellon University

Discourse Synthesis: Creating Texts from Texts

*This study examined an act of discourse synthesis in which writers con-
structed meaning for their own texts by reading multiple source texts. Forty
university-level students performed a synthesis task requiring them to write
reports based on three informative texts on a single topic. In writing these
reports, all writers were quite selective, choosing only a subset of the material
cued by the sources, and they all generated the same general type of organizational pattern appropriate for a descriptive report. Although they produced
texts that had some commonalities in content as well as in overall organizational patterns, the writers varied in how they chunked the material, how
much material they selected as relevant, and how they connected the material
for the reader. Of the group, those writers who were more accomplished
readers produced texts that were more tightly organized, that were more
elaborate, and that had clearer connections between ideas. Their texts were
also rated higher for overall quality. The study illustrates connections
between reading and writing in the construction of meaning, and it also
extends research in literate activities to multitext situations.*

Much writing is accomplished through *discourse synthesis,* constructing
meaning from multiple texts to produce a new, unique text (Spivey, 1983,
1984). In this kind of composing, a writer is also a reader, building meaning
from the texts that are read *for* the text that is being written. This constructive
process of reading and writing is characterized by its selectivity and its
integrativeness: It is selective because a writer must choose content that is
relevant to the text being written from the composite of source material, and it
is integrative because a writer must provide coherence to material from
diverse sources and perspectives. Synthesis texts, a common type of written
discourse, take various forms. They appear in elementary schools as reports
written by children following their teachers' instructions to use more than one
source. They appear in secondary schools and colleges as essays, arguments,

research papers, and literature reviews and in the workplace as business, technical, and clinical reports. Many books as well are synthesis texts, combining in an organized and coherent way information linked to numerous textual sources.

I am using the term *discourse synthesis* to characterize those acts of literacy in which writers actually read extant texts for the purpose of writing their own texts and use the sources rather directly as they produce their own discourse. The term, if not limited in these ways, could embrace virtually any act of writing. This is, of course, because writers draw from their own experiences when they write, using their knowledge of discourse conventions and options, their knowledge of topic and domain, their world knowledge, and so on—much of it gained from interactions with other writers' texts. As several theorists (e.g., Bakhtin, 1981; Riffaterre, 1980) have pointed out, texts have traces, pieces, influences of other texts, making a text a unit in a more inclusive intertext.

Constructive Processes of Writing and Reading

Because discourse synthesis, as defined here, includes both reading the source texts and writing the synthesis texts, an examination of this process does not belong exclusively to writing research or to reading research. Instead, it is a logical and necessary extension of both lines of inquiry and falls within the larger arena of meaning construction, which includes both production and comprehension. In this larger view of literacy, a person responding to discourse goals in either role, reader or writer, or in both roles is thought to be engaged in a constructive process, building a cognitive representation of meaning or, put another way, creating a "text world" (Petofi, 1982).

Meaning Construction in Writing

When composing, a writer builds a mental representation of meaning for the text being written. The representation has semantic content that is structured in some fashion, although the content and form may change considerably over the course of composing as the writer generates and organizes material and sets goals (Flower & Hayes, 1984; Witte, 1985). The meaning being built may become more structured or may be structured differently. Some content may drop out, additional content may be generated, and certain content may gain a prominence that it did not previously have. The writer, actively building this mental meaning, uses graphic marks to provide signals to that meaning—signals to content and its relative importance, to organizational patterns, and to relations among units of content.

Thus, texts themselves are not meaning but are merely sets of cues to meaning. They are cues for readers to use in constructing meaning of their own, and they are also cues to the writer's mental construct.

To gain insights into a writer's representation of meaning, researchers often use some kind of verbal product, which might be oral or written. It might be a protocol from a think-aloud procedure, responses to interview questions, or some other kind of verbal report. But it might also be the text that the writer has generated. As Bereiter and Scardamalia (1983) argue, the text itself can provide information about the writer's constructive processes: "Whatever lawfulness is found in a text must reflect lawful behavior on the part of the writer because the physical properties of the text impose no requirements of lawfulness" (p. 11). By examining texts in systematic ways, researchers can study the effects of various factors—factors within the writing context, such as audience, or within the writers themselves, such as topic knowledge, upon the text produced. Because no prior template exists for evaluating the textual products, writing researchers often create their own in the form of subjective quality ratings (Cooper, 1977) or use quantitative measures believed to be related to quality (e.g., Hunt, 1965; Stahl, 1974). Instead of focusing only on the textual product, researchers sometimes choose to look at the relation of the product to other data, as from think-alouds or interviews (e.g., Flower & Hayes, 1981; Hayes & Flower, 1980; Sommers, 1980).

Meaning Construction in Reading

No longer thought of as passive reception of information, reading comprehension is today viewed as an active process of constructing meaning from the signals that writers put in textual form (Kintsch, 1974; Rumelhart, 1977). As in composing, comprehending discourse presupposes building a mental representation of meaning. But in reading, the meaning-maker operates from cues signaled by an extant text. For the past 15 years or so, reading researchers in the constructivist tradition, hearkening to Bartlett's (1932) *Remembering* investigations, have been studying discourse comprehension as readers' building of mental representations by integrating content signaled by source texts with material generated from previously acquired knowledge.

To gain insights into the representation of meaning, reading researchers (like writing researchers) often use written or oral verbal products. In the case of reading, these products might take such forms as response statements, answers to questions, or think-aloud protocols. But sometimes researchers have readers generate products more isomorphic to the total text they read— recalls of the text (e.g., Meyer, 1975; Thorndyke, 1977). The researcher can

471

then compare the content of readers' recalls with the content of the original text, as Bartlett (1932) did. The asymmetry between the two provides evidence of readers' constructivity, such as changes in organizational patterns, the selection of particular content and omission of other content, and the addition of elaborative material. For studies of constructive processes in reading, the original texts (as parsed by the researcher) can provide templates against which the comprehension product can be measured.

Meaning Construction in Discourse Synthesis

The situation becomes more complex in discourse synthesis because the reader (writer) uses cues from more than one text to construct a representation of meaning for the text being written. Even though the source texts suggest possible methods of organizing, prioritizing, and linking content, the writer must supply new connections and possibly new organizational patterns to integrate the information for the synthesis. For insights into the writer's constructive processes, researchers can compare the structural characteristics and content of the synthesis texts to those signaled by the source texts. To do so, they can develop composite templates with contributions from each of the original texts.

Reading-Writing Connections

Relevant to a study of discourse synthesis is a growing body of knowledge about reading-writing connections—a topic that researchers have approached from various perspectives. One group of studies has demonstrated that genre structures and text conventions internalized through reading appear in subsequent writing (e.g., Bereiter & Scardamalia, 1984). Another group of studies has demonstrated that instructional intervention in one process, reading or writing, can affect performance in the other (e.g., Taylor & Beach, 1984). A third group has shown correlations between reading comprehension scores and various measures of writing proficiency (reviewed by Stotsky, 1983). In longitudinal research conducted over a 13-year period, Loban (1976) discovered consistent relationships between students' reading and writing abilities. Students who were less fluent in their reading tended to produce writing that was disorganized and rambling, and students who excelled in reading seemed to have unity in their writing and superior command of connective words.

Particularly relevant to discourse synthesis is a fourth group of studies that have used the read-recall paradigm, mentioned earlier, to study readers' representations of meaning. While providing information about comprehen-

472

sion, recalls also provide information about production because they are texts that readers generate. These read-recall studies suggest differences that are associated with reading ability in the representations of meaning the readers build and in the texts they produce that signal those representations. These differences have been shown in the *organizing, selecting,* and *connecting* of content—three operations that are involved in discourse synthesis.

Organizing as a constructive operation entails supplying global patterns, such as cause-effect, comparison, sequence, collection, and problem-solution, to shape semantic material in large units, or clusters (Frederiksen, 1977; Meyer, 1975). Addressing the operation of organizing, Meyer, Brandt, and Bluth (1980) compared recalls of good and poor comprehenders in the ninth grade. The researchers found that the better comprehenders not only recalled more of the content but were also more likely to use the author's top-level organizational pattern to guide recall. The less accomplished comprehenders, who recalled less, tended to produce recalls that were poorly organized collections of information. Similarly, Taylor (1980) found differences in recall between groups of sixth-grade readers, with better readers organizing their recalls according to the organizational pattern suggested by the text that was read.

Like organizing, selecting is important to meaning construction. A reliable finding in much discourse research focused on text comprehension has been the "levels effect," readers tending to select for memory the content staged prominently in the text hierarchy (Johnson, 1970; Kintsch, 1974; Meyer, 1975). However, in selecting content, able and less able readers respond differently to the structural importance of information. For example, Eamon (1978-79) found that college students identified as better readers recalled more topical than nontopical information after reading, but poorer readers' recalls did not reveal this difference. Differences in selecting content have often been obtained in studies with younger groups of students. Smiley, Oakley, Worthen, Campione, and Brown (1977) found the recall of good seventh-grade readers to be a function of the structural importance of information but did not find the same relation between importance and the recall of the less skilled readers. McGee's (1982) study with fifth graders demonstrated an interaction between reading ability and level of importance. Although good readers recalled more superordinate ideas than subordinate ideas, poor readers showed no differences in the structural importance of information recalled.

In addition to the coherence that organizational patterns help provide at the global level, meaning construction also requires connecting content at more local levels—relating one idea to the next. Readers (and writers) must generate material to make a connected text base (Kintsch & van Dijk, 1978). Here, in regard to the connecting of content, two studies suggest differences associated with reading ability, as those differences are reflected in recalls of texts. Connecting information in recall protocols was one focus of a study by Marshall and Glock (1978-79). The researchers manipulated, among other things, the explicitness of the relations among ideas and found that the manipulation had differential effects for two groups of college students, fluent and less fluent readers. It increased the less fluent readers' recalls but did not affect the recalls of the truly fluent readers, who were able to supply their own connections. For the written protocols, the fluent readers produced true connected discourse containing propositions from the logical network that was signaled and implied by the source text. Similar findings were reported by Meyer, Brandt, and Bluth (1980) in their study with younger students.

This set of studies, though focused on discourse comprehension, is also relevant to discourse production because all the researchers used texts produced from texts as the basis for making inferences about mental representations. These inquiries provide evidence of some links between reading ability and text generation in the organizing, selecting, and connecting of content.

The discourse synthesis study reported here was intended to provide additional insights into connections between reading and writing. It also was intended to contribute to knowledge about a common (but little understood) type of writing and to extend previous single-text research in reading to a multitext situation. The study examined university-level students' performance on a task requiring each writer to select and combine information from three descriptive reports in order to write a single report on the same topic. Four measures were derived from analyses or ratings of the texts themselves: *content* in terms of its quantity, *organization* of the material, *connectivity* among ideas, and overall *quality* of the text. Three additional measures were elaborateness of *written plan*, extensiveness of *textual revisions*, and *time* spent on the task. The study investigated differences associated with reading ability in writers' performance on these measures and also examined differences in their selection of content.

Method

Participants

The participants in the study were 40 adult readers, juniors and seniors recruited and selected from four education classes at a private university in the

474

Southwest. Students from three of the classes substituted participation in the study for one of their course requirements, and students from the other class received extra credit in their course. Two pools of potential subjects, able and more able readers, were formed from all students who participated in the testing and writing sessions. The basis of pool assignment was whether an individual's raw score on the Comprehension Subtest of the Nelson-Denny Reading Test, Form E, was above or below the group mean of 52, a score falling within the 5th stanine for the Nelson-Denny's normative sample of juniors in 4-year colleges and universities (Brown, Bennett, & Hannah, 1981). Because the Nelson-Denny is considered most valuable as a survey and screening test (Cummins, 1981), the reading scores served merely as a basis for classification of students into groups. The pools were stratified according to the sex of the student and according to the college in which the student was enrolled within the university. Eliminated from the pools were 6 students, 3 with scores above the mean and 3 with scores below the mean, whose compositions consisted of intact excerpts from the textual sources that they used during the study.

Subjects were selected from the pools so that the groups of able readers and more able readers were equivalent in the two selection variables of gender and course of study. Each of the two groups was composed of 8 females from the college of arts and sciences, 3 males from the college of arts and sciences, 6 females from the college of business, 2 males from the college of business, and 1 female from the college of fine arts. The mean score on the Comprehension Subtest for the able comprehenders selected was 43.9 (SD = 6. 34), and the mean score for the more able comprehenders was 60 (SD = 4.47) . The equivalence of the two groups was checked for prior knowledge of the topic by having students spend 5 minutes jotting down the facts they knew about armadillos, the subject matter of the texts they would be reading. All students had some general knowledge of armadillos, the number of facts averaging about nine. Analyses revealed no significant differences between the two groups in number of facts.

Materials: The Textual Sources

The three source texts (see Appendix) for the synthesizing task were descriptive texts on the topic of "the armadillo" selected from the following encyclopedias: *McGraw-Hill Encyclopedia of Science and Technology* (Curtin, 1982), *Encyclopedia Americana* (Tate, 1982), and *Collier's Encyclopedia* (Goodwin, 1983). Word counts for the three, respectively, were 373, 546, and 443. The students read unidentified typed versions of the texts.

Within the three texts, 277 content units were identified through a procedure of parsing the semantic content of the sources into text bases. The procedure used for parsing was a modification of Turner and Greene's (1978) procedure, based on Kintsch's (1974) propositional theory. Like Kintsch's propositions, each included a relation and its arguments. In the parsing, some propositions were embedded as arguments in other propositions to form complex propositions that could be presented as informative facts to the intended audience of readers. For instance, (PART OF, ARMADILLO, TONGUE) and (CYLINDRICAL, TONGUE) were combined to form the complex proposition (PART OF, ARMADILLO, (CYLINDRICAL, TONGUE)). Three other procedures were used in the parsing: (1) Propositions that stood in conjunctive relations with each other were considered to be separate units if each one could appear without the other in the synthesis texts. For instance, "The armadillo's tongue is cylindrical and viscous" was two separate content units: (PART OF, ARMADILLO, (CYLINDRICAL, TONGUE)) and (PART OF, ARMADILLO, (VISCOUS, TONGUE)). A writer could choose to include one attribute but not the other. (2) Some content units were elaborations extending the information appearing in other units. In the parsing, both the one without the elaborated information and the one with the elaborated information were considered as separate units because either could individually be presented as an informative fact. For example, the text base for the Collier's article contains both (5 IN. LONG, FAIRY ARMADILLO) and (ONLY, (5 IN. LONG, FAIRY ARMADILLO)). (3) Following Kintsch and van Dijk (1978) and Crothers (1979), the text bases included other propositions strongly implied by the texts but not explicitly signaled. For example, the unit (COMPRISE, ARMADILLO, (DIFFERENT, KIND)), which was rather explicit in the Collier's text was implied in the McGraw-Hill text by the unit (COMPRISE, ARMADILLO, (21, SPECIES)). It was included in the text bases for both.

These content units varied in their structural importance, which was determined through a hierarchical analysis. Grimes's (1975) rhetorical relations, as summarized by Meyer (1975), were used in arranging the content units into hierarchical structures. Grimes has identified a set of hypotactic, or subordinate, relations that one unit can have with another: specification, evidence, attribution, equivalence, explanation, analogy, setting, manner, adversative, and identification. In the parsing of information explicitly cued by the text, a content unit perceived as having one of the hypotactic relations with another unit was placed at a lower level in the text base. For example, the sentence from the Collier's text, "The name armadillo, meaning 'little armored thing,' was given to the animal by the Spanish when they invaded the

New World," was parsed into three units arranged in two levels:

    1 (GIVE, SPANISH, NAME, ARMADILLO)

       2 ("LITTLE ARMORED THING," ARMADILLO)

       2 (WHEN, (GIVE SPANISH, NAME, ARMADILLO),

             (INVADE SPANISH, NEW WORLD))

The procedure yielded eight semantic levels within the source texts.

Of the 277 source units, some units were unique to a single text, some were linked to two texts, and some were linked to all three. Roughly synonymous information signaled by two texts was considered a repetition. Table 1 provides information about the textual materials: number of content units, repetitions of content units, and hierarchical level of units.

Procedures for Data Collection

Data were collected in two writing sessions, the first held one evening and the second held the next day. At the first session, after being pretested for prior knowledge of the topic, students received their assignment. Each received a packet containing a sheet of directions, typed versions of the three source texts appearing in random order, sheets of paper for their drafts, and sheets labeled "scratch paper." The assignment was a composition *case* in which the writers were to synthesize information from the three articles to

Table 1

Sources and Heights of Content Units

Content units	McGraw-Hill	Americana	Collier's
		Text	
This text only	48	95	72
This text and one of the other texts	31	31	18
The text and both of the other texts	22	22	22
Repeated within this text	0	4	3
Total	101	152	115
Structural level 1	33	36	33
Structural level 2	39	31	41
Structural level 3	25	34	28
Structural level 4	4	24	12
Structural level 5 or lower	0	27	1

make it accessible as a single text for 12th-grade students. The ostensible purpose was that the teachers of these 12th graders felt that none of the articles was complete enough. Students were told to write a draft in no more than 1-1/2 hours, to put the information in their own words, but not to use footnotes.

The following day, the regularly scheduled 50-minute class periods were devoted to preparing a final version of the report. At these sessions, students were given their materials from the previous evening along with paper for writing the final text.

These sessions yielded the following sources of data: the final reports which could be studied for various text features; two (or more) versions of the same report, which could be examined for evidences of textual revisions; and the source texts and scratch paper, which could be studied for elaborateness of written plan.

Procedures for Data Analysis

The research employed four measures based on the analyses or ratings of the final text—measures for content, organization, connectivity, and overall quality. Three additional measures—elaborateness of a written plan, extensiveness of textual revisions, and time spent on the discourse synthesis task—were also employed.

Content. The content units for a writer's text were totaled by scoring the text against a composite template showing abbreviated versions of the 277 units identified by parsing the three textual sources. In addition to providing the total units, the template, as illustrated in the excerpt in Table 2, provided the following quantitative information about each student's synthesis: number of content units linked to only one text, number of content units linked to two source texts, and number of content units linked to all three source texts.

A composite importance score for each unit was also included in the template, as shown in the excerpt in Table 2. First the unit was given points according to its structural level in one text, which, as mentioned earlier, could range from Level 1 to Level 8. A unit at Level 1 in the text received 5 points for that text; Level 2, 4 points; Level 3, 3 points; Level 4, 2 points; Level 5 through 8, 1 point. If it was not signaled by that text, it received no points. Next it was given points according to its structural level in the second text and then the third text. Finally, after points were calculated for the unit for each of the three texts, the points were added across texts to yield the composite score. Content Unit 6, for example, was not associated with the McGraw-Hill text but was associated with both the Americana and the Collier's articles—at the second level for the former and at the third level for the latter. This unit, thus, had the composite score of 9 (0+4+5) points. The range of points for the various content units was 15 to 1: A unit with 15 points (which is the case for units 2, 4, and 12 in the excerpt in Table 2) would be at a prime level in all three texts; a unit with 1 point would be a detail in only one text.

The composite template had built-in scoring rules footnoted at appropriate points. As a check on reliability, two raters independently scored 10 students' texts selected at random, and the scoring procedure for total content was found to have a reliability of .97 (Pearson's r).

Organization. The organization of the synthesis text was measured with a breadth-depth ratio based on thematic chaining and chunking. Ratio of breadth to depth (cf. Collins & Gentner, 1980; Nold & Davis, 1980; Vipond, 1980) was viewed as a way to quantify organization for descriptive texts, which often have no fixed or ideal order for presentation of information. Content units on the composite template had been tagged for the following themes:

     X: PRONUNCIATION
     C: CLASSIFICATION
     H: HABITAT
     N: NAME
     E: FOLKLORE
     A: ARMOR
          Ab: BANDS
     Q: BEHAVIOR TRAITS
     V: SIZE
     K: HAIR
     T: TEETH
     M: MOUTH (SNOUT & TONGUE)
     L: LEGS & CLAWS
     B: BURROWING/DIGGING
     F: FLEXIBILITY PROTECTION
     D: DIET
     I: IMPACT ON HUMANS
     R: REPRODUCTION
     O: ANCIENT ARMADILLO (LIKE) FORMS
     S: SPECIES
          S^1: FAIRY ARMADILLO
          S^2: GIANT ARMADILLO
          S^3: NINE-BANDED ARMADILLO
          S^4: OTHER SPECIES & GENERA

Table 2
Excerpts from Composite Template

	Text			Importance
	M-H	A	C	
PRONUNCIATION				5
1X ARMADILLO PRONOUNCED ar-me-dil-o		X		5
CLASSIFICATION				
2C MAMMAL	X	X	X	15
3C FAMILY DASYPODIDAE		X		5
4C ORDER EDENTATA	X	X	X	15
5CT EDENTATA: LACKING TOOTH ENAMEL	X			4
6CT EDENTATA: TOOTHLESS		X	X	9
7CT GROUP WITH FEW OR NO TEETH		X		5
HABITAT				
8H HABITAT: AMERICAS	X	X		10
9H HABITAT: SOUTH AMERICA	X	X	X	14
10H HABITAT: SOUTH AMERICA ORIGINALLY			X	4
11H HABITAT: SOUTH AMERICA ESPECIALLY	X			3
12H HABITAT: UNITED STATES	X	X	X	15
13H HABITAT: SOUTHERN UNITED STATES	X		X	8
14H HABITAT: SOUTH-CENTRAL UNITED STATES		X		4
15H HABITAT: SOUTHEASTERN UNITED STATES		X		4
16H HABITAT: CENTRAL AMERICA		X		5
NAME				
17N NAME GIVEN BY SPANISH (OR NAME FROM SPANISH)			X	5
18N NAME "LITTLE ARMORED THING"			X	4
19N NAME GIVEN WHEN SPANISH INVADED NEW WORLD			X	4

For the analysis of organization, vertical chains of thematic tags were formed from the content units identified in a synthesis text. To demonstrate the scoring procedure, the following student text, in which added information has been underlined, will serve as an example:

> The armadillo is a member of the *Edentata* family, which is a family of mammals characterized by a lack of teeth. The animal originally came from South America, has made its way north, and is now found all the way to Oklahoma. In the U.S., the armadillo has spread from the Rio Grande area to Oklahoma and as far east as Louisiana. There are about 20 species of armadillo, which are distinguishable by the number of thin, movable bands of plates along the back. The most common species is the nine-banded armadillo, or *Dasypus*. However, there are other species with 12, 11, 6, and 3 bands. They are called *Xenurus, Cabassores, Euphractus*, and *Tolypeutes*, respectively. Armadillo species range in size from the giant armadillo, or *Priodontes*, which measures five feet in length, to the *Chlamyphorus truncatus*, which only measures five to six inches in length.
>
> Armadillos have been around since prehistoric times. Fossils have been found in both North and South America. It is thought that the present-day armadillo evolved from a huge "armadillo-like" animal the size of an ox.
>
> Although true edentates lack teeth, armadillos have several small and practically useless teeth. The armadillo's soft body is protected by a hard shell. Its "armor" is made up of bony plates with sharp coverings and is hardened within the skin. The plates connect to form two shields; one covers the shoulders and the other covers the haunches. The two shields come together and hinge across the middle of the back to allow the animal to move freely. In some species, the tail also has an armor and the face is shielded. The three-banded species has the ability to roll into a ball, kind of like a turtle, so that all body parts can be protected by a shield. The shield is nature's way of protecting this animal from flesh-eaters, since it is harmless, feeding only on insects and vegetable matter.
>
> The armadillo is a timid animal. To protect itself, it uses its legs and claws, which are adapted for burrowing, and digs itself into a hole.
>
> This burrowing technique is also used when birth is about to take place. The young are born at the end of the burrow. Armadillo breeding season begins in late July, and the young are born in March or April of the following year. Baby armadillos are always born in quadruplets; the fertilized egg divides into four parts to form four babies, identical in every way. They are born with soft shells, which harden the following year.

481

> The armadillo is an interesting animal. While we in Texas consider the armadillo our state's official animal, the South Americans eat certain species of them for their delicate taste and the Mayan Indians believe that blackheaded vultures turn into armadillos at their deaths.

Section A of Figure 1 shows the thematic chaining for that student text. After listing chains, the analyst looked for boundaries between thematic units. A boundary was tentatively identified when there was no overlapping content for more than two content units. Although thematic boundaries sometimes coincided with paragraph boundaries (Koen, Becker, & Young, 1969), very often they did not. Longacre (1979) has argued that the larger structural units in text are characterized by their thematic unity and that they are not the same as orthographic paragraphs, which are often determined by "eye appeal."

When a boundary was tentatively identified, the analyst read the composition to see if the writer had constructed a link between chains by adding information. The following list of six links (cf. D'Angelo, 1975; Frederiksen,1977; Grimes, 1975; Holley & Dansereau, 1984; Kline, 1977; Schallert, Ulerick, & Tierney, 1984), though not comprehensive for all writing, covered the types of links used by the students in their synthesis texts. An example from one of the students' syntheses is included for each:

1. contrastive: Two chains are linked by pointing out some kind of contrast between the content of the two.
   "Despite their unattractive appearance, armadillos are of great benefit to man."
2. similarity: Two chains are linked by pointing out some kind of similarity between the content of the two.
   "The armadillo has other interesting physical characteristics besides its armorlike shell. The armadillo's snout is long."
3. causal: Two chains are linked by supplying a cause-effect relationship between the content of the two.
   "The armadillo does have teeth. Since they are small, peglike and without roots, they are almost useless. Therefore, the armadillo feeds mainly on insects, carrion, and vegetable matter."
4. instrumental: Two chains are linked because the elements in one are used to do something with or to the elements in the other.
   "The armadillo has a long tongue as well as sharp claws, all of which it uses to find its main food sources: insects, carrion, and vegetable matter."
5. temporal: Two chains are linked by some kind of time relationship.
   "The armadillo is an animal that has survived for many years."

6. attribute-possessor: An attribute chain is linked to a possessor chain.
   [A discussion of the different armadillo species precedes this description.]
   "All of these armadillos have their defensive armor which protects them from predators. It consists of small rounded bony plates."
7. A seventh type of link was a syntactical embedding link, which involved syntactically burying a small composite of information within a longer chain:
   "These timid, nocturnal animals are both a hazard and a benefit to man."
   [The two behavioral traits, timid and nocturnal, which had not been mentioned earlier and are not discussed further, are buried within a discussion of hazards and benefits, which is itself held together with a contrastive link.]

Each chain can also be portrayed as a chunk, as illustrated in Section B of Figure 1. When two chains were connected with a link, the larger unit created was considered a single thematic unit. The global units 6 and 7 in the figure illustrate combined chunks in the organizational structure of the same student's text.

This type of scoring was reliable. When two scorers divided the same 10 sets of thematic chains into numbers of chunks, the reliability was .96 (Pearson's r). The organization score was derived by dividing the number of chunks (the breadth) by the number of content units (the depth) to yield a ratio. The number indicates how many chunks there are per 100 content units. A text with 10 chunks and 77 content units would have an organization score (10 / 77) of .13—13 chunks per 100 content units. In contrast, the more tightly organized text illustrated in Figure 1 with its 8 chunks and 95 content units would have an organization score (8 / 95) of .08—8 chunks per 100 content units. This ratio measure for organization is thus inversely related to the construct it is intended to represent: A lower number represents a more tightly organized text.

Connectivity. A reader-based measure of connectivity was used. Three raters independently read all 40 of the synthesis texts, and, as they read, marked each of the syntheses for points at which they felt a reader's flow of reading would be interrupted because of an unusual burden of constructive processing. Though rather subjective in nature, the measure was conceptually related to Kintsch and van Dijk's (1978) and Kintsch and Vipond's (1979) notion of resource-consuming operations. It was intended to cover various problems in students' writing that disrupt the connective flow. So that the readers could focus on semantic content and connections, the versions of the compositions that they read were typed with spelling and punctuation errors

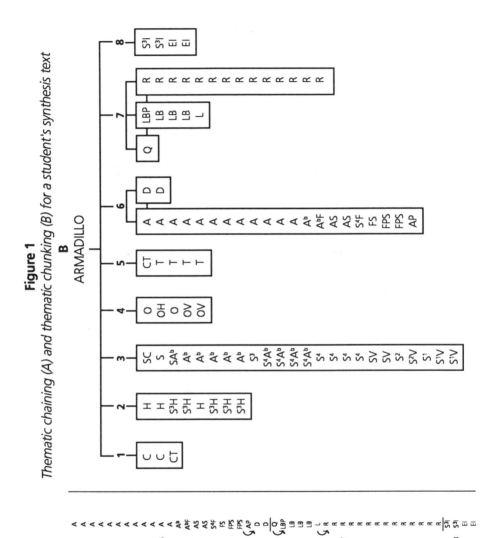

Figure 1

Thematic chaining (A) and thematic chunking (B) for a student's synthesis text

removed. Before reading and marking the participants' syntheses, raters practiced the scoring procedure with other students' texts requiring connective operations. (See Spivey, 1983, 1984, for a more detailed description of the measure.) The following are examples of problematic situations requiring connective operations:

- The reader must work through illogical comparisons or modifications.
- The reader must infer why the writer has used a particular connective word. The connection is not clear, or it is not logical.
- The reader must resolve contradictory information.

Interrater reliability for total counts of connective operations was .80 (Cronbach's alpha).

Like the organization score, the connectivity score was based on a ratio. It was calculated by dividing the average number of perceived connective operations (for the three raters) by the number of content units scored. For example, a text with an average of 7 connective operations and with 86 content units would have a connectivity score (7 / 86) of .08—8 connective operations per 100 content units. As was the case with the organization measure, the resulting score was inversely connected to the construct it was intended to represent. Thus, a lower number reflects a better connected text.

Quality. Another kind of text measure was a holistic quality rating of the synthesis text by three science educators. Two raters were university faculty members in a science education program, and one was a state science curriculum supervisor. The three raters trained with practice papers representing the range of quality for the sample. Using a 6-point scale, with 6 being high in quality and 1 being low, the raters received no predetermined set of criteria and arrived at their own criteria through discussing the practice papers. The scoring system was a form of general impression marking (Cooper, 1977), in which the rater tried to combine into one score aspects of thoroughness and accuracy of content with aspects of communicative effectiveness. As in the connectivity scoring, the raters used typed copies of the texts that had spelling and punctuation errors removed to control bias for what Diederich (1974) calls "Remondino's factor"—handwriting, neatness—and for mechanical errors. To minimize bias from reader fatigue, the compositions were ordered so that a particular synthesis text would appear in the first third of one rater's stack, in the second third of another rater's stack, and in the last third of another rater's stack.

Each synthesis received three independent ratings, and the holistic quality score used in the analysis was the sum, which ranged from 3 to 18. Interrater reliability was .76 (Cronbach's alpha). The reliability coefficient, not as high as sometimes obtained for composition ratings, was perhaps reflective of the different group of raters and the different type of rating task in this study. The raters, who had backgrounds in science rather than in English composition, were each repeatedly reading much of the same information in different texts. As content specialists, they may have begun developing their own individual sets of criteria for content that should be included.

Written plan. The measure for extensiveness of a written plan had two components. The first was based on the extensiveness of textual marking—the underlining, numbering, scratching out, and bracketing that students did on the textual sources. A 4-1evel scale, based on extensiveness of marking, was used for this component of the measure. Values ranged from 0, no marking, to 3, extensive marking. The other component of the planning measure was elaborateness of a written sketch of potential structure and content for the text, a sketch that might take such forms as a formal outline, an ordered list of topics, or some kind of graphic diagram. Again, a 4-1evel scale was used, this time with 0 for no artifact of this type and 3 for a very elaborate one. When the values for this scale were added to those for textual marking, the students had scores for visible planning that ranged from 0 to 6. Interrater reliability for two raters assessing all students' materials for the combined scores was .95 (Pearson's *r*).

Textual revisions. The study also examined numbers of changes that were made in the texts. Changes that were counted included those that affected content (a change that resulted in the addition or deletion of a semantic item), organization (a change that would affect chunking), and connectivity (a change related to one of the connective operations), as defined in this study. Surface changes, such as correcting the spelling of a word, were not counted. Textual revisions were counted within each of the two versions (the draft and the final text) and across the two versions (cf. Bridwell, 1980) in terms of number of content units directly affected. Interrater reliability for two raters scoring 20 of the texts was .88 (Pearson's *r*).

Time. The final measure was the total number of minutes each writer spent on the discourse synthesis task. Time spent on the task was recorded for each session, and the amounts for the two sessions were totaled.

Results

Overall Results

How did participants in the study perform on the synthesis task? Some answers to this question are available in the results of the descriptive data analysis. These results, as summarized in Table 3, show that the writers were selective in regard to content for their syntheses. They averaged about 85 content units, or 31% of the 277 units available to them, with the content ranging in density from 45 units in one student's report to 132 in another student's report. The writers all organized their texts, as might be expected, with a collection type of global structure—clustering content thematically—an organizational pattern similar in kind to the pattern of organization suggested by the sources. On the measure quantifying organization with a breadth-depth ratio (number of thematic chunks divided by number of content units), the writers averaged 10 chunks per 100 content units, which would be about 8 for an average length text. The writers tended to produce writing that created some problems for readers; the texts averaged 8 perceived connective operations per 100 content units, which would be about 7 for a text of medium length. As would be expected, their texts varied in overall quality. Raters scoring the texts for holistic quality used the whole range of the scale available to them, 3 to 18, but the average of 9 was somewhat below the midpoint of the scale.

All 40 writers produced some evidence of a written plan, which might have been marking or noting some material on the source texts or actually writing a sketch of content and structure. All except 2 of them marked the text in some way, and 21 made a separate sketch of content and structure on scratch paper. In general, the writers made numerous textual revisions, averaging 20. And it took them an average of 93 minutes to complete their reports, but the times ranged from 60 to 129 minutes.

Table 4 shows the intercorrelations between pairs of these seven measures. I should point out that scores for two measures, organization and connectivity,

Table 3
Overall Performance on the Measures

	Mean	Standard deviation
Content	84.53	21.40
Organization	.10	.03
Connectivity	.08	.05
Quality	9.15	3.37
Written plan	3.15	1.56
Textual revisions	20.15	8.06
Time	92.53	20.07

were transformed linearly for this report of correlations. The organization score and connectivity score for each writer were both transformed by subtracting each from 1 so that higher numbers would reflect, in the case of organization, a more tightly organized text or, in the case of connectivity, a more clearly connected text. The purpose of the data transformation was to eliminate potentially confusing negative correlations for these two measures.

Some relationships are suggested by the correlations, particularly among the variables derived from analyses and ratings of the text—content, organization, connectivity, and quality. Among these four variables, positive correlations appeared to exist between all pairs, but the values were not so high as to indicate that the variables were measuring the same constructs. The series of correlations also suggest positive relationships between time and content, between time and quality, and between time and extensiveness of the written plan. Extensiveness of textual revisions did not correlate well, either positively or negatively, with any of the other measures.

Differences Between Groups

Analyses were then conducted to see if differences in performance might be associated with reading ability. A multivariate analysis of variance (MANOVA) was conducted first because the inquiry involved several depen-

---

Table 4

Intercorrelations among Variables

	2	3	4	5	6	7
1. Content	.60***	.45**	.53***	.18	.22	.42**
2. Organization		.49***	.48**	.01	.02	.28
3. Connectivity			.49***	-.07	-.04	.20
4. Quality				.11	.02	.42**
5. Written plan					-.06	.36*
6. Textual revisions						.14
7. Time						

*p <.05   **p <.01   ***p <.001

Note: In the correlations the values for organization and connectivity have been transformed linearly by subtracting from 1 so that they are positively, rather than negatively, related to the constructs they represent, tight organization of the text and clear connections among ideas.

dent measures that were intercorrelated, and the MANOVA would allow multiple variables in concert to serve as the dependent measure. Table 5 provides the means and standard deviations on the individual measures for the two groups.

The MANOVA showed that the overall difference between groups was statistically significant, $F(7, 32) = 4.04$, $p < .005$. Follow-up univariate F-tests, for which results are summarized in Table 6, indicated significant differences between groups on four specific dependent measures. All four—quality, organization, connectivity, and content—were text measures.

The results show that, on this comparison, the groups performed differently both on overall performance and on the various measures for characteristics of their texts. The better readers were also better writers, producing texts that were scored higher for quality by content-area experts. They wrote texts that were more unified, or globally coherent, with fewer thematic chunks per content unit, and that were better connected, with fewer connective operations required per content unit. Though no student came close to including all 277 of the available content units, the texts of the more able group were more elaborate. While the groups performed differently on all four of the text measures, the variables showing most difference between groups were holistic quality, organization, and connectivity. The groups' performance on the measures for written plan, textual revisions, and time did not differ significantly. Both groups had similar means on the planning scale and had a similar number of textual revisions. Although the more able readers averaged 9 minutes longer on the task, this difference was not significant on a univariate test.

Further Inquiry into the Selection of Content

The next analysis pursued the question of how writers selected content. Were writers more likely to include content that was signaled more prominently across the source texts? Figure 2 illustrates the data used to provide answers to this question. The vertical axis in the graph is for the percent of the available content that writers included, and the horizontal axis is for the relative importance of content units to the composite. For this analysis, available content units had been grouped into five sets by combining the units on the basis of their composite importance scores (derived by totaling points across the sources, as described earlier). Set 1 was units with 1-3 composite points; Set 2, units with 4-6 points; Set 3, units with 7-9 points; Set 4, units with 10-12 points; and Set 5, units with 13-15 points.

Table 5
Means and Standard Deviations by Group

	Group				
	More able			Able	
	M	SD		M	SD
Content	92.10	20.05		76.95	19.95
Organization	.08	.04		.12	.03
Connectivity	.06	.02		.10	.05
Quality	11.25	2.75		7.05	2.54
Written plan	3.15	1.69		3.15	1.46
Textual revisions	19.75	7.24		20.55	8.98
Time	96.65	22.19		88.00	17.29

Table 6
Multivariate Analysis of Variance and Follow-up Tests

Source of variation	Variable	MS between groups	Univariate F[b]
Discourse synthesis[a]	Content	2295.23	5.60*
	Organization	.01	11.51**
	Connectivity	.02	11.36**
	Quality	176.40	25.13***
	Written plan	0.00	.00
	Textual revisions	6.40	.10
	Time	680.63	1.72

[a]Multivariate F (7, 32) = 4.04, $p < .005$.
[b]$df = 1, 38$.
*$p < .05$ **$p < .01$ ***$p < .001$

An analysis of variance (ANOVA) examined whether or not there was an increasing tendency for writers to include content as the content became more important to the composite. This linear-trend analysis tested whether or not the lines on the graph for the groups of writers had a straight *slant* upward. This ANOVA with two factors—reading ability and importance of information—did find a significant linear trend for importance, $F(1, 38) = 981.25$, $p < .001$, showing that writers were more and more likely to include content as it became more and more important to the composite. The ANOVA also found that the slopes for the two groups were significantly different, $F(1, 38) = 4.37, p < .05$. As the graph shows, the slopes differ (and the gap gets wider between the two groups) because the more able readers included increasingly greater proportions of content as the information became more important to the composite.

Figure 2

Linear trends for groups in selection of content from different levels of importance

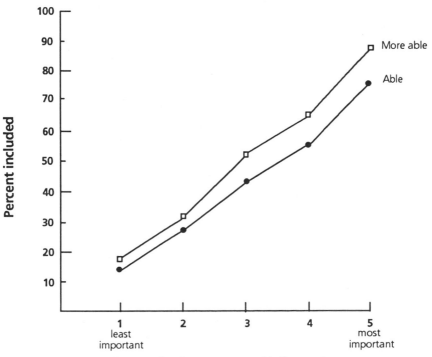

491

Summary of the Findings

On this task writers dismantled textual material and reconfigured it to form
new unique texts. Differences associated with reading ability were apparent
in the following characteristics of the texts: content, organization, connectivity,
and overall quality. There were also differences associated with reading
ability in patterns of selecting intertextually important content. However, no
significant differences associated with reading ability were found in elaborateness of text plans, extensiveness of textual revisions, or total time spent.

Discussion

The study reported here was an initial exploration into a discourse process
that involves both reading and writing—creating texts from other texts. What
do the findings suggest about meaning construction through reading and
writing? What do they say about factors contributing to high-quality syntheses? Where should future research efforts in discourse synthesis be directed?

Synthesis as Organizing

Although all writers employed the same kind of organizational pattern—a
collection pattern of the same type as signaled by the sources—they varied in
how they grouped content items within that pattern. The better readers—who
were also the better writers—wrote syntheses with more content, but they did
so without using a greater number of thematic chunks to organize their
compositions. Without increasing the number of chunks, they constructed
these more elaborate texts in two ways. One was the development of individual topics, the creation of longer thematic chains and thus larger thematic
chunks. They tended to develop a more elaborated discussion of an attribute,
such as armor, species, or teeth, by giving more detailed information about it.

For example, the following excerpt from one of the more successful
syntheses developed only two thematic chunks. One chunk was about
habitat, and the other was a description of armor that integrated and incorporated other themes:

> The armadillo can be found in the southern United States but at
> one time was only native to South America. Its name comes from a
> Spanish term meaning "little armored thing" in reference to its
> defensive armor.

> The hard shell encasing the armadillo serves to protect it from
> flesheaters. Other animals would have a hard time getting through
> the roundish bony plates which form shields hardened within the
> skin over the shoulders and haunches. Freedom of motion is
> allowed by crosswise movable plates. It is the number of thin

492

bands of plates which distinguish the various types of armadillos. These bands allow the mammal to roll itself into a ball, thus protecting its tender underparts.

The better readers (writers) tended to develop the topics that they introduced, as illustrated in Figure 3, a graphic for this excerpt. These writers tended to produce relatively long chains and rather large chunks, resulting in the kind of writing that Witte's (1983a, 1983b) research indicates that readers prefer, writing that is focused through development of topics that are introduced.

That excerpt can be contrasted with another written by a less accomplished reader. This paper introduces many different themes without focusing on any of them for very long:

Figure 3

Thematic chunks suggested by excerpt from student's text

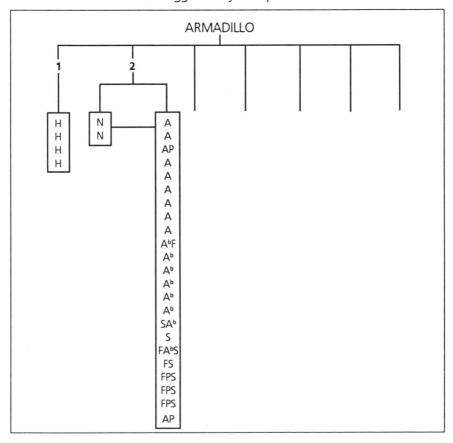

Armadillo. There are 21 species of the mammal. Armadillo, meaning "little armored thing," are found primarily in the southern United States. The armadillo is best characterized by the number of bands on its armor. They range in size from five inches to five feet, although there was a fossil found indicating one as large as six feet in length. This armor is made of horny, dermal scales, unlike most mammals that are covered by hair.

This student's synthesis continued on in much the same way, moving rapidly from topic to topic and even back again to a previously mentioned topic, offering little for its reader in regard to focus or development. This text, with its excerpt illustrated in Figure 4, might fit Collins and Gentner's (1980) characterization of *too flat a structure* and Nold and Davis's (1980) characterization of *too broad a structure*.

The second way in which the better readers (writers) included more information without increasing the number of chunks was creating more integrated structures with larger thematic units. They did so by providing linkages to combine thematic chunks into larger macrochunks. In the first example above, the writer signaled a link, "in reference to," which connected the chunk about name with the chunk about armor. Another writer connected a chunk about the armadillo's name, "little armored thing," with a chunk about species and sizes by adding, "However, all armadillos aren't little," before going on to discuss the sizes of various armadillo species. As in summarizing studies (e.g., Day, 1980; Winograd, 1984), some writers constructed macropropositions (van Dijk, 1977), subsuming ideas that held together more detailed content. For example, one student who had the

Figure 4

Undeveloped thematic chunks creating a flat structure

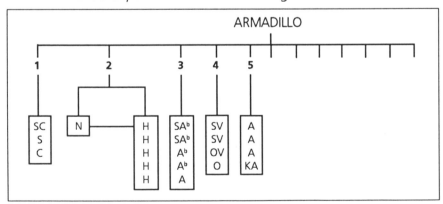

following topics on a formal outline for the final section of his paper

III. Specific Armadillos

    A) Fairy Armadillo

    B) Banded

        3, 6, 9

    C) Giant

    D) Prehistoric

wrote a well-integrated discussion of ancient armadillo-like forms and current species beginning with a macroproposition that he added, "The armadillo is an animal that has survived for many years in different forms." As illustrated in Figure 5, the writer not only added this superordinate contrastive-temporal link holding together the content but also reordered the content from his original plan and meshed together the information from the different sources.

Figure 5

Interlinked thematic chunks

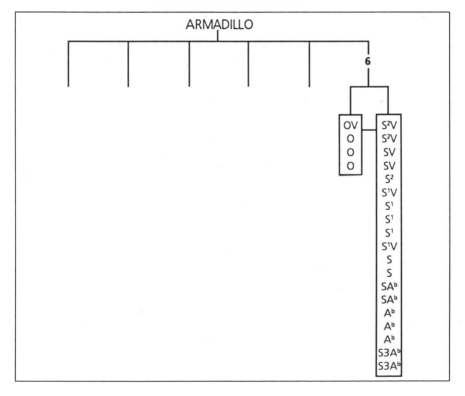

In general, the writers in this study tended to be rather text-bound, staying with content suggested by the sources. The major role of added elements was to provide interchunk links. The result of supplying these links at the top levels of the textual structure was an increase in the global coherence, or unity, of the text. The students who added the links were apparently able to infer relations among the thematic units, to signal those inferences through their texts, and thereby to create more unified structures, often embedding causal or contrastive patterns. Those who did not add links tended to write texts with broad, shallow, loosely connected structures. The texts reveal different kinds of *framing*—to borrow a term used by Bracewell, Frederiksen, and Frederiksen (1982) for the writer's active creation of a structure for a composition. This difference in framing can probably help to explain the difference in quantity of information. Without integrative frameworks to hold together the information, the less able readers (writers) had difficulty incorporating as much material.

Synthesis as Selecting

All writers in the study were selective regarding content for their syntheses. No one came close to using all the source material. What criteria did writers employ for selecting some content and not other content? They seemed to be selecting material, to some extent anyway, on the basis of an intertextual criterion of importance. In this study involving more than one textual source, importance had to be defined in terms of composite importance, a combined value determined both by height in the text base of a single text and by repetition across texts. Under this definition, an item associated with only one text, even though staged at a high level, was considered moderately important to the composite. An item associated with all three texts but staged at a medium level in all received a higher value. The students writing these syntheses seemed to be operating under an importance principle in selecting information for their texts. As the information became more important to the composite, they were more likely to include it.

Thus, the levels effect, which has been well supported by previous research with recall of single-text sources (Goetz & Armbruster, 1980), was also demonstrated in discourse synthesis—on a multitext task when the sources were actually present. At all levels of importance, however, there was a gap associated with reading ability because the more able group was including more information. As the information became progressively more important to the composite, the gap grew wider, revealing a significant interaction between importance and group. As in previous studies, the better readers evidenced a greater sensitivity to importance of information (cf. Vipond, 1980); however, here it was sensitivity to importance defined in intertextual terms.

Synthesis as Connecting

In composing their synthesis texts, writers had to produce new connected discourse by combining thematically related material across the three source texts. In accomplishing this integration, the better readers (writers) produced texts that were better connected not only at the global level, as shown through their thematic chunking, but also at the local level, as shown through the measure for connectivity. Their texts required a reader to stop fewer times to consciously work at making the ideas connect. On the other hand, the reports produced by the less skilled readers were not as "considerate"—to use Kantor's (1978) term—and not as "reader-based"—to use Flower's (1979) term.

The following illustration of poorly connected text comes from a report produced by a writer in the less proficient group. It occurs at a point where the writer is dealing with diverse information about the armadillo's teeth. The source texts have suggested that the armadillo belongs to a group with few or no teeth, that armadillos are edentates, that edentates are toothless, and that edentates have teeth lacking tooth enamel. The texts have also said that the armadillo's teeth are numerous, small, nearly useless, molariform, peglike, and simple; the teeth are missing roots and enamel; and the teeth are placed well back in the mouth. In the following sentences, the writer combines much of the information about teeth but leaves the reader the burden of making sense of what is said:

> The animal is known for its lack of teeth. Actually, the armadillo has numerous small, molariform, and peglike teeth. However, because of their uselessness and lack of roots, it is often misconstrued.

That illustration contrasts with an excerpt from a better connected text. A reader would not have as much difficulty with the following sample of student writing that presents similar information in a more reader-based form. The contradiction in the information is not actually resolved, but it is acknowledged. Although the reader may still wonder why armadillos have teeth if they are classified as edentatas, he or she does not have to expend great conscious effort before moving on:

> Armadillos have been given the order name Edentata (meaning toothless); however, they are not a toothless mammal. Their teeth are rootless and have no enamel on them.

497

Reading one's own writing from the perspective of another person seems to require a special kind of metacognitive reading skill—an ability to anticipate readers' constructions and to provide what is needed for them to construct connected representations. In reading one's own writing, a writer must be aware of potential readers' cognitive products as well as one's own—a kind of awareness associated with social cognition (Rubin, 1984, cf. Kroll, 1978). The more able readers in this study seemed to be more successful, through their writing, at producing texts that would help readers construct coherent meanings as well as being more successful, through their reading, at constructing their own meanings. Their texts not only had tighter, more integrated structures and better developed content but also had fewer points at which readers would have difficulty connecting ideas.

Suggestions for Further Research

This discourse synthesis study considered only one learner variable, reading ability; only one text type, descriptive discourse; only one kind of subject matter, armadillos; and only one task, combining information from three texts to make a "complete one." Further research is needed into all these kinds of variables: other learner variables, such as developmental level and extent of topic knowledge; other text types, such as arguments and narratives; other subject matters, such as issues in a particular discipline. Certainly other tasks should be examined. This task, which asked writers to provide a comprehensive treatment of the topic in report form, privileged an intertextual criterion for the selection of content and a collection pattern for the organization of content. Examinations of other tasks will probably show different relevance criteria and different ways of transforming texts. For investigating discourse synthesis, two methods of data analysis designed for this study seem especially promising, the composite template and the organization measure. The composite template provided a great deal of information about text variables: the source of a particular content unit, the extent of a unit's repetition across sources, and its composite importance. Analysis of thematic chaining and chunking yielded a quantitative measure for organization, which has always been difficult to measure objectively and quantitatively (Stahl, 1974) in the absence of a conventionally ordered structure, such as a story. At least, the chaining and chunking procedure worked well with descriptive texts.

Like much research in reading comprehension, the study had a product emphasis, using the final product to infer constructive processes. Thus, while providing information about the nature of the constructivity in discourse synthesis, the study does not have much to say about how meaning is built over time. There was a measure for total time and there were measures for development of a written plan and extent of textual revision, but these measures were rather static. The measure for extensiveness of textual revisions was particularly uninformative. It did not discriminate between groups, and it was not correlated with any of the other measures, either positively or negatively. Although the correlational analyses suggested correlations between time and quantity of content and between time and quality, the study cannot explain these correlations. What were writers doing during that larger expanse of time that contributed to these more elaborate texts that raters judged to be of better quality? This will have to be a question for further studies that employ other methods. Possible approaches to examining the online process of meaning construction include observational methodologies, such as videotaping (Matsuhashi, 1981) and self-report methodologies, such as think alouds (cf. Hayes & Flower, 1983; Olson, Duffy, & Mack, 1984) already being used to study writing and reading. Data collected through such procedures should reveal more about the processes of synthesis as they relate to the evolving synthesis product.

This study does, however, offer some glimpses into how writers seem to have gone about the task. These glimpses come from their marked copies of the source texts and their scratch paper. Although marking of the source texts was common among the students (only 2 of the 40 students did not mark them), writers had different styles of marking—not only underlining and bracketing but other marks as well. Figure 6 illustrates how one writer marked the Collier's Text. As they read, some students apparently marked passages of content that they selected for inclusion in their syntheses and then scratched through the passages after the information was incorporated. When reading the sources, many of the students wrote labels for recurrent topical themes—*habitat, species, food, armor*—in the margins; and some used numbers keyed to topical headings listed on separate written plans. Reading and marking for these students seemed to be a process of "frame generation" (Bracewell et al., 1982) for the discourse that would be produced, a process that involved identifying thematic topics and often labeling or numbering what was selected. Half of the students produced some kind of written sketch of content and structure—a finding that contrasts with previous research in other types of composition suggesting that students tend not to write out their plans (Emig, 1971; Pianko, 1979; Stallard, 1974). In this study, some were brief sketches with four or five main topics, but others were extremely detailed, extending to as many as three pages.

In addition to research examining the synthesis process over the course of composing, we also need pedagogical research to explore various methods of teaching students how to synthesize material. Synthesis appears critical to successful learning from text as well as to effective writing. According to Spiro (1980), comprehension research has incorrectly focused on the "compartmentalized" reading of a single text when it should be giving more attention to "transitational integration" and "knowledge updating." His criticism might be extended to much reading instruction because it, too, has often emphasized compartmentalized comprehension of single texts rather than the synthesizing of information from various texts. At this point, one can only speculate about optimal methods and environments for teaching discourse synthesis in reading and writing because little empirical evidence exists to guide instructional decisions.

Although the research reported here has provided answers to some initial questions about discourse synthesis, many more questions need to be answered before we can begin to understand the cognitive processing that occurs and the variable forms that syntheses take when writers create texts from texts. Discourse synthesis, a dynamic, recursive process of framing and building, involves complex strategies and conscious decisions. The writer not only makes decisions about content and structure but also balances rhetorical concerns, such as appropriateness of the text for the intended reader. Further research into discourse synthesis can provide valuable insights into the operations of organizing, selecting, and connecting that are integral to construction of meaning in reading and writing and that are essential to learning from text.

Figure 6
Sample of a student's textual marking

ARMADILLO, an insect-eating mammal of the
order Edentata, having an armorlike shell encasing
its back. The name armadillo, meaning "little armored thing," was given to the animal by the Spanish
when they invaded the New World. Its original home
is South America, but it is now also found in the
southern United States.

name
original home

The armadillo is not toothless as its order
name, Edentata, implies; its teeth are simple, rootless pegs placed well back in the mouth. The shell
covering of its back is made up of numerous bony
plates with horny coverings that are often fused together. Across the middle of the back, there is a
hinge between the front and hind sections which permits the animal freedom of action. In some species
the face is shielded and the tail is encased in armor.
The armor is a protection against flesh-eaters.

teeth
shell

The breeding season of the armadillo begins in the
latter part of July, but the young are not born until
March or April of the following year. Although they
resemble the parents at birth, their shells do not
completely harden until they are full grown. There
are up to four young in a litter. All are of the
same sex, being derived from one egg, a phenomenon
called polyembryony.

breeding season — young

In prehistoric times huge armadillo-like animals,
the glyptodonts, were as big as oxen. Some were
armed with a formidable spiked club at the end of
the tail which could be used as a weapon against
such predators as the saber-toothed tiger. Today,
there are many different kinds of armadillos. The
common and best known species is the nine-banded armadillo or peba, Dasypus. It is about the size of
a house cat and has a long, sharply tapered tail.
There is a three-banded armadillo, Tolypeutes, and
also a six-banded armadillo, Euphractus. The nakedtailed armadillo, Cabassores, has eleven bands. The
great armadillo, Priodontes, has an over-all length
of 5 feet (150 cm). The third toe on its forefoot
is armed with a great sicklelike claw used to tear
rotten logs or to rip apart termite nests. The
smallest armadillo is the fairy armadillo, Chlamyphores, a dainty creature that lives underground like
a mole and is only 5 inches (13 cm) long. Others
include the weasel-faced armadillo and the hairy,
the greater, and the lesser peludo.

glyptodonts
types

Armadillos are of benefit to mankind since they
devour large quantities of termites and other injurious insects as well as scorpions. They also eat
snakes, poultry, fruit, and eggs.

purpose to man

Such a strange creature as the armadillo could
hardly escape folklore. The Mayan Indians, for instance, believe that the blackheaded vulture does not
die of old age but changes into an armadillo.

folklore

References

Bakhtin, M. M. (1981). *The dialogic imagination* (trans. & ed. by M. Holquist & C. Emerson). Austin: University of Texas Press.

Bartlett, F. C. (1932). *Remembering: A study in experimental and social psychology.* Cambridge, England: Cambridge University Press.

Bereiter, C., & Scardamalia, M. (1983). Levels of inquiry in writing research. In P. Mosenthal, L. Tamor, & S.A. Walmsley (Eds.), *Research on writing: Principles and methods* (pp. 3-25). New York: Longman.

Bereiter, C., & Scardamalia, M. (1984). Learning about writing from reading. *Written Communication, 1,* 163-188.

Bracewell, R. J., Frederiksen, C.H., & Frederiksen, J. D. (1982). Cognitive processes in composing and comprehending discourse. *Educational Psychologist, 17,* 146-164.

Bridwell, L. S. (1980). Revising strategies in twelfth grade students' transactional writing. *Research in the Teaching of English, 14,* 197-222.

Brown, J. I., Bennett, J. M., & Hannah, G. (1981). *The Nelson-Denny reading test, forms E and F: Examiner's manual.* Boston: Riverside.

Collins, A., & Gentner, D. (1980). A framework for a cognitive theory of writing. In L.W Gregg & E.R. Steinberg (Eds.), *Cognitive processes in writing* (pp. 51-72). Hillsdale, NJ: Erlbaum.

Cooper, C. R. (1977). Holistic evaluation of writing. In C.R. Cooper & L. Odell (Eds.), *Evaluating writing: Describing, measuring, judging* (pp. 3-31). Urbana, IL: National Council of Teachers of English.

Crothers, E. J. (1979). *Paragraph structure inference.* Norwood, NJ: Ablex.

Cummins, R. P. (1981). The Nelson-Denny reading test, forms E and F. *Journal of Reading, 36,* 54-59.

Curtin, C. B. (1982). Armadillo. *McGraw-Hill Encyclopedia of Science and Technology, 1,* 705-706.

D'Angelo, F.J.(1975). *A conceptual theory of rhetoric.* Cambridge. MA: Winthrop.

Day, J. D. (1980). *Teaching summarization skills: A comparison of training methods.* Unpublished doctoral dissertation. University of Illinois, Urbana.

Diederich, P. B. (1974). *Measuring growth in English.* Urbana, IL: National Council of Teachers of English.

Eamon, D. B. (1978-1979). Selection and recall of topical information in prose by better and poorer readers. *Reading Research Quarterly, 14,* 244-257.

Emig, J. (1971). *The composing processes of twelfth graders* (NCTE Research Rep. No. 13). Urbana, IL: National Council of Teachers of English.

Flower, L. (1979). Writer-based prose: A cognitive basis for problems in writing. *College English, 41,* 19-37.

502

Flower, L., & Hayes, J. R. (1981). A cognitive process theory of writing. *College Composition and Communication, 32,* 365-387.

Flower, L., & Hayes, J. R. (1984). Images, plans, and prose: The representation of meaning in writing. *Written Communication, 1,* 120-160.

Frederiksen, C. H. (1977). Semantic processing units in understanding text. In R.O. Freedle (Ed.), *Discourse production and comprehension* (pp. 57-87). Norwood, NJ: Ablex.

Goetz, E., & Armbruster, B. B. (1980). Psychological correlates of text structure. In R.J. Spiro, B. C. Bruce, & W. F. Brewer (Eds.), *Theoretical issues in reading comprehension* (pp. 201-220). Hillsdale, NJ: Erlbaum.

Goodwin, G. G. (1983). Armadillo. *Collier's Encyclopedia, 2,* 66.

Grimes, J. E. (1975). *The thread of discourse.* The Hague: Mouton.

Hayes, J. R., & Flower, L. (1980). Identifying the organization of writing processes. In L. W. Gregg & E. Steinberg (Eds.), *Cognitive processes in writing* (pp. 3-30). Hillsdale, NJ: Erlbaum.

Hayes, J. R., & Flower, L. (1983). Uncovering cognitive processes in writing: An introduction to protocol analysis. In P. Mosenthal, L. Tamor, & S.A. Walmsley (Eds.), *Research on writing: Principles and methods* (pp. 206-220). New York: Longman.

Holley, C. D., & Dansereau, D. F. (1984). Networking: The technique and the empirical evidence. In C. D. Holley & D. F. Dansereau (Eds.), *Spatial learning strategies: Techniques, applications, and related issues* (pp. 81-108). New York: Academic Press.

Hunt, K. W. (1965). *Grammatical structures written at three grade levels* (NCTE Research Rep. No. 3). Urbana, IL: National Council of Teachers of English.

Johnson, R. E. (1970). Recall of prose as a function of the structural importance of the linguistic units. *Journal of Verbal Learning and Verbal Behavior, 9,* 12-20.

Kantor, R.N. (1978). The management and comprehension of discourse connections by pronouns in English (Doctoral dissertation, Ohio State University, 1977). *Dissertation Abstracts International, 38,* 4790A.

Kintsch, W. (1974). *The representation of meaning in memory.* Hillsdale, NJ: Erlbaum.

Kintsch, W., & van Dijk, T. A. (1978). Toward a model of text comprehension and production. *Psychological Review, 85,* 363-394.

Kintsch, W., & Vipond, D. (1979). Reading comprehension and readability in educational practice and psychological theory. In L.G. Nilsson (Ed.), *Perspectives in memory research* (pp. 329-365). Hillsdale, NJ: Erlbaum.

Kline, C. R. (1977, March-April). *Meaning and significance: The hermeneutic as isomorph.* Paper presented at the meeting of the Conference on College Composition and Communication, Kansas City. (ERIC Document Reproduction Service No. ED 151 838).

Koen, F., Becker, A., & Young, R. E. (1969). The psychological reality of the paragraph. *Journal of Verbal Learning and Verbal Behavior, 8,* 49-53.

Kroll, B. M. (1978). Cognitive egocentrism and the problem of audience awareness in written discourse. *Research in the Teaching of English, 12,* 269-281.

Loban, W.D. (1976). *Language development: Kindergarten through grade twelve* (NCTE Research Rep. No. 18). Urbana, IL: National Council of Teachers of English.

Longacre, R.E. (1979). The paragraph as a grammatical unit. In T. Givon (Ed.), *Syntax and semantics: Vol. 12, Discourse and syntax* (pp. 115-134). New York: Academic Press.

Marshall, N., & Glock, M. D. (1978-1979). Comprehension of connected discourse: A study into the relationships between the structure of text and information recalled. *Reading Research Quarterly, 14,* 10-56.

Matsuhashi, A. (1981). Pausing and planning: The tempo of written discourse production. *Research in the Teaching of English, 15,* 113-134.

McGee, L. M. (1982). Awareness of text structure: Effects on children's recall of expository text. *Reading Research Quarterly, 17,* 581-590.

Meyer, B. J. F. (1975). *The organization of prose and its effects on memory.* Amsterdam: North Holland.

Meyer, B.J. F., Brandt, D. M., & Bluth, G. J. (1980). Use of top-level structure in text: Key for reading comprehension of ninth-grade students. *Reading Research Quarterly, 16,* 72-103.

Nold, E. W., & Davis, B. E. (1980). The discourse matrix. *College Composition and Communication, 31,* 141-152.

Olson, G. M., Duffy, S. A., & Mack, R. L. (1984). Thinking-out-loud as method for studying real-time comprehension processes. In D.E. Kieras & M.A. Just (Eds.), *New methods in reading comprehension research* (pp. 253-286). Hillsdale, NJ: Erlbaum.

Petofi, J. S. (1982). Representation language and their function in text interpretation. In S. Allen (Ed.), *Text processing.* Stockholm: Almquist & Wiksell.

Pianko, S. (1979). A description of the composing processes of college freshman writers. *Research in the Teaching of English, 13,* 5-22.

Riffaterre, M. (1980). La trace de l'intertexte. *La Pensee, 215,* 4-18.

Rubin, D. L. (1984). Social cognition and written communication. *Written Communication, 1,* 211-245.

Rumelhart, D. E. (1977). Toward an interactive model of reading. In S. Dornic (Ed.), *Attention and performance VI* (pp. 573-603). New York: Halsted Press.

Schallert, D. L., Ulerick, S. L., & Tierney, R. J. (1984). Evolving a description of text through mapping. In C.D. Holley & D.F. Dansereau (Eds.), *Spatial learning strategies: Techniques, applications, and related issues* (pp. 255-276). New York: Academic Press.

Smiley, S. S., Oakley, D. D., Worthen, D., Campione, J.D., & Brown, A. L. (1977). Recall of thematically relevant material by adolescent good and poor readers as a function of written versus oral presentation. *Journal of Educational Psychology, 69,* 381-387.

Sommers, N. (1980). Revision strategies of student writers and experienced adult writers. *College Composition and Communication, 31,* 378-388.

Spiro, R. J. (1980). Constructive processes in prose comprehension and recall. In R. J.Spiro, B. C. Bruce, & W. F Brewer (Eds.), *Theoretical issues in reading comprehension* (pp. 245-278). Hillsdale, NJ: Erlbaum.

Spivey, N. N. (1983). *Discourse synthesis: Constructing texts in reading and writing.* Unpublished doctoral dissertation, University of Texas, Austin.

Spivey, N. N. (1984). *Discourse synthesis: Constructing texts in reading and writing* (Outstanding Dissertation Monograph Series). Newark, DE: International Reading Association.

Stahl, A. (1974). Structural analysis of children's compositions. *Research in the Teaching of English, 8,* 184-205.

Stallard, C. K. (1974). An analysis of the writing behavior of good student writers. *Research in the Teaching of English, 8,* 206-218.

Stotsky, S. (1983). Research on reading/writing relationships: A synthesis and suggested directions. *Language Arts, 60,* 627-642.

Tate, G.H.H. (1982). Armadillo. *Encyclopedia Americana, 2,* 328-329.

Taylor, B.M. (1980). Children's memory for expository text after reading. *Reading Research Quarterly, 15,* 399-411.

Taylor, B. M., & Beach, R. W. (1984). The effects of text structure instruction on middle-grade students' comprehension and production of expository text. *Reading Research Quarterly, 19,* 134-146.

Thorndyke, P. W. (1977). Cognitive structures in comprehension and memory of narrative discourse. *Cognitive Psychology, 9,* 77-110.

Turner, A., & Greene, E. (1978). Construction and use of a propositional text base. *JSAS Catalog of Selected Documents in Psychology, 8,* 58 (MS no. 1713).

van Dijk, T. A. (1977). Semantic macrostructures and knowledge frames in discourse comprehension. In M.A. Just & P.A. Carpenter (Eds.), *Cognitive processes in comprehension* (pp. 3-22). Hillsdale, NJ: Erlbaum.

Vipond, D. (1980). Micro- and macroprocesses in text comprehension. *Journal of Verbal Learning and Verbal Behavior, 19,* 276-296.

Winograd, P. N . (1984). Strategic difficulties in summarizing texts. *Reading Research Quarterly, 19,* 404-425.

Witte, S.P. (1983a). Topical structure and revision: An exploratory study. *College Composition and Communication, 34,* 313 -341.

Witte, S.P. (1983b). Topical structure and writing quality: Some possible text-based explanations of readers' judgments of students' writing. *Visible Language, 17,* 177-205.

Witte, S. P. (1985). Revising, composing theory, and research design. In S. W. Freedman (Ed.), *The acquisition of written language* (pp. 250-284). Norwood, NJ: Ablex.

Author Notes

This report is based on a study I conducted for my doctoral dissertation, *Discourse Synthesis: Constructing Texts in Reading and Writing*, completed at the University of Texas in 1983 and published as a monograph with the same title by the International Reading Association in 1984. Once again I would like to thank my dissertation committee for their guidance in the project: Charles R. Kline, Jr., Michael Strange, Connie Juel, Diane Schallert, and Stephen Witte. I am also grateful to the following people for their assistance in data collection and analysis: E. Dale Davis, Donald Cox, Jan Teddlie, Richard Bouton, Mary Olson, Kerry Segal, Frank Crawley, Barbara tenBrink, and Tom Koballa; and I appreciate Mark Sadoski's editorial suggestions on the monograph.

Appendix

McGraw-Hill Text

ARMADILLO

The name for 21 species of mammals of the order Edentata, a group characterized by the lack of enamel on their teeth. They are indigenous to the New World, especially South America.

The nine-banded armadillo (*Dasypus novemcinctus*) is the best-known species and ranges from South America to the southwestern and southern United States. It is the only edentate which inhabits the United States. This species is adaptable, and has extended its range from the Rio Grande area to Oklahoma and eastward along the coast to Louisiana during the last century. It is of public health importance, since it is a reservoir host for *Trypanosoma cruzi*, the causative organism of Chagas' disease.

Armadillos range in size from the lesser pichiciego or fairy armadillo (*Chlamyphorus truncatus*), in which the adult is about 5 in. long, to the giant armadillo (*Priodontes giganteus*), which is about 4 ft. in length. The body is covered with horny dermal scales that replace the hair common to most mammals and overlay bony plates. These structures fuse to form rigid shields covering the anterior and posterior ends of the animal, whereas in the midregion they form jointed bands allowing a certain amount of flexibility. The number of bands varies for different species. The teeth, which are small, molariform, and peglike, lack roots and enamel. The giant armadillo has about 100 teeth, more than any other land mammal. The snout is long, and the tongue is cylindrical and viscous to assist in capturing food. The toes are clawed and are used by the animal to dig into ant and termite colonies for food, as well as for

506

burrowing. When disturbed, many species roll into a ball or wedge themselves into a burrow opening. In both instances the dermal plates serve as a protection.

The nine-banded armadillo has been studied because of its unusual life cycle. Four young are born in a den or chamber at the end of the burrow. The young are always of the same sex and are identical quadruplets, all arising from the division of a single egg. This multiple-birth condition, or polyembryony, is natural for these animals and the exception in other mammals. The young are well developed at birth and are weaned at about 8 weeks of age.

Americana Text

ARMADILLO, ar-m -dil o is any one of a group of mammals with few or no teeth. They are found in the south-central and southeastern United States and South and Central America. Armadillos are notable for their defensive armor. The armor consists of small roundish bony plates. hardened within the skin. In most members of the group the plates are united to form solid shields one over the shoulders, and one over the haunches. Between these shields are crosswise bands of movable plates that protect the body but leave freedom of motion to it. These plates are overlaid by a thin horny covering, and between them grow hairs varying in length and amount with the species, from almost none in some to a distinct coat hiding the shell in others. The unarmored undersurface is also hairy. The head has a shield entirely separate from that of the shoulders. In some species even the tail is protected by concentrically overlapping rings of armor. In others (the soft-tailed armadillos) the tail contains only scattered plates that are not firmly united to each other.

The armadillo belongs to the family Dasypodidae; there are 9 genera and about 20 species. The various species of armadillos are distinguished largely by the number of movable thin bands of plates lying between the large fixed anterior and posterior shields, up to as many as a dozen in the cabassous (*Xenurus*). Those of the genus *Tolypeutes* increase the value of the armor by their ability to roll themselves up into a ball so that the tender underparts of the body are completely protected. This ability depends upon the number of bands in the central portion of the armor case.

Although true edentates (mammals lacking teeth), armadillos have numerous small, nearly useless teeth, without true roots. The tongue is covered with a sticky fluid like that secreted by the tongue of an anteater.

507

Armadillos are timid, nocturnal animals, living on insects, carrion, and vegetable matter. Their legs and claws are adapted to burrowing, and when pursued they usually bury themselves more quickly than the pursuer can follow them. One of the most interesting of them all is the pichiciago (*Chlamyphorus truncatus*) found in Argentina, which lives entirely underground like a mole, and exhibits many peculiar structures. The body has a truncated appearance, as if the rear part had been cut squarely off, instead of ending in curved lines. It is very small, only five to six inches (12 1/2 to 15 cm) long. The giant armadillo (*Priodontes giganteus*) measures three feet, exclusive of the tail. Some of the armadillos range north and south as far as Texas and Argentina; among these is the nine-banded armadillo (*Tatusia novemcincta*). They are eaten by the South Americans and are considered to have a delicate taste.

Reproduction in *Dasypus novemcinctus*, a nine-banded form, is peculiar. The young, unless some mishap has taken place, are invariably quadruplets of the same sex. It is believed that the fertilized egg divides and redivides into four parts before each part becomes organized into a young armadillo.

Fossil armadillos have been found in both North and South America. One fossil species was six feet (1.8 meters) long. Another genus was *Eutatus*, which had a shield formed of 36 distinct bands, of which the last 12 were fused together.

Collier's Text

ARMADILLO, an insect-eating mammal of the order Edentata, having an armorlike shell encasing its back. The name armadillo, meaning "little armored thing," was given to the animal by the Spanish when they invaded the New World. Its original home is South America, but it is now also found in the southern United States.

The armadillo is not toothless as its order name, Edentata, implies; its teeth are simple, rootless pegs placed well back in the mouth. The shell covering of its back is made up of numerous bony plates with horny coverings that are often fused together. Across the middle of the back, there is a hinge between the front and hind sections which permits the animal freedom of action. In some species, the face is shielded and the tail is encased in armor. The armor is a protection against flesh-eaters.

The breeding season of the armadillo begins in the latter part of July, but the young are not born until March or April of the following year. Although they resemble the parents at birth, their shells do not completely harden until they are full grown. There are up to four young in a litter. All are of the same sex, being derived from one egg, a phenomenon called polyembryony.

In prehistoric times huge armadillo-like animals, the glyptodonts, were as big as oxen. Some were armed with a formidable spiked club at the end of the tail which could be used as a weapon against such predators as the saber-toothed tiger. Today, there are many different kinds of armadillos. The common and best known species is the nine-banded armadillo, or peba, *Dasypus*. It is about the size of a house cat and has a long, sharply tapered tail. There is a three-banded armadillo, *Tolypeutes*, and also a six-banded armadillo, *Euphractus*. The nakedtailed armadillo, *Cabassores*, has eleven bands. The great armadillo, *Priodontes*, has an over-all length of 5 feet (150 cm). The third toe on its forefoot is armed with a great sicklelike claw used to tear rotten logs or to rip apart termite nests. The smallest armadillo is the fairy armadillo, *Chlamyphores*, a dainty creature that lives underground like a mole and is only 5 inches (13 cm) long. Others include the weasel-faced armadillo and the hairy, the greater, and the lesser peludo.

Armadillos are of benefit to mankind since they devour large quantities of termites and other injurious insects as well as scorpions. They also eat snakes, poultry, fruit, and eggs.

Such a strange creature as the armadillo could hardly escape folklore. The Mayan Indians, for instance, believed that the blackheaded vulture does not die of old age but changes into an armadillo.

Note. "Armadillo" by G.G. Goodwin, *Collier's Encyclopedia*, 1983, *2*, 66. Copyright 1983 by Macmillan Educational Company, a Division of Macmillan, Inc. Reprinted by permission.

Author's Comment—Nancy Nelson Spivey

What you see here is the second major transformation of this report. Its first form was my doctoral thesis, *Discourse Synthesis: Constructing Texts in Reading and Writing*, which I completed in 1983 at the University of Texas at Austin and which is available only through the library there and through University Microfilms. Next it was a more condensed version, a research monograph published with the same title in 1984 by the International Reading Association. And now it is in article form as a chapter in this book. When Hayes, Young, Hajduk, Cochran, McCaffrey, and Matchett asked me to contribute to this volume, I was, of course, delighted to have the opportunity to turn the monograph into an article and to report the study in a more accessible form.

All I would do, I thought, was trim it down a bit—compress it even more. However, when I began cutting it, I could not resist making other revisions. The new title—slightly different from the title of the thesis—signals the change. Some sections dropped out, mainly those involving additional data analyses, and some others that remain have become somewhat more elaborate, as I have attempted to provide more explanation. There are also changes in wording. For instance, now the participants in the study are "able" and "more able" readers instead of "less able" and "able." (Of course, the students in the study were *able*; all were performing well enough in reading the material for their university courses. Why did I label them the other way originally?) Now that the rewriting is completed, I would like to share some of the story behind the study.

Why did I decide to conduct this particular study? To begin to answer that question, I should explain that back in the late 70s and early 80s, when I was pursuing my doctoral studies, reading comprehension was receiving much attention—new attention—from people in various disciplines. It was a very exciting time for people studying discourse processes, as I have pointed out in a recent theoretical review (Spivey, 1987). I was intrigued by the discourse-analysis methods that some reading researchers, such as Bonnie Meyer (1975), Carl Frederiksen (1975), and Walter Kintsch and Teun van Dijk (Kintsch & van Dijk, 1978) were using to examine texts and readers' recalls of those texts. They were performing these careful analyses in order to gain insights into how readers construct representations of meaning from textual cues. Although the

510

studies of reading comprehension at that time focused on readers' understandings of single texts—usually fairly brief texts—I was becoming interested in
reading and learning based on multiple texts—the intertextual connections
that people make when they integrate material from different sources. I
wanted to study what I called "discourse synthesis": to see the commonalities
and the variability that might result when people of different verbal abilities
used the same source texts to create their own meanings. To do so, I needed
a realistic task that invited synthesis. A writing task made sense because
writing often entails using multiple sources and building meaning from the
composite. I was also very interested in the process of composing, and I
wondered why researchers were not studying this very common approach to
writing.

How did the study go? Overall my *data collection* went smoothly mainly
because I had conducted a pilot study to try out the procedure and materials
but also because I had colleagues at Southern Methodist University in Dallas
who were very cooperative. One of them let me use his classes, and he built
the assignment into the course. When I began analyzing data, there were
some some humorous moments, for instance, when I read some of the *facts*
the students listed for the prior knowledge measure—such items as the "fact"
that armadillos eat Lone Star Beer trucks and the "fact" that armadillos are
"always laying dead on the highway." But *data analysis* was a formidable
task because I had numerous dependent measures and those measures were
counts of many little things, such as propositions. (At that point, I thought I
had learned why researchers had not been investigating this very common
process of writing a text.) When I went from Dallas to Austin to run my data
on the mainframe at the University of Texas, I didn't know when (or if) I
would return.

What would I change? Since I can't change the study now, I am quite
happy to leave it as it is. (I could, however, change the report of the study,
and so I did change *it* a bit.) Even though, in general, I feel good about this
study, I could critique it if pushed to do so, and I would then perhaps point
out how the measures for revision and planning were probably too quantitative in emphasis and may have missed important qualitative differences and
how the topic was rather artificial for that class and not as ecologically valid as
it might have been. But instead of taking a revisionist stance or a critical
stance on this one study, I prefer to think about how the study relates to
subsequent work. I see this study as a start—the first study in my career as a
researcher. With it, I established a method for studying a reading-writing task
that is an important kind of literate practice—a literate practice that needs

511

much further investigation (see Spivey, 1990). In subsequent work I have continued to build on the basis of the first study to examine the operations of organizing, selecting, and connecting as people perform other kinds of reading, writing, and synthesis tasks. Now, of course, I explore different issues, and my work is informed to some extent by different bodies of work. And now I have colleagues in various parts of this country and also abroad who are studying discourse synthesis too. Several of them are doctoral students conducting *their* first studies.

What continually impresses me as I read our research literature and conduct my own studies is the *lineage* of a research report—the studies that precede it and the studies that follow it. I have become more conscious of intertextual links in my own work, and I look for intertextual connections when I read the work of others.

References

Frederiksen, C. (1975). Representing logical and semantic structure of knowledge acquired from discourse. *Cognitive Psychology, 7*, 317-458.

Kintsch, W., & van Dijk, T. A. (1978). Toward a model of text comprehension and production. *Psychological Review, 85*, 363-394.

Meyer, B. J. F. (1975). *The organization of prose and its effects on memory.* Amsterdam: North Holland.

Spivey, N. N. (1983). *Discourse synthesis: Constructing texts in reading and writing.* Unpublished doctoral dissertation. University of Texas at Austin.

Spivey, N. N. (1984). *Discourse synthesis: Constructing texts in reading and writing* (Outstanding Dissertation Monograph Series). Newark, DE: International Reading Association.

Spivey, N. N. (1987). Construing constructivism: Reading research in the United States. *Poetics, 16*, 169-192.

Spivey, N. N. (1990). Transforming texts: Constructive processes in reading and writing. *Written Communication, 7*, 256-187.

Chapter 20 Is Writing a Gift? The Impact on Students Who Believe It Is

Some theoretical claims that were considered quite radical when they were introduced have been transformed with the passage of time into common sense beliefs. Some of Freud's claims, e.g., that mental illness has its origin in early childhood sexual conflicts and that slips of the tongue are unconsciously motivated, have been transformed in this way. However, the acceptance of a claim into the canons of common sense is no guarantee of its validity. Psychologists, for example, have long since rejected the main body of Freudian theory, and, in particular, now attribute serious mental illness to chemical imbalances rather than to childhood sexual conflicts.

In their article, Palmquist and Young describe a survey study of another theoretical claim which has found its way into folk wisdom — the claim made by romantic literary theorists that the ability to write well is a gift that can't be taught. The authors find that this belief is related to other important beliefs and attitudes about writing, such as writing anxiety, and suggest that it may have important impact on students' approaches to writing instruction. They note that ". . . teachers must remember that their students come to them freighted with rhetorical lore, not all of which is sound, and some of which may impede their ability to learn to write better."

Although their data collection method was a relatively simple survey, Palmquist and Young's analysis of their data was quite complex. In fact, their article has been placed last in this volume because of the complexity of their data analysis. Not only do the authors make use of ANOVAs, MANOVAs, and post-hoc tests, they also use factor analysis and linear regression analysis — two techniques that have not been discussed previously in this volume. As a result, this is a challenging article. Readers who can understand the main points of the Palmquist and Young article should be able to "get the meat out of" most of the empirical studies that they are likely to encounter in the field of literacy.

Notes on Technical Issues

The purpose of **regression analysis** is similar to that of analysis of variance. Both techniques are designed to identify significant relationships between a dependent variable and one or more independent variables.

However, the two techniques are appropriate for different sorts of independent variables. In analysis of variance, the independent variables are categorical variables. That is, they are variables such as 'gender' which consists of the categories male and female, or 'treatment group' which consists of categories such as experimental group, control group #1, etc. In contrast, in regression analysis, the independent variables are interval variables. That is, they are variables such as age or IQ which can be measured on an interval scale.

The following figure will help in understanding the nature of regression analysis:

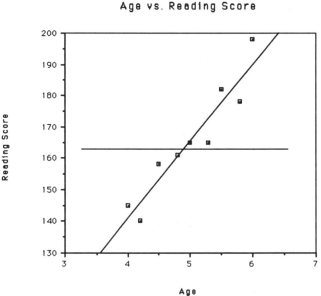

Age vs. Reading Score

The points in the figure represent ages and reading scores for individual children. The sloping line, called the regression line, is the line that fits the data points most closely. A line which slopes up, as this one does, represents the tendency of reading scores to increase with age. A line which sloped down would represent a tendency for reading score to decrease with age. If the line were horizontal, we would say that there was no relation between reading score and age (since the reading score would not tend to increase or decrease with age). What regression analysis tells us is whether the sloped line is different enough in slope from a horizontal line to consider the relation between age and reading score a significant one.

Significance levels for regression analyses are reported in the same way as for analyses of variance, that is, either with an ANOVA table or with an expression such as (F=10.15, df=1,39, p <.003) indicating values of the F-statistic, degrees of freedom, and p-value. Sometimes researchers also report Pearson correlations between independent and dependent variables, e.g., R= 0.454.

Palmquist and Young made use of a technique called **factor analysis** to assess the adequacy of the first 19 questions in their questionnaire. The purpose of these questions was to measure four traits: the belief that writing is a gift, writing anxiety, self assessed writing ability, and experience with writing teachers. As is considered good practice in the construction of questionnaires, Palmquist and Young asked more than one question to assess each of the traits. For example, they included five questions that they thought would reflect writing anxiety, and four that they thought would reflect the belief that writing is a gift.

Even with the best intentions, it is possible for a researcher to construct questionnaires which fail to work the way they were intended to. To check whether or not a questionnaire has worked well, researchers should determine if their results meet the following criteria:

1. All of the questions intended to measure the same trait should be highly correlated with each other and less highly correlated or uncorrelated with questions designed to measure other traits. For example, most participants who agree that "Good writers are born, not made" (Question 1) should also agree that "Writing cannot be taught" (Question 3) because both are intended to measure the belief that writing is a gift. However, these same participants may be evenly split on their answers to Question 15 ("I avoid writing.") because this question is intended to measure a different trait, writing anxiety.
2. One cluster of questions should correspond to each trait being measured. Thus, if four traits are being measured, there should be four highly correlated clusters of questions.
3. Each of the questions should be included in just one of the clusters.

Factor analysis provides the researcher with a systematic way to see if these criteria have been met. The factor analysis which Palmquist and Young applied to their questionnaire indicated that, in most ways, the questionnaire worked as it was designed to work. However, this analysis also revealed two problems. Five of the questions didn't correspond to any of the traits being measured, and one question designed to measure one trait, writing anxiety, proved to be a better measure of a different trait, self-assessed writing ability. Identification of these problems allowed Palmquist and Young to reassess their questionnaire data and to avoid drawing potentially misleading conclusions from them.

Michael Palmquist
Colorado State University

Richard E. Young
Carnegie Mellon University

The Notion of Giftedness and Student Expectations About Writing

Abstract

Research reported by Daly, Miller, and their colleagues suggests that writing apprehension is related to a number of factors we do not yet fully understand. This study suggests that included among those factors should be the belief that writing ability is a gift. Giftedness, as it is referred to in the study, is roughly equivalent to the Romantic notion of original genius. Results from a survey of 247 post-secondary students enrolled in introductory writing courses at two institutions indicate that higher levels of belief in giftedness are correlated with higher levels of writing apprehension, lower self-assessments of writing ability, lower levels of confidence in achieving proficiency in certain writing activities and genres, and lower self-assessments of prior experience with writing instructors. Significant differences in levels of belief in giftedness were also found among students who differed in their perceptions of the most important purpose for writing, with students who identified "to express your own feelings about something" as the most important purpose for writing having the highest mean level of belief in giftedness. Although the validity of the notion that writing ability is a special gift is not directly addressed, the results suggest that belief in giftedness may have deleterious effects on student writers.

> Throughout all my schooling I was led to believe that creative talent was the possession of only a few "gifted and artistic" individuals. Thus, the rest of us were resigned to concentrate on the mechanical aspects of writing and producing well researched and well supported term papers. I can't recall ever being allowed to express my thoughts about a topic I was interested in.
>
> — Graduate student in rhetoric commenting on her previous instruction in writing

The expectations of learners and teachers powerfully influence what happens in school. If we do not already know this in our bones, we can find it documented in studies of learning. It is a truth both reassuring and disturbing, reassuring because it reminds

517

us that not all students who have been judged academically inferior are necessarily or natively so, disturbing because however unsound such judgments may be at the outset, they do tend gradually to fulfill themselves, causing students to lag behind their peers a little more each year until the gap that separates the groups begins to seem vast and permanent.

— Mina Shaughnessy, <u>Errors and Expectations</u> (275)

Introduction

It will come as no surprise to those who teach composition that a large proportion of students enter the classroom believing that the ability to write well is a gift.[1] By "writing well," students seem to mean something like writing with accuracy, grace, and originality or creativity, although the students we have talked with are seldom very precise, assuming apparently that everyone knows and agrees on what "writing well" means. They are no more precise about giftedness. By "gift," they seem to mean an innate ability, such as perfect pitch, with which only a few are born and for which, if absent, no amount of study or practice can adequately compensate. For music students, lack of perfect pitch does not appear to put an end to their efforts to become musicians. For writing students, however, the notion of giftedness appears to play a different role. Students who believe they lack the gift for writing are often anxious about their writing and may turn, when they can, to other studies for which the ability to write well is not a requirement. If you can't write well, they seem to believe, why keep beating your head against a wall?

As we use the term in this article, *gift*—or *giftedness*—is roughly equivalent to the Romantic notion of original genius. "Genius," said Hugh Blair (1965), who doubtless had much to do with the introduction of the term into the vocabulary of popular criticism as well as into the teaching of writing, "is used to signify that talent or aptitude which we receive from nature, for excelling in any one thing whatever .... By art and study, no doubt it can be improved; but by them alone it cannot be acquired" (p. 41). *Giftedness* and *genius*, like such related terms as *originality, imagination,* and *creativity,* are in popular usage today pale descendants of what were almost technical terms in Romantic poetics (Smith, 1925). All are often associated now with a vague and unattributed group of esthetic assumptions widely shared in our society. As Willinsky (1987) argued, "The once-radical philosophy of Romanticism has taken on the forcefulness of common sense, turning almost invisible in the process of becoming the most sensible way of imagining what children should be doing in language" (p. 268). Although the schools no doubt have been the primary conduit of these conceptual traditions, the terms are widely used in

518

popular discourse, providing a common although not especially precise way of thinking and talking about exceptional performance in writing and in other activities that are not conventional and routine.

If we assume for the moment that the ability to write well is, in fact, a gift, then the retreat of the ungifted into more manageable pursuits seems not only understandable but reasonable and prudent. Expecting students who believe they lack the requisite gift to expend the effort required to become good writers is expecting them to spend substantial time and effort trying to achieve a goal that they believe to be unreachable. So put, the expectation is both contrary to reason and quite likely to be a source of anxiety for the student. Daly and Miller's landmark studies of writing apprehension (1975a, 1975b; see also Hillocks' [1986] review of writing apprehension pp. 49-51) directed attention to the potential effects of writing apprehension among student populations. Drawing on previous work in communication anxiety (e.g., Phillips, 1968; Clevenger, 1959; Daly & McCroskey, 1975), they noted that writing apprehension affects a "large proportion of the population" and that highly apprehensive individuals "tend to select occupations that they perceive to require less communication" (1975a, p. 243). Perhaps more important, from the perspective of those associated with writing instruction, Daly and Miller suggest that writing apprehension "might have powerful effects on individuals' attitudes towards, and behavior in, writing courses" (1975b, p. 250). This finding appears to hold not only for writing students but for writing teachers as well. Reporting on a more recent series of studies, Daly, Vangeliste, and Witte (1988) suggested that teachers' writing apprehension may affect the way they value and respond to student writing.

The research conducted by Daly, Miller, and their colleagues, as well as our own experience in the classroom, suggests that writing apprehension is related to a number of factors that are not yet fully understood. In this article, we argue that the belief that writing ability is a gift should be included among those factors. In presenting our findings, however, we do not claim that the belief in giftedness alone leads to writing apprehension. Rather, our results indicate that belief in giftedness, insofar as it affects writing apprehension, does so within a context of beliefs and attitudes, such as an individual's assessment of his or her writing ability and prior experience with writing teachers.

We do not address the question of whether the ability to write with accuracy, grace, and originality is a product of nature or nurturing, except to note that the question is left unresolved after centuries of debate—indicating, perhaps, that the question is not well framed. We do argue, however, that if the ability to write well is not an innate gift and is instead something that can be acquired through study and practice, then students may be doing themselves a disservice by turning away from or minimizing the importance of writing instruction. The notion of giftedness may have an influence like that of the "rigid rules" and "inflexible plans" Rose (1980) described in his study of students struggling with writer's block. If this is the case, it would seem possible—as it was with the student writers Rose observed—to work with students to overcome whatever difficulties may arise from their belief in giftedness.

We see our inquiry as an exploratory study—an initial attempt to map the relationships among a constellation of attitudes and beliefs about writing that have, to a large extent, gone unacknowledged in discussions of writing and writing instruction. Specifically, we address the following questions:

1. What relationships, if any, exist among students' belief in giftedness, their apprehension about writing, and their self-assessments of their writing ability?
2. What relationships, if any, exist between students' belief in giftedness and their confidence in achieving proficiency in specific writing activities and genres?
3. What relationships, if any, exist between students' belief in giftedness and their prior experiences in writing classrooms?
4. What relationships, if any, exist between students' belief in giftedness and their perceptions of the purpose for writing?

Methods

Participants

Students enrolled in thirteen sections of freshman-level writing courses at the University of Pittsburgh and Robert Morris College were surveyed concerning their beliefs and expectations about writing; 119 students in seven sections from the University of Pittsburgh and 128 students in six sections from Robert Morris College completed the questionnaire. The courses at both institutions emphasized a process-oriented approach to the teaching of writing. Of the students from Robert Morris College, 35 were enrolled in two sections that met in the evening; according to their instructors, students in these courses were generally older, nontraditional students. Surveying students at two institutions allowed us to determine if the measures we used in the study would generalize beyond a single group of respondents.

Materials

Students responded to a 32-item questionnaire (see Appendix A). Nineteen items asked for a response to a six-point Likert scale that ranged from "strongly disagree" to "strongly agree." Ten items asked for a true-false response. One item asked for a multiple choice response. And two items asked students to indicate which of several writing activities they felt they could perform at a specified level of proficiency.

Procedure

The questionnaires were distributed to a representative from each institution, who subsequently distributed them to the instructors of the individual sections. The questionnaires were either completed in class or distributed in one class meeting and collected at the next, depending on the preference of the instructor.

Development of Measures

To address our four questions, we set out to compose a questionnaire that would allow us to assess students' belief in giftedness and expectations about writing. After completing a preliminary version of the questionnaire, we asked students and faculty at our own and other institutions to fill out and criticize it. As a result of their responses, some questions were revised and others dropped. After deciding upon a final version of the questionnaire, it was administered to students at the University of Pittsburgh and Robert Morris College. Based on responses from the students, a principal components factor analysis with orthogonal rotations was used to develop four measures—belief in giftedness, writing apprehension, self-assessment of writing ability, and previous experience with writing teachers. The factor loadings were first established using responses from students at Robert Morris College and subsequently tested using responses from students at the University of Pittsburgh. This step resulted in the exclusion from further analysis of five items from the questionnaire. The remaining measures used in the study— measures of student confidence, prior classroom experience, and perceptions of the purpose for writing—were based on multiple-choice and true/false statements. Below, each of the measures is discussed in detail.

Measures of Students' Belief in the Notion of Giftedness: In our initial factor analysis on responses from students at Robert Morris College, four items related to belief in the notion of giftedness loaded on the same factor.

521

Roughly put, this means that student responses to the four items correlated with each other more strongly than they did with other items in the questionnaire. The first two items focus on the extent to which the respondent believes that writing can be learned; the third and fourth focus on the extent to which the respondent believes that writing can be taught (the numbers of the four items below correspond to the item numbers in our questionnaire):

1. Good writers are born, not made.
2. Some people have said, "Writing can be learned but it can't be taught." Do you believe it can be learned?
3. Do you believe it can be taught?
13. Good teachers can help me become a better writer.

A second factor analysis using responses from students at the University of Pittsburgh indicated that the four items loaded on the same factor (see Appendix B for factor loadings).

Measure of Writing Apprehension: To assess writing apprehension, five items from Daly and Miller's (1975a) writing apprehension questionnaire were included in our questionnaire:

15. I avoid writing.
16. I enjoy writing.
17. Writing is a lot of fun.
18. Discussing my writing with others is an enjoyable experience
19. I'm no good at writing.

A recent study indicated that these five statements accurately predict the writing apprehension scores yielded by the entire questionnaire (Hartman, 1989). To develop our measure of writing apprehension, we followed the same procedure used to develop our measure of belief in the notion of giftedness. The factor analysis indicated that four of the five items loaded on the same factor and a fifth (item 19) loaded with items we used to measure students' self-assessment of their writing ability (see below). Although shifting this item out of the measure of writing apprehension reduces the extent to which we can compare our assessment of writing apprehension to assessments obtained via the Daly and Miller instrument, we believe that making the shift is desirable for two reasons. First, the wording of the statement is more consistent with statements we had developed for the self-assessment measure (see 8, 12, 14, 19 below), among which was the contrasting statement, "I am a good writer." Second, factor analysis subsequently showed that it correlated more strongly with the self-assessment measure than with the writing apprehension measure (see Appendix B).

Measure of Students' Self-Assessment of their Writing Ability: We followed the same procedure used to develop the measures of belief in the notion of giftedness and writing apprehension to develop this measure. Factor analysis indicated that four items from the questionnaire associated with students' assessment of their writing ability loaded on the same factor:

8. I am a good writer.
12. I believe I was born with the ability to write well.
14. I have always been a good writer.
19. I'm no good at writing.

Measures of Student Confidence: We assessed students' confidence in their ability to achieve proficiency in various writing activities and genres by analyzing their responses to two items on the questionnaire. Item 31 stated, "Given enough time, hard work, and desire, I could become an expert (that is, I could attain the proficiency of a first class publishable writer) in the following: (check all that apply)." The 15 activities listed in Item 31 ranged from spelling to creating good metaphors. Item 32 stated, "Given enough time, hard work, and desire, I would be able to write well enough to have the following types of writing published: (check all that apply)." The 22 genres listed in Item 32 ranged from business letters to lyric poetry. Each activity and genre was weighted according to a difficulty score based on ratings provided by 20 faculty in the English Department at Colorado State University. All of the faculty who provided ratings either were teaching or had taught freshman composition. The faculty were asked to rate each activity and genre on a 1-to-5 scale, with five corresponding to the highest level of difficulty. Each activity and genre was given a difficulty score based on the mean rating assigned to that activity by the faculty. The confidence scores for students were subsequently calculated by summing the difficulty scores of each activity and genre in which students indicated they could attain proficiency. Higher scores indicate greater confidence in gaining proficiency as a writer.

Our measures of writing confidence were designed to assess students' confidence in their ability—at least potentially—to write well, that is, to write with accuracy, grace, and originality. To make the notion of writing well more concrete and, hence, more accessible to students, we asked whether they could achieve proficiency in specific writing activities and genres. Rather than asking whether students thought they could achieve proficiency in "writing," we asked whether they could achieve proficiency in activities such as punctuating and inventing effective metaphors and in writing in various genres such as the novel and the business letter. We also tried to make the standard for good writing more accessible to students by asking them, in Item 31, whether they had the potential to write as well as a "first class publishable writer" and, in Item 32, well enough to have specific types of writing published. Moreover, to better understand the role that practice and familiarity might play in student writing confidence, we included in our list of writing genres both those with which we expected students to have had extensive writing practice (e.g., school-sponsored writing such as personal essays and critical analyses of literature) and those with which we expected them to have had little writing practice (e.g., novels, plays, and lyric poetry).

Measures of Prior Experience in Writing Classrooms: We assessed four aspects of students' prior experience in writing classrooms: (1) students' response to their prior experience with writing teachers; (2) the extent to which students had received writing instruction that was typical of process-oriented curricula; (3) the extent to which students indicated that they had received writing instruction that focused primarily on grammar, spelling, and punctuation; and (4) the extent to which students indicated that they had received writing instruction that stressed the importance of creativity.

The measure of students' response to their prior experience with writing teachers was developed using the same procedure used to develop the measure of belief in the notion of giftedness. We included several items on the questionnaire that we thought would allow us to assess students' beliefs about the best ways to learn how to write. Of these items, however, only two loaded on the same factor in our factor analysis. Both of these items dealt with students' prior experience with teachers:

> 10. Some of the things my former writing teachers said made
>   me believe I could become a good writer.
> 11. Some of my former writing teachers encouraged me to keep
>   working on my writing.

We used these two items as the basis for a measure of prior response to writing teachers and excluded the items that did not load on the factor analysis from further consideration in the study.

The three other measures of prior classroom experience were based on true/false statements. We derived the scores each student received for these measures by summing the number of responses for each type of instruction (true = 1, false = 0).

To assess the extent to which students had received instruction consistent with process-oriented curricula, we summed responses from the following statements:

21. In past writing classes, I have engaged in "freewriting."
22. In past writing classes, I have engaged in "pre-writing."
25. Some of my former writing teachers required me to submit rough drafts of my papers.
27. In previous writing classes, I've had to revise my papers.

To assess the extent to which students had received instruction consistent with product-oriented curricula, we summed responses from the following statements:

23. Some of my former teachers acted as though the most important part of writing was spelling, punctuation, and grammar.
26. I've taken some courses that focused primarily on spelling, grammar, and punctuation.

To assess the extent to which students had received instruction that stressed the importance of creativity, we summed responses from the following statements:

24. Some of my former writing classes emphasized creativity.
28. Some of my previous writing teachers were more interested in my ideas than in my spelling, punctuation, and grammar.

Measure of Student Perceptions of the Purpose for Writing. We based this measure on students' response to item 30. Item 30 stated, "The most important purpose for writing is: (1) to inform others of your own ideas, (2) to persuade others to believe something that you believe, (3) to come to understand yourself better, or (4) to express your own feelings about something." This item was designed as a multiple-choice statement not because we assume that writing can be said to have a single purpose—a proposition we strongly reject—but rather because we suspected that, in the course of their prior writing instruction, students might have gained a sense that writing was primarily intended for a particular purpose. By designing responses that corresponded to, respectively, current traditional rhetoric, classical rhetoric, and the two dominant strands of expressionist rhetoric, we hoped to determine whether differences existed among students in their attitudes and beliefs about writing.

Validation of Measures

Because we did not collect information that would allow us to assess, for instance, respondents' writing and reading practices, gender, and scores on standardized achievement tests, we were unable to validate our measures externally. We were able, however, to conduct internal tests of validity for several measures used in the study. For the measures developed using factor analysis, we first established and then tested the factor loadings on two groups of students, one from each institution. This process indicated that the factor loadings we had observed on students from the first group of students were not random. In addition, we used Cronbach's Alpha on the three measures developed using factor analysis that involved responses from more than two items on the questionnaire. Scores for the measures of belief in giftedness, writing apprehension, and self-assessment of writing ability, each of which was based on responses to four items, were .669, .822, and .768, respectively.

Results and Discussion

Descriptive Statisticss

With the exception of the measure of students' perceptions of the purpose for writing—for which we did not derive a numerical score for individual students—the mean scores for each of the measures used in this study are presented in Table 1. Scores for the measures of belief in giftedness, writing apprehension, self-assessment of writing ability, and prior experience with teachers are based on a 1-to-6 scale. In contrast, the scores for the remaining measures were derived by summing the number of responses in each category. Because the maximum number of responses in each category varied, student responses were converted to percentages of the maximum possible score for each category. The scores for the measures of prior classroom experience reflect the percentage of the maximum number of responses in each category. The maximum number of responses are: process-oriented instruction = 4; product-oriented instruction = 2; instruction that stressed creativity = 2. The scores for the measures of student confidence reflect the percentage of the maximum possible weighted difficulty scores in each

Table 1
Means and Standard Deviations for Measures
of Belief in Giftedness and Expectations about Writing
(n = 247)

	Mean	SD
Belief in Giftedness	2.65	0.83
Writing Apprehension	3.77	1.12
Assessment of Writing Ability	3.31	0.99
Writing Activities	51.0	28.5
Writing Genres	22.75	15.5
Process-Oriented Instruction	72.6	26.9
Grammar-Oriented Instruction	68.5	36.6
Instruction Stressing Creativity	70.7	36.4
Experience with Writing Teachers	4.04	1.14

category. The maximum possible scores are: writing activities = 42.32; writing genres = 68.36.

Differences Between the Two Student Populations

As we noted above, we collected responses from students at the University of Pittsburgh and Robert Morris College because we wanted to see if our measures would generalize across students from different educational contexts. Although both institutions draw students from the same area (Western Pennsylvania and the surrounding region), their educational emphases differ. The University of Pittsburgh is a large public university with a strong liberal arts tradition, while Robert Morris College is a small private college with a strong vocational orientation.

To determine whether significant differences existed between the two groups of students, we conducted a MANOVA on the measures described above. We found significant differences between students at the two institutions on the multivariate analysis (Wilks' lambda = .909; $F = 2.459$; $df = 9, 222$; $p < .011$). Despite evidence of a statistically significant difference between the institutions, we were skeptical of the indicated difference because the value of Wilks' lambda was quite high (Wilks' lambda varies from zero to one, with one indicating no difference). Subsequent univariate analysis and comparison of mean values and standard deviations for the measures indicated that the University of Pittsburgh students responded more positively to their prior experience with writing teachers than did the Robert Morris students ($F = 6.230$; $df = 1$, 230; $p < .013$; means were 4.231 vs. 3.865 and standard deviations were 1.058 and 1.191, respectively, on a 1-to-6 scale) and that students at Robert Morris had a higher mean score on the measure of process-oriented instruction than did the University of Pittsburgh students ($F = 4.118$; $df = 1$, 230; $p < .042$; means were 3.039 and 2.750 and standard deviations were 1.097 and 1.037, respectively, on a 0-to-4 scale). These relatively small differences, however, in combination with the standard deviations of the scores, suggested to us that the differences being reported, while statistically significant, were not of practical importance. Subsequent comparisons of differences between institutions for each of the four questions discussed below confirmed our conclusion. As a result, in the analyses reported below, we combined responses from the two institutions.

Question One: What relationships, if any, exist among students' belief in giftedness, their apprehension about writing, and their self-assessments of their writing ability?

A series of linear regressions indicated that students' level of belief in the notion of giftedness was moderately correlated with their apprehension about writing and their self-assessments of their writing ability. (For an explanation of our characterization of small, medium, and high correlations in this study, see Cohen's [1987] discussion of effect sizes in the behavioral sciences, pp. 78-81.) Students who believed more strongly that writing ability is a gift tended to have (1) higher levels of writing apprehension ($R = 0.375$; $R^2 = .141$; $F = 39.237$; $df = 1$, 240; $p < .001$) and (2) lower self-assessments of their ability as writers ($R = -.306$; $R^2 = .094$; $F = 24.658$; $df = 1$, 238; $p < .001$).

An additional linear regression indicated a strong correlation between the measures of writing apprehension and self-assessment of writing ability. Students with higher levels of writing apprehension tended to have lower levels of self-assessment ($R = -.569$; $R^2 = .324$; $F = 114.615$; $df = 1$, 239; $p < .001$).

Post-Hoc Analysis: Although these results indicate that students' belief in the notion of giftedness is correlated with their writing apprehension and their self-assessment of their writing ability, they also indicate that belief in the notion of giftedness can explain, at best, only a moderate amount of the variance in the other measures: level of belief in the notion of giftedness

528

accounts for 14.1 and 9.4 percent of the variance in students' writing appre-hension and self-assessment, respectively. These results led us to consider a post-hoc analysis. Despite the negative regression slope between self-assessment and giftedness, it might be the case that some students who believe that writing ability is a gift might also consider themselves gifted and thus have a higher level of writing confidence. If this was the case, the contribution to the regression made by these "gifted" students would affect our results.

To explore this possibility, we conducted a linear regression on our measures of writing apprehension and level of belief in the notion of gifted-ness, using self-assessment as a grouping factor.

We compared students whose self-assessment scores fell more than one standard deviation from the mean, those who, relative to their peers, consid-ered themselves strong writers and those who, relative to their peers, consid-ered themselves weak writers. Among students with relatively low assess-ments of their writing ability, level of belief in the notion of giftedness ac-counted for a much higher amount of variance in writing apprehension than

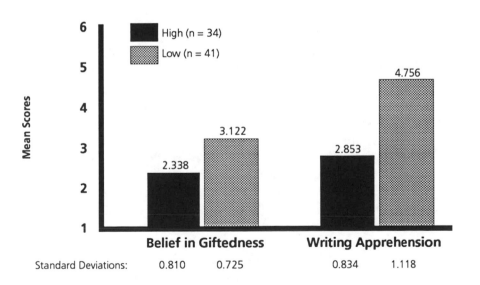

Figure 1
Level of Belief in Giftedness by Response to Item 30
(Means and Standard Deviation)

was the case for all students considered as a group ($R = 0.454$; $R^2 = .207$; $F = 10.150$; $df = 1, 39$; $p < .003$). In contrast, among students with relatively high assessments of their writing ability, the regression analysis indicated no significant association between writing apprehension and belief that writing ability is a gift. An ANOVA comparing the regression coefficients indicated a significant difference between the slopes of the regression line, supporting our expectation that the correlation between writing apprehension and level of belief in the notion of giftedness would differ between the two groups ($F = 22.666$; $df = 2, 71$; $p < .001$).

Further comparisons of the two groups of students showed strong differences in level of belief in the notion of giftedness and level of writing apprehension (see Figure 1). A MANOVA indicated that students with relatively low self-assessments of their writing ability had (a) a significantly higher level of belief in the notion of giftedness than did their peers who had relatively high self-assessments ($F = 19.103$; $df = 1, 73$; $p < .001$) and (b) a significantly higher level of writing apprehension than did their peers who had relatively high self-assessments ($F = 71.146$; $df = 1, 73$; $p < .001$).

The post-hoc analysis indicates that, among students with relatively low self-assessments of their writing ability, level of belief in the notion of giftedness moderately predicts writing apprehension. Among this group of students, belief in giftedness accounts for 20.7 percent of the variance in writing apprehension, suggesting that the belief itself may contribute to these students' apprehension about writing. Such apprehension is likely to have several causes; however, the fact that belief in giftedness accounts for more than 20 percent of the variance in these students' writing apprehension suggests that we should not discount the impact that belief in the notion of giftedness may have upon students' perceptions of writing.

Question Two: What relationships, if any, exist between students' belief in giftedness and their confidence in achieving proficiency in specific writing activities and genres?

A linear regression indicated a low correlation between students' belief in giftedness and their confidence in achieving proficiency in specific writing activities and genres. The measures of writing confidence are based on student responses to Items 31 and 32, which ask students to indicate the activities and genres in which they could become proficient. The measures of relative difficulty are based on ratings provided by 20 faculty in the English Department at Colorado State University. A preliminary regression equation involving the measures of writing confidence in activities and genres indicated that, although the two measures were moderately correlated, they did not appear to be equivalent; the regression equation accounted for only 16 percent of the variance ($R = .400$; $R^2 = .160$; $df = 1, 245$; $F = 46.621$; $p < .001$). Because the two measures appeared to be measuring different types of confidence, we used both as predictors in the regression equation involving the measure of belief in giftedness. The regression indicates that students who had relatively lower levels of belief in giftedness were more confident of their ability to achieve proficiency in writing ($R = -.203$; $R^2 = .041$; $df = 2, 241$; $F = 5.195$; $p < .006$).

The Notion of Relative Difficulty: Student responses to Items 31 and 32 and the difficulty ratings assigned to each activity and genre by faculty provide strong evidence of a consensus on the relative difficulty of the writing activities and, to a lesser degree, the writing genres. For the writing activities, a strong consensus exists among both faculty and students: students were less likely to indicate that they could achieve proficiency in writing activities rated as more difficult by the faculty ($R = -.591$; $R^2 = .349$; $df = 1, 12$; $F = 6.433$; $p < .026$; see Table 2). For the genres, a consensus appears to exist among students and among faculty, but the two groups appear to differ in their estimation of the difficulty of composing the various genres: regression analysis involving the genres failed to detect a significant relationship between student response and faculty difficulty ratings ($R = -.317$; $R^2 = .100$; $df = 1, 20$; $F = 2.232$; $p < .151$; see Table 3).

Although the regressions indicate that faculty and students tended to agree about the relative difficulty of the writing activities, two activities—organizing a paper and coming up with good ideas—stand out as areas of disagreement. Organizing a paper, the activity that received the greatest number of responses, is arguably difficult to master. It seems possible, however, that students interpreted the notion of organizing a paper in a less sophisticated sense than did faculty or perhaps as a routine, mechanical activity. The students might, for instance, have been thinking along the lines of the five-paragraph essay. It also seems possible that students and faculty were applying different criteria to the notion of "good" ideas.

An explanation of the general lack of agreement between faculty and students concerning the relative difficulty of various genres might be found in students' familiarity with the genres. The genre with which students would be expected to have the most experience as writers, the personal essay, received the highest number of responses. The genre receiving the second highest number of responses, the short story, was rated as relatively difficult

531

Table 2
Frequency of Response and Difficulty Ratings for Responses to Item 31: "Given enough time, hard work, and desire, I could become an expert (that is, I could attain the proficiency of a first-class publishable writer), in the following: (check all that apply)"

n = 247

Writing Activity (in ascending level of difficulty)	Difficulty Rating	Student Response
Spelling	1.61	156
Grammar and Punctuation	1.95	131
Finding a Good Topic	2.32	136
Good Word Choice	2.32	145
Composing Good Paragraphs	2.68	118
Composing Good Sentences	2.84	134
Organizing a Paper	3.00	160
Adapting my Writing to a Particular Audience	3.05	114
Coming up with Good Ideas	3.74	146
Revising a Paper	3.84	110
The Handling of Evidence	3.90	90
Coming up with Good Metaphors	4.00	76
The Ability to Refute Someone's Argument	4.26	121
The Ability to Articulate a Problem Well	4.42	111

by the faculty—but again it may be that students' school experience in writing narrative may have contributed to students' confidence. Finally, two genres—haiku and limericks—received few responses from students despite their comparatively low difficulty ratings. It seems possible that students' unfamiliarity with these genres may have contributed to the low frequency of response.

Despite these differences, the results suggest a consensus among students and faculty concerning the relative difficulty of the writing activities and a lack of consensus concerning the genres. The reasons for these findings, however, are open to interpretation. It may be that one or another of the activities and genres is actually more difficult because extensive knowledge is a prerequisite or that more complex psychological processes are involved. Or it may be that proficiency does require a special gift. Still another possible explanation is that the general attitude toward at least some of these activities and genres stems from our cultural heritage. Certainly, the attitude toward metaphor has

Table 3
Frequency of Response and Difficulty Ratings for Responses to Item 32: "Given enough time, hard work, and desire, I would be able to write well enough to have the following types of writing published: (check all that apply)"

n = 247

Writing Activity (in ascending level of difficulty)	Difficulty Rating	Student Response
Business Letters	1.33	99
Letters of Application to a Job	1.50	128
Letters to the Editor	1.67	115
Lab Reports	1.72	58
Limericks	2.17	13
Newspaper Articles	2.28	101
Harlequin Romances	2.33	26
Technical Manuals	2.78	31
Political Speeches	3.06	37
Feature Reports for Magazines	3.06	85
Heiku	3.06	10
Textbooks	3.17	11
Research Papers	3.33	112
Personal Essays	3.39	148
Historical Novels	3.67	24
Critical Reviews of Literature	3.83	37
Free Verse Poetry	3.89	36
Science Fiction Novels	4.00	41
Short Stories	4.06	129
Plays	4.61	25
Lyric Poetry	4.67	31
Novels	4.78	42

been shaped, directly or indirectly, both by Aristotle's view of metaphor as the one rhetorical ability that cannot be taught (1959, III, ii, 6-15) and by a tradition in poetics, especially prominent among the Romantics and contemporary critics, in which metaphor plays a central role in the creative act (e.g., Wimsatt & Brooks, 1959, pp. 399-401, 749-750; Warren, 1950, pp. 18-20, 32-34).

This notion about the relative difficulty of certain writing activities and genres finds expression in the familiar distinction between *art* and *craft*, a distinction that appears to be part of our cultural inheritance, principally from Romantic esthetic theory. Activities that both faculty and students indicated were easier are usually associated with the craft of writing, that is, those skills that have to do with deliberate choice, generally shared conventions, and the mechanics of good prose; because such conventions are explicit, they would seem to be easier to teach and learn. In contrast, activities that faculty and students indicated were more difficult are usually associated with the art of writing, that is, with abilities that are more personal, unconventional, ill-defined, and not wholly under the conscious control of the writer; hence, they are more difficult to learn and are perhaps unteachable (Young, 1982; Kaufer & Young, 1983).

Cultural traditions and values may also play a role in the assessment of the relative difficulty of writing various genres. Every age seems to value strongly certain genres and devalue others, although the reasons for preferences vary from one time to another. The more valued genres may be seen as placing greater demands on the artistry of the writer, or as more appropriate vehicles for exceptional truths, or as playing a more significant role in the maintenance of a civilized society. The responses of the faculty concerning the relative difficulty of the writing genres listed in Item 32 appear to reflect a rather ill-defined hierarchy operating in our own society, one that valorizes artistic performance over rhetorical performance and art over craft; for example, the lyric poem, the novel and the play appear to be regarded as "higher" forms of discourse (i.e., more difficult, requiring special abilities) than the more mundane research paper, public speech, and magazine article, which are apparently considered both learnable and teachable.

Question Three: What relationships, if any, exist between students' belief in giftedness and their prior experiences in writing classrooms?

A series of linear regressions indicates a significant correlation between students' belief in giftedness and only one of our measures of prior classroom experience. We found no significant correlations between belief in giftedness and our measures of process-oriented instruction, product-oriented instruction, and instruction that emphasized creativity. The regression equation involving belief in giftedness and the measure of prior experience with writing teachers indicated a moderate correlation: students who had relatively higher levels of belief in giftedness reported less positive experiences with their previous writing teachers ($R = -.313$; $R^2 = .098$; $F = 25.886$; $df = 1, 239$; $p < .001$).

Question Four: What relationships, if any, exist between students' belief in giftedness and their perceptions of the purpose for writing?

To address this question, we conducted an ANOVA on students' belief in giftedness using the responses to Item 30 as a grouping factor. Item 30 stated, "The most important purpose for writing is: (1) to inform others of your own ideas, (2) to persuade others to believe something that you believe, (3) to come to understand yourself better, or (4) to express your own feelings about something." The ANOVA indicated that level of belief in the notion of giftedness differs significantly among students who have different perceptions of the purpose for writing ($F = 4.592$; $df = 3, 240$; $p < .004$). A comparison of the means for the four categories of response shows that students who chose the fourth response, "to express your own feelings about something," as the most important purpose for writing had a higher level of belief in giftedness than students who chose any of the other three categories (see Figure Two).

We designed the four responses to reflect the divergent emphases writing has received in writing curricula. We thought that the first response, "to inform others of your own ideas," reflected an emphasis characteristic of current-traditional rhetoric. We thought that the second response, "to persuade others to believe something that you believe," was characteristic of neo-classical rhetoric. We thought that the third and fourth responses, "to come to understand yourself better," and "to express your own feelings about something," reflected emphases characteristic of Romantic approaches to the teaching of writing.

As we attempted to develop a measure of students' perceptions of the purpose for writing, we found ourselves wrestling with the obvious objection that the notion of a single purpose for writing is at odds with what we teach in our own writing classes. Because each rhetorical situation is unique, the purposes for which we engage in writing are—literally—endlessly varying. Yet we also wanted to assess—in a way somewhat analogous to a word-association test—what it was that students, when pressed, would indicate is a key reason for writing. We thought that students' response to this item would indicate something of their understanding of what it means to be a writer. As a result, although we had reservations about asking students to identify a single purpose for writing, we finally decided to use Item 30 as it is stated above.

Given the important role self-expression has played in writing curricula, we expected that a large number of students would select the fourth response. This expectation was confirmed (see Figure Three). The majority of students—153 of the 247 students surveyed or 61.9 percent—identified expressing their feelings about something as the most important purpose for writing.

These results underscore the extent to which Romantic theory appears to have shaped students' attitudes toward writing. Over 72 percent of the students surveyed in the study identified self-expression and coming to know themselves as the most important purposes for writing. But these results also point up the importance of avoiding a monolithic conception of Romantic theory. It might be tempting to argue on the basis of these results that students who are influenced by Romantic theory are more likely to believe in the notion of giftedness. But making that argument would have to be tempered

Figure 2

Level of Belief in Giftedness by Response to Item 30
(Means and Standard Deviation)

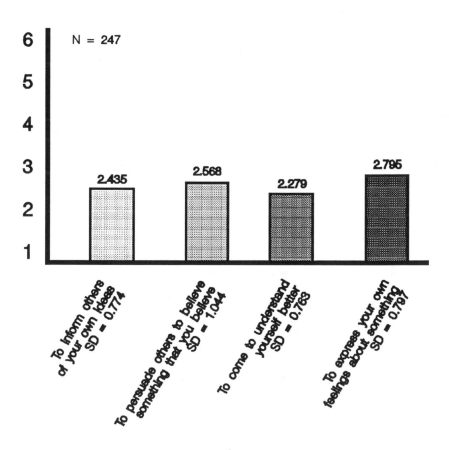

by the fact that students who identified coming to know themselves as the primary purpose for writing had, as a group, the lowest level of belief in the notion of giftedness. As a result, we think it is more reasonable to argue that it is not explicit theories that need to be reexamined but rather a set of presuppositions that have strongly influenced our conceptions of the nature of writing ability. Specifically, we might ask what it is about assumptions associated with Romantic theory that might lead students to view writing ability as an innate rather than an acquired ability.

Discussion

The results of this study indicate that belief in the notion of giftedness plays an important role in students' expectations about writing. It seems clear, however, that belief in giftedness alone does not lead to increased writing apprehension or relatively lower self-assessments of writing ability. Instead, the notion of giftedness appears to make an important, though largely unacknowledged contribution to a constellation of expectations, attitudes, and beliefs that influence the ways in which students approach writing. The role of belief in giftedness is perhaps best illustrated by our comparison of students whose responses placed them at the far ends of the continuum of writing self-assessment. Among students with relatively high self-assessments of their

Figure 3

Frequency of Response to Item 30:
"The most important purpose of writing is:"

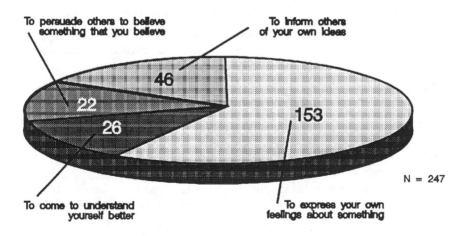

To persuade others to believe something that you believe

To inform others of your own ideas

46

22

26

153

N = 247

To come to understand yourself better

To express your own feelings about something

writing ability, belief in giftedness seemed to be unrelated to our measure of writing apprehension. Among students with relatively low self-assessments of their writing ability, however, a high level of belief in giftedness was strongly correlated with a high level of writing apprehension. We find these results particularly important because they suggest that those students who may be most in need of additional writing instruction may fail to seek it out. Students who believe that they lack a requisite gift for writing may choose not to enroll in writing classes or, if they find themselves in a required composition course, may choose not to put forth the effort needed to improve their writing. Moreover, given Daly and Miller's (1975a) findings concerning the relation-ships between writing apprehension and career choice, we suspect that these students may be making vocational decisions based on erroneous assump-tions—specifically, the assumption that they are not gifted and thus would be unsuccessful in endeavors in which success depends upon the ability to write well.

Although the nature of our inquiry does not allow us to make causal claims about the relationships among the measures explored in this study, our findings nonetheless encourage a serious consideration of the role giftedness might play in shaping student expectations about writing, especially writing apprehension. Thus, although our results do not provide the basis for causal claims, they raise the possibility that belief in giftedness may be educationally damaging.

Our results also suggest that a potential objection to our argument—that belief in giftedness has no relation at all to student expectations about writ-ing—may have little or no merit. Our findings that students with relatively low self-assessments of their writing ability had significantly higher levels of belief in giftedness than did students with relatively high assessments of their writing ability indicate that the notion of giftedness is not uniformly distributed across the students surveyed in this study. If there were no relation between belief in giftedness and self-assessment of writing ability, one group of writers would not be expected to have a higher level of belief in giftedness than another. Findings to the contrary, as well as the evidence of strong correlations be-tween belief in giftedness and writing apprehension among students with low self-assessments of their writing ability, strongly support our claim that the belief in giftedness, in combination with other factors, can play an important role in shaping student expectations about writing.

Because the correlations permit it, one could object that, if there is in fact a causal relation among low self-assessments, writing apprehension, and belief in giftedness, the causation works in the other direction. That is, low self-assessment and apprehension about writing might lead students to a belief in giftedness as a way of rationalizing poor performance (e.g., "I'm not to blame, my parents are; you shouldn't really expect me to do better"). Our findings neither support nor refute this objection. However, regardless of whether low self-assessment and writing apprehension lead to a belief in giftedness or belief in giftedness leads to low self-assessment and writing apprehension, we think that the careful teacher would attend to the relationship as a possible impediment to learning. Years ago, Thorstein Veblen argued that people are sometimes inadvertently trained to fail, that at times people are in effect taught that they are incapable of carrying out activities at which, with proper training, they might otherwise succeed. Ironically, the results of this questionnaire suggest that the notion of giftedness, one of the most pervasive of the modern explanations for exceptional writing performance, may be in some way associated with attitudes that subvert writing performance.

The role teachers might play in shaping those attitudes is also suggested by the results of this study. Our findings indicate that belief in giftedness is moderately—and negatively—correlated with our measure of prior experience with writing teachers. Students who indicated a higher relative level of belief in giftedness reported that their experience with previous writing teachers was less positive than that of their peers with lower levels of belief in giftedness. Again, although the nature of this study precludes making causal inferences, this relationship suggests some interesting avenues of further research.

This study clearly shows that students enter the college classroom with an elaborate set of assumptions about writing and with expectations related to those assumptions about their own ability to perform as writers. Clearly, they are not empty vessels waiting to be filled with rhetorical knowledge. To the extent that their assumptions are faulty, misperceptions and dissonances in the classroom dialogue seem inevitable. As an example, we note the high number of students identifying the most important purpose for writing as self-knowledge and self-expression—72 percent of the total sample. The difficulty we find with these beliefs is not that writing isn't or shouldn't be used for improving self-knowledge or for self-expression; the difficulty is that these purposes are relatively limited given the demands made upon students in their writing both in and out of the classroom. Students who believe that these are the primary purposes for writing may find themselves working at cross-purposes with a teacher who has built a course on, say, classical rhetoric, for which persuasion is the primary purpose. When such expectations seem likely to impede students' efforts in the classroom, teachers may find it useful to hold the expectations up for scrutiny before they proceed with their pedagogical agendas.

Another noteworthy finding concerns student beliefs about the purposes for writing. Students who identified self-expression as the most important purpose for writing had a significantly higher level of belief in giftedness than students who identified other purposes as most important. This finding suggests that students are strongly influenced by assumptions most often associated with the Romantic theory of original genius. Considered in the context of student responses to our measures of writing confidence—responses that suggest that students consider literary, or creative, forms of discourse beyond their ability to master—the likelihood that students are being influenced by those assumptions seems even greater.

Conclusion

Our analyses suggest that belief in the notion of giftedness may have deleterious effects on student writers. It may have deleterious effects on teachers as well. Daly, Vangeliste, and Witte (1988) recently called attention to the ways in which the writing apprehension of teachers can influence the way they value and respond to student writing. We suspect that belief in the notion of giftedness may influence the way they value and respond to students themselves. As Mina Shaughnessy (1977) observed, "unless [the teacher] can assume that his students are capable of learning what he has learned, and what he now teaches, the teacher is not likely to turn to himself as a possible source of his students' failures. He will slip rather into the facile explanations of student failure that have long protected teachers from their own mistakes and inadequacies. But once he grants the intelligence and the will they need to master what is being taught, the teacher begins to look at his students' difficulties in a more fruitful way" (292).

Looking at students' difficulties in the writing classroom in a more fruitful way may require a reconsideration of the nature of writing ability. And that entails at some point, we would argue, re-examining the notion of giftedness. We have tried to leave open the question of the existence of giftedness, even though serious objections have recently been raised to the assumption that in order to account for exceptional performance it is necessary to posit special creative ability (e.g., Perkins, 1981, pp. 245-274). But whatever the theoretical acceptability of the notion, teachers must remember that their students come to them freighted with rhetorical lore, not all of which is sound, and some of which may well impede their ability to learn to write better. As Rose (1980)

540

has argued, close attention to and evaluation of such beliefs may be in many cases a prerequisite to effective rhetorical education (pp. 399-400). Conceivably, one might grant the existence of a creative gift and even that teacher and student can reliably detect its presence or absence, but doing so does not necessarily carry with it the implication that without such a gift the student cannot hope to become a good writer. Once both student and teacher believe that the ability to write at least competently can be learned and taught, they can get on with what is surely one of the most difficult tasks in education.

References

Aristotle. (1959). The "art" of rhetoric. (J. H. Freese, Trans.). Cambridge: Harvard University Press.

Blair, H. (1965). Lectures on rhetoric and belles lettres. H. F. Harding (Ed.) Carbondale, IL: Southern Illinois University Press. (Original work published in 1783).

Clevenger, T. R. (1959). A synthesis of experimental research in stage fright. Quarterly Journal of Speech, 55, 124-145.

Cohen, J. (1987). Statistical power analysis for the behavioral sciences. Hillsdale, NJ: Lawrence Erlbaum Associates.

Daly, J. A., & McCroskey, J. C. (1975). Occupational choice and desirability as a function of communication apprehension. Paper presented at the Annual Convention of the International Communication Association, Chicago, April.

Daly, J. A., & Miller, M. D. (1975a). The empirical development of an instrument to measure writing apprehension. Research in the Teaching of English, 9(3), 242-249.

Daly, J. A., & Miller, M. D. (1975b). Further studies in writing apprehension: SAT scores, success expectations, willingness to take advanced courses and sex differences. Research in the Teaching of English, 9(3), 250-256.

Daly, J. A., Vangeliste, A., & Witte, S. P. (1988). Writing apprehension in the classroom context. In B. A. Rafoth & D. L. Rubin (Eds.), The social construction of written communication, 147-171. Norwood, NJ: Ablex.

Hartman, K. (1989). Personal communication.

Hillocks, G. (1986). Research on written composition: New directions for teaching. Urbana, IL: ERIC Clearinghouse on Reading and Communication Skills and National Conference on Research in English.

Kaufer, D. S., & Young, R. E. (1983). Literacy, art, and politics in departments of English. In W. B. Horner (Ed.), Composition and rhetoric: Bridging the gap, 148-158. Chicago: University of Chicago Press.

Perkins, D. N. (1981). The mind's best work. Cambridge: Harvard University Press.

Phillips, G. M. (1968). Reticence: Pathology of the normal speaker. Speech Monographs, 35, 39-49.

Rose, M. (1980). Rigid rules, inflexible plans, and the stifling of language: A cognitive analysis of writer's block. College Composition and Communication, 31(4), 389-400.

Shaughnessy, M. P. (1977). Errors and expectations: A guide for the teacher of basic writing. New York: Oxford University Press.

Smith, L. P. (1925). Words and idioms: Studies in the English language. London: Constable.

Warren, A. (1950). English poetic theory: 1825-1865. Princeton: Princeton University Press.

Willinsky, J. M. (1987). The seldom-spoken roots of the curriculum: Romanticism and the new literacy. Curriculum Inquiry, 17, 268-291.

Wimsatt, W. K. Jr., & Brooks, C. (1959). Literary criticism: A short history. New York: Knopf.

Young, R. E. (1982). Concepts of art and the teaching of writing. In J. J. Murphy (Ed.), The rhetorical tradition and modern writing, 130-141. New York: Modern Language Association.

Appendix A: Writing Survey

Please darken the number that indicates the extend to
which you agree or disagree with the following questions:

① Strongly Disagree ② Disgree ③ Disagree Slightly ④ Agree Slightly ⑤ Agree ⑥ Strongly Agree

1. Good writers are born, not made. ①②③④⑤⑥
2. Some people have said, "Writing can be learned, but it can't be taught" ①②③④⑤⑥
    Do you believe it can be learned?
3. Do you believe it can be taught? ①②③④⑤⑥
4. The best way to learn how to write well is to learn how to think well. ①②③④⑤⑥
5. The best way to learn how to write well is to read a lot. ①②③④⑤⑥
6. The best way to learn how to write well is to write a lot. ①②③④⑤⑥
7. Hard work, desire, dedication, and enough time are all I need to become a ①②③④⑤⑥
    good writer.
8. I am a good writer. ①②③④⑤⑥
9. No matter how hard I try, I will never be a good writer. ①②③④⑤⑥
10. Some of the things my former writing teachers said made me believe ①②③④⑤⑥
    I could become a good writer.
11. Some of my former writing teachers encouraged me to keep working on ①②③④⑤⑥
    my writing.
12. I believe I was born with the ability to write well. ①②③④⑤⑥
13. Good teachers can help me become a better writer. ①②③④⑤⑥
14. 1 have always been a good writer. ①②③④⑤⑥
15. I avoid writing. ①②③④⑤⑥
16. I enjoy writing. ①②③④⑤⑥
17. Writing is a lot of fun. ①②③④⑤⑥
18. Discussing my writing with others is an enjoyable experience. ①②③④⑤⑥
19. I'm no good at writing. ①②③④⑤⑥

Please respond true or false to the following statements,

20. In past writing classes I wrote many impromptu essays. True False
21. In past writing classes I have engaged in freewriting. True False
22. In past writing classes I learned about "pre-writing." True False
23. Some of my former teachers acted as though the most important True False
    part of writing was spelling, punctuation and grammar.
24. Some of my former writing classes emphasized creativity. True False
25. Some of my former writing teachers required me to submit rough True False
    drafts of my papers.

26. I've taken some courses that focused primarily on spelling, grammar and punctuation.   True   False

27. In previous writing courses I've had to revise my papers.   True   False

28. Some of my previous writing teachers were more interested in my ideas than in my spelling, punctuation and grammar.   True   False

29. I've taken classes in which the teacher made me feel that trying to become a good writer would be a waste of time.   True   False

30. The most important purpose for writing is: (please check one)

_____to inform others of your own ideas.

_____to persuade others to believe something that you believe.

_____to come to understand yourself better.

_____to express your own feelings about something.

31. Given enough time, hard work, and desire I could become an expert (that is, I could attain the proficiency of a first class publishable writer) in the following: (check all that apply)

_____punctuation   _____composing good sentences

_____organizing a paper   _____the ability to articulate a problem well

_____coming up with good metaphors   _____coming up with good ideas

_____spelling   _____composing good paragraphs

_____the ability to refute someone's argument   _____grammar and punctuation

_____good word choice   _____revising a paper

_____the handling of evidence   _____finding a good topic

_____adapting my writing to a particular audience

32. Given enough time, hard work, and desire I would be able to write well enough to have the following types of writing published: (check all that apply)

_____the novel   _____Harlequinn romances   _____critical reviews of literature

_____limericks   _____composition textbooks   _____haiku

_____short stories   _____historical novels   _____plays

_____research papers   _____science fiction novels   _____business letters

_____personal essays   _____newspaper articles   _____free verse poetry

_____letters of application to a job   _____lyric poetry   _____letters to the editor

_____technical manuals   _____feature reports for magazines

Note: Please circle any of the items in questions 31 & 32 which you can already do well.

Appendix B: Factor Analysis with Orthogonal Rotations using Four Factors

Entire sample: n=247

Rotated Loadings

Items	Factor 1	Factor 2	Factor 3	Factor 4
1	-0.034	-0.637	-0.200	0.013
2	0.019	0.663	0.094	0.233
3	0.127	0.794	-0.016	-0.075
8	0.252	0.188	0.371	0.699
10	0.133	0.166	0.808	0.281
11	0.172	0.128	0.839	0.030
12	0.059	-0.071	0.038	0.770
13	0.365	0.607	0.094	0.074
14	0.269	0.066	0.072	0.767
15	-0.658	-0.221	0.103	-0.364
16	0.835	0.206	0.190	0.187
17	0.850	0.069	0.088	0.157
18	0.700	0.011	0.401	0.072
19	-0.427	-0.267	-0.353	-0.485

Variance Explained by Rotated Components

	2.858	2.099	1.899	2.207

Percent of Variance Explained

	20.415	14.994	13.564	15.767

[1] We wish to thank Gilbert Findlay, Doug Flahive, John R. Hayes, George Hillocks, Kate Kiefer, and Christine Neuwirth for their helpful comments on drafts of this article.

Institution: University of Pittsburgh

n=119

Rotated Loadings

Items	Factor 1	Factor 2	Factor 3	Factor 4
1	0.142	-0.661	-0.339	-0.102
2	0.030	0.656	0.014	0.053
3	-0.078	0.784	-0.057	0.110
8	0.765	0.072	0.355	0.139
10	0.218	-0.022	0.819	0.111
11	0.082	0.044	0.812	0.165
12	0.747	-0.137	0.042	0.143
13	0.300	0.479	-0.107	0.301
14	0.772	-0.084	0.003	0.239
15	-0.429	-0.269	-0.058	-0.591
16	0.216	0.195	0.138	0.858
17	0.242	0.149	0.060	0.839
18	0.074	0.012	0.220	0.804
19	-0.590	-0.365	-0.343	-0.263

Variance Explained by Rotated Components

	2.554	2.011	1.778	2.757

Percent of Variance Explained

	18.240	14.361	12.702	19.691

Institution: Robert Morris College
n=128

Rotated Loadings

Items	Factor 1	Factor 2	Factor 3	Factor 4
1	-0.021	-0.599	-0.137	-0.070
2	0.057	0.607	0.407	0.175
3	0.084	0.800	-0.036	0.079
8	0.378	0.269	0.563	0.350
10	0.155	0.263	0.345	0.748
11	0.116	0.186	0.026	0.863
12	0.003	-0.044	0.766	0.037
13	0.372	0.705	-0.088	0.189
14	0.355	0.160	0.697	0.125
15	-0.714	-0.209	-0.296	0.185
16	0.813	0.232	0.124	0.269
17	0.820	0.010	0.042	0.180
18	0.590	-0.033	0.060	0.576
19	-0.565	-0.169	-0.397	-0.364

Variance Explained by Rotated Components

	2.967	2.196	1.968	2.124

Percent of Total Variance Explained

	21.191	15.686	14.055	15.170

Authors' Comment—Richard Young

During the spring semester of 1989 we (i.e., Palmquist and Young) had been reading intensively in eighteenth century rhetorical and literary theory. Many of the readings focused on the concepts of talent, original genius, imagination, taste, and creativity, that is, on theoretical notions about special abilities that enable the creation of original discourse. The concepts were precursors of more fully elaborated assumptions in Romantic poetic theory.

One day toward the end of the semester, a graduate student left a note for Young that included the following statement (which eventually became the first of the two epigraphs in our article):

> Throughout all my schooling I was led to believe that creative talent was the possession of only a few "gifted and artistic" individuals. Thus, the rest of us were resigned to concentrate on the mechanical aspects of writing and producing well researched and well supported term papers. I can't recall ever being allowed to express my thoughts about a topic I was interested in.

It was at that point that two ideas began to occupy our thinking: First, that the concepts we had been exploring in our reading seemed to be still very much alive in the minds of many in our society. In particular, imagination and original genius, in the sense of special abilities that some have and not others, both of which seemed to be captured in the more general notion of gifted-ness, seemed to us to be widely shared in our society, even by those who had never read the texts in which the concepts were originally stated. Second, that the concepts are not inert in people's minds but appear to have significant consequences. For example, they seemed to us to underlie certain attitudes and practices on the part of both students and teachers. Among these are the ones the student mentioned in her note, that is, attitudes and practices that tend to exclude students from activities ordinarily thought to be creative.

Metaphorically speaking, we had become a paper waiting to be written, in the sense that the reading we had been doing prepared us to find the student's statement interesting and worth further inquiry. It seems unlikely that we would have responded as we did had she written the note prior to the reading project. Jerome Bruner remarks somewhere that "discovery, like surprise, favors the well-prepared mind." We set about developing a survey questionnaire that would give us a better understanding of the extent to which the notion of giftedness and related beliefs had become part of our society's cultural inheritance. (By "cultural inheritance" we mean the beliefs passed down to us that have become so fully assimilated into our mental life that we hardly know they are there but that nevertheless influence the way we experience the world and think about it.) The questionnaire was also designed to reveal whether these beliefs were in one way or another related to the attitudes people had toward writing and their own abilities as writers.

Although the survey questionnaire still seems to us reasonably sound, we see the conduct of the survey as a weak spot in the research project. We began the project rather casually, not realizing how involved with it we would eventually become. We distributed a pilot version of our questionnaire first to any doctoral students who happened to be handy as a way of checking whether there were problems in the formulation of the various questions. After making revisions we arranged with friends at the University of Pittsburgh and Robert Morris College to administer the questionnaire to their students. Obviously, we should have taken more care in determining what population should be surveyed and the sampling methods to be used; however, questioning a fairly large number of students at two quite different schools seemed to us at the time sufficient. So our initial, rather casual attitude led to a more casual implementation of the survey than in retrospect we would wish for. But by the time we became more deeply involved with the project it was too late to tighten up the survey procedures. On the other hand, what we learned from the survey is certainly significant enough to warrant more carefully designed replications and other kinds of follow-up studies.

Part 3

Glossary

Analysis of covariance (ANCOVA)

A variety of **analysis of variance** using **covariates** to enable the researcher to account for some of the effects of uncontrolled variables. p373.

Analysis of variance (ANOVA)

A statistical procedure widely used to test the significance of differences among two or more groups. It makes use of the **F-statistic**. p318, 319, 405.

One-way (univariate) ANOVA

An analysis of variance in which groups are arrayed on a single dimension or variable. For example, first-, second-, and third-graders are three groups that are arrayed on a single dimension, grade level. The results of a one-way ANOVA of scores for first-, second-, and third-graders would indicate whether or not there were significant differences among the grades. However, the ANOVA would not indicate where the differences are. The differences may be located by using post hoc tests.

Two-way ANOVA

An analysis of variance in which groups are arrayed on two dimensions. For example, the four groups: first-grade boys, first-grade girls, second-grade boys, and second-grade girls, can be arrayed on the two dimension, grade level and gender. The results of an ANOVA on the scores of first- and second-grade boys and girls will indicate whether there was a significant difference between first- and second-graders, whether there was a significant difference between boys and girls, and whether there was a significant **interaction** between these two variables.

Arithmetic average

The group of a set of scores divided by the number of scores. P38, 320.

Auto-ethnographic study

A kind of **ethnographic study** in which the group being studied participates in the study both by providing observations and by critiquing the conclusion being drawn. p135, 177.

Bias

In an empirical study, observations are said to be biased if they are not representative of the population that the researcher claims to describe. For example, if researchers uses phone interviews to assess people's opinions about health care, the results may be biased because they do not include the opinions of the homeless and of people currently in hospitals. There are many sources of bias that researchers must take into account in designing studies. See, for example, **observer bias, sampling bias**, and **halo effect**. p26.

Binomial test (Sign test)
A statistical test based on the assumption that positive scores are just as likely as negative scores if the **null hypothesis** is true. p435.

Blind grading
Evaluation of performance in which the graders are unaware of the treatment condition of the individuals being graded. p29.

Case studies
Studies which involve the detailed description of one or a few students, class-rooms, or situations. Usually used for exploratory or descriptive purposes. p91.

Chi-square test
A statistical test used to measure the strength of the relation between two or more **nominal** variables. p321, 405.

Concurrent events
Events occurring during a study that could lead to differences among the groups being studied. For example, suppose that researchers were studying the writing abilities of students in an inner-city school and a suburban school and that during the study, the budget for the English department was cut in the inner-city school. That cut is a concurrent event which must be taken into account when interpreting the result. p33, 349.

Concurrent measure
A measure which provides information about task performance while the task is being carried out. **Protocol analysis** is a concurrent measure. Contrasted with **retrospective measures**. p247.

Confounding factor
A variable which is not manipulated as an independent variable but which varies with one or more of the independent variables in a study. When there are confounding factors, it may be unclear whether observed effects on the dependent variables are due to changes in the independent variables or to changes in the confounding factors. For example, racial groups often differ not only in race, but also in such confounding factors as wealth and educational opportunity. Thus, apparent differences among racial groups may actually be attributable to differences in wealth or educational opportunity. p31, 407.

Constructivist
A tradition that emphasizes the active role of readers in constructing meaning from text. p467.

Control group

A group in an **experimental study** which does not receive the experimental treatment. It is used as a basis of comparison for establishing the effectiveness of the experimental variable. p32.

Correlation

A measure of the relationship of two variables which takes on values between +1.0 and -1.0. Correlations close to 0 indicate little or no relationship between two variables, while correlations close to +1.0 (or -1.0) indicate strong positive (or negative) relationship. p25, 39, 230.

Cohen's Kappa

A correlation measure using **nominal** data. For example, Cohen's Kappa would be appropriate for measuring the correlation between two raters who are sorting the problems in students' papers into categories. p39, 230.

Pearson's product-moment correlation

A correlation measure using **interval** data. For example, this measure would be appropriate for relating the number of items correctly spelled on pretest to the number correctly spelled on posttest. The Pearson product-moment correlation is the most frequently used measure of correlation. p39, 230.

Spearman's Rho

A correlation measure using ranked (**ordinal**) data. For example, this measure would be appropriate for assessing the agreement between two judges who rank ordered the same set of papers. p39, 350.

Correlational study

A study in which the researchers examine relations among variables but do not manipulate them. For example, a study of differences in spelling skills in second-, third-, and fourth-grade students would be a correlational study because it examines the relation between skill and grade level without attempting to change either. p17, 318.

Counterbalancing

A procedure for reducing **order effects** which might bias the results of a study. A frequently used counterbalancing technique is to require half of the participants to experience Condition A before Condition B and the other half, to experience the conditions in the reverse order. p34.

Counter-example

An example or case which contradicts a claim or belief. p92.

Covariates

In an experimental study, there may be many uncontrolled variables that can influence the dependent variables. For example, in evaluating a new teaching method for third-grade students, the results may be influenced by variations in I.Q and age. To account for some of the variation, researchers may measure one or more of these variables so that their influence on the results may be assessed. Such variables are called covariates. p372.

Cronbach's Alpha

A type of **correlation** measure used to assess the reliability of the ratings of groups of judges. P318, 319.

Degrees of freedom

The number of degrees of freedom in a data table is the number of cells that can be filled in arbitrarily without changing the row and column sums. In the table on the left below, there is just one degree of freedom because once one value is chosen arbitrarily (see middle table), the values of the rest can be calculated from that value and the values of the row and column sums (see right hand table).

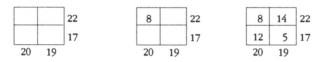

The degrees of freedom of a column of N numbers with a fixed sum is N-1. p386.

Descriptive studies

A study in which the goal of the researchers is to describe or to explore rather than to answer a specific, yes or no, question. Often contrasted to **hypothesis testing studies**. p17

Drop-outs

Drop-outs are participants who fail to complete a study. Researchers must be concerned when drop-out rates are high, especially if they are higher in some conditions than in others. For example, suppose that researchers compared a very dull teaching method with an interesting one. Suppose further that the dull method caused all but the best, most motivated students to drop out of the study. Tests of the participants who remain in the study might suggest that the dull procedure was better than the interesting procedure if researchers failed to take the differential drop-out rate into account. p32, 350.

Ethnographic research

The objective of ethnographic research is to answer the question "what is the culture of this group?" It may involve very detailed description of the actions and artifacts of the group. In ethnographic studies, data is often collected through **participant observation**. p177.

Experimental study

A study in which researchers manipulate some variables (called the **independent variables**) to examine their effect on others (called the **dependent variables**). For example, a study in which researchers manipulate by assigning some students to write narratives, and others to write arguments so that the researchers can examine the effect on writing quality is an experimental study. p17, 318.

Exploratory study

Same as a **descriptive study**.

Factor analysis

A statistical procedure that allows one to reduce a large number of variables to a smaller, representative set of variables called "factors." p404, 515.

F-Statistic

The F-statistic, named after the statistician, Sir Ronald Fisher, is the basis for statistical testing in many statistical procedures including **analysis of variance, analysis of covariance, regression analysis, and multiple analysis of variance**. p321.

"Halo" effect

The tendency of a rater to score individuals higher (or lower) than their performance would warrant because the rater knows that they performed well (or badly) in the past. p26.

Hedging

The practice of pointing out to one's audience the limitations of one's claims. p212, 319, 351.

Hypothesis testing study

A study in which the researcher's goal is to test a clearly stated question such as "Does the new training procedure work better than the standard procedure?" or "Do people write better organized essays with computers than with pen and paper?" Hypothesis testing studies are contrasted to **descriptive studies.** p17.

Independence

Observations are independent if they are unrelated to each other. Successive flips of a coin are independent in the sense that how the coin comes down on the second flip (heads or tails) is unrelated to how it comes down on the first flip. p35, 36.

Interaction

Two independent variables are said to interact if the effect of either of them on a dependent variable depends on the value of the other. p318, 320.

Likert scale
A scale, often used in attitude or opinion polling, on which respondents check one of five alternatives ranging from "strongly disagree" to "strongly agree", to indicate their opinion on an issue. p157, 287.

Main effect
In an **analysis of variance** with more than one variable, a main effect is the effect of one of the independent variables averaged over all of the values of the other independent variables. For example, in a study of first- and second-grade boys and girls, the main effect for grade is the effect of grade averaged over boys and girls. p320.

Manipulation
The purposeful modification of independent variables to produce conditions for an **experimental study**.

Mann-Whitney test
A statistical test for comparing two groups on the basis of ranked (**ordinal**) data. p351.

Maturation
Changes that occur with the passage of time such as growth, aging, and accumulation of experience. In conducting studies that involve a long interval between pretest and posttest, the researcher must recognize that some changes might be expected on the basis of maturation. p32, p349.

Mean
The same as the **arithmetic average**. p38, 320.

Measures of central tendency
These are measures intended to identify the center of a group of measurements. The **mean**, the **median**, and the **mode** are the most frequently used measures of central tendency. p38.

Measures of variability
These are measures of the spread of a group of measurements. The **standard deviations** is the most frequently used measure of variability, but the **range** is also used on some occasions. p38.

Median
The middle measurement in the group of measures. p38.

Metacognition
The ability to think about one's own mental activities. p433.

Metacognitive knowledge
Knowledge of one's own cognitive processes. p433.

Metacognitive skill
Ability to exercise deliberate control over one's own cognitive activities. p433.

Mode
The most frequently occurring measurement in a group of measurement. p38.

Multiple analysis of variance (MANOVA)
A form of analysis of variance designed to reveal the effects of the independent variables on the dependent variables taken as a group. p386.

Null hypothesis
The hypothesis that there is no difference between the treatment and control groups.

Order effects
When participants in a study have to do two or more tasks, the order in which they do them may matter. For example, in a study of persuasion that requires participants to read a pro and a con argument, it may make a difference whether they read the pro or the con argument first. A common way to take order effects into account is to use **counterbalancing**. p34.

Participant observation
A research method in which a group is observed by a participating member of the group. p18, 135.

Participant effects
The results one obtains in a study may be influenced by the participants' responses to being studied. For example, if participants are told they are in the experimental group, they may feel flattered and work especially hard to produce the result that they think the researcher wants to find. p30.

Pre-post differences/gains
The difference between an individual's post-test score and pre-test score. p34.

Post hoc tests
After performing a statistical test such as an analysis of variance which has revealed significant differences among three or more groups, researchers often want to determine which of the differences between pairs of groups are significant. For example, suppose that **analysis of variance** has revealed that there are significant differences among three training groups and a control group. Post hoc tests could be used to determine which of the training groups was significantly different in performance from the control group. p387, 405.

Duncan test
One of several post hoc tests. p387.

Newman-Keuls test
One of several post hoc tests. p387.

Process measure
A measure that reflects the properties of the process or procedure by which the participant carried out a task. p467.

Product measures
A measure which reflects the properties of the final product of a task. p467.

Random assignment
Assignment of participants to experimental conditions by a random procedure such as drawing names from a hat, rolling dice, or using a table of random numbers. p18.

Random sample
A sample selected from a population by a random procedure. p27.

Range
The difference between the largest and the smallest of a group of measurements. p38.

Reactivity
The degree to which the act of observation is likely to influence the phenomena being observed. p29, 75.

Readability tests
A test based on text features such as sentence length and word frequency intended to predict the readability of texts. p156.

Regression analysis
A statistical procedure, closely related to correlation, used for assessing the strength of relations among variables. p513.

Reliability
The extent to which a measure is repeatable. p15, 136, 405.

Observer/rater reliability
The degree to which independent observers can agree on a set of judgments or observations. p24, 25, 318.

Test-retest reliability
The degree to which repeated measurements yield the same result. p25.

Statistical reliability
Same as **stability**. p26.

Replication
A study which substantially repeats another study. p25.

Strict replication
A replication study which matches the original study as closely as possible. p229.

Modified replication
A replication study which is similar to an original study in most ways but differs from it in certain important features. p229.

Researcher bias
When scoring the results of a study, researchers may unconsciously bias the result in favor of their hypothesis. For example, in scoring essays, researchers may be more inclined to give "the benefit of the doubt" to those in the experimental group. A good way to reduce experimenter effects is to use **blind grading**. p28.

Researcher effects
Extensive research has shown that researchers can inadvertently influence the results of the study. For example, without intending to, the researcher may behave in a friendlier, more interested way to the participants in the experimental group than to those in the control group. p29.

Retrospective measure
A measure of task performance conducted after the task has been completed. Interviews of participants conducted after they have completed a task are retrospective measures. p247.

Rival hypothesis
Rival hypotheses are plausible alternatives to a current hypothesis for interpreting observations. For example, suppose that researchers observes that students' conversational skills are better after a year of nursery school than before. Their current hypothesis is that the social experience of nursery school has caused the change. A rival hypothesis is that **maturation**, that is, growth that occurs with the passage of time, may account for the change. p17, 349.

Sample
A portion of a population that is taken as representative of the entire population. p26.

Sample size

The number of individuals included in the sample. p92.

Sampling bias

In an unbiased sample, every member of the population has an equal chance of being included. Any method of data collection that gives some parts of the population a better chance of being included than others is said to suffer from sampling bias. For example, if a researcher attempts to assess students needs for a writing center by surveying students in morning classes, the sample is likely to be biased in the sense that it will miss part-time students who take courses in the evening. p26, 350.

Scales -

Nominal scale

One that assigns individuals to categories without implying that the categories have any order among them. The numbers on football players uniforms form a nominal scale. p287.

Ordinal scale

A scale in which scale values are ordered but successive values are not equidistant. The familiar grading scale (A through E) is an ordinal scale. "A" is better than "B" and "B" is better than "C" but the interval between "A" and "B" is not necessarily equal to the interval between "B" and "C". p287.

Interval scale

A scale which specifies an ordered set of equal intervals or units. Numbers of items answered correctly on a test can be described on an interval scale. p287.

Scientism

Practice of taking on the superficial trappings of science in order to share in its prestige. p385.

S. D.

An abbreviation for standard deviation. p38.

Self-selection bias

A bias introduced into an experimental study by allowing participants to assign themselves to study conditions. For example, students who choose to be in the experimental group may be more adventurous than average. p21, 28.

Significance -

Practical

A difference between two conditions is practically significant if it is large enough to be important to someone. p15, 349.

Statistical

A difference between two conditions is statistically significant if it would occur by chance only rarely, e.g., one time in 20. p15.

Sign test

A statistical test based on the signs of differences between conditions. Same as the **binomial test**. p435.

Social constructionism

An approach to research that emphasizes the role of the social environment in shaping individual behavior. p467.

Stability

Stability refers to the replicability of observations. Suppose that a researcher observed two boys and two girls and found that the boys spelled better than the girls. This result may have little stability in the sense that in the next group of boys and girls, the girls may spell better than the boys. However, if the researcher had found the same result by observing a thousand boys and a thousand girls, the result would be more stable. That is, another sample of the same size is more likely to yield the same result as the first if the sample size is large. In general, the stability of a result increases with the number of observations on which the result is based. p24.

Standard deviation

A measure of the spread of observations. A large standard deviation indicates that observations are widely spread. The standard deviation is the sum of the squared differences between each observation and the mean of the observations divided by the number of observations minus one. p24.

Statistical power

The probability that a statistical test will find a difference when one is actually present. The power of a test increases with the magnitude of the difference and with the number of observations, n. p156.

Test practice effects

When people take the same kind of test more than once, they tend to improve their performance with each retest. This is true even when the tests are "parallel forms" consisting of similar but different test items. Researchers need to design studies so that they can distinguish testing practice effects from improvements due to the experimental treatment. p33, 350.

Triangulation

Using multiple sources of information, e.g., self report, performance, and teacher judgment, to provide converging evidence. p28.

Transfer
The effect that previous learning has on subsequent performance. p371.

t-test
A statistical procedure used to test the significance of the difference between two groups. p411.

Unit of analysis
The units in a study whose properties are being measured, e.g., individual students, classrooms, schools, etc. p410.

Validity
The degree to which a procedure or a study measures what it is claimed to measure. p136, 211.

External validity
A study is externally valid if its results can be generalized beyond the sample actually studied. For example, a study that sampled only private school students would have low external validity compared to a study which sampled students from a wide variety of schools.

Internal validity
The internal validity of a study refers to the extent to which the relations which the researcher claims to have observed in the study are not the product of confounding factors or observational errors. A study has high internal validity if there are no plausible **rival hypotheses** to the researcher's claims. p349.

Variable - p18, 136, 211.
Dependent variable
A variable measured by the researcher to determine if it is influenced by manipulation of the independent variable or variables. p18.

Independent variable
A variable manipulated by a researcher in an experimental study. p18.

Additional Readings

Research Design: General Discussion

Berger, R.M., & Patchner, M.A. (1988). *Planning for Research*. Newbury Park, CA: Sage.

Howard, G.S. (1985). *Basic Research Methods in the Social Sciences*. Glenview, IL: Scott, Foresman and Company.

Huck, S.W., & Sandler, H.M. (1979). *Rival Hypotheses*. New York: Harper & Row.

Kamil, M.L., Langer, J.A., & Shanahan, T. (1985). *Understanding Research in Reading and Writing*. Newton, MA: Allyn & Bacon.

Kraemer, H.C., & Thiemann, S. (1987). *How Many Subjects?* Newbury Park, CA: Sage.

Marshall, C., & Rossman, G.B. (1989). *Designing Qualitative Research*. Newbury Park, CA: Sage.

Patton, M.Q. (1990). *Qualitative Evaluation and Research Methods*. (second edition) Newbury Park, CA: Sage.

Webb, E.J., Campbell, D.T., Schwartz, R.D., Sechrest,, L., & Grove, J.B. (1981). *Nonreactive Measures in the Social Sciences*. Boston: Houghton Mifflin.

The Case Study

Yin, R.K. (1984). *Case Study Research: Design and Methods*. Newbury Park, CA: Sage.

The Ethnographic Study

Atkinson, P. (1990). *The Ethnographic Imagination*. New York: Routledge.

Experimental and Correlational Studies

Campbell, D.T., & Stanley, J.C. (1966). *Experimental and Quasi-Experimental Designs for Research*. Boston, MA: Houghton Mifflin Company.

The Survey

Babbie, E.R. (1973). *Survey Research Methods*. Belmont, CA: Wadsworth Publishing.

Backstrom, C.H., & Hursh, G.D. (1963). *Survey Research*. Evanston, IL: Northwestern University Press.

Fowler, F.J., Jr. (1988). *Survey Research Methods*. Newbury Park, CA: Sage.

Fowler, F.J., Jr., & Mangione, T.W. (1990). *Standardized Survey Interviewing*. (Volume 18). Newbury Park, CA: Sage.

Statistical Methods

Glass, G.V., & Hopkins, K.D. (1984). *Statistical Methods in Education and Psychology* (second edition). Englewood Cliffs, NJ: Prentice-Hall.

Jaeger, R.M. (1983). *Statistics: A Spectator Sport.* Beverly Hills,CA: Sage.

Kleinbaum, D.G., & Kupper, L.L. (1978). *Applied Regression Analysis and other Multivariable Methods.* Belmont, CA: Wadsworth Publishing

Rowntree, D.(1981). *Statistics Without Tears.* New York: Scribner's Sons.

Tanur, J.M., Mosteller, F., Kruksal, W.H., Lehmann, E.L., Link, R.F., Pieters, R.S., & Rising, G.R. (1989). *Statistics: A Guide to the Unknown.* Pacific Grove, CA: Wadsworth & Brooks.

Visual Communication

Cleveland, W.S. (1985). *The Elements of Graphing Data.* Monterey, CA: Wadsworth Publishing.

Tufte, E.R,. (1983). *The Visual Display of Quantitative Information.* Cheshire, CT: Graphics Press.

Tufte, E. R. (1990). *Envisioning Information.* Cheshire, CT: Graphics Press.

White, J.V. (1984). *Using Charts and Graphs.* New York: R.R. Bowker Company.

565